Trials of Nature

Focusing on John Milton's *Paradise Lost*, this book investigates the metaphorical identification of nature with a court of law – an old and persistent trope, haunted by ancient aporias, at the intersection of jurisprudence, philosophy and literature.

In an enormous variety of texts, from the Greek beginnings of Western literature onward, nature has been described as a courtroom in which an all-encompassing trial takes place and a universal verdict is executed. The first, introductory part of this study sketches an overview of the metaphor's development in European history, from antiquity to the seventeenth century. In its second, more extensive part, the book concentrates on Milton's epic *Paradise Lost* in which the problem of the natural law court finds one of its most fascinating and detailed articulations. Using conceptual tools provided by Hannah Arendt, Walter Benjamin, Hans Blumenberg, Gilles Deleuze, William Empson and Alfred North Whitehead, the study demonstrates that the conflicts in Milton's epic revolve around the tension between a universal legal procedure inherent in nature and the positive legal decrees of the deity. The divine rule is found to consolidate itself by Nature's supplementary shadow government; their inconsistencies are not flaws, but rather fundamental rhetorical assets, supporting a law that is inherently "doubleformed". In Milton's world, human beings are thus confronted with a twofold law that entraps them in its endlessly proliferating double binds, whether they obey or not. The analysis of this strange juridical structure can open up new perspectives on Milton's epic, as well as on the way legal discourse tends to entangle norms with facts and thus to embed itself in human life.

This original and intriguing book will appeal not only to those engaged in the study of Milton, but also to anyone interested in the relationship between law, history, literature and philosophy.

Björn Quiring is an Assistant Professor at the School of English, Trinity College Dublin. He has also published *Shakespeare's Curse: The Aporias of Ritual Exclusion in Early Modern Royal Drama* (2014).

Part of the
DISCOURSES OF LAW
series

For information about the series and details of previous and forthcoming titles, see https://www.routledge.com/Discourses-of-Law/book-series/SE1036

The publisher gratefully acknowledges the support of the Jacob Burns Institute for Advanced Legal Studies of the Benjamin N. Cardozo School of Law to the series *Discourses of Law*.

A GlassHouse Book

Trials of Nature

The Infinite Law Court of Milton's *Paradise Lost*

Björn Quiring

Routledge
Taylor & Francis Group
LONDON AND NEW YORK

First published 2021
by Routledge
2 Park Square, Milton Park, Abingdon, Oxon OX14 4RN

and by Routledge
52 Vanderbilt Avenue, New York, NY 10017

Routledge is an imprint of the Taylor & Francis Group, an informa business

British Library Cataloguing-in-Publication Data
A catalogue record for this book is available from the British Library

Library of Congress Cataloging-in-Publication Data
A catalog record has been requested for this book

ISBN: 978-0-367-34442-9 (hbk)
ISBN: 978-0-429-34492-3 (ebk)

Typeset in Times New Roman
by Newgen Publishing UK

Contents

Acknowledgements

This book had a long gestation and has incurred too many debts to mention. First and foremost, Andreas Höfele and Claudia Olk generously, diligently and patiently supported the work. Anselm Haverkamp gave it its impetus and much good advice. Joachim Küpper and Stephan Laqué read the book when it was still a habilitation thesis and gave kind and constructive reviews. Peter Goodrich and Colin Perrin helped to reconceptualize the thesis as a book for the *Discourses of Law* series; and the anonymous reviewers for the series provided helpful criticism. Sage Anderson prepared the bibliography. Sanford Budick, Rüdiger Campe, Philip Lorenz, Julia Lupton, Noam Reisner and Nigel Smith generously provided ideas, encouragement and diverse forms of hospitality. Gordon Teskey welcomed me during my stay as a visiting scholar in Harvard and gave useful hints during the final phase of writing. Iain Hamilton Grant's ideas are floating around in the dark background areas of the text. Among the people who, by criticism, support, inspiration or all of the above, contributed to the book, I would furthermore like to thank, somewhat synecdochically, Armen Avanessian, Ronja Bodola, Ray Brassier, Michael Cisco, Philip Coleman, Ralf Eckschmidt, Stephen M. Fallon, Stephen Greenblatt, Anne Kockelkorn, Darri Lorenzen, Christoph Menke, Bernhard Metz, Jane O. Newman, Christopher Pye, Christopher Ricks, Gianluca Solla, Barbara Ventarola, Ema Vyroubalová, Daniel Weidner, Brian Williams, Richard Wilson and my colleagues and students at Ludwig Maximilian University Munich, the Peter Szondi Institute in Berlin and the School of English at Trinity College Dublin, as well as the respondents to my presentations at the International Milton Symposia in Tokyo and Strasbourg. The research groups *Pluralization and Authority in the Early Modern Period* and *The Role of Nature in Conceptualising Political Order: Ancient – Medieval – Early Modern* at Ludwig Maximilian University were an indispensable help in my efforts to sneak across some disciplinary boundaries. I am also grateful to the German Research Foundation (DFG), the German Academic Exchange Service (DAAD), the Alexander von Humboldt Foundation and the Talma Yzraely Memorial Fund for financing my research and attendant travels. Many kinds of support were provided by my parents, Klaus and Marga Quiring. My greatest thanks go to Elizabeth M. Bonapfel for conversations, revisions and the experience of sharing a life.

Abbreviations

Paradise Lost is cited by book and line, according to Alastair Fowler's edition:

> *Paradise Lost*, edited by Alastair Fowler, London and New York: Routledge, 2013.

References to other works by John Milton employ the following standard abbreviations:

CPEP	*The Complete Poetry and Essential Prose of John Milton*, edited by William Kerrigan, John Rumrich and Stephen M. Fallon, New York: Modern Library, 2007.
CPW	*Complete Prose Works*, edited by Don M. Wolfe, et al., New Haven: Yale University Press, 1953–1982.
CW	*The Complete Works*, edited by Thomas N. Corns and Gordon Campbell, Oxford: Oxford University Press, 2008 ff.
DC	*De Doctrina Christiana*, in *The Complete Works*, Vol. 8, edited by John K. Hale, J. Donald Cullington, Thomas N. Corns and Gordon Campbell, Oxford: Oxford University Press, 2012.

Spelling has been modernized.

References to the Bible generally follow the King James Version which Milton owned and used. The particular edition cited in this volume is:

> *The Bible: Authorized King James Version with Apocrypha*, edited by Robert Carroll and Stephen Prickett, Oxford: Oxford University Press, 1997.

Introduction: the divine contradiction

In the eleventh book of *Paradise Lost*, the reader is confronted with a strange passage: Adam and Eve have eaten the fruit of the Tree of Knowledge, and God has consequently condemned them to death, lifelong misery and exile from Eden. Contrite, the human couple prays and begs for forgiveness. But when the Son asks God the Father to be merciful toward them and let them stay in Paradise, the Father denies the favour with the words:

> But longer in that Paradise to dwell,
> The law I gave to Nature him forbids:
> Those pure immortal elements that know
> No gross, no unharmonious mixture foul,
> Eject him tainted now, and purge him off
> As a distemper, gross to air as gross,
> And mortal food, as may dispose him best
> For dissolution wrought by sin, that first
> Distempered all things, and of incorrupt
> Corrupted.
> (11.48–57; capitalization added)[1]

With these words, God the Father disclaims responsibility for man's expulsion from Paradise and instead points to the law of Nature whose enforcement seems to restrict him in his decisions. Any appeal against the divine decree is blocked by a nature functioning by rules that seem to be independent of God's will – either because he cannot change them or because he could but

1 Researching the uses of "nature" in *Paradise Lost*, one must deal with the attendant problem of Milton's use of minuscules and majuscules. In the 69 occurrences of "nature" and its derivatives within the epic, Milton, or, more specifically, his scribes, do not use lower and upper case consistently. In the two original editions, which were supervised by Milton himself, the capitalization of "nature" is irregular. The general tendency of editions with modernized spelling is to write "nature" in lower case, except when it clearly designates an allegorical or divine figure. However, it is often impossible to tell whether Milton refers to an allegory, to an abstract entity, to a goddess or to an actual, encompassing being; every clarification entails an interpretation. I will generally follow the edition of Alastair Fowler, but will also modify it, frequently in order to emphasize the role of Nature as a volatile allegorical deity.

will not, perhaps because he feels bound by his own legislation, just like a terrestrial constitutional sovereign would.[2] Furthermore, he claims that paradisiacal nature itself enacts this law automatically: neither God nor angel drive Adam and Eve out of Eden; it is the garden itself, whose pure elements cannot support man's new-found impurity which threatens to contaminate it. Paradise thus instigates an autoimmune reaction that God cannot or will not modify. This statement is peculiar for several reasons. First, Milton's God is normally represented as omnipotent: an entity not bound by the laws of his creation and able to suspend them, for example by way of miracles. In the seventh book, God himself boasts: "[N]ecessity and chance/ Approach not me, and what I will is Fate" (7.172–173). Second, the divine remark is mysterious since it is contrafactual and incongruent with God's own behaviour. The nature of Paradise does not actually expel postlapsarian humankind, for if it did, there would be no need for God to send out Michael with his troop in order to dislodge Adam and Eve. There is indeed no sign whatsoever that the garden's natural purity grows incompatible with the impurity of fallen man. On the contrary, the epic describes how man's fall triggers the decay of Eden: after God has sent his angels to spread "influence malignant" (10.662) throughout the cosmos, conflict and corruption enter Paradise; the harmony between the animals is destroyed, and they begin to chase and devour each other. And when the angelic troops finally arrive in Eden, they come with the Sword of God whose intense heat makes the garden wilt and wither:

> The brandished sword of God before them blazed
> Fierce as a comet; which with torrid heat,
> And vapour as the Libyan air adust,
> Began to parch that temperate clime […].
> (12.633–636)

Even after the expulsion, the purge will continue: the archangel Michael announces to Adam that the garden will be destroyed by the Flood

> To teach thee that God attributes to place
> No sanctity, if none be thither brought
> By men who there frequent, or therein dwell.
> (11.836–838)

2 In Milton's other works, it is sometimes asserted, sometimes denied that God restricts himself by his own laws. In the *Doctrine and Discipline of Divorce*, Milton states that God "binds himself like a just lawgiver to his own prescriptions, gives himself to be understood by men, judges and is judged, measures and is commensurate to right reason" (*CPW* 2.292, spelling modernized). However, in *Samson Agonistes*, the chorus disparages those who "would confine th'interminable,/ And tie him to his own prescript,/ Who made our laws to bind us, not himself,/ And hath full right to exempt/ Whom so it pleases him by choice/ From national obstriction, without taint/ Of sin, or legal debt;/ For with his own laws he can best dispense." (*Samson Agonistes* 307–314, *CPEP*, pp. 719–720).

The supposed purity of the Edenic elements seems to be forgotten at this point. Adam does not protest, but the contradictions are blatant; and they all seem to have a common denominator: on the one hand, the law that nature enacts seems to be an iron necessity that invariably asserts itself in all circumstances. On the other hand, it seems to be a positive, variable law that must be instituted and enforced by an executive God and is subject to changes in divine politics. Since the contradiction is never resolved, the impression arises that God might seek excuses for his denial of mercy in factual constraints and – insofar as he is the One True God – can find none. Either the Father cannot oppose the forces of nature, then he is not the omnipotent God he claims to be; or he can do so, but does not want to, and in this case his attempts to justify his unforgiving position by natural restraint appear as disingenuous apologetics. The epic, however, never decides to promote one version over the other; rather, it causes the two to entwine, but never to merge, suggesting that there is an underlying, latent unity to both juridico-theological notions. Since this unity remains inaccessible to them, Adam, Eve and the reader must resign themselves to be judged according to an inconceivable, "double-formed" law, which they are supposed to know, but from which they are also kept apart. As William Empson has first pointed out, Milton, in this and other respects, should be considered as a precursor to Kafka: the position of Adam and Eve bears some striking resemblances to that of Josef K. and other protagonists of Kafka's works.[3]

The following study proposes that this double law is not just a flaw in the divine self-presentation of *Paradise Lost*, but rather a fundamental theological and political asset whose usefulness dominates this particular epic. The legislative discrepancies are symptomatic of a necessary ambivalence in the relation between divine law and natural law that becomes particularly poignant in the early modern era. Milton's epic relies on an overdetermined notion of nature, which, on the one hand, assumes that the processes and trials of nature are instigated and completely controlled by God, but on the other hand presupposes that they unfold in ways that are to a certain extent independent of his will. The conflicts in *Paradise Lost* revolve around the tension between a cosmic legal procedure inherent in nature and the positive legal decrees of the divinity.[4] It will become apparent that they are to be considered as two expressions of God's sovereignty which are incompatible, but nevertheless complement each other. The double law of the cosmos is only tenable when God does double duty; the Father must take the role both of the limitless, omnipotent entity of Christian theology and of a rather pagan divinity whose claim to superiority is mainly based on his superior fire power and who closely

3 William Empson, *Milton's God*, Westport, CT: Greenwood Press, 1978, pp. 13, 146.

4 A similar argument in Althusserian terminology is made in Eric Dunnum, "The Bipartite System of Laws in *Paradise Lost*", *Rocky Mountain Review* 64:2 (2010), pp. 151–169.

resembles both Zeus/Jupiter and the Hobbesian Leviathan. The double face of divine jurisdiction unifies his two bodies,[5] and as a result, law enforcement must be an essential component of God's identity. Consequently, it turns out to structure the whole of his creation: *Paradise Lost* depicts a cosmos that is also a legal system, constructed around an inaccessible centre and pervaded by a vehement passion of judging that affects all characters. The very essence of Milton's notion of divine rule is a self-enhancing, boundlessly proliferating jurisdiction that absorbs traditional notions of Nature's primordial judgment into itself. The following pages will also demonstrate that allegoresis is the preferred method of this proliferation.

Milton's epic focuses on two breaches of divine law, the one causing the Fall of the rebel angels and the other the Fall of mankind. Remarkably, his treatment of these two transgressions and the attendant condemnations also opens the question of the law's legitimacy: Milton's declared goal is to write a theodicy, justifying the ways of God to men (1.26). The narrator thus takes the position of God's lawyer.[6] John Stachniewski states that this endeavour to defend God on the issue of original sin was rather unprecedented:

> No one, I think, much before Milton had spoken of justifying God. The idea arose when it did because of the aggressive insistence of Calvinists, aimed at countering protest at the doctrine of predestined reprobation, that God should not be brought to the bar of human justice. [...] Milton at once announces his rejection of the Calvinist position that God's justice cannot be measured by human understanding [...].[7]

Stachniewski's assumption must be regarded as inaccurate, since God's justice had already been questioned and justified in late antiquity.[8] Furthermore, the very form of the epic enforces this questioning: even though "considerations of representability haunt the poem",[9] Milton's God remains deeply anthropomorphic, a God who is enveloped in the flow of narrative, like any other character. And if it is the goal of the epic to justify his ways, they must be justified by the same criteria as those that would apply to any other epic protagonist. He automatically stands in judgment, as William Empson asserts:

5 Concerning this concept, see, first and foremost, Ernst H. Kantorowicz, *The King's Two Bodies: A Study in Mediaeval Political Theology*, Princeton: Princeton University Press, 1997.

6 According to Harold Skulsky, *Paradise Lost* itself assumes the form of an attorney's plea in an open court. Harold Skulsky, *Milton and the Death of Man, Humanism on Trial in* Paradise Lost, Newark and London: University of Delaware Press, 2000.

7 John Stachniewski, *The Persecutory Imagination: English Puritanism and the Literature of Religious Despair*, Oxford: Oxford University Press, 1991, p. 333.

8 See e.g. René van Woudenberg, "A Brief History of Theodicy", in: *The Blackwell Companion to the Problem of Evil*, ed. Justin P. McBrayer and Daniel Howard-Snyder, Chichester: Wiley-Blackwell, 2013, pp. 177–191.

9 Christopher Kendrick, *Milton: A Study in Ideology and Form*, New York and London: Methuen, 1986, p. 122.

> If God is to be shown acting in a story, we have something better to do than take his status for granted. The fundamental purpose of putting elaborate detail into a story is to enable us to use our judgement about the characters; often both their situation and their moral convictions [...] are very unlike our own, but we use the detail to imagine how they feel when they act as they do [...]. Understanding that other people are different is one of the bases of civilization, and this use for a story is as much a culture-conquest as the idea of God. Milton, therefore could not have made God automatically good in the epic; God is on trial [in *Paradise Lost*] [...]; and the reason is that all the characters are on trial in any civilized narrative.[10]

The harmonization of Milton's brand of theology with the form of the epic thus demands that God assume a double role, both as the eternal judge and as the eternal defendant.

However, Stachniewski is not altogether wrong, insofar as it was indeed the general tendency of seventeenth-century theology, Catholic as well as Protestant, to assert that God was unaccountable by any humanly intelligible conception of law. Martin Luther did so, for example, referring to the postlapsarian corruption of nature as the reason for this divine immunity:

> Solche Erbsünde ist eine so ganz tiefe, böse Verderbnis der Natur, daß sie keine Vernunft kennt, sondern sie aufgrund der Offenbarung der Schrift geglaubt werden muß [...].[11]
>
> This original sin has caused such a deep, evil corruption of nature that reason does not comprehend it; rather, it must be believed on the basis of revelation from the Scriptures [...].[12]

On this issue, the Protestant patriarchs echoed both Augustine[13] and, most importantly, a passage in the very birth document of Christianity, namely Paul's letter to the Romans:

> τῷ Μωϋσεῖ γὰρ λέγει Ἐλεήσω ὃν ἂν ἐλεῶ, καὶ οἰκτιρήσω ὃν ἂν οἰκτίρω. ἄρα οὖν οὐ τοῦ θέλοντος οὐδὲ τοῦ τρέχοντος, ἀλλὰ τοῦ ἐλεῶντος Θεοῦ. λέγει γὰρ ἡ γραφὴ τῷ Φαραὼ ὅτι Εἰς αὐτὸ τοῦτο ἐξήγειρά σε, ὅπως ἐνδείξωμαι ἐν σοὶ τὴν δύναμίν μου, καὶ ὅπως διαγγελῇ τὸ ὄνομά μου ἐν πάσῃ τῇ γῇ. ἄρα

10 Empson, *Milton's God*, p. 94.

11 Martin Luther, "Die Schmalkaldischen Artikel", in *Luther Deutsch: Die Werke Martin Luthers in neuer Auswahl für die Gegenwart*, Vol. 3: *Der neue Glaube*, ed. Kurt Aland, Göttingen: Vandenhoeck and Ruprecht, 1983, p. 350.

12 Martin Luther, *The Schmalkald Articles*, trans. William R. Russell, Minneapolis: Fortress, 1995, p. 16. See also e.g. Martin Luther, *The Bondage of the Will*, trans. J. I. Packer and A. R. Johnston, Old Tappan, NJ: Revell, 1957, pp. 97–99.

13 Augustine, "De diversis quaestionibus ad Simplicianum I 2", in *Logik des Schreckens: die Gnadenlehre von 397*, trans. and ed. Kurt Flasch, Mainz: Dieterich, 1990, pp. 148–239.

> οὖν ὃν θέλει ἐλεεῖ, ὃν δὲ θέλει σκληρύνει. Ἐρεῖς μοι οὖν Τί ἔτι μέμφεται; τῷ γὰρ βουλήματι αὐτοῦ τίς ἀνθέστηκεν; ὦ ἄνθρωπε, μενοῦνγε σὺ τίς εἶ ὁ ἀνταποκρινόμενος τῷ Θεῷ; μὴ ἐρεῖ τὸ πλάσμα τῷ πλάσαντι Τί με ἐποίησας οὕτως; ἢ οὐκ ἔχει ἐξουσίαν ὁ κεραμεὺς τοῦ πηλοῦ ἐκ τοῦ αὐτοῦ φυράματος ποιῆσαι ὃ μὲν εἰς τιμὴν σκεῦος, ὃ δὲ εἰς ἀτιμίαν [...].
>
> For he saith to Moses, I will have mercy on whom I will have mercy, and I will have compassion on whom I will have compassion. So then it is not of him that willeth, nor of him that runneth, but of God that sheweth mercy. For the scripture saith unto Pharaoh, Even for this same purpose have I raised thee up, that I might shew my power in thee, and that my name might be declared throughout all the earth. Therefore hath he mercy on whom he will have mercy, and whom he will he hardeneth. Thou wilt say then unto me, Why doth he yet find fault? For who hath resisted his will? Nay but, O man, who art thou that repliest against God? Shall the thing formed say to him that formed it, Why hast thou made me thus? Hath not the potter power over the clay, of the same lump to make one vessel unto honour, and another unto dishonour?
>
> (Romans 9.15–21)

Although he often vacillates on this question, Milton repeatedly states that he does consider God eligible for judgment. In his great theological Summa, *De Doctrina Christiana*,[14] for example, Milton states that the divine condemnation of man for original sin would be unjust, if God had not bestowed a free will on him:

> [A]t si per decretum Dei non potuit non labi [...] profecto iam non ad gratiam, sed ad iustitiam Dei pertinuit necessario lapsu lapsum restituere.
>
> But if through God's decree he did not have the power not to fall [...], then assuredly it was not the concern of God's grace but of his justice to restore one who fell by a necessary fall.
>
> (*DC* 76/77)

14 The *Doctrina Christiana* has a special status, insofar as Milton's authorship is still questioned by a minority of scholars. But a group of researchers has made a book-length case for Milton's authorship which is hard to find unconvincing, since it not only painstakingly reconstructs the manuscript's provenance but also uses stylometry and diverse other methods in order to demonstrate the compatibility of both its form and content with Milton's other works. (See Gordon Campbell, Thomas N. Corns, John K. Hale and Fiona J. Tweedie, *Milton and the Manuscript of* De Doctrina Christiana, Oxford: Oxford University Press, 2007.) This is not to say that one can map the theology of the *Doctrina* straight onto *Paradise Lost*. For one, it has been demonstrated that Milton inserted deliberate ambiguities into *Paradise Lost* in order to make his heretical philosophical and theological positions more palatable to his readers without altogether denying them. (See e.g. Phillip J. Donnelly, "'Matter' versus 'Body': The Character of Milton's Monism", *Milton Quarterly* 33:3 (1999), p. 81.) And it will be demonstrated that the demands of the epic form occasionally impinge on Milton's representation of his doxa. Thus, while it is certainly legitimate to use the *Doctrina Christiana* in order to gain a better understanding of Milton's theological convictions, one must not assume that *Paradise Lost* is altogether bound by it.

Generally, Milton seeks to exonerate the deity and to harmonize his actions with human notions of justice, and the introduction of free will seems to accomplish this goal. However, the success of Milton's justification project has frequently been doubted: many of Milton's most astute readers have found his way of justifying the ways of God unconvincing even by his own standards.[15] It bears emphasizing that these doubts did not begin in the nineteenth century, with William Blake and Percy B. Shelley, but have been voiced from the beginning of the epic's reception history.[16] The goal of this study is not to swell the ranks of the jury members who feel entitled to condemn the behaviour of the Almighty, but rather to put forward a supplementary thesis: regardless of how the divine jurisdiction is evaluated, an epic that puts God on trial will tend to expose a quandary which has always been latent in Christianity. The Christian God's sovereign rule and judicial function have always been unable to rid themselves from the workings of a shadow government whose monarch has been given various names, among which "Nature" is certainly one of the most prominent. In the following pages, it will be demonstrated that the representation of nature's legal dominion touches upon a central problem that has affected literary, philosophical, theological and juridical discourses since antiquity – a problem on the border of ethics and epistemology that finds one of its most poignant elaborations and provisional solutions in *Paradise Lost*.

While this study owes some other obvious debts to William Empson, his concept of ambiguity will prove particularly useful in the subsequent pages. "Nature" is more than a word with many meanings: between these meanings, relationships establish themselves, complex dynamisms in a semantic forcefield. Empson speaks of the "body" of a word in this context.[17] In *Paradise Lost*, these "aggregates of thought"[18] frequently display some inherent contradictions: consistent logical inconsistencies that appear again and again in various guises. Empson classifies most of them as symptoms of an ambivalence both in the author's mind and in the discursive order that

15 See e.g. Empson, *Milton's God*; A. J. A. Waldock, Paradise Lost *and Its Critics*, Cambridge: Cambridge University Press, 1966; and J. B. Savage, "Freedom and Necessity in *Paradise Lost*", *ELH* 44:2 (1977), p. 291.

16 For example, shortly after its first publication in 1667, the clergyman John Beale called *Paradise Lost* "too full of the devil". (John Beale, *Letter 63* (August 31, 1667), British Library Add. MS 78312, quoted in: William Poole, "The Early Reception of *Paradise Lost*", in: *Literature Compass* 1.1 (2004), p. 7.) In his book *The History of Sin and Heresy* (1698), Charles Leslie criticizes Milton's epic as a "licentious fancy [by which] the truth has been greatly hurt". (Charles Leslie, *The History of Sin and Heresie*, London: Hindmarsh, 1698, quoted in: *John Milton: The Critical Heritage, Vol. 1: 1628-1731*, ed. John T. Shawcross, London: Routledge, 1970, p. 117.) See also C. Q. Drummond, *In Defence of Adam: Essays on Bunyan, Milton and Others*, eds. John Baxter and Gordon Harvey, Norfolk: Brynmill Press/Edgeway, 2004, p. 66.

17 William Empson, *Seven Types of Ambiguity*, New York: New Directions, 1947, p. 5.

18 Empson, *Seven Types of Ambiguity*, p. 68.

dominates the society to which he belongs.[19] An analysis of the complexities and ambiguities of the word "nature" will enable further inquiries into this internal conflict.

When one starts to investigate the semantics of "nature", one must soon acknowledge that one moves on uncertain ground. The teeming obscurities of the term are notorious: David Hume writes that no word is "more ambiguous and equivocal".[20] Friedrich Nicolai states: "The word 'nature' is a real wild card."[21] And Raymond Williams calls "nature" "the perhaps most complex word in the language".[22] Nature seems almost to be defined by the inability of semantics to circumscribe it. To avoid the somewhat fruitless listing of its diverse meanings (Arthur Lovejoy enumerates no less than 19 senses of the word in the field of poetics and normative aesthetics alone),[23] the first step will be to examine to what extent etymology and conceptual history can help to clear this undergrowth.

"Nature" derives from the Latin "nasci", signifying "to be born", "to be generated": "natura" is that which is born.[24] To be grammatically more precise: it is that which is about to be born or generated; the word thus always involves a future perspective. "Natura" originally was introduced into the Latin language as the translation of the Greek term "physis" (φύσις), which derives from "φύειν", a verb that can signify "to develop", "to appear", "to grow" or "to procreate".[25] Roughly speaking, there are five main meanings that the word has accumulated in the course of antiquity and which are still fundamental:

1) the generation, growth and decay of things; the motion of their appearance, persistence and disappearance;
2) the inherent cause of this continual generation and dissolution, the force at the origin of all things' movements;
3) inversely, the goal that is inherent in each thing's motion: that toward which it tends;
4) the undiluted essence of each thing;
5) the entirety of all things and forces.

19 Empson, *Milton's God,* p. 115.

20 David Hume, *A Treatise on Human Nature*, Vol. 1, ed. David Fate Norton, Oxford: Clarendon Press, 2007, p. 304.

21 "Das Wort 'Natur' ist ein wahrer Scherwenzel." Friedrich Nicolai, *Leben und literarischer Nachlass*, ed. Leopold von Göckingk, Berlin: Nicolaische Buchhandlung, 1820, p. 136.

22 Raymond Williams, "Nature", in *Keywords: A Vocabulary of Culture and Society*, Oxford and New York: Oxford University Press, 1983, p. 219.

23 Arthur O. Lovejoy, "'Nature' as Aesthetic Norm", *Modern Language Notes* 42:7 (1927), pp. 444–450.

24 C. S. Lewis, *Studies in Words*, Cambridge: Cambridge University Press, 1967, p. 25.

25 Lewis, *Studies in Words*, p. 34.

The meanings blend into each other, so that nature appears both as the subject and the object of a universal *poiesis*: it is not only that which appears and again recedes, but also the invisible source of these temporary appearances and the ungraspable *telos* toward which they tend.[26]

Around this semantic conglomerate, other meanings have subsequently accumulated. It stands to reason that nature, according to its manifold senses, also has numerous antonyms, such as culture, art, technology, law, chaos, the human and the partial. However, none of these terms qualifies as an unqualified antonym, since they all can also be ascertained as parts of nature, due to be reabsorbed by it in one way or another. Since nature, according to the fifth of the listed meanings, encompasses absolutely everything, the word can have no proper antonym. In the concise formulation of Schelling: "If we want to talk about nature in absolute terms, we have to understand it as the universe without an opposite."[27] That is also why any supposed conflict between natural and supernatural forces tends to end up in their collaboration. The term thus furnishes all it touches with a certain *sfumato* quality; it seems designed to blur distinctions and generate vagueness rather than differentiate one thing from another. Accordingly, there have always been efforts to either determine the word's real, unequivocal meaning or to get rid of it altogether.[28] But the term is nevertheless still going strong in everyday language, in the culture industries, in philosophy, in politics, in literature, and even occasionally in the "natural sciences" (where it is, however, comparatively neglected). As Lorraine Daston and Fernando Vidal put it: "No amount of well-intentioned intellectual and political hygiene is likely to get rid of nature."[29] But why exactly has the term not faded away, after being severely questioned, criticized and deconstructed again and again over the course of several centuries? Why have all these assaults apparently caused no more than slight irritations concerning the use of "nature"? Perhaps because a place where all distinctions become blurry is "bon à penser", good to think

26 Lewis, *Studies in Words*, pp. 33–42. See also Pierre Hadot, *The Veil of Isis: An Essay on the History of the Idea of Nature*, trans. Michael Chase, Cambridge, MA: Belknap Press of Harvard University Press, 2006, pp. 17–26.

27 "Wenn wir von der Natur absolut reden wollen, so verstehen wir darunter das Universum ohne Gegensatz." Friedrich Wilhelm Joseph Schelling, *Vorlesungen über die Methode des akademischen Studiums*, ed. Walter E. Ehrhardt, Hamburg: Meiner, 1974, p. 111. Translation BQ.

28 One of the best-known and most elaborate attempts can be found in Robert Boyle, *A Free Enquiry into the Vulgarly Received Notion of Nature,* eds. Edward B. Davis and Michael Hunter, Cambridge: Cambridge University Press, 1996. Recently, Bruno Latour (who, like Boyle, seems to be motivated by religious considerations) has followed in his footsteps. See Bruno Latour, *Politics of Nature: How to Bring the Sciences into Democracy*, trans. Catherine Porter, Cambridge, MA: Harvard University Press, 2004.

29 Lorraine Daston and Fernando Vidal, "Doing What Comes Naturally", in *The Moral Authority of Nature*, eds. Lorraine Daston and Fernando Vidal, Chicago and London: University of Chicago Press, 2004, p. 12.

with,[30] or rather, "bon à ne pas penser", good to stop thinking: it figures as a supposed point of convergence and unity where thought seems to find rest. However, it is a very specific resting place to which appertains a precipitant, harmonizing gesture of reassurance. One can focus nature's many meanings provisionally by assembling them around this purported reconciliation of a central contradiction: nature is both part and whole, an equation between distinction and indistinction.[31] Positioned at the border between facticity and normativity, the expression designates the essential dynamism inherent in each single thing, but also the all-encompassing (and hence imperceptible) developmental order of all things. The normative supposition that inheres in the common term is a supposed compatibility: some form of harmony must exist between the natural tendency of each palpable thing and the impalpable whole of all things. Nature connects the things themselves to the universe of forces that generate, sustain and destroy them, or as the Neoplatonist Proclus expressed it: "Nature gives the lead to the whole cosmos [...], everywhere securing links between partial entities and wholes."[32] Every single separate thing relates to a whole and expresses a facet of it; and this holism indeed seems to be the central epistemic wager of the term "nature".

If every particular object has the potential to stand in for Nature as the Whole, this representation must involve a form of metaphorical relation, a synechdochal ur-metaphor, one might say. And the poets, prophets and philosophers of nature have generally tended to privilege a particular object or concept, or a limited number of them, to stand in for the whole. As a result, all of nature has been ascribed the characteristics of these objects and concepts. As E. D. Hirsch puts it, "nature is [...] the whole of reality viewed as having a particular sort of structure and value".[33] And many specific things have ended up impersonating the whole. For example, nature has been metaphorized as a tree,[34]

30 Appropriating an expression in Claude Lévi-Strauss, *Le Totémisme aujourd'hui,* Paris: Presses universitaires de France, 1965, p. 128.

31 A similar argument is developed in Niklas Luhmann, "Über Natur", in *Gesellschaftsstruktur und Semantik: Studien zur Wissenssoziologie der modernen Gesellschaft*, Vol. 4, Frankfurt am Main: Suhrkamp, 1995, p. 10.

32 Proclus, *Commentary on Plato's* Timaeus, Vol. 1, trans. Harold Tarrant, Cambridge: Cambridge University Press, 2006, p. 105 [1.11]. "[...] πανταχοῦ δὲ τὰ μερικὰ συνυφαίνουσα τοῖς ὅλοις." Proclus, *In Platonis Timaeum Commentaria*, Vol. 1, ed. Ernst Diehl, Leipzig: Teubner, 1903, p. 11.

33 Eric Donald Hirsch, *Wordsworth and Schelling: A Typological Study of Romanticism*, New Haven: Yale University Press, 1960, p. 53. In the last few centuries, the term "nature" has therefore been closely related to the poetological term "symbol" as well as to the process by which symbols are generated and which has often been characterized as "*naturwüchsig*", i.e. "naturally developing". On symbols and their "Naturwüchsigkeit", see e.g. Gerhard Kurz, *Metapher, Allegorie, Symbol*, Göttingen: Vandenhoeck and Ruprecht, 2009, pp. 70–89.

34 See e.g. Howard E. Gruber, "Darwin's 'Tree of Nature' and Other Images of Wide Scope", in *Creativity, Psychology and the History of Science*, eds. Howard E. Gruber and Katja Bödeker, Boston Studies in the Philosophy of Science, Dordrecht: Springer, 2005, pp. 241–258. See also

a person,[35] a book,[36] a social community,[37] a battlefield,[38] a marketplace,[39] clockwork,[40] a steam engine,[41] a computer,[42] and so on. More precisely, it has been metaphorized as the processes that define these objects (such as growth, creation, communication, production, recognition, combat, trade, information processing, etc.). The focus of the following pages is one of these metaphors, namely the identification of nature with a law court and the associated process of judgment. When the all-encompassing development of nature is equated with a juridical trial, the result, however, is an apparent absurdity: since nature is absolutely everything, there is no outside of this law court; hence the actual objects of its juridical procedures – an outside world to which the law of nature could refer and in which it could actually be transgressed and enforced – seem to disappear. By constituting itself, this law court also constitutes everything that is subject to its procedures. Therefore, the judgment of nature must bend back upon itself. However, that self-suppression is one of the most interesting aspects of this peculiar metaphor: according to Hans Blumenberg's dictum, "metaphorical dissonances are metaphorological entry points".[43] The inconsistencies will allow us to grasp the function of this metaphor more precisely.

In order to do so, the tendency to identify nature with a normative order that autonomously enforces itself will be investigated in Milton's influential synthesis of diverse religious, literary and philosophical traditions. But before the study starts to concentrate on the specificity of *Paradise Lost* as a cultural item, an erratic, necessarily cursory walk through the history of the concept of "nature" and its status as a process of legal judgment will be useful, for it will show the very diverse layers of commonplaces that were at Milton's disposal. The history

Gilles Deleuze and Félix Guattari, *A Thousand Plateaus*, trans. Brian Massumi, Minneapolis and London: University of Minnesota Press, 2005, pp. 3–25.

35 See e.g. Hadot, *The Veil of Isis.* See also Wolfgang Kemp, *Natura: Ikonographische Studien zur Geschichte und Verbreitung einer Allegorie*, Dissertation, Tübingen 1973.

36 See e.g. Erich Rothacker, *Das Buch der Natur: Materialien und Grundsätzliches zur Metapherngeschichte,* ed. Wilhelm Perpeet, Bonn: Bouvier, 1979. See also Hans Blumenberg, *Die Lesbarkeit der Welt*, Frankfurt am Main: Suhrkamp, 1986.

37 See e.g. Alfred North Whitehead, *Process and Reality: An Essay in Cosmology: Gifford Lectures Delivered in the University of Edinburgh During the Season 1927–28*, eds. David Ray Griffin and Donald W. Sherburne, New York: Free Press, 1985.

38 See e.g. Herbert Spencer, *Social Statics*, in *Nineteenth-Century Science: A Selection of Original Texts*, ed. Alan S. Weber, Peterborough, ON and Orchard Park, NY: Broadview Press, 2000, pp. 192–201.

39 See e.g. Jean-Christophe Agnew, *Worlds Apart: The Market and the Theater in Anglo-American Thought*, Cambridge: Cambridge University Press, 1986.

40 See e.g. Boyle, *A Free Enquiry into the Vulgarly Received Notion of Nature*.

41 See e.g. M. Norton Wise and Crosbie Smith, "Work and Waste: Political Economy and Natural Philosophy in Nineteenth Century Britain (3)", *History of Science* 28:3 (1990): pp. 221–261.

42 See e.g. Norman Margolus, "Looking at Nature as a Computer", *International Journal of Theoretical Physics* 42:2 (2003): pp. 309–327.

43 "Metaphorische Unstimmigkeiten sind metaphorologische Einstiege." Hans Blumenberg, *Die Lesbarkeit der Welt*, p. 221. Translation BQ.

of nature's legislation is a very long one and involves much more than legal and literary history in the narrow sense: in an enormous variety of texts, from the Greek beginnings of Western philosophy onward, nature has been described as a court room in which an all-encompassing trial takes place and a universal judgment is executed. Even in works that reject any notion of transcendence and of a Last Judgment, nature often figures as an omnipotent sovereign, an institution that punishes what is dangerous for the integrity of its constitution, and rewards those that comply with it. Natural processes generate everything and by this very act determine the rules that everything must follow. In this context, nature frequently appears not only as a courthouse, but also as its legislator, its law enforcement agency and its legal code, as execution grounds and as instrument of punishment, as witness, judge, jury, police, executrix and defendant. Nature is the groundwork of reality, and therefore the judgment of nature encompasses or overrules all other acts of jurisdiction. The natural process of legislation does not need legitimation by any of its legal subjects, since it has produced them in the first place; rather, it tends to legitimize itself by referring to its official, yet ever-elusive, goal, which is, according to most discourses, justice.[44]

While the origins of the metaphor of nature's law court are hard to determine, some interesting anthropological speculations have been made in this context, which offer an alternative to the common tendency to imagine that a primordial social contract stands at the origin of the legal order. In his book *Arbeit am Mythos* (translated as *Work on Myth*),[45] Hans Blumenberg has introduced a tentative "limit-concept"[46] that might prove useful for our purposes. According to him, at the very beginning of history, human beings were exposed to an environment whose conditions they could not control and of which they could not make sense. Deprived of animal instincts, they were reduced to an altogether powerless and extremely vulnerable position in which they had to accept all outside impositions without any option to negotiate or defend themselves. Blumenberg designates this situation as an "absolutism of reality" ("Absolutismus der Wirklichkeit");[47] on one occasion, he also uses the term "state of nature" ("Naturzustand").[48] But perhaps "totalitarianism of reality/nature" would be a more appropriate term, since Blumenberg describes not so much an autocratic tyranny of arbitrary natural forces, but rather a pervasive, inscrutable and overwhelming reign of diffuse terror that dominates every aspect of life and makes it impossible for its subordinates to assert themselves or even to develop any form of individuality.[49] The first

44 Panu Minkinnen, *Thinking without Desire: A First Philosophy of Law*, Oxford: Hart Publishing, 1999, pp. 113 ff.

45 See Hans Blumenberg, *Arbeit am Mythos,* Frankfurt am Main: Suhrkamp, 2006; Hans Blumenberg, *Work on Myth*, trans. Robert M. Wallace, Cambridge, MA: MIT Press, 1990.

46 Blumenberg, *Work on Myth*, p. 4.

47 See Blumenberg, *Arbeit am Mythos*, pp. 10 ff.; and *Work on Myth*, pp. 4 ff.

48 Blumenberg, *Arbeit am Mythos*, p. 9; and *Work on Myth*, p. 3.

49 Concerning the difference between absolutism and totalitarianism, see e.g. Hannah Arendt, *The Origins of Totalitarianism*, San Diego and New York: Harcourt, 1985, p. 389 et passim.

act of "resistance" against this reign is indeed an attempt to turn total domination into absolutist rule: the disenfranchised human beings try to identify a supremely terrifying entity in which all their terrors are encapsulated and thus to turn an all-pervasive angst into the fear of something or somebody specific.

> Das geschieht primär nicht durch Erfahrung und Erkenntnis, sondern durch Kunstgriffe, wie den der Supposition des Vertrauten für das Unvertraute, der Erklärungen für das Unerklärliche, der Benennungen für das Unnennnbare.[50]
>
> This occurs primarily not through experience and knowledge, but rather through devices such as the substitution of the familiar for the unfamiliar, of explanations for the inexplicable, of names for the unnameable.[51]

The overwhelming terror of the real is mitigated when one is at least able to name and address it, either as a thing, or as a person, or as an organized group or institution. Blumenberg calls this ability to be addressed "appellation capacity" ("Appellationsfähigkeit").[52] To this invocable Other, specific properties and regular behaviours can be ascribed that allow for a certain degree of reliability: if lightning strikes an object, this event may no longer be seen as a terrifying manifestation of an inscrutable power, but as the articulation of a rule or regularity – which is still inscrutable, but might be figured out if one manages to correctly extrapolate its causes from its effects. This is the foundation on which the complex constructions of myth will be raised. Blumenberg's speculation might be extrapolated further: could not the mythical institutions that are imputed to cause change in the world be the primordial law courts of mankind? (Giambattista Vico has already presented a similar speculation.)[53] The creation of actual legal institutions such as law courts with their judges, defendants, and so on, would thus have to be accounted for not as specifically human inventions, but rather as attempts to mimic the mysterious executions imposed from beyond. According to this notion, it is neither the acknowledgement of the world's injustices and the need for their containment and redemption that lie at the origin of jurisdiction, nor the Will to Power of privileged individuals who are able to impose their desires on the community by way of legislation. (Bleak though the latter account may sound, it still would confine the oppressive power of the law within the limits of individual malignancy.) Rather, the human practice of law in its original form would have to be regarded as an act of ritual and mythical representation, imitating and adapting a presumed primordial, natural jurisdiction that is thought to be

50 Blumenberg, *Arbeit am Mythos*, p. 11.
51 Blumenberg, *Work on Myth*, p. 5.
52 Blumenberg, *Arbeit am Mythos,* p. 22.
53 Giambattista Vico, *The New Science*, trans. Thomas Bergin and Max Fish, Ithaca, NY and London: Cornell University Press, 1984, pp. 352–353 [4.10.1].

both mysterious and absolutely limitless in its potential.[54] Legislators and judges would have the priestly task to contain this potential and channel it in appropriate ways. A community's willingness to judge and be judged would thus be dependent on the goal of attaining a sense of familiarity with the "totalitarianism of reality". It stands to reason that the attainment of this sense would entail the overcoming of a fundamental anxiety, and therefore an affect of relief and satisfaction – a libidinal discharge inherent to the juridical process and contributing to its perpetuation.[55]

Of course, quasi-mythical speculations such as these do not meet the standards of scientific enquiry. They concern periods lost in time, and they are necessarily simplistic: the contributing factors to a legal system are too numerous and too heterogeneous to consider any foundational narrative as the unadulterated truth. Still, it might be worthwhile to ponder this alternative version of law's genesis narrative, if only to shake up the certainties and commonplaces that accompany the hegemony of the narratives that the legal institutions like to tell about themselves – whether they assert that law springs from a divine revelation or from an innate sense of justice, whether some primal and binding precepts are supposed to have emerged from an assembly that once came together in order to ward off diverse calamities,[56] or whether the legal system is thought to be based on a primal, collective act of aggression against an ancestor and the resultant feelings of guilt.[57] It has been pointed out that all of these stories, to a greater or lesser degree, presuppose what they pretend to explain.[58] The alternative narrative that is sketched here is no exception, but it will prove interesting insofar as it helps to elucidate some peculiarities of particular cultural products that more dominant foundation myths cannot account for. Against this background, the question deserves to be asked: to what extent were and are representations of law determined by the latent supposition of a primordial entanglement between natural and legal processes that precedes any possible transgression?

This study aims to sketch how this law court metaphor functions and how it structures *Paradise Lost*, in its interaction with juridical, theological and

54 On the ritual foundations of jurisdiction, see e.g. Gerhard Thür, "Oaths and Dispute Settlement in Ancient Law", in *Greek Law in its Political Setting*, eds. Lin Foxhall and A. D. E. Lewis, Oxford: Clarendon Press, 1996, pp. 57–72.

55 One of the few extensive studies of a libidinal investment in the legal act of judging and the form of the trial can be found in Paul Reiwald's obscure study *Die Gesellschaft und ihre Verbrecher*, Zurich: Pan, 1948. To a less extensive degree, the topic is touched upon by Émile Durkheim. See Émile Durkheim, *The Division of Labour in Society*, trans. W. D. Halls, Basingstoke and London: Macmillan, 1984, pp. 31–67.

56 Thomas Hobbes, *Leviathan*, ed. J. C. A. Gaskin, Oxford: Oxford University Press, 1998.

57 Sigmund Freud, *Totem und Tabu: Einige Übereinstimmungen im Seelenleben der Wilden und der Neurotiker*, Stuttgart: Fischer, 1991, pp. 195–196.

58 Regarding Hobbes, see, for example, Matthias Bohlender, *Die Rhetorik des Politischen. Zur Kritik der politischen Theorie*, Berlin: Akademie, 1995; and Björn Quiring, *Shakespeare's Curse: The Aporias of Ritual Exclusion in Early Modern Royal Drama*, trans. Michael Winkler

philosophical discourses. Some further preliminary remarks must be made in this context: first, it should be noted that "nature as first and last judgment" is an absolute metaphor in Blumenberg's sense, which also means: a metaphor for the absolute and therefore the imperceptible. Absolute metaphors are antecedent to concept formation and condition it:

> Ihr Gehalt bestimmt als Anhalt von Orientierungen ein Verhalten, sie gibt einer Welt Struktur, repräsentiert das nie erfahrbare, nie übersehbare Ganze der Realität. Dem historisch verstehenden Blick indizieren sie also die fundamentalen, tragenden Gewißheiten, Vermutungen, Wertungen, aus denen sich die Haltungen, Erwartungen, Tätigkeiten und Untätigkeiten, Sehnsüchte und Enttäuschungen, Interessen und Gleichgültigkeiten einer Epoche regulierten.[59]
>
> By providing a point of orientation, the content of absolute metaphors determines a particular attitude or conduct; they give structure to a world, representing the nonexperienceable, nonapprehensible totality of the real. To the historically trained eye, they therefore indicate the fundamental certainties, conjectures, and judgments in relation to which the attitudes and expectations, actions and inactions, longings and disappointments, interests and indifferences of an epoch are regulated.[60]

Blumenberg himself has pointed out that these metaphors need not even be explicitly invoked; they can operate more effectively in a state of implicit presumption.[61] In this context, it should be added that Blumenberg's use of the term "metaphor" might suggest an illicit simplification of the issue at hand, which should be avoided: it bears repeating that the trial of nature is not to be regarded as the mere projection of a preexistent, man-made jurisdiction outward into nature, as a simplistic ideology critique would tend to do. For the situation is more complicated: there is traffic in both directions. As far back as the sources go, juridical practice has never been unaffected by the assumption that it articulates a law-positing and law-preserving process that is not man-made (and that is frequently, but not necessarily, equated with the course of "justice").[62] The circumstance that discussions about the notion of "natural law" still persist in diverse contexts supports the hypothesis that the natural

and Björn Quiring, London and New York: Routledge, 2014, pp. 63–68. Regarding Freud, see Claude Lévi-Strauss, *The Elementary Structures of Kinship*, trans. James Harle Bell, John Richard von Sturmer and Rodney Needham, Boston: Beacon, 1969, pp. 491–492.

59 Hans Blumenberg, *Paradigmen zu einer Metaphorologie*, Frankfurt am Main: Suhrkamp, 1998, p. 25.

60 Hans Blumenberg, *Paradigms for a Metaphorology*, trans. Robert Savage, Ithaca, NY: Cornell University Press, 2010, p. 14.

61 Blumenberg, *Paradigmen zu einer Metaphorologie*, p. 25.

62 Concerning the difference between "law-positing" and "law-preserving", see Walter Benjamin, "Critique of Violence", trans. Edmund Jephcott, in *Selected Writings*, Vol. 1, eds. Marcus Bullock, Michael Jennings et al., Cambridge, MA: Belknap Press, 1996, pp. 238–252.

and the human court of law are dependent upon one another, even though their relationship has always been strained.

With Gilles Deleuze and Félix Guattari, who sometimes complement Blumenberg in unexpected ways, one might call this uneasy alliance between human and natural law courts a "collective assemblage of enunciation" ("agencement collectif d'énonciation"), an aggregation of heterogeneous objects, discourses and processes for the production of judgments.[63] Upon closer inspection, however, this assemblage reveals itself to be quite unstable; law turns out to be a less definite and univocal entity than one is often led to believe. It is neither a rational nor an altogether human creation. It is more presupposed than posited; it is read before it is written (from the flight of birds, if nothing else is available).[64] The order of positive law, in one form or another, depends on a trial that transcends it and that human law courts can only imitate, or at best slightly emendate. One obvious reason for this conception is to be found in the circumstance that human societies have never been absolutely autonomous: their ability to rule and to judge was and is dependent upon conditions they cannot manufacture or control, involving, on the most basic level, the weather, gravity, the presence of air to breathe, food, and so on. Somehow they have to concede this dependence in their representations of sovereign legislative and legal power; frequently, this dependence becomes itself moralized in the process. A world order is supposed that the political and legal order must not only acknowledge, but also integrate and hopefully bring to perfection.

However, it generally remains unclear and controversial what the laws of nature actually demand: legitimacies and illegitimacies are supposed to become legible in natural processes, but they can only be deciphered provisionally and exemplarily, primarily from the expiatory punishments that nature inflicts (such as an avenging thunderbolt striking and executing a notorious transgressor). Such decipherments always remain questionable, since nature can never be perceived directly, but only by way of synecdoche: this or that particular event is supposed to articulate the will of nature. Where was the punitive thunderbolt in all the years before, during which the transgressor behaved just as badly as in the hour of his demise? Is the former non-appearance of the punishment the sign of a tacit acquiescence

For some theological underpinnings of this idea, see Rémi Brague, *The Law of God: The Philosophical History of an Idea*, trans. Lydia G. Cochrane, Chicago: University of Chicago Press, 2007.

63 See esp. Gilles Deleuze and Félix Guattari, *A Thousand Plateaus*, trans. Brian Massumi, Minneapolis and London: University of Minnesota Press, 2005, pp. 7, 22, 78–90. In the original: Gilles Deleuze and Félix Guattari, *Mille Plateaux*, Paris: Éditions de Minuit, 1980, pp. 13, 33, 99–114. See also Graham Livesley, "Assemblage", in *The Deleuze Dictionary*, Revised Edition, ed. Adrian Parr, Edinburgh: Edinburgh University Press, 2005, pp. 18–19.

64 See e.g. Federico Santangelo, "Law and Divination in the Late Roman Republic", in *Law and Religion in the Roman Republic*, ed. O. Tellegen-Couperus, Leiden and Boston: Brill, 2012, pp. 31–54.

or endorsement? In most cases, the representatives of the ruling classes, for example a caste of priests, ascribe to themselves the task to select and read the signs that nature transmits and derive positive demands and laws from it. Often, rivals make themselves heard, and conflicts over interpretational sovereignty are the consequence. Logically and grammatically, the gap between fact and commandment is obviously just a matter of modalities: each and every descriptive statement can be turned into a imperative.[65] The result may be a proliferation of competing systems of natural law, a process which Ludger Schwarte has termed "hypernomia".[66] But even in places where only one self-contained and supposedly all-encompassing law code exists, the question to what degree it coincides with the true law of nature inevitably arises. Positive law has a palpably arbitrary, creative component that cannot be eradicated altogether.[67] Every time this creativity becomes obvious, the frontiers between jurisdiction and other discourses are blurred. And this is also the moment when literary forms such as tragedy and epic may join in the hypernomian rivalries: some of its most enthusiastic proponents describe literature as a better, more humane influence on and organon of jurisdiction, a supplement by which the world can be judged more accurately.[68] This claim is frequently

65 Ralf Dreier, *Zum Begriff der "Natur der Sache"*, Berlin: de Gruyter, 1965, p. 97.

66 Ludger Schwarte, *Vom Urteilen: Gesetzlosigkeit, Geschmack, Gerechtigkeit*, Berlin: Merve, 2012, p. 11.

67 See e.g. Alexandre Lefebvre, *The Image of Law: Deleuze, Bergson, Spinoza*, Stanford, CA: Stanford University Press, 2008.

68 See e.g. Friedrich Schiller: "Die Gerichtsbarkeit der Bühne fängt an, wo das Gebiet der weltlichen Gesetze sich endigt. Wenn die Gerechtigkeit für Gold verblindet, und im Solde der Laster schwelgt, wenn die Frevel der Mächtigen ihrer Ohnmacht spotten, und Menschenfurcht den Arm der Obrigkeit bindet, übernimmt die Schaubühne Schwert und Waage, und reißt die Laster vor einen schrecklichen Richterstuhl. Das ganze Reich der Phantasie und Geschichte, Vergangenheit und Zukunft stehen ihrem Wink zu Gebot. Kühne Verbrecher, die längst schon im Staub vermodern, werden durch den allmächtigen Ruf der Dichtkunst jetzt vorgeladen, und wiederholen zum schauervollen Unterricht der Nachwelt ein schändliches Leben. Ohnmächtig, gleich den Schatten in einem Hohlspiegel wandeln die Schrecken ihres Jahrhunderts vor unsern Augen vorbei, und mit wollüstigem Entsetzen verfluchen wir ihr Gedächtnis. Wenn keine Moral mehr gelehrt wird, keine Religion mehr Glauben findet, wenn kein Gesetz mehr vorhanden ist, wird uns Medea noch anschauern, wenn sie die Treppen des Palastes herunter wankt, und der Kindermord jetzt geschehen ist. Heilsame Schauer werden die Menschheit ergreifen, und in der Stille wird jeder sein gutes Gewissen preisen, wenn Lady Macbeth, eine schreckliche Nachtwandlerin, ihre Hände wäscht, und alle Wohlgerüche Arabiens herbeiruft, den häßlichen Mordgeruch zu vertilgen." (Friedrich Schiller, "Was kann eine gute stehende Schaubühne eigentlich wirken?", in *Die Entwicklung des bürgerlichen Dramas im 18. Jahrhundert: Ausgewählte Texte*, ed. Jürg Mathes, Tübingen: Niemeyer, 1974, p. 105.) "The jurisdiction of the stage begins where that of the law ends. When justice is blinded by gold and revels in the wages of sin. when the crimes of the mighty mock its impotence and human fear ties the hands of authority, the stage takes up the sword and scales and drags vice before a terrible seat of judgment. The whole realm of the imagination and of history, of past and future, is at its command. Bold criminals, who have long since moldered in the grave, are summoned by the all-powerful call of poetry to reenact their shameful lives for the instruction of a horrified posterity.

accompanied by the assertion that true poetry is the most direct articulation of nature's voice. One of the first uses of the term "nature" within poetry touches upon this idea: in Pindar's Second Olympian Ode, the singer praises his own perfections as natural, not acquired. He knows "many things by nature" ("σοφὸς ὁ πολλὰ εἰδὼς φυᾷ").[69] Over the centuries, this claim has frequently been repeated[70] and has instigated real and fictional involvements of the poet with legislation.[71] In this context, it needs to be stressed that law and literature do no only compete with each other (as scholars of law and literature frequently assume), but also cooperate and work into each others' hands, together exploring and obstructing political as well as poietic potentialities.[72] The transition area between jurisprudence and ethics is a particularly popular site of such cooperations. For example, the vague moral suggestions that one *should* already know the unknown law of nature, and that our ignorance is the symptom of a guilt-ridden unnaturalness, have been a crucial literary topic, especially under the conditions of a hegemonic Christianity. However, the topic is not exclusively Christian: Deleuze and Guattari,[73] Walter Benjamin[74] and Giorgio Agamben[75] have drawn on the work of Nietzsche[76] to develop the thesis that even secular law needs this supposition of a primordial guilt and of the mythical need for atonement in order to function. According to

Impotent, like shadows in a concave mirror, they reproduce the terrors of their century before our eyes, and, in an ecstatic state of horror, we curse their memory. When morality is no longer taught, religion no longer finds adherents, and law no longer avails, we will still shudder at the sight of Medea as she staggers down the palace steps, the murder of her children accomplished. When Lady Macbeth, in a frightful somnambulistic trance, washes her hands and calls upon all the perfumes of Arabia to eradicate the repellent stench of murder, humanity will be seized with a wholesome sense of horror, and every spectator will silently rejoice in his own good conscience." (Friedrich Schiller, "The Stage Considered as a Moral Institution", in: *Sources of Dramatic Theory, Vol. 2: Voltaire to Hugo*, ed. Michael Sidnell, trans. Jean Wilson, Cambridge: Cambridge University Press, 2014, p. 157.)

69 Pindar, "Zweite Olympische Ode", in *Oden,* trans. Eugen Dönt, Stuttgart: Reclam, 1986, pp. 18/19.

70 Besides Wordsworth, see e.g. Thomas Carlyle, "Shakespeare", in *Selections*, ed. A. H. R. Ball, Cambridge: Cambridge University Press, 2014, p. 15. See also Christoph J. Steppich, *Numine afflatur: Die Inspiration des Dichters im Denken der Renaissance*, Wiesbaden: Harrassowitz, 2002.

71 See e.g. Roger Pearson, *Unacknowledged Legislators: The Poet as Lawgiver in Post-Revolutionary France*, Oxford: Oxford University Press, 2016, pp. 20–24.

72 Björn Quiring, "A Consuming Dish: Supplementing Raffield", *Law and Literature* 17.3 (2005), pp. 397–404.

73 Gilles Deleuze and Félix Guattari, *Anti-Oedipus: Capitalism and Schizophrenia*, trans. Robert Hurley, Mark Seem and Helen R. Lane, Minneapolis: University of Minnesota Press, 1983, pp. 185–200; 211–217.

74 Walter Benjamin, "Critique of Violence", in *Selected Writings,* Vol. 1, pp. 238–252.

75 Giorgio Agamben, *Homo Sacer: Sovereign Power and Bare Life*, trans. Daniel Heller-Roazen, Stanford, CA: Stanford University Press, 1998.

76 Friedrich Nietzsche, *Zur Genealogie der Moral*, in *Zur Genealogie der Moral/Götzen-Dämmerung*, ed. Claus-Artur Scheier, Hamburg: Meiner, 2013, pp. 47–87 [2. Abhandlung, 1–21].

this notion, the identity of a legal subject is *per se* laden with guilt. And this guilt is caused neither by deeds committed in the past nor by a sinful interiority; instead, it is ascribed to the subject from the outside in order to make it adressable by the legal system.[77] Hence, it is not the norm that establishes the basis of guilt; it is an original guilt that makes the norm and its transformations possible, as Agamben avers:

> Guilt refers not to transgression, that is, to the determination of the licit and the illicit, but to the pure force of the law, to the law's simple reference to something.[78]

This indissoluble, semiotically necessary culpability lays the groundwork for any justification of death and pain inflicted on legal subjects, be it by a human sovereign or by avenging Nature.

There is, however, a problem with these Nietzschean surveys: they generally affirm that the questionable guilt of mere existence can and must be overcome and replaced by a notion of existential innocence and/or justification. It stands to reason that this verdict to end all verdicts merely perpetuates or even enhances the juridical pattern: it establishes a new imperative, an eleventh commandment, so to speak, requisitioning all subjects to overcome guilt and subsequently live their lives free from this taint. Deleuze and Guattari approvingly quote Henry Miller: "We are all guilty of crime, the great crime of not living life to the full."[79] Thus, the notions of law and transgression that had been thrown out of the front gate tend to sneak back in through the servants' entrance. The natural law court cannot be suspended so easily; more indirect and craftier methods will be needed. To figure them out, one might start with a closer look at the discursive terrain which shows that the notion of nature's juridical powers is more deeply embedded and more widely disseminated than one would think.

The literature of antiquity frequently gives the natural process of birth and decay a legal form, so that its causal chains themselves appear to be the binding and penalizing law of nature. This topic is modulated in diverse myths,[80] but also in philosophical texts, for example the Presocratic dictum of Anaximander:

77 See e.g. Walter Benjamin, "Fate and Character", trans. Edmund Jephcott, in *Selected Writings*, Vol. 1, pp. 201–206.

78 Agamben, *Homo Sacer*, p. 27.

79 Henry Miller, *Sexus*, New York: Grove Press, 1965, pp. 429–430, quoted in Deleuze and Guattari, *Anti-Oedipus*, p. 334. Deleuze's own article "Pour en finir avec le jugement" is another example. (In Gilles Deleuze, *Critique et clinique,* Paris: Minuit, 1990, pp. 158–169.)

80 In a Christian context, the myth of the Fall is most dominant, but there are also pagan analogues. See e.g. Walter Benjamin, "Critique of Violence", in *Selected Writings*, Vol. 1, pp. 248–249.

> ἐξ ὧν δὲ ἡ γένεσίς ἐστι τοῖς οὖσι, καὶ τὴν φθορὰν εἰς ταῦτα γίνεσθαι κατὰ τὸ χρεών διδόναι γὰρ αὐτὰ δίκην καὶ τίσιν ἀλλήλοις τῆς ἀδικίας κατὰ τὴν τοῦ χρόνου τάξιν.[81]
>
> The things that are perish into the things out of which they come to be, according to necessity, for they pay penalty and retribution to each other for their injustice in accordance with the ordering of time.[82]

Seneca takes up the theme when he describes dying as a payment that every living creature must render, under supposition of a debt/guilt that inheres in the mere fact of being alive; hence death is the very law of nature – "mors naturae lex est".[83] Analogously, in Plato's *Timaeus*, it is said that what goes against nature causes pain, and what returns to nature causes joy.[84] Pain thus is treated as a penalty imposed by nature's omnipresent court. The metaphor that comprehends nature as a universally normative, self-perpetuating and unifying force of judgment and sentencing delineates the form of an absolute law that is indiscernible from its area of application. The resulting debates still continue today, in the humanities as well as in legal studies and jurisprudence,[85] not least since natural rights today still have a role to play in texts that carry the force of law.[86] In order to prevent jumping to premature conclusions about the reasons for this adherence, it will be necessary to analyse it more thoroughly. It has comic as well as tragic aspects which will be partly unfolded in what follows, first and foremost insofar as they influence the poetological and political dimensions of Milton's epic.

Generally, the epic form entertains a particularly interesting relation to the law court of nature, for among the genres of literature, it stands closest to foundational myth: it works on myth, just like myth seems to work on

81 Anaximander, "Fragment 110", in *Die vorsokratischen Philosophen*, eds. G. S. Kirk, J. E. Raven and M. Schofield, trans. Karlheinz Hülser, Stuttgart and Weimar: J. B. Metzler, 2001, p. 128.

82 Anaximander, "Fragment", in *Introductory Readings in Ancient Greek and Roman Philosophy*, eds. C. D. C. Reeve and Patrick L. Miller, Indianapolis: Hackett, 2006, p. 2.

83 Seneca, *Naturales Quaestiones/Naturwissenschaftliche Untersuchungen*, ed. and trans. M. F. A. Brok, Darmstadt: Wissenschaftliche Buchgesellschaft, 1995, S. 410 f. [6.12].

84 "An unnatural disturbance that comes upon us with great force and intensity is painful, while its equally intense departure, leading back to the natural state, is pleasant" (Plato, *Timaeus*, trans. Donald J. Zeyl, Indianapolis: Hackett, 2000, p. 58 [64c–d]).

85 For the jurisdiction of the Federal Republic of Germany, including the Federal Court of Justice (*Bundesgerichtshof*) and the Federal Constitutional Court (*Bundesverfassungsgericht*), references to natural law (e.g. in the form of the well-known "Radbruch formula") played a significant role, especially in the years after the Second World War. See Lena Foljanty, *Recht oder Gesetz: Juristische Identität und Autorität in den Naturrechtsdebatten der Nachkriegszeit*, Tübingen: Mohr Siebeck, 2013, esp. pp. 51–95.

86 See e.g. Art. 6, Paragraph 2 of the German constitution (*Grundgesetz*). The invocation of "the Laws of Nature and of Nature's God" in the American Declaration of Independence might also be considered in this context, although the Declaration is not, strictly speaking, a legal document.

the totalitarianism of reality. In the terminology of Stephen Greenblatt: the analysis of epics opens the broadest view on the complex negotiations and renegotiations of society's mythical inheritance.[87] While keeping mythopoeic forces present within public discourse and deriving part of their authority from them, epics also keep them at a certain distance.[88] Georges Dumézil has described the epic as the historicization of myth.[89] This contamination with history allows the epic narrator to reintroduce uncertainties and ambiguities into the authoritative representation of religious, political and juridical relations. As a result, the acts of competing parties in a divine or human conflict may all be described as equally understandable and justifiable: Hannah Arendt speaks of a "Homeric impartiality"[90] which distinguishes the *Iliad* and which has even been enhanced in subsequent epics.[91] Does this impartiality also involve a more objective assessment of divine and natural jurisdiction? To what degree is the history of the epic entangled with the history of the natural law court metaphor?

To obtain a more precise notion of the connection between natural judgment and the epic, the following chapter will take a closer, historicist and necessarily selective look at the juridical capacities of Nature in diverse literary and non-literary discourses, starting with Greek antiquity and ending in Milton's lifetime. Obviously, this overview will be both schematic and partial, focusing on some topical aporias. For example, the problematic relation between Nature's and God's legal office will often be thematized. Additionally, the overview also will demonstrate the enormous breadth and variety of the metaphor. The procedural law of nature's court is in constant flux and the relationships between the parties and institutions involved in her trials also turn out to be incessantly changing. While the absolute metaphor of nature as a law court seems to ground the legal order in the order of things, it also keeps transforming ideas of jurisdiction and sometimes leads its proponents down unexpected paths.

87 On this terminology see Stephen Greenblatt, *Shakespearean Negotiations*, Berkeley, CA: University of California Press, 1988, pp. 1–20.

88 "Epos und Tragödie setzen eine 'entspannte' Qualität ihrer mythologischen Substrate bereits voraus und geben ihr Bestand: Es ist schwer vorstellbar, daß Homer seine Götter einem Publikum hätte zumuten können, das an sie 'glaubte'." (Hans Blumenberg, "Wirklichkeitsbegriff und Wirkungspotential des Mythos", in *Ästhetische und metaphorologische Schriften*, ed. Anselm Haverkamp, Frankfurt am Main: Suhrkamp, 2001, p. 392.) "Epic and tragedy presuppose and substantiate that the relationship to their mythological substrates has become noncommittal. It is hard to imagine that Homer would have been allowed to present his gods to an audience that actually 'believed' in them." (Translation BQ.)

89 Georges Dumézil, *The Destiny of a King*, trans. Alf Hiltebeitel, Chicago and London: University of Chicago Press, 1973, pp. 3–12.

90 "Impartiality, and with it all true historiography, came into the world when Homer decided to sing the deeds of the Trojans no less than those of the Achaeans, and to praise the glory of Hector no less than the greatness of Achilles" (Hannah Arendt, *Between Past and Future: Six Exercises in Political Thought*, New York: Viking, 1961, p. 51).

91 Hannah Arendt, *The Promise of Politics*, ed. Jerome Kohn, New York: Schocken, 2005, pp. 173–176.

1 A short history of the primordial law court of nature

1.1 Hermetic and Dionysian roots

Significantly, the very first documented appearance of the word *physis* is to be found in one of the foundational epics of Western literature, namely in Homer's *Odyssey*.[1] On his way to Circe, Ulysses encounters Hermes who hands him a certain herb called *moly*, a *pharmakon* that will save him from being turned into a pig:

> ὣς ἄρα φωνήσας πόρε φάρμακον ἀργεϊφόντης
> ἐκ γαίης ἐρύσας, καί μοι φύσιν αὐτοῦ ἔδειξε.
> ῥίζῃ μὲν μέλαν ἔσκε, γάλακτι δὲ εἴκελον ἄνθος:
> μῶλυ δέ μιν καλέουσι θεοί: χαλεπὸν δέ τ᾽ ὀρύσσειν
> ἀνδράσι γε θνητοῖσι, θεοὶ δέ τε πάντα δύνανται.
>
> So saying, Argeïphontes gave me the herb, drawing it from the ground, and showed me its nature. At the root it was black, but its flower was like milk. Moly the gods call it, and it is hard for mortal men to dig; but with the gods all things are possible.[2]

Apparently, the plant's *physis* here signifies its characteristic growth: the white flower that grows from the hidden black root over which only the privileged gods possess discretionary power. It is tempting to interpret this episode as the primal scene of nature's epistemology:[3] the *physis* of a thing are the properties that are presented to us, but whose root origins remain inaccessible; humans cannot freely dispose of them, while it is supposed that some privileged (divine) others can. As an invisible force subtending natural appearances,

1 Jenny Strauss Clay, *The Wrath of Athena: Gods and Men in the* Odyssey, London: Rowman and Littlefield, 1997, p. 158.

2 Homer, *Odyssey*, Vol. 1, translated by A. T. Murray, Cambridge, MA: Harvard University Press and London: Heinemann, 1945, pp. 366/367 [10.302–307].

3 Regarding the concept of "primal scene" ("Urszene"), see Sigmund Freud, *Aus der Geschichte einer infantilen Neurose*, in *Zwei Krankengeschichten*, Frankfurt am Main: Fischer, 1996, pp. 164–242.

nature is an entity that remains beyond the grip of human power, enclosing a constitutive zone of latency. Its characteristic movement springs from the unknown and passes back into the unknown. (Thus, nature has frequently been defined as that which is generated without the contribution of man.)[4]

Accordingly, Sophocles' Oedipus, after his divine punishment for a crime he did not intend, laments his horrible, guilt-ridden origins, which were hidden from him for too long, as "δεινὰ φύσις" ("horrible nature"), before mysteriously disappearing from the hill of Colonus.[5] At best, nature is partially accessible to man; in Aeschylus' *Prometheus Bound*, Prometheus claims to have shown to Man (more precisely, to a few priests) the *physis* of birdflight, insofar as it is auspicious or inauspicious.[6] It still takes a while for the appearance of *physis* without a qualifier, a nature that is not the nature of a specific object, such as moly, Oedipus or birdflight, but is instead Nature *per se*. One early instance can be found in a Euripidean fragment which refers to "eternal nature's ageless order" ("ἀθανάτου φύσεως κόσμον ἀγήρων") to which men should accommodate themselves.[7]

The use of the word in Greek drama and epic remains rather infrequent and incidental for a long time, though; it is in philosophy, with the Presocratics of the fifth century BCE, that the term first takes centre stage. For this reason, most of the earliest philosophers were called *physiologoi* or *physikoi* (e.g. by Aristotle).[8] The Presocratics are "natural philosophers" first and foremost in the sense that they are "everywhere securing links between partial entities and wholes", in other words, enquiring into the original basic elements whose specific properties rule the entirety of all cosmic processes. The first philosophical statements about nature as a whole are ascribed to Heraclitus,[9] and one of the most prominent of these statements asserts:

4 See e.g. Hannah Arendt, *The Human Condition: Second Edition*, Chicago and London: University of Chicago Press, 1998, p. 150. Id., *Vita activa oder vom tätigen Leben*, Munich and Zurich: Piper, 1987, p. 177.

5 Sophocles, *Oedipus at Colonus*, in *Antigone, The Women of Trachis, Philoctetes, Oedipus at Colonus*, ed. and trans. Hugh Lloyd-Jones, Cambridge, MA and London: Harvard University Press, 1994, p. 436 [212].

6 Aeschylus, *Prometheus Bound*, in *Persians. Seven against Thebes. Suppliants. Prometheus Bound*, ed. and trans. Alan H. Sommerstein, Cambridge, MA and London: Harvard University Press, 2008, p. 496 [489–490].

7 Euripides, *Fragments: Aegeus-Meleager*, eds. and trans. Christopher Collard and Martin Cropp, Cambridge, MA: Harvard University Press, 2008, pp. 226–227. See Dieter Bremer, "Von der Physis zur Natur: Eine griechische Konzeption und ihr Schicksal", *Zeitschrift für philosophische Forschung* 43:2 (1989), p. 250.

8 See e.g. Martha C. Nussbaum, "Philosophy and Literature", in *The Cambridge Companion to Greek and Roman Philosophy*, ed. David Sedley, Cambridge and New York: Cambridge University Press, 2003, pp. 214–215.

9 F. P. Hager, "Natur", in *Historisches Wörterbuch der Philosophie*, Vol. 6, eds. Joachim Ritter and Karlfried Gründer, Darmstadt: Wissenschaftliche Buchgesellschaft, 1984, col. 422.

φύσις κρύπτεσθαι φιλεῖ.[10]

Pierre Hadot offers several possible translations for this maxim; in their sum, they amount to the assertion that nature loves or has a tendency to hide or to disappear.[11] From her hideout, the figure of nature both tempts and threatens. Just like the aphorism itself, it remains enigmatic, therefore inviting divergent interpretations. Thus the aphorism, in the *terrain vague* between the said and the unsaid, generates its own evidence. Even though this strategy shows similarities to that of mystic speech,[12] it bears emphasising that the term "nature" hardly appears in genuinely religious texts and that its religious and cultic use only starts in some syncretisms of Late Antiquity. Contrariwise, nature-philosophy at this time frequently involves a critique of religion, although its criticisms are not so much directed against the state-sponsored cults as against mythological poetry, especially against Homer and Hesiod. At this point, the tasks of the *physiologoi* also involve a certain amount of literary criticism.[13] The question that dominates a large part of Presocratic discourse is: if we cannot rely on mythological accounts, what are the essential parts and processes that constitute the whole of natural objects? Some Presocratics, mingling synecdoche and metaphor, propose the workings of water, the workings of fire and the entanglement and disentanglement of the four elements. In this context, Democritus, Antiphon and others start to involve juridical concepts in their natural speculations, for example, by contrasting man's natural bent, his *physis*, with the civil law, i.e. with *nomos*, a term that denotes both positive laws and also customs qua "unwritten laws".[14] Antiphon, for example, states:

> τὰ μὲν γὰρ τῶν νόμων ἐπίθετα, τὰ δὲ τῆς φύσεως ἀναγκαῖα. καὶ τὰ μὲν τῶν νόμων ὁμολογηθέντα οὐ φύντ' ἐστίν, τὰ δὲ τῆς φύσεως φύντα οὐχ ὁμολογηθέντα.
>
> For the laws are imposed, whereas nature is necessary; and the laws are not born but agreed upon, whereas nature is not agreed upon but born.[15]

In addition to stating that the law is in opposition to nature, Antiphon also states that law imposes bounds upon nature ("δεσμοι τῆς φύσεώς").[16] Here

10 Heraclitus, "Fragment 123", in *Die vorsokratischen Philosophen*, eds. G. S. Kirk, J. E. Raven and M. Schofield, trans. Karlheinz Hülser, Stuttgart and Weimar: J. B. Metzler, 2001, p. 210.

11 Pierre Hadot, *The Veil of Isis: An Essay on the History of the Idea of Nature*, trans. Michael Chase, Cambridge, MA: Belknap Press of Harvard University Press, 2006, pp. 9–10.

12 See Alois M. Haas, *Mystik als Aussage: Erfahrungs-, Denk- und Redeformen christlicher Mystik*, Frankfurt am Main: Suhrkamp, 1996, pp. 110 ff.

13 See e.g. Maureen Quilligan, *The Language of Allegory: Defining the Genre*, Ithaca, NY: Cornell University Press, 1979, p. 29.

14 See Rémi Brague, *The Law of God*, pp. 19–20.

15 Antiphon the Sophist, *The Fragments*, ed. Gerard J. Pendrick, Cambridge: Cambridge University Press, 2002, pp. 160/161 [Fragment 44a].

16 Antiphon the Sophist, *The Fragments*, pp. 166/167 [Fragment 44a].

the discourse on nature begins to touch upon the field of human jurisdiction. However, a controversy soon develops: some disputants emphasize that nature itself has also established laws that should be followed, on pain of natural atonement. Thus the aforementioned Heraclitus demands that one should act and make things according to nature ("ποιεῖν κατά φύσιν"), even though he also stresses nature's impenetrability.[17] One can discern a general tendency in literature from fifth- and fourth-century Athens to seek a reliable foundation of the legal order in mysterious nature, especially in times of crisis.[18] This tendency also makes itself felt within the theatre, for example, in the *Bacchae* of Euripides when the chorus reprimands the sacrilegious Pentheus and avers:

> οὐ
> γὰρ κρεῖσσόν ποτε τῶν νόμων
> γιγνώσκειν χρὴ καὶ μελετᾶν.
> κούφα γὰρ δαπάνα νομί-
> ζειν ἰσχὺν τόδ' ἔχειν,
> ὅ τι ποτ' ἄρα τὸ δαιμόνιον,
> τό τ' ἐν χρόνῳ μακρῷ νόμιμον
> ἀεὶ φύσει τε πεφυκός.
>
> Never should a man's thought and practice
> Rise above the laws
> For it costs but little to believe
> That these have sovereign power:
> The might of heaven, whatever it be,
> And what through long ages has ever been lawful
> And upheld by nature.[19]

Characteristically, the law upheld by nature is here supposed to ratify the institution of the Dionysia, that is, an orgiastic feast and temporary state of anarchy: an impermanent disorder that expresses a higher order. And that this order is able to assert itself against all decrees promulgated by the sovereign becomes evident by the awful end of Pentheus, whose head is torn off by his own mother. Subsequently, Aristotle assumes that he can discern the same opposition between two orders of justice in the work of Sophocles. He writes in his *Rhetoric* about *Antigone*:

> ἔστι γάρ τι ὃ μαντεύονται πάντες, φύσει κοινὸν δίκαιον καὶ ἄδικον, κἂν μηδεμία κοινωνία πρὸς ἀλλήλους ᾖ μηδὲ συνθήκη, οἷον καὶ ἡ Σοφοκλέους

17 Heraclitus, "Fragment 112", in *Die Fragmente der Vorsokratiker, griechisch und deutsch*, Vol. 1, ed. Hermann Diels, Berlin: Weidmann, 1906, p. 77.

18 See W. K. C. Guthrie, *A History of Greek Philosophy,* Vol. 3: *The Fifth Century Enlightenment*, Cambridge and New York: Cambridge University Press, 1969, pp. 55–60.

19 Euripides, *Bacchae*, in *Bacchae/Iphigenia at Aulis/Rhesus*, ed. and trans. David Kovacs, Cambridge, MA: Harvard University Press, 2002, pp. 98/99 [891–896].

> Ἀντιγόνη φαίνεται λέγουσα, ὅτι δίκαιον ἀπειρημένου θάψαι τὸν Πολυνείκη, ὡς φύσει ὂν τοῦτο δίκαιον [...].
>
> In fact, there is a general idea of just and unjust in accordance with nature, as all men in a manner divine, even if there is neither communication nor agreement between them. This is what Antigone in Sophocles evidently means, when she declares that it is just, though forbidden, to bury Polynices, as being naturally just.[20]

Subsequently, Aristotle quotes the lines 456–457 of the play:

> οὐ γάρ τι νῦν γε κἀχθές, ἀλλ' ἀεί ποτε
> ζῇ ταῦτα, κοὐδεὶς οἶδεν ἐξ ὅτου 'φάνη.
>
> For neither today, nor yesterday, but from all eternity, these statutes live and no man knoweth whence they came.[21]

The connection of Antigone's assertion to the topic of natural law appears questionable, however, not least because the term *physis* does not appear in the quotation.[22] Instead, Antigone pits the "unwritten, eternal divine laws" ("ἄγραπτα κἀσφαλῆ θεῶν νόμιμα") against the decrees of Creon.[23] From this circumstance, it can be concluded that the laws of nature in Aristotle's time tend to be identified with laws imposed by the gods.[24] This association of the precepts of nature with a divine judgment was already implicit in the quoted passage from Euripides. Over the centuries, it will be postulated and contested again and again, in various forms.[25]

20 Aristotle, *The Art of Rhetoric*, trans. John Henry Freese, Cambridge, MA: Harvard University Press and London: Heinemann, 1967, pp. 138–141 [1373b].

21 Aristotle, *The Art of Rhetoric*, pp. 140/141 [1373b].

22 When the term "physis" and its derivates appear in *Antigone* (ll. 523, 642, 659 etc.), the meaning of the term is always "birth", "parentage", "provenance". Sophocles, *Antigone*, in *Antigone, The Women of Trachis, Philoctetes, Oedipus at Colonus*, ed. and trans. Hugh Lloyd-Jones, Cambridge, MA and London: Harvard University Press, 1994. For a more detailed consideration of the status of natural law in *Antigone*, see Tony Burns, "Sophocles' *Antigone* and the History of the Concept of Natural Law", *Political Studies* 50:3 (2002), pp. 545–557.

23 Sophocles, *Antigone*, p. 44 [454–455].

24 However, *Antigone* is interesting for the topic, since it depicts a world in which a transgression of the divine (ritual) law within the *polis* produces effects far beyond the *polis*. That Polynices remains unburied also has results in the nonhuman environment: according to Teiresias, the land becomes impure, the birds stop singing and start to attack each other, apparently mimicking human warfare and iniquity. Since the birds are used for augury, this eruption of avian violence also interrupts the communication with the gods (1001–1013).

25 See e.g. Brague, *The Law of God*, pp. 234–242.

1.2 Plato: the impossible artifice of the *Phytourgos*

The Sophists seem to have adopted another facet of the physiologists' heritage, namely the Antiphonean commonplace of an inherent conflict between the bent of nature and the customary law. In Plato's dialogues, this conflict is thematized by Socrates' sophist interlocutors several times. For example, in the *Gorgias*, a certain Callicles sketches a concept of just, natural law ("νόμον […] φύσεως"[26] or "δικαίου φύσει")[27] which equates it more or less with the law of the strongest, for example that the possessions of the weaker should be appropriated by the stronger. He contrasts the purely conventional law with this order of nature:

> ὡς τὰ πολλὰ δὲ ταῦτα ἐναντί' ἀλλήλοις ἐστίν, ἥ τε φύσις καὶ ὁ νόμος […] φύσει μὲν γὰρ πᾶν αἴσχιόν ἐστιν ὅπερ καὶ κάκιον, τὸ ἀδικεῖσθαι, νόμῳ δὲ τὸ ἀδικεῖν.[28]
>
> Now, for the most part, these two, nature and convention, are antagonistic to each other. […] For by nature everything that is worse is more shameful, suffering wrong for instance, but by convention it is more shameful to do it.[29]

According to Callicles, codified jurisdiction has been designed in order to keep the strong from their natural prerogative, namely to lord it over the weak; in this context, he invokes the authority of a (lost) ode by Pindar. Socrates, however, objects: united, the many who are weak and establish conventional laws are evidently more powerful than the few who are strong. Thus, their rule is also sanctioned by nature, according to Callicles' own argumentation.[30] The reasoning of Callicles neutralizes itself, for his natural right of the strongest becomes indiscernible from the conventional law that is already executed within the power games of the *polis*. However, Plato's Socrates does not abandon "natural law" because of this result. Instead, he shifts the meaning of the term, and by this shift ascribes a special competence of natural judgment to the philosopher; for he has the tendency to ally or even equate *physis* with the immutable world of ideas.[31] Not only the artist and craftsman, but also the politician must accommodate themselves to the world of ideas if they are to produce anything worthwhile: the ideal state that is outlined in the *Politeia* is a

26 Plato, *Gorgias*, in *Werke*, Vol. 2, ed. Gunther Eigler, Darmstadt: Wissenschaftliche Buchgesellschaft, 1973, pp. 378/379 [483e].

27 Plato, *Gorgias*, ed. Eigler, pp. 380/381 [484c].

28 Plato, *Gorgias*, ed. Eigler, pp. 376/378 [482e/483a–b].

29 Plato, *Gorgias*, trans. W. D. Woodhead, in *The Collected Dialogues*, eds. Edith Hamilton and Huntington Cairns, Princeton, NJ: Princeton University Press, 1973, p. 266 [482e/483a–b].

30 Plato, *Gorgias*, ed. Eigler, pp. 392/393 [488d].

31 E.g. in Plato, *Kratylos*, in *Werke,* Vol. 3, ed. Gunther Eigler, Darmstadt: Wissenschaftliche Buchgesellschaft, 1974, pp. 414–417 [389 b–c]; Plato, *Politeia*, in *Werke*, Vol. 4, ed. Gunther Eigler, Darmstadt: Wissenschaftliche Buchgesellschaft, 1971, pp. 800/801 [597d].

state determined by the world of ideas; it is also a state "established according to nature" ("κατὰ φύσιν οἰκισθεῖσα πόλις").[32] This naturally ordered *polis* would also be a just *polis*, its law oriented toward the attainment of the Good.[33]

In the tenth book of Plato's *Laws*, this thought is expanded and slightly varied: here the Athenian Stranger (who is conventionally regarded as a representation of Plato himself) protests against the tendency, common since Empedocles, to equate nature with the four elements, that is, to see water, air, fire and earth as the source of all things, whereas the real, original cause of everything is the soul qua self-generating movement.[34] Accordingly, *physis* is not a blind, material process, but a τέχνη, a divine art. Thus, Plato reintroduces the association between nature and divinity; as the Stranger expresses it in *Sophistes*:

> ἀλλὰ θήσω τὰ μὲν φύσει λεγόμενα ποιεῖσθαι θείᾳ τέχνῃ, τὰ δ' ἐκ τούτων ὑπ' ἀνθρώπων συνιστάμενα ἀνθρωπίνῃ [...].[35]
>
> I will only lay it down that the products of nature, as they are called, are works of divine art, as things made out of them by man are works of human art.[36]

This identification of "products of nature" with "works of divine art" finds its most extensive elaboration in the enormously influential cosmology of the *Timaeus*. Symptomatically, medieval and early modern editions of the *Timaeus* were often given the title or subtitle *Peri Physeōs* (*On Nature*), even though the word "nature" itself is not particularly prominent in the text.[37] And when the term does appear, it is used mainly to designate specific inherent properties and tendencies of a determinate thing ("the nature of x"), rather than to designate a common cause which sustains the movement of all things. Nevertheless, the *Timaeus* is very important for the history of the natural law court metaphor: it introduces the figure of the *demiurgós* (a term that signifies "craftsman", "creator" as well as "magistrate") who crafts the cosmos from pre-existent chaotic raw materials in a feminized receptacle[38] and administers his creation. This creative and administrative

32 Plato, *Politeia*, pp. 306/307 [428e].

33 Plato, *Politeia*, pp. 360/361 [444d].

34 Plato, *Nomoi*, in *Werke*, Vol. 8.2, ed. Gunther Eigler, Darmstadt: Wissenschaftliche Buchgesellschaft, 1977, pp. 278–309 [889b–899a].

35 Plato, *Der Sophist*, in *Werke*, Vol. 6, ed. Gunther Eigler, Darmstadt: Wissenschaftliche Buchgesellschaft, 1970, p. 392 [265e3].

36 Plato, *Sophist*, trans. F. M. Cornford, in *The Collected Dialogues*, p. 1013 [265e3].

37 See e.g. Diogenes Laertius, *Leben und Meinungen berühmter Philosophen,* trans. Otto Apelt and Hans Günter Zekl, ed. Klaus Reich, Hamburg: Meiner, 2015, p. 164 [3.1.60].

38 See e.g. Emanuela Bianchi, *The Feminine Symptom: Aleatory Matter in the Aristotelian Cosmos*, New York: Fordham University Press, 2014, pp. 85–113. Concerning the receptacle, see also Jacques Derrida, "Khōra", in: *The Derrida Reader: Writing Performances*, trans. Ian McLeod, ed. Julian Wolfreys, Lincoln: University of Nebraska Press, 1998, pp. 231–262.

work also has a political dimension, since the demiurge has to "persuade" the recalcitrant matter of chaos to be moulded into a beautiful, all-encompassing order, just like lower-class citizens have to be convinced by their superiors to serve the general good of the state.[39] The demiurge thus establishes a cosmic order which might be described as a totality of "natural laws", although Plato himself does not use the term in this context; on one occasion, he speaks of a "law of destiny" instead.[40] The cosmos he creates is a rational being, equipped with a "world soul" that has subsequently been equated with Nature by Plotinus.[41] In Plato, however, nature is not created, but eternal. Furthermore, what the demiurge does, namely create and administer the cosmos, will precisely become the business of the goddess Natura in medieval allegories.[42]

However, there is one problem with Plato's neat solution: in the *Politeia*, he uses the term φυτουργός, which generally means "planter" or "gardener", but in its context demands the translation "nature-maker".[43] Dealing with the question where nature came from in the first place, Plato suggests it has been created, perhaps by a *creatio ex nihilo*.[44] This figure remains surprisingly undeveloped in Plato's work, and has been largely ignored in its reception. In one of the few texts devoted to the topic, Jean-Claude Nilles comes to the conclusion that the *phytourgos* cannot be accorded an ontological status, since this would result in a contradiction: the ideas are eternal and therefore uncreated.[45] The contradiction can only be sublated when one acknowledges the *phytourgos* to be a mythical figure. But since Plato's own argument demands this figure, *mythos* is found to contaminate his *logos*:

39 Plato, *Timaios*, in *Werke*, Vol.7, ed. Gunther Eigler, Darmstadt: Wissenschaftliche Buchgesellschaft, 1972, pp. 82–85 [48a]. See also Peter Adamson, "State of Nature: Human and Cosmic Rulership in Ancient Philosophy", in *Menschennatur und politische Ordnung*, eds. Andreas Höfele and Beate Kellner, Paderborn: Wilhelm Fink, 2016, pp. 89–90.

40 Plato, *Timaios*, p. 67 [41e].

41 Plotinus, "On Nature and Contemplation and the One", in *Ennead III*, trans. A. H. Armstrong, Cambridge, MA and London: Harvard University Press, 1967, pp. 360–401 [3.8]. See also Carolyn Merchant, *Autonomous Nature: Problems of Prediction and Control from Ancient Times to the Scientific Revolution,* New York and London: Routledge, 2016, p. 34 ff.

42 Edgar C. Knowlton, "The Goddess Nature in Early Periods", *The Journal of English and Germanic Philology,* 19:2 (1920), p. 225.

43 Plato, *Politeia*, in *Werke,* Vol. 4, ed. Gunther Eigler, Darmstadt: Wissenschaftliche Buchgesellschaft, 1971, pp. 800/801 [597d].

44 See also Hans Blumenberg, "'Imitation of Nature': Toward a Prehistory of the Idea of the Creative Being", trans. Anna Wertz, *Qui Parle* 12:1 (2000), p. 27. Id., "'Nachahmung der Natur': Zur Vorgeschichte der Idee des schöpferischen Menschen", in *Ästhetische und metaphorologische Schriften*, ed. Anselm Haverkamp, Frankfurt am Main: Suhrkamp, 2001, p. 22.

45 Jean-Claude Nilles, "Approche mythique du Bien, du Phytourgos et du Démiurge" in *Revue Internationale de Philosophie* 40:1 (1986), p. 129.

> L'usage du *phytourgos* et du Bien, connus comme des figures mythiques indique que seul le mythe permet d'assumer les contradictions introduites par le logos, et d'expliquer la co-présence du sensible et de l'intelligible.[46]
>
> The fact that Plato refers to the *phytourgos* and the Good, which are both generally known as mythical figures, indicates that only myth can handle the contradictions the logos has introduced and that only myth can explain the co-presence of the sensible and the intelligible.[47]

The *phytourgos* marks a place where Plato's philosophy borders on its mythical antecedents and cannot overcome them.

1.3 Aristotle and the judgment of the organism

Plato maintains that the *téchne* of the demiurge always remains bound by the eternal law of *physis*, and Aristotle basically confirms this hierarchy. According to Aristotle, *téchne* is also a derivation and imitation of *physis*;[48] the workings of nature are paradigmatic for any other works, including the works of God and of man (such as poetry, rhetoric and jurisdiction). However, Aristotle conceives of nature quite differently from Plato, and his conceptions have been even more influential than those of his teacher: the Aristotelian conception of nature and his philosophy in general have been hegemonic for centuries.[49] In fact, in early modern times, his philosophy was so dominant that it was occasionally designated as the "ratio naturalis".[50] Even in modern times, the discourse on nature sometimes looks like an extended footnote to Aristotle's *Physics*. So it is worthwhile investigating his attempts to conceptualize nature and natural jurisdiction more extensively. In his *Physics*[51] and *Metaphysics*,[52] Aristotle discusses the many senses of the term "nature". And he elaborates a basic definition that synthesizes them when he defines nature as "the principle and cause of motion and rest to those things, and those things only, in which she inheres primarily, as distinct from incidentally",[53] or elsewhere as "the essence of those things which contain in themselves as

46 Jean-Claude Nilles, "Approche mythique du Bien, du Phytourgos et du Démiurge", p. 131.

47 Translation BQ.

48 "ἡ τέχνη μιμεῖται τὴν φύσιν [...]." Aristotle, *The Physics*, Vol. 1. trans. Philip H. Wicksteed and Francis Cornford, Cambridge, MA: Harvard University Press and London: Heinemann, 1963, p. 120/122 [194a].

49 See e.g. Dieter Bremer, "Von der Physis zur Natur", p. 249.

50 Eckhard Keßler, "Naturverständnisse im 15. und 16. Jahrhundert", in *Naturauffassungen in Philosophie, Wissenschaft, Technik*, Vol. 2, eds. Lothar Schäfer and Elisabeth Ströker, Freiburg and Munich: K. Alber, 1994, pp. 15–16.

51 Aristotle, *The Physics*, Vol. 1, esp. pp. 106–127 [192b–194b].

52 Aristotle, *The Metaphysics*, Vol. 1, trans. Hugh Tredennick, Cambridge, MA: Harvard University Press and London: Heinemann, 1961, esp. pp. 218–223 [1014b–1015a].

53 "Ὡς οὔσης τῆς φύσεως ἀρχῆς τινὸς καὶ αἰτίας τοῦ κινεῖσθαι καὶ ἠρεμεῖν ἐν ᾧ ὑπάρχει πρώτως καθ' αὑτὸ καὶ μὴ κατὰ συμβεβηκός." Aristotle, *The Physics*, Vol. 1, pp. 108/109 [192b].

such a source of motion".[54] In another place, nature is also defined as "that which each thing is when its growth is completed".[55] Aristotle's conception of "nature" is thus threefold: he characterizes it as the inherent movement of self-moving things, as well as the original cause of this movement and as its telos. "Physis" unites the movement which appears with that which has already passed and that which has not yet appeared. Being an end in and of itself, nature always returns upon itself, thus perpetuating itself. It has already been pointed out by John Protevi and others that Aristotle, according to this self-perpetuating definition, comprehends nature not only as dynamic and circular, but also implicitly as organic.[56] It is insinuated that a tendency both of self-preservation and of self-reproduction inheres in nature, two properties that later came to define the "organism."[57] Aristotle, one might say, "organifies" nature. Accordingly, he focuses his natural research on living organisms, even though nature's inherent tendencies for him include the disposition of anorganic beings to find the location appropriate to them, for example the inclination of a handful of earth to fall toward the earth's centre,[58] as well as the inherent tendencies of abstract entities, for example the propensity of tragedy to develop until it attains its proper perfection with Aeschylus and Sophocles.[59] In this context, Aristotle's differentiation between natural and violent motion should be briefly noted. Since everything in the universe has its assigned, organic position in the cosmic order, every movement either directs an object toward this assigned position and therefore is natural, or removes it from this place and therefore is violent. For example, the proper place of the element earth is the centre of the universe, therefore a stone, which mainly consists of earth, falls naturally downward; the proper place of fire is at the periphery of the world, therefore it naturally rises. If one throws

54 "ἡ οὐσία ἡ τῶν ἐχόντων ἀρχὴν κινήσεως ἐν αὑτοῖς ᾗ αὐτά." Aristotle, *The Metaphysics*, Vol. 1, pp. 222/223 [1015a].

55 "οἷον γὰρ ἕκαστόν ἐστι τῆς γενέσεως τελεσθείσης, ταύτην φαμὲν τὴν φύσιν εἶναι ἑκάστου [...]." Aristotle, *Politics*, trans. H. Rackham, Cambridge, MA: Harvard University Press and London: Heinemann, 1944, pp. 8/9 [1252b].

56 John Protevi, "The Organism as the Judgment of God: Aristotle, Kant and Deleuze on Nature (that is, on Biology, Theology and Politics)", in *Deleuze and Religion*, ed. Mary Bryden, London and New York: Routledge, 2001, pp. 30–41. The juridical and the organic conception of order are not necessarily opposed, as Michael Hampe, among others, assumes. (See Michael Hampe, *Eine kleine Geschichte des Naturgesetzbegriffs*, Frankfurt am Main: Suhrkamp, 2007, p. 55.)

57 See e.g. Thomas Lemke, *Biopolitics: An Advanced Introduction,* New York and London: New York University Press, 2011, p. 48.

58 See e.g. Aristotle, *The Nicomachean Ethics*, trans. H. Rackham, Cambridge, MA: Harvard University Press and London: Heinemann, 1962, pp. 70/71 [1103a]. Aristotle, *The Physics*, Vol. 2, pp. 306/307 [254b].

59 "καὶ πολλὰς μεταβολὰς μεταβαλοῦσα ἡ τραγῳδία ἐπαύσατο, ἐπεὶ ἔσχε τὴν αὑτῆς φύσιν." Aristotle, *Poetics*, trans. Stephen Halliwell, in Aristotle, *Poetics*, Longinus, *On the Sublime*, Demetrius, *On Style*, Cambridge, MA: Harvard University Press, 1999, pp. 42/43 [1449a].

a stone upward, one forces it to move against its natural inclination, thence it is a violent motion.[60] This organicist worldview obviously privileges organic life and encourages thought in biological terms. Consequently, nature *per se* is conceived of as a vast organism by Aristotle, whose interlocking parts are all determined by their inherent purposes; he thus firmly consolidates the many natures of the individual things into the one, all-encompassing Nature.[61]

Aristotelian nature functions as a kind of feedback loop: the telos that inheres in natural things causes them to sustain and reproduce themselves, so their future is already contained in their present which was contained in their past. Nature unfolds its self-similiarity over time within a dynamism that is not disposable in the present moment and, as it were, brackets the present, sublating it within an eternal time frame. It is only consequent that in some late antique conceptions of nature that were influenced by Aristotle (for example in Cicero's *De natura deorum*), nature is either designated as the playwright of the *theatrum mundi*[62] or equated with providence.[63] According to Aristotle though, it is not personified Nature herself, but rather the "unmoved mover" ("ὃ οὐ κινούμενον κινεῖ") who coordinates natural movements by his powers of attraction.[64] The eternally animated order of nature is directed toward this equally eternal mover who is also referenced as "the God" ("ὁ θεός"), the goal of all things.[65] Nature can be described as the universal pull toward this perfection; and as such it is likewise eternal and uncreated.[66] In their inclination

60 Aristotle, *The Physics*, Vol. 2, pp. 306/307 [254b]. Mechanics in antiquity was understood as the art to produce movements against nature; however, it was understood that all things moving against nature were bound to wear away and disintegrate sooner or later (Horst-Heino Borzeszkowski und Renate Wahsner, *Die Natur technisch denken? Zur Synthese von* technē *und* physis *in der Newtonschen Mechanik oder das Verhältnis von praktischer und theoretischer Mechanik in Newtons Physik*, Berlin: Max-Planck-Institut für Wissenschaftsgeschichte/Preprint, 1998, p. 2). Through the centuries, this notion persisted in various forms. We even re-encounter it in Copernicus, who also considered gravity as a form of natural appetition (Nicolaus Copernicus, *De revolutionibus I*, in *Das neue Weltbild, Lateinisch-Deutsch*, Hamburg: F. Meiner, 1990, p. 123). Only Descartes and Galilei effectively refuted the distinction between "natural" and "violent" movements (Friedrich Steinle, "From Principles to Regularities: Tracing 'Laws of Nature' in Early Modern France and England", in *Natural Law and Laws of Nature in Early Modern Europe: Jurisprudence, Theology, Moral and Natural Philosophy*, eds. Lorraine Daston and Michael Stolleis, Farnham and Burlington, VT: Ashgate, 2008, p. 218).

61 See also Arnaud Macé, "La naissance de la nature en Grèce ancienne", in *Anciens et Modernes par-delà nature et société*, eds. Arnaud Macé and Stéphane Haber, Besançon: Presses universitaires de Franche-Comté, 2012, pp. 80–81.

62 Marcus Tulius Cicero, *Cato Maior*, in *Cato Maior und Laelius, Lateinisch-deutsch*, ed. Rainer Nickel, Berlin: Akademie, 2011, S. 42 [2.5].

63 Marcus Tulius Cicero, *De natura deorum/Über das Wesen der Götter, Lateinisch-deutsch*, trans. Ursula Blank-Sagmeister, Stuttgart: Reclam, 1995, pp. 166–169 [2.57–2.58].

64 Aristotle, *The Metaphysics*, Vol. 2, pp. 146/147 [1072a]. However, Aristotle seems to conceive this unmoved mover as a part of nature. See Aristotle, *The Metaphysics*, Vol. 1, p. 12/13 [982b].

65 See e.g. Aristotle, *The Metaphysics*, Vol. 2, pp. 150/151 [1072b].

66 See also Protevi, "The Organism as the Judgment of God", p. 32.

to assimilate themselves to the Godhead as far as possible, the natures of all singular things are unified in the universal nature of the cosmos. The deity is the objective of all things, and they differ from each other according to the degree in which they are able to reach this objective. This differentiation determines which place in the hierarchy of nature is accorded to each singular thing. Nature thus establishes relations of domination and legislation, according to which, for example, organs exist for the sake of the organism, the inorganic exists for the sake of the organic, plants exist for the sake of the animals, and animals exist for the sake of men.[67] Analogously, women are subordinated to men in consequence of their natural "deformity" "in the ordinary course of nature".[68] In Aristotle, not only is hierarchy organic, but the organism qua organism is a self-preserving hierarchy between lower and superior components.[69] If this hierarchy is not respected, the telic operations of the body and of the state are interrupted and disorder ensues, which, like an afflicting disease, leads either to a recovery or condemns the organism to death "under the governance of divine justice".[70] In this schema, the organism is conceived of as politico-juridical form, as Deleuze and Guattari have pointed out: "the organism is [...] the judgment of God".[71] And Nature figures as God's bailiff, one might add. However, the hierarchical relation between God and Nature remains unclear; Nature certainly appears as the more active party in the relationship between the two. It is, incidentally, remarkable how frequently Aristotle personifies Nature and compares her, implicitly or explicitly, to a good housekeeper: she exercises her craft sensibly, always aims for the best, does nothing without a purpose and never throws anything away if it can still be used.[72] However, it should be noted that Aristotle also takes pains not too feminize Nature too strongly.[73] In this context, it bears pointing out in passing that the personified Natura/Physis is not always depicted as female, but occasionally also appears as androgynous or male.[74]

Aristotle's organic and goal-oriented conception of Nature provides a framework for the establishment of his notion of political order: in the *Politics*, he regards the human community as the realization of human nature.

67 Aristotle, *Politics*, pp. 36/37 [1256b].

68 "ἀναπηρίαν [...] φυσικήν." Aristotle, *Generation of Animals*, trans. A. L. Peck, Cambridge, MA: Harvard University Press; and London: Heinemann, 1943, pp. 460/461 [775a].

69 Aristotle, *Politics*, pp. 18/19 [1254a].

70 Kostas Kalimtzis, *Aristotle on Political Enmity and Disease: An Inquiry into Stasis*, Albany: State University of New York Press, 2000, p. 22.

71 Deleuze and Guattari, *A Thousand Plateaus*, p. 159. "L'organisme, c'est déjà ça, le jugement de Dieu", Gilles Deleuze and Félix Guattari, *Mille Plateaux*, p. 197.

72 See e.g. William Keith Chambers Guthrie, *Aristotle: An Encounter, A History of Greek Philosophy* Vol. 6, Cambridge: Cambridge University Press, 1981, p. 107.

73 See Emanuela Bianchi, *The Feminine Symptom: Aleatory Matter in the Aristotelian Cosmos*, p. 64.

74 Hans Leisegang, "Physis", in *Paulys Realencyclopädie der classischen Altertumswissenschaft*, Half-Volume 39, eds. Georg Wissowa, Wilhelm Kroll and Karl Mittelhaus, Stuttgart: Druckenmüller, 1941, col. 1130.

The *polis*, as the natural telos of the human being, is engendered through an organic process originating from the germ of the basic societal unit, namely the community between man and woman in the service of procreation.[75] The state is therefore a natural entity. Since human society develops organically from the nature of the species "man", a "natural law" to a certain degree always realizes itself within the law of a *polis*, just like every organism attains its inherent telos more or less perfectly. Hence, Aristotle also does not consider *physis* and *nomos* as opposites, but as linked. However, as Merio Scattola has pointed out, no Aristotelian system of natural law exists, only assorted remarks.[76] The best-known and most influential passage is to be found in the *Nicomachean Ethics*:

> τοῦ δὲ πολιτικοῦ δικαίου τὸ μὲν φυσικόν ἐστι τὸ δὲ νομικόν, φυσικὸν μὲν τὸ πανταχοῦ τὴν αὐτὴν ἔχον δύναμιν, καὶ οὐ τῷ δοκεῖν ἢ μή, νομικὸν δὲ ὃ ἐξ ἀρχῆς μὲν οὐδὲν διαφέρει οὕτως ἢ ἄλλως, ὅταν δὲ θῶνται, διαφέρει [...].
>
> Political justice is of two kinds, one natural, the other conventional. A rule of justice is natural that has the same validity everywhere, and does not depend on our accepting it or not. A rule is conventional that in the first instance may be settled in one way or the other indifferently, though having once been settled it is not indifferent [...].[77]

The law of nature is here distinguished from positive law by its omnipresence: it is enforced everywhere and men have no discretionary power over it. Aristotle has the tendency to equate this natural law with justice; it is what gives everybody what is to due to him or her.[78] However, his remarks on the topic are sparse, and hence the relation between positive law and natural law in Aristotle is still under discussion.[79] A few points are certain though, for example, the fact that Aristotle in his *Politics* defends slavery as a natural institution. And once more, his argument is developed with the help of organic analogies: in every whole, there is that which rules and that which is ruled. The master relates to the slave as soul relates to body, as old relates to young, as male relates to female.[80] All of these hierarchies are asserted *a priori*. For example, Aristotle knows very well that there are at least some species of animals in which the female is stronger and more dominant than the male, but he asserts nevertheless that males are stronger "by nature".[81] In this context, "nature" is obviously not a

75 Aristotle, *Politics*, pp. 4–13 [1252a–1253a].

76 Merio Scattola, *Das Naturrecht vor dem Naturrecht: Zur Geschichte des* ius naturae *im 16. Jahrhundert*, Tübingen: Niemeyer, 1999, pp. 9, 21.

77 Aristotle, *The Nicomachean Ethics*, pp. 294/295 [1134b].

78 Aristotle, *The Nicomachean Ethics*, pp. 292/293 [1134a/b].

79 On the current state of the discussion, see Tony Burns, *Aristotle and Natural Law*, London and New York: Continuum, 2011.

80 Aristotle, *Politics*, pp. 18–23, 60–63 [1254a–b, 1260a].

81 Aristotle, *Politics*, pp. 58/59 [1259b].

descriptive concept, but one that is normatively posited.[82] And the prevailing legal order can be more or less accurately adapted to this norm, that is, be more or less "natural" in its constitution. The more *physis* and *nomos* coincide, the more those whom nature has destined to serve are also legally bound to the role of serfs or slaves.[83] Aristotle asserts what Kurt Flasch has called a fragile unity of fact and norm,[84] but what one might also designate as a norm that the empirical facts are bound to imitate or "represent".[85] The world is a theatre of justice in which nature does not precede mimesis, but constantly and imperfectly mimics itself in its feedback loops. The role ascribed to *physis* is that of a planning, ordering and legislating power, and it is still largely conceptualized in terms of this role today.[86]

Of course, the circumstance that the facts frequently deviate from the norm must be explained. Aristotle therefore insists on the contingency that nature frequently aims for a greater perfection than is obtainable under the given circumstances. Due mostly to the resistance of recalcitrant matter, the loop can be interrupted, so that a thing fails to reach its telos, for example, an organism cannot preserve or reproduce itself.[87] A hierarchy between successful and failed natures is thereby established that superimposes itself on the hierarchy of higher and lower natures – an uneasy coexistence marked by interferences. At this point, human art/craftsmanship (*téchne*) becomes relevant: *téchne* has the general function to serve nature and to help her out in case of her faltering or failure in the attainment of her inherent goals.[88] Blumenberg notes:

> [D]as Aufnehmen des von der Natur Liegengelassenen fügt sich doch der Vorzeichnung der Natur, setzt bei der Entelechie des Gegebenen an und vollstreckt sie. Dieses Einspringen der "Kunst" für die Natur geht so weit, daß Aristoteles sagen kann: Wer ein Haus baut, tut nur genau das, was die Natur tun würde, wenn sie Häuser sozusagen "wachsen" ließe.[89]

82 Geoffrey E. R. Lloyd, "Greek Antiquity: The Invention of Nature", in *Nature: Critical Concepts in the Social Sciences*, Vol. 1, eds. David Inglis, John Bone and Rhoda Wilkie, London and New York: Routledge, 2005, p. 40. See also Emanuela Bianchi, *The Feminine Symptom: Aleatory Matter in the Aristotelian Cosmos*.

83 Aristotle, *Politics*, pp. 22/23 [1254b]. See also Geoffrey E. R. Lloyd, *Aristotelian Explorations*, Cambridge and New York: Cambridge University Press, 1999, p. 201.

84 Kurt Flasch, "Ars imitatur naturam: Platonischer Naturbegriff und mittelalterliche Philosophie der Kunst", in *Parusia: Studien zur Philosophie Platons und zur Problemgeschichte des Platonismus: Festgabe für Johannes Hirschberger*, ed. Kurt Flasch, Frankfurt am Main: Minerva, 1965, p. 297.

85 What is against nature ("παρὰ φύσιν"), is also against order ("παρὰ τάχιν"). Aristotle, *Generation of Animals*, pp. 424/425 [770b].

86 Dieter Bremer, "Von der Physis zur Natur", p. 250.

87 See e.g. Aristotle, *Generation of Animals*, pp. 480–483 [778a]; Aristotle, *Politics*, pp. 26/27 [1255b].

88 Aristotle, *The Physics*, Vol. 1, pp. 120–125. [194a/b].

89 Hans Blumenberg, "'Nachahmung der Natur': Zur Vorgeschichte der Idee des schöpferischen Menschen", pp. 9–10.

> The task of picking up where nature leaves off is carried out after all, by closely following nature's prescription, by taking what is inherently given and carrying it out. This interchangeability of art for nature extends so far that Aristotle can say that the builder of a house only does exactly what nature would do, if it were able, so to speak, to "grow" houses.[90]

The problems in the relation between art and nature converge in the concept of mimesis: nature is an automimetic process that is imitated by heteromimetic arts, namely by the mechanical arts and the performing arts, by poetry as well as statecraft.[91] According to Aristotle, the art of non-self-reproductive mimesis (just like language) is based on a natural inclination of man, so even this form of mimesis is subsumed to nature, incorporated as its supplement.[92] Mimesis is what separates nature and art, but it also connects them. In this arrangement, the contours of nature as an all-encompassing court of law are discernible in which man judges and corrects the other forces of nature, but in which they also judge and correct him.

1.4 The universal poetic administratrix of Late Antiquity

After Aristotle, this mutual dependence of human and natural legislation becomes a common topic: with increasing frequency, nature is identified with a cosmic normativity. First and foremost, the influential school of the Stoics, from their founder Zeno of Citium (c. 334–262 BCE) to Seneca (c. 4 BCE–65 CE), takes up the topic: they ontologize the law of nature, representing it as a creative force immanent in the world as a whole and in all its parts.[93] The Stoic notion of natural law also asserts that the state of nature is one of harmony, of a good cosmic society in which all mutual obligations are met and every subject can realize its inherent telos.[94] Reviving Plato's mythic *phytourgos*, Cleanthes the Stoic describes Zeus as the "founder of nature" ("φύσεως ἀρχηγέ"), who controls everything in accordance with his law ("νόμου μέτα πάντα κυβερνάν").[95] In the first centuries of the new era, this new conception increasingly seems to

90 Hans Blumenberg, "'Imitation of Nature': Toward a Prehistory of the Idea of the Creative Being", p. 18, referring to *Politics* 1337a and *Physics* 199a.

91 See e.g. Aristotle, *Poetics*, pp. 100–103 [1460b].

92 Aristotle, *Poetics*, pp. 12–15 [1448b].

93 The Neoplatonists take a similar route: Plotinus identifies "physis" with that "what has been ordained by universal soul": "ἡ γὰρ φύσις τὸ ὑπὸ ψυχῆς τῆς πάσης ταχθέν" (Plotinus, "On the Movement of Heaven", in *Ennead II*, trans. A. H. Armstrong, Cambridge, MA: Harvard University Press; and London: Heinemann, 1966, pp. 44/45 [2.2.1]). There is no consensus on the question of whether "physis" is to be regarded as a hypostasis in Plotin's cosmic hierarchy (See e.g. Sui Han, *Der Begriff des Nichtseienden bei Plotin*, Wiesbaden: Springer VS, 2016, pp. 83–84).

94 See A. A. Long, *Stoic Studies*, Berkeley, CA and London: University of California Press, 1996, pp. 22–23; and John Sellars, *Stoicism*, Berkeley, CA: University of California Press, 2006, p. 125.

95 *Stoicorum Veterum Fragmenta*, ed. Johannes von Arnim, Stuttgart: Teubner, 1964, p. 121 [537].

impose itself, under the auspices of Rome's imperial ideology and the formulation of the *ius gentium* (law of nations), both of which must have rendered the thought of a cosmic jurisdiction more plausible, as a sanctified, transcendent double of Roman hegemony in the Mediterranean world.[96] Positive legislation, according to Cicero, is subordinated to this phantasm:

> Ergo est lex iustorum iniustorumque distinctio, ad illam antiquissimam et rerum omnium principem expressa naturam, ad quam leges hominum diriguntur, quae supplicio inprobos adficiunt, defendunt ac tuentur bonos.
>
> Therefore Law is the distinction between things just and unjust, made in agreement with that primal and most ancient of all things, Nature; and in conformity to Nature's standard are framed those human laws which inflict punishment upon the wicked and protect the good.[97]

Nature's law, being "of universal application, unchanging and everlasting", is identified with the highest reason – and occasionally also with Roman law.[98] At this point, a question arises: if the law of nature is both reasonable and also expresses the will of Zeus, does Zeus will it because it is reasonable, or is it reasonable because Zeus wills it? Different philosophers provide different answers: early Stoics from Greece take the former route, but later Roman Stoicism tends to prefer the latter, voluntarist option which is more harmonious with the absolutist rule of the empire.[99]

Furthermore, since the Stoics identify obedience to natural law and rational behaviour, it follows that they consider any affects and passions that have the power to override reason as unnatural.[100] Diogenes Laertius quotes Zeno as asserting that passion is an "an irrational movement of the mind, contrary to nature".[101] Nature will not fail to provide punishments for these transgressions:

96 See Edgar Zilsel, *Die sozialen Ursprünge der neuzeitlichen Wissenschaft*, ed. Wolfgang Krohn, Frankfurt am Main: Suhrkamp, 1976, p. 72.

97 Cicero, *On the Laws*, in *On the Republic/On the Laws*, trans. C. W. Keyes, Cambridge, MA and London: Harvard University Press, 2000, pp. 384–387 [2.13].

98 Cicero, *De Re Publica/The Republic*, in *De Re Publica/De Legibus*, trans. C. W. Keyes, Cambridge, MA: Harvard University Press, 1943, p. 211 [3.22.33]. "Roman praetors charged with implementing *ius gentium* (*praetor peregrinus*) did nothing of the sort. Instead they made assumptions regarding what was rational and what was reasonable, concluding that the rational and reasonable must be common to all polities. Because by the first century BCE Roman jurists tended to consider their own legal system (*ius civile*) as embodying pure, atemporal, universal, and permanent reason, they began identifying *ius civile* with *ius gentium* and both with natural law." (Tamar Herzog, *A Short History of European Law: The Last Two and a Half Millennia*, Cambridge, MA and London: Harvard University Press, 2018, p. 153.)

99 Jacob Klein, "Stoic Eudaimonism and the Natural Law Tradition", in *Reason, Religion, and Natural Law: From Plato to Spinoza*, ed. Jonathan A. Jacobs, Oxford and New York: Oxford University Press, 2012, pp. 69–72.

100 Dieter Bremer, "Von der Physis zur Natur", p. 258.

101 Diogenes Laertius, *Lives and Opinions of Eminent Philosophers* [7.110]; quoted in Malcolm Schofield, *The Stoic Idea of the City*, Chicago: University of Chicago Press: 1999, p. 29.

> Cui qui non parebit, ipse se fugiet ac naturam hominis aspernatus hoc ipso luet maximas poenas, etiamsi cetera supplicia, quae putantur, effugerit [...].
>
> Whoever is disobedient is fleeing from himself and denying his human nature, and by reason of this very fact he will suffer the worst penalties, even if he escapes what is commonly considered punishment [...].[102]

Congruously, the Stoics' political demands are mostly limited to the exhortation that the positive law should differ from the law of nature as little as possible.[103] So the relation between citizen and *polis* is dissolved into that between individual and cosmos, occluding the actual political powerlessness of most late antique *cives Romani*.[104] It might be seen as another symptom of this depoliticization that the rhetoric of Stoic treatises is more focused on the individual goal of human happiness and less focused on the general structure and welfare of the cosmopolis.[105]

In Late Antiquity, the topic of nature as a law court also finds its way into juridical texts. In the *Institutiones Iustiniani*, the first part of the *Corpus Iuris Civilis* – that is, the fundamental manual of late antique Roman law – the notion of a *ius naturale* is introduced at the very beginning. And, just as in Aristotle, the relation between male and female is understood to be its basic building block. Not only human beings are subordinate to this law, however:

> Ius naturale est quod natura omnia animalia docuit. nam ius istud non humani generis proprium est, sed omnium animalium, quae in caelo, quae in terra, quae in mari nascuntur. hinc descendit maris atque feminae coniugatio, quam nos matrimonium appellamus, hinc liberorum procreatio et educatio: videmus etenim cetera quoque animalia istius iuris peritia censeri.
>
> The law of nature is the law instilled by nature in all creatures. It is not merely for mankind but for all creatures of the sky, earth and sea. From it comes intercourse between male and female, which we call marriage; also the bearing and bringing up of children. Observation shows that other animals also acknowledge its force.[106]

According to the *Institutiones*, natural laws apply universally, and divine providence ("divina providentia") is to be regarded as their author.[107] Law is

102 Cicero, *De Re Publica/The Republic*, pp. 210/211.
103 See e.g. Schofield, *The Stoic Idea of the City*, p. 110.
104 See e.g. Hans Jonas, *Gnosis: Die Botschaft des fremden Gottes*, ed. Christian Wiese, Frankfurt am Main and Leipzig: Insel, 1999, p. 295.
105 Klein, "Stoic Eudaimonism and the Natural Law Tradition", p. 69.
106 *Justinian's Institutes*, trans. Peter Birks and Grant McLeod, London: Duckworth, 1987, pp. 36/37 [1.2].
107 *Justinian's Institutes*, pp. 38/39 [1.2.11].

thus adopting Stoic commonplaces. In this context, jurisprudence is conceived as an art which basically imitates nature. For example, any legal subject is prohibited from adopting another who is older than her- or himself, since legal adoption is supposed to imitate natural parenthood:

> Minorem natu non posse maiorem adoptare placet: adoptio enim naturam imitatur et pro monstro est ut maior sit filius quam pater.
>
> It is rightly held that a younger person cannot adopt an older one. Adoption imitates nature. A son older than a father would outrage nature.[108]

The civil law procedure of adoption imitates the natural law procedure of procreation. But since imitation implies nonidentity, positive jurisprudence does not simply merge into natural jurisprudence; it merely pretends to become its shadow image. A boundary that actually does grow unstable during Late Antiquity however, is that between natural law and natural legislator: Nature and/or the law of nature are frequently identified with the supreme Godhead in Late Antiquity.[109] The old political commonplace that identifies the king as the "living law" here seems to have been transferred to the cosmocrator.[110] For example, Plutarch asserts:

> εἰ δὲ δεῖ ταῦτ' εἰκάζειν, ὁ μὲν Ζεὺς οὐκ ἔχει τὴν Δίκην πάρεδρον, ἀλλ' αὐτὸς Δίκη καὶ Θέμις ἐστὶ καὶ νόμων ὁ πρεσβύτατος καὶ τελειότατος.
>
> I should say that Zeus does not have Justice to sit beside him, but is himself Justice and Right and the oldest and most perfect of laws [...].[111]

Of course, more traditional notions that the supreme deity is "the author of this law, its promulgator, and its enforcing judge"[112] also prevail. Furthermore, many Stoics, among them Epictetus and Seneca, describe the enforcer of the world order as a kind of secondary goddess who bears the name of Natura/Physis and whose status remains somewhat unclear: sometimes she appears merely as an allegorical figure without proper agency, but sometimes as a

108 *Justinian's Institutes*, pp. 44/45 [1.11.4].

109 For example, Seneca: "Quid enim aliud est natura quam deus et divina ratio toti mundo partibusque eius inserta?" "For what else is Nature but God and the Divine Reason that pervades the whole universe and all its parts?" (Seneca, *De Beneficiis*, in *Moral Essays,* Vol. 3, trans. John W. Basore, Cambridge, MA: Harvard University Press, 1935, pp. 216/217 [4.7.1].) See also the anonymous Stoic tractate *De Mundo*, trans. E. S. Forster, Oxford: Clarendon Press, 1914, pp. 22–23 [400b].

110 Brague, *The Law of God*, p. 25.

111 Plutarch, "To an Uneducated Ruler", in *Moralia*, Vol. 10, trans. Harold North Fowler, Cambridge, MA: Harvard University Press and London: Heinemann, 1969, pp. 60/61.

112 Cicero, *De Re Publica/The Republic* p. 211 [3.22.33].

created, yet autonomous and intelligent force.[113] The description of Stoic theology in Cicero's *De natura deorum* can be regarded as exemplary in this context: the Stoic Balbus defines nature as "the sustaining and governing principle of the world"[114] and describes her relation with the cosmos partly as that of a political sovereign toward his dominion, partly as that of an artist/ craftsman toward his or her materials:

> Ipsius vero mundi, qui omnia conplexu suo coercet et continet, natura non artificiosa solum sed plane artifex ab eodem Zenone dicitur, consultrix et provida utilitatum oportunitatumque omnium, atque ut ceterae naturae suis seminibus quaeque gignuntur augescunt continentur, sic natura mundi omnis motus habet voluntarios, conatusque et adpetitiones, quas ὁρμὰς Graeci vocant, et is consentaneas actiones sic adhibet ut nosmet ipsi qui animis movemur et sensibus. Talis igitur mens mundi cum sit ob eamque causam vel prudentia vel providentia appellari recte possit – Graece enim πρόνοια dicitur –, haec potissimum providet et in is maxime est occupata, primum ut mundus quam aptissimus sit ad permanendum, deinde ut nulla re egeat, maxume autem ut in eo eximia pulchritudo sit atque omnis ornatus.
>
> The nature of the world itself, which encloses and contains all things in its embrace, is styled by Zeno not merely "craftsmanlike" but actually "a craftsman" whose foresight plans out the work to serve its use and purpose in every detail. And as the other natural substances are generated, reared and sustained each by its own seeds, so the world-nature experiences all those motions of the will, those impulses of conation and desire, that the Greeks call *hormae*, and follows these up with the appropriate actions in the same way as do we ourselves, who experience emotions and sensations. Such being the nature of the world-mind, it can therefore correctly be designated as prudence or providence (for in Greek it is termed *pronoia*); and this providence is chiefly directed and concentrated upon three objects, namely to secure for the world, first, the structure best fitted for survival; next, absolute completeness; but chiefly, consummate beauty and embellishment of every kind.[115]

Balbus describes nature as an ordering force, a "mens mundi" that, while not identical with the entirety of all things, pervades them all and gives them orientation, mediating between what is possible and what is real, and drawing all extremes toward a middle position, "ad medium rapit et convertit extrema",

113 See e.g. Giorgio Agamben, *Herrschaft und Herrlichkeit: Zur theologischen Genealogie von Ökonomie und Regierung*, trans. Andreas Hiepko, Frankfurt am Main: Suhrkamp, 2010, pp. 143–144; Hager, "Natur", col. 435.

114 Cicero, *De Natura Deorum*, in *De Natura Deorum/Academica*, trans. Harris Rackham, Cambridge, MA: Harvard University Press and London: Heinemann, 1967, p. 203 [2.32].

115 Cicero, *De Natura Deorum*, pp. 178/179 [2.22].

punishing those who overstep the bounds of nature by the very processes of nature.[116] Once again, nature appears both as a force of universal attraction and as a force of referential connectivity, providing the universe with a sense of unity and a unity of sense. It is remarkable that beauty ("pulchritudo") seems to be its most important goal in this process. Natura is an aesthete.[117] Cicero also describes nature as a creative fire ("ignis artificiosus")[118] and personifies it as the playwright ("poeta") of the *theatrum mundi.*[119] Thus, *téchne* and *nomos* are identified under the auspices of a poetic Nature.[120] Consequently, in Ovid's eclectic *Metamorphoses*, we find similar references to a personified "Natura" who orders Chaos.[121]

In contrast to this rather absolutist (if aestheticist) conception of cosmic enforcement, the Epicureans suppose that the natural order was constituted not from above, but from below; it was not forced upon the world by its sovereign, but developed spontaneously from the "democratic" interaction of its parts. In *De rerum natura,* Lucretius speaks repeatedly of a "foedus naturae", a sort of social contract among all things that establishes order in the universe and differentiates among the species.[122] However, in the same

116 Cicero, *De Natura Deorum*, pp. 232/233 [2.45].

117 On the latent aesthetic aspirations of law in general see e.g. Peter Goodrich, *Legal Emblems and the Art of Law:* Obiter Depicta *as the Vision of Governance*, Cambridge: Cambridge University Press, 2013.

118 Cicero, *De Natura Deorum*, pp. 176/177 [2.22].

119 "[…] in hoc sumus sapientes, quod naturam optimam ducem tamquam deum sequimur eique paremus; a qua non veri simile est, cum ceterae partes aetatis bene discriptae sint, extremum actum tamquam ab inerti poeta esse neglectum". Cicero, *Cato Maior*, p. 42 [2.5].

120 Klein, "Stoic Eudaimonism and the Natural Law Tradition", p. 79.

121 "Hanc deus et melior litem natura diremit;/ nam caelo terras et terris abscidit undas/ et liquidum spisso secrevit ab aere caelum./ quae postquam evolvit caecoque exemit acervo,/ dissociata locis concordi pace ligavit […]". "God – or kindlier Nature – composed this strife; for he rent asunder land from sky, and sea from land, and separated the ethereal heavens from the dense atmosphere. When thus he had released these elements and freed them from the blind heap of things, he set them each in its own place and bound them fast in harmony". Ovid, *Metamorphoses*, Vol. 1., ed. Frank Justus Miller, Cambridge, MA: Harvard University Press and London: Heinemann, 1971, pp. 2–5 [1.21–1.25].

122 "[…] res quaeque suo ritu procedit et omnes/ foedere naturae certo discrimina servant". "[…] but each thing proceeds after its own fashion, and all by fixed law of nature preserve their distinctions". Lucretius, *De rerum natura*, trans. W. H. D. Rouse and Martin Ferguson Smith, Cambridge, MA: Harvard University Press, 1992, pp. 450/451 [5.922–924]. See also: "Denique iam quoniam generatim reddita finis/ crescendi rebus constat vitamque tenendi,/ et quid quaeque queant per foedera naturai,/ quid porro nequeant, sancitum quandoquidem extat/ nec commutator quicquam, quin omnia constant […]". "Again, since a limit has been fixed for the growth of things after their kind and for their tenure of life, and since it stands decreed what each can do by the ordinances of nature, and also what each cannot do, and since nothing changes, but all things are constant […]". Lucretius, *De rerum natura*, pp. 48/49 [1.584–588]. Occasionally, the metaphor is revived; see Bruno Latour, *Politics of Nature: How to Bring the Sciences into Democracy*, trans. Catherine Porter, Cambridge, MA: Harvard University Press, 2004.

text, nature is also personified as creator ("natura creatrix"),[123] pilot ("natura gubernans"),[124] sovereign[125] and orator.[126]

Whether all these diversely personifying statements about nature are always meant to be taken allegorically becomes increasingly unclear. One might say that Nature has had a career that inverted those of the Olympian gods: she was an allegorical figure before she became a goddess. It is only in the third century CE that an actual cult of Natura/Physis, can be ascertained: an Orphic hymn praises her as the universal mother, the eldest of all gods, who engendered herself and is the origin of all movement; she brought forth all things, keeps forming them and makes them gyrate in her cycles. She sees everything and reigns supreme over everything, especially over marriage and generation, but also over the subsequent decay of that which has reached maturity.[127] From this emphasis on her relation to fertility springs the tendency to identify her with Aphrodite, Hera or Isis.[128] But in the hymn she is also addressed as personified justice (δίκη) who rewards her followers and punishes the wicked. In addition, paradoxical attributes like that of a dark bringer of light and of an endless end ("ἀτελής τε τελευτή"), which might echo Aristotelian conceptions, are ascribed to her. However, the Orphic cults are not to be regarded as *bona fide* religions; they are mystery cults, that is, syncretistic artifices designed for alienated citizens of the Roman Empire – one might categorize them as the ancient equivalent of the Californian New Age movements.[129] Christian writers of Late Antiquity such as Lactantius and Prudentius err when they consider Natura as a vanquished pagan divinity: she is the back projection of a figure who only developed a cult following in the age of an expanding Christendom.[130] And it is only in the subsequent period that the shape of the goddess Natura is actually fleshed out. Around the year 400, in the panegyric epic *De consulatu Stilichonis*, Claudian places Natura on the threshold between latency and evidence: she is stationed as the guardian at the entrance of the Cave of Time, from which the ages proceed and to which they return. Beside her, an old man sits who prescribes their paths to the stars and thus its fortunes to the world.[131] In this context, Nature is described as

123 Lucretius, *De rerum natura*, p. 52 [1.629].

124 Lucretius, *De rerum natura,* p. 384 [5.77].

125 "[…] natura videtur/libera continuo dominis privata superbis,/ipsa sua per se sponte omnia dis agere expers […]". "[…] nature is seen to be free at once and rid of proud masters, herself doing all by herself of her own accord, without the help of the gods". Lucretius, *De rerum natura*, pp. 178–181 [2.1090–1092].

126 Lucretius, *De rerum natura*, pp. 260–273 [3.931–1052].

127 "Φύσεως/To Physis", in *The Orphic Hymns*, ed. Apostolos N. Athanassakis, Missoula, MT: Scholars Press for the Society of Biblical Literature, 1977, pp. 16–19.

128 Ernst Robert Curtius, *Europäische Literatur und lateinisches Mittelalter: Götter – Menschen – Rituale*, Bern and Munich: Francke, 1965, p. 116. See also Hadot, *The Veil of Isis*.

129 See e.g. Hans Kloft, *Mysterienkulte der Antike*, Munich: Beck, 2003.

130 Curtius, *Europäische Literatur und lateinisches Mittelalter*, p. 117.

131 "Est ignota procul nostraeque impervia menti,/ vix adeunda deis, annorum squalida mater,/ inmensi spelunca aevi, quae tempora vasto/ suppeditat revocatque sinu. […]/ vestibuli custos

extremely beautiful, despite her advanced age. But that is all the depiction the reader is offered; more extensive descriptions of Mother Natura/Physis only appear about 700 years later, in the twelfth century.[132] Of course, there are references to a personified Nature in other works that were written between the third and the twelfth century, but they remain occasional and sketchy.[133] It is in keeping with this descriptive restraint, that a common topos of late Latin literature purports Nature to be a goddess who likes to veil herself, be it out of modesty or because she has something to hide, for example that she is ugly.[134] The Heraclitean saying that nature loves to hide itself is revived in this context. All man can certainly know about her is that she has mysterious judicial and administrative tasks. She might also be a poet, but the opinions on that subject are divided.

1.5 Christian doublings

This is the situation of the discourse on nature's jurisdiction at the end of the fourth century, when Christianity attains the status of a state religion. Early Christianity revises this legacy in a somewhat undecided manner. A coordination problem arises from the circumstance that there is almost no reference to nature in the Bible; there is no equivalent word in the Old Testament, and the word *physis* accordingly never occurs in the Septuagint.[135] Likewise, *physis* hardly ever makes an appearance in the New Testament; the few instances are mainly to be found in the letters of Paul who is intervening in discussions about natural

vultu longaeva decoro/ ante fores Natura sedet, cunctisque volantes/ dependent membris animae. mansura verendus/ scribit iura senex, numeros qui dividit astris/ et cursus stabilesque moras, quibus omnia vivunt/ ac pereunt fixis cum legibus". "Far away, all unknown, beyond the range of mortal minds, scarce to be approached by the gods, is a cavern of immense age, hoary mother of the years, her vast breast at once the cradle and the tomb of time. [...] Before the entrance sits Nature, guardian of the threshold, of age immense yet ever lovely, around whom throng and flit spirits on every side. A venerable old man writes down immutable laws: he fixes the number of stars in each constellation and causes these to move and those to be at rest, whereby everything lives or dies by pre-ordained laws". Claudian, *On Stilicho's Consulship*, in *Works*, Vol. 2, ed. Maurice Platnauer, Cambridge, MA and London: Harvard University Press, 1922, pp. 32–35 [2.424–427; 2.431–436].

132 Wolfgang Kemp, *Natura: Ikonographische Studien zur Geschichte und Verbreitung einer Allegorie*, pp. 9–11.

133 See e.g. Boethius: "Quantas rerum flectat habenas/ Natura potens, quibus immensum/ Legibus orbem provida servet/ Stringatque ligans inresoluto/ Singula nexu, placet arguto/ Fidibus lentis promere cantu". Boethius, *Consolatio Philosophiae/Trost der Philosophie*, eds. and trans. Ernst Gegenschatz and Olof Gigon, Zurich: Artemis and Winkler, 2004, p. 98 [3.2.c]. For further examples, see George D. Economou, *The Goddess Natura in Medieval Literature*, Cambridge, MA: Harvard University Press, 1972, pp. 28–52.

134 Pierre Hadot, *The Veil of Isis*, p. 31.

135 Charles A. Anderson, *Philo of Alexandria's Views of the Physical World*, Tübingen: Mohr Siebeck, 2011, p. 105.

law that were rampant at his time.[136] Paul mainly uses the topos normatively and apodictically: in most of his letters, natural law is equated with Aristotelian prescriptions, for example when Paul declares homosexuality and men who wear their hair long to be unnatural.[137] But there is a passage in Romans in which his treatment of Aristotelian and Stoic traditions becomes more complex: in order to justify the integration of Gentiles into the Christian community, he writes:

> ὅταν γὰρ ἔθνη τὰ μὴ νόμον ἔχοντα φύσει τὰ τοῦ νόμου ποιῶσιν, οὗτοι νόμον μὴ ἔχοντες ἑαυτοῖς εἰσιν νόμος. οἵτινες ἐνδείκνυνται τὸ ἔργον τοῦ νόμου γραπτὸν ἐν ταῖς καρδίαις αὐτῶν, συμμαρτυρούσης αὐτῶν τῆς συνειδήσεως καὶ μεταξὺ ἀλλήλων τῶν λογισμῶν κατηγορούντων ἢ καὶ ἀπολογουμένων, ἐν ἡμέρᾳ ὅτε κρινεῖ ὁ θεὸς τὰ κρυπτὰ τῶν ἀνθρώπων κατὰ τὸ εὐαγγέλιόν μου διὰ Χριστοῦ Ἰησοῦ.[138]
>
> For when the Gentiles, which have not the law, do by nature the things contained in the law, these, having not the law, are a law unto themselves: which shew the work of the law written in their hearts, their conscience also bearing witness, and their thoughts the mean while accusing or else excusing one another, in the day when God shall judge the secrets of men by Jesus Christ according to my gospel.[139]

Remarkably, the law that naturally guides the Gentiles is here associated both with their inborn conscience (συνείδησις) of good and evil and with the final judgment of God. In this context, Paul combines elements appropriated from Stoic philosophy[140] with the notion of Yahweh's terminal law court appropriated from the prophetic traditions of Judaism.[141] However, it remains unclear how exactly both are supposed to relate to one another: conscience might anticipate the divine judgment,[142] but Paul's teachings on the subject remain sparse and imprecise.[143]

136 See Michael Bertram Crowe, *The Changing Profile of the Natural Law*, The Hague: Nijhoff, 1977, pp. 52–55. 2 Peter 1.4 mentions a "divine nature" ("θείας [...] φύσεως") in which man might participate.

137 Romans 1.26–27; 1 Corinthians 11.14.

138 Romans 2.14–16. The Greek text of the New Testament is cited according to *Das Neue Testament, Interlinearübersetzung Griechisch-Deutsch*, trans. Ernst Dietzfelbinger, Neuhausen: Hänssler, 1998.

139 Romans 2.14–16.

140 "Paul probably adopted the term συνείδησις from popular Hellenistic philosophy. Here συνείδησις mostly means the awareness that one's own actions are morally condemned or approved." (Udo Schnelle, *Apostle Paul: His Life and Theology*, trans. M. Eugene Boring, Grand Rapids, MI: Baker, 2005, p. 528.)

141 See also e.g. Romans 14.10–12. On the Hebrew notion of a divine final judgment see C. D. Elledge, *Resurrection of the Dead in Early Judaism, 200 BCE–CE 200*, Oxford: Oxford University Press, 2017.

142 Wilhelm Schmidt-Biggemann, *Philosophia Perennis: Historical Outlines of Western Spirituality in Ancient, Medieval and Early Modern Thought*, Dordrecht: Springer, 2004, p. 370.

143 According to Matthias Konradt, Paul's conceptions of divine judgment are inconsistent. (Matthias Konradt, *Gericht und Gemeinde: Eine Studie zur Bedeutung und Funktion von*

Subsequently, the church fathers attempt to link the Christian and the Greco-Roman worldviews in more meticulous ways. Early Christian conceptions of nature are generally Aristotelian, with smatterings of Stoicist motives: from Augustine all the way to Albertus Magnus and Thomas Aquinas, nearly everybody repeats the Aristotelian definition of nature as the principle or the force inhering in each thing and in all things.[144] This conception is supplemented by the Platonic/Stoicist commonplace that nature is the manifestation of divine reason and artfulness.[145] However, the fathers' teachings diverge on the question whether God himself is part of nature and thus subject to its restrictions, or whether he transcends it. In some cases, only the sublunary sphere is called "nature",[146] but in others God is subsumed under the term. Since Philo of Alexandria tried to reconcile the Jewish heritage with Stoicism by designating the God of the Old Testament as the highest and best *physis*, this identification has been rather common; but it has always remained an uneasy amalgamation.[147] Both Augustine and Scotus Eriugena comprehend God as a part of nature: Augustine calls him "natura creatrix", as opposed to his creation, "natura creata";[148] Eriugena develops a

Gerichtsaussagen im Rahmen der paulinischen Ekklesiologie und Ethik im 1 Thess und 1 Kor, Berlin and New York: De Gruyter, 2003.) "As to the suggestion sometimes made that Paul attended one of the universities, such as that of Tarsus, one can only say that it is most unlikely. Paul shows as little sign of being learned in the Hellenistic as in the Jewish sense. Except for a citing of what Moffatt calls a 'popular tag' from Menander in 1 Cor. 15.33, Paul never quotes from the Greek philosophers and poets nor so much as refers to them. It is Luke (Acts 17.28) and the writer of the Pastoral epistles (Tit. 1.12) who attribute such references to Paul, and such vague reminiscences of philosophical language as may be found in his writings, as possibly some echoes of Aristotle in Rom. 2.14–15, can be fully accounted for by his having heard, as he could hardly have avoided, the popular Stoic-Cynic preachers who taught philosophy to any who would listen in the markets and streets of any large Hellenistic city. [...] That Paul was a man of active, alert mind and great intellectual capacity, that he had had some contact with Greek philosophy and that he had some knowledge of rabbinical theology must be fully granted. But there is no evidence of advanced formal training either in Hellenistic wisdom or in scribal learning." (John Knox, *Chapters in a Life of Paul: Revised Edition*, ed. Douglas Hare, Macon: Mercer University Press, 1987, p. 54.)

144 For an exemplary, if unremarkable, summary of the Aristotelian commonplaces on nature and art, as perpetuated and modified by medieval Christian scholarship, see John of Salisbury, *The Metalogicon: A Twelfth-Century Defense of the Verbal and Logical Arts of the Trivium*, trans. Daniel D. McGarry, Philadelphia: Paul Dry Books, 2009, pp. 28–52.

145 See e.g. Aquinas' commentary on Aristotle's *Physics*: "Unde patet quod natura nihil est aliud quam ratio cuiusdam artis, scilicet divinae, indita rebus, qua ipsae res moventur ad finem determinatum." Thomas Aquinas, *De Physico Auditu*, in *In Aristotelis Stagiritae Nonnullos Libros Commentaria*, Parma: Petrus Fiaccadorus, 1865, p. 289 [Liber 2, Lectio 14].

146 See Michael Hampe, *Eine kleine Geschichte des Naturgesetzbegriffs*, p. 31.

147 See Anderson, *Philo of Alexandria's Views of the Physical World*, pp. 148–154. See also Hager, "Natur", col. 436–437.

148 Augustine, *De Trinitate (Bücher VIII–XI, XIV–XV)*, ed. Johann Kreuzer, Hamburg: Meiner, 2001, pp. 248/249 [15.1.1].

more complex differentiation between nature that creates and is not created, nature that is created and creates, nature that is created and does not create and nature that is not created and does not create.[149] Mutual absorptions of God and Nature such as these make it easier for the church fathers to integrate the trials of nature into Christian theology. This task is simplified by the circumstance that God's role as sole legitimate legislator of the world, as well as claimant, prosecutor, witness and judge is already a dominant theme in the Bible, especially in the prophetic books.[150] Significantly, when God appears, he is often accompanied by ministering angels, taking the roles of prosecutors and attorneys.[151] Occasionally, even the sun, the moon, the stars, the sea and the long-suffering earth are integrated into the divine courtroom, appearing as accusers of man's ungodliness in early Christian apocrypha.[152]

On closer inspection, God's jurisdiction turns out to be enacted in two courts. On the one hand, a fair amount of stories in the Bible support the claim that the divine tribunal realizes itself through all the things that happen on earth: God's justice frequently determines that transgressors will come to bad ends, as Pharaoh, Ahab and Jezebel did. Consequently, Hellenized Jews and early Christians frequently equate divine legislation with natural law, just as the Stoics did.[153] On the other hand, this legal order is supplemented by a final judgment that will only come at the end of history and will administer punishments a lot more terrible than anything natural circumstances are able to inflict.[154] This notion of an ultimate trial that settles all cases is only mentioned in passing in the Old Testament, but is fleshed out extensively in Jewish and Christian apocalyptic texts, of which the Revelation of John has been the most influential.[155] From the beginning of its history, Christianity has installed a bifurcated jurisdiction in the name of the both natural and supernatural divine.

The biblical emphasis on God's omnipotence occasions a stronger emphasis on his legislative autonomy. When Cicero approximates Zeus and the Natural Law, he still leaves it undecided whether the supreme God himself is subject to the order of nature. But when Augustine uses the term "law of God", he explicitly emphasizes that God himself is not bound to this law while his creatures

149 "Videtur mihi divisio naturae per quattuor differentias quattuor species recipere: quarum prima est in eam, quae creat et non creatur; secunda in eam, quae creatur et creat; tertia in eam, quae creatur et non creat; quarta, quae nec creat nec creatur". (The fourth option is subsequently rejected as impossible.) John Scotus Eriugena, *Divisione della Natura*, ed. and trans. Nicola Gorlani, Milan: Bompiani, 2013, pp. 156/157 [441 B].

150 See Brague, *The Law of God*.

151 Meira Z. Kensky, *Trying Man, Trying God: The Divine Courtroom in Early Jewish and Christian Literature*, Tübingen: Mohr Siebeck, 2010, p. 5.

152 Kensky, *Trying Man, Trying God*, p. 272.

153 Anderson, *Philo of Alexandria's Views of the Physical World*, p. 154.

154 Kensky, *Trying Man, Trying God*, p. 259.

155 L. Pinomaa and U. Dierse, "Gericht", in *Historisches Wörterbuch der Philosophie*, Vol. 3, ed. Joachim Ritter, Darmstadt: Wissenschaftliche Buchgesellschaft, 1989, col. 339.

are.[156] Frequently, this supreme legislative power is legitimated – in a Pauline, but quite un-Aristotelian fashion – by God's creative power, the circumstance that he has created both man and the world out of nothing.[157] This Christian belief perpetuates the Stoic notion that God's office of legislating and judging extends over all of creation. In this sense, Eusebios of Caesarea writes:

> παιδεύει τοιγαροῦν ἀρχόμενος τοῦτον ἡγεῖσθαι μὴ μόνον τῶν πρὸς αὐτοῦ σμικρὸν ὕστερον διαταχθησομένων ἀνθρώποις νόμων αὐθέντην εἶναι καὶ κύριον, ἀλλὰ καὶ τῶν ἐν τῇ φύσει τῶν ὅλων.
>
> So Moses teaches from the beginning that God must not only be recognized as the originator and master of the laws which were prescribed to men shortly afterwards, but also as the originator and master of the laws of the universe which subsist in nature.[158]

In this context, the reception of the Book of Job is particularly important because it asserts that God, among other things, "made a decree for the rain".[159] In his *Homilies on the Hexaemeron*, Basil of Caesarea interprets Genesis 1.9 to mean that the natural properties of water were instituted by a commandment of God, promulgated on the third day of creation, when God ordered the waters to assemble in one place. This gathering of the waters at the lowest point is not merely natural, he writes:

> Ἴσως δ' ἄν τις κἀκεῖνο πρὸς τούτοις ἐπιζητήσειε. Πρῶτον μὲν, διὰ τί ὃ κατὰ φύσιν ὑπάρχει τῷ ὕδατι φέρεσθαι πρὸς τὸ κάταντες, τοῦτο ἐπὶ τὸ πρόσταγμα τοῦ δημιουργοῦ ὁ λόγος ἀνάγει; Ἕως μὲν γὰρ ἂν ἐπὶ τοῦ ἰσοπέδου κείμενον τύχῃ τὸ ὕδωρ, στάσιμόν ἐστιν, οὐκ ἔχων ὅπου μεταρρυῇ· ἐπειδὰν δέ τινος πρανοῦς λάβηται, εὐθὺς ὁρμήσαντος τοῦ προάγοντος, τὸ συνεχὲς αὐτῷ τὴν βάσιν τοῦ κινηθέντος ἐπιλαμβάνει, καὶ τὴν ἐκείνου τὸ ἐφεπόμενον· καὶ οὕτως ὑπεκφεύγει μὲν ἀεὶ τὸ προάγον, ἐπωθεῖ δὲ τὸ ἐπερχόμενον· καὶ τοσούτῳ ὀξυτέρα ἡ φορὰ γίνεται, ὅσῳπερ ἂν καὶ τὸ βάρος ᾖ πλεῖον τοῦ καταφερομένου, καὶ τὸ χωρίον κοιλότερον, πρὸς ὃ ἡ ἐπίρρυσις. Εἰ οὖν οὕτω πέφυκε τὸ ὕδωρ, παρέλκοι ἂν τὸ πρόσταγμα τὸ κελεῦον συναχθῆναι εἰς συναγωγὴν μίαν. Ἔμελλε γὰρ πάντως, διὰ τὸ κατάρροπον τῆς φύσεως, ἐπὶ τὴν πάντων κοιλοτέραν χώραν αὐτομάτως συνδίδοσθαι, καὶ μὴ πρότερον

156 Augustine, *Der Gottesstaat/De Civitate Dei,* Vol. 2, trans. Carl Johann Perl, Paderborn: Ferdinand Schöningh, 1979, pp. 750/751 [22.2]. Rémi Brague, *The Law of God,* p. 214.

157 See Romans 9.18–24.

158 Eusebios of Caesarea, *La préparation évangelique*, Livre VII, trans. Guy Schroeder, Paris 1975, pp. 202/203 [7.9.4]; translation BQ.

159 Job 28.25–26, The Vulgate translates: "ponebat pluviis legem". Luther translates: "als er dem Regen ein Gesetz gegeben". However, other Bible passages also play a role, for example Ezekiel 6.3. See Jean-Robert Armogathe, "Deus Legislator", in *Natural Law and Laws of Nature in Early Modern Europe*: *Jurisprudence, Theology, Moral and Natural Philosophy*, eds. Lorraine Daston and Michael Stolleis, Farnham and Burlington, VT: Ashgate, 2008, p. 276.

> στήσεσθαι πρὶν ὁμαλισθῆναι τὰ νῶτα. […] ὅτι μάλιστα μὲν σὺ μετὰ τὸ πρόσταγμα τὸ δεσποτικὸν ἐπέγνως τοῦ ὕδατος τὰς κινήσεις, ὅτι τε περιρρεπές ἐστι καὶ ἀστήρικτον, καὶ πρὸς τὰ πρανῆ καὶ κοῖλα φέρεται κατὰ φύσιν· πρὸ τούτου δέ, πῶς εἶχε δυνάμεως πρὶν αὐτῷ τὸν ἐκ τοῦ προστάγματος τούτου ἐγγενέσθαι δρόμον, οὔτε εἶδες αὐτὸς, οὔτε ἰδόντος ἤκουσας. Νόησον γὰρ ὅτι Θεοῦ φωνὴ φύσεώς ἐστι ποιητική, καὶ τὸ γενόμενον τότε τῇ κτίσει πρόσταγμα τὴν πρὸς τὸ ἐφεξῆς ἀκολουθίαν τοῖς κτιζομένοις παρέσχετο. Ἡμέρα καὶ νὺξ ἅπαξ ἐδημιουργήθη, καὶ ἐξ ἐκείνου καὶ νῦν ἀλλήλας διαδεχόμεναι, καὶ κατ' ἰσομοιρίαν διαιρούμεναι τὸν χρόνον οὐκ ἀπολήγουσι. […] Ἐκελεύσθη τρέχειν τῶν ὑδάτων ἡ φύσις, καὶ οὐδέποτε κάμνει τῷ προστάγματι ἐκείνῳ κατασπευδομένη διηνεκῶς.[160]
>
> Perhaps you will ask me new questions. And first, is it not a law of nature that water flows downwards? Why, then, does Scripture refer this to the fiat of the Creator? As long as water is spread over a level surface, it does not flow; it is immovable. But when it finds any slope, immediately the foremost portion falls, then the one that follows takes its place, and that one is itself replaced by a third. Thus incessantly they flow, pressing the one on the other, and the rapidity of their course is in proportion to the mass of water that is being carried, and the declivity down which it is borne. If such is the nature of water, it was supererogatory to command it to gather into one place. It was bound, on account of its natural instability, to fall into the most hollow part of the earth and not to stop until the levelling of its surface. […] Since God's command, you know perfectly well the motion of water; you know that it is unsteady and unstable and falls naturally over declivities and into hollow places. But what was its nature before this command made it take its course? You do not know yourself, and you have heard from no eye-witness. Think, in reality, that a word of God makes the nature, and that this order is for the creature a direction for its future course. […] It was ordered that it should be the natural property of water to flow, and in obedience to this order, the waters are never weary in their course.[161]

The law of nature is here obviously conceived not just as a norm, but as a force, namely a force that coincides to a large extent with God's executive power of language. The natural order coincides with the sum of God's primordial speech acts at the time of creation. The laws of language thus must be considered to preexist the laws of nature.

160 Basil of Caesarea, *Homilien zum Hexameron*, New Series, *Die griechischen christlichen Schriftsteller der ersten Jahrhunderte*, Vol. 2, eds. Emmanuel Amand de Mendieta and Stig Y. Rudberg, Berlin: Akademie, 1997, pp. 59–60 [Homily 4.2–3].

161 Basil of Caesarea, *The Hexaemeron*, in *Letters and Select Works*, *Nicene and Post-Nicene Fathers:* Second Series, Vol. 8, eds. Philip Schaff and Henry Wallace, New York: Cosimo, 2007, pp. 72–73 [Homily 4.2–3].

How does God's biblical legislation relate to this natural legislation? At first, this problem is rather sparsely treated, beyond the general assumption of their compatibility.[162] Frequently, the church fathers had identified natural law with the law that was given to Adam or with the Noahide laws.[163] But this identification sidesteps several central issues. For one, it is a central topos of the New Testament that all former laws have been superseded by the death of Christ. To what extent does this also entail a supersession of the law of nature? On the one hand, Christian rhetoric tends to suggest that the destructive paradoxes of nature's law court have been supplanted by a new covenant of love in which at least the true believer attains the privilege to pass beyond nature's confines. (Not only the Christian emphasis on a transcendent eternal life, but also the emphasis on the apostolic workings of miracles in the early church might be considered as symptomatic in this context.) But on the other hand, natural law seems to remain alive and healthy in early Christianity: echoing the Stoics, Augustine asserts that divine law coincides both with divine reason and also with the natural order of things.[164] And according to Origen, a certain part of Mosaic law coincided with natural law, and only this part was not rendered superfluous by Christ's sacrifice.[165] The issue remains largely undecided, but, somewhat awkwardly, a continuity with Aristotelian and Stoic notions of natural law is maintained, rendering palpable once more that Christianity is an uneasy compromise formation between paganism and Judaism on almost every level.[166] When Christianity inserted the Jewish notion of an apocalyptic divine judgment into the pagan conception of a cosmos that is its own law, further contortions were necessary. According to Augustine, the Last Judgment will only bring the First Judgment of the cosmos to perfection:

> Ideo autem, cum diem iudicii Dei dicimus, addimus ultimum vel novissimum, quia et nunc iudicat et ab humani generis initio iudicavit dimittens de paradiso et a ligno vitae separans primos homines peccati magni perpetratores; immo etiam quando angelis peccantibus non pepercit, quorum princeps homines a se ipso subversus invidendo subvertit, procul dubio iudicavit; nec sine illius alto iustoque iudicio et in hoc aerio caelo et in terris et daemonum et hominum miserrima est vita, erroribus aerumnisque plenissima. Verum etsi nemo peccasset, non sine bono rectoque iudicio universam rationalem creaturam perseverantissime

162 Brague, *The Law of God*, p. 213.

163 Alexander Passerin d'Entrèves, *Natural Law: An Introduction to Legal Philosophy*, New Brunswick, NJ and London: Transaction, 1994, p. 39.

164 Brague, *The Law of God*, p. 215.

165 Origen, *Commentaria in Evangelium secundum Matthaeum*, 2.9 and 6.12, cited in Brague, *The Law of God*, p. 212.

166 See e.g. Bernhard Lang, *Jesus der Hund: Leben und Lehre eines jüdischen Kynikers*, Munich: Beck, 2010.

sibi suo Domino cohaerentem in aeterna beatitudine retineret. Iudicat etiam non solum universaliter de genere daemonum atque hominum, ut miseri sint propter primorum meritum peccatorum; sed etiam de singulorum operibus propriis, quae gerunt arbitrio voluntatis. Nam et daemones ne torqueantur precantur, nec utique iniuste vel parcitur eis vel pro sua quique inprobitate torquentur; et homines plerumque aperte, semper occulte, luunt pro suis factis divinitus poenas sive in hac vita sive post mortem: quamvis nullus hominum agat recte, nisi divino adiuvetur auxilio; nullus daemonum aut hominum agat inique, nisi divino eodemque iustissimo iudicio permittatur. Sicut enim ait apostolus, non est iniquitas apud Deum; etiam sicut ipse alibi dicit, inscrutabilia sunt iudicia eius et investigabiles viae eius. Non igitur in hoc libro de illis primis nec de istis mediis Dei iudiciis, sed de ipso novissimo, quantum ipse tribuerit, disputabo, quando Christus de caelo venturus est vivos iudicaturus et mortuos. Iste quippe dies iudicii proprie iam vocatur, eo quod nullus ibi erit inperitae querellae locus, cur iniustus ille sit felix et cur ille iustus infelix. Omnium namque tunc nonnisi bonorum vera et plena felicitas et omnium nonnisi malorum digna et summa infelicitas apparebit.[167]

Also, when we speak of the day of God's judgment, we add the word "last" or "final"; for God is judging even now. He has been judging from the beginning of the human race, when He expelled the first human beings from Paradise and cut them off from the tree of life as perpetrators of a great sin. Indeed, He undoubtedly gave judgment even before that, when He did not spare the angels who sinned, whose prince, himself seduced, seduced man in his envy. Also, it is by nothing else than the deep and just judgment of God that the life of the demons in the air, or in the sky, and the life of men on earth, is most miserable, and so full of errors and fears. Moreover, even if no one had sinned, the whole rational creation could not have been maintained in eternal blessedness by persevering in its adherence to the Lord without His good and righteous judgment. Again, not only does He pass judgment universally on the whole race of demons and men, condemning them to misery as the deserved punishment of their first sins; also, He judges the personal acts of individuals performed by the free choice of their will. For even the demons beseech that they may not be tormented; and it is certainly not without justice that they are spared or tormented according to the degree of wickedness exhibited by each. Men also are punished by God for what they do, often openly, always secretly, either in this life or after death; although no man acts rightly unless he is sustained by divine aid, and no demon or man acts wickedly unless permitted to do so by he same divine and most just judgment. For, as the apostle says, "There is no unrighteousness with God"; and, as he says elsewhere, "His judgments are inscrutable, and His

167 Augustine, *Der Gottesstaat/De Civitate Dei*, Vol. 2, pp. 518/520 [20.1].

> ways past finding out". In this book, then, I shall speak, as far as God permits, not of those first judgments, nor of the intervening judgments of God, but of the last judgment itself, when Christ will come from heaven to judge the living and the dead. For that day is properly called the Day of Judgment because, when it comes, there will no longer be occasion for the ignorant to ask why this unjust man is happy and that just man unhappy. It will then become clear that true and full happiness belongs to none but the good, while all the wicked, and only the wicked, are to suffer deserved and supreme unhappiness.[168]

The *City of God* spells out that, in the jurisdiction of the Christian God, two courts are superadded to one another – one open, one secret – to produce an awkward synthesis: the miseries, errors and fears of this life are judgments, and men will be delivered from them by another judgment. This judgment will be based on another, not quite compatible, verdict, since the divine aid which only some angels and men receive and which will enable them not to sin is described as a form of judgment, although one that strikes the creature as rather capricious. Indeed, since God is not under the law and therefore not obliged to be just to his creatures, one might say that even the final judgment, be it nominally just or not, is not an act of justice, but a gratuitous act of sheer arbitrariness, "past finding out". Divine judgment does not seem to be a means to an end, but an end in and of itself, since even in the absence of sin, "His good and righteous judgment" would proceed incessantly. Thus, the trials of nature are officially absorbed by divine justice, but a bone turns out to be stuck in the throat of theology: God's judgment takes on the form of an infinite process of inscrutability. The creatures have to live with the doubt, already articulated in Job and the Psalms[169] whether God's mysterious notion of justice will happen to coincide with their own.

1.6 Fleshing out medieval allegories

The absolutist rule of the Christian God is consolidated when his competitors are first dethroned and then transformed into allegorical figures. According to Walter Benjamin, Christian allegoresis of pagan traditions is a method of Christianization that seeks to suppress the lingering remnants of polytheism.[170] But allegoresis not only exorcises the pagan gods, it also preserves

168 Augustine, *The City of God Against the Pagans*, ed. and trans. R. W. Dyson, Cambridge and New York: Cambridge University Press, 1998, pp. 965–966 [20.1].

169 See e.g. Psalm 89.

170 Walter Benjamin, *The Origin of German Tragic Drama*, trans. John Osborne, London: Verso, 1998, p. 223. See also Jeffrey Burton Russell, *The Prince of Darkness: Radical Evil and the Power of Good in History*, Ithaca, NY: Cornell University Press, 1992, pp. 17–20.

them; in general, it both mortifies and saves at once.[171] Nature is one of the figures subjected to this treatment. In medieval times, Christian nature, just like Stoic nature, is not only codified, but also anthropomorphized, without being identified with the sovereign God: Natura reappears in some allegorical short epics from Northern France and England, and she appears as a goddess to whom God has assigned juridical as well as administrative tasks. First and foremost, however, she takes the role of a primordial plaintiff and judge who wails, accuses and condemns in the cosmic courtroom. The *Cosmographia* (c. 1145) by Bernardus Silvestris is the first text to reestablish the topos: it opens before the creation of the cosmos, with Natura (whose outer appearance is not described) appearing before God and complaining to Divine Providence about the chaotic state of matter, the "generationis uterus indefessus".[172] She demands that chaos be replaced by a state of order, for the beautification of the world:

> Natura ad Noym, id est dei providentiam, de prime materie confusione conquerens inducitur, et ut mundus pulcrius poliatur humiliter implorat.[173]
>
> Nature [...] makes complaint to Noys, or Divine Providence, about the confused state of the primal matter, or Hyle, and pleads that the universe be more beautifully wrought.[174]

She claims to speak in the name of everything: "Pro Mundo Natura rogo [...]".[175] ("It is for the universe that I, Nature, appeal [...]".)[176] Noys/Nous adjudges that her appeal is appropriate in every respect since it conforms to higher laws ("supernis legibus").[177] Thereupon, Noys instigates the separation of the four elements and further measures, until the cosmos in its entirety is clearly structured. The second book describes the creation's crowning achievement, namely the manufacture of the microcosm that is man. Throughout these processes, Natura plays only an initiating, but not an active, creative role, mostly imploring and demanding. All the other allegorical figures carry out her organizing requests. Basically, she mediates between the divine commands (with which she exhibits a peculiar harmony) and the material world. As the sky deity Urania expresses it:

> Supremi decreta dei, Natura, reportas,
> Quid ve recens fieri sacra mens velit.[178]

171 Benjamin, *The Origin of German Tragic Drama*, p. 223.
172 Bernardus Silvestris, *Cosmographia*, ed. Peter Dronke, Leiden: Brill, 1978, p. 100.
173 Silvestris, *Cosmographia*, ed. Dronke, p. 95.
174 Bernardus Silvestris, *The Cosmographia of Bernardus Silvestris*, trans. Winthrop Wetherbee, New York and London: Columbia University Press, 1973, p. 65.
175 Silvestris, *Cosmographia*, ed. Dronke, p. 98.
176 Silvestris, *Cosmographia*, trans. Wetherbee, p. 69.
177 Silvestris, *Cosmographia*, ed. Dronke, p. 99.
178 Silvestris, *Cosmographia*, ed. Dronke, p. 126.

> You bring, O Nature, the decrees of the most high God, and what the divine mind has even now willed to come about.[179]

In keeping with her mediating and mediumistic function, it is Natura's special task in the creation of man to establish the connection between body and soul ("corporis et anime formativa concrecio").[180] Strangely, among her underlings, one also encounters the more earthy master craftswoman Physis who lives at the centre of the earth and forms the material creatures with her own hands. Once again, nature seems to do double duty; and once again, just as in Aristotle, her operations in the world take the form of a great feedback loop:

> Influit ipsa sibi mundi natura, superstes,
> Permanet et fluxu pascitur usque suo:
> Scilicet ad summam rerum natura recurrit
> Nec semel – ut possit sepe perire – perit.[181]

> The nature of the universe outlives itself, for it flows back into itself, and so survives and is nourished by its very flowing away.[182]

Whereas this Natura still remains a somewhat abstract *gestalt*, her namesake in Alan of Lille's Menippean prosimetrum *De Planctu Naturae* (*c.* 1165) is depicted very concretely and meticulously. In both form and content, Alan of Lille's text is modelled on the *Consolatio Philosophiae* by Boethius, with Natura taking the role that Boethius gave to Philosophia. The narration begins with the narrator complaining about the proliferation of homosexual practices, whereupon he is graced with a vision: an extraordinarily beautiful woman descends weeping from heaven. On her head, she wears a crown on which the planets and the zodiac are represented. On her dress, whose colours are constantly changing and which is torn in one place, all the animals of the world are depicted; on her shoes and undergarments, all the plants. All creatures spontaneously humble themselves in front of this apparition who introduces herself to the narrator as Natura, the deputy of God ("uicaria dei").[183] Later on, she describes her status more specifically as "his substitute, his vice-regent, the mistress of his mint".[184] And throughout her subsequent

179 Silvestris, *Cosmographia*, trans. Wetherbee, p. 97.

180 Silvestris, *Cosmographia*, ed. Dronke, pp. 126, 142.

181 Silvestris, *Cosmographia*, ed. Dronke, pp. 154–155.

182 Silvestris, *Cosmographia*, trans. Wetherbee, p. 126.

183 Alan of Lille, *The Plaint of Nature*, trans. James J. Sheridan, Toronto: Pontifical Institute of Mediaeval Studies, 1980, p. 117. Alan of Lille, *De Planctu Naturae*, ed. Nikolaus M. Häring, Spoleto: Centro italiano di studi sull'alto medioevo, 1978, p. 825.

184 Alan of Lille, *The Plaint of Nature*, p. 146. "Me igitur tanquam pro-deam, tanquam sui uicariam, rerum generibus sigillandis monetariam destinauit." (Alan of Lille, *De Planctu Naturae*, p. 840.)

speech, she emphasises her subordinate status: she was created by God ("Ille faciens, ego facta")[185] and she follows his orders in everything she does.[186] She proceeds to lament the disobedience of man; all creatures follow her laws with that one exception:

> Cum omnia lege sue originis meis legibus teneantur obnoxia michique debeant ius statuti uectigalis persoluere, fere omnia tributarii iuris exhibitione legitima meis edictis regulariter obsequuntur. Sed ab huius universalitatis regula solus homo anomala exceptione seducitur [...].[187]
>
> As all things by the law of their origin are held subject to my laws and are bound to pay me the tribute rightly imposed, practically all obey my edicts as a general rule, by bringing forward the rightful tribute in the manner appointed by law. However, from this universal law man alone exempts himself by a nonconformist withdrawal.[188]

She complains about man's proclivity toward the seven deadly sins, but first and foremost about male homosexuality which distracts from the natural imperative of procreation. Thereupon, she announces that man is going to be punished for his transgressions. However, her power in that respect seems clearly limited, since she cannot punish man but only deliver him to divine punishment by an excommunication ritual. She declares:

> De contingentibus igitur nichil omittens, in me fine proprium consecuta, prout ualeo brachium mee potestatis extendere, eos uindicta uicio respondente percutiam. Sed quia excedere limitem mee uirtutis non ualeo nec mee facultatis est huius pestilentie uirus omnifariam extirpare, mee possibilitatis regulam prosecuta, homines predictorum uiciorum anfractibus irretitos anathematis cauteriabo caractere.[189]
>
> Accordingly, ignoring no pertinent fact and finding the proper motivation in myself, in so far as I can extend the arm of my power, I will smite men with a punishment commensurate with their crimes. However, since I cannot pass the limits of my strength and it is not in my power to eradicate completely the poison of this pestilence, I will attain what is allowed my power and will burn with the brand of anathema men who are ensnared in the tangle of the vices that I have mentioned.[190]

One of her "subdelegates" with the name Genius, who is apparently to be understood both as an allegory of generative force and also as an allegory of

185 Alan of Lille, *De Planctu Naturae*, p. 829.
186 Alan of Lille, *The Plaint of Nature*, p. 146.
187 Alan of Lille, *De Planctu Naturae*, p. 829.
188 Alan of Lille, *The Plaint of Nature*, p. 131.
189 Alan of Lille, *De Planctu Naturae*, pp. 870–871.
190 Alan of Lille, *The Plaint of Nature*, pp. 205–206.

art,[191] carries out in her name this ceremony of anathematization against all those men who have sinned against Nature and her imperatives. Surrounded by twelve allegorical maidens (apparently standing in for the twelve priests who traditionally assisted a bishop in ceremonies of anathematization),[192] he proclaims:

> O Natura, non sine interne inspirationis afflatione diuina a tue disretionis libra istud inperiale processit edictum, ut omnes, qui abusiua dissuetudine nostras leges obsoletas reddere moliuntur, non in nostre sollempnitatis feria feriantes, anathematis gladio feriantur. [...] Auctoritate superessentialis Vsye eiusque Notionis eterne, assensu celestis milicie, coniuncte Nature etiam ceterarumque officialium uirtutum monisterio suffragante, a superne dilectionis osculo separetur ingratitudinis exigente meito, a Nature gracia degradetur, a naturalium rerum uniformi concilio segregetur omnis qui aut legitimum Veneris obliquat incessum aut gulositatis naufragium aut ebrietatis sentit insomnium aut auaricie sicientis experitur incendium aut insolenis arrogantie umbratile ascendit fastigium aut precordiale patitur liuoris exicium aut adulationis amorem comitatur ficticium.[193]
>
> O Nature, it is not without the divine breath of interior inspiration that there has come from your balanced judgement this imperial edict, to the effect that all who strive to make our laws obsolete by misuse and desuetude, by not keeping holiday on our solemn days of rest, should be struck with the sword of anathema. [...] By the authority of the super-essential Usia and his eternal Idea, with assent of the heavenly army, with the combined aid and help of Nature and the other recognised virtues, let everyone who blocks the lawful path of Venus, or courts the shipwreck of gluttony or the nightmares of drunkenness, or indulges the fire of thirsty avarice, or scales the shadowy heights of insolent arrogance, or submits to the death of the heart in envy, or makes a companion of the hypocritical love of flattery – let every such be separated from the kiss of heavenly love as his ingratitude deserves and merits, let him be demoted from Nature's favour, let him be set apart from the harmonious council of the things of Nature.[194]

No attempt is made to depict Natura as a secular entity who is immanent to creation: she resides in heaven, as supreme deputy of the supreme being, a mediating angelic figure who, in some respects, resembles the Virgin Mary. Accordingly, the punishment she deals out is mainly a spiritual

191 Barbara Newman, *God and the Goddesses: Vision, Poetry and Belief in the Middle Ages*, Philadelphia: University of Pennsylvania Press, 2003, p. 69.

192 Lester K. Little, *Benedictine Maledictions: Liturgical Cursing in Romanesque France*, Ithaca, NY and London: Cornell University Press, 1993, p. 38.

193 Alan of Lille, *De Planctu Naturae*, p. 878.

194 Alan of Lille, *The Plaint of Nature*, pp. 219–220.

punishment: the excommunicates will no longer enjoy the benefits of the law which they have transgressed. The consequences, however, remain unclear.[195] Is her excommunication ritual a good Christian rite or an extra-ecclesiastical, secular curse (which is officially forbidden at the time of Alan of Lille)?[196] The church authorities tend to insist that they hold a monopoly on cursing, for excommunication is one of their most powerful judicial and religious instruments.[197] Besides its legal consequences (i.e. expulsion from the community of the faithful),[198] the anathema also represents the enormous spiritual power of the church, since it is staged as an anticipation of the final judgment (involving acts such as an erasure of the name of the condemned from the "book of life", alluding to Rev. 20.15).[199] Yet despite these performances ripe with suggestions of omnipotence, there has always been a strange oscillation between power and powerlessness inherent in the act of cursing: Natura acknowledges it when she declares that helplessness lies at the base of her execration. The curse performs a condemnation and at the same time presupposes it: since God perceives everything and judges only rightly, the condemnable deed itself has already brought a pre-existent divine condemnation down on the doer to which the execrator merely lends his voice in repetition. Through the curse, he or she affirms an order of the world in which the accursed has already been singled out for punishment, which makes the work seem ritualistically tautological. Yet on the other hand, the same imprecator also aspires to carry out this condemnation himself through the curse, thereby insinuating that, at the moment of its utterance, divine judgment and world do not coincide after all. Interestingly, the curse of Genius involves the verdict that the damned be "demoted from Nature's favour", even though this disfavour was

195 On the aporias resulting from this ceremonial form of "inclusive exclusion", see Quiring, *Shakespeare's Curse*, pp. 40–58.

196 Justifications of this prohibition are to be found e.g. in Thomas Aquinas, *Summa Theologiae Secunda Secundae, 1–91*, Latin/English Edition, trans. Laurence Shapcote, Lander, WY: Aquinas Institute, 2012, pp. 693–695 [Summa 2.2, Quaestio 76, Art. 1]. It might be taken as symptomatic that the greater part of her curse is freely invented and does not use ecclesiastical formulas which tend to consist almost entirely of appropriated, refunctionalized, and rearranged biblical and patristic quotes.

197 Jürgen Stein, "Excommunication", in *The Encyclopedia of Christianity*, Vol. 1., eds. Erwin Fahlbusch and Geoffrey William Bromiley, Grand Rapids, MI: Eerdmans and Leiden: Brill, 2001, p. 236.

198 For example, even though the church does not lose its jurisdiction over him or her, a person anathematized is forbidden from instituting legal proceedings or to stand before a court as a witness or an advocate. See e.g. Thomas Aquinas, *Summa Theologica: Die deutsche Thomas-Ausgabe*, Vol. 32: *Supplement, Quaestiones 17–40*, trans. Dominicans and Benedictines of Germany and Austria, Graz [etc.]: Styria, 1985, pp. 95–97 [Supplement, Quaestio 22, Art. 6]. See also Elisabeth Vodola, *Excommunication in the Middle Ages*, Berkeley: University of California Press, 1986, p. 162. At times, the exclusion of excommunicates from secular jurisdiction had a Catch-22 effect insofar as the quest for absolution would have meant an admission of guilt in exactly the matter that would have to be deliberated in court (see Vodola, *Excommunication in the Middle Ages,* pp. 109–110).

199 Quiring, *Shakespeare's Curse*, pp. 43–44.

already a given at the beginning of the prosimetrum. In its entanglements of description and prescription, it remains questionable what consequences the curse of Natura and Genius will have. And this ambivalence shows a problem of divine judgment that turns out to be problem of natural judgment too: in a social situation, its omnipotence is almost indiscernible from impotence.

Later, Alan of Lille wrote a sequel to the *Planctus Naturae*, titled *Anticlaudianus*, in which Nature with her assistants creates a perfect man who will redeem creation, an act whose historical reference remains unclear; some critics think the perfect man is Jesus Christ, some think it is Philip II of France, some think it is just a utopian figure.[200] In any case, it is remarkable that Nature seems to conceive the plan for this redemptive generation on her own accord, without any apparent instigation from God.[201] Despite her proclaimed dependency on God, she appears remarkably autonomous, as if she was not a servant, but a supplementary ruler. It is generally supposed that Natura does God's bidding, but the way he communicates with her is not altogether obvious.

Further texts from the same period also make use of the allegorical figure of Natura, but they mainly repeat the patterns that Bernardus and Alan have established, not adding much that could be considered original.[202] For example, in the anonymous *Altercatio Ganimedis et Helene*, another discourse on the unnaturalness of homosexuality is developed. Ganymede and Helena argue about the prospective merits of homo- and heterosexuality; Nature and Reason subsequently take the role of judges and, unsurprisingly, declare the procreative union between man and woman far superior to any other form of sexual bonding.[203] The close association between Natura and sexual normativity is perpetuated in other texts: in Jean de Meun's part of the *Roman de la Rose* (*c.* 1275), we find another lament of beautiful Natura over disobedient man, heavily indebted to Alan of Lille.[204] Again, Natura judges man in her function as *vicaria dei*, and her complaint is once more followed by an excommunication ceremony, headed by Genius. However, this time Natura condemns (against all Pauline and monastic tradition) not only sodomites, but also celibates for their denial of the forces of generation and their disobedience to their own natural inclinations.[205] At this point, the divine law and the law of Nature diverge appreciably. Nevertheless, her insistence on

200 Newman, *God and the Goddesses*, pp. 81–83.
201 Newman, *God and the Goddesses*, p. 81.
202 Newman, *God and the Goddesses*, p. 90 ff.
203 Newman, *God and the Goddesses*, pp. 90–91.
204 In the *Roman de la Rose*, Natura also has a more artisanal role to play in man's creation and perpetuation: she forges humans in her workshop. Guillaume de Lorris and Jean de Meun, *Le Roman de la Rose*, Vol. 4, ed. Ernest Langlois, Paris: Firmin-Didot, 1922, pp. 128–129 [16005–16012].
205 Guillaume de Lorris and Jean de Meun, *Le Roman de la Rose*, Vol. 5, ed. Ernest Langlois, Paris: Firmin-Didot, 1924, p. 12 [19701–19708]. See also Newman, *God and the Goddesses*, p. 109; George D. Economou, *The Goddess Natura in Medieval Literature*, p. 112.

universal law justifies Barbara Newman's verdict that medieval Natura is the "goddess of the normative".[206] One might add: the biopolitical normative.[207] In order to legitimate herself, Jean de Meun's Natura asserts that man owes her an eternal debt for the gift of sexuality:

> Mais pour ceus don Amours se plaint,
> Car j'en ai bien oï le plaint,
> Je meïsmes, tant con je puis,
> M'en plaing e m'en dei plaindre, puis
> Qu'il me renoient le treü
> Que trestuit ome m'ont deü
> Et toujourz deivent et devront,
> Tant com mes oustiz recevront.[208]

> But of those of whom love complains (for I have indeed heard the complaint) I complain myself, as much as I can, and I should do so, because they have denied me the tribute that all men have owed me, and always do and always will owe me as long as they receive my tools.[209]

Again, she summons Genius as her "priest" and spokesman, and he proceeds to promise damnation to the disobedient and Paradise to those of Nature's subjects who keep her laws:

> De l'auctorité de Nature
> Qui de tout le monde a la cure,
> Come vicaire et conestable
> A l'empereeur pardurable
> Qui siet en la tor souveraine
> De la noble cité mondaine
> Don il fist Nature menistre,
> Qui touz les biens i amenistre
> Par l'influence des esteles,
> Car tout est ordené par eles
> Selonc les dreiz emperiaus
> Don Nature est officiaus,
> Qui toutes choses a fait naistre,
> Puis que cist mondes vint en estre.
> E leur dona terme ensement
> De grandeur et d'acreissement; [...]

206 Newman, *God and the Goddesses*, p. 90.
207 See e.g. Thomas Lemke, *Biopolitics: An Advanced Introduction*.
208 Lorris and Meun, *Le Roman de la Rose*, Vol. 4, pp. 264–265 [19327–19334].
209 Guillaume de Lorris and Jean de Meun, *The Romance of the Rose*, trans. Charles Dahlberg, Princeton, NJ: Princeton University Press, 1995, pp. 318–319.

> Seient tuit escomenié
> Li desleial, li renié,
> Et condannné senz nul respit,
> Qui les euvres ont en despit,
> Seit de grant gent, soit de menue,
> Par cui Nature est soutenue.
> Et cil qui de toute sa force
> De Nature garder s'efforce,
> E qui de bien amer se peine,
> Senz nule pensee vilaine,
> Mais qui leiaument i travaille,
> Flouriz en paradis s'en aille;
> Mais qu'il se face bien confès,
> I'en preing seur mei trestout son fais
> De tel poeir con jou puis prendre,
> Ja pardon n'en portera mendre.[210]

> By the authority of nature, custodian of the whole world, vicar and constable of the eternal emperor who sits in the sovereign tower of this noble city, the world, and who made nature its minister, to administer all its riches through the influence of the stars (for everything is ordered by the stars, according to the imperial right exercised by Nature); by her authority who has brought all things to birth since this world began, and likewise given them their allotted time for growth and increase [...]; by the authority of Nature, let all those disloyal renegades, great or humble, who scorn those works by which Nature is maintained, be excommunicated and ruthlessly condemned. But if a man strives with all his might to preserve Nature, keeps himself from base thoughts and toils and struggles faithfully to be a true lover, let him go to paradise crowned with flowers. Provided he make a good confession, I will take the whole burden of it upon myself with all the power at my disposal, and he will take away with him no less a pardon than that.[211]

Again, Natura's power over the stars whose influence regulates the events on earth is emphasised. But here, the might of Natura starts to resemble the intercessionary might of the Virgin Mary, although her precepts appear to be very different – a madonna of procreation. And her intercession takes the form of an accusation: most medieval representations of Natura seem to involve a trial of man's wicked ways. Man is not only sinful before God, he is also sinful before Natura, although for different reasons. Natura does not

210 Lorris and Meun, *Le Roman de la Rose*, Vol. 5, pp. 4–6 [19505–19520; 19527–19542].

211 Guillaume de Lorris and Jean de Meun, *The Romance of the Rose*, trans. Frances Horgan, Oxford and New York: Oxford University Press, 1999, p. 301.

restrict the order to be fruitful and multiply to those who "cannot contain", but applies it to all, Gen. 1.28 apparently trumping 1 Cor. 7.9 again.[212] In some subsequent allegorical epics, the conflict between natural and divine law is made explicit: Dame Nature threatens the order of the Christian cosmos. In Guillaume de Deguileville's *Pèlerinage de la vie humaine* (*c.* 1330), for example, Dame Nature hubristically accuses Dame Grace of having taken liberties with the laws of nature by causing the virgin birth and the eucharistic transformation of wine into blood. A disputation ensues, and in the end, defeated by the *ex auctoritate* arguments of Grace, Nature has to acknowledge her subservient, sublunary status in the divine hierarchy. Grace compares her to a "porc sauvage".[213]

In fourteenth-century England, Natura again takes on a judicial role on issues of sexuality, but its verdicts have become more ambivalent: approximately 100 years after *De Planctu Naturae*, Chaucer's epic *Parlement of Foules* (*c.* 1380) also describes a dream vision, once again strongly inspired by Alan of Lille, as Chaucer himself acknowledges.[214] In the beautiful Garden of Love, the narrator passes some allegorical figures, associated with the rewards and dangers of love, before he finally encounters Dame Nature in a naturally grown palace:

> [...] ther sat a quene
> That, as of light the somer-sonne shene
> Passeth the sterre, right so over mesure
> She fairer was than any creature.
> And in a launde, upon an hille of floures,
> Was set this noble goddesse Nature;
> Of braunches were hir halles and hir boures,
> Y-wrought after hir craft and hir mesure;
> Ne ther nas foul that cometh of engendrure,
> That they ne were prest in hir presence,
> To take hir doom and yeve hir audience.[215]

Nature bids all the birds that surround her to take their proper place, then makes a speech in which she emphasizes that the birds have arrived on her orders, in the interest of mate selection:

212 See also Jeremy Cohen, *Be Fertile and Increase, Fill the Earth and Master It: The Ancient and Medieval Career of a Biblical Text*, Ithaca, NY: Cornell University Press, 1989, pp. 271–305.

213 See Rebecca Davis, Piers Plowman *and the Books of Nature*, Oxford: Oxford University Press 2017, pp. 69–76.

214 Geoffrey Chaucer, *The Parliament of Fowls*, in *Dream Visions and Other Poems*, ed. Kathryn L. Lynch, New York and London, W. W. Norton and Co., 2007, p. 106 [316].

215 Chaucer, *The Parliament of Fowls*, p. 105 [298–308].

By my statut and through my governaunce,
Ye come for to chese – and flee your way –
Your makes, as I prik yow with plesaunce.[216]

The rhyme of "governaunce" und "plesaunce" here seems significant, suggesting even by the assonance that the mating instinct and its expressions are a manifestation of Nature's law in action. Since Nature also insists on social hierarchy as another manifestation of natural order, the eagles, as the noblest birds, will begin with the choice of their mates. Immediately, a problem arises since three male eagles vie for the affection of the same female eagle, using the rhetoric of courtly love. Several birds from the lower ranks grow tired of the ensuing discussion, protesting that they have their own mates and do not want to be dragged into the useless discussions of their superiors. Incompatibilities between the demands of aristocratic courtly love and the natural demands of procreation articulate themselves. Instigated by Nature, the birds decide that the she-eagle herself must decide the case, but the latter asserts that she cannot make a choice and needs another year to resolve herself. Her request is granted by Nature, the other birds all pair off, and the vision ends. In Chaucer's text, Nature is less insistent on the imperative to be fruitful and multiply, at least as far as the most elevated members of the natural community are concerned. Thus, she establishes a provisional harmony between the demand for procreation and the social rules that govern the aristocracy.

In William Langland's *Piers Plowman* (*c.* 1380), Nature/Kynde makes a more sublime and frightening appearance; the figure is male and, in the tradition of Augustine and Eriugena, largely identified with God, or at least a representative of God. He sends Death, Old Age and diverse diseases to punish human disobedience:

"Kynde," quod Wit, "is creatour of alle kynnes þynges,
Fader and formour of al þat euere was maked –
And þat is þe grete God þat gynnyng hadde neuere,
Lord of lif and of liȝt, of lisse and of peyne.
Aungeles and alle þyng arn at his wille,
Ac man is hym moost lik of marc and of shafte". […]
Kynde Conscience þo herde, and cam out of þe planetes,
And sente forþ his forreyours – feueres and fluxes,
Coughes and cardiacles, crampes and tooþaches,
Rewmes and radegundes and roynouse scalles,
Biles and bocches and brennynge agues,
Frenesies and foule yueles – forageres of Kynde,
Hadde ypriked and prayed polles of peple;
Largeliche a legion lees hir lif soone.

216 Chaucer, *The Parliament of Fowls*, p. 108 [387–390].

There was "Harrow!" and "Help! Here comeþ Kynde,
With Deeþ þat is dredful, to vndo vs alle!"[217]

"Nature," said Intelligence, "contrived all things,
He's the father who formed every facet of life,
The God so great that he had no beginning,
God of light and life, of pleasure and pain,
And angels and all things are at his will,
Though man most resembles him in stature and shape". [...]
Nature heeded Conscience and came from the cosmos
And sent out his foragers, fevers and fluxes,
Cardiac cramps and toothaches and coughs,
Colds and sores and suppurating scabs,
Boils and blotches and burning palsies,
Fits and spasms and vile diseases,
Which settled on people's scalps and skins,
Till a legion of sufferers lost their lives.
"Help!" folk hollered. "Here comes Nature
With dreadful Death to undo us all!"[218]

But this dreadful image remains an exception. In almost all other allegories, Natura does double duty as a positive figure, representing not only universal law and divine order but also procreative fertility (occasionally including intellectual creativity).[219] The assertion that these very different vocations harmonise conflict with the passages in the New Testament that denounce procreation in favour of a truly religious life (e.g. 1 Cor. 7). In the *Roman de la Rose*, the service to nature by way of procreation is nevertheless designated as the true act with which to worship God and enact his will:

Ainz veulent Nature destruire
Quant ses enclumes veulent fuire,

217 William Langland, *Piers Plowman, A Parallel-Text Edition of the A, B, C and Z Versions*, Vol. 1, ed. A. V. C. Schmidt, London and New York: Longman, 1995, pp. 372/724 [B 9.26–31; B 20.80–89].

218 William Langland, *Piers Plowman: A Modern Verse Translation*, trans. Peter Sutton, Jefferson: McFarland, 2014, pp. 101/244 [9.26–31; 20.82–91]. See also Rebecca Davis, *Piers Plowman and the Books of Nature*. Another prominent appearance of Dame Nature in Middle English poetry occurs in John Lydgate's fragmentary allegory *Reason and Sensuality*. However, the text of this admirer of Chaucer is very much in the tradition of Alan of Lille and rather unoriginal: a beautiful Dame Nature appears to the poet in a dream vision and presents herself as God's supreme servant, both inducing and policing man's inclinations. See John Lydgate, *Reson and Sensuallyte*, ed. Ernst Sieper, London: Kegan Paul, Trench, Trübner and Company, 1901. See also Edgar C. Knowlton, "Nature in Middle English", *The Journal of English and Germanic Philology* 20:2 (1921), pp. 192–194.

219 Natura seems to make her first appearance as a Muse figure in *L'Avision-Christine* by Christine de Pizan. See Newman, *God and the Goddesses*, p. 122.

E ses tables e ses jaschieres,
Qu'el fist precieuses et chieres,
Pour les choses continuer,
Que Mort ne les peüst tuer.
Bien deüssent avoir grant honte
Cil desleial don je vous conte
Quant il ne deignent la main metre
En tables pour escrivre letre,
Ne pour faire empreinte qui pere; [...]
Vis les puisse l'en enfoïr,
Quant les oustiz osent foïr
Que Deus de sa main entailla
Quant a ma dame les bailla,
Qui por ce les li vost baillier,
Qu'el seüst auteus entaillier
Pour doner estres pardurables
Aus creatures corrompables.[220]

> The false ones will not [...] serve and honour Nature; instead they wish to destroy her by fleeing the anvils, tablets and fallow fields that she has made so rich and dear, so that things might be continued and Death prevented from killing them. They ought to be deeply ashamed, those disloyal ones of whom I speak, who will not deign to put their hands to the tablets to write a letter nor to make any visible mark upon them. [...] These people should be buried alive for daring to neglect the tools that God fashioned with his own hand and gave to my lady. He chose to give them to her so that she would be able to make similar ones and so give eternal life to mortal creatures.[221]

The eternal life that is promised here is that of the species; its paradise inheres in the joys of love that propagate humankind. In this way, the natural world and the kingdom of God are unified; however, the kingdom of God seems to have been secularized in the process. Divine chastity has become a form of sexual deviance. It is particularly interesting in this context that procreation is insistently metaphorized not only as an agricultural activity, as ploughing or sowing, but also as a performative act of inscription on materials, as writing or minting. (Shakespeare's sonnets will perpetuate both metaphors.)[222] Once

220 Lorris and Meun, *Le Roman de la Rose*, Vol. 5, pp. 6–7 [19555–19565; 19575–19582].

221 Lorris and Meun, *The Romance of the Rose*, trans. Horgan, pp. 301–302.

222 See e.g. Sonnet 3 and Sonnet 11: "Let those whom nature hath not made for store,/ Harsh, featureless and rude, barrenly perish./ Look whom she best endowed she gave the more,/ Which bounteous gift thou shouldst in bounty cherish./ She carved thee for her seal, and meant thereby/ Thou shouldst print more, not let that copy die". William Shakespeare, Sonnet 11, in *The Norton Shakespeare*, ed. Stephen Greenblatt, New York and London: W. W. Norton and Co., 1997, pp. 1926–1927.

more, the production of significant artefacts and the production of children are equated. Even more conspicuously than in the *Planctus Naturae*, Natura seems strangely powerless for so formidable and high-ranking a deity. She can be attacked by mere mortals: for Nature to be immortal in the full sense of the word, man must collaborate with her. Thus, both Nature and man must take measures to defend themselves against antinatural behaviour; this strife for divine self-perpetuation seems to be their common foremost political priority. On the one hand, Nature asserts the harmony between the resultant law of procreation and the individual desires. On the other hand, the plot of these short epics develops from the germinal fact that there are inherent tensions between both forces. In all cases, these tensions find their expression in a peculiar trial with religious overtones and an uncertain outcome – a trial that tends to be represented in epic form.

In a more metaphysical mood, the reader reencounters Dame Nature and her all-embracing jurisdiction in the seventh book of Edmund Spenser's *Faerie Queene*, namely the "Mutabilitie Cantos", published posthumously in 1609. Again, Nature appears as a supreme judge, but by now it is explicitly asserted that she has legal authority even over the pagan gods and Titans. The conflict she has to decide upon is one over precedence: the female Titan Mutabilitie, who always has had a tendency to break "the lawes of Nature", starts an insurrection.[223] She leaves the sublunar sphere and, on her way to heaven, attacks the moon goddess Cynthia, pushing her off her throne. When Mercury comes to investigate, she challenges him and Jove, claiming supremacy by primogeniture in the ensuing discussion, whereas Jove claims supremacy by right of conquest.[224] Mutabilitie appeals to the higher authority of Nature to decide the issue:

> But thee, ô Ioue, no equall Iudge I deeme
> Of my desert, or of my dewfull Right;
> That in thine owne behalfe maist partiall seeme:
> But to the highest him, that is behight
> Father of Gods and men by equall might;
> To weet, the God of Nature, I appeale.
> There-at Ioue wexed wroth, and in his spright
> Did inly grudge, yet did it well conceale;
> And bade Dan Phoebus Scribe her Appellation seale.[225]

223 Edmund Spenser, *The Faerie Queene*, ed. A. C. Hamilton, Harlow: Longman, 2001, p. 692 [7.6.5–6].

224 This conflict between primogeniture and the right of conquest has a long history and was a frequent topic in Spenser's time. See e.g. Kristin M. S. Bezio, *Staging Power in Tudor and Stuart English History Plays: History, Political Thought, and the Redefinition of Sovereignty*, Farnham: Ashgate, 2015, pp. 64–65.

225 Spenser, *The Faerie Queene*, p. 697 [7.6.35].

For the ensuing trial, all living creatures assemble around a mountain in Ireland. On the mountain's top, in a pavilion which "th'earth her self of her owne motion,/ Out of her fruitfull bosome made to growe",[226] Nature appears, veiled:

Then forth issewed (great goddesse) great dame Nature,
With goodly port and gracious Maiesty;
Being far greater and more tall of stature
Then any of the gods or Powers on hie:
Yet certes by her face and physnomy,
Whether she man or woman inly were,
That could not any creature well descry:
For, with a veile that wimpled euery where,
Her head and face was hid, that mote to none appeare.

That some doe say was so by skill deuized,
To hide the terror of her vncouth hew,
From mortall eyes that should be sore agrized;
For that her face did like a Lion shew,
That eye of wight could not indure to view:
But others tell that it so beautious was,
And round about such beames of splendor threw,
That it the Sunne a thousand times did pass,
Ne could be seene, but like an image in a glass.[227]

It remains not only unclear whether the reason for her Heraclitean concealment is extreme beauty or extreme frightfulness. Even her gender is in doubt: although she is constantly addressed with female pronouns, Mutabilitie also designates her as "Father".[228] Nature remains a figure of latency throughout, "vnseene of any, yet of all beheld".[229] And, in explicitly referring to his precursors Chaucer and Alan of Lille, Spenser links this characteristic to the circumstance that she has become a figure in a covert literary tradition.[230] Just as in the *Planctus*, Spenser's Nature first receives the spontaneous adoration of all living beings before the trial begins. Subsequently, Mutabilitie repeats the accusation that Jove is usurping her sovereignty and appeals to Nature's strong sense of justice. To prove her point, she holds forth

226 Spenser, *The Faerie Queene*, p. 702 [7.7.8].
227 Spenser, *The Faerie Queene*, p. 702 [7.7.5–6].
228 Spenser, *The Faerie Queene*, p. 697 [7.6.697].
229 Spenser, *The Faerie Queene*, p. 703 [7.7.13].
230 "So hard it is for any liuing wight,/ All her array and vestiments to tell,/ That old *Dan Geffrey* (in whose gentle spright/ The pure well head of Poesie did dwell)/ In his *Foules parley* durst not with it mel,/ But it transferd to *Alane*, who he thought/ Had in his *Plaint of kindes* describ'd it well:/ Which who will read set forth so as it ought,/ Go seek he out that *Alane* where he may be sought". Spenser, *The Faerie Queene*, p. 702 [7.7.9].

extensively on the mutability of all things. When it is Jove's turn, he asserts briefly that it is precisely the rule of the gods that causes all these changes. Mutabilitie retorts that this rule is not evident. Another thing is evident, however: not only all mortal things, but even the gods are subject to change – for example, they were all born at some point in time. Nature ponders the question for a while, and then predictably decides in favour of Jove. The reason for the decision is interesting, however:

> I well consider all that ye haue sayd,
> And find that all things stedfastnes doe hate
> And changed be: yet being rightly wayd
> They are not changed from their first estate;
> But by their change their being doe dilate:
> And turning to themselues at length againe,
> Doe worke their owne perfection so by fate:
> Then ouer them Change doth not rule and raigne;
> But they raigne ouer change, and doe their states maintaine.[231]

Remarkably, it is the supposed subordination of all things to the inherent feedback processes of nature that finally decides the question of precedence. Nature itself/herself/himself traditionally figures precisely as this constant sublation of change into an eternal framework of laws, hence as an interested party in the trial: her assertion of Jove's superiority is actually an act of self-assertion. Somewhat abruptly, as if aware of this partiality in her argument, Nature inserts a snippet of additional Christianity into the pagan context, namely a reference to the Last Judgment: "But time shall come that all shall changed bee,/ And from thenceforth, none no more change shall see".[232] However, it is the legitimacy of any authoritative divine judgment that Mutabilitie has challenged in the first place, and thus Nature's argument is clearly circular. Nonetheless, on this note, the trial and the poem ends. In their insistence on Nature's circularity and latency, they seem to reaffirm the Aristotelian position. Only the association of Nature with desire and procreation is less pronounced in Spenser. Yet it is all the more central in Nature's numerous appearances within other early modern allegorical poems: for example, in Robert Chester's "Love's Martyr",[233] she frequently appears as a spokesperson or governor of love, but always either as a mourning accuser or as a judge and administratrix.

This literary history of personified Natura is complemented by developments in iconography. Whereas the juridical function of Nature seems to become ever more prominent in late medieval and early modern epic and

231 Spenser, *The Faerie Queene*, p. 711 [7.7.58].
232 Spenser, *The Faerie Queene*, p. 711 [7.7.59].
233 Robert Chester, *Love's Martyr or Rosalin's Complaint*, ed. Alexander B. Grosart, London: Trubner, 1878.

poetry, it is rendered increasingly invisible in art. A good exemplification of this tendency can be found in the history of Cesare Ripa's *Iconologia* (1603), a work that codified the iconographical tradition and was enormously influential over the next few centuries.[234] According to Ripa, Natura's official dress is no longer merely torn, she is completely denuded and also seems to be stripped of her administrative office. His description of her reads:

> Donna ignuda, con le mammelle cariche di latte, & con vn' auoltore in mano, come si vede in vna Medaglia d'Adriano Imperatore, essendo la Natura, come diffinisce Aristotile nel 2. della Fisica, principio in quella cosa, oue ella si ritroua del moto, & della mutatione, per la quale si genera ogni cosa corruttibile./ Si farà donna, & ignuda, & diuidendosi questo principio in attiuo, & passiuo, l'attiuo dimandorono con il nome di forma, & con nome di materia il passiuo./ L'attiuo si nota con le mammelle piene di latte, perche la forma è che nudrisce, & sostenuta tutte le cose create, come con le mammelle la donna nutrisce, & sostenta li fanciulli./ L'auoltore vccello auidissimo di preda, dimostra particolarmente l'altro principio dimandato materia, la quale per lo appetito della forma mouendosi, & alterandosi strugge à poco à poco tutte le cose corruttibili.[235]
>
> Naked woman, with breasts full of milk and with a vulture in her hand, as depicted on a medal of the Emperor Hadrian; this is Nature, as Aristotle defines it in the second book of his *Physics*, in which it is posited as the origin of movement and change by which all corruptible things are generated. This principle is to be depicted as as woman and as naked, dividing itself into an active and a passive principle, the active receiving the name of form, the passive the name of matter. The active shows itself in the breasts filled with milk, because it is the form which nourishes and sustains all created things, as the woman nourishes and sustains the children with her breasts. The vulture, a rapacious bird, represents the other principle which is called matter; moving and changing by the hunger of form, it slowly consumes all perishable things.[236]

The Aristotelian notion of nature involved both growth and corruption, frequently represented as the administration of natural rewards and punishments. In Ripa's image, the bad, corrosive and "material" side of Nature is exteriorized in the form of the vulture, and in subsequent icons, this destructive shadow is subtracted, for the vulture very rarely appears in

234 Kemp, *Natura: Ikonographische Studien zur Geschichte und Verbreitung einer Allegorie*, pp. 21, 23.

235 Cesare Ripa, *Iconologia*, Rome: Lepido Faci, 1603, pp. 351–352.

236 Translation BQ. It might be mentioned in passing that the "medal of the Emperor Hadrian" which is mentioned apparently never existed and just serves to suggest that this description is based on the *sapientia veterum*. (Kemp, *Natura: Ikonographische Studien zur Geschichte und Verbreitung einer Allegorie*, p. 22.)

other representations of Natura. Much more common is the sole image of the *Natura lactans*: a beautiful young woman from whose breasts squirt milk – a maternal image of seductive sexuality.[237] Sometimes Natura was even depicted with multiple breasts, resembling the famous statue of Artemis/Magna Mater from Ephesus.[238]

This sexualized maternal image also found its way onto the stages of public ceremony where we encounter it occasionally in pageants and court masques. When Henry VI returned to London after his coronation as King of France in 1431, he was received with a pageant in the course of which Dame Nature addressed him with a poetical eulogy.[239] This power play spawned many successors, for example, the interlude *Nature* (published between 1529 and 1535) by Henry Medwall, in which Nature introduces herself as God's "minister" who "should, perpetually,/ His creatures in such degree maintain/ As it hath pleased His grace for them to ordain".[240] But in the play, she is reduced to offering some motherly admonitions to Man. Nature acts in a similar fashion in the masque *The Visit of the Nine Goddesses* (1621) in which she offers her protection to James I.[241] One of her most notable appearances in a court masque occurs in Ben Jonson's *Mercury Vindicated* (1615) which also emphasizes the role of Nature as a provider who endows the court, and first and foremost the ruler, with sexual, artistic and political power.[242] One play in which Nature comes to act as judge is *The Woman in the Moon* by John Lyly (1597), a rewriting of the Pandora myth. Nature here is described as the supreme deity, the "only Queen"[243] of the cosmos. It is never said that she takes orders from God; instead, she seems to have taken over his titles: she is addressed as "author of the world,/ Of all that was, or is, or shall be framed".[244] Not restricted to the sublunary sphere, she claims to have "ordained" the motions of the planets who are equated with

237 Kemp, *Natura: Ikonographische Studien zur Geschichte und Verbreitung einer Allegorie*, pp. 17–25.

238 Kemp, *Natura: Ikonographische Studien zur Geschichte und Verbreitung einer Allegorie*, pp. 25–29. See also Hadot, *The Veil of Isis*, illustrations 2, 7, 9, 11 and 14.

239 Enid Welsford, *The Court Masque: A Study in the Relationship Between Poetry and the Revels*, Cambridge: Cambridge University Press, 1927, pp. 50–51.

240 Henry Medwall, "Nature", in *Recently Recovered "Lost" Tudor Plays with Some Others*, ed. John S. Farmer, London: English Drama Society, 1907, p. 43. Interestingly, Nature in this play occasionally refers to Aristotle as to her "philosopher elect" (Id., p. 45). (Medwall's interlude seems to be partly inspired by John Lydgate's poem *Reason and Sensuality* in which Nature has a similar role. See W. Roy Mackenzie, "A Source for Medwall's *Nature*", *PMLA* 29:2 (1914), pp. 189–199.)

241 C. E. McGee, "'The Visit of the Nine Goddesses': A Masque at Sir John Crofts's House", *English Literary Renaissance* 21:2 (1991), pp. 371–384.

242 Ben Jonson, *The Complete Masques*, ed. Stephen Orgel, New Haven, CT: Yale University Press, 1969, pp. 221–223.

243 John Lyly, *The Woman in the Moon*, ed. Leah Scragg, Manchester/New York: Manchester University Press, 2006, p. 52 [Prologus, 6].

244 Lyly, *The Woman in the Moon*, p. 55 [1.1.31–32].

the Olympian gods.[245] All living beings are said to "yield themselves to follow Nature's doom"[246] and they behave accordingly, although they occasionally try to disobey her. Thus Nature is represented as the world's supreme administratrix and judge, as well as the great creatrix. At the beginning of the play, instigated of some shepherds, she creates woman as her creation's crowning glory. Nature calls this first human female Pandora and endows her with inward and outward gifts, while warning her: "Use all these well, and Nature is thy friend,/ But use them ill, and Nature is thy foe".[247] The planetary gods, who are depicted as aristocrats at Nature's court, envy the perfection of the new creation and consider themselves diminished by Pandora's excellencies. When they complain, however, Nature sees no need to justify her creation: "It was my will, and that shall stand for law".[248] She even threatens the gods:

> But I have means to end what I begun,
> And make Death triumph in your lives' decay.
> If thus you cross the meed of my deserts,
> Be sure I will dissolve your harmony,
> When once you touch your fixèd period.[249]

The planetary gods feel slighted and decide to sabotage the new creation while Nature is absent, spreading bad planetary influences which lead Pandora into delusions, entanglements and diverse conflicts with her adoring entourage of shepherds. At the end of the play, Nature returns and castigates everyone except Pandora, whom she sees as a victim of her surroundings and elevates to the status of a moon goddess. In accordance with Nature's condemnations, Pandora's servant is transformed into a hawthorn bush and her jealous husband into the unhappy and enslaved Man in the Moon. And with this verdict, the play ends.

However, Nature as sovereign judge never became a stock character in the repertoire: after Lyly, she no longer appears in the theatres as an adjudicator and punisher, but assumes a thoroughly maternal and nourishing role, generously showering her aristocratic children with gifts and indulging their whims. This image of the *Magna Mater* is still present in the ceremonies of the eighteenth century; it was even adapted by the masterminds of the French Revolution when a great statue of the figure was built for the anniversary of the monarchy's abolition in 1793.[250]

245 Lyly, *The Woman in the Moon*, p. 60 [1.1.122].
246 Lyly, *The Woman in the Moon*, p. 52 [Prologus, 10].
247 Lyly, *The Woman in the Moon*, p. 59 [1.1.105–106].
248 Lyly, *The Woman in the Moon*, p. 59 [1.1.120].
249 Lyly, *The Woman in the Moon*, p. 60 [1.1.125–128].
250 Kemp, *Natura: Ikonographische Studien zur Geschichte und Verbreitung einer Allegorie*, pp. 170–175.

Before finishing this iconographical overview and refocusing on the field of medieval philosophy, a side remark is in order: since nature, from its antique beginnings, is not only conceived as a legislator, but also as the law itself, another conventional metaphor would be worth investigating in this context, namely that of the Book of Nature, which is first and foremost a book of law, supplementing the Bible. In his study *Die Lesbarkeit der Welt*, Hans Blumenberg has outlined the career of this metaphor from its first elaboration by Augustine to its resumption by Ernst Schrödinger, and little can be added to his account.[251] Blumenberg already hints at the problem that Nature's book of law tends to coincide with its own area of application.[252] However, one might emphasize another aspect of the book metaphor more than Blumenberg has done: in the most dominant Christian version of the metaphor, nature represents something beyond it, namely the divine will. All things are to be regarded as signs which emanate from God and whose ultimate signified is God as the ultimate Good.[253] Often, the manifestation of God's grandeur is thought to be the most important motivation for the world's creation, and one might term this an aesthetic goal. Accordingly, God is often presented as *deus poeta* in medieval times, and the whole of nature as his great artwork – a kinetic installation, one might say.[254] He is the only true poet, since human poetry relies on nature, whereas divine art creates "ex nihilo".[255] Just as Dame Nature asserts a harmony between law and healthy desire, the Book of Nature asserts a harmony between created beauty and legality, echoing Stoicist conceptions of *natura poeta* in the process.

1.7 Scholasticism: legal affirmations *ex nihilo*

Medieval philosophy represents the world both as an artwork and as a state in which God rules as lawgiver and eternal sovereign.[256] Divine jurisdiction

251 Blumenberg, *Die Lesbarkeit der Welt*.

252 See e.g. Blumenberg, *Die Lesbarkeit der Welt*, p. 57.

253 As Susannah Ticciati expresses it: "[A]ll creatures of God, as uttered by God, remain signs of God for God". Susannah Ticciati, *A New Apophaticism: Augustine and the Redemption of Signs*, Leiden and Boston: Brill, 2013, p. 179. Again, Augustine plays an important role in the development of this topic. See also Peter Harrison, *The Bible, Protestantism, and the Rise of Natural Science*, Cambridge: Cambridge University Press, 1998, pp. 28–33.

254 Philo of Alexandria seems to have been the first to present the works of nature as God's poem. Philo of Alexandria, *Quod deterius potiori insidiari soleat*, ed. Irène Feuer, Paris: Éditions du Cerf, 1965, pp. 96/97 [§§ 124–125]. He could refer to the Nicene Creed and to the Septuagint, since in both God is designated as the ποιητής of the world. Nicene Creed: "Πιστεύομεν εἰς ἕνα θεόν, πατέρα, παντοκράτορα, πάντων ὁρατῶν τε και ἀοράτων ποιητήν." John Norman Davidson Kelly, *Altchristliche Glaubensbekenntnisse: Geschichte und Theologie*, Göttingen: Vandenhoeck und Ruprecht, 1972, p. 215. Gen. 1.1: "Ἐν ἀρχῇ ἐποίησεν ὁ θεὸς τὸν οὐρανὸν καὶ τὴν γῆν." *Septuaginta,* ed. Alfred Rahlfs, Stuttgart: Deutsche Bibelgesellschaft, 1979, p. 1. See also Hadot, *The Veil of Isis*, p. 201.

255 Flasch, "Ars imitatur naturam", pp. 267–268.

256 Curtius, *Europäische Literatur und lateinisches Mittelalter*, p. 127. John Scotus Eriugena speaks of a "republica naturarum", in which God introduces order: "Si enim Deus

seems to thoroughly determine the proceedings in nature's court: the Lord's role as the legislator of nature has been treated extensively by scholasticism, and in this context, scholastic thinkers such as Gratian, William of Auxerre, Roger Bacon and Thomas Aquinas perpetuate and modify the natural law discourses of antiquity.[257] The reworkings of Aquinas and Duns Scotus have been particularly influential; the former even had a decisive impact on Christian epics, such as Dante's *Divina Comedia*.[258] For our purposes, the most interesting feature of Aquinas' theory is the strange way in which it entangles divine and natural jurisdiction: the *Summa Theologica* differentiates between the *lex aeterna* (the eternal law enclosed within the mind of God) and the *lex naturalis* (the limited part of the eternal law which is discernible to God's creatures). This natural law is perceptible in the creatures' inherent inclination toward the good. In man, most prominently, inheres an inbuilt dynamism toward sociality, knowledge, self-preservation, procreation, and the recognition of God – all limited by the constraints of reason.[259] God himself has installed this *inclinatio naturalis* into each thing and thus directs it by its internal dynamics:

> [N]ecessitas naturalis inhaerens rebus quae determinantur ad unum, est impressio quaedam Dei dirigentis ad finem, sicut necessitas qua sagitta agitur ut ad certum signum tendat, est impressio sagittantis, et non sagittae. Sed in hoc differt, quia id quod creaturae a Deo recipiunt, est earum natura; quod autem ab homine rebus naturalibus imprimitur praeter earum naturam, ad violentiam pertinet.
>
> The natural necessity inherent in those beings which are determined to a particular thing, is a kind of impression from God, directing them to their end; as the necessity whereby an arrow is moved so as to fly towards a certain point is an impression from the archer, and not from the arrow. But there is a difference, inasmuch as that which creatures receive from

aequaliter, absque ulla ordinum diversorum differentia et proprietate et ascensione et descensione variorum graduum universitatem conditam faceret, et nullus fortassis ordo in republica naturarum fieret". John Scotus Eriugena, *Expositiones super Ierarchiam caelestem S. Dionysii*, in *Opera*, Vol. 1, ed. Heinrich Joseph Floss, Paris: Migne, 1865, col. 212.

257 Brague, *The Law of God*, p. 218. Gratian affirms that natural law is part of biblical law, since the Golden Rule, which he designates as the essence of the *ius naturae*, is stated in the New Testament (Cornelia Schweiger, *Die Naturrechtskonzeption des Antoninus von Florenz OP: Ein Spiegel theoretischen Erbes oder praktischer Erfordernisse?*, Berlin: Lit, 2012, p. 74).

258 Whether he read Aquinas or not, Dante's conception of law in his theoretical tractates and his poetry can generally be regarded as Thomistic. See e.g. Hans Kelsen, "Die Staatslehre des Dante Alighieri", in *Veröffentlichte Schriften 1905–1910 und Selbstzeugnisse,* ed. Matthias Jestaedt, Tübingen: Mohr Siebeck, 2007, p. 187. See also Hugo Friedrich, *Die Rechtsmetaphysik der Göttlichen Komödie*, Frankfurt am Main: V. Klostermann, 1942, pp. 96–98.

259 Thomas Aquinas, *Summa Theologiae Prima Secundae, 71–114*, Latin/English Edition, trans. Laurence Shapcote, Lander, WY: Aquinas Institute, 2012, pp. 228–230 [Summa 2.1, Quaestio 94, Art. 2].

> God is their nature, while that which natural things receive from man in addition to their nature is somewhat violent.[260]

Divine and natural law are supplemented by the positive law, *lex humana*, which is merely the human attempt to imitate the natural law, best aided by the revealed law of the Bible, the *lex divina*.[261] According to Aquinas, the supreme maxim of the natural law from which all other precepts of nature derive is the blanket statement that "good should be done" ("bonum est faciendum").[262] Duns Scotus specifies that the central commandment that logically generates all others more specifically postulates that "God should be loved".[263] This imperative includes the self-love of God, a natural inclination to which God is bound by law.[264] Duns Scotus further elaborates that the creaturely natural inclination should neither be unrestrainedly indulged in nor altogether suppressed, but moderated in a way that is consistent with the will of God:

> Quando ergo accipitur, quod voluntas consona voluntati naturali semper est recta quia et illa semper est recta; respondeo et dice, quad si consonat sibi in eliciendo actum (sicut illa eliceret si ex se sola ageret) non est recta, quia habet aliam regulam in agenda quam illa non haberet si ex se sola ageret; tenetur enim sequi voluntatem superiorem in moderando illam inclinationem naturalem, ex quo in potestate eius est moderari, vel non moderari quia in potestate eius est non summe agere, vel non tantum quantum potest.[265]
>
> As for the assumption, then, that a will conformed to a natural will [or appetite] is always right, because what is natural is always right, I reply by saying this. If in eliciting its act, the will behaves as it would if it were acting solely on its own, then it is not right, for it has another rule for

260 Thomas Aquinas, *Summa Theologiae Prima Pars, 50–119*, Latin/English Edition, trans. Laurence Shapcote, Lander, WY: Aquinas Institute, 2012, p. 492 [Summa 1, Quaestio 103, Art. 1].

261 However, many scholastics emphasize that the secular positive law, made by worldly rulers, does not merge with the law of God. The *ius consuetudinis* of the commonwealth might assuage the effects of the Fall, but it is not an absolute Good in itself. Gratian points out that Cain was the founder of the first state. See Peter Landau, "Der biblische Sündenfall und die Legitimität des Rechts", in *Die Begründung des Rechts als historisches Problem, Schriften des Historischen Kollegs 45*, ed. Dietmar Willoweit and Elisabeth Müller-Luckner, Munich: Oldenbourg, 2000, pp. 204/210.

262 Thomas Aquinas, *Summa Theologiae Prima Secundae, 71–114*, p. 229 [Summa 2.1, Quaestio 94, Art. 2].

263 John Duns Scotus, "Ordinatio, 4.46.1", cited in Richard Cross, "Natural Law, Moral Constructivism, and Duns Scotus's Metaethics: The Centrality of Aesthetic Explanation", in *Reason, Religion, and Natural Law: From Plato to Spinoza*, ed. Jonathan A. Jacobs, Oxford and New York: Oxford University Press, 2012, p. 183.

264 Cross, "Natural Law, Moral Constructivism, and Duns Scotus's Metaethics", p. 184.

265 John Duns Scotus, "Ordinatio 2, Distinctio 6", in *Commentaria Oxoniensa*, Vol. 4.2, Florence: Ad Claras Aquas, 1914, p. 393 [Quaestio 2, Art. 1].

> acting than it would have if it were to act solely on its own. For it is bound to follow a higher will [viz. that of its Creator], from whom it was given the power to moderate or not moderate this natural inclination, for it has the power not to act in the most passionate and forceful way that it could.[266]

Thus, God again turns out to have instituted two natural laws, the one that is higher modifying and surpassing the lower one. And it is, unfortunately, the higher, surpassing one that is not immediately evident to the creature.[267] However, it is the law that all creatures are called to constantly execute on God's behalf. Therefore, it needs mediators who promulgate it. The question who exactly the supreme mediator is constitutes a point of contention. But the scholastics are less interested in that question than the early moderns; sometimes Christ takes the role, sometimes the Bible, sometimes the pope, sometimes the king.[268] In the scholastic disputes on the legal system of nature, another issue takes centre stage: how free is God in his determination of the laws of nature? Is his own power curtailed by the establishment of these laws? To answer this question, scholasticism differentiates between *potentia absoluta* and *potentia ordinata*, a theological differentiation that was influenced by political developments and influenced them in its turn.[269] Once again, Duns Scotus summarizes the issue lucidly:

> In omni agente per intellectum et voluntatem, potente conformiter agere legi rectae et tamen non necessario conformiter agere legi rectae, est distinguere potentiam ordinatam a potentia absoluta; et ratio huius est, quia potest agere conformiter illi legi rectae, et tunc secundum potentiam ordinatam (ordinata enim est in quantum est principium exsequendi aliqua conformiter legi rectae), et potest agere praeter illam legem vel contra eam, et in hoc est potentia absoluta, excedens potentiam ordinatam. Et ideo non tantum in Deo, sed in omni agente libere – qui potest agere secundum dictamen legis rectae et praeter talem legem vel contra eam – est distinguere inter potentiam ordinatam et absolutam; ideo

266 John Duns Scotus, "Ordinatio 2, Distinctio 6", in *On the Will and Morality*, eds. and trans. Allan B. Wolter and William A. Frank, Washington DC: Catholic University of America Press, 1997, pp. 300–301 [Quaestio 2, Art. 1].

267 A more modern variation of this theme can be found in John Fortescue, *De Natura Legis Naturae*, in: id., *Works*, ed. Thomas Fortescue, Lord Claremont, London: private distribution, 1869, pp. 63–336.

268 See e.g. Thomas Aquinas, *Über die Herrschaft der Fürsten*, trans. Friedrich Schreyvogl, Stuttgart: Reclam, 1990. Ewart Lewis, *Medieval Political Ideas*, Vol. 1, Abingdon and New York: Routledge, 2013, pp. 28–30.

269 See e.g. Giorgio Agamben, *Herrschaft und Herrlichkeit*, p. 130; William J. Courtenay, *Capacity and Volition: A History of the Distinction of Absolute and Ordained Power*, Bergamo: P. Lubrina, 1990, pp. 92–95.

> dicunt iuristae quod aliquis hoc potest facere de facto, hoc est de potentia sua absoluta, – vel de iure, hoc est de potentia ordinata secundum iura.[270]
>
> In every agent acting intelligently and voluntarily that can act in conformity with an upright or just law but does not have to do so of necessity, one can distinguish between its ordained power and its absolute power. The reason is that either it can act in conformity with some right and just law, and then it is acting according to its ordained power (for it is ordained insofar as it is a principle for doing something in conformity with a right or just law), or else it can act beyond or against such a law, and in this case its absolute power exceeds its ordained power. And therefore it is not only in God, but in every free agent that can either act in accord with the dictates of a just law or go beyond or against that law, that one distinguishes between absolute and ordained power; therefore, the jurists say that someone can act *de facto*, that is according to his absolute power, or *de jure*, that is, according to his ordained legal power.[271]

Whereas *potentia absoluta* designates the boundless divine omnipotence, *potentia ordinata* comprises the spectrum of things that God can do without transgressing the laws which he himself has posited – first and foremost, the covenant with the faithful which is interpreted as a contract by which God has agreed to bind himself to certain rules, as an absolute monarch may be bound by an oath. This covenant not only comprises the New Covenant instituted by Christ, but also the Noahide Covenant, which was made with all creatures and sealed by the rainbow. Expressly, it regulates the behaviour of the elements, that of men, animals and plants, but also that of God himself:

> And God blessed Noah and his sons, and said unto them: Be fruitful, and multiply, and replenish the earth. And the fear of you and the dread of you shall be upon every beast of the earth, and upon every fowl of the air, upon all that moveth upon the earth, and upon all the fishes of the sea; into your hand are they delivered. Every moving thing that liveth shall be meat for you; even as the green herb have I given you all things. But flesh with the life thereof, which is the blood thereof, shall ye not eat. And surely your blood of your lives will I require; at the hand of every beast will I require it, and at the hand of man; at the hand of every man's brother will I require the life of man. Whoso sheddeth man's blood, by man shall his blood be shed: for in the image of God made he man. And you, be ye fruitful, and multiply; bring forth abundantly in the earth, and multiply therein. And God spake unto Noah, and to his sons with him, saying: And I, behold, I establish my covenant with you, and with your seed after you;

270 John Duns Scotus, "Ordinatio 1, Distinctio 44", in *Opera Omnia*, Vol. 6, Vatican City: Typis Polyglottis Vaticanis, 1963, pp. 363–364.

271 John Duns Scotus, "Ordinatio 1, Distinctio 44", in *On the Will and Morality*, p. 191.

and with every living creature that is with you, of the fowl, of the cattle, and of every beast of the earth with you; from all that go out of the ark, to every beast of the earth. And I will establish my covenant with you, neither shall all flesh be cut off any more by the waters of a flood; neither shall there any more be a flood to destroy the earth. And God said, This is the token of the covenant which I make between me and you and every living creature that is with you, for perpetual generations: I do set my bow in the cloud, and it shall be for a token of a covenant between me and the earth. And it shall come to pass, when I bring a cloud over the earth, that the bow shall be seen in the cloud: and I will remember my covenant, which is between me and you and every living creature of all flesh; and the waters shall no more become a flood to destroy all flesh. (Gen. 9.1–15)

That "life" ["נֶפֶשׁ"/"nephesh"] seems to have a similar intermediate status here as "physis" and "natura" in the Greco-Roman context needs only to be remarked in passing at this point. At the moment, it is more important that God, in the cited passage, seems not only to renew his ancient command to be fruitful and multiply (Gen. 1.22, 1.28) and to establish a cosmic hierarchy and social rules between all living creatures, but also to submit to his own law which is henceforth as binding upon himself as upon all other parties. Opinions diverge on the question whether God would be morally condemnable if he would transgress this law, and even whether his decision never to destroy the earth is contingent upon his creatures' obedience.[272] Again, the situation remains unclear. And an even more mysterious question is also hotly debated in this context: how far does God's *potentia absoluta* extend? Are there natural and moral limits to it? Does it include an ability to do things that are inconceivable to human reason, such as the creation of a round triangle and other logically impossible objects? This discussion surmounts mere scholastic quibbling, since it has consequences for the question of whether the acts and laws of God are compatible with human reason (understood to be an imperfect and partial participation in divine reason).[273] Aquinas, echoing Plato, Aristotle and the Stoics, insists that God's acts and laws always accord or are even identical with divine reason:

> Impossibile est Deum velle nisi quod ratio suae sapientiae habet. Quae quidem est sicut lex iustitiae, secundum quam eius voluntas recta et iusta est. [...] Deus autem sibi ipsi est lex.

272 David Novak, *Natural Law in Judaism*, Cambridge and New York: Cambridge University Press, 1998, pp. 149 ff.

273 See e.g. Thomas Aquinas, *Summa Theologiae Prima Secundae, 71–114*, p. 206 [Summa 2.1, Quaestio 91, Art. 3].

> For God to will anything except what is held in the exemplar of his wisdom is out of the question. It is here that the law of justice lies whereby his will is right and fair. [...] God is a law unto himself.[274]

But Duns Scotus and William of Ockham, among others, object that this unduly limits God's power and authority. According to them, the natural order is not dependent on divine reason, but on divine will. And his will surpasses his reason; it involves his ability to change basic natural laws as well as to determine logical and mathematical truths.[275] Thus, the contingency of the natural, spiritual and even of the moral order is emphasized. Ultimately, according to this voluntarist position, absolutely everything depends on the divine will. Notoriously, Ockham asserts that acts such as murder and adultery would be good if God commanded them:

> Licet odium Dei, furari, adulterari habeant malam circumstantiam annexam et similia de communi lege quatenus fiunt ab aliquo qui ex precepto divino obligatur ad contrarium: [...] ista nomina significant tales actus non absolute: sed connotando vel dando intelligere quod faciens tales actus per preceptum divinum obligatur ad oppositum [...]. Si autem caderent sub precepto divino: tunc faciens tales actus non obligaretur ad oppositum et per consequens tunc non nominaretur furtum, adulterium etc.
>
> Although the hate of God, theft and adultery are qualified as bad – as are acts that under the common law are similar to them – because carried out by persons who by divine precept are bound to the contrary conduct: [...] these terms do not designate such acts in any absolute sense, but rather by implying or getting us to understand that the author of the same acts is obligated by divine precept to hold the opposite behaviour: [...] Whereas, if these acts were to be commanded by God, then their authors would not be bound to the opposite behaviour, and then, also, these acts would not in consequence be called "theft", "adultery" and so forth.[276]

However, even in the voluntarist worldview of Duns Scotus, the autonomy of God is limited. Richard Cross has demonstrated that the Scotist God is not altogether arbitrary in the selection of the laws that bind his creation: the construction and maintenance of the universe is not determined

274 Thomas Aquinas, *Summa Theologiae Prima Pars, 1–49*, p. 236 [Summa 1, Quaestio 21, Art. 1]. See also Thomas Aquinas, *Summa Theologiae Prima Secundae, 71–114*, p. 228–230 [Summa 2.1, Quaestio 94, Art. 2].

275 See e.g. Alister E. McGrath, *The Intellectual Origins of the European Reformation*, Malden, MA: Blackwell, 2004, p. 21.

276 William of Ockham, *Quaestiones in Librum Secundum Sententiarum* (a), q. 19, cited in Enrico Pattaro, *The Law and the Right: A Reappraisal of the Reality that Ought to Be*, Dordrecht: Springer, 2005, p. 74.

by moral intentions and restrictions, however, but by considerations of beauty and appropriateness.[277] Scotus develops an aesthetically inclined voluntarism that has had just as great an influence on some late medieval and early modern thinkers as the more Aristotelian conceptions of Aquinas.[278] Likewise, Ockham's theories of natural law also have had a considerable impact, despite their anti-telological and anti-essentialist tendencies.[279] According to Ockham, natural laws are occasionally subject to inscrutable divine revisions,[280] God's sole constraints being the requirements of internal consistency and non-contradiction which prevent the deity from becoming incoherent.[281] This emphasis on a mutable and unfathomable divine will at the heart of all things has often been interpreted as the harbinger of a more uncertain and dynamic worldview; consequently, Ockham is supposed to have influenced early modern thinkers such as Descartes and Jean Bodin, as well as Luther.[282] Hans Blumenberg writes in this context:

> The God who is subject only to the logical principle of contradiction is at the same time the God who can contradict himself, whose creation does not exclude the will to destruction, who stands over every present as the uncertainty of the future, in other words, finally, the God whose activity does not allow us to assume immanent laws and who puts all rational "constants" in question. The God who places no constraints on himself, who cannot be held accountable for any consequence of his

277 Cross, "Natural Law, Moral Constructivism, and Duns Scotus's Metaethics", p. 188.

278 Jonathan A. Jacobs, "Introduction", in *Reason, Religion, and Natural Law: From Plato to Spinoza*, ed. Jonathan A. Jacobs, Oxford and New York: Oxford University Press, 2012, p. 23.

279 Wolfgang Achtner, *Vom Erkennen zum Handeln: Die Dynamisierung von Mensch und Natur im ausgehenden Mittelalter als Voraussetzung für die Entstehung naturwissenschaftlicher Rationalität*, Göttingen: Vandenhoeck und Ruprecht, 2008, pp. 298–312.

280 See e.g. "Si enim sint simpliciter precepta iuris naturalis, nullus casus excipi debet propter quamcumque necessitatem vel utilitatem, nisi Deus specialiter aliquem exciperet (quemadmodum, non obstante precepto iuris meri naturalis de nullo innocente scienter interficiendo, Deus precipiendo Abrahe ut immolaret filium suum specialem exceptionem fecit)". "If they are simply commandments of natural law, no case should be excepted for any necessity or utility whatever, unless God specially excepted some case (as, notwithstanding the commandment of purely natural law about not knowingly killing the innocent God made a special exception in commanding Abraham to sacrifice his son)". William of Ockham, "A Dialogue", in *A Letter to the Friars Minor and Other Writings*, ed. Arthur Stephen McGrade and John Kilcullen, Cambridge: Cambridge University Press, 1995, p. 289 [3.1.2.24].

281 See e.g. "Omnipotens tamen potest efficere omne factibile quod non includit contradictionem [...]". "The omnipotent can effect everything doable that does not include an contradiction". William of Ockham, *Scriptum in librum primum sententiarum, Ordinatio, Distinctiones XIX–XLVIII*, ed. Girard Etzkorn and Francis Kelley, New York: The Franciscan Institute of St. Bonaventure University, 2000, p. 36.

282 See Wolfgang Achtner, *Vom Erkennen zum Handeln*, pp. 182–183. Francis Oakley, "Medieval Theories of Natural Law: William of Ockham and the Significance of the Voluntarist Tradition", *Natural Law Forum/The American Journal of Jurisprudence* 6.1 (1961), p. 75.

> manifestations, turns time into a dimension of utter uncertainty. This affects not only the identity of the subject, the presence of which at any given moment does not guarantee it any future, but also the persistence of the world, whose radical contingency can transform it, from one moment to the next, from existence into mere appearance, from reality into nothingness. Temporality becomes the crucial handicap of the human spirit. The philosophical impact of these considerations becomes clearest when one perceives in them the central motivation of Descartes's experiment in doubt in the *Meditations* [...].[283]

It is doubtful whether Ockham and his successors did really understand divine will in such disconcerting terms: several authors have criticized Blumenberg for exaggerating the bleak topicality of fourteenth-century nominalist thought.[284] However, Ockham's focus on the contingency of natural law certainly influenced subsequent discourses on the tribunals of Nature and their unfathomability.

Another area in which traces of voluntarist discourse can be ascertained is the differentiation between the normal ways of the world and their extraordinary, "supernatural" interruption by way of miracles.[285] In late medieval discourse, miracles are considered as communicative acts, divine proclamations in which God often emphasizes precisely that universal law which the miracle seems to have violated. Thus he indicates to his creatures that he himself is not subject to these natural laws and that his *potentia absoluta* is able to overcome nature.[286] This also touches upon the old and complex problem of divine inspiration under the conditions of Christianity: it would have been considered as heretical if poets had claimed to be inspired by the divinity in the same miraculous way in which the prophets and evangelists were inspired; therefore, poets such as Petraca and Boccaccio in their poetics distinguish between natural and supernatural inspiration and claim only the former.[287] That is, they assume that divine inspiration may also manifest itself through

283 Hans Blumenberg, *The Legitimacy of the Modern Age*, trans. Robert M. Wallace, Cambridge, MA and London: MIT Press, 1985, pp. 161–162 (translation modified). In the original: id., *Die Legitimität der Neuzeit*, Frankfurt am Main: Suhrkamp, 1996, pp. 180–181.

284 See e.g. Jürgen Goldstein, *Nominalismus und Moderne: Zur Konstitution neuzeitlicher Subjektivität bei Hans Blumenberg und Wilhelm von Ockham*, Freiburg and Munich: Karl Alber, 1998. Achtner, *Vom Erkennen zum Handeln*, p. 305. Wilhelm Vossenkuhl, "Vernünftige Kontingenz: Ockhams Verständnis der Schöpfung", in *Die Gegenwart Ockhams*, ed. Wilhelm Vossenkuhl and Rolf Schönberger, Weinheim: VCH Acta Humaniora, 1990, pp. 77–79.

285 On miracles in Duns Scotus, see Richard Cross, *The Metaphysics of the Incarnation: Thomas Aquinas to Duns Scotus*, New York and Oxford: Oxford University Press, 2002, p. 155. On miracles generally see e.g. Lorraine Daston and Katharine Park, *Wonders and the Order of Nature: 1150–1750*, New York: Zone, 1998.

286 Francis Oakley, *Natural Law, Laws of Nature, Natural Rights: Continuity and Discontinuity in the History of Ideas*, New York: Continuum, 2005, p. 57. See also Carl Schmitt, *Politische Theologie. Vier Kapitel zur Lehre von der Souveränität*, Berlin: Duncker und Humblot, 1996, p. 43.

287 Steppich, *Numine afflatur*, p. 363.

natural channels, namely in the impulsive workings of nature within the poet's mind. In this context, Boccaccio emphasises that the poet's art does not imitate the products of nature, but the powers and processes by which nature creates them and which the poet mediates.[288]

In the fifteenth century, however, this pattern is increasingly encroached upon by a growing emphasis on the artist's originality which competes with the mimetic ways of nature. Nicholas of Cusa's work takes some steps into this direction: in his *Idiota de mente*, a layman who carves spoons for a living asserts that, in doing so, he imitates no form in nature, but God's "inifinita et divina ars":[289]

> Non enim in hoc imitor figuram cuiuscunque rei naturalis. Tales enim formae cocleares, scutellares et ollares sola humana arte perficiuntur.
>
> For in this, I do not imitate the form of any natural thing. Such forms of spoon, bowls and pots are exclusively produced by human art.[290]

Creative acts such as these may rely on nature and participate in it, but they are not entirely derivable from it; the same applies to the production of speech, for example in the naming of things and persons.[291] The distinction between the artificial and the natural turns out to be relative however: in God, "ars" and "natura" become altogether indistinguishable.[292] In conceptions such as these, Cusanus achieves a new synthesis of Aristotelianism and Platonism which will become important for modernity.[293] After him, the notion of a poetic originality that is both natural and independent from nature spreads further and becomes increasingly more assertive.

It is hard to identify an origin of this development; Ernst Kantorowicz, however, in his article "The Sovereignty of the Artist", offers a provocative proposal.[294] According to him, the process begins in an area beyond the field of metaphysics or poetics, namely in the jurisprudence of the thirteenth century: some canonists, first and foremost the influential law professor Tancred of Bologna, attributed to the pope the power of creation *ex nihilo*,

288 "[E]go honorabilissimum reor opus, in id scilicet arte conari quod agit natura potentia." Giovanni Boccaccio, *Genealogia Deorum Gentilium*, 14.17, cited in Gregory B. Stone, *The Ethics of Nature in the Middle Ages*, New York: St. Martin's Press, 1998, p. 44.

289 Nicholas of Cusa, *Idiota de mente,* in *Philosophisch-theologische Werke*, Vol. 2, ed. Renate Steiger, Hamburg: Meiner, 2002, pp. 12/13 [2.59].

290 Nicholas of Cusa, *Idiota de mente*, pp. 14/15 [2.62]. Translation BQ.

291 Nicholas of Cusa, *De coniecturis*, in *Philosophisch-theologische Werke*, Vol. 2, ed. Winfried Happ and Josef Koch, Hamburg: Meiner 2002, pp. 154–157 [2.12].

292 Nicholas of Cusa, *De coniecturis*, pp. 154/155 [2.12].

293 Jürgen Mittelstraß, "Das Wirken der Natur: Materialien zur Geschichte des Naturbegriffs", in *Naturverständnis und Naturbeherrschung, Philosophiegeschichtliche Entwicklung und gegenwärtiger Kontext*, ed. Friedrich Rapp, Munich: Wilhelm Fink, 1981, p. 45.

294 Ernst Kantorowicz, "The Sovereignty of the Artist: A Note on Legal Maxims and Renaissance Theories of Art", in *De artibus opuscula XL: Essays in Honor of Erwin Panofsky*, ed. Millard Meiss, New York: New York University Press, 1961, pp. 267–279.

conveyed to him by God: the pope (in his role as *vicarius Dei*) can create actualities by establishing or suspending laws and legalities.[295] For example, when he institutes a jurisdiction or when he, by his decree, legitimates a formerly illegitimate act, he *ex officio* changes nature, supposedly under divine inspiration. That is one way for the transcending potency of God to manifest itself within creation. According to Kantorowicz, Tancred's conception of a human *creatio ex nihilo* was afterwards taken over by poetics, first in Dante's work, later in Petrarch's.[296] Particularly since the Renaissance, the biblical commonplace that man is made in God's image has been interpreted in the sense that the human capacity to re-create the world is divine. A humanist of the fifteenth century, Gianozzo Manetti, consequently involves man in God's aesthetic project, by ascribing him the task of beautifying and perfecting nature.[297] This was subsequently juxtaposed with discourses on natural law of which the humanist poetologists were well aware.[298] In his great task, the poet does act not so much generatively as legislatively; he creates judgments *ex nihilo*. For example, when Julius Caesar Scaliger calls the poet "another God", "alter deus", this is not so much because he creates another world, but because he "founds" the world as it should be: "condere" is the word Scaliger uses.[299] In a similar vein, Sidney declares that all men are "actors and players, as it were, of what nature will have set forth". Only the poet is free from the restrictions of nature, hence able to sovereignly create "another nature", tendentially a paradisiacal one, both highlighting and sublating man's fall.[300] Correspondingly, George Puttenham in his *Arte of English Poesie* insists that only the creation of the poet is a human creation that does not proceed by "copy or example" and hence compares with the divine creation *ex nihilo*.[301]

295 Kantorowicz, "The Sovereignty of the Artist", pp. 271–272.

296 Kantorowicz, "The Sovereignty of the Artist", pp. 276–277.

297 Eckhard Keßler, "Naturverständnisse im 15. und 16. Jahrhundert", in *Naturauffassungen in Philosophie, Wissenschaft, Technik*, Vol. 2, eds. Lothar Schäfer and Elisabeth Ströker, Freiburg and Munich: K. Alber, 1994, pp. 27–29.

298 See e.g. Conal Condren, *Argument and Authority in Early Modern England: The Presupposition of Oaths and Offices*, Cambridge: Cambridge University Press, 2006, p. 89; and Robert E. Stillman, *Philip Sidney and the Poetics of Renaissance Cosmopolitanism*, Aldershot and Burlington, VT: Ashgate, 2008, p. xii et passim.

299 Julius Caesar Scaliger, *Poetices libri septem: Sieben Bücher über die Dichtkunst*, Vol. 1, eds. Luc Deitz and Gregor Vogt-Spira, Stuttgart-Bad Cannstatt: Frommann-Holzboog, 1994, pp. 70–73. Apparently Scaliger is echoing the humanist Cristoforo Landino in this context (Luc Deitz, "Einleitung zum ersten Buch", in Julius Caesar Scaliger, *Poetices libri septem*, p. 49).

300 Philip Sidney, "The Defence of Poesy", in *Sidney's "The Defence of Poesy" and Selected Renaissance Literary Criticism*, ed. Gavin Alexander, London and New York: Penguin, 2004, pp. 8–9.

301 "A poet is as much to say as a maker. […] Such as (by way of resemblance and reverently) we may say of God, who without any travail to his divine imagination made all the world of nought, nor by any pattern or mold as the Platonics with their Ideas do fantastically suppose. Even so the very poet makes and contrives out of his own brain both the verse

The jurist, the sage and the statesman are to be considered subordinate to the poet in this respect.[302]

To this story of the sovereign artist as the voice of nature beyond nature, there is an interesting supplement: due to his endorsement of "delation" as an admissible instrument of legal procedure, the same Tancred was also an influential trailblazer for the establishment of the modern "inquisitorial" form of the legal trial, of which the famous Holy Roman Inquisition was the most prominent exponent.

> Tancred (*c.* 1185 – *c.* 1236), an influential law professor at Bologna, then Europe's leading law school, proposed that judges could count a delation as a half-proof. A delation differed from testimony because it was a statement of belief, not knowledge. The person who made a delation did not claim to have seen or heard the defendant commit the alleged offence. Rather the delator simply asserted his or her belief that a crime had occurred and that the defendant had committed it. Because a delation was a sworn statement of belief, rather than of knowledge, it failed to meet the critera of proof, but Tancred maintained that it nonetheless ought to have some evidentiary weight. Tancred asserted that a sworn delation should count as a half proof, or in other words that it ought to carry half the weight of full proof, which, as we have seen, meant the testimony of two actual witnesses to the perpetration of a criminal act.[303]

Subsequently, the delation, in other words, denunciation, became "probably the most important phase of any trial, but especially one by the Inquisition".[304] The legal system of antiquity and the early medieval period had basically regarded criminal trials as conflicts between a miscreant and a victim; it therefore retained an "adversarial" form which required that legal procedures could only be initiated through an official accusation by the person or persons who had been wronged.[305] The later Middle Ages, however, saw the rise of the *processus per inquisitionem* which functioned very differently and in which delations (which also could be made anonymously) were used as the decisive instruments:[306]

and matter of his poem, and not by any foreign copy or example [...]." George Puttenham, *The Art of English Poesy: A Critical Edition*, eds. Frank Whigham and Wayne A. Rebhorn, Ithaca, NY and London: Cornell University Press, 2007, p. 93.

302 Puttenham, *The Art of English Poesy*, pp. 96–99.

303 James Brundage, "Sin, Crime, and the Pleasures of the Flesh: The Medieval Church Judges Sexual Offences", in *The Medieval World*, eds. Peter Linehan and Janet L. Nelson, London and New York: Routledge, 2003, p. 302.

304 Thomas F. Mayer, *The Roman Inquisition: A Papal Bureaucracy and Its Laws in the Age of Galileo*, Philadelphia: University of Pennsylvania Press, 2013, pp. 168–169.

305 Mirjan R. Damaška, *The Faces of Justice and State Authority: A Comparative Approach to the Legal Process,* New Haven, CT: Yale University Press, 1986, p. 186.

306 See e.g. Brian Pullan, *The Jews of Europe and the Inquisition of Venice: 1550–1620*, London: Tauris, 1997, pp. 92–93.

> The relentlessly expanding and more powerful central authorities, especially those of the church, soon began to covet powers much wider than those of conflict resolution: the ambit of governmental action expanded. [...] To use a contemporary phrase, criminal "excesses" were now expected to be "corrected" even in the absence of a complaining victim or of a dispute to engage the forum. As a result of these changing ideas on both the agenda of government and the nature of crime, a spin-off occurred from the essentially conflict-absorbing justice of early medieval times; an officially controlled and propelled procedure of inquiry (*processus per inquisitionem*) emerged. Even if nobody came forward as an accuser, the judge was now obliged to begin a unilateral search for the truth about the possible incidence of a crime. Toward this end he was empowered to examine witnesses and to gather other types of evidence, either personally or through officials appointed by him. [...] This ecclesiastical procedure was soon taken up with enthusiasm by secular continental rulers, so that it continually gained ground at the expense of the old adversarial form of criminal prosecution.[307]

This new self-generating legal procedure, that sprang from the bosom of the church, soon spread all over Europe, and modern forms of the criminal trial to a substantial degree came to be based on it.[308] Could this new entitlement/obligation of legal authorities to begin legal proceedings, on the basis of mere sovereign suspicion, not be seen as the legal analogon of the developing sense of entitlement in the realm of humanist poetics?[309] It certainly constituted a capacity to generate trials and legal judgments *ex nihilo* and a warrant never to cease doing so, thus complementing the unceasing legal procedures of divine nature.

1.8 Early modern nature: the order of disorder

In the sixteenth century, the history of natural legislation and law enforcement became even more complicated, first and foremost because of the Reformation. The legal concept of "natural law" was intensely discussed, and both Catholics and Protestants claimed to act on its behalf.[310] There are important confessional differences, however: for example, in the late scholasticism of Francisco Suárez and others, nature itself was considered to be *natura*

307 Damaška, *The Faces of Justice and State Authority*, p. 187.

308 Damaška, *The Faces of Justice and State Authority*, p. 188.

309 The relationship of these new legal procedures to the discourses of the "pastorate" would be worth investigating. See Michel Foucault, *Security, Territory, Population: Lectures at the Collège de France, 1977–78*, trans. Graham Burchell, eds. Michel Senellart, François Ewald and Alessandro Fontana, Basingstoke and New York: Palgrave Macmillan, 2007.

310 See e.g. Perez Zagorin, *Hobbes and the Law of Nature,* pp. 9–10.

pura, neither fallen nor to be restituted. According to the definition of the Council of Trent, nature is a "precondition of grace, substantially unaffected by sin".[311] The salvation destined for man is a "donum superadditum" to this natural existence, and it is only this celestial destiny (expressed in man's natural tendency toward divine virtue and justice) that was lost by man's fall.[312] This conception harkens back to Thomas Aquinas, who writes:

> Bona naturalia, prout in esse naturae absolute considerantur, remanent integra post peccatum, tamen pervertuntur quantum ad rectum ordinem quem habebant in gratia vel virtute [...].
>
> Insofar as one considers natural goods absolutely, in their natural being, they remain intact after sin. Nevertheless, they are perverted with respect to the right order they had toward grace or virtue [...].[313]

Thus, medieval theology differentiated between the *status naturae integrae* and the *status naturae lapsae*.[314] But since fallen nature has not been corrupted altogether by sin, it can still convey readable revelations about the eternal world; the world is able to function as an allegory of heaven.[315] (Dante tends to agree with Aquinas on that issue, too.)[316] By contrast, many Protestant teachers take nature itself to be essentially darkened and corrupted through original sin. In his commentary on Genesis, Luther writes:

> Manifestum est naturalia non mansisse integra sicut Scholastici delirant [...].[317]
>
> It is manifest that no qualities or properties or powers of nature remain perfect and sound, as the schoolmen madly dream.[318]

311 "Die in der Substanz durch die Sünde unangetastete Voraussetzung der Gnade". Blumenberg, *Die Lesbarkeit der Welt*, p. 107. Blumenberg does not give a precise indication of his source.

312 Francisco Suárez, *Tractatus de Gratia Dei*, in *Opera Omnia*, Vol. 7, ed. Charles Berton, Paris: Vives, 1857, p. 133 [Prol. 2, Cap. 3].

313 Thomas Aquinas, *On Love and Charity: Readings from the Commentary on the Sentences of Peter Lombard*, Washington, DC: Catholic University of America Press, 2008, p. 86 [In II Sententiarum, d. 3, q. 4]. For a more extensive treatment of the topic, see Thomas Aquinas, *Summa Theologiae Prima Secundae, 71–114*, pp. 145–148 [Summa 2.1, Quaestio 85, Art. 1–2].

314 Pat Moloney, "Leaving the Garden of Eden: Linguistic and Political Authority in Thomas Hobbes", in *History of Political Thought*, 18.2 (1997), p. 244.

315 Blumenberg, *Die Lesbarkeit der Welt,* p. 107.

316 Dante, *Purgatorio*, trans. Jean Hollander and Robert Hollander, New York: Random House, 2003, pp. 626–629 [28.88–144].

317 Martin Luther, *Text der Genesisvorlesung*, in *Werke: Kritische Gesamtausgabe*, Vol. 42, ed. G. Koffmane and Otto Reichert, Weimar: Hermann Böhlaus Nachfolger, 1911, pp. 125.

318 Martin Luther, *On the Creation: A Critical and Devotional Commentary on Genesis*, Vol. 1, trans. Henry Cole and John Lenker, Minneapolis: Lutherans in All Lands, 1904, p. 261.

For Luther and other Protestants, internal and external nature have been proscribed together with man and are henceforth "multis modis corrupta", first and foremost as a means of punishing man, but also as a means of admonishing him.[319] So even though Nature is corrupt and all her verdicts are condemnations, her law is nevertheless to be respected. This becomes palpable when God curses the ground for Adam's sake (Gen. 3.17). Luther comments:

> Ubi igitur Adam ante peccatum inter fecundissimas arbores, in amenissimis pratis, in floribus et rosis ambulavit, ibi nunc urticae, sentes et alia molesta germina pullulant, cum tanta copia, ut fere, quae bona sunt, obruantur.[320]
>
> In those very places where Adam before his sin used to walk among the most fruitful trees, over most fertile meadows and in the midst of roses and flowers of every kind, there nettles and briers, and other annoying plants abound; and in such quantities that the good and useful plants are well nigh choked by them.[321]

Calvin similarly asserts that the elements, the animals and all of nature have been corrupted by the sin of man.[322] This does not imply that nature can no longer serve as a legal order; its all-embracing deterioration must be understood as a condemnation, a divine act of justice. For Calvin, Luther and Melanchthon, postlapsarian natural law first and foremost consists of men's spontaneous inward awareness that their nature is corrupted and that all their inclinations are evil, a truth written into the human heart in the form of conscience, in order to render man inexcusable. As Calvin expresses it: "Finis ergo legis naturalis est, ut reddatur homo inexcusabilis".[323] ("It is the goal of natural law to render man inexcusable".) This remainder of natural law has therefore nothing to do with the Thomist "inclinatio naturalis" toward the good; it is unrelated to salvation, a mere recognition of man's and nature's guilty state that must be supplemented by the Bible and by faith.[324] Philipp Melanchthon, on a rather circular argumentative basis, assumes that this inner "voice of conscience" announces the same verdict to everyone.[325]

319 See e.g. Johann Arndt and Anne-Charlott Trepp, "Natural Order and Divine Salvation: Protestant Conceptions in Early Modern Germany (1550–1750)", in *Natural Law and Laws of Nature in Early Modern Europe: Jurisprudence, Theology, Moral and Natural Philosophy*, eds. Lorraine Daston and Michael Stolleis, Farnham and Burlington, VT: Ashgate, 2008, p. 130.

320 Martin Luther, *Text der Genesisvorlesung*, p. 153.

321 Martin Luther, *On the Creation: A Critical and Devotional Commentary on Genesis*, Vol. 1, p. 314.

322 Charles Partee, *Calvin and Classical Philosophy*, Leiden: Brill, 1977, p. 48.

323 John Calvin, *Institutio Christianae Religionis in Libros Quattuor*, Geneva: Robert Estienne, 1559, p. 91 [2.2.22].

324 See e.g. Antti Raunio, "Divine and Natural Law in Luther and Melanchthon", in *Lutheran Reformation and the Law*, ed. Virpi Mäkinen, Leiden and Boston: Brill, 2006, pp. 46–47.

325 Merio Scattola, *Das Naturrecht vor dem Naturrecht*, pp. 42–43.

On the question of how the law of conscience relates to positive law, both Luther's and Calvin's positions are somewhat inconsistent. But their general tendency is to echo Romans 13.1 and assert that all political and juridical orders come from God, and that sinful man must therefore submit to them, if such a submission is not contradicted by the Bible.[326] In practical respects, natural law is therefore mainly seen as the precondition of positive law and otherwise suspended. However, a fair number of Protestant writers, somewhat inconsistently, still tend to personify Nature and assume that she is still provided with an active judicial power that surpasses the mere force of conscience. The Protestant humanist Conrad Lycosthenes, for example, asserts that "we know that Nature is God's minister in matters both favorable and unfavorable, and that through her agency he aids the pious and punishes the impious, according to their different conditions".[327]

The multi-phased English Reformation established a peculiar mixture between Protestantism and Catholicism that can in many respects be characterized as a compromise formation. The question of natural jurisdiction was treated accordingly. Richard Hooker, for example, in his *Of the Laws of Ecclesiastical Polity* (1593) admits that there is a postlapsarian "defect in the matter of things natural" and that its cause is "divine malediction, laid for the sin of man upon these creatures which God had made for the use of man".[328] However, he assures his reader that these "swervings" have not fundamentally changed the natural law, defined with Thomas Aquinas as the part of eternal law "which ordereth natural agents".[329] Taking his cues from scholastic theology, Hooker goes on to develop a more complex network of all-embracing legal systems: to the eternal laws, natural laws, human laws and divine laws of Aquinas, he adds celestial laws, laws of reason and others.[330] This plethora might be qualified as metaphysical analogue of the legislative patchwork that was Elizabethan England. According to Edward Coke, 16 independent legal systems were in force in the country around 1600.[331]

326 See e.g. Luther: "Das weltliche herrschafften, Keiserthumb, Königreich, Fürstenthumb, Stete, Rat und gemeine auff erden stehen und gehen inn irer ordnung, das ist nicht menschlich thun noch vermögen, sondern Gottes Regiment. [...] Wer hellt nu hie das Regiment, das ein eitzeler mensch soviel köpffe unter im hat, die im müssen unterthan sein, und so viel land und leute im zwang halten sol? Freilich niemand denn Gott alleine, Darumb sol man ihm dafur lob und danck sagen, wo es stehet und bleibt [...]". Martin Luther, "Predigt 41" (1534), in *Werke: Kritische Gesamtausgabe*, Vol. 37, ed. O. Brenner, Weimar: Böhlau, 1910, p. 443.

327 Lycosthenes, *Chronicon, Dedicatory Epistle*, n. p., cited in Daston and Park, *Wonders and the Order of Nature*, p. 183.

328 Richard Hooker, *Of the Laws of Ecclesiastical Polity: Preface, Book 1 and 8*, ed. Arthur Stephen McGrade, Cambridge: Cambridge University Press, 1989, p. 61 [1.3.3].

329 Hooker, *Of the Laws of Ecclesiastical Polity*, p. 58 [1.3.1].

330 Hooker, *Of the Laws of Ecclesiastical Polity*, p. 58 [1.3.1].

331 Alison A. Chapman, *The Legal Epic:* Paradise Lost *and the Early Modern Law*, Chicago and London: University of Chicago Press, 2017, p. 48.

> Contemporaries also complained about the coexistence of a multiplicity of dramatically different jurisdictions, courts, and normative systems on the island. Common law and equity were the systems followed by royal courts, but parallel to them were hundreds of feudal, ecclesiastic, and municipal courts, each obeying radically different rules, procedures and norms.[332]

This multiplicity was nothing new, but it was increasingly denounced as impractical.[333] In the ensuing efforts to unify the English legal system, a favourite argument of the competing parties striving for hegemony was the assertion that their jurisdiction was more natural (and therefore more just) than that of the others.[334] The natural law doctrine of the Roman jurists was thus perpetuated by the Elizabethan jurists, whether they were trained in the common law, in Roman law or in canon law.[335] And since common law had grown "organically", by way of precedent, it could somewhat convincingly be defended as the form that natural law had taken in England.[336] That might be one of the reasons why the authority of common law steadily increased in the course of the seventeenth century.[337] But the conflict persisted, and there were diverse attempts to contain it. John Selden came to argue against the intuitively evident character of natural law[338] and to equate it with the positive law that was promulgated by God:

> I cannot fancy to myself what the law of nature means, but the law of God. How should I know I ought not to steal, I ought not to commit adultery, unless somebody had told me so? Surely 'tis because I have been told so. 'Tis not because I think I ought not to do them, not because you think I ought not; if so, our minds might change. Whence then comes the restraint? From a higher power, nothing else can bind. I cannot bind

332 Herzog, *A Short History of European Law*, p. 134.

333 Herzog, *A Short History of European Law*, p. 134.

334 The introductory works on English law written in the sixteenth and seventeenth century generally referred to the law of nature as a source of common law, not as its alternative, and in the courts it was treated accordingly. Sometimes, the jurists had to admit that divergences between common law and natural law existed, but the cases in which natural law prevailed over codified law were rare. Generally, the more subordinate the courts and officials were that had made a legal decision, the more easily they could be overruled by references to natural law. R. H. Helmholz, *Natural Law in Court: A History of Legal Theory in Practice*, Cambridge, MA and London: Harvard University Press, 2015, pp. 89–90, 98, 113, 117, 176.

335 Helmholz, *Natural Law in Court*, pp. 132, 184.

336 Many a jurist since the Reformation (Christopher St. German, for example) considered English Common Law an amplification of natural law. See e.g. John Hamilton Baker, *An Introduction to English Legal History*, London: Butterworths, 1979, p. 147.

337 Chapman, *The Legal Epic*, p. 53.

338 Arthur P. Monahan, *The Circle of Rights Expands: Modern Political Thought after the Reformation, 1521 (Luther) to 1762 (Rousseau)*, Montreal and Ithaca, NY: McGill-Queen's University Press, 2007, p. 118.

> myself, for I may unbind myself again; nor an equal cannot bind me, for we may untie one another. It must be a superior power, even God Almighty.[339]

This identification of *lex divina* and *lex naturalis* is already moving toward a new conception of natural law that Hobbes will express most poignantly: minimizing the difference between prelapsarian and postlapsarian nature[340] and between divine and human law,[341] Hobbes asserts that "the law of nature, and the civil law, contain each other, and are of equal extent".[342] Obedience to the civil laws is demanded by the laws of nature, even though Hobbes, unlike Aristotle, does not consider man a political animal by inclination.[343] According to Hobbes, the dominant natural law of any commonwealth is to obey the sovereign who takes the position of the supreme being in the political domain. "The law is a command", he writes, "and a command consisteth in declaration or manifestation of the will of him that commandeth".[344] Whenever this central law is not kept, society tends to degenerate into the state of nature in which there is no palpable sovereign and in which therefore everybody has the right to do all that which he is able to do in order to preserve him- or herself – just as the great fish have the power to eat the small, and therefore have the right to do it.[345] Several commentators have pointed out that this state of natural rights is not annihilated and replaced by the Hobbesian state of society but persists within it; the two orders do not oppose but complement each other, together constituting the natural order of modernity which the sovereign represents.[346] This new rule of nature's law, which is, after all, not so different from the old, is the place where theological and

339 John Selden, *The Table Talk*, ed. Samuel Harvey Reynolds, Oxford: Clarendon, 1892, p. 101.

340 According to Hobbes, Adam and Eve were not immortal by nature, but only because they regularly ate the fruits of the Tree of Life. Hobbes, *Leviathan*, p. 410 [4.44.14].

341 James Bernard Murphy, *The Philosophy of Positive Law: Foundations of Jurisprudence*, New Haven, CT and London: Yale University Press, 2005, p. 152.

342 Hobbes, *Leviathan*, p. 177 [2.26.8].

343 Giovanni Fiaschi, "The Power of Words: Political and Theological Science in Thomas Hobbes", in *Hobbes Studies* 26 (2013), pp. 35, 63.

344 Hobbes, *Leviathan*, p. 179 [2.26.12]. There are, of course, other natural laws in Hobbes, but they are contingent on the first – except for the right to self preservation whose practical importance within the functioning state is, however, negligible. It is the right of the delinquent to struggle while he is led to the gallows.

345 Remarkably, Hobbes also asserts that nature forces us to escape from the state of nature: "[B]y natural necessity every man seeks his own good, but no one believes that the war of all against all which naturally belongs to such a state, is good for him. And so it comes about that we are driven by mutual fear to believe that we must emerge from such a state and seek allies; so that if we must have war, it will not be a war against all men nor without aid". Thomas Hobbes, *On the Citizen*, ed. and trans. Richard Tuck and Michael Silverthorne, Cambridge: Cambridge University Press, 1997, p. 30 [1.13].

346 See Werner Hamacher, "Wilde Versprechen: Die Sprache *Leviathan*", in *Die Ordnung des Versprechens*, ed. Manfred Schneider, Munich: Wilhelm Fink, 2005, p. 192; and Agamben, *Homo Sacer,* pp. 35–36.

political voluntarism meet and where God thrones over all creation as the supreme sovereign who is just as unaccountable and perhaps just as legitimately capricious as the Leviathan. Hobbes explicitly stresses that God may and occasionally does punish creatures just because he can, not because they have transgressed any law: "God may afflict by a right derived from his omnipotence, though sin were not".[347] It should be emphasised in this context that Hobbes in his *Leviathan* also perpetuates the Stoic notion that Nature herself punishes those who transgress her boundaries by what he calls "natural punishments":

> There is no action of man in this life, that is not the beginning of so long a chain of consequences, as no humane providence is high enough, to give a man a prospect to the end. And in this chain, there are linked together both pleasing and unpleasing events; in such manner, as he that will do any thing for his pleasure, must engage himself to suffer all the pains annexed to it; and these pains, are the natural punishments of those actions, which are the beginning of more harm than good. And hereby it comes to pass, that intemperance is naturally punished with diseases; rashness, with mischances; injustice, with the violence of enemies; pride, with ruin; cowardice, with oppression; negligent government of princes, with rebellion; and rebellion, with slaughter. For seeing punishments are consequent to the breach of laws; natural punishments must be naturally consequent to the breach of the laws of nature; and therefore follow them as their natural, not arbitrary effects.[348]

Thus, Nature's administration of justice complements all other legislations. And while she seems to dispense her punishments by way of well-established causal chains, it is hard to see why she should not also be entitled to the same privilege of arbitrary legislation as all other sovereigns. Her ways thus sustain the distribution of power that creates man's greatest artwork, a creation analogous to God's natural creation and legislation of the cosmos:

> Nature, the art whereby God hath made and governs the world, is by the "art", of man, as in many other things, so in this also imitated, that it can make an artificial animal. [...] For by art is created that great "Leviathan" called a "Commonwealth" or "State", in Latin *civitas*, which is but an artificial man, though of greater stature and strength than the natural.[349]

In his thoroughly voluntarist position, Hobbes is at odds with another of the great natural law theoreticians of the seventeenth century, namely the

347 Thomas Hobbes and John Bramhall, *On Liberty and Necessity*, ed. Vere Chappell, Cambridge and New York: Cambridge University Press, 1999. p. 29.

348 Hobbes, *Leviathan*, p. 244 [2.31.40].

349 Hobbes, *Leviathan*, p. 7 [Introduction].

Arminian Hugo Grotius in his work *De jure belli ac pacis* (1625, translated into English in 1654).[350] Implicitly relying on the work of Thomas Aquinas,[351] Grotius explicitly states that God acts like a judge who must remain loyal to a natural legal codex: the supreme being is bound by the laws of ethics as well as by the laws of reason:

> Est autem ius naturale adeo immutabile, ut ne a Deo quidem mutari queat. Quanquam enim immensa est Dei potentia, dici tamen quaedam possunt, ad quae se illa non extendit; quia, quae ita dicuntur, dicuntur tantum, sensum autem qui rem exprimat nullum habent, sed sibi ipsis repugnant. Sicut ergo ut bis duo non sint quattor ne a Deo quidem potest effici, ita ne hoc quidem, ut quod intrinseca ratione malum est, malum non sit.[352]
>
> The law of nature, again, is unchangeable – even in the sense that it cannot be changed by God. Measureless as is the power of God, there can nevertheless be said to be some things to which that power does not extend; for things of which this is said are spoken only, having no sense corresponding with reality and being mutually contradictory. Just as even God cannot cause that two and two should not make four, so even He cannot cause that that which is intrinsically evil should not be evil.[353]

Grotius goes so far as to assert that natural law would remain valid even if God did not exist.[354]

One would assume that this conception of unbreakable natural laws was conducive the development of the natural sciences. However, not only many early modern jurists, but also many founding fathers of modern science, including Isaac Newton, were not "rationalists", as the Thomist/Grotian position has come to be called, but voluntarists.[355] René Descartes, for example, in his *Principia Philosophiae* (1644), seems to have been the first to coherently use the term "natural law" in the "scientific" sense of "physical law" in which it is mostly understood today.[356] And, as the good voluntarist

350 Helmholz, *Natural Law in Court*, p. 90.

351 Douglas M. Johnston, "The Heritage of Political Thought in International Law", in *The Structure and Process of International Law: Essays in Legal Philosophy, Doctrine, and Theory*, eds. Ronald St. John Macdonald and Douglas M. Johnston, The Hague and Boston: Nijhoff, 1983, p. 208.

352 Hugo Grotius, *De jure belli ac pacis: Libri tres, in quibus jus naturae et gentium, item juris publici praecipua explicantur*, Amsterdam: Joan Blaeu, 1646, p. 4 [1.1.10].

353 Hugo Grotius, *On the Law of War and Peace*, trans. Francis W. Kelsey, ed. Stephen C. Neff, Cambridge and New York: Cambridge University Press, 2012, pp. 29–30 [1.1.10].

354 Grotius, *On the Law of War and Peace*, p. 4 [Prologue].

355 Of course, there were also rationalists among them; Leibniz, for example.

356 René Descartes, *Principia Philosophiae*, Amsterdam: Elsevir, 1644, pp. 54–59 [2.37–44]. See also Catherine Wilson, "From Limits to Laws: The Construction of the Nomological Image of Nature in Early Modern Philosophy", in *Natural Law and Laws of Nature in Early Modern Europe*, eds. Lorraine Daston and Michael Stolleis, Farnham and Burlington, VT: Ashgate, 2008, pp. 23–24. It should be added that Descartes thereby eliminates the

he is, he conceives these laws as the consequences of God's free and sovereign decision; thus they are contingent and dependent on divine legislation – and so are the mathematical and logical precepts that impose themselves on the mind of man.[357] Descartes writes:

> Mihi autem non videtur de ulla unquam re esse dicendum ipsam a Dei fieri non posse; cum enim omnis ratio veri et boni facti ab eius omnipotentia dependeat, nequidem dicere ausim, Deum facere non posse ut mons sit sine valle, vel ut unum et duo non sint tria; sed tantum dico illum talem mentem mihi indidisse, ut a me concipi non possit mons sine valle, vel aggregatum ex uno et duobus quod non sint tria, etc., atque talia implicare contradictionem in meo conceptu.[358]
>
> I do not think we should ever say of anything that it cannot be brought about by God. For since every basis of truth and goodness depends on his omnipotence, I would not venture to say that God cannot make an uphill without a downhill, or that one and two should not be three. But I merely say that he has given me a mind of such a nature that I cannot conceive an uphill without a downhill, or a sum of one and two which is not three, and that such things involve a contradiction in my conception.[359]

Frequently, like Hobbes, early modern natural philosophers relate the laws of nature to the laws of the state, the sovereignty of God to the sovereignty of the prince. But while they approximate them, they also tend to differentiate them. For example, when Galileo Galilei formulates his laws of motion, he, like Descartes, abolishes the Aristotelian categorical difference between natural and unnatural (i.e. "violent") motions, as well as that between celestial and terrestrial, "sublunary", "natural" objects.[360] This unification offers one more reason for him to call Nature "a most careful executrix of God's orders"

Aristotelian distinction between "natural" and "violent" ("artificial") movement. With Descartes, all movements are "violent" and "artificial". See Dennis Des Chene, "Forms of Art in Jesuit Aristotelianism (with a Coda on Descartes)", in *The Artificial and the Natural*, eds. Bernadette Bensaude-Vincent and William R. Newman, Cambridge, MA: MIT Press, 2007, pp. 142–143.

357 Oakley, *Natural Law, Laws of Nature, Natural Rights*, p. 41.

358 René Descartes, Pour Arnauld, Paris, 29 Juillet 1648, in *Correspondance avec Arnauld et Morus*, ed. Geneviève Lewis, Paris: J. Vrin, 1953, p. 92. Notation modified.

359 René Descartes, Letter to Arnauld, 29 July 1648, in *The Philosophical Writings, Vol. 3: The Correspondence*, trans. John Cottingham, Robert Stoothoff, Dugald Murdoch and Anthony Kenny, Cambridge: Cambridge University Press, 1991, pp. 358–359. Translation slightly modified.

360 See Alexandre Koyré, *Galileo Studies*, trans. John Mepham, Atlantic Highlands, NJ: Humanities Press, 1978, p. 174. See also Marco Piccolino and Nicholas J. Wade, *Galileo's Visions: Piercing the Spheres of the Heavens by Eye and Mind*, New York and Oxford: Oxford University Press, 2014, p. 156. Galilei's laws (which he never designated as "laws" but as "rules") thus dehierarchize (and decenter) the cosmos.

("osservantissima esecutrice de gli ordini di Dio");[361] God has given laws to Nature, which, in contrast to the biblical laws, are not accommodated to human understanding.[362] Galileo goes on to emphasise that the human state aparatuses have no right to participate in Natura's procedural acts: according to Galilei, nature "laughs about the constitutions and decrees of princes, emperors and monarchs, in virtue of which it would not alter even an iota of its laws and statutes".[363] In Galileo's formulation, the reference to the divine sovereign and his court serves to deflate the aspirations of the earthly ruler.

While Galileo thus distances the political from the natural law courts, Francis Bacon, by contrast, has the tendency to approximate them, and his great project is to make them coincide, under the auspices of an all-encompassing statute that is both human and natural. The ground in England was well-prepared for such a move, since English common law had often been described as an amplification of natural law.[364] And Bacon's official career was that of a jurist.[365] According to him, wise laws and true jurisprudence must accord with the laws of nature.[366] Based on this project and a pragmatic methodology, Bacon develops in his novel *New Atlantis* the utopia of a society based on the natural sciences.[367] Once the mysteries of nature have been solved by way of induction and experimentation, man's "right over nature" can be reasserted.[368] This new rule even involves a promise of regaining Paradise and of overcoming original sin; Bacon writes that "the true ends of knowledge" are "a restitution and reinvesting (in great part) of man to the sovereignty and power [...] which he had in his first state of creation".[369] Accordingly, the roles in this law court are reversed: by the artful production of situations in which nature is forced to reveal herself, man rises to the position of nature's

361 Galileo Galilei, Lettera à Padre Benedetto Castelli, in *Opere,* Vol. 5, ed. Antonio Favaro, Florence: Barbèra, 1968, p. 282.

362 Galilei, Lettera à Padre Benedetto Castelli, p. 282.

363 Galileo Galilei, Lettera à Sig. Francesco Ingoli, in *Opere,* Vol. 6, ed. Antonio Favaro, Florence: Barbèra, 1968, p. 538; cited in: Friedrich Steinle, "The Amalgamation of a Concept: Laws of Nature in the New Sciences", in *Laws of Nature: Essays on the Philosophical, Scientific and Historical Dimensions*, ed. Friedel Weinert, Berlin and New York: Walter de Gruyter, 1995, p. 321.

364 John Hamilton Baker, *An Introduction to English Legal History,* London: Butterworths, 1979, p. 147.

365 On the relation between Bacon's jurisprudence and his philosophical ideas, see Daniel R. Coquillette, *Francis Bacon*, Stanford, CA: Stanford University Press, 1992.

366 "I find the wisdom of the law, by imitation of the course of nature [...]". Francis Bacon, "The Case of Impeachment of Waste", in *The Works,* Vol. 7, eds. James Spedding, Robert Leslie Ellis and Douglas Denon Heath, London: Longman [etc.], 1861, p. 529.

367 Francis Bacon, *New Atlantis and The Great Instauration*, ed. Jerry Weinberger, Arlington Heights: H. Davidson, 1989.

368 Francis Bacon, *The New Organon*, eds. Lisa Jardine and Michael Silverthorne, Cambridge and New York: Cambridge University Press, 2000, p. 101.

369 Francis Bacon, *Valerius Terminus*: *Of the Interpretation of Nature*, in *The Works,* Vol. 3, eds. James Spedding, Robert Leslie Ellis and Douglas Denon Heath, London: Longman [etc.], 1854, p. 220.

judge in an inquisitorial trial. The scientific experiment is metaphorized as a torture chamber into which she is led for interrogation, "so nature exhibits herself more clearly under the trials".[370] Creation becomes a tribunal in which man figures as the judge and executioner who extorts confessions from the defendant or witness Natura. Here, "nature" obviously designates both the dynamic properties of singular objects and the unity of all things. Like his predecessors, Bacon assumes that both are harmonious and that, by way of this harmony, Natura can fall under the dominion of man. In the testimony that nature dictates under torture, the true order of the world is articulated: an order to which man must accommodate himself, since nature can only be ruled by submission to her rules[371] – rules that seem to sanction the violent seizure of judicial powers. This investigative usurpation is bound to reconstitute the Adamic language, that is to say, the true names in which the essence of each named object is expressed (as torture frequently tends to be oriented toward the ascertainment of names). And by this knowledge of the true names, power over their referents is attained.[372] Once this process is established, the law book of nature begins to report on the power of man; it is absorbed into the book of history, as Blumenberg expresses it.[373] And thus creation will be brought to perfection and all strife will end. Under the guidance of Man, the law court of Nature will finally be all in all.

This politico-theological heritage of the early modern natural philosophers overdetermines the developing scientific notion of natural law; this law is both the palpable order of creation and the divinely prescribed order of the lordly human spirit.[374] So when the term becomes firmly established in the natural sciences, after the foundation of the Royal Society in 1660, "law of nature" can refer both to an empirically determined regularity and to a law that can be *a priori* deduced by the use of reason alone.[375] The most influential scientific book of the epoch largely decides to ignore the difference: in Newton's *Principia Mathematica* (1687), the term "law" designates axiomatic principles as well as empirical regularities.[376] This indistinctiveness serves the

370 Francis Bacon, *Of the Dignity and Advancement of Learning*, in *The Works*, Vol. 4, eds. James Spedding, Robert Leslie Ellis and Douglas Denon Heath, London: Longman [etc.], 1858, p. 298. Bacon was not the first to use this image: "As early as the end of the fifth century BCE, the author of the Hippocratic treatise *On Art* was certainly thinking of this judicial model when he declared that one must do violence to Nature to make her reveal what she is hiding from us [...]" (Hadot, *The Veil of Isis*, p. 93).

371 "Natura enim non nisi parendo vincitur". Francis Bacon, *Neues Organon, Lateinisch-deutsch*, ed. Wolfgang Krohn, Hamburg: Meiner, 1999, p. 80.

372 "[...] for whensoever [man] shall be able to call the creatures by their true names he shall again command them [...]". Bacon, *Valerius Terminus*, p. 220. See also Blumenberg, *Die Lesbarkeit der Welt*, p. 87.

373 Blumenberg, *Die Lesbarkeit der Welt*, p. 91.

374 See Dieter Groh, *Göttliche Weltökonomie: Perspektiven der wissenschaftlichen Revolution vom 15. bis zum 17. Jahrhundert*, Berlin: Suhrkamp, 2010.

375 Steinle, "From Principles to Regularities", p. 223.

376 Steinle, "From Principles to Regularities", p. 227.

novae scientiae well, since their claim to power remains equally unclear, oscillating uncertainly between prescription and description.[377] Thus, it allows the embattled Royal Society to give scientific research a vaguely religious sheen; their reflections about the status of scientific natural laws frequently entail some references to the divine lawgiver and an assertion that man's quest for knowledge about nature's laws is itself a divinely legitimated process. For example, Milton's friend Henry Oldenburg characterizes the Royal Society (whose secretary and founding member he was) as "not taking up old fame, or flying reports, upon too easy trust; nor straining for other kinds of wonders, than the most wise author of nature hath allowed, but attending closely to the strict measures of natural truth, and to the useful contrivances of art".[378] Accordingly, some members of the Royal Society suggest that their work may complement the work of biblical exegesis.[379] The new discourse of science delineates the functioning of God's law-positing will that manifests itself within creation: Richard Bentley, for example, describes the Newtonian force of gravity as "the immediate *fiat* and finger of God, and the execution of divine law", as well as the source of natural laws.[380] In the background of statements like this, a continuity between the scientific process and the process of divine judgment is implied. Studies in the history of science have demonstrated that the natural philosophers' choice of religious terminology was, at least to a certain extent, politically and juridically motivated: according to a thesis that Friedrich Steinle has formulated, the concept of natural law in this context served to inconspicuously extend the area of competence over which the new sciences could claim dominion into the field of religion.[381] Perhaps the strangest flower of this amalgamation is the system of Leibniz which equates *ius naturale* and *lex naturalis* and unfolds this equation into a system.[382]

Proceedings in the political arena were strongly influenced by all these controversies: in the English Civil Wars, all the contending parties tended to regard their own position as sanctioned by natural law – monarchists as well as parliamentarians, Presbyterians, Puritans, Anglicans, Levellers and Ranters. The term "natural law" can be found in key passages of parliamentary papers, in the transcripts of the Putney debates and in Digger manifestos. The leading intellectuals and politicians engaged with the term: Robert Filmer,

377 Steinle, "From Principles to Regularities", p. 229.

378 Henry Oldenburg, "A Preface to the Third Year of These Tracts", in *Philosophical Transactions of the Royal Society 2* (1666), p. 410. Spelling modernized.

379 See e.g. Robert Boyle, *The Excellency of Theology Compared with Natural Philosophy*, in *The Works*, Vol. 4, ed. Thomas Birch, London: J. and F. Rivington [etc.], 1777, pp. 6–66.

380 Richard Bentley, *The Works, Vol. 3, Theological Writings*, ed. Alexander Dyce, London: Macpherson, 1838, pp. 74–75.

381 See e.g. Steinle, "From Principles to Regularities", p. 229.

382 See e.g. Klaus Luig, "Leibniz's Concept of Jus Naturale and Lex Naturalis – Defined 'with Geometric Certainty'", in *Natural Law and Laws of Nature in Early Modern Europe: Jurisprudence, Theology, Moral and Natural Philosophy*, eds. Lorraine Daston and Michael Stolleis, Farnham and Burlington, VT: Ashgate, 2008, pp. 183–198.

Gerrard Winstanley, John Lilburne, Samuel Rutherford and even Charles I and Oliver Cromwell himself.[383] Poetry and drama also joined the debate; one of the most developed examinations of "nature" and its law can be found in Shakespeare's *King Lear*, amounting to a rigorous deconstruction: Lear naturalises the law of the land, and the result of this political decision is an unravelling of the social net and of the supposedly divine legal order.[384] In the course of these appropriations and controversies, natural law becomes a hopelessly overdetermined concept:

> The entanglement of the law of nature with vaguely understood concepts like the laws of nations, of reason, and of God, betrays the mounting prestige and the declining clarity of the concept. It was fast becoming a transcendent principle of essentially emotional appeal. All groups regarded it sanctioning their dearest political convictions.[385]

All these overdetermined constructions are vulnerable to criticism, and there was no lack of conservative and progressivist detractors. Blumenberg was not the first to regard "natural law" as a metaphor:[386] Francisco Suárez[387] and Oldenburg's correspondent Spinoza[388] did the same in the seventeenth century. In this context, it was also pointed out – by Robert Boyle, for example – that the metaphor is strangely inappropriate: while the natural laws of the sciences are supposed to be universal, immutable and inexorably enforced, usually none of these three attributes applies to the laws of the courts. The latter depend on the contingent and limited acts of legislative, judicative and executive organs and are prone to inconsistencies, variations and violations.[389] However, this very inconsistency is usually hidden, since jurisdiction has the tendency to claim a foundation in the infallible and eternal law court of Nature or God. The early modern "laws of nature" thus reconstruct an old supplement of jurisdiction that has always tended to shadow its instantiation

383 See e.g. Merritt Y. Hughes, "Introduction" in *CPW* 3:68–70.

384 See Björn Quiring, *Shakespeare's Curse: The Aporias of Ritual Exclusion in Early Modern Royal Drama*, trans. Michael Winkler and Björn Quiring, New York: Routledge, 2014, pp. 167–251.

385 Merritt Y. Hughes, "Introduction" in *CPW* 3:68.

386 Hans Blumenberg, *Geistesgeschichte der Technik*, Frankfurt am Main: Suhrkamp, 2009, p. 19.

387 "Unde haec tertia acceptio [i.e. lex naturalis] metaphorica est; nam res carentes ratione non sunt proprie capaces legis, sicut nec obedientiae. Efficacia ergo divinae virtutis et necessitas naturalis, quae in his rebus inde resultat, per metaphoram lex appellatur". Francisco Suárez, *Tractatus de legibus et legislatore Deo*, in *Opera Omnia*, Vol. 5, ed. Charles Berton, Paris: Vives, 1856, p. 1 [1.1].

388 "Verum enimvero quoniam nomen legis per translationem ad res naturales applicatum videtur [...]". Baruch de Spinoza, *Tractatus Theologico-Politicus*, in *Oeuvres*, vol. 3, eds. Fokke Akkerman and Pierre-François Moreau, trans. Jacqueline Lagrée and Pierre-François Moreau, Paris: Presses universitaires de France, 1999, p. 182 [Cap. 4].

389 Robert Boyle, *A Free Enquiry into the Vulgarly Received Notion of Nature*, p. 24 [Sec. 2].

in actual court proceedings. In the teeming discourses of the seventeenth century, its close, uncomfortable entanglement with science, jurisdiction, theology, rhetoric, poetics and politics manifests itself.

This short historical overview must remain unsatisfactory in many ways, but it shows that the history of natural jurisdiction is not a coherent development, as intellectual history tends to represent it, but an amalgamation of heterogeneous processes, in which very different, often contradictory notions are employed at the same time. The law enacted by nature is characterized as both eternal and contingent, both divine and secular, both political and transpolitical, both moral and amoral, depending on the gaps it needs to fill in the legal and metaphysical system in each particular situation. Because of social and functional differentiations, this heterogeneity comes to a head in the early modern period. That is the state of things at the time when Milton enters the scene with an epic that aspires to "justify the ways of God to men". In the course of this apologetic project, it soon turns out that the poet also has to take account of the jurisprudences of Nature. Serving himself freely from the store of available concepts and images, appropriating whatever suits him best in his strife for maximum effect, he *nolens volens* exposes the conflicts of his age.

2 Milton's wager

2.1 Between Puritanism, humanism and the Scientific Revolution

It is useful to remember that the time of *Paradise Lost* is also a time of "paradigm lost":[1] Christopher Ricks has pointed out that the second half of the seventeenth century in which Milton worked is just the period during which biblical myths lose their unquestioned revelatory status.[2] Milton's life overlapped with those of many proto-enlightenment thinkers, and he wrote his great works at a time in which efforts to find a new, coherent view of the world were underway. The first version of *Paradise Lost* was probably completed in the same year 1666 which is designated as the *annus mirabilis* of Newton.[3] John Rumrich has pointed out that Milton and Newton also shared the heresy of Arianism and numerous other peculiarities.[4] Although the two never became acquainted, Milton knew some other members of the Royal Society personally, thus witnessing a fundamental change in cosmology from a close range. Having long been a backwater in the area of "natural philosophy", England "became, arguably, 'the major centre for organized scientific activity in Europe'" in the course of the seventeenth century.[5] This stupendous scientific activity was mostly conducted within the context of the Royal Society, whose members included Milton's friend Henry Oldenburg and his former pupil Richard Jones (who, incidentally, was also a nephew of

1 See Niklas Luhmann, *Paradigm Lost: Die ethische Reflexion der Moral*, Festvortrag anlässlich der Verleihung des Hegel-Preises der Landeshauptstadt Stuttgart am 23. November 1988 im Neuen Schloß Stuttgart, Stuttgart: Enke, 1988.

2 Christopher Ricks, "Introduction", in John Milton, *Paradise Lost,* ed. Christopher Ricks, London: Penguin, 1989, p. xxii.

3 Barbara Kiefer Lewalski, *The Life of John Milton: A Critical Biography,* Oxford, and Malden, MA: Blackwell, 2003, p. 444; and Richard S. Westfall, *Never At Rest: A Biography of Isaac Newton*, Cambridge: Cambridge University Press, 1980, p. 143 f.

4 John P. Rumrich, *Milton Unbound: Controversy and Reinterpretation,* Cambridge: Cambridge University Press, 1996.

5 John Henry, "The Scientific Revolution in England", in *The Scientific Revolution in National Context*, eds. Roy Porter and Mikuláš Teich, Cambridge: Cambridge University Press, 1992, p. 178.

Robert Boyle).[6] Another associate, Theodore Haak, the first to translate parts of *Paradise Lost* into German, was not only a member of the Society, but also of the Hartlib circle, a correspondence network that treated questions of natural philosophy.[7] One of these scientifically inclined acquaintances, the clergyman John Beale (another member of both the Royal Society and the Hartlib circle), even attempted to claim Milton and his poetical talents for the cause of the natural sciences, although these efforts proved to be in vain.[8] Milton had acquaintances in common with Hobbes and John Locke (e.g. John Dryden), and in Henry Oldenburg, he even shared one with Spinoza.[9] In the span of seven years between the first and the second edition of *Paradise Lost*, Spinoza's *Tractatus Theologico-Politicus* was published, the first treatise to opt for a secularized society on the basis of a thorough historical critique of the Bible.[10] Milton was very much involved with the political reverberations of these paradigm shifts: his political career as a pamphleteer and civil servant depended on his critique of church dogma and of the divine right of kings. He thus contributed to a delegitimation of religiously sanctioned authority, which marked an important stage in the transition from feudal to capitalist society. However, his goal was certainly not the abolition, but the radicalization of political theology: Milton proposes a society in which God himself rules instead of his questionable representatives, a theocracy whose organization does not depend on the institutions of church and state, but on Christian individuals and their (biblically informed) consciences.[11] In the *Doctrina*, Milton emphasizes that

> Verùm […] aeternae salutis viam non nisi propriae cuiusque fidei Deus aperuerit postuletque hoc à nobis, ut qui salvus esse vult, pro se quisque credat […].
>
> God has opened the way of eternal salvation solely to each person's individual faith, and demands from us that whoever wants to be saved must have a personal faith of their own […].
>
> (*DC* 4/5)

And the responsibility of individual faith includes that of jurisdiction. Milton states that "nothing can be more essential to the freedom of a people than to

6 Lewalski, *The Life of John Milton*, pp. 302–303; 332–333; and Angelica Duran, *A Concise Companion to Milton,* Oxford and Malden, MA: Blackwell, 2007, p. 69.

7 Pamela R. Barnett, *Theodore Haak, F. R. S. (1605–1690): The First German Translator of* Paradise Lost, The Hague: Mouton, 1962.

8 Lewalski, *The Life of John Milton*, p. 458.

9 See Baruch de Spinoza, *The Letters*, trans. Samuel Shirley; eds. Steven Barbone, Lee Rice and Jacob Adler, Indianapolis: Hackett, 1995, p. 8.

10 Baruch de Spinoza, *Theological-Political Treatise*, trans. Michael Silverthorne and Jonathan Israel, Cambridge: Cambridge University Press, 2007.

11 See e.g. Sharon Achinstein, *Milton and the Revolutionary Reader*, Princeton, NJ: Princeton University Press, 1994, pp. 164–166.

have the administration of justice [...] in their own election and within their own bounds" (*CPW* 7.383–384). According to him, "the plain authority of Scripture" and "the reason of justice and equity" always lead to the same conclusions (*CPW* 1.868),[12] and state legislation should just follow their common lead:

> The judicial law can serve to no other end than to be the protector and champion of religion and honest civility [...] and is but the arm of moral law, which can no more be separate from justice than justice from virtue.
>
> (*The Doctrine and Discipline of Divorce, CPW* 2:321–322)

While Milton tends to respect both Roman and common law, he subordinates both of them to the judgment of faithful reason.[13] Ultimately, good Christian communities should always "make their own judicial laws, and execute them by their own elected judicatures" (*CPW* 7.383).

And the resultant laws can always be renegotiated. In his most radical treatises, such as *The Ready and Easy Way to Establish a Free Commonwealth*, he proposes a constant reformation of the Reformation, a "Trotskyite" religious commonwealth of permanent revolution.[14] Although his political views in some aspects resemble those of his Puritan contemporaries, it would be wrong to label him a Puritan, as Catherine Gimelli Martin has shown.[15] It would be slightly more accurate, if also problematic, to label him a humanist; the influence of Erasmus of Rotterdam on him is particularly pervasive.[16] Accordingly, he keeps pleading for tolerance among dissenting opinions:

> Quod si inter eos qui fideles videntur esse, de scripturae sensu [n]on convenit, tolerare alii alios debebunt, donec Deus, quod verum sit, omnibus revelaverit.

12 See also Alison A. Chapman, *The Legal Epic:* Paradise Lost *and the Early Modern Law*, Chicago and London: University of Chicago Press, 2017, p. 44.

13 Chapman, *The Legal Epic*, p. 58.

14 David Hawkes seems to have been the first to draw the parallel between Milton and Trotsky. See David Hawkes, *John Milton: A Hero of Our Time*, Berkeley, CA: Counterpoint, 2009, p. 179. Hawkes' book stands in the tradition of Christopher Hill, *Milton and the English Revolution*, Harmondsworth: Penguin, 1979. However, it should be noted that Milton did not envisage any redistribution of property in his political projects. See Chapman, *The Legal Epic*, pp. 111–112.

15 Catherine Gimelli Martin, *Milton among the Puritans: The Case for Historical Revisionism*, Farnham and Burlington, VT: Ashgate, 2010.

16 Rosemary Masek, "Desiderius Erasmus", in *A Milton Encyclopedia*, Vol. 3, ed. William B. Hunter Jr., Lewisburg, PA: Bucknell University Press and London: Associated University Presses, 1978, pp. 65–68.

> But if there is disagreement amongst the seemingly faithful about the sense of scripture, their duty will be to tolerate one another until God shall reveal to all what is true [...].
>
> (*DC* 804/805)

On the other hand, he condones and even advocates the unleashing of religious violence, especially against Catholics whom he regards as intolerant and idolatrous heretics aspiring to worldly power. In his writings, he repeatedly asserts that all measures are justified against the enemies of faith. Sometimes, he even seems to revel in real and phantasmatic cruelties; in a sonnet praising Cromwell, he approvingly refers to the Lord Protector's rather ruthless military campaigns:

> And on the neck of crownèd Fortune proud
> Hast reared God's trophies and his work pursued,
> While Darwen stream with blood of Scots imbrued,
> And Dunbar field resounds thy praises loud [...].[17]

In his treatise *Of Reformation*, in rather disconcerting terms, he wishes all misfortunes in this life and the next to come upon ambitious heretics:

> But they contrary, that by the impairing and diminution of the true faith, the distresses and servitude of their country, aspire to high dignity, rule, and promotion here, after a shameful end in this life (which God grant them), shall be thrown down eternally into the darkest and deepest gulf of hell, where, under the despiteful control, the trample and spurn of all the other damned, that in the anguish of their torture, shall have no other ease than to exercise a raving and bestial tyranny over them as their slaves and negroes, they shall remain in that plight forever, the basest, the lowermost, the most dejected, most underfoot, and downtrodden vassals of perdition.
>
> (*Of Reformation, CPW* 1:616–617)

Diverse tendencies that were characteristic of his age intersect in Milton's work, and he sometimes seems to be stunningly unconcerned about the resulting contradictions. A certain eclecticism characterizes him, which may not only be due to his extremely wide reading in religion, literature and the sciences, but also to his biographical situation. He was not only a scholar and savant, but also very much influenced by the realities of the worldly professions. That he was steeped in the world of politics is obvious by the considerable number of his political pamphlets and his position as Cromwell's foreign secretary. But it must also be remembered that Milton's family was "in

17 "Sonnet 16: To the Lord General Cromwell, May 1652", in *CPEP*, p. 153.

trade", that his father was a moneylender and stockholder of diverse companies (among them the Shakespearean Blackfriars Theatre).[18] He himself to a certain degree continued the tradition, partly supporting himself by moneylending, as well as proving a writer with a shrewd business sense. (Apparently, he was the first English author to contractually claim the property rights to his work and then to cause the stationer to buy him out.)[19] This context has to be taken into account, for example, when we perceive that Milton tends to read problems of law and ethics as problems of debt and indebtedness. The ethical question for him is almost always: what is owed to whom? Furthermore, Milton's life-world was also steeped in secular law: his father worked as a scrivener, a profession that required a considerable amount of legal knowledge; his brother Christopher studied law and eventually became Judge of the Common Pleas; and his brother-in-law Edward Phillips worked in the office of Chancery.[20] And there were more jurists in the extended family and in Milton's circle of friends.[21] Last not least, he was close to James Bradshaw, the judge who presided at Charles I's trial and condemned the king to death.[22]

Milton himself was obviously interested in legal philosophy and secular jurisprudence. He owned treatises on law by Plato, Aristotle, Cicero, Justinian, Thomas Aquinas, Henry de Bracton, Richard Hooker and Edward Coke. And in his work, one can also find references to other legal philosophers and jurists such as Gratian and John Fortescue.[23] In his pedagogical treatise *Of Education*, he declares secular legal history to be a central part of any pupil's curriculum (*CPW* 2:398–399). The jurist whom he seems to have admired the most is Hugo Grotius. In Milton's work, references to Grotius and his theory of natural law are always reverential; the exiled Dutch jurist is designated as a "man of these times, one of the best learned" (*CPW* 2:238). Milton apparently not only read his *De jure belli ac pacis* (1625) and his poetry, such as *Adamus exul*.[24] He also "ardently desired to meet" their author (*CPW* 4.1:615), and, during his Grand Tour in 1638, seems to have managed to pay his respects to him in Paris.[25]

When Milton began to engage in politics and when he held office as foreign language secretary, he often had to deal with questions of law, including

18 Roy Flannagan, *John Milton: A Short Introduction*, Oxford and Malden, MA: Blackwell, 2002, pp. 1–4.
19 Lewalski, *The Life of John Milton*, p. 453.
20 Helen Darbishire, *The Early Lives of Milton*, London: Constable and Co., 1932, p. 53.
21 Chapman, *The Legal Epic*, p. 18.
22 Gordon Campbell and Thomas N. Corns, *John Milton: Life, Work and Thought*, Oxford: Oxford University Press, 2008, pp. 207, 290.
23 Chapman, *The Legal Epic*, pp. 20–21
24 Christopher N. Warren, "John Milton and the Epochs of International Law", *The European Journal of International Law* 24. 2 (2013), p. 567.
25 Lewalski, *The Life of John Milton*, p. 89.

international law.[26] And some of his remarks hint that he considered his legal and political work closely linked to his poetical works. In *The Reason of Church Government*, for example, he states that legislation should always be framed by persuasion and narration:

> In the publishing of human laws, which for the most part aim not beyond the good of civil society, to set them barely forth to the people without reason or preface, like a physical prescript, or only with threatenings, as it were a lordly command, in the judgement of Plato was thought to be done neither generously nor wisely. His advice was, seeing that persuasion certainly is a more winning and more manlike way to keep men in obedience than fear, that to such laws as were of principal moment, there should be used as an induction, some well-tempered discourse, showing how good, how gainful, how happy it must needs be to live according to honesty and justice, which being uttered with those native colours and graces of speech, as true eloquence the daughter of virtue can best bestow upon her mother's praises, would so incite, and in a manner, charm the multitude into the love of that which is really good, as to embrace it ever after, not of custom and awe, which most men do, but of choice and purpose, with true and constant delight. But this practice we may learn from a better and more ancient authority than any heathen writer hath to give us, and indeed being a point of so high wisdom and worth, how could it be but we should find it in that book within whose sacred context all wisdom is enfolded? Moses therefore the only lawgiver that we can believe to have been visibly taught of God, knowing how vain it was to write laws to men whose hearts were not first seasoned with the knowledge of God and of his works, began from the book of Genesis, as a prologue to his laws; which Josephus right well hath noted. That the nation of the Jews, reading therein the universal goodness of God to all creatures in the creation and his peculiar favour to them in his election of Abraham their ancestor, from whom they could derive so many blessings upon themselves, might be moved to obey sincerely by knowing so good a reason of their obedience.
>
> (*The Reason of Church Government, CPW*, 1:746–747)

In his prose works as well as in his poetry, Milton seems to promote a poetics of persuasion by accumulation. To some of the legal and religious controversies of this time, Milton offered a solution in *Areopagitica*, promoting a culture of toleration, but not of pluralism: he asserts that the truth will always emerge from the juxtaposition of all the arguments brought forth by all the contending parties:

26 See e.g. Christopher N. Warren, *Literature and the Law of Nations, 1580–1680*, Oxford: Oxford University Press, 2015, p. 170.

> And though all the winds of doctrine were let loose to play upon the earth, so Truth be in the field, we do injuriously, by licensing and prohibiting to misdoubt her strength. Let her and Falsehood grapple; who ever knew Truth put to the worse in a free and open encounter. Her confuting is the best and surest suppressing. [...] For who knows not that Truth is strong next to the Almighty; she needs no policies, nor stratagems, nor licencings to make her victorious, those are the shifts and the defences that error uses against her power: Give her but room, and do not bind her when she sleeps, for then she speaks not true, as the old Proteus did, who spake oracles only when he was caught and bound, but then rather she turns herself into all shapes, except her own, and perhaps tunes her voice according to the time, as Micaiah did before Ahab, until she be adjured into her own likeness. Yet is it not impossible that she may have more shapes than one.
>
> (*Areopagitica, CPW* 2:561–563)

Milton propagates scholarly discussion and literary agon both as a struggle and as a redemptory mediation between the diverse factions. One might compare this approach with Spinoza's maxim "verum index sui et falsi".[27] But Milton here also seems to echo a belief that was common among early modern scholars, namely the supposition that the paradisiacal nature-language of Adam and Eve could be reconstructed by the analysis and re-synthesis of the post-Babelian languages.[28] According to this notion of scholarly and poetical redemption, the writer (re)integrates, rather than creates. Milton's literary work, and *Paradise Lost* first and foremost, might be understood as a literary exploration of this topic, not only because of his Latinisms, Hebraisms and other polylingualisms that seem always to strive for the integration of other languages into English.[29] More importantly, as William Hazlitt pointed out, Milton's epic generally seems to be woven from fragments of other texts, an encyclopaedic web of quotes,[30] one might say: an allegory of reading. Generally, classical antiquity seeps into his theology not merely by the official road of its Christianized philosophical heritage, but also in disconcertingly

27 The formulation "index sui et falsi" derives from Baruch de Spinoza, *Ethica/Die Ethik*, trans. Jacob Stern, Stuttgart: Reclam, 1977, pp. 214/215 [2.43, Scholium].

28 See e.g. Umberto Eco, *The Search for the Perfect Language,* trans. James Fentress, Malden and Oxford: Blackwell, 1995, pp. 73–116; see also Björn Quiring, "'With Real Hunger to Transubstantiate': Die Dispersion der Eucharistie in John Miltons *Paradise Lost*", *Mitteilungen des Sonderforschungsbereichs 573, "Pluralisierung und Autorität in der Frühen Neuzeit"* 1 (2011).

29 John K. Hale, *Milton's Languages: The Impact of Multilingualism on Style*, Cambridge: Cambridge University Press, 1997.

30 William Hazlitt, "On Shakespeare and Milton", in *The Complete Works of William Hazlitt,* Vol. 5, eds. P. P. Howe, A. R. Waller and Arnold Glover, London and Toronto: J. M. Dent and Sons, 1930, p. 58; cited in Gordon Teskey, *Delirious Milton*, Cambridge, MA and London: Harvard University Press, 2006, p. 123.

direct references to Greek and Roman poets in questions of theology. For example, in the *Doctrina Christiana*, Milton quotes not only the Bible and a few theologians, but also Homer's *Odyssey* in order to deal with a question of theodicy (*DC* 116/117); and he quotes Euripides to reinforce his mortalist position (*DC* 454/455). Milton's imagination is intertextual; this is why *Paradise Lost* resembles a "gigantic cultural memory".[31] The literary forms and citations compete with each other and overwrite each other, so that complex palimpsests are generated. This plurivocity is what makes the poetry of *Paradise Lost* inherently dramatic.[32] However, a peculiar problem arises: as a zealous Christian, Milton wagers that true Christianity will emerge as evidently truthful and victorious on all levels in the course of these competitions. Thus, the way of God will be justified to men. But the case turns out to be not so easy: when he appropriates the trappings of paganism (such as the form of the epic) and other snippets of unbelief in order to convey a biblical message, it turns out that the heathen elements threaten to overwhelm the teachings of the One True Faith, despite the narrator's protestations to the contrary. Occasionally, Milton's evident fascination with pagan antiquity prompts him to construct hybrids between Greco-Roman and Judeo-Christian imagery that more orthodox contemporaries might have considered blasphemous. For example, in the Latin elegy for Charles Diodati, Milton declares that his dear departed friend in heaven will forever participate in "orgiastic feasts" that "have their Bacchic celebration under the thyrsus of Zion" ("Festa Sionaeo bacchantur et Orgi thyrso").[33] Normally, though, the poet manages to check himself and discredit the unchristian traditions on which he nevertheless relies. The uneasy reliance on pagan predecessors, which constituted a general problem of Christian epic,[34] is very pronounced in Milton's work. As Linda Gregerson elucidates:

31 "[Ü]berdimensionales kulturelles Gedächtnis". Anselm Haverkamp, "Distant Information: Die komparatistische Bedeutung Miltons", *Deutsche Vierteljahrsschrift für Literaturwissenschaft und Geistesgeschichte* 68:4 (1994), p. 639.

32 William Empson, *Milton's God*, pp. 209–210.

33 "Epitaphium Damonis", in *CPEP*, p. 242 [219].

34 For this reason, some poetologies recommended the total avoidance of Christian subjects when the epic form is used. Nicolas Boileau's *L'Art poétique* (1674) is a prominent example:

> C'est donc bien vainement que nos auteurs déçus,
> Bannissant de leurs vers ces ornements reçus,
> Pensent faire agir Dieu, ses saints et ses prophètes,
> Comme ces dieux éclos du cerveau des poètes;
> Mettent à chaque pas le lecteur en enfer,
> N'offrent rien qu' Astaroth, Belzébuth, Lucifer…
> De la foi d'un chrétien les mystères terribles
> D'ornements égayés ne sont point susceptibles:
> L'Évangile à l'esprit n'offre de tous côtés
> Que pénitence à faire et tourments mérités;
> Et de vos fictions le mélange coupable
> Même à ses vérités donne l'air de la fable.

> While the younger religion lays claim to legitimacy at the expense of the elder, it remains imaginatively dependent upon the system of belief it displaces. The epic similes of *Paradise Lost*, which summarize and displace a lofty poetic heritage, constituting a kind of house arrest for the likes of Homer, Virgil, and Ovid, notoriously preserve and perpetuate the tales they make much show of discrediting.[35]

Thus Milton is confronted with a problem that is not only his own, but haunts the whole history of the Christian religion: Christianity is a hybrid between a Hebrew and a Greco-Roman heritage, claiming to supersede both traditions, but still remaining dependent on them. Ever since pagan temples were turned into Christian churches and pagan holidays became Christian ones, the Roman Empire has persisted not only as the Other of the church, the Great Whore of Babylon, but also as its disavowed progenitor.[36] Even the seemingly pure Christianity of the Middle Ages never managed to rid itself of polytheistic remnants.[37] In the constant struggle to subdue the uncannily familiar spectres of the Roman Empire, many theologians have tried to appropriate the pagan cultural heritage by constructing biblical precedents from which they supposedly degenerated. This tradition was started in Late Antiquity, first and foremost by Tertullian and Origen. For example, they pointed out that the texts of the Old Testament frequently make use of rhetorical devices. And since these texts are older than Homer and Plato, it follows that the pagan authors must have stolen their rhetorical knowledge from Moses and the other prophets.[38] In this construction of precedence out of belatedness, the biblical text is nonetheless evaluated according to literary and rhetorical standards that were laid down by Aristotle, Horace and Quintilian. To this extent, one might say that the church fathers have paganized the Bible by Christianizing culture.[39] And under the conditions of the late seventeenth century, namely rampant religious controversy, increasing secularization and

> Et quel objet, enfin, à présenter aux yeux
> Que le diable toujours hurlant contre les cieux,
> Qui de votre héros veut rabaisser la gloire,
> Et souvent avec Dieu balance la victoire!

See Nicolas Boileau, "L'Art poétique" in *Art poétique, épîtres, poésies diverses, odes, et epigrammes*, ed. Sylvain Menant, Paris: Flammarion, 1969, p. 103 [3.193–208]. This reproach is first and foremost directed against Tasso, but it is even more applicable to Milton.

35 Linda Gregerson, *The Reformation of the Subject: Spenser, Milton, and the English Protestant Epic*, Cambridge and New York: Cambridge University Press, 1997, p. 257.

36 See e.g. Christopher P. Jones, *Between Pagan and Christian*, Cambridge, MA: Harvard University Press, 2014.

37 See e.g. Jean Seznec, *The Survival of the Pagan Gods: The Mythological Tradition and its Place in Renaissance Humanism and Art,* Princeton, NJ: Princeton University Press, 1981.

38 Dietmar Till, *Das doppelte Erhabene: Eine Argumentationsfigur von der Antike bis zum Beginn des 19. Jahrhunderts,* Tübingen: Niemeyer, 2006, p. 134.

39 Till, *Das doppelte Erhabene*, p. 139.

epistemological uncertainty, these repressed inheritances make their presence felt particularly vehemently. Milton certainly did not think of himself as a secularizer; but nonetheless he articulates the modernizing developments of his time. For example, he could have written an epic in which Satan and the pagan deities following him are so univocally evil that its author would never have been suspected to be "of the devil's party without knowing it".[40] His precursor Tasso certainly did so.[41] What he does instead, is "to yield himself, at the critical moments, to the full imaginative promptings of his subject", as Waldock put it.[42] Milton was first and foremost a poet and rhetorician who chose his words for maximum impact. The result is a formidable *argumentum in utramque partem*. William Empson speculates that Milton might have learned how to put himself in the position of his diverse opponents when he worked as a propagandist for the cause of the English republic.[43] Whether one is convinced by this speculation or not, there are good reasons to regard *Paradise Lost* as an "echoing chamber for the whole mind of his period",[44] as Empson did. As John Stachniewski put it:

> Milton is doing more in *Paradise Lost* than dramatizing the theology to which he consciously subscribed, the theology of *De Doctrina*; he is imaginatively heightening aspects of the spiritual experience of his day, aspects which had no less social reality for having sprung from doctrines he rejected.[45]

Thus, while Milton aspires to synthesize diverse strands of discourse under the auspices of his own theology and poetics, he has difficulties containing the contradictions that articulate themselves. Most prominently, the descriptions of the proceedings and the narrator's explicit evaluations of them tend to clash, as Waldock has emphasized:[46] the better Satan's lines, for example, the keener the narrator is to draw a *cordon sanitaire* of denigration around them:

> There is hardly a great speech of Satan's that Milton is not at pains to correct, to damp down and neutralize. He will put some glorious thing in Satan's mouth, then, anxious about the effect of it, will pull us gently by the sleeve, saying (for this is what it amounts to): "Do not be carried

40 William Blake, "The Marriage of Heaven and Hell", in *The Complete Poetry and Prose of William Blake*, ed. David V. Erdman, New York and London: Doubleday, 1988, p. 35; spelling modified.

41 Torquato Tasso, *Jerusalem Delivered (Gerusalemme liberata)*, trans. Anthony M. Esolen, Baltimore: Johns Hopkins University Press, 2000, pp. 72–75 [4.1-19].

42 A. J. A. Waldock, Paradise Lost *and Its Critics*, Cambridge: Cambridge University Press, 1966, p. 51.

43 Empson, *Milton's God*, p. 123.

44 Empson, *Milton's God*, p. 210.

45 John Stachniewski, *The Persecutory Imagination*, p. 384.

46 Waldock, Paradise Lost *and its Critics*, p. 78.

> away by this fellow: he sounds splendid, but take my word for it. ..." We have in fact, once again, the two levels: the level of demonstration or exhibition, and the level of allegation or commentary; and again there is disagreement.[47]

Among the contradictions that unfold in *Paradise Lost* are also those of the term "nature": the domain of nature is sometimes represented as boundless, encompassing the infinite spaces of Chaos and hell (see e.g. 2.624–625), sometimes it seems to be restricted to the circumscribed area of heaven and earth (2.1037–1038). Sometimes it is described as an (allegorical?) person (9.782–784), sometimes as a mere abstraction (8.153). Sometimes it seems to be under God's direct command (6.176), sometimes to act independently of him (11.48–49). Sometimes, nature seems to fall with Adam and Eve (9.782–784); sometimes it seems to remain unaffected (11.836–838). Thus the epic offers a compendium of contradictory commonplaces that Milton tends to position for maximum rhetorical and poetical effect. His treatment of nature is highly contradictory, but, as Deleuze and Guattari have pointed out, no one and nothing ever died from contradictions. Contrariwise, "social machines make a habit of feeding on the contradictions they give rise to, on the crises they provoke, on the anxieties they engender, and on the infernal operations they regenerate".[48] Empson has already pointed out that in *Paradise Lost* the contradictory conceptions of nature, which put "her above, equal to and below man", do actually reinforce each other and "work together" despite their discrepancies.[49]

2.2 Milton's poetics: the problem of inspiration

One of the fields in which these contradictory conceptions of nature end up working hand in hand is that of poetics, which Milton relates to the problem of inspiration: the double role of God – above nature and within nature – complements the double role of the poet who, on the one hand, is free in his creative work, but, on the other hand, is officially being dictated to by his "heavenly Muse". First, it needs to be pointed out that the narrator of *Paradise Lost* claims divine inspiration, but does so in a context and at a time in which divine inspiration has become highly questionable. The status of the Muses was never altogether uncontested: belief in them and their agency has been doubtful and problematic ever since they first appeared in literary history.[50] Ernst Robert Curtius asserts that their invocation had already become

47 Waldock, Paradise Lost *and its Critics*, p. 78.

48 Gilles Deleuze and Félix Guattari, *Anti-Oedipus: Capitalism and Schizophrenia*, trans. Robert Hurley, Mark Seem and Helen R. Lane, Minneapolis: University of Minnesota Press, 1983, p. 151.

49 William Empson, *Some Versions of Pastoral*, New York: New Directions, 1974, p. 187.

50 See e.g Paul Veyne, *Did the Greeks Believe in Their Myths? An Essay on the Constitutive Imagination,* trans. Paula Wissing, Chicago: University of Chicago Press, 1988, pp. 28–29.

an altogether empty convention in the days of the Roman Empire under Augustus; for that very reason, in Late Antiquity many cultivated Christian poets saw no problem with addressing the Muse at the beginning of their works.[51] Despite its pointedly pagan roots, the invocation of the inspiring Muse has subsequently found its way into almost all Christian epics, for example into Dante's *Divine Comedy*[52] and into Tasso's *Jerusalem Delivered*.[53] In all cases, however, it seems to signify something slightly different: there were many attempts to integrate the Muses into a Christian worldview, but none of them was successful enough to establish a binding tradition.[54] Some Christians even seem to have taken the existence of the Muses more seriously than the pagans; several patristic allegorists, for example, tried to integrate the Muse into the Christian worldview through euhemeristic interpretation,[55] while Iuvencus, the first Christian epic poet, equated her with the Holy Spirit.[56] Milton continues the latter tradition, but also stresses a continuity with paganism: while the narrator identifies his Muse with the Holy Spirit (1.6–22),[57] he also addresses her as the classical pagan Muse Urania (7.1). Furthermore, he declares this Muse to be the sister of the personification of Wisdom that is mentioned in Proverbs 8 and thus integrates her, in a rather awkwardly eclectic move, into the Holy Family (7.7–12). Indeed, Milton's Muse is a thoroughly and irreducibly eclecticist personage, as Philip Edward Phillips has demonstrated: throughout the epic, she keeps accumulating both pagan and Christian attributes and relies on them both for operating.[58]

This abundance of contradictory influences casts some doubt upon the seriousness of the narrator's claim to divine inspiration – all the more since this claim generally had shrunken not only to a mere convention in Milton's time, but also to a target of ridicule. We find parodies of the topos in Rabelais' *Pantagruel*[59] and in Shakespeare's Sonnet 38 which addresses the beloved as

51 Ernst Robert Curtius, "Die Musen im Mittelalter, Erster Teil: Bis 1100", *Zeitschrift für romanische Philologie* 59:1 (1939), pp. 140–141.

52 See e.g. Dante, *Purgatorio*, trans. Jean Hollander and Robert Hollander, New York: Random House, 2003, pp. 644/645 [29.40–42].

53 Tasso, *Jerusalem Delivered,* p. 17 [1.2].

54 See e.g. Curtius, "Die Musen im Mittelalter", p. 131.

55 Ernst Robert Curtius, *European Literature and the Latin Middle Ages*, trans. Willard R. Trask, Princeton, NJ: Princeton University Press, 2013, p. 236.

56 Curtius, *European Literature and the Latin Middle Ages,* p. 235.

57 See also: "Taught by the heavenly Muse to venture down/ The dark descent, and up to reascend" (3.19–3.20); and "If answerable style I can obtain/ Of my celestial patroness, who deigns/ Her nightly visitation unimplored,/ And dictates to me slumbering, or inspires/ Easy my unpremeditated verse" (9.20–9.24).

58 Philip Edward Phillips, *John Milton's Epic Invocations: Converting the Muse*, New York: Peter Lang, 2000, pp. 98, 118. This ecumenical acquisitiveness also expresses itself by a formal eclecticism: Milton's invocations most closely resemble not those of his Christian contemporaries, but those of Virgil. See Phillips, *John Milton's Epic Invocations*, p. 99.

59 See e.g. François Rabelais, *Pantagruel*, in *Oeuvres complètes*, ed. Mireille Huchon, Paris: Gallimard, 1994, p. 315 [ch. 28].

"the tenth Muse, ten times more in worth/ Than those old nine which rhymers invocate".[60] Likewise, Spinoza derides the biblical claims of inspiration,[61] and Hobbes asserts:

> I can imagine no cause but a reasonless imitation of custom, of a foolish custom, by which a man, enabled to speak wisely from the principals of nature and his own meditation, loves rather to be thought to speak by inspiration, like a bagpipe.[62]

Thus, Milton's use of the topos raises a number of questions. One might think that at least the appeal to the Holy Spirit clears the Miltonian invocations from any suspicion of frivolity; but it should be kept in mind that this Spirit is actually a contested entity in Protestantism generally, and in Milton's theology in particular. In the *Doctrina Christiana,* Milton denies that the Holy Spirit exists as a separate, determinate entity and points out that the term oscillates between several meanings, being occasionally also applied to angels and to the human mind (*DC* 244/245). He even demands that no one should invoke the Holy Spirit in religious ceremonies, since it is an altogether derivative and ephemeral entity which therefore is not to be worshipped (*DC* 266/267). Literary critics who stress Milton's Christian univocity tend to ignore this problem,[63] but the status of the Muse spirit in *Paradise Lost* remains unclear.

In order to see this status with greater clarity, it is worthwhile to investigate what Milton's general position on literary inspiration is: how does he assume poetry is made? His preliminary remarks on "The Verse" in *Paradise Lost* convey the impression that he carefully selected his formal poetological restraints and calculated their effects, instead of being in the thrall of religious inspirations in which some supernatural entity dictated to him. When we look at his other (surprisingly rare) poetological statements, we find that Milton universalizes, but at the same time secularizes inspiration in his *Art of Logic*; it may be divine, but not more divine than all other events:

> I am supposing that no one doubts that the primary efficient source of art is God, the author of all wisdom. Even the ancient philosophers were aware of this. The ministerial causes were the talented and divinely instructed men who in the past discovered the various arts.
>
> (*Art of Logic, CPW* 8:213)

60 William Shakespeare, "Sonnet 38", in *The Norton Shakespeare* ed. Stephen Greenblatt, New York and London: W. W. Norton and Co., 1997, p. 1936.

61 Baruch de Spinoza, *Theological-Political Treatise*, pp. 13–26.

62 Thomas Hobbes, "The Answer to the Preface", in William Davenant, *The Works*, London: T.N. for Henry Herringman, 1673, p. 23.

63 See e.g. Stanley E. Fish, *Surprised By Sin: The Reader in* Paradise Lost, Cambridge, MA: Harvard University Press, 1997, p. 206.

If God is the primary cause of all the arts, then all art might obviously be designated as divinely inspired – including the arts of natural history, pottery, horsemanship, dicing, and so on. Reflections on the products of the human intellect are thus enveloped by a theological truism: whatever happens, was ultimately caused by God, since he is at the absolute origin of all causal chains. Milton here inscribes himself in a poetological tradition that does not regard inspiration as a divine intervention into the chain of natural causality, but as a force operating within and through this causality:

> Kennzeichnend für diese Alternative zum biblisch-hagiographischen Modell ist, daß sie unter Gott, sofern er auf den Dichter einwirkt, nicht in erster Linie den Gott der biblischen Offenbarung versteht, der Aussagen über sich selber oder seine die Menschheit betreffenden Absichten macht und sich zum Zwecke dieser Selbstmitteilung bzw. zur Eröffnung seines Heilsplanes eigens erwählter menschlicher Instrumente bedient, sondern den Schöpfergott, von welchem, als der Ersten Ursache, alle Geschöpfe, einschließlich der Menschen und einschließlich der Dichter, in ihrem je eigenen Sein und Wesen und bei der Verwirklichung ihres je eigenen Tuns ursächlich abhängig sind. Die göttliche Beeinflussung des Dichters erscheint dabei als eine lediglich besonders ins Auge gefaßte Form jener seinsgebenden, welterhaltenden und alle geschöpfliche Aktivität erst ermöglichenden allgemeinen Kausalität, die von der göttlichen Ersten Ursache auf die einzelnen Kreaturen ausgeübt wird und bei diesen zu unterschiedlichen Wirkungen führt.[64]
>
> It is characteristic for this alternative to the biblical-hagiographic model that it does not conceptualize the God who inspires the poet as the God of biblical revelation who discloses himself and his intentions regarding mankind and who chooses particular human subjects for this revelatory purpose. Instead, this model depends on God as supreme creator, the First Cause, on whom all creatures, including all humans, including all poets, depend in their being, their essence and their actions. Thus, the divine influence on the poet appears as no more than a specific form of this general creative and world-sustaining causality that the divine origin impresses on each generated thing, enabling and effectuating creaturely activity in all its manifold forms.[65]

In this line of thought, inspiration turns out to be a rather ordinary, natural occurrence; and it becomes sensible (and even modest) to assert that the force that causes the creation of a poem is also the force that creates and orders the universe.

64 Christoph J. Steppich, *Numine afflatur: Die Inspiration des Dichters im Denken der Renaissance*, Wiesbaden: Harrassowitz, 2002, p. 99. Dante was among Milton's precursors in that respect. See e.g. Steppich, *Numine afflatur*, p. 363.

65 Translation BQ.

On the other hand, the narrator of *Paradise Lost* still claims the prophetic role, comparing himself to Moses and other biblical prophets (see e.g. 1.6–13; see also *CPW* 1:816). Thence, he also plays with the *frisson* of a transcendence that would directly assert itself in the field of everyday experience, as it did in the time of the ancient prophets, interrupting the causal chains of nature in the forms of miracles.. (One may discern a similarity to the scholastic differentiation between grace that works "praeter ordinem rebus inditum" and grace that unfolds according to the "ordo naturae".)[66] In Milton's time, this was a dangerous assertion to make: under certain circumstances it still could lead to an accusation of blasphemy, since similar statements had led to political turmoil not too long ago.[67] A tension between natural and heavenly inspiration persists in Milton's poetics: he positions himself in the grey area between them.[68] It is in this zone that the narrator's poetical persona unfolds, dealing strategically with both notions, asserting them both, preferring sometimes the one, sometimes the other, according to the occasion.[69] As a result, *Paradise Lost* relies on a poetics in which, as Joanna Picciotto has expressed it, divine and human agency are "inextricably confused".[70] The voice of the Muse and the voice of the poet mingle, sometimes awkwardly, sometimes elegantly. This allows the narrator to assume a double role, one that is both unaffected and affected by the Fall, an elevated and illuminated spirit soaring freely through the prelapsarian cosmos, but also a fallen, suppressed, isolated, blind and withered human being, "with dangers compassed round" (7.27). Inspiration causes the first voice to manifest itself within the second, brightening up an otherwise dreary life. It remains unclear however, whether the resultant poetic joys of supralunar illumination and cosmic flight are the result of natural causes, an act of unfathomable divine grace or a compensatory act of divine justice, indemnifying the narrator for his unbroken faith and for his opposition to ungodly "hirelings" (4.193) and royalist "revelers" (7.33). Thus, even in this regard the narrative allows the narrator to inhabit a grey zone between the inspired pagan poet – who did not have to be a particularly virtuous man – and the biblical prophet – who was thought to be chosen by God for his "life of almost unapproachable excellence".[71]

66 See Thomas Aquinas, *Summae Contra Gentiles/Summe gegen die Heiden*, Vol. 3.2, ed. and trans. Karl Allgaier, Darmstadt: Wissenschaftliche Buchgesellschaft, 1996, p. 378 [3.161].

67 Christoph J. Steppich, *Numine afflatur*, p. 363; and Keith Thomas, *Religion and the Decline of Magic: Studies in Popular Beliefs in Sixteenth- and Seventeenth-Century England*, London: Penguin, 1991, pp. 474–480.

68 It is worth noting in this context that Milton also tended to mingle the doctrines of predestination and free will in peculiar ways. See Stephen M. Fallon, *Milton's Peculiar Grace: Self-Representation and Authority*, Ithaca, NY: Cornell University Press, 2007.

69 See e.g. John M. Steadman, *Moral Fiction in Milton and Spenser*, Columbia, MO: University of Missouri Press, 1995, p. 6.

70 Joanna Picciotto, *Labors of Innocence in Early Modern England*, Cambridge, MA and London: Harvard University Press, 2010, p. 443.

71 See. e.g. Origen, *Contra Celsum, Books II–VIII*, trans. Frederick Crombie, Edinburgh: T. and T. Clark, 1872, p. 430 [7.7].

In this perspective, the double status of inspiration and the double status of nature reinforce each other: the oscillation of inspiration between immanence and transcendence is connected to its ambiguous envelopment in a nature that is both above and indistinguishable from man. It seems all the more appropriate that the Muse Urania is traditionally associated with the goddess Natura: Eike Barmeyer has pointed out that the Muses, ever since Hesiod, have frequently been depicted as nature deities, associated with mountains and the sources of certain rivers, like the nymphs.[72] In the *Georgica*, Virgil does not ask the Muses for poetic inspiration, but for knowledge of natural laws.[73] And in the *Cosmographia* of Bernardus Silvestris, Urania is explicitly represented as a feudatory of the goddess Natura.[74] Generally, Nature is often the name given to the place where the question of inspiration's theological status has not been answered.

2.3 The epic of God

Milton's project of synthesizing the pagan and the Christian heritage by rewriting the Bible in the form of a classical epic unfolds under the auspices of this encompassing and poetical Nature.[75] One of the narrator's goals, as he demonstrates again and again (see e.g. 1.740–748; 7.39), is to show the superiority of biblical truth over pagan deception. Subsequent difficulties develop, even though Milton approaches the task rather flexibly. Throughout his work, Milton is rather unorthodox in his dealings with the Bible: like any good Protestant, he assumes that the true Christian doctrine must be gathered from Holy Scripture (*DC* 794–801). And yet, like a good humanist, he asserts that over the ages the biblical text has been repeatedly corrupted by interested parties (*DC* 810/811). While he declares himself bound by the framework of the Bible, he takes remarkable liberties with it, as he also does in his prose works, most famously in the divorce tracts, in which he declares marital union dissoluble and invokes for confirmation passages such as Matthew 5.31–32 and 19.3–9 which were generally thought to affirm the very opposite (see e.g. *Tetrachordon*, *CPW* 2:636–680). In *Paradise Lost*, he takes similar liberties with the first three chapters of Genesis, and in this instance he cannot avoid taking them. For by translating the biblical text into the form of an epic,

72 Eike Barmeyer, *Die Musen: Ein Beitrag zur Inspirationstheorie*, Munich: Wilhelm Fink, 1968, pp. 67–68.

73 Virgil, *Georgica/Vom Landleben,* trans. and ed. Otto Schönberger, Stuttgart: Reclam, 1994, pp. 66–69 [2.475–482]. See also: Curtius, *European Literature and the Latin Middle Ages*, p. 230.

74 Bernardus Silvestris, *Cosmographia,* ed. Peter Dronke, Leiden: Brill, 1978, p. 127 [5.1].

75 Milton owned and used the King James Version of the Bible, although, of course, he also worked with other English Bible translations, as well as Latin, Greek and Hebrew versions of Holy Scripture. See Matthew S. Stallard, "Editorial Preface", in John Milton, *Paradise Lost: The Biblically Annotated Edition*, ed. Matthew S. Stallard, Macon, GA: Mercer University Press, 2011, p. xxix.

Milton has to flesh it out. Famously, Erich Auerbach has contrasted the continuous and detailed narrative style of Homer's epics with the discontinuous and laconic style of the Bible:

> Auf der einen Seite ausgeformte, gleichmäßig belichtete, ort- und zeitbestimmte, lückenlos im Vordergrund miteinander verbundene Erscheinungen; ausgesprochene Gedanken und Gefühle; mußevoll und spannungsarm sich vollziehende Ereignisse. Auf der anderen Seite wird nur dasjenige an den Erscheinungen herausgearbeitet, was für das Ziel der Handlung wichtig ist, der Rest bleibt im Dunkel; die entscheidenden Höhepunkte der Handlung werden allein betont, das Dazwischenliegende ist wesenlos; Ort und Zeit sind unbestimmt und deutungsbedürftig; die Gedanken und Gefühle bleiben unausgesprochen, sie werden nur aus dem Schweigen und fragmentarischen Reden suggeriert […].[76]
>
> On the one hand, externalized, uniformly illuminated phenomena, at a definite time and in a definite place, connected together without lacunae in a perpetual foreground; thoughts and feeling completely expressed; events taking place in leisurely fashion and with very little suspense. On the other hand, the externalization of only so much of the phenomena as is necessary for the purpose of the narrative, all else left in obscurity; the decisive points of the narrative alone are emphasized, what lies between is nonexistent; time and place are undefined and call for interpretation; thoughts and feeling remain unexpressed, are only suggested by the silence and the fragmentary speeches […].[77]

Auerbach draws this characterization of biblical style from a close reading of Gen. 22, but his description also applies to Gen. 1–3: the Bible does not provide God with a motivation for creating the world; neither is it clear why and when the serpent seduces the woman or why exactly her mate also eats of the fruit. But if Milton wants to "justify the ways of God to men" according to the conventions of classical epic and humanism, he has to answer these questions. In obeisance to tradition, he does this mainly by making his narrator flesh out the events or by making his characters explain themselves, causing them to express their feelings and thoughts; the very form of the epic forces this device upon him. C. Q. Drummond has pointed out that, knowingly or not, Milton was confronted with unforeseen consequences of this procedure, quietly sabotaging his project:[78]

76 Erich Auerbach, *Mimesis: Dargestellte Wirklichkeit in der abendländischen Literatur*, Tübingen and Basel: Francke, 2001, pp. 13–14.

77 Erich Auerbach, *Mimesis: The Representation of Reality in Western Literature,* trans. Willard Trask, Princeton, NJ: Princeton University Press, 1953, p. 11.

78 Drummond, *In Defence of Adam*, p. 85.

> God may possibly be justified if he recedes into an infinite abyss of background so that he is unknowable in his motives and inscrutable in his purposes; this is, I believe, the God of Genesis or at least the God of Genesis as interpreted by sophisticated theology. But can a God who himself explains his motives and outlines his purposes in epic speeches of self-justification be said to be even the same character?[79]

When Dante encounters the Holy Trinity in the *Divina Comedia*, the epic must end, because this encounter surpasses all words.[80] But Milton represents God as a protagonist within an epic narrative, thus inserting him into a chain of causes and effects that renders him less inscrutable. By conferring the form of an epic on the biblical proceedings, *Paradise Lost* therefore makes them appear "natural rather than miraculous".[81] This result confirms Blumenberg's dictum that the epic tends to work as a device that secularizes myth:

> Der Dichter sorgt seinerseits entscheidend für die *Unbestimmtheit* der Tradition, die er vorfindet, und zwar paradoxerweise gerade durch die Wahrnehmung jenes Anreizes für eine Phantasie, die frei geworden ist, dem vorgefundenen Substrat *Überbestimmtheit* zu geben. Homer und Hesiod wußten gleichsam zu viel von den Göttern, zu Genaues über ihre Genealogien und Geschichten, als daß diesem noch so etwas wie "Glauben" hätte entgegengebracht werden können.[82]
>
> The poets decisively advance the *indeterminacy* of the tradition that precedes them; paradoxically, they do so by granting their imagination the liberty to *overdetermine* the preexistent materials. One might say that Homer and Hesiod knew too much about the gods, too many particulars about their genealogies and their histories, for their narratives to inspire anything like "belief" in their hearers.[83]

If the epic generally tends to counteract the mythical claims to faith, Milton reinforces this function by his "myth corrections", his frequent emendations of Greco-Roman mythology in the style of: "thus they relate,/ Erring" (1.746–747).[84] By the constant use of these revisionary interventions, Milton inscribes himself in a long literary tradition among whose earliest and most important

79 Drummond, *In Defence of Adam*, p. 90.

80 Dante, *Paradiso*, trans. by Jean Hollander and Robert Hollander, New York: Random House, 2007, pp. 820–827 (33.55–145).

81 Joseph Frank, "John Milton's Movement Toward Deism", *Journal of British Studies* 1.1 (1961), p. 43.

82 Hans Blumenberg, "Wirklichkeitsbegriff und Wirkungspotential des Mythos", in *Ästhetische und metaphorologische Schriften*, ed. Anselm Haverkamp, Frankfurt am Main: Suhrkamp, 2001, p. 346.

83 Translation BQ.

84 See *Mythenkorrekturen: Zu einer paradoxalen Form der Mythenrezeption*, eds. Martin Vöhler, Bernd Seidensticker and Wolfgang Emmerich, Berlin and New York: Walter de Gruyter, 2005.

representatives is Lucretius, with his notoriously anti-mythical didactic poem *De Rerum Natura*.[85] In his *Life of Milton*, Edward Phillips points out that his uncle John taught this "egregious" poet to his two young nephews,[86] and in his tractate *Of Education* Milton advises all pedagogues to do the same (*CPW* 2:395). And he did this at a time when it was hotly debated whether the philosophical, poetical and rhetorical devices that Lucretius had used to undermine belief in the Olympians might not also be turned against the God of Abraham, Isaac and Jacob.[87] Like Petrarch, Milton is confident that the indubitable truths of Christianity cannot be endangered by the metaphysical speculations of Epicureanism.[88] However, it has been pointed out before and will repeatedly be shown in the next chapters that Milton's appropriations of Lucretius occasionally also threaten to undermine the Christian logic of *Paradise Lost*.[89]

The same applies to another characteristic (and characteristically two-edged) device of the epic, namely the use of metanarratives.[90] Several crucial events of the story are not represented directly, but merely narrated by the characters, first and foremost by the archangels Raphael and Michael. And these narrators occasionally emphasize that they are speaking allegorically of primal and celestial things, "likening spiritual to corporal forms,/ As may express them best" (5.573–574). To a certain extent, this device successfully seems to remove the ways of heaven from the causal chains of nature and from human scrutiny, reinstating a suggestion of divine sublimity. However, the use of metadiegetic narrators instantly generates another problem: can the reader be sure of their veracity? This problem also has a long tradition in the reception history of the epic genre and even affects the *Odyssey*: Homer "brackets" the diegetical existence of mythical creatures such as the Sirens and the Cyclops by confining their appearances to a story which is narrated by the "cunning" Ulysses and which might very well be merely a lie.[91] Just in the same way, the divine act of Creation in *Paradise Lost* is removed from direct scrutiny and put into metadiegetic quotation marks: generally, divine creativity is never directly

85 Philip Hardie, "The Presence of Lucretius in *Paradise Lost*", in *Milton Quarterly* 29:1 (1995), p. 18.

86 Edward Phillips, "The Life of Milton", in John Milton, *Complete Poems and Major Prose*, ed. Merritt Y. Hughes, Indianapolis: Sheridan Books, 2003, p. 1029.

87 See Ada Palmer, *Reading Lucretius in the Renaissance*, Cambridge, MA: Harvard University Press, 2014.

88 Palmer, *Reading Lucretius in the Renaissance*, p. 71.

89 See e.g. Harold Bloom, *The Anatomy of Influence: Literature as a Way of Life*, New Haven, CT: Yale University Press, 2011, p. 141.

90 On the term see Gérard Genette, *Narrative Discourse: An Essay in Method*, trans. Jane E. Lewin, Ithaca, NY: Cornell University Press, 1980, p. 228.

91 See. e.g. Seth L. Schein, "Introduction", in *Reading the* Odyssey*: Selected Interpretive Essays*, ed. Seth L. Schein, Princeton, NJ: Princeton University Press, 1996, pp. 18–20.

represented as part of the diegetic action; instead, representations of God's generative powers are restricted to stories within the story, pre-eminently that of the Father, the Son, Raphael and Michael, but also that of Adam. Moreover, the narrator of *Paradise Lost* sometimes gives the reader reason to doubt the accuracy of these second-hand stories, for example when Raphael vividly narrates events he cannot actually have witnessed, most prominently the creation of Adam (compare 7.524–530 and 8.229–234). The absolute precedence and omnipotence of God is likewise never made manifest, but only asserted, first and foremost by God himself. When the eternal Father and his Son do make their immediate presence felt in the epic, it is either their superior fire power or their juridical and administrative authority that distinguishes them from the other protagonists. This is not to suggest that the narrator implies the falsity of the doctrine of divine creation; rather, he parallelizes the uncertain position of the epic's human protagonists with that of the reader him- or herself for whom divine creation must also be an object of faith. Satan, for his part, has not witnessed the divine creation of the heavens and the angels, and from this circumstance he deduces that it may well never have taken place: "who saw/ When this creation was?" (5.856–857). The narrator repeatedly suggests to the reader that she/he should have a firmer belief in the works of God than the devil, but the poem thus also implies that the reader finds her-/himself in a position of uncertainty about the world's origins which is analogous to that of Satan. The epic form automatically contextualizes all claims to precedence, prompting the narrator to issue direct and indirect commands to believe. For narratives always raise the questions: who uttered them when, to whom, and why? And *Paradise Lost* never univocally declares that the answers to these questions are beyond human understanding.

The representation of God as an epic character necessarily runs into problems. God and his traditional attributes were thought to be beyond representation, not only because of limited human perceptive and intellectual capacities, but because these attributes are situated beyond the very structure of logic. Apparent failings of God do not pose a problem for theology: the latter can refute them with the blanket statement that the ways of God are beyond all human comprehension. But an epic has to deal with them differently, as long as it treats God as an anthropomorphic subject. In *Paradise Lost*, Milton finds a political solution to this problem: since the transcendent status of God cannot be demonstrated within the empirical world, it must be treated as an article of faith and therefore as an ethical and theologico-political issue. This is exactly how it is largely treated in *Paradise Lost*: not as a matter of ontology, but as a matter of obligatory pious acknowledgement. When Satan starts to doubt that God is transcendent, omniscient, omnipotent and eternal, God can, *per definitionem*, provide no proof; according to a dilemma that Kant analysed, omnipotence, omniscience, eternity and other attributes of transcendence can never become the object of a finite, conditioned experience.[92] Thus, the epic largely deals with the political impact of God's supremacy as a doctrine that God himself constantly proclaims and defends against satanic counter-doctrines by political means. The divine omniscience and omnipotence have an impact as articles of faith, first and foremost, so God's power basically is reduced to the power to make his creatures believe in him: he is omnipotent, and this is demonstrated when they do not act against his will, and omniscient, which is demonstrated when he can prescribe them their view of the world. That is why Milton describes creation first and foremost as a poetical and political project. It may also explain the diagnosis of Walter Raleigh:

> [Milton's] heresies may be reduced to a single point; the ultimate basis on which he rests the universe is political, not religious. [...] He fell back on Law as the naked assertion of Will.[93]

From this perspective, the representation of God in *Paradise Lost*, which has caused many irritations, starts to make a new kind of sense:

> We encounter a deity neither inaccessible nor abstract, but distinctly anthropomorphic, individual, vocal, and to all appearances mutable. So while the deity does boast the impersonal, diagrammatic qualities the narrator and the critics ascribe to him, the Father as epic character turns out to be much more (or less) than an assembly of abstract functions, religious platitudes, or articles of faith.[94]

If the God of *Paradise Lost* resembles the Zeus/Jupiter of the *Iliad*, *Odyssey* and *Aeneid* more than the God of Dante's *Comedy*, this must be regarded not as a bug, but as a feature: *Paradise Lost* deals in its own way with a general problem of the monotheistic heritage. Judaeo-Christian monotheism slowly and gradually developed from an "Israelite polytheistic heritage".[95] Yahweh

92 As Kant put it succinctly in the "Transcendental Dialectic": "[...] die Ewigkeit, ohne Bedingungen der Zeit, die Allgegenwart, ohne Bedingungen des Raumes, die Allmacht usw. sind lauter transzendentale Prädikate, und daher kann der gereinigte Begriff derselben, den eine jede Theologie so sehr nötig hat, bloß aus der transzendentalen gezogen werden". (Immanuel Kant, *Kritik der reinen Vernunft*, ed. Wilhelm Weischedel, Frankfurt am Main: Suhrkamp, 1974, p. 563 [B 669–670]). "[...] eternity without conditions of time, omnipresence without conditions of space, omnipotence, etc.: all of these are transcendental predicates; and hence the purified concept of them, which any theology needs so very much, can be obtained only from transcendental theology". (Immanuel Kant, *Critique of Pure Reason*, trans. Werner S. Pluhar, Indianapolis: Hackett, 1996, p. 616 [B 669–670].)

93 Walter Raleigh, *Milton*, London: Edward Arnold, 1900, p. 128.

94 J. Allan Mitchell, "Reading God Reading 'Man': Hereditary Sin and the Narrativization of Deity in Paradise Lost, Book 3", *Milton Quarterly* 35:2 (2001), p. 73.

95 Mark S. Smith, *God in Translation: Deities in Cross-Cultural Discourse in the Biblical World*, Grand Rapids, MI: Eerdmans, 2010, p. 159; and Jack Miles, *God: A Biography*, New York: Alfred A. Knopf, 1995.

was originally a weather god among others, and he resembled Zeus in many respects; the biblical text still bears marks of these origins.[96] One might venture to say that the Christian God never altogether overcame this heritage, and his behaviour in Milton's epic could be viewed as a symptom of this. Over the centuries, diverse attempts have been made to unify the very diverse biblical conceptions of God, and to harmonize them with contemporary notions of the divine. *Paradise Lost*, which draws sustenance from diverse strands of this long tradition, therefore must confront the reader with a deity who is a highly complex character; indeed, he is so complex and so much at the centre of everything that happens in the epic, that it is fair to consider him its true protagonist. Surprisingly, this has never been done, as far as I can see; instead, almost every other character has been thought to be the principal hero of *Paradise Lost* at one time or another: Dryden assumed it was Satan; Addison thought the Son to be the hero; Jonathan Richardson asserted that it was Adam;[97] and John Collier proposed it was Eve.[98] Contrariwise, it is one of the theses to be unfolded in the following chapters that *Paradise Lost* is primarily not the tragic epic of man's or Satan's fall, but the imperial epic of God's rise and of the consolidation of his hegemony. And this saturation is facilitated by the attainment of a new synthesis between the Father's roles as both Zeus and Elohim. God attains his theological goal of absolute rule by legislative and political means that include the downfall of his creatures. Thus, one can designate *Paradise Lost* as a juridico-political theogony.

In the process of his hegemonization, the Father never altogether resolves the contradictions of his position, but he manages to install a system in which these contradictions work in his favour. One strategy he uses (just like Milton himself, according to Harold Bloom)[99] is to make an antecedence out of a belatedness. Many of his utterances and actions are to be understood as efforts to represent himself as the very origin of time and space, as attempts at discursive self-transcendentalization. God transcendentalizes his claims to power, but "the transcendentality is a function of the claim itself" (as Judith Butler writes in another context).[100] The hypothesis that will be developed in the following chapters is that God, to bolster his claims of transcendence by political means, propagates his double law, namely a positive law, supplemented by a natural law – with all the condensations and displacements that the latter concept undergoes in the seventeenth century. The politics in

96 See e.g. Reinhard Müller, *Jahwe als Wettergott: Studien zur althebräischen Kultlyrik anhand ausgewählter Psalmen*, Berlin and New York: Walter de Gruyter, 2008.

97 Joseph H. Summers, *The Muse's Method: An Introduction to* Paradise Lost, London: Chatto and Windus, 1962, p. 37.

98 John Collier, *Milton's* Paradise Lost*: Screenplay for Cinema of the Mind*, New York: Knopf, 1973, p. ix.

99 Harold Bloom, "Introduction", in *John Milton: Bloom's Modern Critical Views*, ed. Harold Bloom, New York and Philadelphia: Chelsea House, 2004, p. 12.

100 Judith Butler, *Antigone's Claim: Kinship Between Life and Death*, New York: Columbia University Press, 2000, p. 43.

Paradise Lost revolve around the tension between both laws: both the fall of Satan and the fall of man are partly caused by the uncertainty of how these two legal orders – the law which states what should be and the law which states what is – relate to each other. Together, they turn the world into a constant trial over which God can claim to preside as supreme and sole judge. While he thus consolidates his power, it should be remarked that Milton's epic theogony-cum-theodicy only functions if God does not become the God of the theologians, but retains some Jovian attributes, and if some perspective of a possible theomachy is retained. For example, William Empson has rightly pointed out that the social order of heaven is heavily organized and restricted and that these constraints of heaven are sorely lacking in justification, precisely because God is supposed to be all-powerful. For this reason, they compare unfavourably to the constraints of an army, a hospital or of a tourist party on a skiing holiday:

> The crowds who go to the seaside on a public holiday would be annoyed if someone tried to organize them, because they want to sit around and let the kids make sand-castles; but in a Butlin camp or a skiing hotel people will put up with a surprising amount of being organized, because they see some point in it, such as learning a new trick. Heaven, surely, is not usually visualized as like a Butlin camp, let alone a hospital; a variety of mystical writers have said, always with beauty I think, that it is like being at the seaside. It is that immortal sea where the children sport upon the shore. Thus to describe the God of Milton as "legalistic" is too charitable; what we are offered is a parody of legalistic behaviour, a thing in itself often necessary and reassuring, but also often suspected of being employed to gratify the privileged few; and it is evidently used in Heaven for that purpose alone.[101]

Both with and against Empson, it might alternatively be argued that the epic leaves open the possibility that Milton's God (despite his own infallible claims) resembles the Zeus of Nonnus and Pseudo-Apollodorus in that he can theoretically be overcome by military might, so that the martial order of heaven remains morally defensible. It is precisely an altogether omnipotent God whose ways cannot be justified. Therefore, God must remain positioned in a shadowy region between transcendence and immanence. And for the generation of this shadow, "nature" has an essential function to perform, as a power that seems to be the executive organ of the Lord, but also to be eluding his grasp. It will be demonstrated that this ambiguity is indeed necessary to *Paradise Lost*: it is Nature as first and last judgment that holds the epic's whole theologico-political edifice together and stabilizes the rule of God, even though it seems to be the one thing over which he has no power. By this

101 Empson, *Milton's God*, pp. 108–109.

utilization of nature, Milton has found a savvy solution for the problem of his great work's internal tensions; but it must be noted that it is a political, not a theological solution.

2.4 The miraculous draught of fish and the Hobbesian *Palintropos Harmonia*

In the course of the topic's investigation, a strange amalgam of theoretical perspectives will be useful. Since the main impetus of the analysis remains metaphorological and focused on ambiguities, Blumenberg and Empson will often be consulted. But frequently, they will interact with unaccustomed partners, for the text will also often refer to concepts developed by Walter Benjamin, especially his concept of allegory, and by Gilles Deleuze and Félix Guattari, especially in their book *Mille Plateaux*. These concepts, despite some shortcomings, will prove eminently useful for the investigation of the ways in which transcendence is created in a field of competing epistemologies by political means; for it is a central component of Deleuze's and Guattari's common project "to think transcendence within the immanent".[102] Their complex, idiosyncratic terminology describes a world of pure processes that stratify in a complex network of power relations, involving physical, social and linguistic structures. Thus subtracting pre-existent objects and subjects from their world leads these thinkers almost inevitably to the use of terms with a prominent theological heritage, despite their declared atheism.[103]

If *Paradise Lost* is analysed under these auspices, the text's modernity becomes obvious. In recent times, this modernity has often not been particularly emphasized. Rather, there has been a tendency to treat *Paradise Lost* as a repository of the Anglo-American cultural heritage in its connection with ancient cultural and religious traditions. As a consequence, the identification of possible cultural influences on Milton has been a major occupation of Milton studies for quite a long time.[104] Although the results are no doubt valuable, one might wonder whether this cultural asset management does not neglect what is unique about *Paradise Lost*. In the words of William Kerrigan:

> Some of what passes for historical scholarship committed to restoring or recollecting intentional meaning in fact levels off this meaning by giving undue weight to artificially constructed "traditions" and "conventions",

102 Gilles Deleuze and Félix Guattari, *What is Philosophy?*, trans. Hugh Tomlinson and Graham Burchell, New York: Columbia University Press, 1994, p. 47.

103 On the affinity and incompability of Deleuzean philosophy and theology, see e.g. Philip Goodchild, "Why Is Philosophy so Compromised with God?", in *Deleuze and Religion*, ed. Mary Bryden, London and New York: Routledge, 2001; F. LeRon Shults, *Iconoclastic Theology: Gilles Deleuze and the Secretion of Atheism*, Edinburgh: Edinburgh University Press, 2015.

104 See for example the assessment of William E. Cain, "Reflections on the Milton Industry", *Modern Language Notes* 96: 5 (1981): pp. 1121–1133.

> forcing the sense of great texts into a simplistic redundance of past commonplaces [...].[105]

One of the most influential representatives of this tendency is without doubt C. S. Lewis who tried his best to make a good Anglican out of Milton, often simplifying the involved traditions in the process.[106] Another representative is Stanley Fish with his study *Surprised by Sin: The Reader in* Paradise Lost, which largely reduces Milton's epic to a mixture of medieval theology, Ramist logic and the didactic rhetoric of Puritan preachers. Fish dealt with the obvious contradictions within the epic (which had been foregrounded by A. J. Waldock) by his own, rather reductive, brand of reader-response criticism, asserting that they are all meant to lure the reader into a trap deliberately set by Milton for educational purposes.[107] Whenever the narrator seems to contradict what Fish supposes to be Milton's worldview, he must actually teach the reader to recognize the contradictory statement as an illusion or deception from which to free him- or herself. The unified narratorial voice that is thus constructed is then proclaimed to be "an authority who is a natural ally against the difficulties of the poem".[108] In the course of his analysis, Fish chooses not only to ignore some contradictions that do not fit easily into his pattern, but also some extensive narrative passages of the epic. The realm of Chaos, for example, and the diverse questions it raises are treated rather curtly and undecidedly.[109] It is easy to see that Fish's argument is circular and self-supporting – which does not invalidate it, insofar as this question-begging is to be understood as a politically savvy performative rather than an interpretive argument. In his "strong" reading of *Paradise Lost*, Fish proceeds much like Milton's God, enforcing a code of doubtful, yet useful, univocities within the text, just like the Father establishes them within the cosmos. This mimetic relationship to the epic's main subject might partly explain the success of *Surprised by Sin* in the field of Milton criticism. However, one can see that something is missing from Fish's account of *Paradise Lost* by merely looking at the opening of the third book:

105 William Kerrigan, *The Sacred Complex: On the Psychogenesis of* Paradise Lost, Cambridge, MA and London: Harvard University Press, 1983, p. 3.

106 C. S. Lewis, *A Preface to* Paradise Lost, Oxford: Oxford University Press, 1969. See also Elmer Edgar Stoll, "Give the Devil His Due: A Reply to Mr. Lewis", *Review of English Studies* 20 (1944); B. A. Wright, Review of *A Preface to* Paradise Lost by C. S. Lewis, *The Review of English Studies*, 20.77 (1944); Peter C. Herman, "C. S. Lewis and the New Milton Criticism", in *Milton Quarterly* 45.4 (2011).

107 On the limitations of Fish's conception of reader-response theory, see Robert Crosman, "Some Doubts about 'The Reader of *Paradise Lost*'", *College English*, 37.4 (1975). See also Wolfgang Iser, "Talk like Whales: A Reply to Stanley Fish", *Diacritics*, 11.3 (1981).

108 Fish, *Surprised by Sin*, p. 47.

109 See Fish, *Surprised by Sin*, pp. 147–149. Lewis, for his part, decides to ignore the problem of Chaos altogether in his *Preface*.

Hail, holy light, offspring of heaven first-born,
Or of the eternal co-eternal beam
May I express thee unblamed? since God is light,
And never but in unapproached light
Dwelt from eternity, dwelt then in thee,
Bright effluence of bright essence increate.
Or hearst thou rather pure ethereal stream,
Whose fountain who shall tell?

(3.1–8)

Never an epic so tentative. The narrator is reduced to listing mutually exclusive alternatives: either light was created by God or it is uncreated; either it is identical with the Eternal or it differs from him; either it is a thing or an attribute. Oscillating between the alternatives, the narrator obviously is neither sufficiently authoritarian to decide on them nor humble enough to shy away from undue curiosity in such divine matters. Nor is it clear to him whether he is allowed to address the light, and if so, how. The ignorance about the light's character may be booked as a symptom of mankind's fallen state from which the narrator does not claim to be exempt; but his inability to determine how to relate to it is a sign that he is not even certain about the implications of his fallen state. It is hard to see how utterances such as these could be considered characteristic of a "controlling and inspired mind"[110] in full possession of all available knowledge about the human condition and always on the ready to rap the reader's sin-infested knuckles with it.[111] Instead, Milton's epic style in this passage is characterized by an insecurity which cannot be found in Homer, Virgil or Dante. Peter Herman asserts that the word "or" is the most important word in *Paradise Lost*.[112] But this very indecision allows the narrator to hover over mutually exclusive worldviews, never settling down on one of them, but never abandoning one of them either. It will be demonstrated that this hovering can be considered as another form of control, differing markedly from the bullying univocity that Fish ascribes to the epic.

Fish localizes Milton mainly in the company of Puritan preachers and represents *Paradise Lost* as an extended sermon. But comparisons to the work of less orthodox theologians and philosophers can provide an access to *Paradise Lost* which is just as instructive; the work of Thomas Hobbes, for example.[113] In many respects, it seems that Hobbes and Milton are

110 Fish, *Surprised by Sin*, p. 207.

111 See also Tobias Gregory, "In Defense of Empson: A Reassessment of *Milton's God*", in *Fault Lines and Controversies in the Study of Seventeenth-Century English Literature*, ed. Claude J. Summers and Ted-Larry Pebworth, Columbia and London: University of Missouri Press, 2002, p. 79.

112 Peter C. Herman, "*Paradise Lost*, the Miltonic 'Or', and the Poetics of Incertitude", *Studies in English Literature 1500–1900* 43:1 (2003).

113 Of course, the two writers have been compared before. See e.g. Timothy Rosendale, "Milton, Hobbes, and the Liturgical Subject", *Studies in English Literature, 1500–1900* 44:1 (2004),

positioned at opposite ends of the literary, political and theological spectrum of seventeenth-century England: Milton is seen as a republican idealist who insisted forcefully on the idea of human freedom; Hobbes was a royalist, materialist and determinist. Milton was a theocrat, propagating a rule of the saints, while Hobbes' major work *Leviathan* is firmly set against the traditional notions of theocracy. However, on closer inspection, things turn out to be more complicated, since one can also detect remarkable similarities in their worldviews: after the publication of *Leviathan*, Hobbes fell out with the English royalists as well as with the court, for it turned out that his absolutism was pragmatic. If he prefers monarchy to other state forms, it is mainly for practical reasons; accordingly, the sovereign ruler can legitimately also be a group, it can even be "the people". Hobbes advises the subject to submit to whoever is in power and in the process brushes away all tenets of the "divine right of kings" and other transcendent justifications of royalty.[114] He thus tends to secularize the political discourse with his notion of the social contract, creating a blueprint for modern society. Consequently, his royalism fell into doubt; English monarchists tended to burn copies of the *Leviathan* on special occasions, and they might have burned Hobbes too, if the king had not protected his former tutor.[115] The Royalist Edward Hyde, Earl of Clarendon, writes of "the most mischievous principles, and most destructive to the peace both of church and state, which are scatter'd through that book of his *Leviathan*".[116] He might have characterized Milton's regicide tracts with just the same words. On other levels, one can also perceive strange convergences.[117] Milton and Hobbes were not personally acquainted, however, although they knew of each other. All Hobbes ever wrote about Milton is a remark in *Behemoth*: without mentioning Milton's name, Hobbes characterizes his pamphlet *Pro Populo Anglicano Defensio*, which justifies the execution of Charles I, as a combination of "very good Latin" and "very ill reasoning".[118] Milton's work, in turn, never explicitly mentions Hobbes (although it is very

pp. 149–172. Fish himself does not ignore Hobbes altogether; but in *Surprised by Sin* he uses his texts merely as a repository of seventeenth-century truisms about language. See Fish, *Surprised by Sin*, pp. 109, 116, 122.

114 Norberto Bobbio, *Thomas Hobbes and the Natural Law Tradition*, Chicago: University of Chicago Press, 1993, p. 86.

115 Jeffrey R. Collins, *The Allegiance of Thomas Hobbes*, Oxford and New York: Oxford University Press, 2005, p. 2.

116 Edward Hyde, Earl of Clarendon, *A Brief View and Survey of the Dangerous and Pernicious Errors to Church and State in Mr. Hobbes's Book, entitled Leviathan*, Oxford: Printed at the Theater, 1676, p. 5 (spelling modernized).

117 For a more extensive treatment of this subject, see Björn Quiring, "Milton's God and Hobbes' Leviathan: Elective Affinities", in *Natur und Herrschaft: Analysen zur Physik der Macht*, eds. Kay Peter Jankrift, Alexander Kagerer, Christian Kaiser and María Ángeles Martín Romera, Berlin and Boston: Walter de Gruyter, 2016, pp. 273–284.

118 Thomas Hobbes, *Behemoth, or The Long Parliament*, ed. Paul Seaward, Oxford: Clarendon Press, 2010, p. 329.

likely that he read the *Leviathan*, since it was a bestseller in his time).[119] There are possible allusions, however, first and foremost the passage in *Paradise Lost* in which the "arch-fiend" Satan is compared to "that sea-beast/ Leviathan" (1.200–201), drawing sailors who mistake it for *terra firma* into the depths. Apart from vague echoes such as this, only a posthumous reference exists: one of the first Milton biographies, John Aubrey's *Minutes of the Life of Mr. John Milton*, contains fragments of an interview with Milton's widow, among them the sentence:

> His widow assures me that Mr. T. Hobbes was not one of his acquaintances, that her husband did not like him at all, but he would acknowledge him to be a man of great parts, and a learned man.[120]

This grudging appreciation of a political opponent is atypical for Milton: normally, he represents his opponents as both evil and stupid. This mild verdict might be the symptom of an "oppositional harmony" (*gegenstrebige Fügung*)[121] which is not merely of antiquarian interest: by his rather wide-ranging subtraction of transcendent norms from the realm of politics and the juxtaposition of a Leviathanic sovereign and a state of nature, Hobbes has created what one might call the political myth of modernity.[122] And Milton's *Paradise Lost*, published 16 years after the *Leviathan*, might be read as a reworking of that myth, which has also been very influential, although in a more subterranean and roundabout way. Considering these Hobbesian echoes will also remind us to take Milton's materialism seriously which insists on the tangibility of the events in all the realms of the universe. As a result, this study will develop an interpretation of *Paradise Lost* that makes it occasionally resemble a science fiction novel. Christopher Ricks, occasionally wondered whether *Paradise Lost* might not be "our greatest work of science fiction".[123] To treat it as such produces an alienation effect that might be helpful if one wants to gain awareness of the specificity and specific strangeness of Milton's epic.

This emphasis on materiality does not contradict the allegorical status of some of the events and personages in *Paradise Lost* (the strange couple Sin and Death, first and foremost). Instead, it calls for a materialist reading of allegory in the Benjaminian vein:[124] as will be demonstrated, allegoresis must

119 Quentin Skinner, "The Ideological Context of Hobbes's Political Thought", *The Historical Journal* 9:3 (1966), p. 294.

120 John Aubrey, "Minutes of the Life of Mr. John Milton", in *CPEP*, p. xxx.

121 Jacob Taubes used this Heraclitean term to designate his interest in Carl Schmitt. See Jacob Taubes, *Ad Carl Schmitt: Gegenstrebige Fügung*, Berlin: Merve, 1987.

122 See Michael Oakeshott, *Hobbes on Civil Association*, Indianapolis: Liberty Fund, 2000, pp. 159–163.

123 Christopher Ricks in the *Sunday Times*, according to a blurb of the Vintage edition (John Milton, *Paradise Lost*, ed. Gordon Campbell, London: Vintage, 2008).

124 Catherine Gimelli Martin's study *The Ruins of Allegory:* Paradise Lost *and the Metamorphosis of Epic*, Durham, NC: Duke University Press, 1998 moves into the same

be regarded as a concrete administrative practice, adopted by God and others. The subsequent chapters will show that *Paradise Lost* is an abyss of allegory – and "how violently the movement of dialectics roars within this abyss".[125]

"Nature" and "natural law" are central but ambiguous terms in Milton, not least because they straddle this abyss of allegory. With William Empson, this ambiguity is assumed not to be a deficit, but an asset: the porous borders between the diverse senses of "nature", and the strategical uses of these borders, are decisive, if one wants to gain a better understanding of this facet of *Paradise Lost.* It will be shown that the ambiguity of "nature" and "natural law" in Milton is mostly of the seventh Empsonian type. This ambiguity "occurs when the two meanings of the word, the two values of the ambiguity, are the two opposite meanings defined by the context, so that the total effect is to show a fundamental division in the writer's mind".[126] And while this division may affect the mind of the poet, it is in this case also to be read as a symptom of his society's general schizophrenia.

After a more precise exposition of the relations between God and Nature in *Paradise Lost*, the following analysis will delineate the six different territories that together constitute the epic's universe: Chaos, heaven, hell, the cosmos created for man, Paradise and the postlapsarian earth. Each of them is provided with a specific administrative and legal system in which natural and divine judgment are exercised in their own way. While the study passes through these spaces, it will be seen that an inner logic connects them: the constraints of one territory develop from the predicaments of the others, so that the whole unfolds the early modern ambiguities of nature's law court and its divine appropriations in all their complexity.

direction, but her book, although impressive, is in many respects unsatisfactory. See e.g. Neil Forsyth, Review of *The Ruins of Allegory: Paradise Lost and the Metamorphosis of Epic Convention* by Catherine Gimelli Martin, *International Journal for the Classical Tradition* 7:3 (2001): pp. 478–480.

125 "Wie gewaltig in diesem Abgrund der Allegorie die dialektische Bewegung braust". Walter Benjamin, *Ursprung des deutschen Trauerspiels*, in *Gesammelte Schriften*, Vol. 1, ed. Rolf Tiedemann, Frankfurt am Main: Suhrkamp, 1977, p. 342. Translation BQ.

126 William Empson, *Seven Types of Ambiguity,* New York: New Directions, 1947, p. 192.

3 The primordial nature of God

3.1 God's firm body and fragile mind

The God of *Paradise Lost* is supposed to have given a law to all things, and this law is repeatedly associated with nature (3.125–127; 5.508–514; 6.176). But it has been pointed out that, on the other hand, nature sometimes does not seem to follow the divine law.[1] Nature remains a shady, vacillating figure with indistinct contours in Milton's epic, despite her frequent appearances. Reliable information about her can only be described as sparse. To better understand this obscurity, we will take a closer look at the origins of God's legal rule and at his ontological status. It is hard, however, to discern his divine origins or non-origins: *Paradise Lost* begins *in medias res*, as every good epic should, according to Aristotle. We get access to the very beginning only through the narrations of the angels, of the devils and of God himself. The narrator himself tends to circumvent the question of origins,[2] so the reader is sent back to his/her own preconceptions. In this situation, it is useful to first look at Milton's official theology as developed in *De Doctrina Christiana*. But we soon find that in his theological treatise, Milton also seems to vacillate on the question of how much we can know about God: on the one hand, he states that God far surpasses human knowledge but has condescended to partly reveal himself through scripture but also through nature (*DC* 24–27). On the other hand, Milton insists that God, according to the authoritative Bible, resembles man more than the theological tradition assumes, that he has, for example, passions resembling those of humans, or at least that we are obliged to think so:

> [S]i post sex dierum operam quiete refici, Exod. 31.17, si "metuere indignationem ab inimico", Deut. 32.27, dicitur Deus, credamus dolere quod dolet; credamus eo refici quo refectus est; id metuere quod metuit,

1 Richard Strier, "Milton's Fetters, or, Why Eden is Better Than Heaven", *Milton Studies* 38:1 (2000), p. 188.

2 See Peter C. Herman, "*Paradise Lost*, the Miltonic 'Or', and the Poetics of Incertitude", *Studies in English Literature 1500–1900* 43:1 (2003), pp. 181–211.

non esse infra Deum: longo licet interpretationis ambitu heac et huiumodi de Deo dicta lenire tentaveris, eodem res redibit, si "creasse hominem Deus dicitur ad imaginem suam, ad similitudinem suam", Gen. 1.26, idque non animo solum sed forma etiam externa, nisi eadem verba idem non significant quod postea, cap. 5.3, ubi Adam "ad similitudinem suam, ad imaginem suam filium genuit", et Deus humana membra ac speciem passim sibi tribuit, quid est quod nos quae ipse sibi tribuit, eadem tribuere vereamur, dummodo quod in nobis imperfectum ac debile est, id Deo sicubi tribuatur, perfectissimum atque pulcherrimum esse credamus [...].

If God is said after six days' labour "to be refreshed by rest", Exod. 31.17, and "to fear the truculence of the enemy", Deut. 32.27, let us believe that it is not beneath God to be grieved at what grieves him, to be refreshed by what refreshes him, to fear what he fears. Try as you may to soften these and similar statements about God with long, roundabout explanations, the result will be the same. If God is said "to have created man after his own image, after his of likeness", Gen 1.26 – and not just a spiritual one either, but an outward physical one too, unless the same words do not mean the same as later, ch. 5.3, where Adam "begot a son after his own likeness, after his own image" – and if God assigned himself a thoroughly human body and aspect, why should we be afraid to assign him what he assigned himself, so long as we believe that what is imperfect and feeble in us is most perfect and beautiful wherever assigned to God?

(*DC* 30/31)

Milton proceeds to build theological arguments on the supposition of God's emotionality, intelligibility and familiarity; for example, the incomprehensible doctrine of trinitarianism must be rejected because of them (*DC* 34/35). However, Milton's insistence that the divinity has revealed himself as an anthropomorphic being soon starts to conflict with others of God's attributes: both in *Paradise Lost* and in the *Doctrina Christiana*, God is described as a spirit (1.17–18; *DC* 34/35), as eternal (2.46; *DC* 34/35), infinite (3.373; *DC* 34/35), omnipresent (7.590; *DC* 38/39), immutable (3.373; *DC* 36/37), omniscient (10.227; *DC* 44/45) and omnipotent (3.372; *DC* 38/39). God's power, encompassing both reality and possibility, is only limited insofar as it is "not engaged in the sort of things that involve a contradiction" (*DC* 38/39). On the other hand, Milton's epic God acts very much as an empirical, hence delimited and somewhat material, person; he appears as finite, mutable, emotional and frequently even as capricious and devious.[3] On several occasions divine body parts are mentioned, such as his eye (2.189, 3.58), his ear (3.193, 5.626), his hand (2.174) and even his nostrils (9.196). God has an emotional life, for he occasionally smiles (5.718) and pities (5.220). As

3 See e.g. J. Allan Mitchell, "Reading God Reading 'Man': Hereditary Sin and the Narrativization of Deity in *Paradise Lost*, Book 3", *Milton Quarterly* 35:2 (2001), pp. 72–86.

A. J. A. Waldock has pointed out, Milton's God is said to be omnipotent, but sometimes Milton uses the word so that it seems to be no more than a "grandiloquent synonym for 'supreme'".[4] In a similar vein, Raphael first affirms that the affairs of heaven resemble those of earth much more than man is inclined to think (5.574–576), only to declare later the utter incomprehensibility of the transcendent realm, "surpassing human measure" (7.640) which makes it necessary to accommodate celestial events to earthly understandings. In the background of these inconsistencies hover unresolved tensions that have long plagued the history of Christian theology, especially regarding the question how to deal with some very anthropomorphic descriptions of God in the Bible:

> If God is exactly as he represents himself, the "theory of accommodation" falls to the ground; no accommodation has occurred; if on the other hand he is not such as he represents himself to be then, once we understand this, it is only through (of all things) a pious bad faith that we can continue to believe what is evidently untrue.[5]

This problem is not resolved by Milton; instead, it is further aggravated by his declared monism and the resultant need to reconcile it with more conventional theological conceptions that insist on God's thoroughly transcendent status. According to the *Doctrina*, all things once were part of the unity and simplicity of God and subsequently proceeded from him, including matter:

> Verum Materia [...] incorruptibilis ex Deo prodiit, post peccatum etiam quoad essentiam incorruptibilis manet.
>
> The fact is, Matter [...] proceeded incorruptible from God: even since the fall it remains incorruptible as far as concerns its essence.
>
> (*DC* 292/293)

This notion is obviously connected to the thought, expressed in *Paradise Lost* as well as in the *Doctrina Christiana*, that the whole of divine creation is a creation not *ex nihilo* but *ex deo*; that is, that God has generated all things out of himself. (The elusive proto-elements of Chaos perhaps excepted, since they do not clearly qualify as matter.)[6] Nothing exists in nature that was not "first from God and in God" (*DC* 294/295). Hence, matter and spirit are not contraries with distinct essences; rather, in a universal continuum, which also involves God, spirit figures as a more perfect state of matter; and, since it has

4 A. J. A. Waldock, Paradise Lost *and Its Critics*, Cambridge: Cambridge University Press, 1966, p. 68.

5 A. D. Nuttall, *Overheard by God: Fiction and Prayer in Herbert, Milton, Dante, and St. John*, London: Methuen, 1980, p. 100.

6 See the next chapter.

a higher degree of excellence in the cosmic hierarchy, includes and subsumes matter within itself:

> Spiritus enim, ut substantia excellentior, substantiam utique inferiorem virtualiter, quod aiunt, et eminenter in se continet, ut facultas facultatem spiritualis et rationalis corpoream, sentientem nempe et vegetativam. Nam neque virtus et efficientia divina potuisset iuxta communem sententiam corpora ex nihilo producere, nisi vis corporea quaedam in substantia Dei fuisset; nemo enim dat quod non habet. Quin et corporale quiddam Deo attribuere non ipse dubitavit Paulus Coloss. 2.9, "in eo habitat omnis plenitudo Deitatis corporaliter".
>
> Spirit, being the more excellent substance, virtually (as they say) and eminently contains within itself what is undoubtedly the inferior substance – just as the spiritual and rational faculty contains the corporeal one, that is, the sentient and vegetative faculty. For not even God's virtue and efficiency could have produced bodies from nothing as the conventional wisdom says he did, unless there had been some corporeal power in his own substance; for no one gives what he does not have. Besides, Paul himself did not hesitate to attribute something corporeal to God, Col. 2.9: "in him dwells all the fullness of Deity corporeally".
>
> (*DC* 294/295)

It must be remarked that Paul is actually not talking about God in Col. 2.9, but about Christ; and in other places of the *Doctrina*, Milton even acknowledges this.[7] There might be a slight ambiguity in the text, but Milton's interpretation is clearly forced. As this somewhat questionable, but vehemently assertive attempt at a biblical reinterpretation demonstrates, the supposition that spiritual beings, and even the divine being, also have a material component is important to Milton's thought.[8] In *Paradise Lost*, Milton hints at it on diverse occasions, that of Raphael digesting and "transubstantiating" earthly food being one of the most prominent among them (5.433–443). Admittedly, the formulation "vis corporea quaedam in substantia Dei" (*DC* 294) does not necessarily entail that God himself is a material being. But by a careful exegesis John Reesing has shown that the *Doctrina* enforces precisely this conclusion, even at the price of certain inconsistencies.[9] Milton is, of course, not the first Christian to have asserted the materiality of God. Tertullian is among his precursors in that respect,[10] and among his early modern contemporaries

7 See John Reesing, "The Materiality of God in Milton's *De Doctrina Christiana*", *Harvard Theological Review* 1:3 (1957), p. 168.

8 See Reesing, "The Materiality of God", p. 160.

9 See Reesing, "The Materiality of God", pp. 159–173.

10 "Quis enim negabit deum corpus esse, etsi deus spiritus est? Spiritus enim corpus sui generis in sua effigie" (Tertullian, *Adversus Praxean/Treatise against Praxeas*, ed. Ernest Evans, London: SPCK, 1948, p. 96).

we also find Spinoza[11] and Hobbes who seems surprisingly close to Milton when he affirms God to be a bodily substance[12] – a claim for which he was frequently labelled an atheist.[13] Generally, Hobbes' materialism and Milton's emanationist idealism converge in the common form of monism: Hobbes asserts that spirit is basically a body that is not "visible or palpable",[14] while Milton takes bodies to be a inferior component of spirit. Phillip J. Donnelly has introduced the useful but problematic differentiation between "matter" and "body" (i.e. "formed matter") into the debate in order to separate Milton's material God from the bodily God of more radical monists such as Spinoza and Hobbes.[15] But whatever the merits of the differentiation, Milton's monism still seems unorthodox enough. Most importantly, in the *Doctrina*, Milton implies that the spirit of God and the spirit of his creatures are not different in their essence. Neil D. Graves has analysed the argumentative drift:

> Milton argues: "Moreover spirit, being the more excellent substance, virtually, as they say, and eminently contains within itself what is clearly the inferior substance; *in the same way* as the spiritual and rational faculty contains the corporeal, that is, the sentient and vegetative faculty" (*CPW* 6:309; emphasis NDG). What is vital are the subjects to which the two parts of the analogy refer. In the first sentence the spirit in question is unquestionably God himself, for the context is of the creation of the universe by the emanation of body from God's spirit. In the second sentence the spiritual and rational faculty that contains the sentient and vegetative faculty must refer either to God Himself or to aspects of His creation such as angels or men. Now if it refers to God, this immediately clarifies the issue by stating that God's faculty does "contain the corporeal" and thus God possesses not only material cause but also materiality. If instead it refers to aspects of God's creation, which in fact I think it does, then Milton has established an analogy between the two realms he has posited to elucidate the nature of God. It is clear from even a cursory consideration of Milton's metaphysics that in the created universe all things belong in a monist hierarchical scale of nature wherein the higher form of substance called spirit includes within itself the lower form of body. Accordingly, as I have noted above, Miltonic angels are spirits and

11 "Extensio attributum Dei est, sive Deus est res extensa" (Baruch de Spinoza, *Ethica/Die Ethik*, trans. Jacob Stern, Stuttgart: Reclam, 1977, p. 114 [2 prop. 2]).

12 In the Latin version of *Leviathan*, Hobbes explicitly states that God is (a) body. See Thomas Hobbes, *Leviathan, sive De Materia, Forma et Potestate Civitatis Ecclesiasticae et Civilis*, in *Opera Philosophica Omnia*, Amsterdam: Joan Blaeu, 1668, p. 360.

13 See e.g. George MacDonald Ross, *Starting with Hobbes*, London and New York: Continuum, 2009, pp.150–161.

14 See Thomas Hobbes, *Leviathan*, ed. J. C. A. Gaskin, Oxford: Oxford University Press, 1998, p. 447 [4.46.15].

15 Phillip J. Donnelly, "'Matter' versus 'Body': The Character of Milton's Monism", *Milton Quarterly* 33:3 (1999), pp. 79–85.

> yet, composed of matter, are possessed of corporeality. The result is that Milton in this analogy has equated the concept of God as spirit with that of spirit in the created universe, and he has implied that God does possess materiality in the same way that created spirits possess materiality.[16]

Thus, Milton has effectively forfeited divine transcendence in favour of an all-encompassing continuum of hierarchical graduations. Divine infinity is "one with the boundlessness of the universe God pervades".[17] In Milton's world, everything is therefore divine, some things more, some less. Thus, it appears that Milton's God is not essentially different from his creatures, but merely possesses a lot more power and knowledge than they do. This concentration of power distinguishes him from his creatures, but, like the gnostic demiurge, he does not surpass his creatures in his very essence. The slip that has the narrator of *Paradise Lost* designate the Father himself as a "[c]reated thing" (2.679) is certainly suggestive in this context.

Is God therefore no more than an ambitious ancestral Jove? Did he develop from Chaos, like the pagan gods? *Paradise Lost* refuses to give a definitive answer, but the similarities between the Father and Zeus are conspicuous throughout. They are thematized not only by Satan who keeps designating God as the "thunderer" (2.28), and as the one "whom thunder hath made greater" (1.258), thus translating Zeus' customary epithet "Brontios" (see e.g. 2.28; 5.491),[18] but occasionally also by the narrator (e.g. 1.386; 1.740–748). Belial also refers to God's "red right hand" (2.174), an allusion to an Ode of Horace in which Jove's "rubente dextera" is mentioned.[19] It is the very structure of the epic that assigns to the Father the same supreme administrative function of steering the world and the plot that Zeus/Jupiter holds in the works of Homer and Virgil.[20]

This also implies that Satan's insurrection is not a mere category mistake, despite the narrator's protestations to that effect (1.44–49). He has a Greco-Roman precursor in Typhon, who managed to attack Olympus and endanger the reign of Zeus, according to Nonnos[21] and Pseudo-Apollodorus.[22] The

16 Neil D. Graves, "'The Whole Fulness of the Godhead Dwells in Him Bodily': The Materiality of Milton's God", *Christianity and Literature* 52:4 (2003), pp. 510–511.

17 D. Bentley Hart, "Matter, Monism and Narrative: An Essay on the Metaphysics of *Paradise Lost*", *Milton Quarterly* 30:1 (1996), p. 21.

18 See Arthur B. Cook, *Zeus: A Study in Ancient Religion*, Cambridge: Cambridge University Press, 1925, pp. 833–839.

19 Horace, *Oden und Epoden: Lateinisch/Deutsch*, trans. and ed. Bernhard Kytzler, Stuttgart: Reclam, 2000, p. 6 [1.2.3–4].

20 On Zeus as planner of the epic plot in Homer, see Gregory Nagy, *Homer the Preclassic*, Berkeley and Los Angeles: University of California Press, 2010, pp. 113–115.

21 Nonnos, *Dionysiaca*, Vol. 1, trans. W. H. D. Rouse, Cambridge, MA and London: Harvard University Press, 1940, pp. 2–97 [Books 1 and 2].

22 Apollodorus, *The Library*, Vol. 1, trans. James George Frazer, London: Heinemann and New York: Putnam's Sons, 1921, pp. 146–151 [1.6.3].

devils' victory would not be ontologically inconceivable, but only immensely improbable, because of God's vastly superior fire power and reconnaissance capacities. And this is indeed how not only Satan and his minions (see e.g. 1.248–249), but also how God himself occasionally describe things. For example, the Father's remark to the Son on the eve of battle, in which God seems to confess to a certain amount of vulnerability (5.711–732), seems ironical, especially when we consider the Son's reaction, but this very irony, as William Empson has pointed out, "does not suggest a transcendent God whose Godhead is mysteriously identical with Goodness".[23] As often, irony here points to different levels of meaning that it simultaneously affirms as incompatible and relates to each other.[24]

Occasionally, it is suggested that Milton's God rules not only because of his sheer superior force, but also because of his moral supremacy. In the *Doctrina Christiana*, Milton states that God is "by supreme justness and his own merit sovereign Lord of all" ("iure quidem summo et merito suo dominus omnium supremus", *DC* 46/47). However, it is remarkable that, while belief in God's goodness and justice is constantly demanded and professed by men and angels, *Paradise Lost* steadfastly prefers not to provide conclusive diegetic evidence for these divine attributes. Even God's most devoted spokesmen are alert to his potential for unjust, irrational behaviour: the angel Abdiel as well as Raphael express anxiety over the Father's capacity to lose control of himself in anger: Abdiel professes to flee Satan's camp out of fear of the divine temper, not out of fear of Satan: he apprehends that God's "wrath/ Impendent, raging into sudden flame" might "[d]istinguish not" between the good and the bad angels in Satan's entourage (5.890–892). Likewise, Raphael narrates that the angels had to seal off God from any disturbance while he was creating the world, "[l]est he incensed at such eruption bold,/ Destruction with creation might have mixed" (8.235–236). His angelic creatures assume that God cannot control his boundless wrath when anybody dares to treat him with insufficient subservience and that his punishments might also be visited upon the innocent.[25] His actions are thus hard to justify by any code of ethics except the one that declares God as unaccountable to his creatures and not subject to the laws he posits. Provoked by Satan's teasing, Abdiel admits as much, despite his protestations of God's evident benevolence (5.818–825). Indeed, as Joseph Jenkins has pointed out, only the creatures are held to the standards of reason and ethics in the epic, not God himself; consequently, the reference

23 William Empson, *Milton's God*, Westport, CT: Greenwood Press, 1978, p. 97. Generally, the Father's penchant for irony (what Empson calls God's "eerie jokes", p. 108) may be partly explicable by his ambiguous status.

24 See Wayne C. Booth, *A Rhetoric of Irony*, Chicago and London: University of Chicago Press, 1975.

25 Empson, *Milton's God*, p. 111.

to "reason" in several passages of *Paradise Lost* tends to function as an "emerging site of authority effects".[26]

When all is said and done, God is tacitly positioned above the law, not because of any ontological, spiritual, intellectual or ethical supremacy, but because of his superior political and physical potency. The other divine attributes, such as omniscience, seem to be contingent on God's power: he can predict man's fall because he disposes of superior forces that he mainly employs to expedite it, by his instructions to the unfallen angels, by his policy toward Adam and Eve, and even by the way he structures and administrates hell and the cosmos. The God of *Paradise Lost*, for all practical purposes, appears as a jealous Jove with cosmic political sovereignty, constituting an ambivalent point of orientation and identification.

One strange result of Milton's theological and aesthetic choices is the circumstance that the immortal Father, stripped of his unquestioned transcendence, over the course of the narrative increasingly resembles not only Zeus, but also the sovereign Leviathan as depicted by Thomas Hobbes. The Hobbesian ruler must be able to hold on to supreme power in his domain; this, and nothing else, defines him and will make him a "mortal God".[27] He is accountable only to God and may freely alter his own rights as well as the rights of everyone else, thereby deciding on what is to be considered right and wrong in the commonwealth.[28] However badly the despot may handle these privileges, Hobbes asserts that the results will be not as bad as the original state of chaotic civil war. It has already been pointed out (by Alexander Passerin d'Entrèves, among others) that the Hobbesian political notion of the Leviathan very much resembles Calvin's theological notion of God as "legibus solutus".[29] Giovanni Fiaschi has pointed out that, in Hobbes' theory, social order and sovereign power are not built on the overbearing force of the ruler, whether human or divine, but on the belief of all subjects in this overbearing force and the resultant fear. God's unrestricted power can therefore be reduced to a limit toward which human sovereignty converges.[30]

For our purposes, it is largely irrelevant, whether in this context jurisprudential and political theory have influenced theology (as Passerin d'Entrèves assumes) or vice versa (as Carl Schmitt assumes).[31] What interests us is the zone of overlap toward which both theories tend and which *Paradise Lost*

26 Joseph S. Jenkins, *Inheritance Law and Political Theology in Shakespeare and Milton: Election and Grace as Constitutional in Early Modern Literature and Beyond*, Burlington, VT: Ashgate, 2012, p.123.

27 Hobbes, *Leviathan*, p. 114 [2.17.13].

28 Hobbes, *Leviathan*, p. 222 [2.30.1].

29 Alexander Passerin d'Entrèves, *Natural Law: An Introduction to Legal Philosophy*, New Brunswick and London: Transaction, 1994, p. 70.

30 Giovanni Fiaschi, "The Power of Words: Political and Theological Science in Thomas Hobbes", *Hobbes Studies* 26 (2013), pp. 52, 55.

31 Carl Schmitt, *Politische Theologie: Vier Kapitel zur Lehre von der Souveränität*, Berlin: Duncker und Humblot, 1996, p. 43 ff.

occupies: a world ruled by an absolutely sovereign deity who, on the one hand, is subject to the laws of nature, but who, on the other, positions himself above them. This ambivalence articulates itself, for example, in the previously-cited passage 11.48–57. We will encounter other examples. Christopher Kendrick has expressed it concisely:

> God as character constantly oscillates between imposing his own will or reality principle on all the other agents and observing the dictates of an anterior reality principle which seems to have programmed the whole Godly (or theological) narrative in advance.[32]

For Milton's way of justifying the ways of God, this oscillation is a necessity: just like in the work of Hobbes, it is not decisive whether the almighty Father is in fact the best of all possible rulers; it is not even verifiable that he really has the divine attributes he claims: omnipotence, omniscience and omnipresence cannot be conclusively demonstrated to finite creatures anyway. However, it is decisive that he be treated as if he was in all respects superior to all his competitors in the interests of a harmonic, unified cosmos and a general peace of mind. In both cases, the abolition of this monopoly would have catastrophic consequences: politics would have to be disconnected from theology, unable to set bounds to the civil wars that pervade the realm of Chaos. The Hobbesian absolutism and its contradictions thus find themselves (re-) transferred into the realm of the divinity. It is ultimately the concept of nature and its oscillation between autonomy and subordination that enables Milton to keep the resultant epistemological tensions under control.

3.2 Nature as God's motherly daughter and as the eternal word

In *Paradise Lost*, Nature is sometimes treated as an abstract principle (4.667), but generally as more than that. There is no doubt that she frequently functions as a deity; the narrator and the protagonists often personify her: she has at least one hand (3.455; 8.27) with which to paint (5.24), create (8.28), work (8.506–507) and play (5.295), but also a mouth with which to ordain (6.175–176), to call (8.458–459), to sigh (9.782–783) and to groan (9.1001); she has her own will (4.633) and desire (5.45), and she is "wise and frugal" (8.26), but needs to rest occasionally (5.109). One might object that in most or even all of these instances, Nature merely appears as an allegorical figuration, not as a living, breathing entity. But this objection relies on a distinction that is contested in this particular epic. It has been pointed out repeatedly that allegories have a tendency to incarnate in *Paradise Lost*, most prominently the unholy pair of Sin and Death whose interactions with the rest of the world are

32 Christopher Kendrick, *Milton: A Study in Ideology and Form*, New York and London: Methuen, 1986, pp. 113–114.

only all too palpable. Nature is likewise represented as a person, although her allegorical status is never actually abrogated. And like Sin, she is extremely fertile, taking the role of the first-engendered progenitrix of everything. The building blocks of the universe, namely the four elements, are called "the eldest birth/ Of Nature's womb" (5.180–181). Everything was made after her, since Mother Nature first enclosed all of creation within herself. She would thereby assume the role of the *magna mater* with whom she has often been equated.[33] The Goddess Physis first appears on the scene as a primordial mother goddess; accordingly, the characterization of Chaos as the "womb of Nature" (2.911; capitalization added) could be read as a *genitivus subiectivus*; this would mean that Nature has a womb which is Chaos and from which everything else is born.

Nature's personifications in *Paradise Lost* are not without precedent in Milton's work: she also makes personal appearances in "On the Morning of Christ's Nativity" (32–36), *Paradise Regained* (e.g. 2.331–336) and *Comus* (esp. 706–780). In Milton's political tractates she is referred to in rhetorical flourishes, as a God-fearing, but autonomous goddess (Nature generally being female in his texts) who must be treated in the right way. In *Tetrachordon*, for example, he maintains that the failure of a marriage is sometimes not due to a moral lapse of either party but can be ascribed to "blameless Nature":

> For Nature hath her Zodiac also, keeps her great annual circuit over human things as truly as the sun and planets in the firmament; hath her anomalies, hath her obliquities in ascensions and declinations, accesses and recesses, as blamelessly as they in heaven. And sitting in her planetary orb with two reins in each hand, one straight, the other loose, tempers the course of minds as well as bodies to several conjunctions and oppositions, friendly and unfriendly aspects, consenting oftest with reason, but never contrary.
>
> (*Tetrachordon*, *CPW* 2:680–681, spelling modernized)

This Nature resembles the Great Coordinatrix of the Stoics much more than the Great Mother of the iconological tradition synthesized by Cesare Ripa (although Milton apparently knew Ripa's work).[34] In a rather conventional procedure, Nature's personification is mitigated by turning her into a sphere of influence, as if she was a planetary goddess. But first and foremost, the description takes up the ancient notion of "nature" as individual, spontaneous inclination and universalizes and personifies it in the way of Stoicism, insinuating that there is a global harmonizing administratrix of all singular passions, just like there is to the forces that move the stars in the firmament.

33 Mechthild Modersohn, *Natura als Göttin im Mittelalter: Ikonographische Studien zu Darstellungen der personifizierten Natur*, Berlin: Akademie, 1997, p. 25.

34 Marcia R. Pointon, *Milton and English Art*, Manchester: Manchester University Press, 1970, p. 57.

And, since the impulses by which she reigns are basically good and even divine, they should be obeyed. There are other texts in Milton's oeuvre, however, in which the rule of Nature is represented as a mere interregnum, to be overcome and superseded by the rule of Man. In one of his early prolusions, Milton professes faith in the salvific potential of the sciences, which expresses itself in a rather Baconian pathos:[35]

> Sic tandem, auditores, cum omnimoda semel eruditio suos orbes confecerit, non contentus iste spiritus tenebricoso hoc ergastulo eousque late aget se, donec et ipsum mundum, et ultra longe divina quadam magnitudine expatiata compleverit. Tum demum plerique casus atque eventus rerum ita subito emergent, ut ei, qui hanc arcem sapientiae adeptus est, nihil pene incautum, nihil fortuitum in vita possit accidere; videbitur sane is esse, cujus imperio et dominationi astra obtemperent, terra et mare obsecundent, venti tempestatesque morigerae sint; cui denique ipsa parens Natura in deditionem se tradiderit, plane ac si quis deus abdicato mundi imperio, huic jus ejus, et leges, administrationemque tanquam præfectori cuidam commisisset.[36]

> So at length, my hearers, when universal learning has once completed its cycle, the spirit of man, no longer confined within this dark prison-house, will reach out far and wide, till it fills the whole world and the space far beyond with the expansion of its divine greatness. Then at last most of the chances and changes of the world will be so quickly perceived that to him who holds this stronghold of wisdom hardly anything can happen in his life which is unforeseen or fortuitious. He will indeed seem to be one whose rule and dominion the stars obey, to whose command earth and sea hearken, and whom winds and tempests serve; to whom, lastly, Mother Nature herself has surrendered, as if indeed some god had abdicated the throne of the world and entrusted its rights, laws, and administration to him as governor.[37]

According to this passage, one must not be swayed by divine, natural inclinations, but gain control over them; Nature must abdicate and submit

35 Milton quotes Francis Bacon in several passages of his work and refers to him as to an authority in the *Apology for Smectymnuus* as well as in *Areopagitica*. See e.g. "The state shall be my governors, but not my critics; they may be mistaken in the choice of a licencer, as easily as this licencer may be mistaken in an author: this is some common stuff: and he might add from Sir Francis Bacon, that such authorized books are but the language of the times [...]." And "The punishing of wits enhances their authority, saith the Viscount St. Albans, and a forbidden writing is thought to be a certain spark of truth that flies up in the faces of them who seek to tread it out" (*Areopagitica*, *CPW* 2:534, 2:542, spelling modernized).

36 John Milton, "In Sacrario habita de Arte", *The Works in Verse and Prose*, Vol, 7, ed. John Mitford, London: Bicker and Bush, 1863, p. 463.

37 John Milton, "Delivered in the College Chapel in Defence of Learning an Oration", *CPW* 1:296. Translation by Phyllis Tillyard.

to a (male) human will. In *Areopagitica*, this self-empowerment by way of knowledge acquisition is even associated with salvation and an apocalyptic "second coming".[38] Milton thus demonstrates an ambivalent attitude toward Nature in his prose works: on the one hand, she is a benevolent, legitimate and legitimating ruler, but on the other hand she must ultimately be dethroned by Baconian saints, initiating the foundation of a New Jerusalem.

This ambivalence must partly be ascribed to the shady, vacillating status that the goddess Natura/Physis has always held; Heinz Schott calls her a hybrid figure.[39] It is indeed remarkable, even given her syncretistic origins, how many antique goddesses have been identified with her: not only Venus and Isis,[40] but also, more interestingly for us in this context, the (equally syncretistic) goddesses Sophia/Wisdom, Heimarmene/Fate and Tyche/Fortuna/Fortune.[41] These identifications are relevant in our context, because they tend to reverse the hierarchy of the Goddess and the Jovian God: in ancient treatments of Greco-Roman myth, Zeus/Jupiter is generally thought to be subject to the exigencies of Nature and Destiny.[42] Whereas Homer remains ambivalent on the question,[43] Hesiod asserts that the Moirai pursue the transgressions of both men and gods,[44] and Aeschylus' Prometheus affirms that Zeus has less power than the Fates.[45] In Ovid's *Metamorphoses* the narrator likewise states that no

38 *CPW* 2:549. See also Björn Quiring, "'With Real Hunger To Transubstantiate': Die Dispersion der Eucharistie in John Miltons 'Paradise Lost'", *Mitteilungen des Sonderforschungsbereichs 573, "Pluralisierung und Autorität in der Frühen Neuzeit"* 1 (2011), p. 16.

39 "Mischfigur". Heinz Schott, "Natur und Gott im Menschenbild des Paracelsus", in *Nova Acta Paracelsica 19*, eds. Urs Gantenbein and Pia Holenstein, Bern: Peter Lang, 2005, p. 13.

40 Modersohn, *Natura als Göttin im Mittelalter*, p. 117; Pierre Hadot, *The Veil of Isis: An Essay on the History of the Idea of Nature*, Cambridge, MA: Belknap Press of Harvard University Press, 2006, pp. 233–238.

41 See Hans Leisegang, "Sophia", in *Paulys Realencyclopädie der Classischen Altertumswissenschaft*, Second Series, Fifth Half-Volume, eds. Georg Wissowa, Wilhelm Kroll and Karl Mittelhaus, Munich: Druckenmüller, 1927, col. 1027; Modersohn, *Natura als Göttin im Mittelalter*, p. 181; Alessandro Linguiti, "Physis as Heimarmene: On Some Fundamental Principles of the Neoplatonic Philosophy of Nature", in *Physics and Philosophy of Nature in Greek Neoplatonism*, eds. Riccardo Chiaradonna and Franco Trabattoni, Leiden and Boston: Brill, 2009, pp. 173–178.

42 See e.g. Gerard Naddaf, *The Greek Concept of Nature*, Albany, NY: State University of New York Press, 2005, p. 57. See also Cicero, *De Natura Deorum/Über das Wesen der Götter: Lateinisch/Deutsch*, trans. and ed. Ursula Blank-Sagemeister, Stuttgart: Reclam, 1995, pp. 42/43 [1.15.40].

43 Concerning Homer, see e.g. Adam Drozdek, *Greek Philosophers as Theologians: The Divine* Arche, Aldershot and Burlington, VT: Ashgate, 2007, p. 2. In the *Theogony*, Hesiod positions Zeus both above and below the Fates/Moirai, who are, in some versions of the myth, daughters of Night/Nyx (Hesiod, *Theogonie, Griechisch/Deutsch*, trans. and ed. Otto Schönberger, Stuttgart: Reclam, 1999, pp. 68/69 [901–906]; see also Pausanias, *Description of Greece*, ed. W. H. S. Jones, Cambridge, MA: Harvard University Press, 1918, pp. 214/215 [1.40.4]).

44 Hesiod, *Theogonie*, pp. 18–21 [217–222].

45 Aeschylus, *Prometheus Bound*, in *Persians. Seven against Thebes. Suppliants. Prometheus Bound*, edited and translated by Alan H. Sommerstein, Cambridge, MA and London: Harvard University Press, 2008, pp. 498/499 [515–518].

one can break the decrees of the Fates, not even the Olympians.[46] Herodotus[47] and Nonnos[48] tend to agree. In Virgil's *Aeneid*, Jupiter is basically just the administrator of the all-powerful *Fatum*.[49] Even in a Christian context, Fate has, in the words of Odo Marquard, been God's "competitor for omnipotence" ("Allmachtskonkurrent") for quite some time.[50]

Like Nature, Fate and Wisdom play important roles in *Paradise Lost*. Personified Fate is called upon by the narrator and by Raphael when unpleasant events occur that might be the will of God, but might also be caused by another power (2.610–613; 3.33; 6.869–870; 11.181–189).[51] And personified Sophia/Wisdom is occasionally mentioned by Raphael (8.562–564), but also invoked by the narrator next to her "sister" Urania during his central appeal to the Muse in the seventh book:

> heav'nly born,
> Before the hills appeared, or fountain flowed,
> Thou with eternal wisdom didst converse,
> Wisdom thy sister, and with her didst play
> In presence of the almighty Father, pleased
> With thy celestial song.
> (7.7–12)

The central source for this passage is, however, not to be found in the pagan, but in the Jewish Wisdom tradition.[52] Particularly, the narrator here echoes a passage in the Book of Proverbs in which Wisdom/*Chokma* herself speaks:

46 Ovid, *Metamorphoses*, Vol. 2, trans. Frank Justus Miller, London: Heinemann and New York: Putnam's Sons, 1916, pp. 420/421 [15.780–781].

47 Herodotus, *The Persian Wars*, Vol. 1, trans. A. D. Godley, London: Heinemann and New York: Putnam's Sons, 1920, pp. 116/117 [1.91].

48 Nonnos, *Dionysiaca*, Vol. 1, trans. W. H. D. Rouse, Cambridge, MA and London: Harvard University Press, 1940, pp. 296/297 [8.351].

49 See e.g. Heinz-Günther Nesselrath, "Wenn Zeus an seine Grenzen kommt: Die Götter und das Schicksal bei Homer", in *Vorsehung, Schicksal und göttliche Macht: Antike Stimmen zu einem aktuellen Thema*, eds. Reinhard G. Kratz and Hermann Spieckermann, Tübingen: Mohr Siebeck, 2008, p. 82.

50 Odo Marquard, "Ende des Schicksals? Einige Bemerkungen über die Unvermeidlichkeit des Unverfügbaren", in *Abschied vom Prinzipiellen: Philosophische Studien*, Stuttgart: Reclam 1991, p. 71.

51 For a more thorough, but somewhat superficial overview over the most prominent uses of the word "fate" in *Paradise Lost*, see Ben Gray Lumpkin, "Fate in *Paradise Lost*", *Studies in Philology* 44:1 (1947): pp. 56–68.

52 On Sophia/*Chokma* in the Jewish wisdom tradition see e.g. Hans Leisegang, "Sophia", in *Paulys Realencyclopädie der Classischen Altertumswissenschaft*, Second Series, Fifth Half-Volume, eds. Georg Wissowa, Wilhelm Kroll and Karl Mittelhaus, Munich: Druckenmüller, 1927, cols. 1031–1032.

> The Lord possessed me in the beginning of his way, before his works of old. I was set up from everlasting, from the beginning, or ever the earth was. When there were no depths, I was brought forth; when there were no fountains abounding with water. Before the mountains were settled, before the hills was I brought forth [...]. When he prepared the heavens, I was there: when he set a compass upon the face of the depth [...]. When he gave to the sea his decree, that the waters should not pass his commandment: when he appointed the foundations of the earth: then I was by him, as one brought up with him: and I was daily his delight, rejoicing always before him [...].
>
> (Proverbs 8.22–30)

Significantly, this Wisdom figure also assigns to itself the function to convey to mankind the right notion of God's law, thereby assuming the role Thomas Aquinas gave to Nature:

> By me kings reign, and princes decree justice. By me princes rule, and nobles, even all the judges of the earth. [...] I lead in the way of righteousness, in the midst of the paths of judgment [...].
>
> (Proverbs 8.15–20)

Philo of Alexandria was one of the first to identify this Jewish figure of Wisdom with the Hellenistic goddess Sophia. In the process, her birth is compared to the birth of Athena from the head of Zeus.[53] It is this strange amalgamation of very diverse female figurations of Wisdom, Fate and Chance from which the Christian iconography of Nature has grown and from which Milton liberally supplies himself.

In *Paradise Lost*, we therefore encounter similarly uncertain entities that mediate between the extremes, partly blending into abstraction and allegory, but also blending with dark, uncertain, yet very palpable eternal forces. Accordingly, the narrator repeatedly suggests that personified Nature has two parents: she is the offspring of both God and Chaos, with Chaos assuming the maternal, God the paternal, impregnating role. When Milton feminizes Chaos as "the womb of Nature" (2.911; capitalization added), he echoes Hesiod's *Theogony* in which Chaos is the Primal Progenitor. But, whereas the Hesiodic children of Chaos seem to develop by spontaneous parthenogenesis, Nature finds a second, paternal forebear in God: in the seventh book, the divine creation of the cosmos is described by Adam as an organic process, a "rising birth/ Of Nature from the unapparent deep" (7.102–103; capitalization added). And several passages of *Paradise Lost* imply that Nature emerges from cosmic activities that resemble titanic sexual acts: Raphael's history of creation involves an episode in which the Holy Spirit – who, according to

53 Leisegang, "Sophia", col. 1033.

the *Doctrina*, might be God himself, God's power or "a minister to God […] produced from God's substance" – pours his fertilizing "virtue" into Chaos (see *DC* 248/249; 250/251; 270/271).

> His brooding wings the Spirit of God outspread,
> And vital virtue infused, and vital warmth
> Throughout the fluid mass […].
> (7.235–237)

Note the sexual charge of this terminology (e.g. the proximity between "virtue" and the Latin "virtus", i.e. "manhood"). In another place, the Holy Spirit is addressed even more explicitly, as the one who

> with mighty wings outspread
> Dovelike satst brooding on the vast abyss,
> And mad'st it pregnant […].
> (1.20–22)

The spirit seems to adapt a vaguely hermaphroditic position since it not only inseminates but also takes on the more feminine task of "breeding". Similarly, Chaos appears to be double-sexed, since he is also allied to the female "consort" Night (2.963). As with the angels, they seem to be able to "either sex assume" (1.424), depending on the power relationship they find themselves in. Nature as common progeny of God and Chaos is caught between them and retains an attachment to her chaotic as well as to her divine heritage. It is not an easy position to be in: the relation of God and Chaos does not resemble that of a harmonious, matrimonial union, but rather that of permanent warfare, a face-off between two sovereign beings attempting to subdue and conquer each other. Milton has resexualized Genesis; and in this war of the sexes, intercourse appears as an act of aggression and appropriation. The cosmology he sketches begins to resemble that of the Mesopotamian creation myths from which the creation myth of Genesis is partly derived.[54] There are several passages in the Old Testament in which Yahweh is represented as engaged in a fight with a (female) dragon and in which this fight is related to the creation of the world.[55] One predecessor myth bears particular mention in this context, namely the Babylonian *Enuma Elish*,[56] in which the supreme god Marduk kills

54 See e.g. Hermann Gunkel, *Creation and Chaos in the Primeval Era and the Eschaton*, trans. K. William Whitney Jr., Grand Rapids, MI: Eerdmans, 2006.

55 Bruce K. Waltke, *Creation and Chaos: An Exegetical and Theological Study of Biblical Cosmogony*, Portland, OR: Western Conservative Baptist Seminary, 1974, p. 5.

56 Translated in Alexander Heidel, *Babylonian Genesis: The Story of the Creation*, Chicago: University of Chicago Press, 1972. Regina Schwartz and others have already made the connection. See Regina M. Schwartz, *Remembering and Repeating: On Milton's Theology and Poetics*, Cambridge and New York: Cambridge University Press, 1988, p. 28.

the monstrous, primeval mother goddess Tiamat, rips her apart and builds the earth and the sky from her two halves – a violent act that Paul Ricoeur approximates to a rape.[57] Marduk's sexually charged aggression serves not only to establish the authoritarian order of Babylon, but also to occupy and consolidate the territory over which the order is to extend.[58] Milton's God proceeds similarly, without altogether eliminating the female competition. Accordingly, Milton's universe is permeated by a latent sexual tension: "two great sexes animate the world", as Raphael gives to understand (8.151). That these sexual undertones are difficult to harmonize with the official monotheist doctrine causes cosmological as well as ethical problems, the latter first and foremost in the relationship between Adam and Eve. The reader may well wonder whether these problems are not the decisive cause for the Fall of Man; we will come back to this question extensively in Chapters 7 and 8.

The creation of Nature is not only a matter of mysterious divine procreations though, but also the result of God's omnificent decrees. And in this more orthodox context, the approximation of Nature, Wisdom and Fate also proves useful: Milton designates Nature as the fateful word of God, or rather the material force of this word. This is made most explicit in two passages from the *Doctrina Christiana* that associate nature, fate and divine speech. Milton here denies that nature and fate control the ways of the world autonomously:

> Nonnulli naturam aut fatum supremum quoddam in rebus esse argutantur: sed natura natam se fatetur aut proprie rem nullam significat, sed vel rei essentiam, vel communem illam legem, qua nascuntur omina atque agunt; et fatum quid nisi effatum divinum omnipotentis cuiuspiam numinis potest esse?
>
> Some people babble that nature or fate has supremacy over events, but nature declares that it was born – or else, strictly, it means nothing except the essence of a thing, or the universal law governing the birth and action of everything. And what can fate [fatum] be but the divine decree [effatum] of some almighty deity?
>
> (*DC* 24/25)

In the second passage, Milton identifies this fatum/effatum/natura with the "providentia Dei ordinaria", a common identification since Boethius:[59]

57 Paul Ricoeur, *Finitude et culpabilité II: La symbolique du mal*, Paris: Aubier, 1960, pp. 170–172.

58 John Rumrich, "Milton's God and the Matter of Chaos", *PMLA* 110:5 (1995), p. 1039.

59 "Omnium generatio rerum cunctusque mutabilium naturarum progressus et quiequid aliquo movetur modo, causas, ordinem, formas ex divinae mentis stabilitate sortitur. Haec in suae simplicitatis arce composita multiplicem rebus regendis modum statuit. Qui modus cum in ipsa divinae intellegentiae puritate conspicitur, providentia nominatur; cum vero ad ea quae movet atque disponit refertur, fatum a veteribus appellatum est." Boethius, *Consolatio Philosophiae/Trost der Philosophie*, ed. and trans. Ernst Gegenschatz and Olof Gigon, Zurich: Artemis und Winkler, 2004, p. 204 [4.6]. "The generation of all things, and the whole course of mutable natures and of whatever is in any way subject to change, take their causes, order, and forms

> Providentia Dei est ordinaria vel extraordinaria. Ordinaria, qua Deus constantem illum causarum ordinem qui ab ipso constitutis in principio est, retinet ac servat. Haec vulgo et nimis etiam frequenter Natura dicitur, neque enim aliud quicquam natura esse potest, nisi mirifica illa vis et efficacia divinae vocis primitus emissae, cui dehinc omnia veluti mandato perpetuparent.
>
> God's providence is ordinary or extraordinary. The ordinary kind is that whereby God maintains and preserves that consistent order of causes which was established by himself in the beginning. This is commonly, and also too frequently, called Nature, for indeed nothing else can be nature except that marvellous force and efficacy of the divine voice sent forth at first, which thenceforth all things obey just like a perpetual command.
>
> (*DC* 338/339)

According to this definition, Nature is the divine verbal force ordering matter – the primordial performative, one might say. When the Father in *Paradise Lost* approximates "Nature" to his "high decree" (3.126), he seems to echo this passage. A command that was promulgated at the beginning of time persists within creation as something that does not stop to be obeyed. But how is this all-pervasive obedience to be imagined? God's creation is not a creation *ex nihilo*, which implies that the divine word is imposed on a pre-existent, inherently dynamic proto-matter. And is language perhaps also pre-existent to the divine command? A major problem with God's absolute power and precedence persists in this context: it remains unclear, even in the *Doctrina Christiana*, whether God himself created language. Might language, like Chaos, Nature and possibly the Holy Light, be co-original with God, or even have preceded him? If so, it must have come naturally to the Almighty to use language for a primordial speech act. We can be sure that Milton took language to be a material entity or process, since absolutely everything is material in Milton's universe; but otherwise, he remains silent on this particular issue.[60] The reason for this silence might be Milton's epistemological humility before the mystery of divine revelation,[61] but the proliferating paganisms that surround the resultant blur keep suggesting the alternative notion of Language as an autonomous and eternal entity. The "universal

from the unchanging mind of God. This divine mind established the manifold rules by which all things are governed while it remained in the secure castle of its own simplicity. When this government is regarded as belonging to the purity of the divine mind, it is called Providence; but when it is considered with reference to the things which it moves and governs, it has from very early times been called Fate [...]." Boethius, *The Theological Tractates: The Consolation of Philosophy*, trans. H. F. Stewart and E. K. Rand, London: Heinemann, 1973, p. 341.

60 D. C. Allen, "Some Theories of the Growth and Origin of Language in Milton's Age", *Philological Quarterly* 28 (1949), pp. 5–16.

61 Besides Allen, "Some Theories of the Growth and Origin of Language in Milton's Age", see Stanley E. Fish, *Surprised By Sin: The Reader in* Paradise Lost, Cambridge, MA: Harvard University Press, 1997, p. 127.

hubbub" which traverses Chaos suggests that language might pre-exist creation in a disordered state (2.951). In his creative works, God would then act as a poet or a human sovereign, transforming a given reality by means of a given language.

All in all, the statements about the relation between God and Nature in *Paradise Lost* remain elusive and conflicting, because Milton's monism condenses several heterogeneous origin myths and conceptions into a volatile mixture. The power of his sovereign deity over nature seems to transcend all temporal and spatial boundaries; but it also appears to be both hemmed in and complemented by the uncertain, yet very palpable forces of Chaos. First and foremost, Nature's relation to the realm of this dark precursor therefore deserves to be investigated more thoroughly.

4 The vacuous trials of Chaos

4.1 Competing ancestries

At first sight, the figure of Chaos in *Paradise Lost* appears to be even more ambiguous and vacillating than that of Nature: the name denotes a location, a kingdom, an abstract principle, as well as a person of uncertain gender (sporting both a male pronoun[1] and a female consort, and yet frequently feminized by epithets such as "wide womb", 2.150). One of the few things of which we can be sure, however, is the profession of personified Chaos: he functions both as a sovereign and as an administrating judge ("umpire", 2.907). Furthermore, since he and his court inhabit a pavilion, that is, a tent[2] and establish their residence where occasion demands in an open space (2.998–999), it is fair to describe them as nomads.[3]

Before we can investigate the intricacies of Chaos' situation, his profession and their relation to those of his offspring, however, we have to confront one major difficulty the reader is faced with when encountering Chaos: *Paradise Lost* is supposedly a Christian epic. However, in commonsensical Christianity, Chaos does not exist (apart from the limited disorder Satan and his minions tend to generate). The word does not appear in the Bible. Milton's primordial Chaos obviously stems from Greco-Roman mythology, particularly Hesiod's *Theogony*, perhaps including its reception in Plato's *Timaeus*,[4] certainly its reception in Ovid's *Metamorphoses*.[5] However, in the archetypal Christian epic, Dante's *Comedia*, Chaos only appears in conjunction with

1 The Greek word is grammatically neuter. Jenny Strauss Clay, *Hesiod's Cosmos*, Cambridge: Cambridge University Press, 2003, p. 15.

2 See "pavilion, n.", *OED Online*. Oxford University Press, June 2016. Web. 20 August 2016.

3 Eric B. Song has pointed out that this association of Chaos and nomadism has parallels in other passages of *Paradise Lost* and in others of Milton's works. See Eric B. Song, *Dominion Undeserved: Milton and the Perils of Creation*, Ithaca, NY and London: Cornell University Press, 2013, p. 14.

4 In this text, the term ἀταξία is used, however. Plato, *Timaios*, in *Werke*, Vol. 7, ed. Gunther Eigler, Darmstadt: Wissenschaftliche Buchgesellschaft, 1972, pp. 38/39 [30a].

5 Ovid, *Metamorphoses*, Vol. 1, trans. Frank Justus Miller, London: Heinemann; and Cambridge, MA: Harvard University Press, 1971, pp. 2/3 and 80/81 [1.5–20 and 2.297–299].

an idle speculation.[6] In the *Summa* of Thomas Aquinas, the very notion is refuted: the cosmos is completely and thoroughly structured, and beyond the cosmos, there is nothing, except God.[7] Admittedly, in the Hebrew Bible, one can find a suggestion of primal disorder, an earth "without form and void" (Gen. 1.2). And this *tohu-wa-bohu* has been equated with Greek Chaos in some hexaemeral works, for example in *La semaine* by Guillaume du Bartas, which Milton apparently knew;[8] however, this Chaos is neither eternal nor is it personified, as is that of Milton.[9] Rather, it is merely a passing phase in the process of creation, preceded by the non-biblical but orthodox *creatio ex nihilo* which has been declared a Christian dogma in the fourth century CE.[10] Since then, theology insists that God created the ordered world not out of pre-existent disordered materials, but out of sheer nothingness. Around 400 CE, Augustine already tends to view any reference to a primordially disordered state of creation as a mere trope. He asserts that nothing existed before creation except formlessness ("informitas sine ulla specie").[11] And, in the Bible, the inconceivability of this primordial nothingness was "insinuated to people of slow apprehensions [...] by some ordinary word".[12] In Milton's time, late Spanish scholasticism differentiates God from Nature by means of this very same *creatio ex nihilo*: "God produces from nothing, Nature from potential being".[13] However, in *De Doctrina Christiana*, Milton interprets the Bible in the very opposite sense: he insists that God's creation was not a *creatio ex nihilo*, but an ordering of primordial (divine) matter. For confirmation, he employs philological arguments:

> Materia autem prima quae fuerit, varie disputatur. Moderni plerique volunt ex nihilo emersisse omnia; unde et ipsorum credo sententia orta est. Primum autem constat, neque Hebraeo verbo אָרָּב, neque Graeco

6 Dante, *Inferno*, translated by Jean Hollander and Robert Hollander, New York: Random House, 2000, pp. 220/221 [12.43].

7 Thomas Aquinas, *Summa Theologiae Prima Pars, 50–119*, Latin/English Edition, trans. Laurence Shapcote, Lander, WY: Aquinas Institute, 2012, pp. 145–148 [I, q. 66, a. 1].

8 See e.g. George Coffin Taylor, *Milton's Use of Du Bartas*, Cambridge, MA: Harvard University Press, 1934.

9 See Guillaume du Bartas, *La Sepmaine ou Création du Monde*, Paris: Michel Gadouleau, 1583, p. 20.

10 See Gerhard May, *Creatio Ex Nihilo: The Doctrine of "Creation out of Nothing" in Early Christian Thought*, trans. A. S. Worrall, London and New York: T. and T. Clark International, 2004.

11 Augustine, *Confessions*, Vol. 2, trans. William Watts, London and New York: William Heineman and Macmillan, 1912, pp. 292/293 [12.3].

12 Augustine, *Confessions*, Vol. 2, pp. 292/293 [12.4].

13 *Commentarii Collegii Conimbricensis Societatis Jesu in octo libros Physicorum Aristotelis Stagyritae*, Vol. 1, Coimbra: A. Mariz, 1591, p. 214; cited in Dennis Des Chene, *Physiologia: Natural Philosophy in Late Aristotelian and Cartesian Thought*, Ithaca, NY and London: Cornell University Press, 1996, p. 244.

> κτίζειν, neque Latino creare, idem quod ex nihilo facere significari: immo vero unumquodque horum idem quod ex materia facere passim significat.
> As to what the original matter was, however, there are various arguments. Most moderns contend that everything emerged out of nothing (out of which nothing, I reckon their own opinion originates!). In the first place it is certain that neither the Hebrew word *bara'* nor the Greek word *ktizein* nor the Latin *creare* means "to make out of nothing". On the contrary, each of them regularly means "to make something out of matter".
> (*DC* 286–289)

He also backs up his point with philosophical statements:

> Actio enim et passio relata cum sint, nullumque agens extra se possit agere, nisi sit quod pati queat, materia nimirum, Deus ex nihilo creare hunc mundum videtur non potuisse non ob virium, aut omnipotentiae defectum, sed quia necesse fuit aliquid iam tum fuisse, quod vim eius agendi potentissimam patiendo reciperet.
> For since "activity" and "passivity" are relational terms, and since no agent can act outside itself unless there exists something to be acted upon, which doubtless is matter, it seems that God could not have created this world out of nothing – "could not", not from any lack of power or omnipotence, but because there had to be something already in existence which by being acted upon might receive the almighty force of his efficacy.
> (*DC* 288/289)

Hence matter cannot be created from nothing, nor annihilated (*DC* 294/295). The process of creation has to be understood as an ordering "dispositio" of God's primordial matter (*DC* 292–295). Similarly, in *Paradise Lost*, Chaos is described as the location in which God, the "almighty maker", finds the raw materials for his creation, "His dark materials to create more worlds" (2.915–916).[14] And this is not an exclusively divine privilege: even other creatures

14 As often, Spenser turns out to be one of Milton's precursors in that respect. In the *Faerie Queene*, all created things are also formed from the raw material of Chaos:

> Daily they grow, and daily forth are sent
> Into the world, it to replenish more,
> Yet is the stocke not lessened, nor spent,
> But still remaines in euerlasting store,
> As it at first created was of yore.
> For in the wide wombe of the world there lyes,
> In hatefull darkenesse and in deepe horrore,
> An huge eternall Chaos, which supplyes
> The substances of natures fruitfull progenyes.
> All things from thence doe their first being fetch,
> And borrow matter, whereof they are made,
> Which when as forme and feature it does ketch,

can create out of Chaos, first and foremost Death and Sin, who build their highway to hell from the "foaming deep" (10.301). Furthermore, Chaos appears to be eternal and infinite, since it is a place where "time and place are lost" (2.894), a place of "*[e]ternal* anarchy, amidst the noise/ Of *endless* wars" (2.896–897, emphasis added). A problem results: how does the temporal and spatial boundlessness of Chaos relate to the temporal and spatial infinity and authority of the sole God? For Milton suggests that Chaos is no mere passive matter: it is a dynamic and self-aware entity, once more contradicting his own arguments in the *Doctrina* in the interest of an epic tradition: God and Chaos seem to enclose one another, and the narrator affirms both their claims to antecedence, even though Milton, in the *Doctrina*, rejects the notion of two infinities (*DC* 152/153). Questions of power and hierarchy pose themselves in this context; and *Paradise Lost* never actually resolves them. God, as "first and last" (2.324) ruler over everything who shall be "all in all" (3.341), must precede and succeed the personified, active Chaos, but how can one precede and succeed something that is eternal? Again, a general tension between the Protestant biblical worldview and an officially suspended, but strangely persistent, Greco-Roman mythical cosmos articulates itself within Milton's text. It has already been noted that the figure of the Father tends to oscillate between the transcendent and incomprehensible God of Protestantism and that of a Homeric supreme godhead such as Zeus, privileged only by his superior powers. God's powers, according to Milton's representation, largely manifest themselves in his powers of arranging and rearranging existing materials, thus constituting consistent, organized territories that he rules and cultivates.[15] Hence, he accomplishes nothing that the other characters could not emulate if their powers over primal matter were equal to his. God's ontological supremacy, however, is not evident. The Father's claims to be infinite are subverted by the epic's tendency to treat him as a character among others who is clearly positioned at a specific, delimited point in space; and about his absolute temporal precedence and its relation to the asserted eternity of Chaos, no conclusive verdict can be reached, since the narrative provides none. The Hesiodic myth of origins, to which *Paradise Lost* remains attached, affirms that Chaos was the first of all gods, after whom the others emerged,[16]

Becomes a body, and doth then inuade
The state of life, out of the griesly shade.

(Edmund Spenser, *The Faerie Queene*, ed. A. C. Hamilton, Harlow: Longman, 2001, p. 347 [3.6.36–37].) But Spenser's Chaos is not personified; and neither is it infinite or uncreated, according to John E. Hankins (John E. Hankins, "Chaos", in *The Spenser Encyclopedia*, ed. A. C. Hamilton, Toronto: University of Toronto Press, 1990, p. 139).

15 Julie Stone Peters, "A 'Bridge over Chaos': *De Jure Belli, Paradise Lost*, Terror, Sovereignty, Globalism, and the Modern Law of Nations", *Comparative Literature* 57:4 (2005): p. 276.

16 Hesiod, *Theogonie, Griechisch/Deutsch*, trans. and ed. Otto Schönberger, Stuttgart: Reclam, 1999, pp. 12/13 [116].

so the Father's claim to have existed from all eternity and to have created everything is accompanied by a subdued counterclaim. The Father's uncertain, transitional relation to the other protagonists, Chaos foremost among them, thus tends to "paganize" the Christian God, threatening to turn him into a god amongst others, a Zeus who tries to consolidate his position by turning into Yahweh. To ward off these threats, God, for his part, denies the mere existence of "uncreated" (2.150) Chaos/Night when he asserts that he himself is

alone
From all eternity, for none I know
Second to me or like, equal much less.
How have I then with whom to hold convérse
Save with the creatures which I made, and those
To me inferior, infinite descents
Beneath what other creatures are to thee?
(8.405–411)

In none of God's utterances is Chaos even mentioned; he once uses the word, but strategically conflates the place with hell, referring to "the gulf/ Of Tartarus, which ready opens wide/ His fiery chaos to receive their [i.e. the devils'] fall" (6.53–55). The nonexistence of Chaos would make Nature the offspring of a single, male parent. But Chaos likewise asserts precedence over God (2.999–1005), and several passages of *Paradise Lost* allow the interpretation that Nature indeed might have been generated by the parthenogenesis of Chaos (e.g. 2.894–895). The resultant contradictions remain unresolved. Joseph Wittreich characterizes *Paradise Lost* as an "arena for conflict, a battleground for warring values";[17] one might also say that, to a certain degree, Milton's epic itself remains chaotic.

4.2 The embryon state of war

It is all the more interesting that Milton often uses a political vocabulary in his descriptions of the disordered state beyond creation: Chaos is not only represented as a self-contradicting person, but also as a conflicted society. For example, the word "anarchy" and its derivatives appears no less than four times in these descriptions (2.896; 2.988; 6.873; 10.283). First and foremost, the Miltonian Chaos is a place where every kind of identity is threatened "with utter loss of being" (2.440), an "abortive gulf" (2.441) where no thing remains what it is. It is not an infinity of entropy however, an undifferentiated, homogeneous mass of dead matter, lying inertly in "utter darkness", but dynamic

17 Joseph Wittreich, "Milton's Transgressive Maneuvers: Receptions (Then and Now) and the Sexual Politics of *Paradise Lost*", in *Milton and Heresy*, eds. Stephen Dobranski and John Rumrich, Cambridge: Cambridge University Press, 1998, p. 244.

and conflictual. It is differentiated within itself, containing, for example, at least one "vast vacuity" (2.932), "clouds" (2.936), and "smoke" (2.928) , even though these differentiations are erratic and all objects apparently unstable. One can frequently read that it is the disorganized four elements that are battling eternally in Milton's Chaos.[18] However, on closer inspection, this is not what Milton says: he describes the eternal process of Chaos thus:

> Hot, Cold, Moist, and Dry, four champions fierce,
> Strive here for mastery, and to battle bring
> Their embryon atoms [...].
>
> (2.898–900)

Hence it is a battle not of the elements, but of the four properties that, according to Aristotle, constitute the elements. He draws the distinction in *De generatione et corruptione* and in *De partibus animalium* where he also calls those properties "powers", or, more precisely, "forces" (δυνάμεις).[19] These forces, due to the extreme volatility of Chaos, constitute mere potentials of materiality, "embryon atoms". Accordingly, Milton later on emphasizes that the "dark materials" of Chaos are

> neither sea, nor shore, nor air, nor fire,
> But all these in their pregnant causes mixed
> Confusedly [...].
>
> (2.912–914)

A further influence might be Plato's *Timaeus* according to which pre-cosmic matter was not thoroughly undifferentiated, but already contained "traces" (ἴχνη) of the elements.[20] Besides Plato and Aristotle, Ovid seems to have been the most important precursor: in the *Metamorphoses*, Chaos is not only described as Nature's first form ("toto naturae vultus"), but also as the "discordia semina rerum":

> Ante mare et terras et quod tegit omnia caelum
> unus erat toto naturae vultus in orbe,
> quem dixere chaos: rudis indigestaque moles
> nec quicquam nisi pondus iners congestaque eodem
> non bene iunctarum discordia semina rerum.

18 See e.g. Maynard Mack, *Milton*, Englewood Cliffs, NJ: Prentice-Hall, 1961, p. 150.

19 Aristotle, *Parts of Animals/Movement of Animals/Progression of Animals*, trans. A. L. Peck and E. S. Foster, London: Heinemann; and Cambridge, MA, Harvard University Press, 1956, pp. 106/107 [646a].

20 Plato, *Timaios*, in *Werke*, Vol. 7, ed. Gunther Eigler, Darmstadt: Wissenschaftliche Buchgesellschaft, 1972, pp. 96/97 [53a–b].

> Before the sea was, and the lands, and the sky that hangs over all, the face of Nature showed alike in her whole round, which state have men called chaos: a rough, unordered mass of things, nothing at all save lifeless bulk and warring seeds of ill-matched elements heaped in one.[21]

Unlike Ovid's, however, Milton's version of Chaos is not a "lifeless bulk", but a dynamic space of pure potentiality; it does not contain inert matter, but consists only of competing forces. His emphasis on the forces' utter instability does not hinder the narrator from personifying them as competing military leaders and the "embryon atoms" as their soldiers, engaged in (confessional?) battles:

> [T]hey around the flag
> Of each his faction, in their several clans,
> Light-armed or heavy, sharp, smooth, swift or slow,
> Swarm populous, unnumbered as the sands
> Of Barca or Cyrenë's torrid soil,
> Levied to side with warring winds, and poise
> Their lighter wings. To whom these most adhere
> He rules a moment [...].
> (2.900–907)

In an offside remark within his magnum opus *Process and Reality*, Alfred North Whitehead has perceptively pointed out that Milton thus revives an old notion of Chaos as a dynamic state preceding the "evolution of matter". Whitehead's philosophy assumes that reality is not made up of substances, but of processes and events and their aggregation into "societies". And he considers this notion to have a precursor in Plato, as well as in Milton:

> In the *Timaeus* the origin of the present cosmic epoch is traced back to an aboriginal disorder, chaotic according to our ideals [...]. Plato's notion has puzzled critics who are obsessed with the Semitic Theory of a wholly transcendent God creating out of nothing an accidental universe. Newton held the Semitic theory. The "Scholium" [by Newton] made no provision for the evolution of matter – very naturally, since the topic lay outside its scope. The result has been that the non-evolution of matter has been a tacit presupposition throughout modern thought. Until the last few years the sole alternatives were: either the material universe, with its present type of order, is eternal; or else it came into being, and will pass out of being, according to the *fiat* of Jehovah. Thus, on all sides, Plato's allegory

21 Ovid, *Metamorphoses*, Vol. 1, trans. Frank Justus Miller, London: Heinemann; and Cambridge, MA: Harvard University Press, 1971, pp. 2/3 [1.5–9].

of the evolution of a new type of order based on new types of dominant societies became a daydream, puzzling to commentators.

Milton, curiously enough, in his *Paradise Lost* wavers between the *Timaeus* and the Semitic doctrine. This is only another instance of the intermixture of classical and Hebrew notions on which his charm of thought depends. In the description of Satan's journey across Chaos, Satan discovers

> The secrets of the hoary Deep – a dark
> Illimitable ocean, without bound,
> Without dimension; where length, breadth, and height,
> And time, and place, are lost; where eldest Night
> And Chaos, ancestors of Nature, hold
> Eternal anarchy, amidst the noise
> Of endless wars, and by confusion stand.

Milton is here performing for Plato the same poetic service that Lucretius performed for Democritus [...]. Both for Plato and for Aristotle the process of the actual world has been conceived as a real incoming of forms into real potentiality, issuing into that real togetherness which is an actual thing. Also, for the *Timaeus*, the creation of the world is the incoming of a type of order establishing a cosmic epoch. It is not the beginning of matter of fact, but the incoming of a certain type of social order.[22]

Whitehead declares Milton to be at least half a Whiteheadian Platonist, hence a poetic precursor of process philosophy. Strangely, the quotation does not seem to be the most apt for the purpose, since Milton's depiction of dynamic, conflictual processes generated by proto-elemental forces which are "neither sea, nor shore, nor air, nor fire" would be a better exemplification of the overlap between process philosophy and the cosmogony of *Paradise Lost*. It is remarkable, however, that both Whitehead and Milton blend a terminology of physical interactions with a terminology of social cooperation and antagonism in order to depict this pre-material world of powers.[23] The noisy disorder of Milton's Chaos is described as an eternal war with unclear, constantly shifting party lines and no conceivable objective;[24]

22 Alfred North Whitehead, *Process and Reality: An Essay in Cosmology: Gifford Lectures Delivered in the University of Edinburgh During the Season 1927–28*, eds. David Ray Griffin and Donald W. Sherburne, New York: Free Press, 1985, pp. 95–96.

23 On Whitehead's use of this terminology of social physics and its implications, see Michael Halewood, *A. N. Whitehead and Social Theory: Tracing a Culture of Thought*, London and New York: Anthem, 2011.

24 A similar point is made in Peters, "A 'Bridge over Chaos'", p. 276.

in Deleuzo-Guattarian terms: a war that is completely deterritorialized.[25] This eternal battle also exhibits remarkable similarities to what Hobbes, in his *Leviathan*, had called a war of all against all, "the first Chaos of violence and civil war":[26] a war that cannot be confined within the usual bounds of military conflict between states – long considered to be the enforcement of natural as well as divine law.[27] In his pre-natural state, Milton develops what Joanna Picciotto has called a "physical correlate of the political state of nature as Hobbes imagined it".[28] Likewise, the Miltonian Chaos reminds John Rogers of "the atomized structure of the originary Hobbesian polity".[29] Rogers additionally points out that this association between physics and politics was common in Milton's time.[30] Evidently, Hobbes himself was not too averse to this mixture between "natural philosophy" and politics, basing the *Leviathan* partly on his treatise on physics, *De Corpore*.[31] Although Milton does not share Hobbes' trust in the natural sciences, the development of the *novae scientiae* influenced his poetry as well as his politics (see *Of Education*, *CPW* 2:389–394, and *Areopagitica, CPW* 2:538). The disorienting suspension of all fixed spatial reference points in his description of Chaos – the loss of "length, breadth, and height,/ And time and place" (2.893–894) – would hardly have been conceivable without the reconceptualization of space that was instigated by Giordano Bruno, Galileo and their successors, and that culminated in what Alexandre Koyré designated as the passage "from

25 For a relatively lucid exposition of the terms "territorialization" and "deterritorialization", see Gilles Deleuze and Félix Guattari, *What is Philosophy*?, trans. Hugh Tomlinson and Graham Burchell, New York: Columbia University Press, 1994, pp. 67–70.

26 Thomas Hobbes, *Leviathan*, ed. J. C. A. Gaskin, Oxford: Oxford University Press, 1998, p. 290 [3.36.20].

27 See e.g. Frederick H. Russell, *The Just War in the Middle Ages*, Cambridge and New York: Cambridge University Press, 1979, p. 26; and J. A. Fernández-Santamaría, *Natural Law, Constitutionalism, Reason of State, and War: Counter-Reformation Spanish Political Thought*, Vol. 2, New York: Peter Lang, 2006, pp. 247–271.

28 Joanna Picciotto, *Labors of Innocence in Early Modern England*, Cambridge, MA: Harvard University Press, 2010, p. 453.

29 John Rogers, *The Matter of Revolution: Science, Poetry and Politics in the Age of Milton*, Ithaca, NY and London: Cornell University Press, 1996, p. 131. The formulation neglects the difference between atomism and "embryon atomism".

30 "The speculation of an atomistically structured chaos played a special role in the later-seventeenth-century practice of organizational speculation. The theorization of a specifically atomistic abyss permitted the articulation of the relative merits of a liberally organized system of individual, perhaps even equal, elements or particles. It functioned, often explicitly, to ground the philosophical speculation about the promise, or threat, of free-trade economics and democracy, those nonauthoritarian systems of economic and political organization to which the adjective 'chaotic' was most often applied." Rogers, *The Matter of Revolution*, p. 131. Rogers goes on to cite a text by the poet and politician Edmund Waller as an example.

31 Cees Leijenhorst, "Sense and Nonsense about Sense: Hobbes and the Aristotelians on Sense Perception and Imagination", in *The Cambridge Companion to Hobbes's* Leviathan, ed. Patricia Springborg, Cambridge: Cambridge University Press, 2007, pp. 98–99.

the closed world to the infinite universe".[32] Koyré portrays the Scientific Revolution as a dissolution of the world's limits:

> I shall [...] characterize this revolution by two closely connected and even complementary features: (a) the destruction of the cosmos, and therefore the disappearance from science – at least in principle, if not always in fact – of all considerations based on this concept, and (b) the geometrization of space, that is the substitution of the homogenous and abstract – however now considered as real – dimension space of the Euclidean geometry for the concrete and differentiated place-continuum of pre-Galilean physics and astronomy. As a matter of fact, this characterization is very nearly equivalent to the mathematization (geometrization) of nature and therefore the mathematization (geometrization) of science. The disappearance – or destruction – of the cosmos means that the world of science, the real world, is no more seen, or conceived, as a finite and hierarchically ordered, therefore qualitatively and ontologically differentiated whole, but as an open, indefinite, and even infinite universe, united not by its immanent structure but only by the identity of its fundamental contents and laws [...].[33]

Milton is one of the first to transfer this notion of a world of infinite spaces into an aesthetic context and to derive effects of sublimity from it.[34] However, in Milton this boundless, unnatural realm coexists with a traditional, bounded and rounded cosmos, acting as the latter's sombre background and enabling condition. By this manoeuvre, the Aristotelian, hierarchical world picture is partly retained, but subtly decentred. There is only one character in *Paradise Lost* who emphatically insists on the universal applicability of Aristotelian physics, and it is a blatantly misguided devil: when the fallen angels sit in council and discuss ways by which they might return to heaven, Moloch supposes with Aristotle that every thing, according to its composition, has its natural place to which it tends. Therefore, the fallen angels, after their violent overthrow, should have no difficulties in tracing their "natural" way back up through Chaos to heaven:

> in our proper motion we ascend
> Up to our native seat: descent and fall
> To us is adverse. [...]

32 Alexandre Koyré, *From the Closed World to the Infinite Universe*, Baltimore: Johns Hopkins University Press, 1957. The relation has been alluded to before, e.g. in Claire Colebrook, *Milton, Evil and Literary History*, London and New York: Continuum, 2008, p. 132.

33 Alexandre Koyré, *Newtonian Studies*, London: Chapman and Hall, 1965, pp. 6–7.

34 John Donne is another poet who exemplifies this tendency. See William Empson, "Donne the Space Man", in *Essays on Renaissance Literature*, Vol. 1, ed. John Haffenden, Cambridge and New York: Cambridge University Press, 1993, pp. 78–128.

The ascent is easy then […].
(2.75–81)

However, experience does not confirm his hypothesis: on his way through Chaos, Satan does not tend either to heaven or to hell by natural inclination, but loses himself in a volatile space in which even the difference between verticality and horizontality seems to dissolve.[35] When that distinction reasserts itself, it appears in a thoroughly modernised version: as Satan makes his way through the "dark, unbottomed, infinite abyss", he encounters a vacuum, which triggers a second fall:

[He] meets
A vast vacuity: all unawares
Fluttering his pennons vain plumb down he drops
Ten thousand fathom deep, and to this hour
Down had been falling, had not by ill chance
The strong rebuff of some tumultuous cloud
Instinct with fire and nitre hurried him
As many miles aloft […].
(2.931–938)

This fall is remarkable for several reasons: first, it is potentially infinite since it occurs in an "illimitable" space (2.892); in Dante's Aristotelian universe with its clear boundaries, this calamity would be impossible. Admittedly, one can also find notions of infinite universes in the time before Bruno, for example in *De rerum natura* by Lucretius.[36] However, one must acknowledge that Milton's infinite Chaos is a post-Galileian phenomenon. The most obvious symptom of this modernity is the circumstance that Satan's fall occurs in a vacuum in which his wings are useless: within the ancient cosmology, true "vacuities" do not exist.[37] And the circumstance that Satan cannot fly in this void, but only plummet forever despite his wings, is beholden to Galilei's ground-breaking assertion that, due to lack of air resistance, a feather in a vacuum falls just as fast as a piece of lead.[38] Miltonian Chaos apparently observes the natural laws of the *novae scientiae*.[39]

Furthermore, and most importantly, it is not altogether clear whether God's will is realized in the enforcement of these freshly discovered primordial laws. Satan would still fall into the infinite void of Chaos, if the apparently

35 See e.g. 2.950; 2.1047–1052; 3.501–522.

36 Lucretius, *De rerum natura/Welt aus Atomen*, ed. Karl Büchner, Stuttgart: Reclam, 2005, pp. 72–83 [1.951–1113].

37 See e.g. Aristotle, *Physik*, trans. Hans Günter Zekl, Hamburg: Meiner, 1987, pp. 174–203 [213a–217b].

38 Galileo Galilei, *Dialogues Concerning Two New Sciences*, trans. Henry Crew and Alfonso de Salvio, New York: Cosimo Classics, 2010, pp. 72 ff.

39 See also Harinder S. Marjara, "Angelic Motion and Moloch's False Rhetoric", *Milton Quarterly* 19.3 (1985), p. 86.

contingent appearance of a cloud had not saved him by "ill chance" (2.935). Is this chance encounter beyond creation a manifestation of the Father's law-positing will or a thoroughly chaotic event over which he either has no control or chooses to exercise no control? This question is all the more crucial since Satan's lucky deliverance will allow him to enact the Fall of mankind. But Milton leaves it just as open as that of the general ascendancy of Chaos, since both of the possible answers would present him with theological quandaries. In the unstable realm of original anarchy, the arbitrary arbiter Chance, a courtier of Chaos, is said to "govern all" (2.910). Is this paradoxical divinity autonomous on his own constantly shifting turf? Did Milton's God leave the infinite spaces beyond creation to a shady competitor who basically incarnates the random fortunes of the four "pregnant causes"? The Father occasionally seems to assert such a voluntary self-limitation and partial abdication:

> I uncircumscribed my self retire,
> And put not forth my goodness, which is free
> To act or not [...].
>
> (7.170–172)

However, as soon as he has thus spatially delimited himself, he would not actually be infinite anymore, as he claims (7.168–169), and even his boundless sovereignty would seem to be impaired by his "retirement", even though this impairment might be voluntary and temporary. This retirement from Chaos cannot be explained by God's benign decision to make room for his creatures and their free will either, since these creatures do not actually inhabit those outer reaches, except in dire emergencies. On the other hand, if Chance is interpreted as one of his dependent executors, God's government in this particular case seems altogether indistinguishable from that of mere accident: no apparent transgression has caused Satan's second fall into the endless void. In fact, this fall would mar God's proclaimed plans for the execution of justice, at least to the extent that it would save Satan from the fires of hell that have officially been ordained for him. And, likewise, no apparent merit or demerit brings about Satan's subsequent salvation from the depths – which is also a double-edged sword, since it will only help him toward additional damnation (1.215). Perhaps the Father and Chance are subject to a common law that constantly relates them to each other? The epic does not provide the reader with definite answers at this point; the fog of war lies thick over Chaos. However, it has at least become obvious that Chaos is a historically overdetermined area in which remainders that do not fit into the closed cosmos of traditional Christian doctrine lead an uncanny, "incomposed" (2.989) and conflictual existence: primordial deities of pagan antiquity, but also successors such as the uncharted expanses of Galileian science. It stands to reason that Milton's protagonists describe this vast repository of abject non-things as a site of superabundant generativity – qua uterus of nature – as well as of destruction and utter sterility: it is not only designated as a potential "grave" (2.911), but also as "abortive" (2.441) and "wasteful" (2.961); occasionally, it is associated with excrement (e.g. in 7.238).

Since Milton's Chaos is a space of competing potentials, it is only logical that some have conceived it as the true domain of poetry because poetics, since Aristotle, tends to define the poet as a writer who does not describe what is real, but that which might be.[40] Johann Jacob Bodmer, in his *Critische Abhandlung von dem Wunderbaren in der Poesie* (1740), apparently was the first to flesh out this connection: he understands Milton's Chaos as paradigmatic for the realm of *poiesis*.

> Diese Art der Schöpfung ist das Hauptwerck der Poesie, die sich eben dadurch von den Geschichtschreibern und Naturkündigern unterscheidet, daß sie die Materie ihrer Nachahmung allezeit lieber aus der möglichen als aus der gegenwärtigen Welt nimmt. [...] Aber am allerweitesten hat er [i.e. Milton] sich von der Erden entfernet, wo er Himmel und Hölle selbst aus dem Gesicht verlassen, und sich in das Nichts gestürtzet hat, ich will sagen, wo er das Nichts selbst als etwas vorgestellet, und mittelst seiner Erfindungskraft eine Erschaffung vor der Erschaffung beschrieben hat.[41]
>
> This manner of creation is the main task of poetry which differs from any writing on human or natural history insofar as it always prefers to take its subject matter from the possible rather than from the real world. [...] But he [i.e. Milton] removed himself farthest from earth when he left even heaven and hell behind and threw himself into nothing, or rather, when he imagined nothing to be something, thus describing a creation before the creation by the strength of his imagination.[42]

According to Bodmer, every poet penetrates in his work the space of pure potential that is the basis of all reality, the "creation before creation" ("Schöpfung vor der Schöpfung"). Milton's depiction of Chaos as a space of pure potential not only exemplifies this penetrating work of the poet, but it also manifests its supreme achievement. Even his heretical denial of the *creatio ex nihilo* is therefore justified by its sublime poetological context:

40 Aristotle, *Poetik*, trans. Manfred Fuhrmann, Stuttgart: Reclam, 1994, pp. 28/29 [1451b]. Appropriately, a suggestion that the narrator's Muse might be a close relative of Chaos hangs over *Paradise Lost*: while Urania is not equated with the conglomerate entity of Fate/Wisdom/Nature, she is declared to be Wisdom's sister (7.10); and in medieval times, the divine Sophia was indeed invoked in the same function as Urania, i.e. as the Muse of all heavenly and transcendent things (Ernst Robert Curtius, "Die Musen im Mittelalter, Erster Teil: Bis 1100", *Zeitschrift für romanische Philologie* 59:1 (1939): pp. 129–188; here p. 151). This indication of kinship implies that the "pregnant causes" of the infinite abyss are also at work within Milton's epic, covertly co-writing it.

41 Johann Jacob Bodmer, *Critische Abhandlung von dem Wunderbaren in der Poesie und dessen Verbindung mit dem Wahrscheinlichen*, Zurich: Conrad Orell, 1740, pp. 32/163.

42 Translation BQ.

> Ein gewisser Kunstrichter hat dem Poeten [i.e. Milton] hierüber Schuld geben wollen, daß er die Erschaffung aus Nichts geleugnet hätte, alleine wir sehn aus dem, was ich von dieser Erdichtung gesagt habe, daß er dießfalls nicht straffwürdiger ist, als ein jeder Poet, der etwas mögliches als würcklich vorstellet, und die Natur und Schöpfung nachahmet, worinn die poetische Erschaffung bestehet; man könte mit demselben Recht die Poeten anklagen, daß sie dem Schöpfer in sein Ammt greiffen, so oft sie nach ihrer Kunst mittelst der Nachahmung Dinge hervorbringen, die nicht sind; welches Verbrechen nicht anderst, als durch eine gäntzliche Zernichtigung der Poesie könte gebessert werden.[43]
>
> A certain critic has blamed the poet [i.e. Milton] for denying the *creatio ex nihilo*. However, from the things I have said about this poetic fiction we may infer that he is no more culpable in this than any poet who represents something possible as real and imitates Nature and creation, wherein poetical conception consists. With the same right, one might accuse all poets that they encroach upon the function of God whenever their art by imitation produces things that are not – a crime that could not be rectified except by the complete annihilation of poetry itself.[44]

Prolonging Bodmer's argument into the nineteenth century, one might comprehend Chaos as the true realm of aesthetics, since aesthetics traditionally "has to do with things insofar as they cannot be cognized, or subordinated to concepts; and also insofar as they cannot be utilized, or normatively regulated, or defined according to rules".[45]

4.3 The cosmic shadow government

However, Milton's place of "utter darkness" (1.72; 5.614) cannot be regarded as a place of pure non-identity: this Chaos is more than a mere tumult of virtuality, insofar as it has a sovereign (or at least an claimant) who both rules and personifies it, thus unifying it at least on a symbolic level. Hesiod's *Theogony* confronts the reader with a mythical Chaos that is not only a space, but also a vaguely allegorical person (though not a ruler and "umpire"). Milton here touches upon a topos of political theology, namely the identification of a sovereign and his state.[46] Significantly, this ruler of Chaos is positioned on the unstable border of his deterritorialized territory, both defending it and

43 Bodmer, *Critische Abhandlung*, pp. 164–165. See also the sketchy remarks on Bodmer in Hans Blumenberg, "'Nachahmung der Natur': Zur Vorgeschichte der Idee des schöpferischen Menschen", in *Ästhetische und metaphorologische Schriften*, ed. Anselm Haverkamp, Frankfurt am Main: Suhrkamp, 2001, pp. 43–44.

44 Translation BQ.

45 Steven Shaviro, *The Universe of Things: On Whitehead and Speculative Realism*, Minneapolis: University of Minnesota Press, 2014, p. 7.

46 Ernst Kantorowicz, *The King's Two Bodies: A Study in Mediaeval Political Theology*, Princeton: Princeton University Press, 1997, pp. 259–272.

representing it to the outside, retaining some of its disordered characteristics, such as a "visage incomposed", but being endowed at least with a vaguely anthropomorphic form and with the power of speech, even though "faltering" (2.989). For our purposes, it is crucial to gain some further insight into his manner of liminal administration and jurisdiction. We glean some hints from the description of his nomadic court:

> [...] straight behold the throne
> Of Chaos, and his dark pavilion spread
> Wide on the wasteful deep; with him enthroned
> Sat sable-vested Night, eldest of things,
> The consort of his reign; and by them stood
> Orcus and Ades, and the dreaded name
> Of Demogorgon; Rumour next and Chance,
> And Tumult and Confusion all embroiled,
> And Discord with a thousand various mouths.
> (2.959–967)

Among this assembly, there are several deities who stand in an implicit competition with the Father. Most obviously, Chaos in his function as primordial divinity claims antecedence over God: he characterizes the Father's dominion as a recent innovation and territorial conquest that encroaches on his ancient and customary regions (2.1002–1005). And he describes the Father just like Hesiodic Chaos might describe Zeus: as an inimical upstart (2.998–1000).[47] But beside Chaos himself, God's pagan competition in the abyss still has other members: in Demogorgon's very name, a claim to supreme godhead is embedded; it is a variant of Plato's name for the divine creator, *demiurgós*. Apparently, "Demogorgon" first appears as a misreading in a commentary on Statius's *Thebaid* (either stemming from Late Antiquity or from early medieval times); in this commentary, Demogorgon is characterized as the supreme creator God, "summus deus".[48] Subsequently, perhaps due to the name's similarity to that of the monstrous Gorgons, it came to designate a demon who is responsible for the world's disorder. The name seems to have been introduced into the Renaissance tradition by Boccaccio,[49] and it subsequently appears both

47 Some epics of Late Antiquity that narrate the battles between the Olympian Gods and the Titans might be considered as neglected precursors of *Paradise Lost*. The first two books of Nonnos' *Dionysiaca* (in which Chaos also makes a cameo appearance) would be a good example. See Nonnos, *Dionysiaca*, Vol. 1, trans. W. H. D. Rouse, London: Heinemann; and Cambridge, MA: Harvard University Press, 1940.

48 Herbert J. Rose, *Griechische Mythologie: Ein Handbuch*, Munich: Beck, 1982, p. 169. I thank Michael Waltenberger for pointing out this etymology to me.

49 Jean Seznec, *The Survival of the Pagan Gods: The Mythological Tradition and its Place in Renaissance Humanism and Art,* Princeton, NJ: Princeton University Press, 1981, p. 222.

in Marlowe's *Faustus*[50] and in Spenser's *Faerie Queene*.[51] In general, Milton in his epic does not efface the components of Greco-Roman mythology that are incompatible with the traditional Christian doctrine of monotheism; rather, he rewrites the pagan myths as if to make these incompatibilities even more blatant. For example, in Hesiod, Chaos gives birth to Nyx/Night;[52] but Milton makes her his wife instead of his parthenogenetic daughter. Accordingly, the text stresses her primordiality. She is not only called "ancient" and "old", but "eldest" (2.894), "eternal" (3.18) and "unoriginal" (10.477), that is, "without origin", in other words "uncreated". In thus materializing and personifying darkness as a third eternal divinity, Milton goes against the grain of theology since Augustine expounded in his *Commentary on Genesis* that darkness is just an absence of light, a mere lack, instead of an active force (just as Evil is merely a lack of the Good):

> Sed quia ipsi fabulis suis decepti crediderunt gentem esse tenebrarum, in qua et corpora et formas et animas in illis corporibus fuisse arbitrantur, ideo putant quod tenebrae aliquid sint. [...] Sicut autem isti dicunt gentem tenebrarum contra lucem Dei pugnasse; sic potest et alius similiter vanus dicere, gentem silentiorum contra vocem Dei pugnasse.
>
> But they have been taken in by their own fables, and have come to believe that there is a race of darkness, to which bodies belong, in their view, and the forms and souls in those bodies; and that is why they think that darkness is an actual something. [...] But just as these people say that the race of darkness has been fighting against the light of God, so too any other simpleton can likewise say that the race of silence has been fighting against the voice of God.[53]

Again, Milton re-mythologizes and re-personifies an otherness that Christian theology had taken great pains to desubstantiate. In *Paradise Lost*, the celestial realm certainly treats "the realm of Night" like a substantial, autonomous enemy state that must be kept under close surveillance by celestial secret services: it is said that the angels

50 Christopher Marlowe, *The Tragical History of Doctor Faustus*, in *English Renaissance Drama: A Norton Anthology*, ed. David Bevington, New York and London: W. W. Norton and Company, 2002, p. 256 [1.3.19].

51 Edmund Spenser, *The Faerie Queene*, p. 426 [4.2.47].

52 Hesiod, *Theogonie*, pp. 12/13 [123].

53 Augustine, *On Genesis*, in *Works* 1.13, trans. Edmund Hill, ed. John E. Rotelle, Hyde Park, NY: New City Press, 2002, pp. 43–44 [4.7]. Whereas Aquinas agrees with Augustine (Summa 1, Quaestio 5, Art. 48), the reformed theologians were rather reluctant to make binding statements about the essential or non-essential nature of evil, even though Calvin, in *De aeterna Dei praedestinatione*, voices a reserved disagreement with Augustine on the matter. See David J. Marshall, "John Calvin", in *Augustine Through the Ages: An Encyclopedia*, ed. Allan D. Fitzgerald, Grand Rapids, MI: Eerdmans 1999, p. 119.

> oft on the bordering deep
> Encamp their legions, or with óbscure wing
> Scout far and wide into the realm of Night,
> Scorning surprise.
> (2.131–134; capitalization added)

Although this might be another example of the useless tasks with which Father loves to plague his underlings according to Empson,[54] the reader cannot be certain.

In a slightly different vein, it should be noted that two other courtiers of Chaos – Orcus and Ades – bear the names of two punitive judges of the pagan underworld (and of their territories), one of Greek, one of Roman descent. They are shady figures whose function remains unclear, but their presence here strikes the reader at least as curious, as if there were not one, but two or three supplementary hells beyond the hell of orthodoxy from which Satan has just escaped. Do the infinite spaces of Chaos store up primordial pagan doppelgangers not only of the Father, but also of the inferno he created for the enactment of justice?[55]

Five more courtiers and governors under Chaos are mentioned – Rumour, Chance, Tumult, Confusion and Discord – and they all seem to be emblematic, allegorical figures, just like Death and Sin, whom Satan encountered at the gates of hell. However, this estimation is slightly complicated by the fact that these five creatures also appear in Hesiod (or in Pseudo-Hesiod).[56] And in Hesiod, the allegorical status of these deities is not clearly determinable. Hesiod delivers semi-allegories that are still imbued with the *mana* and the lineage of venerated divinities, powers that are not reducible to mere abstractions.[57] Indeed, the very form of allegory itself in Milton's time still bears distant witness to a pagan holy terror, not only according to Walter

54 William Empson, *Milton's God*, Westport, CT: Greenwood Press, 1978, p. 110.

55 We will return to this strange continuity between hell and Chaos in Chapter 6.

56 Chance and Discord are both integrated into the genealogies of the *Theogony* under the names of Tyche and Eris; Rumour as Pheme is maligned in "Works and Days"; and Tumult/Homados and Confusion/Kydoimos are mentioned in the pseudepigraphic "Shield of Heracles". Hesiod, *Theogonie*, pp. 20/21, 30/31 [225/360]; id., *Works and Days*, in *Theogony, Works and Days, Testimonia*, trans. and ed. Glenn W. Most, Cambridge, MA and London: Harvard University Press, 2006, pp. 148/149 [760–764]; id., "The Shield" in *The Shield, Catalogue of Women, Other Fragments*, trans. and ed. Glenn W. Most, 2007, pp. 14/15 [155/156].

57 On the problem of allegorical intentions in Homer and Hesiod, see Gordon Teskey, *Allegory and Violence*, Ithaca, NY: Cornell University Press, 1996, pp. 40 ff. See also Klaus Heinrich, *Gesellschaftlich vermitteltes Naturverhältnis: Begriff der Aufklärung in den Religionen und der Religionswissenschaft*, Dahlemer Vorlesungen 8, Frankfurt am Main: Stroemfeld/Roter Stern, 2007, pp. 53–91. It should be noted that Hesiod's other two primordial divinities, Gaia and Eros, do not appear in this chaotic context, since they will be integrated into *Paradise Lost* in other places. (See Chapters 8 and 9.)

Benjamin,[58] but also according to the seventeenth-century rhetorician and theologian Gerardus Vossius, who writes that allegory "by its obscurity resembles the darkness of night which easily terrifies the fearful" and compares it to the Athenian mystery cults.[59] Traces of this attitude also persist in *Paradise Lost*. In the words of Catherine Gimelli Martin: Milton's allegories emphasize the allegorical entities' "organic and 'efficient' effect on the material continuum".[60] As in many early modern re-imaginings of the pagan gods, they appear as indeterminable entities here, positioned uneasily between the poet's persistent fascination with Greco-Roman religion and its Christian repudiation and secularization by way of allegorization.[61] The personified proto-elements are the appropriate subjects of this emblematic nobility.

The proximity to allegory endows the Court of Chaos with yet another characteristic property: despite all the mythical tensions, the unholy commotion and the noise that envelop it, the Court seems to be a strangely static and lifeless place. Its members are mostly reduced to their names and merely enumerated, provided neither with attributes, nor actual occupations. The impression of atrophy (rather than entropy) is reinforced by the circumstance that Chaos professes himself to be a rather powerless ruler, not only in relation to the neighbouring states, but also respecting his internal affairs. The "anarch" Chaos administrates his realm in a strange way: by definition, he cannot rule it; accordingly, the battle between the proto-elements itself determines who is to rule by the law of combat. Yet, because the competing parties are inherently impermanent entities, victory is always transient: a certain configuration of hot, cold, moist and dry "rules a moment", then dissipates again (2.907). Personified Chaos presides over this unending competition-jurisdiction merely as "umpire", that is as a person who has the authority to judge a conflict, because he is an independent third party (from the Latin "impar").[62] Apparently, he is to decide impartially on the victorious party. The position of personified Chaos is therefore an adjudicative one; he provides a jurisdiction that supplements the rule of the strongest. However, he can only utter a judgment that is already obsolete at the very moment of its promulgation and that has no conceivable consequences within the non-space and non-time of Chaos. The judgment is neither performative nor constative, but altogether void: an empty intervention, itself blown about according

58 Walter Benjamin, *The Origin of German Tragic Drama*, trans. John Osborne, London: Verso, 1998, p. 226.

59 Gerardus Vossius, *Commentariorum rhetoricorum sive oratoriarum institutionum libri VI*, Vol. 2, Leiden 1643, p. 451; cited in Deborah Shuger, *Sacred Rhetoric: The Christian Grand Style in the English Renaissance*, Princeton, NJ: Princeton University Press, 1988, p. 160.

60 Catherine Gimelli Martin, *The Ruins of Allegory:* Paradise Lost *and the Metamorphosis of Epic Convention*, Durham, NC: Duke University Press, 1998, p. 166.

61 See Walter Benjamin, *The Origin of German Tragic Drama*, pp. 220–222. See also Seznec, *The Survival of the Pagan Gods*, pp. 84–121.

62 A. R. Lakshmanan and J. J. S. Wharton, *Wharton's Concise Law Dictionary*, Delhi: Universal Law Publishing, 2009, p. 1065.

to the law of brute force. At best, the utterance of the decision functions as another deployment within the conflict; it "more embroils the fray" (2.908) and thereby complicates it. Personified Chaos imposes a juridical structure on his dominion, but a juridical structure that is indistinguishable from lawlessness. Chaos himself stresses this paradoxical nature of his sovereignty:

> I upon my frontiers here
> Keep residence; if all I can will serve
> That little which is left so to defend
> Encroached on still through our intestine broils
> Weakening the sceptre of old Night.
>
> (2.998–1002)

It must strike the reader as odd that he considers "intestine broils" as detrimental to a reign which "by confusion stand[s]" (2.897). These broils should be the very essence of Chaos, the "fray/ By which he reigns" (2.908–909). But on the other hand, this contradiction is symptomatic: sovereign Chaos not only presides over a universal battle, he also incarnates it. He is the confused ruler of a realm of confusion, attached both to form and to formlessness. The attempt at encapsulating non-identity within identity, at personifying a depersonalizing force, ends in disarray. Allegoresis (along with other methods of representation) has frequently been described as a method of domesticating deviant or unknowable otherness, of seemingly subordinating it to the established symbolic order.[63] But it turns out that Milton's Chaos is not rendered more comprehensible and domesticated by its personification; rather, this personification takes allegoresis to the limit where it begins to founder. King Chaos, with his "visage incomposed", becomes an allegory of a failure of allegoresis, which demonstrates that the symbolic order not only borders on Chaos, but is contaminated by it. As often, allegory thus presents itself as the scene of a problematic "entanglement of nature and history".[64]

This argument can be developed further: it has already been pointed out that Milton's dominion of Chaos may be interpreted as a figuration of society in a combative condition beyond the order of the state.[65] Werner Hamacher

63 "But this allegorization was also part of another process of canonization, namely, domestication. By domestication I mean the ways in which a poem's objectionable or problematic aspects are suppressed or ignored so that it can be shown to conform not only to conventional ethical and religious values, but to artistic ones as well" (Daniel Javitch, *Proclaiming a Classic: The Canonization of* Orlando Furioso, Princeton, NJ: Princeton University Press, 1991, p. 6). See also Walter Benjamin, *The Origin of German Tragic Drama*, pp. 221–223.

64 "Verschränkung von Natur und Geschichte", Walter Benjamin, *Ursprung des deutschen Trauerspiels*, p. 344. Translation BQ.

65 Accordingly, the personifications of Chaos, Rumour, Chance, Tumult, Confusion and Discord did find their way into early modern caricature and satire, as roles ascribed to political opponents. See e.g. Theresa M. Kelley, *Reinventing Allegory*, Cambridge and New York: Cambridge University Press, 1997, p. 54; Philip Hardie, *Rumour and Renown: Representations of Fama in Western Literature,* Cambridge and New York: Cambridge University Press, 2012,

and Giorgio Agamben have pointed out that the relation between this Hobbesian "state of nature" and the Hobbesian "state of commonwealth" is intricately ambiguous. On the one hand, the truculent "state of nature" seems to be incompatible with the instauration of the leviathanic sovereign and of the commonwealth that subjects itself to him. Yet on the other hand, both states are intimately entwined; one might say that either state only persists within the other and becomes inconsistent without it.[66] Just as the Hobbesian war of all against all never altogether disappears from the social field, but keeps sustaining the order of the state, ready to re-emerge at appropriate occasions, so the wars of Chaos sustain the order of the cosmos, fuelling it with its "dark materials". In that respect, the strange and distant law of the unchartered regions of Chaos turns out to be closely connected to the official divine order. Their relation resembles what Deleuze and Guattari describe as the sometimes mutually supportive, sometimes conflictual connection between the state apparatus and the nomadic war machine.[67] In Milton's infinite spaces, order and disorder entwine and contaminate each other. Thus *Paradise Lost* affirms the Christian cosmos, but posits it in a decentred space of latent potentials, in which its place and the conditions of creation must be renegotiated.

pp. 586–587; and Alexander Pope, "The Dunciad" and "Windsor Forest", in *The Poems: A One-Volume Edition of the Twickenham Text with Selected Annotations,* ed. John Butt, New Haven, CT and London: Yale University Press, 1963, pp. 317–459 and p. 210 [414 ff.].

66 See Giorgio Agamben, *Homo Sacer: Sovereign Power and Bare Life*, trans. Daniel Heller-Roazen, Stanford, CA: Stanford University Press, 1998, pp. 35–36. Werner Hamacher, "Wilde Versprechen: Die Sprache *Leviathan*", in *Die Ordnung des Versprechens*, ed. Manfred Schneider, Munich: Wilhelm Fink, 2005, pp. 192–193. See also Andrés Rosler, "Odi et Amo? Hobbes on the State of Nature", in *Hobbes Studies* 24 (2011), pp. 91–111.

67 For example, while the state apparatus imposes its preconceived forms on matter, the nomad war machine develops them out of the inherent dynamics of its materials. See Gilles Deleuze and Félix Guattari, *A Thousand Plateaus*, trans. Brian Massumi, Minneapolis and London: University of Minnesota Press, 2005, pp. 351–423.

5 The eternal word of creation and the regimens of heaven

5.1 God's codings and overcodings

Milton's genesis narrative contains many lacunae: apart from a few suggestive remarks, God's creation of heaven and the angels is not described. The angels themselves have no memory of their own origin, and their divine creation therefore must function as an article of faith among them (5.809–895). The only extensive description of God's creative activities concerns the generation of the earthly cosmos in the seventh book, which occurs after the war in heaven is over. However, the monist metaphysical scheme of the epic strongly suggests that the creation of the heavens must have been accomplished through similar methods as that of earth. And, in conformity with the Bible, Milton's God creates the earth by means of a differentiating force that is both verbal and corporeal, a power in which language and matter are intimately entwined. Angela Esterhammer has outlined the peculiarities of this generative act with the help of Austinian speech act theory. And even though some of her assertions remain problematic,[1] she makes some excellent points. One of them concerns the circumstance that the Miltonian creation of the cosmos starts with the production of univocity.[2] Milton describes Chaos not only as warfare, but also as verbal strife, a "universal hubbub" of discordant voices (e.g. 2.951; 3.710). So the first act of cosmic creation is the establishment of an obedient silence by commanding the nearby roarings and exclamations of Chaos to hush by means of the "omnific Word": "Silence, ye troubled waves, and thou deep, peace,/ Said then the omnific Word, your discord end" (7.216–217). It is only in the ensuing stillness – the silencing of dissonant voices within earshot – that the word of God can resound. The first cosmos-building performative turns out to subtract from the world, rather than add to it. The zone which has thus been pacified is afterwards delimited and ordered by means of divine utterances that are similar to sociopolitical performative

1 See the review of the book by Terence Allan Hoagwood in the *Modern Language Review* 91.4 (October 1996), pp. 974–976.

2 Angela Esterhammer, *Creating States: Studies in the Performative Language of John Milton and William Blake*, Toronto: University of Toronto Press, 1994, p. 104.

speech acts.[3] After God has marked off his territory, he proceeds to introduce internal differentiations into it. By his active word, God thus imposes a system of opposites onto the pre-existent, chaotic matter.[4] Having separated the cosmos from Chaos, he divides light from darkness, dry land from the sea, day from night, and so forth, by designating these distinctions. God creates the world not so much by construction as by separation, "by his divorcing command" (*The Doctrine and Discipline and Divorce*, *CPW* 2:273). Sanford Budick has pointed out that these operations mirror Milton's own poetic and poetological operations, instigated by the "dividing Muse".[5] Esterhammer likewise suggests an analogy between God's work and Milton's work; however, in this context, the limits of a certain use of speech act theory become apparent: instead of really clarifying the relation between sacralized words and actions in *Paradise Lost*, this application of the theory merely assimilates the mystery of divine power with the mystery of poetic creativity.[6] Instead, it might be more instructive to describe the operations that God uses to form a world as "codings" of Chaos, in the sense in which Gilles Deleuze and Félix Guattari use the term. In *Anti-Oedipus* and *A Thousand Plateaus*, coding is described as the most basic operation by which a stable order of determinable things within space and time can establish itself. It encompasses not only speech, but also the full spectrum of semiotic and epistemic operations in the material world.[7]

Deleuze and Guattari incorporate Austin's speech act theory into their own reflections on language, but use a different terminology which allows them to explain the palpable and impalpable effects of utterances in greater detail. According to them, the basic unit of language is the "order word" (*mot d'ordre*): both a command and a password.[8] Order words effect "incorporeal transformations"; for example, a verdict by a law court turns a defendant into a convict; and saying "I do" at a marriage ceremony turns a fiancé into a spouse. In any assemblage of forces, these incorporeal transformations are linked with material processes on which they rely and which they regulate: a policeman applies handcuffs and leads the convict to jail; rings are exchanged. Codings and decodings are always involved in these processes, as well as the transformation of territories (i.e. deterritorializations and reterritorializations). In this context, Deleuze and Guattari use the word "code" to designate an order

3 Esterhammer, *Creating States*, p. 89.

4 Esterhammer, *Creating States*, p. 111.

5 Sanford Budick, *The Dividing Muse: Images of Sacred Disjunction in Milton's Poetry*, New Haven, CT: Yale University Press, 1985, pp. 114–121.

6 See Terence Hoagwood's review in the *Modern Language Review*, pp. 974–976.

7 See esp. Gilles Deleuze and Félix Guattari, *Anti-Oedipus: Capitalism and Schizophrenia*, trans. Robert Hurley, Helen R. Lane and Mark Seem, Minneapolis: University of Minnesota Press, 1983, pp. 139–222. See also Gilles Deleuze and Félix Guattari, *A Thousand Plateaus*, trans. Brian Massumi, Minneapolis and London: University of Minnesota Press, 2005, pp. 40–74.

8 Gilles Deleuze and Félix Guattari, *Mille Plateaux*, Paris: Éditions de Minuit, 1980, pp. 95–139. Deleuze and Guattari, *A Thousand Plateaus*, pp. 75–110.

of distinctions regulating the possible connections between bodies.[9] The convict as well as the new spouse will have to accommodate themselves to other codes in their respective new milieus after the incorporeal transformation. Deleuze and Guattari go beyond Austin's theory by pointing out that language use always has the tendency to "overcode" i.e. engage in "second-degree coding".[10] By imposing the codes that are associated with it, language is set up as the sustaining medium that expresses all codes and therefore dominates them as their origin.[11] The notion that God brings the world into being by his primordial word is an obvious example of this tendency.

Codings, by persistently drawing distinctions within the flow of processes, solidify boundaries and introduce discontinuities (for example, the distinctions between subject and object). In this way, stratified, "molar" forms are generated. Thus, the code organizes the raw materials of experience into determinable bodies to which a univocal name can be ascribed.[12] Frequently, these operations of coding are also designated as "inscriptions".[13] By inscribing persistent boundaries onto and into the shifting altercations of Chaos, God's works establish a primordial form of stable social order; and he also generates identities by this homogenizing coding, conferring personhood on his creatures.[14]

Since these acts of ordering and designating are so intimately entwined with the creation of all things, it stands to reason that the true name of a thing approximates its essence. This might partly explain the narrator's insistence on names and naming in *Paradise Lost*[15] and the abundance of etymological arguments in the *Doctrina Christiana* (e.g. "naturam nate se fatetur"; *DC* 24). In a tractate that criticizes one of Milton's last political treatises, James Harrington reproaches the author for his fixation on words:

> [Y]ou are very solicitous about words as if they were charms, or had more in them than what they signify: For no conjurer's devil is more concerned in a spell than you in a mere word, but never regard the things which it serves to express.[16]

9 Deleuze and Guattari, *A Thousand Plateaus*, pp. 335, 352.

10 Félix Guattari, *The Anti-Oedipus Papers*, trans. Kélina Gotman, ed. Stéphane Nadaud, New York: Semiotext(e); and Cambridge, MA: MIT Press, 2006, p. 416.

11 Deleuze and Guattari, *A Thousand Plateaus*, pp. 62–63.

12 Deleuze and Guattari, *Anti-Oedipus*, p. 144.

13 Deleuze and Guattari, *Anti-Oedipus*, pp. 141–145. See also Gregory Flaxman, *Gilles Deleuze and the Fabulation of Philosophy: Powers of the False, Vol. 1*, Minneapolis and London: University of Minnesota Press, 2012, p. 56; and Ian Buchanan, *Deleuze and Guattari's* Anti Oedipus*: A Reader's Guide*, London and New York: Continuum, 2008, p. 92.

14 See e.g. Deleuze and Guattari, *Anti-Oedipus*, p. 160.

15 This topic is treated extensively in John Leonard, *Naming in Paradise: Milton and the Language of Adam and Eve*, Oxford: Clarendon Press, 1990.

16 James Harrington, *The Censure of the Rota upon Mr. Milton's Book, Intitled* The Ready and Easy Way to Establish a Free Commonwealth etc., London: Paul Giddy, 1660, cited in the appendix of John Milton, *The Ready and Easy Way to Establish a Free Commonwealth*, ed.

When the reader is confronted with the lengthy lists of names for mythical or historical places and persons that are spread all over *Paradise Lost* (see e.g. 1.376–521; 4.268–287; 11.385–411), the impression imposes itself that these names are not merely arbitrary ascriptions, accumulated for the sheer beauty of their sound, but that they express and perpetuate the essence of the designated things, according to God's will. Exemplary for such a form of verbal genesis "from the void and formless infinite" (3.12) is God's second act after he has established the silence of the deep: he starts creating "this world" by demarcating its boundaries, physically drawing the distinction between its inside and its outside and safeguarding this distinction by a divine order:

> He took the golden compasses, prepared
> In God's eternal store, to circumscribe
> This universe, and all created things:
> One foot he centred, and the other turned
> Round through the vast profundity obscure,
> And said, Thus far extend, thus far thy bounds,
> This be thy just circumference, O world.
> (7.225–231)

Significantly, immediately after circumscribing his territory, God proceeds to address it by name with a command, as if its demarcation also entailed its subjectivation and submission. The subsequent homogenizing codings establish categorical dichotomies such as light and darkness, male and female, rational and irrational, owner and property. One term of the two tends to be privileged, but the dichotomization itself is more decisive than the hierarchy. By inscribing borders and thus marking off bodies, addressable unities and territories are constituted.[17] God's creative process thus establishes an enormous network of cosmic dichotomies. In his work, Milton was a vocal proponent of Ramist logic; he frequently referred to Pierre de la Ramée and his works, structured the *Doctrina Christiana* ramistically,[18] and even wrote (i.e. translated and partly re-wrote) a separate book on the subject.[19] The claim of Ramist logic to organize the whole of knowledge in binaries was often seen as an ontological rather than an epistemological achievement: its sentences were taken to be divinely prescriptive rather than descriptive.[20] Some English Ramists claimed that Ramus had worked out the order of ideas in the mind

Evert Mordecai Clark, New Haven, CT: Yale University Press, London: Humphrey Milford and Oxford: Oxford University Press, 1915, p. 179.

17 See also Deleuze and Guattari, *Anti-Oedipus*, p. 144.

18 See John K. Hale and J. Donald Cullington, "Preface", in *DC*, pp. lv–lxii.

19 John Milton, *A Fuller Course in the Art of Logic Conformed to the Method of Peter Ramus*, *CPW* 8: 208–407.

20 Walter J. Ong, *Ramus, Method, and the Decay of Dialogue: From the Art of Discourse to the Art of Reason*, Chicago: University of Chicago Press, 2004, pp. 189, 207.

of God and that the world was just its material counterpart.[21] All forms of reason derive from divine reason, which actively structures the universe by its dichotomies. Accordingly, the structuring *diakosmesis* of Milton's God must be understood as a political and law-positing act of "Landnahme" and power redistribution.[22] It involves the constitution of a territory, an action that Deleuze and Guattari call "territorialization".[23]

When God codes in this way, it is never without inscribing himself into the code as its origin: he not only draws distinctions, but he also signs them by adding a mark that it is he who drew them, so that all codes refer to him as their creator (*DC* 24/25). Hence, his coding involves an overcoding which integrates the different codes and gives them a common denominator in the divine word and the divine body, the unified subject-substance that subtends and dominates them all, saturating and re-constituting itself by their domination.[24] All things are ascribed their place in relation to this body which is posited as an entity that transcends them as their (quasi-)cause.[25] One of his most important methods of overcoding is the imposition of a point of transcendence onto the coded territory. The sovereign spaces of *Paradise Lost* are constituted accordingly: God tends to establish territories with clear frontiers that are structured by and around an eminent centre that represents his power: within Chaos, he establishes the domineering bulwark of heaven; and within heaven, he posits his throne as his centre of command, at the most elevated place. After the fall of the apostate angels, he creates the cosmos at heaven's periphery, within which the earth, as the breeding ground of man, is possibly not the central, but certainly the domineering globe from which heaven shall be replenished. On earth, the most important and most elevated spot is Paradise, the seat of man, the world's ruler; and in the midst of Paradise, we find at its highest elevation the tree of life, next to the tree of knowledge, representing the law of God.[26] In the subsequent chapters, it will be shown more extensively that all these encapsulated command centres function as places of alleged transcendence, from which the rest of the territory is overcoded. They do not constitute a logical proof of the divine supremacy, however, and Satan can still doubt God's transcendence; but the signs are there for everyone to read.

21 Perry Miller and Thomas Herbert Johnson, "Introduction", in *The Puritans: A Sourcebook of Their Writings*, Mineola and New York: Dover, 2001, p. 31.

22 See e.g. F. M. Cornford, *From Religion to Philosophy: A Study in the Origins of Western Speculation*, Princeton, NJ: Princeton University Press, 1991, p. 27. See also Carl Schmitt, *The Nomos of the Earth in the International Law of the Jus Publicum Europaeum*, trans. G. L. Ulmen, New York: Telos Press, 2003, pp. 67–100.

23 See. e.g. Gilles Deleuze and Guattari, *What is Philosophy?*, pp. 67–70.

24 Deleuze and Guattari, *A Thousand Plateaus*, p. 62. See also Mark Bonta and John Protevi, *Deleuze and Geophilosophy: A Guide and Glossary*, Edinburgh: Edinburgh University Press, 2006, p. 122.

25 On the notion of quasi-cause, see Deleuze and Guattari, *Anti-Oedipus*, pp. 10, 194.

26 The Book of Genesis already places the fatal trees in the centre of Paradise. See Gen. 2.8–10.

Interlocking and mutually re-enforcing series of overcodings such as these assign to all things a role that they must play.[27] By ordering a delimited section of Chaos and prescribing codes for it, God has already established a law, a "nomos", insofar as "nomos" originally designates an "exercise of power within spatial or departmental boundaries".[28] "The *nomos* as customary, unwritten law is inseparable from a distribution of space, a distribution in space".[29] Referencing Nietzsche and Claude Lévi-Strauss, Deleuze and Guattari assert that acts of coding not only create identities and territories, but also "distribute prescriptions and prohibitions".[30] For the bodies that are formed by codings are formed "within the debtor-creditor relation":[31] every entity is marked as an investment of God, indebting the creature defined – and thus created – through the codes.[32] All bodies should be what the code says they are; and the divine law is nothing but the juridical form assumed by this debt.[33] Because its very being is at stake in these processes that correlate code, debt, law and form, the creature is endowed with the task of "endless gratitude" (4.52). God as the Great Creditor institutes an infinite debt of obeisance.[34] Insofar as this procedure is successful, he transforms the territory into a state, with himself as the sole ruler.[35] Consequently, throughout *Paradise Lost*, the Father not only claims the position of the creator, but also that of the supreme legislator, prosecutor, judge and jury. Indeed, the role of creator/procreator and that of the supreme judge blend seamlessly into each other, since both functions converge in the act of coding.[36] As Francis Bacon expresses it in another context: "[T]he same action of the mind which inventeth, judgeth".[37]

Since the epic leaves it doubtful whether God can be distinguished from all other beings on an ontological level, his transcendent supremacy must mainly manifest itself by his actions, namely the exercise of his supreme capacity to

27 Deleuze and Guattari, *A Thousand Plateaus*, p. 41.
28 F. M. Cornford, *From Religion to Philosophy*, p. 30.
29 Deleuze and Guattari, *A Thousand Plateaus*, p. 312.
30 Deleuze and Guattari, *Anti-Oedipus*, p. 301.
31 Deleuze and Guattari, *Anti-Oedipus*, p. 180.
32 Mark Bonta and John Protevi use a quote from Augustine's *Confessions* to illustrate this overcoding: "Even the milk of mothers' breasts comes from you, O Lord". See Bonta and Protevi, *Deleuze and Geophilosophy*, p. 70.
33 Deleuze and Guattari, *Anti-Oedipus*, p. 213.
34 For parallel constructions, see Deleuze and Guattari, *Anti-Oedipus*, p. 197.
35 Deleuze and Guattari designate rulers who aspire to thoroughly overcode the social field in order to saturate their absolute hegemony as "despots". See *Anti-Oedipus*, p. 198; and Bonta and Protevi, *Deleuze and Geophilosophy*, p. 122.
36 Similarly, in the *Doctrina Christiana*, Milton asserts that God is the "supreme father and judge of all"/ "summum patrem omnium et iudicem" (*DC* 952/953).
37 Francis Bacon, *The Advancement of Learning*, in *The Major Works*, ed. Brian Vickers, Oxford and New York: Oxford University Press, 2008, pp. 224–225.

create and freely dispose of his creation.[38] In a world whose creation has been accomplished and therefore come to an end, the Father can only manifest his power and thus assert his identity by the enforcement of his laws. This may explain the "permanent need to punish" that John Stachniewski has ascribed to Milton's God.[39] Since the active, combative forces of Chaos remain the raw material sustaining organized matter, the divine influence must constantly counteract creation's inherent resistance to its codes. The divine territories may always be undone and recuperated by "ancient Night" (2.986), as several protagonists of *Paradise Lost* point out (see e.g. 2.980–987; 3.723–732; 4.662–666). An internal tension is installed within creation, and this tension is intimately connected to the concept of nature. By God's word, an order of nature is implemented that is simultaneously a legal, social, religious and physical order; nature, however, also retains a constant tendency to become disorderly, an affinity to Chaos. As John Protevi puts it, "nature is the abstract machine of […] coding/overcoding/decoding. There is a double direction to […] nature, towards unity and towards dispersion, towards capture and towards escape".[40] It is by this double movement toward two opposite poles of creation that the divine trial of all natural things establishes itself.

Milton's God occasionally declares to feel bound by the law that he has established in creation. In two key situations, the Father explains that he will not change the process of nature: one of them was already introduced ("But longer in that Paradise to dwell,/ The law I gave to nature him forbids", 11.48–49), the other can be found in the third book where he insists on man's ineradicable capacity to move between two opposite poles of creation:

> I formed them free, and free they must remain,
> Till they enthrall themselves: I else must change
> Their nature, and revoke the high decree
> Unchangeable, eternal, which ordained
> Their freedom, they themselves ordained their fall.
> (3.124–128)

And in both cases it remains altogether unclear whether the reason for this refusal is his unwillingness or incapacity to change the law of nature. Earlier

38 His status as uncreated creator also seems to be the one distinctive trait of God's eternal dominion in the *Doctrina Christiana*. See Kent R. Lehnhof, "Deity and Creation in the *Christian Doctrine*", *Milton Quarterly* 35 (2001), p. 235.

39 John Stachniewski, *The Persecutory Imagination: English Puritanism and the Literature of Religious Despair*, Oxford: Clarendon Press, 1991, p. 374.

40 John Protevi, "The Organism as the Judgment of God: Aristotle, Kant and Deleuze on Nature (that is, on Biology, Theology and Politics)", in *Deleuze and Religion*, ed. Mary Bryden, London and New York: Routledge, 2001, p. 31. "Machine" is here to be understood as a process, rather than an object. On the term "abstract machine", see Deleuze and Guattari, *A Thousand Plateaus,* pp. 510–514.

theologians, such as St. Augustine, for example, were less reluctant to assume that God is above the law of nature. In *De Civitate Dei*, we read:

> Sicut ergo non fuit impossibile Deo, quas voluit, instituere; sic ei non est impossibile, in quidquid voluerit, quas instituit, mutare naturas.[41]
>
> So, just as it was not impossible for God to set in being natures according to his will, so it is afterwards not impossible for him to change those natures which he has set in being, in whatever way he chooses.[42]

In this respect, the relation of Milton's God to nature is more ambiguous, and hence he appears, once again, as a rather Hobbesian ruler. It has already been pointed out by some of his readers that the world of Hobbes seems to be structured by the strange coexistence of a state dominated by an absolute sovereign on the one hand and a natural state where such a domination remains doubtful on the other.[43] Hobbes not only contrasts, but also equates the rule of nature with the law of the state.[44] When the central natural law to obey the sovereign, is not kept, society tends to degenerate into the anarchic, violent state of nature, which is a war of all against all. Thus, nature seems to do double duty in the world of Hobbes: Chaos and commonwealth are intimately entwined, not only as mutually exclusive, but also as coexistent; one might even say that either state becomes inconsistent without the supposition of the other. And nature appears on both sides of the fence, connecting the two orders.[45] The use of the word "nature" covers up their inconsistencies and mutual dependencies, but also points them out, once one starts paying attention to it, in Milton as well as in Hobbes. In the shadow of allegory, Nature is persistently drawn in two opposite theologico-political directions, but this double drift does not subvert, but sustains the precarious order of Milton's world.

5.2 The celestial decree of gravity

The heaven of *Paradise Lost*, God's first statelike dominion, differs considerably from the traditional medieval version, first and foremost because it is not set in the medieval cosmos. According to the Aristotelian/Ptolemean

41 Augustine, *Der Gottesstaat/De Civitate Dei*, Vol. 2, trans. Carl Johann Perl, Paderborn: Ferdinand Schöningh, 1979, pp. 676–677 [21.8].

42 Augustine, *Concerning the City of God Against the Pagans*, trans. Henry Bettenson, London/New York: Penguin, 2003, p. 982.

43 See e.g. Giorgio Agamben, *Homo Sacer: Sovereign Power and Bare Life*, trans. Daniel Heller-Roazen, Stanford, CA: Stanford University Press, 1998, pp. 35–36. See also Werner Hamacher, "Wilde Versprechen: Die Sprache *Leviathan*", in *Die Ordnung des Versprechens*, ed. Manfred Schneider, Munich: Wilhelm Fink, 2005, pp. 171–198. See also Hobbes *Leviathan*, p. 244 [2.31.40].

44 Hobbes, *Leviathan*, p. 177 [2.26.8].

45 See Agamben, *Homo Sacer*, pp. 35–36; and Hamacher, "Wilde Versprechen", p. 192.

worldview, an unbounded and unmoved mover is posited at the world's periphery, enclosing endlessly circling, ethereal, spirit-driven spheres, which have the earth at their centre.[46] The divinity acts as the eternal centrifugal force, drawing the spheres towards himself and thus causing them to rotate.[47] Under him, objects are distributed naturally according to their lightness and weight, earth being the heaviest and therefore concentrated at the centre of the universe. When this worldview was taken up and varied by Christianity in Late Antiquity and the Middle Ages, it had received an ethical subtext. In Augustine's *Confessions*, we find a moralistic interpretation of weight:

> Corpus pondere suo nititur ad locum suum. pondus non ad ima tantum est, sed ad locum suum. ignis sursum tendit, deorsum lapis; ponderibus suis aguntur, loca sua petunt. oleum infra aquam fusum super aquam attollitur, aqua supra oleum fusa infra oleum demergitur; ponderibus suis aguntur, loca sua petunt. minus ordinata inquieta sunt; ordinantur et quiescunt. pondus meum amor meus; eo feror, quocumque feror. dono tuo accendimur et sursum ferimur; inardescimus et imus. ascendimus ascensiones in corde et cantamus canticum graduum. igne tuo, igne tuo bono inardescimus et imus, quoniam sursum imus ad pacem Hierusalem […].
>
> Our body with its weight strives toward its own place. Weight makes not downward only, but to its own place also. The fire mounts upward, a stone sinks downward. All things pressed by their own weight go towards their proper places. Oil poured in the bottom of the water, is raised above it: water poured upon oil, sinks to the bottom of the oil. They are driven by their own weights, to seek their own places. Things a little out of their places become unquiet: put them in their order again, and they are quieted. My weight is my love; by that am I carried, whithersoever I be carried. We are inflamed by thy gift and are carried upward: we wax hot within, and we go on. We ascend thy ways that be in our heart, and we sing a song of degrees; we glow inwardly with thy fire, with thy good fire, and we go, because we go upward to the peace of Jerusalem […].[48]

Similarly, at the end of Dante's *Comedia*, the will and desire of the narrator who has ascended outward through all the spheres attains a glimpse of God, and his will and desire start to rotate with "l'amor che move il sole e l'altre

46 See e.g. Julian B. Barbour, *The Discovery of Dynamics: A Study from a Machian Point of View of the Discovery and the Structure of Dynamical Theories*, Oxford: Oxford University Press, 2001, pp. 68–69.

47 Aristotle, *The Physics*, Vol. 2. trans. Philip H. Wicksteed and Francis Cornford, Cambridge, MA: Harvard University Press and London: Heinemann, 1963, pp. 405–425 [8.10]. See also id., *The Metaphysics*, Vol. 2, trans. Hugh Tredennick, Cambridge, MA: Harvard University Press and London: Heinemann, 1961, pp. 144–153 [12.7].

48 Augustine, *Confessions*, Vol. 2, trans. William Watts, London and New York: Macmillan, 1912, pp. 390–393 [13.9.10].

stelle".[49] Generally, rational creatures can either be attracted upward to God or downward to Satan, whom Dante places at the very centre of the universe, since his prodigious fall made him crash all the way down to the earth's core. Evil is thus represented as a centripetal force, opposed to the centrifuge of the good. At the end of time, the two contrary forces will have reached their respective *teloi*, and the upper and lower realm will be forever separated.

In *Paradise Lost*, a similar separation is envisaged for the end of time. But, since Milton's God has been transplanted into a chaotic, infinite universe, we are confronted with a spatial inversion: God is not placed, like a framing device, at the enclosing periphery of outer space, but into the midst of heaven qua midst of creation. The result is a theocentric universe whose most striking emblem is the splendid circumambulation of the angels around God's throne, of which Raphael narrates in the fifth book. That these motions take the form of a parade hints at the political structure of God's world: heaven is already a military society before Satan's fall, with the angels assembling before the throne of God in formation, sporting "[t]en thousand ensigns high advanced,/ Standards, and gonfalons twixt van and rear" (5.588–590). In these rallies, they are always arranged strictly according to rank "[o]f hierarchies, of orders, and degrees" (5.591), which "in heaven […] none neglects" (3.737–738). Their procession is explicitly compared to the movement of the spheres:

> That day, as other solemn days, they spent
> In song and dance about the sacred hill,
> Mystical dance, which yonder starry sphere
> Of planets and of fixed in all her wheels
> Resembles nearest, mazes intricate,
> Eccentric, intervolved, yet regular
> Then most, when most irregular they seem:
> And in their motions harmony divine […].
> (5.618–625)

This arrangement mirrors the cosmological developments of the sixteenth and seventeenth century: the society of heaven is structured like a heliocentric planetary system (and comparisons are constantly made in both directions). God, emanating light, force and order, sits immovably on his central throne, and the angels (even though they seem to have their own territories and seats elsewhere)[50] are busy circling around him, thus demonstrating their unwavering obedience and love for him. It might be worthwhile to systematically investigate parallels to the politics of the Sun King Louis XIV, Milton's

49 Dante, *Paradiso*, trans. Jean Hollander and Robert Hollander, New York: Random House, 2007, pp. 826/827 [33.145].

50 Satan, at least, has one (5.755–766).

contemporary and correspondent,[51] who kept his potentially unruly court occupied with state ritual and shufflings for position.[52]

A phantom image of medieval cosmology, however, also survives in Milton's world, causing space to fold in onto itself: the centre that God occupies is said to be not the lowest, but instead the highest point in the universe; the legal, hierarchical and physical eminence of God on his throne, "[h]igh throned above all height" (3.58), is constantly emphasized. Orientation toward the seat of God equals an upward movement; and the farther one is removed from God, the farther down one is located.[53] Milton, like Augustine, stresses the ethical dimension of these positionings: seamless transitions between spatial and moral elevations and downfalls characterize the text. Thus the new disposition of space entails a new disposition of morality, especially a new representation of evil: since God is situated in the centre – the place where the devil used to be in Dante's world – the abyss opens in the place the divine has vacated. Divine creation bathes in an illimitable Chaos; it therefore has a central and uppermost point, but it has no edge and no nadir. In Dante's world, every movement has an end point, either in an appropriate proximity to God or an appropriate location within Satan's estate; no one could fall lower than Satan whose waist eternally occupies the icy hub of the universe. Who tries to climb farther down from there, ends up rising up again.[54] Milton, however, makes visible the perspectives inherent in the post-Aristotelian world, which involve perpetual descents through infinite space and infinite time. When Satan starts to doubt God's legitimacy and physical superiority, he attempts to conquer the divine pinnacle: "[a]spiring/ To set himself in glory above his peers,/ He trusted to have equaled the most high" (1.38–40). As a result, he is "fallen, to disobedience fallen,/ And so from heaven to deepest hell" (5.541–542). But the establishment of a circumscribed hell, a nine-day-drop from heaven, is often hinted to be only provisional. The ways of goodness are restricted, but the rovings of evil are boundless: the good angels as well as the narrator declare on various occasions that the descending paths of the devils will find no end (see e.g. 2.561; 6.172–173). And Satan himself perceives his perdition as a bottomless fall (4.76–78). It has already been mentioned that the narrative indeed represents his fall in the "vast vacuity" (2.932) of Chaos as a potentially endless one. However, here the equation between ethical and physical lowness meets its limits: it has also been pointed out that Satan's encounter with the vacuum and his subsequent rescue from it (2.935–938)

51 Christophe Tournu, "Louis XIV", in *The Milton Encyclopedia*, ed. Thomas N. Corns, New Haven, CT: Yale University Press, 2012, p. 223.

52 See e.g. Peter Burke, *The Fabrication of Louis XIV*, New Haven, CT: Yale University Press, 1992.

53 For one, it would otherwise make no sense for God to say: "In heaven, or earth, or under earth in hell" (3.322).

54 See Dante, *Inferno*, trans. Jean Hollander and Robert Hollander, New York: Random House, 2000, pp. 630–633 [34.70–93].

is not described as a cosmic judgment, but rather as the contingent result of "ill chance" (2.935). A pervasive contingency makes itself felt in this way, but does not supersede God's absolutism; rather, it reinforces the Janus-faced legal structure of the his realm. Once again, Milton presents the reader with a peculiar compromise formation "between worlds and worlds" (5.268).

The divine kingdom of *Paradise Lost* is unusual in other respects, too: it is depicted as an absolutist state, first and foremost, but also as a landscape: Milton's heaven turns out to be less ethereal and more "natural" than most conventional representations. Instead of palatial cloud structures in which to sit down and play the harp,[55] we find a spacious and varied territory of "hill and dale" (6.641), equipped with diverse climates and life forms. "[G]ems, and gold" (6.475), "rocks, waters, woods" (6.645), diverse fruit-bearing trees (5.426–428) and even animals (6.391) are present in the realm beyond the pearly gates – while Aquinas extensively denied that there might be a place in heaven for any creature except for men and angels.[56] And it also appears that the semi-autonomous, dynamic processes of Nature are very much at work in Milton's heaven. Heaven is personified as female, active and organic ("Disburdened heaven rejoiced, and soon repaired/ Her mural breach", 6.878–879); and what Satan says about the workings of a dark, natural force within it is also subsequently borne out:

> Which of us who beholds the bright surfáce
> Of this ethereous mould whereon we stand,
> This continent of spacious heav'n, adorned
> With plant, fruit, flower ambrosial, gems and gold,
> Whose eye so superficially surveys
> These things, as not to mind from whence they grow
> Deep under ground, materials dark and crude,
> Of spiritous and fiery spume, till touched
> With heaven's ray, and tempered they shoot forth
> So beauteous, op'ning to the ambient light.
> These in their dark nativity the deep
> Shall yield us, pregnant with infernal flame [...].
> (6.472–483)

According to this statement, the process of Nature prevails in heaven, in the form of an ongoing creative intercourse between the light (connoted divine and male) and dark, spontaneously responsive elements (connoted chaotic and female). And this reference to a sexualized and generative activity of

55 See e.g. Jeffrey Burton Russell, *A History of Heaven: The Singing Silence*, Princeton, NJ: Princeton University Press, 1997, p. 113.

56 Thomas Aquinas, *Summa Theologica, Vol. 26: Suppl., 87–99*, trans. Dominicans and Benedictines of Germany and Austria, Heidelberg: Kerle and Cologne: Styria, 1961, pp. 449–452 [Summa 3, Quaestio 91, Art. 5].

the celestial raw materials is not a satanic misinterpretation: Raphael also refers to the dark elements as to the "originals of Nature in their crude/ Conception" (6.511–512; capitalization added). Delivered before their time, they support Satan's war, providing gunpowder for his cannons. Thus, the energies of Chaos are still discernible within empyreal Nature and can be extracted from it; this is another characteristic of heaven that makes it look not only secondary, but also eminently vulnerable. Just like God himself, the land of heaven seems to be split: on the one hand, it is a work of God, freely differentiating according to his omnipotent will; on the other hand, it is the unstable result of a conflictual process: the workings of Nature, situated at the border between darkness and light, order and disorder.

It seems that there is not much getting in the way of Nature in heaven: there do not seem to be any celestial cities, for example; even houses are apparently sparse. When the Father calls his dispersed angels, they are to be found in "their blissful bowers/ Of amarantine shade, fountain or spring,/ By the waters of life" (11.077–079). Even God himself has taken his abode not in a temple, but on a mountain. Apart from heaven's ramparts with its pearly gates, Satan's palace is the only heavenly building that Milton mentions, and devilish Mulciber the only angelic architect. In that respect, Milton's heaven does not at all resemble the representation of heaven-on-earth in the biblical Apocalypse: John's "celestial Jerusalem" is thoroughly urban, a gigantic city in cubic form, constantly illumined and temperature-controlled (Rev. 22). The heaven of *Paradise Lost* rather suggests the Greco-Roman afterlife with its Elysian fields; and God's mountain similarly recalls Mount Olympus on which Zeus resides, nourished by ambrosia. Accordingly, "Elisian" (3.359) and "ambrosial" (2.245; 5.427; 6.475) flowers are said to be found within the confines of heaven. Encouraging the association, the Father occasionally addresses the angels as "gods", as if they constituted a pantheon (3.341).

There is still another aspect in which Milton's heaven appears to be "naturalized", and it is connected with Milton's monism: all things celestial, including the angels, are clearly marked as material entities.[57] They therefore can all be destroyed. While the angels do not die a natural death, God is able to punish them with utter annihilation (see e.g. 6.853–855). And they are also equipped with some sort of digestion, for God feeds them during festivities (5.632–641), and Raphael points out that they do need the nourishment (5.407–409). Palpable food, however, is apparently not absolutely necessary to them, for they can undertake feats such as journeys of many days through Chaos (2.129–134; 8.229–234) or ceaseless watches on barren planets (5.587–588), seemingly without provisions. Perhaps they are endowed with the capacity to constantly absorb the subtle, ethereal matter or proto-matter that surrounds them; that would also explain why the devils (except for

57 Stephen M. Fallon, *Milton Among the Philosophers: Poetry and Materialism in Seventeenth-Century England*, Ithaca, NY: Cornell University Press, 1991, p. 195.

ever-hungry Death) seem to be surprisingly unconcerned about the apparent lack of foodstuff in hell. But however these mysteries are to be understood, the circumstances contribute to the impression that life in heaven is only gradually, but not essentially different from life on earth.

5.3 Grotius and the world's final aim

While the natural processes in the circumscribed territory of heaven proceed, so too does God's administrative work of coding. He imposes his own forms upon these processes, and this imposition has both a generative and a juridical side. By generating a celestial day and a dusky celestial night, for example, he also asserts that diurnal and nocturnal activities should be kept separate until further notice and that night should be used for rest:

> Now when ambrosial night with clouds exhaled
> From that high mount of God, whence light and shade
> Spring both, the face of brightest heaven had changed
> To grateful twilight (for night comes not there
> In darker veil) and roseate dews disposed
> All but the unsleeping eyes of God to rest [...].
> (5.642–647)

It is Satan who keeps transgressing this implicit commandment, repeatedly engaging in night-time activities such as the nocturnal decampment of his troops (5.700–701). In that sense, all of God's acts of creation are also judgments, additionally providing the opportunity for further judgments, since they keep indebting his creatures. The divine act of creation in itself entails imposing an obligation on the created, since they owe their existence to God (see e.g. 4.52–57; see also *Paradise Regained* 3.122–129). They can pay off parts of this infinite debt in the form of obedience and praise. That is not only their duty, but also their essential purpose: according to the *Doctrina Christiana*, God creates heaven and the cosmos "in order to make manifest the glory of his power and goodness" ("ad patefaciendam potentiae, et bonitatis suae gloriam", *DC* 280/281). For confirmation, Milton can refer to several passages in the Bible, among them Job 40.25–41.26, which insinuates that God created living beings mainly to demonstrate his supremacy over them. Creation, in order to justify its existence, must constantly acknowledge its divine origins, thus referring itself back to God.

However, the creatures also have the option to act against his divine will by disobedience. The double creation myth that has been sketched suggests that this disobedient counterforce is ascribable to creation's inherent and acknowledged tendency to revert back to the decoded proto-elements of Chaos. But this is not the official doctrine; instead, free will, and its potential to stray from the straight and narrow path, are presented as God's own gift. Thus the forces of Chaos and Nature are subsumed under his divine will, for they are declared not to be a delimiting disturbance of his omnipotence, but rather a concession he himself has granted. This reframing allows the Father to lay a convincing claim to a monopoly on reality. As a result, the metaphysical problem of the disordering counterforce and of its origin (which the epic leaves undecided) is turned into an ethical question. It is symptomatic that the assertion of creaturely free will is always coupled with an assertion of creaturely accountability, the angelic and human capacity to stand in judgment. Every act is subject to the codices of God, to be judged according to its compliance with the divine will. Basically, the self-aware creatures are ascribed the task to close the gap between the processes of nature and the process of divine satisfaction. Since God expressly demands a constant obedience to the divine law as a debt that is due to him, freedom in this context can only be understood in a proto-Kantian way, that is, as a vanishing mediator that is experienced almost exclusively in its sacrificial surrender.[58] Heaven turns out to be a constant trial; as Richard Strier expresses it, celestial life is "based on tests of sincerity and obedience".[59]

Some of his creatures fail these tests, and it is striking that God appears to take pleasure in the these failures. Angels and devils alike are occasionally saddened by the transgressions and by the subsequent damnations that befall God's creatures (see e.g. 1.604–621; 10.17–25), but God himself seems to be always in good spirits. That he keeps executing his juridical office with passion becomes most obvious when he conveys his verdicts in the form of grumpy outbursts (3.96–99) or of sneering slights, tinged with sarcasm (6.715–719; 10.48–54; 11.84–98). He seems to find his joy not only in those who stand, but also in those who fall. In their own manner, these transgressors also contribute to his power: they keep legitimating the Father in his juridical role, for their crimes against his order demonstrate the necessity of his redemptive jurisdiction. So they contribute to the divine satisfaction that is the main reason for their existence. God himself suggests that the universe was created in order to be the abode of angels and humans, and asks about them:

> Not free, what proof could they have given sincere
> Of true allegiance, constant faith or love?
> Where only what they needs must do, appeared,
> Not what they would, what praise could they receive?
> What pleasure I from such obedience paid,
> When will and reason (reason also is choice)
> Useless and vain, of freedom both despoiled,
> Made passive both, had served necessity,

58 See Immanuel Kant, *Kritik der praktischen Vernunft/Grundlegung zur Metaphysik der Sitten*, ed. Wilhelm Weischedel, Frankfurt am Main: Suhrkamp, 1974. See also Sanford Budick, *Kant and Milton*, Cambridge, MA: Harvard University Press, 2010.

59 Richard Strier, "Milton's Fetters, or, Why Eden is Better Than Heaven", *Milton Studies* 38:1 (2000), p. 184.

> Not me. They therefore as to right belonged,
> So were created […].
>
> (3.103–112)

God here not only affirms that his own pleasure is the aim for which heaven and earth were created; he also connects this pleasure to the legal and ethical right that must determine creation. In his first *Defence*, Milton accordingly asserts with Cicero that the divine will "commands what is right and forbids what is wrong".[60] But has God established this particular heavenly and natural order because the order is good in itself, or is this order good *per definitionem*, because God wills it? In the first case, God seems to be restricted in his decision-making, hence not truly sovereign; in the second case, his legal order would be indistinguishable from mere divine caprice. An old problem of theodicy articulates itself in this context, and it is not solved, but merely obfuscated, by the prevalent supposition that God, the Good and the Natural all harmonize perfectly.[61] The faithful angel Abdiel proclaims that "God and Nature bid the same" (6.176; capitalization added), and the proclamation echoes in the prose works, in which Milton likewise asserts that "the law of God does exactly agree with the law of nature".[62] Sometimes, Milton almost sounds like a Thomist, for example when he stipulates "the peculiar sway of nature, which also is God's working" (*CPW* 2:363).[63] However, his treatments of the matter lean more heavily on Hugo Grotius to whom he often refers (see e.g. *CPW* 2:234, 2:238). In Grotius' attempts to reconcile natural and revealed law (as well as voluntarism and rationalism), one finds the same aporias and very similar attempts at solutions as in Milton's theology. Grotius identifies revealed law as "volitional divine law" and emphasizes that "God does not will a thing because it is lawful, but that thing [becomes] lawful – that is obligatory – because God wills it".[64] He contrasts this "volitional divine law" with

60 John Milton, *A Defence of the People of England*, *CPW* 4.1:383.

61 See e.g. Stanley E. Fish, *Surprised by Sin: The Reader in* Paradise Lost, Cambridge, MA: Harvard University Press, 1997, pp. 82–87.

62 Milton, *A Defence of the People of England*, *CPW* 4.1:422.

63 First and foremost in the divorce tractates, Milton emphasizes the ultimate convergence of reason, divine law and natural law, and uses this assertion as an argument with which to question the literal meaning of scripture. For example, despite Matthew 19 and Mark 10, divorce of incompatible spouses must be lawful, since God demands of us nothing that is against our nature; at the heart of it all, there is "a law not only written by Moses, but charactered in us by nature, of more antiquity and deeper ground than marriage itself; which law is to force nothing against the faultless proprieties of nature" (*Doctrine of Divorce*, *CPW* 2:237; spelling modernized). Unnatural laws are always man-made, never divine; Milton even speaks of "the fundamental law book of nature; which Moses never thwarts, but reverences" (*CPW* 2:272). Mosaic law is supposed to be compatible with the gospel, and both are "grounded on [the] moral reason" of natural law (*CPW* 2:264). See also Jason P. Rosenblatt, "Milton, Natural Law, and Toleration", in *Milton and Toleration*, eds. Sharon Achinstein and Elizabeth Sauer, Oxford and New York, Oxford University Press, 2007, p. 136.

64 Hugo Grotius, *On the Law of War and Peace*, trans. Francis Kelsey, Cambridge and New York: Cambridge University Press, 2012, p. 33.

natural law, which is known to man by his innate tendencies and by reason. Ultimately, the distinction turns out to be unsustainable, though: natural law is also a divine law, since God created it, and divine law is also reasonable:

> Et haec jam alia juris origo eft praeter illam naturalem, veniens scilicet ex libera Dei voluntate, cui nos subjici debere intellectus ipse noster nobis irrefragabiliter dictat. Sed et illud ipsum de quo egimus naturale jus, sive illud sociale, sive quod laxius ita dicitur, quamquam ex principiis homini internis profluit, Deo tamen asscribi merito potest, quia ut talia principia in nobis existerent ipse voluit […].[65]
>
> Herein, then, is another source of law besides the source in nature, that is, the free will of God, to which beyond all cavil our reason tells us we must render obedience. But the law of nature of which we have spoken, comprising alike that which relates to the social life of man and that which is so called in a larger sense, proceeding as it does from the essential traits implanted in man, can nevertheless rightly be attributed to God, because of His having willed that such traits exist in us.[66]

The problem is, however, that this divine law of nature is most emphatically not volitional, as was already pointed out in the first chapter; in Grotius' work, the natural law also restricts God so that he cannot change it:

> Ius naturale est dictatum rectam rationis indicans, actui alicui, ex ejus convenientia aut disconvenientia cum ipsa natura rationali, inesse moralem turpitudinem aut neccesitatem moralem, ac consequenter ab auctore naturae Deo talem actum aut vetari aut praecipi. Actus de quibus tale exstat dictatum, debiti sunt aut illiciti per se, atque ideo a Deo necessario praecepti aut vetiti intelliguntur: qua nota distat hoc jus non ab humano tantum jure, sed et a divino voluntario, quod non ea praecipit aut vetat, quae per se ac suapte natura aut debita sunt aut illicita, sed vetando illicita, praecipiendo debita facit. […] Est autem jus naturale adeo immutabile ut ne a Deo quidem mutari queat. Quanquam enim immensa est Dei potentia, dici tamen quaedam possunt ad quae se illa non extendit […].[67]
>
> The law of nature is a dictate of right reason, which points out that an act, according as it is or is not in conformity with rational nature, has in it a quality of moral baseness or moral necessity; and that, in consequence, such an act is either forgiven or enjoined by the author of nature, God. The acts in regard to which such a dictate exists are, in themselves, either obligatory or not permissible, and so it is understood that necessarily they

65 Hugo Grotius, *De jure belli ac pacis: Libri tres, in quibus jus naturae et gentium, item juris publici praecipua explicantur*, Amsterdam: Joan Blaeu, 1646, Prolegomena, 5^{r}.
66 Grotius, *On the Law of War and Peace*, p. 4
67 Grotius, *De jure belli ac pacis,* p. 4.

> are enjoined or forbidden by God. In this characteristic, the law of nature differs not only from human law, but also from volitional divine law; for volitional divine law does not enjoin or forbid those things which in themselves and by their own nature are obligatory or not permissible, but by forbidding things it makes them unlawful, and by commanding things it makes them obligatory. […] The law of nature, again, is unchangeable – even in the sense that it cannot be changed by God. Measureless as is the power of God, nevertheless, it can be said that there are certain things over which that power does not extend […].[68]

But if God is dominated by a natural law that frames and restricts his actions, he seems not to be indispensable for the workings of nature. Francis Oakley indeed asserts that *De jure belli ac pacis* leaves a door open through which atheism will subsequently be able to enter and occupy natural law theory.[69] Grotius points out this tendency of his theory himself:

> Et haec quidem quae iam diximus, locum aliquem haberent etiamsi daremus, quod sine summo scelere dari nequit, non esse Deum, aut non curari ab eo negotia humana.[70]
>
> What we have been saying would have a degree of validity even if we should concede that which cannot be conceded without the utmost wickedness: that there is no God, or that the affairs of men are of no concern to Him.[71]

Thus Grotius claims to reconcile natural and revealed law, but fails to achieve a true synthesis between them; instead, he seems to be caught in a *circulus vitiosus*, in which the one keeps referring to the other as to its true foundation.[72]

The same quandary of a Janus-faced law can also be found in Milton. Stanley Fish's supposition that the tension between voluntarism and naturalism in Milton's work is always resolved in favour of the former is to be regarded as doubtful.[73] The question remains open, and it must remain open if the flexible debt relation between the monist God and his creatures is to be sustained. God does not fail to exploit the resultant uncertainty, since it gives him a remarkable leeway in his actions. For example, by vaguely referring to a "justice" that is not under his will (3.210), he can suggest that the legal

68 Grotius, *On the Law of War and Peace*, p. 29.

69 Francis Oakley, *Natural Law, Laws of Nature, Natural Rights: Continuity and Discontinuity in the History of Ideas*, New York: Continuum, 2005, pp. 66–67.

70 See Grotius, *De jure belli ac pacis*, p. iii.

71 Grotius, *On the Law of War and Peace*, p. 4.

72 For a similar estimation, see e.g. Jon Parkin, *Science, Religion and Politics in Restoration England: Richard Cumberland's* De Legibus Naturae, Woodbridge: Royal Historical Society/Boydell Press, 1999, p. 59.

73 See e.g. Fish, *Surprised by Sin*, p. 256, et passim. See also William Walker, "On Reason, Faith, and Freedom in *Paradise Lost*", *Early Modern Literary Studies* 10:1 (2004): pp. 143–159.

system he upholds is not altogether arbitrary, while it is also acknowledged that his "just avenging ire" (7.184) may overstep its bounds and alight upon the innocent.

5.4 The holy ignorance of the angels

If God wants to retain his hegemonic role that is dependent upon his ambivalent status between immanence and transcendence, he cannot allow his creatures to learn too much about him and about the world in which he lives. And it is indeed easy to see that Milton's angels are remarkably ignorant about their environs, especially compared to the angels of Aquinas, who constantly and intuitively comprehend all of reality, infallibly and non-discursively.[74] From this ideal, Uriel, the "sharpest sighted spirit of all in heaven" (3.691), is far removed, as can be gleaned from the fact that he fails to recognize the disguised Satan, standing right in front of him. Raphael boasts that a superhuman amount of intuition guides the angelic host (5.486–490), but their intuition is not much in evidence. The angels tend to judge by the same outward, sensory appearances and signs of rank that are available to men. Uriel can only think of two ways in which the heavenly cherubs might gather information about Paradise and its inhabitants: by report and by direct experience of their visual sense (3.700–701). Even their the scope of their own prerogatives and competences often appears to escape the angels. For example, Raphael occasionally acts insecure in his conversation with Adam because he does not really know how much he is allowed to say about heaven (5.568–570). Nor are they better informed about their own origins than men; they must engage in speculations, as can be ascertained from the discussion between Satan and Abiel in the fifth book. While Abdiel insists that God created the angels, Satan advances the thesis that the angels generated themselves, as well as the thesis that they were generated by the Fates of heaven:

> That we were formed then sayest thou? […]
> Strange point and new!
> Doctrine which we would know whence learned: who saw
> When this creation was? Rememberst thou
> Thy making, while the maker gave thee being?
> We know no time when we were not as now;
> Know none before us, self-begot, self-raised
> By our own quickening power, when fatal course
> Had circled his full orb, the birth mature
> Of this our native heaven, ethereal sons.
>
> (5.853–5.863)

74 Thomas Aquinas, *Summa Theologiae Prima Pars, 50–119*, Latin/English Edition, trans. Laurence Shapcote, Lander, WY: Aquinas Institute, 2012, pp. 61–71 [Summa 1, Quaestio 58].

Satan counters the official political myth with a counter-myth. Since the original combines two mutually contradictory origin stories, the alternative version does the same: according to Satan, the angels' existence is due both to their own free (and apparently timeless and transcendent) will and to a cosmic law, prescribed by fate. On the one hand, he asserts that the angels autonomously begat themselves, supervising their own birth; on the other hand, he describes them as the result of a preordained, impersonal dynamism inherent within the celestial realm, whose traditional name is, of course, "Nature". The reference to an all-embracing Nature and to subjective autonomy are by Satan used as argumentative weapons in order to counter the claim of an existential liability toward God, but both references remain beholden to God insofar as they mimic the deity's own political strategy of self-empowerment. It is an appropriation of the Father's ideology that allows Satan to demand equal treatment from him and denounce the angels' subservience as unjust. When the upright angel Abdiel opposes this argumentation, he denies Satan the right to demand justice from God (echoing Romans 9.14–24): God is not bound to the law of his creatures, since he is the condition for their existence:

> Shalt thou give law to God, shalt thou dispute
> With him the points of liberty, who made
> Thee what thou art, and formed the powers of heaven
> Such as he pleased, and circumscribed their being?
> (5.822–825)

But the original reproach is not answered, but merely evaded by this counter-reproach, for even God's creative powers are doubtful in the heaven of *Paradise Lost*, and they are explicitly doubted by Satan. Abdiel accordingly tries another argument straightaway:

> Yet by experience taught we know how good,
> And of our good, and of our dignity
> How provident he is [...].
> (5.826–828)

The claim to know by experience that God is good, in this context, avoids the real question, for Abdiel's appraisal is not shared by Satan and a third of all the angels. The angels have no evidence of God's morally superior status; they can only believe in it.[75] No evidence of God's absolute, ontological superiority can be provided. In this context, it is worth noting that God's omniscience is occasionally doubted not only by the future devils, but also by the most upright angels. Satan believes that he can hide his rebellious schemes from God by ways of conspiratorial secrecy (5.682–683). This may be the symptom

75 Even Stanley Fish admits as much. Fish, *Surprised by Sin*, p. xxxv.

of a self-conceited delusion, inhibiting Satan's access to angelic intuition (as Stephen M. Fallon assumes).[76] But Abdiel, despite his own vauntings about divine omniscience (see e.g. 5.884–888), also assumes that Satan's plans must have escaped God: after fleeing the camp of Satan and reaching God's throne, Abdiel finds God's loyalists already assembled in arms; he "found/ Already known what he for news had thought/ To have reported" (6.19–21). Abdiel seems to have had a lapse of faith here; but this does not constitute a problem and is not imputed to him as a sin, as long as he rightly chooses the side that is going to be master in the field and maintain the dominion of heaven.

God's extremely restrictive information policy, which distributes revelation and even basic information very sparsely, sets the angelic rumour mill grinding: it is remarkable how important rumours, conjecture and hearsay remain in the heaven of *Paradise Lost*: Raphael, Satan, Abdiel, Gabriel and Uriel (as well as Adam and Eve) all must rely on second-hand information at one point or another. It even touches the narrator: the prevalent use of the Miltonic "or" suggests his insecurity, despite his frequent claim to be divinely inspired.[77] When all is said and done, the knowledge of the angels seems to be almost as limited as that of fallen humans. Transcendent theological and cosmological structures are not evident to them. The cherubs and seraphs are only temporarily equipped with supersensory knowledge, namely when God provides them directly and purposefully with information. This happens to Michael in the course of the eleventh and twelfth books ("As I shall thee enlighten", 11.115), just as it might happen to a human prophet. In the *Doctrina Christiana*, Milton says as much:

> Angeli boni non intuentur in Deo omnia, ut fingunt Papistae, sed tantum per revelationem ea quas visum est Deo, alia per eminentem quandam ratiocinationem.
>
> The good angels do not see into all things in respect of God, as the Papists imagine, but [see] only, through revelation, those things which God has decided to [reveal], and other things through a certain outstanding process of reasoning.
>
> (*DC* 350/351)

It thence seems fitting that Raphael in conversation with Adam obliquely but repeatedly hints at the fact that life in heaven is not as dissimilar from life on earth, and hence not as sublime, as his human interlocutor assumes. In those few passages in his report in which he really seems to be at a loss for words and is forced to convey his meanings by circumlocutions and metaphors, it is precisely not the utterly transcendent status of heavenly proceedings which is at issue, but rather the contrast between the angel's soldiering life of wars,

76 Fallon, *Milton Among the Philosophers*, p. 218.

77 P. C. Herman, "*Paradise Lost*, the Miltonic 'Or' and the Poetics of Incertitude", *Studies in English Literature 1500–1900* 43:1 (2003), pp. 181–211.

technology and politics and the private and paradisiacal life that his hearers Adam and Eve lead (see e.g. 6.73–76; 6.195–198; 6.311–315; 6.501–506).[78] All angelic claims to superior knowledge and a more spiritual, transcendent life can thus largely be reduced to vain boasting: the heavenly host is a body in a state of epistemological and existential uncertainty, just like Adam and Eve.

By constantly emphasizing their lack of power and comprehension, God efficiently conveys to the angels that they are insufficient and dependent on him. In the *Doctrina*, Milton approvingly quotes Job 4.18: God "imputes folly to his angels" ("angelis suis tribuit stultitiam", *DC* 346/347). Apparently, the resultant insecurity makes God's creatures all the more assertive and officious when they interact with each other. In their social relations, the angels seem to be hemmed in by what Empson has trenchantly described as the "timid, slavish mind" their position generates.[79] The angels are compelled to constantly act as mouthpieces for the higher orders in order to confirm their unanimity with the Father. And the more they have to rely on uncertain information in the process, the more officious they become. Abdiel may serve as an example here, but also Raphael, who narrates the official version of the earth's creation as if from direct experience, even though it later turns out that he was not present at the decisive events (8.228–231).

Where knowledge is lacking, zeal and authoritative gestures take its place. Most conversations of the angels are permeated by extensive evaluations of their interlocutor's religious credentials and behaviour (see e.g. 3.694–697; 4.833–946; 11.251–12.605). In a society that is characterized by these judgments, blissful angelic harmony does not seem to have been attained: in their interactions, the angels display a strict adherence to God's military and administrative codings, a certain corporate spirit, a formal politeness toward their peers and a constant subdued bickering and shuffling for position, but not much else. And the career of Abdiel (his zealous engagement for God apparently raises Abdiel from the rank of a foot soldier in Satan's regiments to a position "[a]mong the mightiest"; see 6.111–112) also indicates that the angels are not fixed in their positions, but may hope to be promoted, in other words to be elevated to a closer proximity to God, if their obedience is ostentatious enough.[80] Just like God and Satan, the angels appear vindictive, power-hungry and narcissistic even in their very gestures of humility. Beyond the facade of self-abnegation, a universal nervous narcissism is discernible, in which everyone is playing for the eye of the others, anxiously trying to be seen in a favourable and dignified light. During his narration of the war in heaven, for example, Raphael asserts that he does not want to list the countless

78 See also John Reichert, *Milton's Wisdom: Nature and Scripture in* Paradise Lost, Ann Arbor: University of Michigan Press, 1992, p. 126.

79 William Empson, *Milton's God*, Westport, CT: Greenwood Press, 1978, p. 111.

80 According to Milton's theology, this seems to involve an *imitatio dei*: the conception of "godliness" in his 1641 pamphlet *Of Reformation* includes the emulation of God: "likeness to God which in one word we call godliness" (*CPW* 1:571 spelling modernized).

names of the angelic heroes because those knightly cherubs are so saintly and modest that they "[s]eek not the praise of men" (6.376). However, among the four champion names he happens to mention, he does not fail to include his own (6.363). In the altercation between Satan and Gabriel's patrol, the angels prove as self-important and thin-skinned as the devil, falling into a vehement rage when their enemy doubts their military prowess and mocks them as servile underlings (4.970–980). Gabriel occasionally reprimands Satan:

> And thou sly hypocrite, who now wouldst seem
> Patron of liberty, who more than thou
> Once fawned, and cringed, and servilely adored
> Heaven's awful monarch? Wherefore but in hope
> To dispossess him, and thyself to reign?
> (4.957–961)

According to Empson, the epic suggests that Gabriel is not entirely free from the desire for accession he ascribes to Satan.[81] At the very least, the archangel's utterance demonstrates that such a hope for the ultimate advancement conceivably can be entertained by the inhabitants of heaven: since there is no manifest ontological gap between God and his creatures, at least some of the heavenly host can be led to believe that the barrier between the One and all the others might be surmountable. A tacit war of all against all still informs the social life of the heavens.

As an antidote, the mutual love and respect among the angels is repeatedly invoked (6.94–95; 8.620–629); yet these affections unfold within a context of divine love, according to the Augustinian ideal. That is, they love the other as a member of the heavenly community, enjoying their commonality in God.[82] As Hannah Arendt has pointed out, this form of love does not take into account the other as an individual being; the other is not loved for his or her own sake, but for the sake of the *gratia Dei*.[83] Arendt describes this affection as harshly circumscribed and degraded, since it is "a love which disowns the loved one as well as the lover".[84] Indeed, a certain debasement of the affective life seems prevalent in heaven, for any affection that could compete with that for God is *a priori* prohibited. Raphael's famous report on angelic sexuality seems to contradict this estimation and affirm a boundless mutual love among the heavenly creatures:

81 Empson, *Milton's God*, p. 111.

82 See e.g. Hannah Arendt, *Der Liebesbegriff bei Augustin: Versuch einer philosophischen Interpretation*, Olms: Hildesheim, 2006. Their communal ceremonies, which resemble the Eucharist, also point in this direction. See Björn Quiring, "'With Real Hunger To Transubstantiate': Die Dispersion der Eucharistie in John Miltons *Paradise Lost*", in *Mitteilungen des Sonderforschungsbereichs* 573, *Pluralisierung und Autorität in der Frühen Neuzeit* 1 (2011), pp. 15–22.

83 Arendt, *Der Liebesbegriff bei Augustin*, p. 123.

84 Arendt, *Der Liebesbegriff bei Augustin*, p. 102.

> Whatever pure thou in the body enjoyst
> (And pure thou wert created) we enjoy
> In eminence, and obstacle find none
> Of membrane, joint, or limb, exclusive bars:
> Easier than air with air, if spirits embrace,
> Total they mix, union of pure with pure
> Desiring; nor restrained conveyance need
> As flesh to mix with flesh, or soul with soul.
> (8.622–629)

According to this report, the angelic way of love is superior to the human because it is a total union under a unified, spiritual will. However, one might ask how one subject can even perceive, let alone love, another without experiencing him or her as other, and how this otherness can be experienced, except as some form of spiritual and material resistance. Otherwise, how would one even know that one is encountering something that is not oneself? At best, the two dissolving and interpenetrating spirits could come to the pure experience of the medium that sustains them both, namely, the word of God. If the result was different, it would have to be censured as "a step away from making 'one individual soul' with God".[85] Hence, one has the impression of being confronted with another of Raphael's empty boasts.

Empson has pointed out that the angels are also denied the option to find fulfilment in their work, because of the latter's futility, at least according to official doctrine. For example, the angels are frequently given jobs as scouts and envoys, but Raphael himself points out that all the work they do for the supposedly all-powerful, all-seeing Godhead is useless except as a test of their prompt obedience (8.237–240). Similarly, they must battle Satan's armies, even though they assume that God "at one blow/ Unaided could have [...] whelmed" these "legions under darkness" (6.140–142). And they are assigned to guard Adam and Eve against a fall that, despite their best efforts, they know must come to pass. Consequently, they seem to harbour a stifled resentment against their position in the scheme of things. One is left with the impression that the angels tend to sabotage their official, senseless tasks, as far as their high self-opinion and their fear of God permits. Uriel, Gabriel and the latter's subordinates certainly prove to be useless or worse in their guardian jobs, as does Raphael in his role as a warning voice. In the process, they make their hierarchical superiority unmistakably clear to the earthlings, treating them in rather haughty and impersonal ways. The affable Raphael is the exception to that rule; however, by his well-meaning admonitions he also ends up aggravating the situation.[86]

85 Empson, *Milton's God*, p. 107.

86 See Empson, *Milton's God*, pp. 147–181, referring to Paul Phelps Morand, *De Comus à Satan: L'Oeuvre poétique de John Milton expliquée par sa vie*, Paris: H. Didier, 1939, p. 192.

The reader increasingly gets the impression that God presides over a gigantic military and administrative apparatus whose primary function is to discipline and to humble its agents. This Miltonian association between administrative apparatuses and angelogy is not accidental: Giorgio Agamben points out that there has always been an intimate relation between conceptualizations of heavenly hierarchies and those of earthly bureaucratic order: sometimes, the structure of earthly administration serves as a model for the angelic host, sometimes the angel choirs provide the pattern to which bureaucrats tried to accommodate themselves.[87] Ceri Sullivan has shown that Milton's work as foreign secretary for the Council of State influenced his depiction of heaven; and the Cromwellian Commonwealth was to a significant extent a bureaucratic as well as a theocratic state.[88] The Father, as he is directly encountered in *Paradise Lost*, is both a sovereign ruler and an administrator. He enforces a regime that frequently legitimizes itself by reference to the "nature of things" – as bureaucratic administrative power, qua rational "power by knowledge", tends to do.[89] In this context, it should also be noted that Milton's divine bureaucracy has some atypical properties. For one, there seems to be a relatively minimal amount of paperwork: mention is made of the "books of life" (1.363) from which the devils' names have been "blotted out and razed" (1.362), thus perpetuating the judgment that has been passed upon them. However, this might be only a metaphor or a rumour. Furthermore, this remark only implies that the eldest and most rudimentary form of celestial record keeping is in place, i.e. listing the names of the elect. Since Augustine, the phantasm of a much more complex system of continuous double bookkeeping had emerged and proliferated,[90] a perpetual judgment that Milton abandons in favour of

87 Giorgio Agamben, *Die Beamten des Himmels: Über Engel. Gefolgt von der Angelologie des Thomas von Aquin*, trans. Andreas Hiepko, Frankfurt am Main: Verlag der Weltreligionen, 2007, p. 13 ff.

88 Ceri Sullivan, *Literature in the Public Service: Sublime Bureaucracy,* New York: Palgrave Macmillan, 2013, pp. 20–64. See also G. E. Aylmer, *The State's Servants: The Civil Service of the English Republic: 1649–1660*, London and Boston: Routledge and Kegan Paul, 1973.

89 See Max Weber, *Wirtschaft und Gesellschaft: Grundriß der verstehenden Soziologie*, Tübingen: Mohr, 1972, pp. 499 ff.

90 "Mit der Durchsetzung substantiell verbürgter Unsterblichkeit aus hellenistischer Metaphysik wird die Funktion des Gerichtstages umfassender: auf Gute und Böse ausgedehnt, also eine doppelte Buchführung benötigend, wo vorher Eintragung oder Löschung des Namens genügte. Diese scheint in Zusammenhang mit der Ausbildung einer himmlischen Funktionärshierarchie zu stehen, denn die Tafeln seiner Freunde und die seiner Feinde führen an Stelle Gottes Buchhalterengel." (Hans Blumenberg, *Die Lesbarkeit der Welt*, Frankfurt am Main: Suhrkamp, 1986, p. 26.) "When the substantial, authenticated immortality that was postulated by Hellenist metaphysics gains general acceptance, the function of the Day of Judgment becomes more encompassing; taking good and evil deeds into account, double-entry bookkeeping is needed where once the simple registration or deletion of a name used to suffice. This development seems to be accompanied by the formation of a hierarchy of celestial functionaries, for the lists of God's friends and enemies are no longer kept up to date by God himself, but by accounting angels." (Translation BQ.) Furthermore, Milton would be sceptical of another interpretation of divine bookkeeping: reality was often implied not to be

an alternative approach, namely the direct inscription of the law onto the creatures' bodies, supplemented by a law that is orally transmitted. His heavenly bureaucracy is kept nebulous, perhaps so that it may not impede God's court-martial legislation.

5.5 The captivating face of the Son

This celestial regime seems to be already firmly installed when the chronologically first extensively narrated event of *Paradise Lost* occurs: the proclamation of the Son, which is also the proclamation of a new political order (5.594–617). We were already confronted with Nature as the mysterious daughter of God, and now we encounter his Son Messiah, who is unfathomable like his sister. As can be seen by the reactions of Abdiel and Satan (5.772–895), the angels are as uncertain about the Son's origin as they are about their own. In his usual manner, God installs a double bind,[91] declaring the Son to have been begotten on that day (5.603–604), but also in other contexts disseminating the doctrine that the Son had already existed before all other creatures were called into being (3.383–384). To the angels, this primordial pre-existence of the Messiah has not been apparent; it is only on the event of his exaltation that he actually becomes manifest to God's other creatures, at least in his function as Son.[92] Whether he has taken a definite form in the stage prior to this exaltation, for example the form of an angel, remains wrapped in darkness.

Once more, it might clarify the issue to take a look at the *Doctrina Christiana*. Milton's Christology refers to the beginning of the Gospel of John in order to reinforce the claim that the Son was the first thing created by God and that he assisted in the creation of all other existents:

> Hoc constat, quicquid moderni quidam contra argutantur, Filium, Verbi sive Sermonis sub nomine, in principio extitisse, rerum creatarum primum fuisse, per quem deinde caetera omnia tam in coelo quam in terra sunt facta.
>
> This is certain – whatever certain revisionists prattle to the contrary – that the Son, under the name of the Word or Speech, existed in the beginning

re-written, but pre-written, in God's books, associating the topic with the Calvinist doctrine of predestination which Milton rejected. (See Blumenberg, *Die Lesbarkeit der Welt*, p. 26. See also Meira Z. Kensky, *Trying Man, Trying God: The Divine Courtroom in Early Jewish and Christian Literature*, Tübingen: Mohr Siebeck, 2010.)

91 On the concept see Gregory Bateson, *Steps to an Ecology of Mind: Collected Essays in Anthropology, Psychiatry, Evolution, and Epistemology*, Chicago and London: University of Chicago Press, 2000, p. 201 ff.

92 Albert Labriola, "The Begetting and Exaltation of the Son: The Junius Manuscript and Milton's *Paradise Lost*", in *Milton's Legacy*, eds. Kristin A. Pruitt, and Charles W. Durham, Selinsgrove, PA and London: Susquehanna University Press and Associated University Press, 2005, pp. 22–32.

and was the first of created things, through whom all the rest were then made […].

(*DC* 128/129)

Accordingly, in *Paradise Lost*, not only Abdiel, but also the other angels assert that the Son is "of all creation first" (3.383) and that the "heaven of heavens and all the powers therein" were created through him (3.390). Milton and his angels are Arians, that is, they assume that the Son is not part of a triune eternal Godhead, but that he was created to express the Godhead, being its reflection and echo. The biblical passage that is decisive for Milton's conception of the Son, as explicated in the *Doctrina Christiana*, is Hebrews 1.1–3, from which he quotes repeatedly:

> Πολυμερῶς καὶ πολυτρόπως πάλαι ὁ Θεὸς λαλήσας τοῖς πατράσιν ἐν τοῖς προφήταις, ἐπ' ἐσχάτου τῶν ἡμερῶν τούτων ἐλάλησεν ἡμῖν ἐν υἱῷ, ὃν ἔθηκεν κληρονόμον πάντων, δι' οὗ καὶ ἐποίησεν τοὺς αἰῶνας, ὃς ὢν ἀπαύγασμα τῆς δόξης καὶ χαρακτὴρ τῆς ὑποστάσεως αὐτοῦ, φέρων τε τὰ πάντα τῷ ῥήματι τῆς δυνάμεως αὐτοῦ, καθαρισμὸν τῶν ἁμαρτιῶν ποιησάμενος ἐκάθισεν ἐν δεξιᾷ τῆς μεγαλωσύνης ἐν ὑψηλοῖς […].
>
> God, who at sundry times and in divers manners spake in time past unto the fathers by the prophets, hath in these last days spoken unto us by his Son, whom he hath appointed heir of all things, by whom also he made the worlds; who being the brightness of his glory, and the express image of his person, and upholding all things by the word of his power, when he had by himself purged our sins, sat down on the right hand of the Majesty on high […].

In the Gospel of John (10.30), Jesus asserts that he and the Father are one. Milton comments that "he [Jesus] declares that he and the Father are one in the same way that we are one with him, and that is definitely not in essence, but in love, in communion, in agreement, in charity, in spirit, and finally in glory" (*DC* 147). One of the key points Milton proceeds to make is that the Son fulfils each created thing's inherent purpose to perfection: he subordinates his free will so completely to that of the Father, that the Father can be mirrored, that is, "substantially expressed" (3.140) in him. The Son is completely obedient, therefore able to become the medium in which God becomes manifest and tangible (*DC* 146/147). Politically, this enables the Son to act as the main representative of the Father, and this is indeed his function in *Paradise Lost*. Sometimes, the Son utters statements to which he could not possibly subscribe in his own voice; they only make sense when he is understood to be the Father's mouthpiece – for example, his claim that he is "alone/ From all eternity, for none I know/ Second to me or like, equal much less" (8.405–407).

Once again, difficulties arise when this theology meets with the demands of a heroic epic. The fact that God in *Paradise Lost* is represented both as a transcendent entity and as an embodied and thoroughly anthropomorphic deity poses yet another problem here: for it remains unclear why the Father would choose to depend on the Son's representation in heaven or on earth; God himself seems manifest enough without a mediating presence, and he alone is perfectly able both to communicate with the angels and also to interfere directly and physically with all celestial processes. When the Son is sent out on his earth-creating mission, this act of delegation is justified by the circumstance that the Father is above going anywhere, since he, being God, is already everywhere:

> The filial power arrived, and sat him down
> With his great Father (for he also went
> Invisible, yet stayed, such privilege
> Hath omnipresence) and the work ordained,
> Author and end of all things […].
> (7.587–591)

But when God is already present where the representative is going and can without any difficulty do all the work by himself, why send a representative in the first place, perfect though he may be? Again, the sole discernible reason for the introduction of a divine representative is a political one: it adds to God's eminent dignity not to do his wondrous works himself, but to be able to delegate them. And this demonstration of divine power through creaturely "strict obedience" contributes to God's general project of ambiguous self-transcendentalization: the stepping forth of the Son into the limelight enables the Father to remain withdrawn in indeterminacy and the darkness of "excessive bright" (3.380). He can render himself less visible by hiding behind his substantial expression: it is now the body and particularly the face of the Son that is emphasized in the descriptions of Raphael and the narrator, while the Father increasingly manifests as a voice and as the source of the light that falls on the Son:

> He said, and on his Son with rays direct
> Shone full, he all his Father full expressed
> Ineffably into his face received […].
> (6.719–721)

Other creatures henceforth will have access to the Father mainly through the Messiah's mediation. This newly inaugurated system could be described as an instance of "faciality" ("visagéité"), a term used by Deleuze and Guattari to describe a way how signs and affects can be distributed in a social field.[93] According to *A Thousand Plateaus*, representations of the visage (first and

93 Deleuze and Guattari, *A Thousand Plateaus*, pp. 167–191.

foremost, the visage of the ruler) fulfil a political function of capture, for the face is both an emitter of signs which overcode bodies and a locus of fascination and subjectivation which tends to capture all the energies that escape the codes.[94] Deleuze and Guattari assume that faciality, with its ingenious combination of absorbing passion and despotic force, is best exemplified in representations of Christ's expressive visage. Hyperbolically, they affirm: "Le visage, c'est le Christ".[95] In the instance of *Paradise Lost*, God re-implements his double eminence via the filial "conspicuous countenance" (3.385), simultaneously assimilating himself to his creatures and placing himself at one more remove from them. However, there is also a danger involved: the audience of the resultant *mise-en-scène* might wonder to what extent the Son really executes the paternal will and to what extent he acts on his own behalf. Lest any such confusion should arise, God occasionally finds it useful to emphasize that the act the Son just performed is exactly the act the Father wanted him to perform (see e.g. 3.170–172; 11.47).

No christological subtleties are explained to the angelic host, however, and the effectiveness of God's declaration partly derives from this lack of explanation. Instead of publishing any long-winded disquisitions, God calls an assembly and rather curtly and harshly declares that he has begotten his only Son and that he appoints him vice-regent, immediately calling down the full weight of the law upon any naysayers:

> Hear all ye angels, progeny of light,
> Thrones, dominations, princedoms, virtues, powers,
> Hear my decree, which unrevoked shall stand.
> This day I have begot whom I declare
> My only Son, and on this holy hill
> Him have anointed, whom ye now behold
> At my right hand; your head I him appoint;
> And by myself have sworn to him shall bow
> All knees in heaven, and shall confess him Lord:
> Under his great vicegerent reign abide
> United as one individual soul
> For ever happy: him who disobeys
> Me disobeys, breaks union, and that day
> Cast out from God and blessed vision, falls
> Into utter darkness, deep engulfed, his place
> Ordained without redemption, without end.
>
> (5.600–615)

94 Deleuze and Guattari, *A Thousand Plateaus*, p. 179.

95 Deleuze and Guattari, *Mille Plateaux*, p. 216. "The face is Christ". Deleuze and Guattari, *A Thousand Plateaus*, p. 176.

As the appointment of a representative, the ceremony is clearly a political act. Accordingly, God designates his announcement as a "decree", i.e. a law pronounced by the celestial head of state. But the implications and, one might say, even the content of the proclamation remain unclear: the event remains an *interpretandum*. For example, the wording leaves it open as to whether the Son was indeed generated on that very day or whether he was pre-existent either in the form of an angel or in the form of a divine attribute and has only recently advanced to a new official position.[96] And if the latter is the case: was his advancement caused by a meritorious deed that he has freely performed, or by some positive property that is an intrinsic part of his identity? Might the angels witness a promotion of an angel who has demonstrated perfect obedience? For the proclamation of the Son can also be interpreted as an act of adoption.[97] The question is further complicated by the circumstance that God occasionally addresses the other angels as "my sons", too (6.46).[98] This merely implies that all of the angels are God's creatures; but how is the contrast between the general sonship of all the angels and the sonship of him whom God declares his "only Son" to be understood? A closer, more, physical bond seems to be involved, exceeding God's general parentage of all celestial beings. This bodily intimacy also finds expression in the terminology that God uses when he addresses the Son, such as "Son of my bosom" (3.169) and "heir of all my might" (5.720). In this context, the term "begotten" is particularly noteworthy and provocative because of its sexual import. By "begotten", an organic genesis is implied in which Nature and/or Chaos may also be involved. By this route, generation is (re)introduced into the world of creation.[99] Of course, the "begetting" of the Son has several biblical precedents and hence a long history of theological treatment; yet it has always remained problematical.[100] Milton's recontextualization renders the term its pagan connotations: the context allows for the suspicion that the Father might have begotten his Son in the same way in which Great Father Jove begat Apollo. Since the angels are equipped with their own form of sexuality, they might logically deduce that there also exists a godly sexuality. And a divine ruler who has recently begotten a son appears to be subject to genealogy and the immanent procreative laws of nature.

Thus, not special merit, but natural inclination would have brought the Son to his elevated position, and there is indeed no mention of merit in the

96 Nothing in the Son's appearance suggests that he cannot be an angel, all the more since the angelic bodies are extremely variable. On such diverse theories, see e.g. Albert C. Labriola, "The Begetting and Exaltation of the Son", pp. 22–32.

97 Neil Forsyth, *The Satanic Epic*, Princeton, NJ: Princeton University Press, 2003, p. 186.

98 He also addresses all of them, just like the Son, with the confidential "thou".

99 On the distinction between generation and creation, see Arendt, *Der Liebesbegriff bei Augustin*, pp. 102–104.

100 For the early history of the term and its repressed pagan heritage, see Michael Peppard, *The Son of God in the Roman World: Divine Sonship in its Social and Political Context*, Oxford: Oxford University Press, 2011.

Father's speech. The interaction between Son and Father suggests that the filial privilege of the former could be based on birthright rather than advancement. The Messiah apparently would thus not attain his privileged position because of his superior obedience, but instead can afford his absolute obedience because he knows he will always remain privileged. For example, his confidence that his loving Father will not leave him "in the loathsome grave" (3.247) after his supreme sacrifice but let him "rise victorious" (3.250) makes this sacrifice appear somewhat commodious and risk-free.[101] In other situations, the Son's meritorious deeds also seem to spring from his privilege; if the Son wins the war in heaven, it is because God enforces this victory:

> Two days are therefore past, the third is thine;
> For thee I have ordained it, and thus far
> Have suffered, that the glory may be thine
> Of ending this great war, since none but thou
> Can end it. Into thee such virtue and grace
> Immense I have transfused, that all may know
> In heaven and hell thy power above compare [...].
> (6.699–705)

It is easily discernible that the Father here engages in a circular argument: he declares that the only the Son can win the war in heaven, because the Son is uniquely gifted; but all the Son's gifts supposedly come from the Father, who has not conveyed similar powers to the other angels.[102] Inevitably, the impression of favouritism and inherited privilege hangs in the air, reinforced by the appearance of a bond between Father and Son that is closer and more natural than God's relation to the other angels.

Of course, *Paradise Lost* does not actually assert that the link between God and Messiah is in fact a blood line, but the suggestion hovers over the proceedings. For the question whether the investiture of the Son is effective, however, it is irrelevant: the son might as well be adopted as biological. The reference to the Son's anointing and the attendant command to unite under his rule emphasize the act's political dimension: the new position of a viceroy who might also be heir to God's throne has been instituted, and all the signs point toward the establishment of an imperial dynasty. Might the Son beget/adopt another Son in time? Where does that leave the other "sons" of God? Has their own sonship been diminished or refuted by this instauration? The heavenly host cannot know, since the elevation of the

101 As Empson remarked: "Death for a day and a half any of us might proffer [...]." Empson, *Milton's God*, p. 128.

102 In the words of Thomas Festa: "I made so you would win the war, because no one but you can win it" (Thomas Festa, "God as Geometer and Architect in *Paradise Lost*", in *Their Maker's Image: New Essays on John Milton*, eds. Mary C. Fenton and Louis Schwartz, Selinsgrove, PA: Susquehanna University Press, 2011, p. 109).

Son is merely posited; it is a pure performative of inscrutability, sustained first and foremost by God's double role in the theology of *Paradise Lost*. The angels are subsequently commanded not only to accept, but also to be happy about an act of state they cannot possibly comprehend. The Father's speech bears all the marks of a provocation: the angels are called upon to exult in an unclear situation, to accept a Janus-faced God, and to accept, as a result, their own uncertain legal and ontological status. God's orders amount to the command: "Thou shalt not comprehend me, and thou shalt not comprehend the law".

By this new command, God also indirectly claims the right to freely dispose of the laws that bind the heavenly hierarchies; this is what causes Satan to secretly protest to his nearest confidant, Beelzebub:

> New laws thou seest imposed;
> New laws from him who reigns, new minds may raise
> In us who serve, new counsels to debate
> What doubtful may ensue [...].
>
> (5.679–682)

His subsequent statements show that Satan also suspects God to be an individual like any other, not a substantially and morally superior being. And the assumption that the supreme ruler only pretends to be transcendent and invincible in order to render his subjects submissive logically derives from it. God could not provide evidence that would effectively allay these suspicions. He has chosen the opposite path, introducing a naturalized vocabulary of "generation", which almost forces the angels to become suspicious.

In his resultant reproach of Satan, Abdiel professes that all things were made by God with the help of the Son, but avoids tackling the question of the Son's own origins (5.836–837). Instead, he diverts the argument to another organic relation: the Father's goal is not only to exalt the Son, but also to unify the angelic community, which is henceforth to form the celestial body politic. But the angels are already a highly organized, centralized and hierarchical military organization, so it is hard to see what advantage this re-organization would bring their commonwealth. Abdiel does not occupy himself with this question, but proceeds to refute Satan's complaint that the Son's elevation to the role of a universal mediator entails a degradation of the other angels. Abdiel retorts that "all honour to him done/ Returns our own" (5.844–845). According to him, God wants to transubstantiate the celestial commonwealth into a united "corpus Christi", with Messiah as the "head" of the angels. *Paradise Lost* here echoes some passages in Paul's epistles, for example 1 Cor. 12.12–27 and Col. 1.18: "And he [Christ] is the head of the body, the church". In the situation, however, it is a speculation not actually warranted by what the Father himself has proclaimed: by him, the angels were not told to unite with the Son, but exclusively to unite "under" him (5.609–611). Abdiel offers an organicist and sacramental misreading of the divine decree. When he encounters Satan again on the battlefield for a trial by combat,[103] the topic is taken up again, and in this context, Abdiel sketches his own conception of the relation between Nature and God. Against Satan's reproach that acquiescence in the Son's new rulership is the mark of a servile mind, he avows:

> Unjustly thou deprav'st it with the name
> Of servitude to serve whom God ordains,
> Or Nature; God and Nature bid the same,
> When he who rules is worthiest, and excels
> Them whom he governs.
> (6.174–178; capitalization added)

Serving the Son not only fulfils a religious duty, but also satisfies Abdiel's natural sense of justice. Of course, the question arises in what way the Son can be reasonably ascertained as naturally superior. It must be an excellence *a priori*, since Messiah has not yet had a chance to prove himself in his position. All Abdiel has so far learned about the Son is that he is linked to the Father more closely than the angels; and he deems this link to be a natural link, because of the organicist terminology the Father has used. Consequently, a perfect harmony between the will of God and the precepts of Nature is supposed that allows Abdiel to avoid the crucial question of which of the two determines the other.

5.6 Filial force triumphant

The declared motivation for the revolt of the satanic hordes is not so much their thirst for divine power than their desire to answer the question that Abdiel dodges, namely to learn whether God is really their absolutely sovereign, omnipotent creator and legitimate ruler, thereby eliminating the theological uncertainty at the base of the celestial community. Retrospectively, they describe their insurrection as a kind of experimental procedure, putting "to proof his high supremacy,/ Whether upheld by strength, or chance, or fate" (1.132–133). One method they use for their "investigation", namely the invention and use of gunpowder and cannons, might be characterized as proto-scientific. However, as the discussion at the beginning of the second book demonstrates, they seem to be uncertain about the key question: what would actually qualify God as legitimate, if his military strength is not deemed sufficient? If God's transcendent status cannot be proven, it cannot be disproved either. Moreover, Satan's monologue at the beginning of the fourth book suggests that there is also a more basic and emotional motivation for his revolt, namely to "quit/ The debt immense of endless gratitude,/ So

103 Alison A. Chapman, *The Legal Epic:* Paradise Lost *and the Early Modern Law*, Chicago and London: University of Chicago Press, 2017, p. 92.

burdensome, still paying, still to owe" (4.51–53). The desire for unmasking God drives him because this delegitimation would relieve him of the burden of obedient self-abnegation. His political goal is largely a negative one; accordingly, his positive programmatic statements prove rather vague. In some passages, he suggests that he plans to replace God's despotism with a more republican political order (e.g. 5.783–786; 6.164–165), but in others he apparently just wants to take the Father's place and become himself a despot, only a better one (e.g. 1.101–102). Even his private statements on the matter are so contradictory that they convey the impression not of an opportunistic demagogue, but of a commander who is not altogether sure of what he wants. His indecision mirrors the ambiguity of the divine order.

When all is said and done, not much difference remains between the two parties' methods of legitimation: both angels and devils accuse the other party of relying exclusively on violence and of neglecting questions of truth and justice; and both have a point. As a result, both parties claim to fight on the side of Nature (just like the diverse parties in the English Civil Wars did). In the process, the question of legitimacy is reduced to a question of superior fire power. All the angels are thus left with is Abdiel's knockout argument:

> Then who created thee lamenting learn,
> When who can uncreate thee thou shalt know.
> (5.894–895)

Accordingly, the Son seems, above all else, eager to enforce the divine hierarchy by forcefully implementing God's word, and to use thunderbolts, not pious arguments, for the purpose. It is unconvincing to conceive of the Son as an epitome of radical passivity:[104] he is largely portrayed as a fawning and pugnacious careerist who is not only obedient to the Father, but also never fails to point out spontaneously and loquaciously his prompt and militant obedience (see e.g. 3.256–257; 5.735–742; 6.723–745; 10.68–72).

The exaltation of the Son effectuates a hard division between the angels: they separate into the group of those who are willing to submit their self-will to that of a God whose legitimacy and ontological status remain questionable, and the group of those who do not want to make that sacrifice. It is understandable that the Father intends to separate the sheep from the goats in this way, for he may deem it necessary for the stability of the heavenly realm. But, one may ask: why be so provocative about it? It is fair to say that God represents the double bind that underlies his reign as undiplomatically as possible, pushing Satan over the edge. Satan's reproach that the Father "tempted" the devils' "attempt" (1.642) by his all-consuming demands and partial revelations is hard to refute. But if God sets up a damnation trap in

104 As, for example, Regina M. Schwartz does (Regina M. Schwartz, *Sacramental Poetics at the Dawn of Secularism: When God Left the World*, Stanford, CA: Stanford University Press, 2008, p. 75).

which a third of the angels are caught, what can be his motivation? As always, he seems first and foremost interested in consolidating his political position as the one true God. A good way to increase his control over heaven is to keep society as militarized and therefore as disciplined as possible. However, the need for military discipline cannot be experienced very keenly in the populace, if all that can be found outside the ramparts of heaven is the rather unthreatening, self-absorbed and self-defeating realm of Chaos. It is said that the angelic soldiers

> oft on the bordering Deep
> Encamp their legions, or with óbscure wing
> Scout far and wide into the realm of night,
> Scorning surprise.
>
> (2.131–134)

But the legions of Chaos seem to be sufficiently occupied with their internal brawls. Furthermore, since King Chaos raises hardly refutable counterclaims to the divine attributes of eternity and infinity, it could be slightly dangerous to draw too much attention to him. Consequently, another enemy and competitor must be found to supplant the primordial otherness of Chaos with a secondary other who can be represented more convincingly as a derivative entity created by God, a *simia dei*.[105] The battle against Satan also gives the Son an opportunity to distinguish himself, thus legitimating the project of a partial *translatio imperii*, which allows the Father to assume an even more transcendent position (see esp. 3.315–322; 3.339–341). This may be one of the reasons why God encourages the revolt; and Satan promptly falls into the baited trap, allowing the Father to Christianize the universe: God's military triumph is accompanied by a theologico-political triumph.

This double victory is reinforced by a propaganda coup: the celestial party also manages to convey the general impression that their supremacy on the battlefield is complemented by their moral superiority. Before he moves into battle, the Son addresses the faithful angelic host and announces that he will rout the rebel angels from heaven:

> That they may have their wish, to try with me
> In battle which the stronger proves, they all,
> Or I alone against them, since by strength
> They measure all, of other excellence
> Not emulous, nor care who them excels;
> Nor other strife with them do I vouchsafe.
>
> (6.818–823)

105 On this term, see Jeffrey Burton Russell, *The Prince of Darkness: Radical Evil and the Power of Good in History*, Ithaca, NY: Cornell University Press, 1992, p. 70.

Strier calls this speech a "brilliant but desperate maneuver", for the Son errs or lies: the rebel angels actually "appreciate many kinds of 'excellence'", as several passages of *Paradise Lost* demonstrate.[106] And the devils do not fail to direct the same accusation against the celestial party, affirming that it is exclusively interested in dominance by brute force (see e.g. 1.245–249; 1.257–260). Their reproaches also simplify the issue, but they do have a point, which is just as good as that of the Son: throughout the fifth and sixth books of *Paradise Lost*, the celestial party represents the Messiah as a ruler "who by right of merit reigns" (6.43). But whenever this praise of the Son's merit assumes a more concrete form, it praises his military prowess. The Father addresses the Son with the assurance that he has "this perverse commotion governed thus,/ To manifest thee worthiest to be heir" (6.706–707). Richard Strier has pointed out that "'worthiest' here can only mean most powerful".[107] God engages in a Hobbesian rhetoric in which might proves right.

After he has expelled the devils, the Son rides through heaven in a triumphal procession:

> Sole victor from the expulsion of his foes
> Messiah his triumphal chariot turned:
> To meet him all his Saints, who silent stood
> Eyewitnesses of his almighty acts,
> With jubilee advanced; and as they went,
> Shaded with branching palm, each order bright,
> Sung triumph, and him sung victorious king,
> Son, heir, and Lord, to him dominion giv'n,
> Worthiest to reign [...].
>
> (6.880–888)

Again, it is hard to fathom what property of the Son the angelic hymn might call "worthiest" here, except the Son's ability to rout the devils. They can afford him no other praise, since he has not had an opportunity to demonstrate any other virtue yet. What is more, his victory does not even demand any superior intellectual or even physical capacities: according to the description, it is largely ascribable to the powers of the "almighty arms" (6.713) with which the Father has equipped him. Milton's monistic worldview strongly suggests that the wonderous force of these dire weapons harnesses the same natural energies as the devilish cannons. Their advantage is not a moral, but a technological one; Zeus or Satan could have prevailed in the same way. Accordingly, the taunts that the celestial party levels against the devils mostly ridicule the latter's weakness. The Son's boast that he will send the devils to hell even though he stands "alone against them" (6.820) is a case in point.[108]

106 Strier, "Milton's Fetters", p. 180.
107 Strier, "Milton's Fetters", p. 180.
108 See also e.g. 4.855–856.

However, a willingness to fight against an enemy who is stronger than oneself is certainly not in every case a sign of moral or intellectual deficiency; it might indeed be the opposite.[109] Again and again, the divine claim to ethical supremacy turns out to be empty: superior fire power proves nothing except superior fire power; it demonstrates neither the legitimacy nor the goodness, nor the justice of the Father and the Son. The good shepherd may assert that his own reliance on physical coercion is a dire necessity, since the other party is utterly incapable of understanding any other language, but this assertion cannot be sustained under scrutiny. But while it does not demonstrate anything, the statement nevertheless successfully suggests a vague "other excellence", transcending the obvious shortcomings of a divine jurisdiction that is based on physical supremacy. Intimations of transcendence such as these characterize the divine rhetoric; they are rhetorical tools that contribute to the general project of confirming the Father in his position as an identification figure beyond all creaturely conceiving.

109 Strier, "Milton's Fetters", p. 178.

6 The growths of hell

After their expulsion to hell, the outlawed devils face a two-pronged attack of divine and natural condemnations which subdues them even more completely than the good angels are subdued by their boundless obedience. Milton's God marks the fallen angels with signs that they have been irrevocably excluded from the divine legal order, which nevertheless still applies to them. The loss of their names (1.361–365), the lack of an official verdict, and the circumstance that all subsequent communication between heaven and the fallen angels assumes snarkily ironical forms all serve as indicators of their exclusion. For example, Satan on his way to earth finds that the drawbridge to the pearly gates has been let down:

> The stairs were then let down, whether to dare
> The fiend by easy ascent, or aggravate
> His sad exclusion from the doors of bliss.
> (3.523–525)

The narrator leaves it open as to whether God merely stages a theatre of punishment or tempts the sinner to undertake another transgression. For it is a stated goal of God to entangle the fallen ever further in sin:

> But hard be hardened, blind be blinded more,
> That they may stumble on, and deeper fall [...].
> (3.200–201)

De Doctrina Christiana provides a political justification for this procedure: God tends to harden the hearts of those who are already in sin and lead them further to their doom in order to "uncover hypocrisy". Their primordial guiltiness thus becomes visible to the general public (*DC* 335). Therefore, this ever-increasing punishment has a deterrent effect: God provides it "to ensure that for the future others would be very afraid to sin in a similar way" (*DC* 335). One might detect a contradiction between these two arguments, for those who only refrain from sinning against God because they are "very afraid" of his Great Revenge might be regarded as hypocritical, since it is not the goodness of their hearts that keeps them on the straight and narrow path. Nevertheless, both arguments have a common denominator, namely what Milton repeatedly calls "patefactio", that is, disclosure: the world is a forensic procedure in which steadfast faithfulness and its rewards as well as wickedness and its penalization are forever displayed. Milton is echoing Calvin in this context: according to the *Institutes of the Christian Religion*, the damned are punished eternally not in order to bring them "to a better mind: but only that, to their great hurt, they should prove God to be a judge and revenger". They were "raised up by the just but inscrutable judgment of God to show forth his glory in their condemnation".[1] Similarly, God tempts the good, because their goodness is clearly demonstrated by their resistance and patience.[2] This performance of virtue is not officially intended for the eye of God since he is already supposed to know all creatures' inner workings and their future, but it is designed to prove their moral value to the other creatures in nature's universal law court. The aim of God is the production of deterrent and polarizing show trials, covering increasingly large areas of the social field. Accordingly, hell has a representative, theatrical function; and it soon becomes evident that it is not only supposed to punish the condemned transgressors, but also to breed ever new transgressions and condemnations so that punishment may keep proliferating and deterring. One symptom is the strange architecture of hell that transforms its inhabitants, *nolens volens*, into performers within allegorical tableaus: it is doubtlessly allegorical that hell is a place of both annihilating barrenness and of prodigious, monstrous generation. The allegory is extended when Sin is found to hold hell's keys, and turns out to be capable of opening, but not of closing, its gates. When the gates are described as extremely wide, so that whole armies can pass through, the narrator obviously echoes the parable of Matthew 7.13 (2.883–889). In accordance with medieval tradition, Milton's hell is designed as an immense allegory of divine maxims.[3]

However, these infernal allegories remain hidden to at least some of their potential addressees: the proceedings of hell are not, like those of earth, in general view from heaven; the angels are only provided with occasional, horrifying glimpses and eavesdroppings, as can be gathered from Raphael's report on his military expedition toward its gates (8.240–245). This restrictive information policy seems to deter and discipline God's faithful subjects all the more effectively. God himself, however, enjoys unlimited access to the infernal regions; he can even actively intervene in their development, and he demonstrates this by transforming Satan and his minions into "the shape he

1 Jean Calvin, *Institutes of the Christian Religion*, trans. Ford Lewis Battles, ed. John T McNeill, Louisville, KY: Westminster John Knox Press, 2006, pp. 662, 981 [3.4.33, 3.24.14].

2 Jean Calvin, *Institutes of the Christian Religion*, p. 828 [3.18.7]. Milton agrees in *DC* 334/335.

3 See e.g. Maureen Quilligan, *The Language of Allegory: Defining the Genre*, Ithaca, NY: Cornell University Press, 1979, p. 112; Joseph L, Koerner, *Bosch and Bruegel: From Enemy Painting to Everyday Life*, Princeton, NJ: Princeton University Press, 2016, p. 318.

sinned after the Fall of Man" (10.506–584). Tellingly, this seasonal intervention to ensure the "deeper fall" (3.201) of the devils also takes the form of a brutalization, depriving them of language and reducing them to the need for food. This strange mixture of allegoresis and naturalization is characteristic of hell. In order to gain a better comprehension of this combination, one must take a closer look at hell's origins. These origins turns out to be characteristically uncertain; it remains unclear when and how Milton's hell was created. When God proclaims the Son as his vicegerent and condemns his adversaries, the place is not mentioned:

> him who disobeys
> Me disobeys, breaks union, and that day
> Cast out from God and blessed vision, falls
> Into utter darkness, deep engulfed, his place
> Ordained without redemption, without end.
> (5.611–615)

According to this pronouncement, damnation seems to entail an endless fall into the illimitable spaces of Chaos, not a fall into a clearly delimited and structured penal colony[4] within it. For, despite certain affinities and uncertain limits between the two, hell cannot be regarded as a part of Chaos: within hell, the four elements have stabilized, and even aboriginal forms of organic life seem to be present.[5] Despite the fact that the angels and Adam tend to confound the two and conflate them by the common denominator of "darkness", both regions compete with each other. When Satan encounters King Chaos, he tells him that the Fall of Man will extend the dominion of Chaos (2.980–987), but this is not what actually happens. Rather, the victory of hell's inhabitants further encroaches upon the unordered regions of Old Night. When Satan's progeny builds the highway from earth to hell, Chaos accordingly roars in "indignation" (10.416–418). The hell of *Paradise Lost* is constantly expanding and impinging upon other spaces. And no serious divine efforts are made to keep the devils in and to stop their expansionary politics. Are they doing God's work in the process? Before we try to answer that question, it first needs to be investigated more closely who or what has produced hell. The first and obvious answer is that God created it by his word:

> A universe of death, which God by curse
> Created evil [...].
> (2.622–623)

4 J. Martin Evans describes hell as the penal colony of God's empire (J. Martin Evans, *Milton's Imperial Epic:* Paradise Lost *and the Discourse of Colonialism*, Ithaca, NY: Cornell University Press, 1996, pp. 35, 146).

5 See e.g. 2.611–612.

But, once again, things turn out to be more complicated on a closer look: this curse of God is a curse that is never pronounced within the epic, and Raphael alternatively states that hell was fixed by Fate:

> Hell heard the unsufferable noise, hell saw
> Heav'n ruining from heav'n and would have fled
> Affrighted; but strict Fate had cast too deep
> Her dark foundations, and too fast had bound.
> (6.867–870; capitalization added)

Both statements may be compatible if we remember the definition of "fate" in Milton's *Doctrina*:

> [E]t fatum quid nisi effatum divinum omnipotentis cuiuspiam numinis potest esse?
>
> And what can fate be but the divine decree of some almighty deity?
>
> (*DC* 24/25)

It should be remembered that the *Doctrina* also equates this divine decree with Nature:

> [N]eque enim aliud quicquam natura esse potest, nisi mirifica illa vis et efficacia divinae vocis primitus emissae, cui dehinc omnia veluti mandato perpetuo parent.
>
> [F]or indeed nothing else can be nature except that marvellous force and efficacy of the divine voice sent forth at first, which thenceforth all things obey just like a perpetual command.
>
> (*DC* 338/339)

If the statements are juxtaposed, the primordial creative order word of God must be acknowledged to involve a hell-raising curse, the curse of Fate/Nature, drawing the line between the godly and the ungodly. Again, the strange double position of both Nature and Fate must be emphasized here: on the one hand, they do God's bidding; but on the other, a certain amount of autonomy is constantly suggested. The devils echo these suggestions: like the mythologists of Ancient Greece and Rome, they consider Fate to be sovereign even above the Thunderer. For example, they "complain that Fate/ Free virtue should enthral to force or chance" (2.550–551; capitalization added), as if Fate had capriciously empowered the God who has condemned them (see also 1.116–117; 2.197–198; 2.809). But it remains not only mysterious whether they are under or above the Lord; it is also unclear how Fate and Nature relate to each other. Are they altogether identical? In any case, they certainly seem to collaborate in hell: while Fate has founded it, Nature makes it grow and flourish, organically generating monsters: in the infernal regions: "Nature breeds,/ Perverse, all monstrous, all prodigious things" (2.624–625; capitalization added). By their very presence, Nature, in her role as daughter of Hesiodic Chaos, and Fate both hint at a pagan component of Milton's inferno and at its close relationship with allegory.[6] Appropriately, the location at first sight very much resembles the Greco-Roman underworld. It should be noted in this context that the Tartarus is not only the designated place of eternal divine punishment, but also the prison of the vanquished Titans after Zeus defeated them.[7] While Milton's God is insistently compared to Zeus, the devils are implicitly equated with the latter's discarded uncles and cousins. The five rivers of ancient Hades – Styx, Acheron, Cocyton, Phlegeton and Lethe – flow in Milton's hell (2.575–583); and when his fallen angels for the first time swarm out in search of more commodious climes, the first expedition finds Lethe not only imbued with the powers of oblivion, but also with a punishing spirit that has already claimed other victims before:

> of itself the water flies
> All taste of living wight, as once it fled
> The lip of Tantalus.
>
> (2.612–614)

Please note that the tale of the infernal expedition is narrated in the present tense, while the reference to the plights of Tantalus is in the past tense. Hell thus seems to open onto a strange, diegetically impossible pagan past: in a time when man has not yet fallen and in which he may not even have been created, when could this "once" have occurred? And furthermore, where have the devils learned about the miraculous power of Lethe, so that they strive "to reach/ The tempting stream, with one small drop to lose/ In sweet forgetfulness all pain and woe"? (2.606–608). Have they read Ovid or Virgil?[8] The narrative here suggests that the hell of *Paradise Lost* succeeds Hades, instead of preceding it as its true model.

Milton's hell is assimilated to Hades in yet another respect: it is not quite as bad as most Christian writers, Dante for example, tend to imagine the place; it is dark, vast and largely too hot, but not (yet) an execution ground of systematic torture. There is no mutual aggression among the devils (the narrator emphasizes that they hold "[f]irm concord", 2.496–497), and the pains they are made to feel are not incapacitating. Accordingly, several forms of infernal

6 See e.g. Mechthild Modersohn, *Natura als Göttin im Mittelalter: Ikonographische Studien zu Darstellungen der personifizierten Natur*, Berlin: Akademie, 1997, pp. 179–183.

7 Hesiod, *Theogonie, Griechisch/Deutsch*, trans. and ed. Otto Schönberger, Stuttgart: Reclam, 1999, pp. 62/63 [810–814].

8 See Ovid, *Metamorphoses*, Vol. 2, trans. Frank Justus Miller, London: Heinemann and New York: Putnam's Sons, 1916, 11.602–604, pp. 162/163. Virgil, *Aeneis*, trans. and ed. Johannes Götte and Maria Götte, Düsseldorf: Artemis und Winkler, 2002, pp. 260/261 [6.703–715].

cultural life can be established: the devils engage in the arts, in politics, in sports and games (the sportive battles in the air possibly alluding to the Wild Hunt of pagan mythology), but also in music and poetry. It is even said that hell is "[s]uspended" (2.554) by the devils' heavenly music. Furthermore, some devils pass the time discussing philosophical topics, publicly speculating about Fate and about what their damnation entails (2.555–569). It is hard to imagine these devils as thoroughly dedicated, raving sadistic torturers: they admittedly want mankind to fall and to "partake" (2.374) with them, but their official motivations are first and foremost political: to get a new power-base and to engage in territorial struggle with heaven (2.360–376). Milton's devils resemble Olympian deities much more closely than the cruel devils one encounters in Dante. Accordingly, in the first book of *Paradise Lost*, Milton takes up an old tradition when he represents all pagan deities, including Jupiter, as devils in disguise, seducing the inhabitants of earth into idolatry:[9] the fallen angels will thus cause the greatest part of mankind "devils to adore for deities" (1.373). Sometimes the narrator himself is apparently also affected; he seems to get carried away and he seems to imagine that he is writing a heroic epic about them. For example, when Belial proposes to the devils that they get accustomed to their place in hell, all the more since their punishment is just, the narrator calls this a proposal of "ignoble ease, and peaceful sloth" (2.227). This is all the more surprising since Belial largely asserts the same thing as the narrator and his God: all the devils' insurrectionary acts only will produce more woe (see e.g. 3.85–86), and not only among the devils: the narrator seems to have momentarily forgotten that the "ignoble peace" Belial recommends would also spare mankind any Satanic temptations; it consequently might have remained unfallen. Either he has been transported beyond the confines of piety and rational consideration by his martial ideals of heroic manliness,[10] or the narrator is indeed keen on the crime and punishment he subsequently laments. In either case, he both requires and condemns the continuation of the Satanic rebellion.

It soon becomes clear that Belial's plans are stillborn anyway, and that the fault is not so much Satan's or God's as Nature's: Greco-Roman goddesses and demons proliferate in hell, such as the Furies and the Gorgons, who are not from the tribe of the fallen angels, but have been bred by Nature and function as a kind of meta-devils, punishing the fallen angels.

> Nature breeds,
> Perverse, all monstrous, all prodigious things,

9 See Walter Benjamin, *The Origin of German Tragic Drama*, trans. John Osborne, London: Verso, 1998, p. 223. See also Jeffrey Burton Russell, *The Prince of Darkness. Radical Evil and the Power of Good in History*, Ithaca, NY: Cornell University Press, 1992, pp. 17–20.

10 See also Neil Forsyth, *The Satanic Epic*, Princeton, NJ: Princeton University Press, 2003, p. 109.

Abominable, inutterable, and worse
Than fables yet have feigned, or fear conceived,
Gorgons and Hydras, and Chimeras dire.
(2.624–628; capitalization added)

Nature populates Milton's empty underworld to make it even more hellish. Besides Gorgons, Hydras and Chimeras, we also encounter the Furies in their role as the executrixes of hell:

Thither by harpy-footed Furies haled,
At certain revolutions all the damned
Are brought: and feel by turns the bitter change
Of fierce extremes, extremes by change more fierce,
From beds of raging fire to starve in ice
Their soft ethereal warmth, and there to pine
Immovable, infixed, and frozen round,
Periods of time, thence hurried back to fire.
(2.596–603)

In the ruminations of Belial, a doubt is articulated whether God may not one day be "satisfied/ With what is punished" (2.212–213), so that the devils will gradually grow accustomed to the fires and "receive/ Familiar the fierce heat" (2.218–219). It turns out that his conception of God's infinite justice is too generous. The epic exposes these almost apocatastatic hopes as unfounded: the Furies will regularly work to revive the sensitivities of the damned. God and Nature connive to make hell a thoroughly nasty, brutish and hopeless place.

According to Milton, Nature's pagan executors grow organically, but also prodigiously, beyond the bounds that are normally prescribed to nature. One might find it peculiar that Nature is present in hell at all, for after Satan has made his way through Chaos and reaches the border area of heaven and man's cosmos, these borders are also defined as the limits of Nature's influence:

But now at last the sacred influence
Of light appears, and from the walls of heaven
Shoots far into the bosom of dim Night
A glimmering dawn; here Nature first begins
Her farthest verge, and Chaos to retire
As from her outmost works a broken foe
With tumult less and with less hostile din […].
(2.1034–1040; capitalization added)

According to this statement, hell is situated far beyond Nature's "farthest verge" (2.1038). And yet, Nature is very active in hell, even though operating out of bounds. As is the custom, even the unnatural must be regarded as an exponent of nature, in the form of a "prodigy" or "wonder".[11] Hell is a "free" zone beyond the regular, encoded jurisdictions of God and Nature, yet both still make their presence and power felt in it. To clarify the implications of this arrangement, it is useful to employ Giorgio Agamben's concepts of "inclusive exclusion" and "exception". Agamben adopts the concept of "exception" via Benjamin from Carl Schmitt's *Political Theology* and makes it the centre of his legal philosophy. According to Schmitt, a state of exception arises when a danger to the order of the state (a *coup d'état*, a revolutionary uprising, a civil war, etc.) requires the suspension of civil laws. In this emergency, the validity of the law becomes so precarious that the sovereign, unconstrained by laws, must first bring about by violent means "a situation in which legal prescriptions can be valid again".[12] By proclaiming a state of exception, the sovereign may declare the order of law to be invalid without being obligated to invoke an existing law that would justify the declaration. Schmitt reverses this definition – the state of exception is the result of a sovereign decision – and defines sovereignty as the authority both to proclaim and to end a state of exception: "Sovereign is he who decides on the exception".[13] In this respect, whoever institutes and guarantees the legal order is the one who is exempt from it and can suspend it, if necessary, in order to replace it with a "state of nature". The institution and the suspension of the law – rule and exception – are united in Schmitt's rather Hobbesian figure of the sovereign. Agamben expands Schmitt's concept by defining the exception as an "inclusive exclusion"[14] and widening its applicability enormously: every law presupposes its own exception *qua* transgression. And it is via this exception that the law manages to include its outside, namely the entirety of social life, within itself and thus to coincide with pure facticity.[15] The concept of exception, when defined in such broad terms, obviously becomes the clandestine paradigm of every legal system. The law puts everything and everyone in a zone of exception by putting them simultaneously inside and outside the juridical order, by abandoning them and then reapplying itself to them. The omnipresent state of exception institutes "a situation that is neither one of fact nor one of right",[16] thereby opening the space in which the positive legal order can prove its efficacy as a modifying force. But this state also pertains in areas that are positioned outside the law, where the law itself decrees that it is suspended.

11 See also Lorraine Daston and Katharine Park, *Wonders and the Order of Nature, 1150–1750*, New York: Zone Books and Cambridge, MA: MIT Press, 1998.

12 Carl Schmitt, *Political Theology: Four Chapters on the Concept of Sovereignty*, trans. George Schwab, Cambridge, MA and London: MIT Press, 1985, p. 13.

13 Schmitt, *Political Theology*, p. 5.

14 Giorgio Agamben, *Homo Sacer*, trans. Daniel Heller-Roazen, Stanford, CA: Stanford University Press, 1998, p. 21.

15 Agamben, *Homo Sacer*, pp. 25–27. See also Giorgio Agamben, *The Time that Remains: A Commentary on the Letter to the Romans*, trans. Patricia Dailey, Stanford, CA: Stanford University Press, 2005, pp. 105–106.

16 Agamben, *Homo Sacer*, p. 18.

Agamben sees the extralegal space of the camp (above all the Nazi concentration camp) as paradigmatic for this development in that the camp is the place where no law rules apart from the pure form of the law, in other words, the state of exception.[17] It turns out that Milton's hell is just such a zone of exception, constituting its inhabitants as *diaboli et homines sacri*: the divine and natural law integrate them by abandoning them.[18]

In representations of hell, there has always been a problem: according to Irenaeus and others, hell was originally created for the punishment of the fallen angels.[19] But on the other hand, the iconography of hell since medieval times depicts the devils not as the victims of hell, but as its supervisors and professional torturers. And they tend to do their job with so much glee and dedication that it is hard to categorize their detention in hell as a punishment. Milton solves this problem by deploying naturally generated deities and semi-deities of classical mythology for their punishment. But are these punishers to be considered free moral agents? It is hard to deny them a conscience, since Greek mythology not only represents the Furies as reasonable creatures, but even as enforcers of the law of bloodlines. This raises the question whether the fires of hell do hurt them. At least at first, this would not seem to be justifiable: hell is not their place of punishment, but their place of birth, so any regular notion of guilt seems to be inapplicable in their case. On the other hand, it is hard to conceive of the hell-born demons with pagan roots as obedient worshippers of the one true God, and this disrespect might justify their condemnation. Furthermore, like Sin, they might come to slacken their penalizing duties or even start to collaborate and fraternize with the fallen angels with whom they share so much. This would make it all the more necessary to punish them. For this purpose, further avenging deities would have to be generated in the womb of Nature, setting in motion an unending spiral of breeding and punishment. The uncertain borders of hell start to make sense in this context: by design, it has the capacity for infinite growth, being the "capital of pain" in more than one sense.[20] This perspective of a teeming hell – forever accumulating misery – also makes it more understandable why all the generated

17 Agamben, *Homo Sacer*, pp. 166–180.

18 Therefore I neither agree with Julie Stone Peters who understands the relation between God and the devils as one determined by the rules of international law nor with Alison Chapman who regards it as a conventional relation between a monarch and the subjects under his jurisdiction (Julie Stone Peters, "A 'Bridge over Chaos': *De Jure Belli*, *Paradise Lost*, Terror, Sovereignty, Globalism, and the Modern Law of Nations", *Comparative Literature* 57.4 (2005), pp. 275–276; Alison A. Chapman, *The Legal Epic:* Paradise Lost *and the Early Modern Law*, Chicago and London: University of Chicago Press, 2017, p. 4).

19 Irenaeus of Lyon, *Adversus Haereses,* Vol. 3, trans. and ed. Norbert Brox, Freiburg: Herder, 1995, p. 286 [23.3].

20 See Paul Éluard, *Capitale de la douleur*, Paris: Gallimard, 1966, alluding to the "città dolente" of Dante, *Inferno*, trans. Jean Hollander and Robert Hollander, New York: Random House, 2000, pp. 46/47 [3.1].

avenging deities and demons are exclusively female: the official doctrine of heaven tends to associate femininity both with transgression and with procreation, as can be seen from the fact that Raphael addresses Eve exclusively as the mother of mankind and is fixated on her powers as a temptress in his discussion with Adam in the eighth book. In this perspective, monstrous mothers would be fitting emblems of an endlessly proliferating Gehenna.

Generally, it is notable that the emergence of hell as a place of abandonment is closely associated with the concretion of the female sex among God's creatures. The potential for femininity is already given in heaven: angels can "either sex assume, or both" (1.424). However, they apparently never choose to do so: the male pronoun is consistently used for all inhabitants of heaven, as well as, of course, for God. (The exceptions are the converging figures of Fate, Urania, Wisdom and Nature, who, however, remain strategically positioned between the status of God's creatures, of mere allegories and that of primordial divine entities). The creatures of Chaos appear as more straightforwardly androgynous: in the preceding chapters, it was repeatedly pointed out that the anarch Chaos and his entourage sometimes assume male and sometimes female attributes. The monsters generated in hell, however, with the sole exception of Death, are all clearly marked as female; and the chronologically first of all monsters also happens to be the first of all terminally female creatures, namely Sin. According to her origin narrative, as narrated by herself, the emergence of Sin is inherently and immediately associated with the emergence of both the female sex and of hell. When Satan encounters her at its gates and professes not to know her, she affirms:

> In heaven, when at the assembly, and in sight
> Of all the Seraphim with thee combined
> In bold conspiracy against heaven's king,
> All on a sudden miserable pain
> Surprised thee, dim thine eyes, and dizzy swum
> In darkness, while thy head flames thick and fast
> Threw forth, till on the left side opening wide,
> Likest to thee in shape and count'nance bright,
> Then shining heavenly fair, a goddess armed
> Out of thy head I sprung [...].
>
> (2.749–758)

It is both strange and consistent with the logic of Miltonian hell-building that this primordial Sin (allegorically representing the pre-existent sin of the conspiracy against God) does not seem to have been created by God, but to have grown spontaneously and organically – by "self-begot" generation (5.860). Again, the forces of Nature are seen to be at work in heaven, supplementing its univocity. The story of Satan's brainchild obviously quotes and parodies the pagan myth of Athena's birth from the head of Zeus. However, by thus constructing another instance of antecedence out of his epigonism,[21] he also alludes to a Renaissance tradition that comprehended the birth of Athena as an allegory of the Son's generation by the divine Father.[22] Moreover, Milton's version is peculiar in that it remains incongruous with everything else that one learns about the (pro)creative powers of the angels. This becomes even more obvious in the sequel of Sin's tale:

> I pleased, and with attractive graces won
> The most averse, thee chiefly, who full oft
> Thyself in me thy perfect image viewing
> Becam'st enamoured, and such joy thou tookst
> With me in secret, that my womb conceived
> A growing burden.
>
> (2.762–767)

This occurrence of procreative sexuality within the confines of heaven seems to be rather unprecedented. The angels' occasional intercourse, to which Raphael refers (8.620–629), seems to be sterile. If the unfallen angels would regularly procreate, God would look incongruous when he, after Satan's fall, solemnly vows to repair the "detriment" (7.153) of a "dispeopled heaven" all by himself (7.151). After all, the angels could then replace the missing third part without any special divine effort – and rather quickly, considering how fast Sin breezes through her two pregnancies. It is hard to gauge whether the obstacles to angelic procreation are organic or legislative, in other words, whether celestial engenderings would violate the natural or the positive law of heaven. In any case, not illicit sexual desire, but sexual difference and reproduction in and of themselves first appear as the consequences and marks of fallenness in Milton's world. And as the fruit of reproduction, shapeless Death is born, transforming Sin's "nether shape" (2.784) into the animalistic shape of a serpent. The allegory is apparently taken from the epistle of James (1.15): "Then when lust hath conceived, it bringeth forth sin: and sin, when it is finished, bringeth forth death". Milton adds another twist, however: subsequently, Death rapes his mother and Sin speedily gives birth to a second generation, a cry of hell hounds:

> of that rape begot
> These yelling monsters that with ceaseless cry
> Surround me, as thou sawst, hourly conceived
> And hourly born, with sorrow infinite

21 Harold Bloom, *A Map of Misreading*, Oxford and New York: Oxford University Press, 2003, p. 131.

22 Victoria Kahn, "Allegory, the Sublime, and the Rhetoric of Things Indifferent in *Paradise Lost*", in *Creative Imagination: New Essays in Renaissance Literature in Honor of Thomas M. Greene*, Binghamton, NY: Medieval and Renaissance Texts and Studies, 1992, p. 189.

> To me, for when they list into the womb
> That bred them they return, and howl and gnaw
> My bowels, their repast; then bursting forth
> Afresh with conscious terrors vex me round,
> That rest or intermission none I find.
>
> (2.794–802)

From this description, which appropriates the myth of Scylla, it is obvious that Sin no longer belongs to the creatures who "can either sex assume, or both". Since her womb is perpetually inhabited and there is continuous, gnawing traffic from the inside to the outside and back, any sex change would prove an impossibility. Sin's femininity is apparently the first that is truly fixed, and fixed in pain, for her vagina merges with a wound, continuously re-inflicted according to the supreme verdicts of God and Nature. The primordial establishment of a determinate female sex thus has to be regarded as a part of the divine punishments of hell, even though it is hard to see for what exactly Sin herself is punished at that point, except for being "vitiated in nature" (10.169) by her blood relation to Satan. It is never implied that she actively participated in the war in heaven (she uses the passive formulation: "fields were fought", 3.768) or in the diverse unholy intercourses to which she has been subjected. Attributing such a violent origin to gender difference implies that the narrator basically perceives it as a relation of domination: persistent womanhood appears on the scene by an act of allegorizing disempowerment.

What exactly is the status of allegory in *Paradise Lost*? And why is allegory so prevalent in hell? Like many Christian writers, Milton appropriates and rewrites pagan myths by allegorizing them.[23] Christian allegoresis of pagan traditions frequently has been an attempt to exorcise the remnants of polytheism,[24] for example by interpreting the outward attributes of pagan deities as an expression of their (low) morals:

> Man lese nur die Erklärungen des Fulgentius und seiner Nachfolger, warum Venus, Cupido, Bacchus nackt gemalt werden, Venus z. B., weil sie ihre Verehrer nackt und bloß heimschickt oder weil das Verbrechen der Wollust sich nicht verhüllen läßt, Bacchus, weil die Trinker sich ihres Besitzes entäußern oder weil der Berauschte seine heimlichsten Gedanken nicht bei sich behalten kann.[25]

23 In his age, this was already a long-standing and common procedure. See Jean Seznec, *The Survival of the Pagan Gods: The Mythological Tradition and its Place in Renaissance Humanism and Art*, Princeton, NJ: Princeton University Press, 1981.

24 Walter Benjamin, *The Origin of German Tragic Drama,* p. 223. See also Russell, *The Prince of Darkness*, pp. 17–20.

25 Friedrich von Bezold, *Das Fortleben der antiken Götter im mittelalterlichen Humanismus*, Bonn and Leipzig: Schroeder, 1922, pp. 31–32; quoted in Walter Benjamin, *Ursprung des deutschen Trauerspiels*, in *Gesammelte Schriften*, Vol. 1, ed. Rolf Tiedemann, Frankfurt am Main: Suhrkamp, 1977, pp. 395–396.

> It is only necessary to read the explanations of Fulgentius and his followers as to why Venus, Cupid, and Bacchus are painted naked; Venus, for instance, because she sends her admirers away stripped bare, or because the crime of lust cannot be concealed; Bacchus, because drinkers throw away all their possessions, or because the drunkard cannot keep his most secret thoughts to himself.[26]

Allegoresis thus implies guilt: "The allegorically significant is prevented by guilt from finding fulfilment of its meaning in itself".[27] Their allegorization turns the pagan gods, especially those of classical antiquity, into illustrations of evil deeds and their consequences.[28] Their resultant evil fortunes henceforth indirectly pronounce the justice and glory of God. Accordingly, Milton's God transmutes the fallen angels into allegories of their transgressions:

> the dire form
> Catched by contagion, like in punishment,
> As in their crime.
>
> (10.543–545)

The association between the process of allegoresis and punishment is very pronounced in *Paradise Lost*. Obviously, this allegoresis not only exorcises paganism, it also inclusively excludes it, as it generally both mortifies and preserves at once.[29] This tendency to subjugate its object explains why allegoresis is so closely associated with the production of immobilized, tortured, fragmented and violently feminized bodies.[30] In *Paradise Lost*, however, the procedure of inculpating allegoresis seems to reach an interior limit, as if the narrator would or could not accomplish its perfection: hell was built to contain, represent and punish sin, yet Sin, of all people, seems to suffer altogether sinlessly in it; when Satan first encounters her, she endures the constant agony of allegorization, but her guilt consists in her mere existence: personified Sin is racked by the law of exception.

Against this background, the criticisms that Milton's introduction of allegorical figures into *Paradise Lost* has received should be considered. Since the eighteenth century, many critics of *Paradise Lost* have complained that this insertion is not only tasteless, confusing and unbiblical, but also seems to put

26 Bezold, *Das Fortleben der antiken Götter*, pp. 31–32; quoted in Benjamin, *The Origin of Tragic Drama*, p. 222.
27 Benjamin, *The Origin of Tragic Drama*, p. 224.
28 Benjamin, *The Origin of Tragic Drama*, pp. 223–226.
29 Benjamin, *The Origin of Tragic Drama*, p. 223.
30 See Benjamin, *The Origin of Tragic Drama*, passim; and Christine Buci-Glucksmann, *Baroque Reason: The Aesthetics of Modernity*, London and Thousand Oaks, CA: Sage Publications, 1994, p. 102.

the literal truth of all the other proceedings into question.[31] In recent times, this criticism has been reframed or rejected by diverse arguments. Some of the most prominent were developed by Stephen M. Fallon who claims that the emergence of allegory in *Paradise Lost* demonstrates not Milton's ineptitude, but Satan's: according to Fallon, the narrator of *Paradise Lost* clearly presents Sin and Death as Satan's "brainchildren" and hence as mere "non-beings", thus emphasizing that the devils' delusional acts can produce nothing but the negativity and vacuity of Satanic allegories.[32] Despite its numerous strengths, this argument is not convincing for the simple reason that Sin and Death are described as independent entities who have the capacity to suffer, to rejoice and to take initiatives, even when Satan is not around. Most importantly, God in the tenth book also sees them, and refers to them as collaborating legal subjects who are to be punished at the end of time (10.610–637). Are we to assume that God is hallucinating too? Furthermore, the devils turn out to be a lot less allegorically inclined than God and the God-given environment they are forced to inhabit. The main allegorist is doubtlessly God, and his troping tendencies are never more in evidence than when he designs the architecture of hell with the help of Nature.[33] Hell consists of allegorical assemblages that are designed to represent and assert the devil's elemental abandonment.[34] Let us return to the infernal Lethe, which is one of these assemblages: according to the narrator, the river has been created in order to present a deceptive hope of oblivion to the inhabitants of hell:

> They ferry over this Lethean sound
> Both to and fro, their sorrow to augment,
> And wish and struggle, as they pass, to reach
> The tempting stream, with one small drop to lose
> In sweet forgetfulness all pain and woe,
> All in one moment, and so near the brink;

31 In broad strokes, the history of this discussion is sketched in Joseph H. Summers, *The Muse's Method: An Introduction to* Paradise Lost, London: Chatto and Windus, 1962, pp. 35–39. "Naturalistic" is used within this context in Sarah R. Morrison, "When Worlds Collide: The Central Naturalistic Narrative and the Allegorical Dimension to *Paradise Lost*", in *Living Texts: Interpreting Milton*, eds. Kristin A Pruitt and Charles W Durhamp, Selingsgrove, PA: Susquehana University Press; and London and Cranbury, NJ: Associated University Presses, 2000, p. 179.

32 Stephen M. Fallon, *Milton Among the Philosophers: Poetry and Materialism in Seventeenth-Century England*, Ithaca, NY: Cornell University Press, 1991, p. 168 ff.

33 Catherine Gimelli Martin has pointed out the close link between Miltonian allegory, violence and irony, but she relates it to the narrator's proto-modern stance and not to the anti-historical stance of Milton's God. See Catherine Gimelli Martin, *The Ruins of Allegory:* Paradise Lost *and the Metamorphosis of Epic Convention*, Durham, NC: Duke University Press, 1998, pp. 58 ff.

34 "The relation of exception is a relation of ban. He who has been banned is not, in fact, simply set outside the law and made indifferent to it but rather abandoned by it, that is, exposed and threatened on the threshold in which life and law, outside and inside, become indistinguishable" (Agamben, *Homo Sacer*, p. 23).

But fate withstands, and to oppose the attempt
Medusa with Gorgonian terror guards
The ford [...].
(2.604–612)

This representation implicitly revises Dante's *Comedy*, which transposes Lethe to the garden of Eden. In Canto 31 of the *Purgatorio*, Dante's immersion into Lethe is equated with the rite of absolution, according to a commentary by Jean and Robert Hollander.[35] The Protestant abolition of the sacrament of penance (an abolition that Milton supports in *De Doctrina Christiana*; *DC* 764/765) implies that the corresponding mythologem must also be put under erasure. Just like good Protestants, the devils are forever trapped with their "umpire conscience" (3.195), which thus is turned into an inexorable instrument of torture. As if to enforce this notion by another vaguely allegorical turn, Medusa, as one of the Nature-bred Gorgons, keeps a mockingly enticing oblivion inaccessible to the fallen angels, with the succour of Fate. It should be noted in this context that Medusa, since she is endowed with the powers of petrification, has often been used as an emblem of Saturnine melancholy.[36]

If the tortures of hell are described in such a thoroughly allegorical fashion, it is easy to regard them as externalizations of interior processes, such as self-destructive, egotistic obsession or remorse. Indeed, this allegorizing procedure is common in apologetic descriptions of hell and is particularly widespread in Protestantism ever since Calvin compared the pangs of conscience to the "inferorum terrores".[37] Jacob Böhme wrote about the (feminized) damned soul:

> Und weil Gottes Licht nicht in ihr scheinet und seine Liebe sie nicht berühret, so ist sie eine große Finsternis und eine peinliche, ängstliche Feuerqual und träget die Hölle in sich, und kann das Licht Gottes nicht sehen. Also wohnet sie in sich selber in der Hölle, und darf keines Einfahrens. Denn wo sie innen ist, so ist sie in der Hölle, und ob sie sich viel hunderttausend Meilen könnte von ihrer Stätte schwingen, so ist sie doch in solcher Qual und Finsternis.[38]
>
> And because God's light does not shine within her and his love does not touch her, she is a great darkness and a painful, fearful, fiery agony and

35 See Dante, *Purgatorio*, trans. Jean Hollander and Robert Hollander. New York: Anchor Books, 2008, p. 707 [31.91–102].

36 See e.g. Benjamin, *The Origin of German Tragic Drama*, p. 154.

37 Calvin, *Institutes*, 3.13.3.

38 Jakob Böhme, *Der Weg zu Christo*, Amsterdam: n.p., 1682, p. 154. Spelling modernized. (Christopher Marlowe and others echo this sentiment. See Christopher Marlowe, *The Tragical History of Doctor Faustus*, in *English Renaissance Drama: A Norton Anthology*, edited by David Bevington, New York and London: W. W. Norton and Company, 2002, pp. 257–258 [1.375–82]. Swedenborg later perfected this strand of thinking; it might even have influenced psychoanalysis.)

> carries hell within herself and cannot see the light of God. Thus she lives in hell within herself and does not have to enter into it. For where she is inside, there she is in hell, and even if she could remove herself many hundreds of thousands of miles from her abode, she nevertheless remains in this darkness and affliction.[39]

The narrator himself occasionally takes this route, presenting hell as a manifestation of Satan's degeneracy:

> within him hell
> He brings, and round about him, nor from hell
> One step no more than from himself can fly
> By change of place [...].
> (4.20–23)

Satan himself chimes in with his own famous statement: "Which way I fly is hell; myself am hell" (4.75). This interpretation of hell has frequently been echoed in Milton criticism, but it turns out to be an altogether unconvincing interpretation when the whole storyline of *Paradise Lost* is considered. The most striking counterargument is, once again, the further career of Sin, for she only becomes sinful after her guiltless punishment, within and by the allegorical arrangements that are imposed on her. To give Satan's daughter the position of hell's gatekeeper and to hand her its keys must be considered a staggeringly bad hiring choice, unless the goal of this recruitment is entrapment, the further accumulation of guilt and the multiplication of emblematic images. Her relationship to Satan is as close as can be, whereas all the Son and the Father ever did for her was to throw her into hell on unspecified charges. So when Satan asks her to open the gates for him, her reaction is altogether understandable:

> But what owe I to his commands above,
> Who hates me, and hath hither thrust me down
> Into this gloom of Tartarus profound,
> To sit in hateful office here confined,
> Inhabitant of heaven and heavenly born –
> Here in perpetual agony and pain,
> With terrors and with clamours compassed round
> Of mine own brood, that on my bowels feed?
> Thou art my father, thou my author, thou
> My being gavest me; whom should I obey
> But thee? Whom follow?
> (2.856–866)

39 Translation BQ.

A primal divine punishment inspires her to consolidate evil deeds with further evil deeds, so that she "may stumble on, and deeper fall" (3.201). The inner life of the fallen angels does not determine their environment, but is pressured to conform to the infernal exteriority they have been assigned so that they may turn into proper hell-raising devils. They even seem to be morally obliged to do so, considering how much the reconciliatory tone of Belial moves the narrator to irritation and further condemnation. The proliferation of hell is the implementation of a divine phantasm, before it becomes a Satanic obsession. In this context, it is to be noted that there are political and juridical techniques of power,[40] which strongly resemble Milton's infernal theatre of punitive allegoresis: it has been noted that legal punishment by secular or ecclesiastical courts in Milton's time has a strong tendency to mirror the crime, to "restage" it in the interest of a retributively balancing justice. Frequently, executions are "carried out at the very place where the crime had been committed" and "with the same instruments".[41] According to Foucault, such an execution effectuates an officially sanctioned allegoresis of the crime, "publishing it in its truth".[42] This mirror construction seems to reduce the role of state violence to the staging of an eternal and just judgment of God. It is useful to add that this technique has frequently been combined with another for which Hannah Arendt has coined the ingenious term "Wahrlügen" ("lying the truth"): the conversion of juridical and political phantasms into truths by political means.[43] "Wahrlügen" has the capacity to "conjure up a lying world of consistency which is more adequate to the needs of the human mind than reality itself".[44] Examples of practices from diverse regions and eras can easily be found. For example, it has always been a common practice to assert that certain groups of people are mentally inferior and consequently to deprive them of an education. Arendt herself gives the example of fascist racism: Nazism declares certain peoples and ethnic minorities to be lower life forms, completely subject to their animal instincts; then it imprisons them in camps and proceeds, by diverse methods of systematic degradation, to reduce them to the animal status they are supposedly already endowed with.[45]

40 On this term see e.g. Michel Foucault, *Abnormal: Lectures at the Collège de France, 1974–1975*, trans. Graham Burchell, eds. Valerio Marchetti and Antonella Salomoni, New York: Picador, 2003.

41 See e.g. Michel Foucault, *Discipline and Punish: The Birth of the Prison*, trans. Alan Sheridan, New York: Vintage Books, 1979, pp. 44–46.

42 Foucault, *Discipline and Punish*, p. 45.

43 Hannah Arendt, "Approaches to the German Problem", in *Essays in Understanding: 1930–1954*, ed. Jerome Kohn, New York: Harcourt, Brace and Co., 1994, p. 111; see also Hannah Arendt, *Zur Zeit: Politische Essays,* trans. Eike Geisel, ed. Marie Luise Knott, Berlin: Rotbuch, 1986.

44 Hannah Arendt, *The Origins of Totalitarianism*, San Diego and New York: Harcourt, 1985, p. 353.

45 Arendt, *The Origins of Totalitarianism*, pp. 454–455.

The theatrical dimension of these degradations has frequently been noted.[46] Likewise, Milton's hell is an environment that is designed not only to punish its inhabitants, but also to justify its institution by bringing out the lowest in them, by making sin visibly proliferate. To further his cause, God temporarily reduces the devils to the status of reptiles and thus enforces their senseless self-condemnation:

> Thus was the applause they meant,
> Turned to exploding hiss, triumph to shame
> Cast on themselves from their own mouths.
> (10.545–547)

The narrator mockingly ascribes their enforced "pronouncement" to the devils themselves: their involuntary, animal articulation is retranslated into socially mediated semantics. Whatever is done to them can thus be imputed to the devils as their own fault. They find themselves in a situation in which they are not only condemned to eternal punishment, but also deprived of the right to do right and to have rights. The devils in hell must exist exclusively as their own embodied, unconditional condemnations.

Generally, the devils struggle not to coincide with the terminal, "natural" place that the architecture of the universe assigns to them. Given that they have little choice in the matter, they resist God's solidified ordinance mainly by strictly separating between inwardness and outwardness. Satan declares:

> The mind is its own place, and in itself
> Can make a heaven of hell, a hell of heaven.
> (1.254–255)

However, this counterstrategy proves altogether unsuccessful: Satan and the devils make feeble attempts to compete with heaven and institute an alternative sovereignty. But punishing pain keeps breaking through the barrier between inside and outside.[47] Satan's statements on the subject therefore remain inconsistent, as has often been remarked, and they tend to change with his outer circumstances.[48] In his official role, among his troops, he confidently designates God as a cruel usurper; but when he finds himself on earth, isolated and somewhat disoriented, he acknowledges God's legitimacy and moral superiority. Satan appears to be ambivalent to the point of schizophrenia, a

46 See e.g. Margaret-Anne Hutton, *Testimony from the Nazi Camps: French Women's Voices,* London and New York: Routledge, 2005, pp. 93–96.

47 See Björn Quiring, "The Greatest Share of Endless Pain: The Spectral Sacramentality of Pain in Milton's *Paradise Lost*", in *Passions and Subjectivity in Early Modern Culture*, eds. Brian Cummings and Freya Sierhuis, Farnham and Burlington, VT: Ashgate, 2013, pp. 253–266.

48 See Stanley E. Fish, *Surprised By Sin: The Reader in* Paradise Lost, Cambridge, MA: Harvard University Press, 1997; and Fallon, *Milton Among The Philosophers.*

disjointedness that is best explained as a symptom of his inclusive exclusion. A. J. A. Waldock took this disjointedness to be a sign of Milton's lack of narrative talent,[49] and Stanley E. Fish interpreted it as a symptom of Satan's moral, religious and intellectual failure.[50] But it might also be taken to be a sign of the ambiguous position in which he has been placed. Satan is not the determined rebel the Romantics liked to see in him, but neither does he assume the role of the incoherent, broken buffoon that the Fish school has tried to force upon him: the contradictions in which he is caught are actually not his own, but those he inherits from heaven. William Empson has pointed out that the atmosphere of heaven necessarily produces sycophancy as well as narcissism.[51] And the disappointed careerist Satan never completely breaks with this heaven; even after his fall, he still upholds the old celestial hierarchy, at least to the degree that he insists on his own elevated position within it. He still addresses the fallen angels with their old titles and, collectively, as the "deities of heaven" (2.11). And when Ithuriel and Zephon try to question him, he retorts:

> Know ye not me? Ye knew me once no mate
> For you, there sitting where ye durst not soar;
> Not to know me argues yourselves unknown,
> The lowest of your throng […].
>
> (4.828–831)

Furthermore, when Abdiel questions the legitimacy of Satan's orders, the latter does not call him "counterrevolutionary", but "seditious" (6.152). Satan thus clings to a political order he professes to despise, and keeps it intact in his new environment, as much as possible. He certainly still considers himself "of the first/ If not the first arch-angel" (5.659–660).[52]

This ambivalence also impinges on the political order that the devils institute among themselves. They establish a council that claims to be governed by the "popular vote" (2.313). However, only the "peers" of hell, "[b]y place or choice the worthiest" (1.759), are admitted to the assembly, while the lower classes must remain outdoors. Furthermore, among these peers, some are more equal than others, foremost the twelve "chief" devils (1.381); and Satan presides over all, seated "[h]igh on a throne of royal state" (2.1), displaying "monarchal pride" (2.428). He justifies his elevated position in rather murky terms:

49 A. J. A. Waldock, Paradise Lost *and Its Critics*, Cambridge: Cambridge University Press, 1966, p. 91.

50 Fish, *Surprised By Sin*, pp. 336–339.

51 William Empson, *Milton's God*, Westport, CT: Greenwood Press, 1978, p. 111.

52 Incidentally, this characterization by Raphael shows that the angels themselves sometimes are uncertain about another angel's exact place within the heavenly hierarchy.

Me though just right, and the fixed laws of heaven
Did first create your leader, next, free choice,
With what besides, in counsel or in fight,
Hath been achieved of merit [...].
(2.18–21)

First, he is leader by "just right and the fixed laws of heaven", whether they are positive laws or natural laws inherent in the cosmos, as the Stoics envisaged it. Second, he is the freely chosen sovereign, elected by general consensus. Third, his supreme position is due to his political and military merits. However, it remains unclear which of these three sources of legitimation he considers decisive; and if all of them would always work in harmony, the war in heaven would never have occurred. In practice, it is obviously the democratic consensus that caves in first. Even within the elect circle of peers, hell is found to be a managed democracy at best: it turns out that the discussion in the council is carefully orchestrated to achieve the result desired by Satan. The "worthiest" devils get to discuss and vote, but it is he, together with his right hand Beelzebub, who gets to determine the topic and to interrupt their discussion, initiating a vote just at the point when the general inclination happens to coincide with his own (2.378–389). Even in that respect, hell's supreme "possessor" feebly imitates the sovereign of heaven: when God calls "to synod all the blest" (11.67), there is no "synod" in the original sense of "general council": the Father just makes an announcement and dispenses commands, while nobody else has a chance to get a word in (11.84–125). The devils in hell do not invent new forms of government; they mimic the old Hobbesian theocracy as well as they can.

Consequently, the organization of hell also mirrors diverse peculiarities of the divine order from which it cannot break away. It is occasionally made obvious that Satan, Sin and Death function as a parody of the Holy Trinity, for example when Sin, speaking to Satan and echoing Mark 16.19, designates earth as the place

where I shall reign
At thy right hand voluptuous, as beseems
Thy daughter and thy darling, without end.
(2.868–870)

And the twelve supreme devils, whom Satan calls to himself at the edge of the fiery lake, prefigure the twelve apostles of Christ.[53] When all is said and done, hell appears merely as a continuation of heaven by other means. The difference is that it is not a machine for the unending accumulation of debt, but one for the unending accumulation of guilt. In this vein, hell provides the

53 See John N. King, *Milton and Religious Controversy: Satire and Polemic in* Paradise Lost, Cambridge and New York: Cambridge University Press, 2000, pp. 52–53.

Father with another advantage besides the one already mentioned, that is to keep at his disposal an enemy who can make his angels stand "confirmed" (11.71) under divine discipline: it also serves God as a demonstration that there is no alternative to his own rule, no outside to his infinite dominion. The angels "freely [...] serve" (5.538), and the devils serve unfreely, under the law of the sovereign exception which presents itself as the law of nature out of bounds. In this zone of cruel allegoresis, under pressure to coincide with their verdict beyond and "without recall" (5.885), the fallen can do nothing but represent and repeat their own condemnation. It will turn out that the foundation of this hell is the condition of possibility for the creation of man and his cosmos – though not quite in the way that the Father officially announces.

7 Cosmic redemptions

7.1 The judgment of Genesis

After the Fall of the devils, a new world is created, and it strongly resembles what has traditionally been called the "cosmos", even though Milton himself does not use that term. According to Alexandre Koyré, the word "cosmos" designated in the seventeenth century the traditional "conception of the world as a finite, closed, and hierarchically ordered whole" "in which the hierarchy of value determined the hierarchy and structure of being, rising from the dark, heavy and imperfect earth to the higher and higher perfection of the stars and heavenly spheres".[1] In most cases, the earth is thought to be situated at the centre of this cosmos.[2] Although strongly indebted to Ptolemaism, Milton's cosmology does not coincide with this traditional Aristotelian-Ptolemaic worldview. Instead, he echoes the scientific developments of his age in emphasizing the decentred status of man's habitat. In this context, the suggestions of heliocentrism that pervade *Paradise Lost* are less relevant than the marginal status of the cosmos itself. It is but a small part of creation, on the border of the inconceivably immense spaces of heaven and hell, which in turn are surrounded by the infinite spaces of Chaos where the very idea of a centre ceases to make sense. The Miltonian cosmos is only a divine colony, an "addition of his empire", according to Raphael (7.555), and a rather negligible one at that: next to the mighty ramparts of heaven, it looks like "a star/ Of smallest magnitude close by the moon" (2.1052–1053). This is appropriate, since its official function is merely that of an incubator. According to God, the cosmos is designed to serve as the breeding ground for prospective angels who are to replace the fallen ones:

> heaven yet populous, retains
> Number sufficient to possess her realms
> Though wide, and this high temple to frequent

1 Alexandre Koyré, *From the Closed World to the Infinite Universe*, Baltimore: Johns Hopkins University Press, 1957, pp. vii, 2.

2 Koyré, *From the Closed World to the Infinite Universe*, p. 277.

With ministries due, and solemn rites:
But, lest his heart exalt him in the harm
Already done, to have dispeopled heaven,
My damage fondly deemed, I can repair
That detriment, if such it be to lose
Self-lost, and in a moment will create
Another world, out of one man a race
Of men innumerable, there to dwell,
Not here, till by degrees of merit raised
They open to themselves at length the way
Up hither, under long obedience tried,
And earth be changed to heaven, and heaven to earth,
One kingdom, joy and union without end.
(7.146–161)

The motivation for the creation of the cosmos appears as self-contradictory: God suggests that the fall of Satan's crew is no loss at all, but he nevertheless proceeds to repair it, apparently in order both to uphold his own non-endangered reputation and to spite the devils' arrogance (even though the devils are supposedly locked away in hell and thus unable to learn about this setback). It furthermore turns out that he does not repair the breach himself, but gives the newly created creatures a chance to do so: unlike the other angels who were created as such, their successors will have to work their way up the great chain of being in order to attain angelic status, as if they had to make the redemptive reparations for Satan's breach that are denied to the fallen angels themselves. Significantly, the cosmos is posited on "that side heaven from whence [Satan's] legions fell" (2.1006), hinting at the presupposed association between both. Men on earth are created as deficitary beings who shall redeem the error of the fallen angels; it is their *telos* to get rid of an innate deficit by trial of their "long obedience". From his first breath, man is under probation, which means that the guilt of the fallen angels is foundational for the cosmos that he is to inhabit – a monument to their disobedience. One might even ask whether or not he is also indebted to Satan, whose rebellion is, after all, the cause of his very existence.[3] In any case, man must both expurgate and incarnate guilt. In conformity with this double obligation, man is confronted with a Janus-headed task: he is both to multiply on earth and also to fly from earth. On the one hand, Raphael asserts that man has the task to leave the cosmos behind and to "winged ascend/ Ethereal" (5.498–499) toward heaven; accordingly, man's sexuality is denigrated (8.579–585). Yet on the other hand, Raphael also claims that Adam and Eve should not neglect their earthly station as breeders; their attempt to soar thus also runs the danger of hubris

3 According to Neil Forsyth, Satan is also a cause of man's salvation. Neil Forsyth, *The Satanic Epic*, Princeton, NJ: Princeton University Press, 2003, pp. 15–17.

(5.388–391; 8.172–174). Caught in this double bind, man is an aprioric target of a divine judgment that condemns his unworthiness. This partly explains why God already knows from the beginning that man will be unable to elevate himself from his habitat, but be ensnared instead (3.95–96).

Man's Fall is not merely a repetition of Satan's Fall, however: unlike the devils, at least some of the fallen men "shall find grace" – if not the grace to ascend to heaven, then at least the grace of not descending into hell (3.131; 12.461–464). The official reason for this partial administration of grace is the fact that man fell because he was deceived by Satan, whereas the devils fell "[s]elf-tempted, self-depraved" (3.130). Harold Skulsky has pointed out that, with the exception of Satan himself, the devils were actually not "self-tempted", but were persuaded to manifest disobedience by their superior's strong rhetoric. But in their case, God does not consider their seduction an extenuating circumstance, and so they have to share Satan's eternal doom.[4] Since this difference in treatment cannot be ascribed to the official reason, the reason for God's grace toward mankind must be sought elsewhere. Definitive answers are, once again, hard to come by, but God's generosity may once again provide him with a strategic advantage and a chance to consolidate his position beyond the reach of his creatures. For the amnesty comes at a price: the happy few humans to whom grace is administered shall know unmistakably that they owe their salvation to God, not to themselves:

> Yet not of will in him, but grace in me
> Freely vouchsafed; once more I will renew
> His lapsèd powers, though forfeit and enthralled
> By sin to foul exorbitant desires;
> Upheld by me, yet once more he shall stand
> On even ground against his mortal foe,
> By me upheld, that he may know how frail
> His fallen condition is, and to me owe
> All his deliverance, and to none but me.
> (3.174–182)

Although men must contribute to their salvation, they cannot ascribe this contribution to themselves. In contrast to the angels who "freely" stand (3.102) so long as they stand, fallen man must be forever propped up. God thus further liberates himself from all claims of legal accountability: men rightfully deserve to be in the same state of inclusive exclusion as the devils; and if they are not, this is a praiseworthy act of divine mercy. Thus, the Father can establish a cosmic legislation that is even more unaccountable and indebting than that of heaven. Moreover, the creation of the cosmos has a side effect that also

4 Harold Skulsky, *Milton and the Death of Man: Humanism on Trial in* Paradise Lost, Newark, NJ and London: University of Delaware Press, 2000, pp. 208–209.

contributes to the transcendentalization of God: he deals with the cosmos only by proxy; earth is principally not visited by God himself, but only by the Son as his representative. Indeed, after the Fall of the devils, the Son's most important function seems to be this negotiation between heaven and earth: in heaven, as far as the reader can gather, the Father keeps ruling and administrating in his own person (see e.g. 10.28–62; 11.67–125). Through the creation of earth, God is put at yet one more remove, appearing ever more inscrutable and disembodied to his creatures. Raphael's assertion that he must liken "spiritual to corporal forms" (5.573) when narrating episodes from celestial history (5.571–574) would also fit this general strategy: Noam Reisner has pointed out that the angelic theory of accommodation is irreconcilable with the narrator's and Raphael's own monism,[5] so one is allowed the suspicion that the divine messenger does not make an effort to render the transcendent accessible, but instead unconditionally asserts divine transcendence where it must remain doubtful, even to himself.

How does the Son as the divine emissary go about the creation and legislation of man's cosmos? It has already been sketched in the fourth chapter that God's generative work involves three hardly reconcilable concepts in Milton's epic: 1) the first and familiar biblical notion of creation by a divine order word; 2) the somewhat more distant, but still traditional, notion of creation by demiurgic manual craftsmanship (see e.g. 8.462–477) as developed extensively in Plato's *Timaeus* and subsequently adopted by Christian theology;[6] and 3) the pagan and in a Christian context rather peculiar notion of divine creation by way of sexualized procreation: a penetrative interaction with a generative chaotic/natural force of uncertain pedigree (see e.g. 1.19–22; 8.234–237). The creation of the cosmos proceeds accordingly: first Chaos is pacified by a speech act (7.216); second, the Son enters the zone that he has pacified and delimits it, thereby manually enacting a territorialization with the help of a tool:

> in his hand
> He took the golden compasses, prepared
> In God's eternal store, to circumscribe
> This universe, and all created things:
> One foot he centred, and the other turned
> Round through the vast profundity obscure,
> And said, Thus far extend, thus far thy bounds,
> This be thy just circumference, O world.
> (7.224–231)

5 Noam Reisner, *Milton and the Ineffable*, Oxford and New York: Oxford University Press, 2009, p. 212.

6 On the relation between creation-by-word and creation-by-deed, see also Hans Blumenberg, *Paradigms for a Metaphorology*, translated by Robert Savage, Ithaca, NY: Cornell University Press, 2010, p. 80.

The Son's intervention generates a limited amount of matter that is no longer inherently dynamic and conflictual but is instead "unformed and void", inertly passive and thus ready to receive forms: it resembles the Aristotelian ὕλη in its pure potentiality.[7] Thereupon, God acts on this passive material neither as a demiurge who forms it with his own hands, nor as a Great Author who continues to structure it by order words. Rather – in the third part of the creation of the cosmos – the Holy Spirit (whom Milton equates with the Father's "virtus et potentia" in the *Doctrina*)[8] copulates with the matter of the cosmos and inseminates it, rendering it "pregnant" (1.22):

> His brooding wings the Spirit of God outspread,
> And vital virtue infused, and vital warmth
> Throughout the fluid mass [...].
>
> (7.235–237)

From this point onward, Milton will often represent the cosmos as an organism. Significantly, the impregnation is supplemented by another expulsion:

> but [the Spirit] downward purged
> The black tartareous cold infernal dregs,
> Adverse to life [...].
>
> (7.237–239)

In early modern natural philosophy, "tartar" is the standard name for "the inassimilable elements purged from the system [of the human body] in the process of digestion".[9] In the works of Paracelsus und Helmont, the term furthermore designates the evil principle within matter.[10] Since Chaos is described as a "desert" (2.973) and the court of Chaos as nomadic,[11] the alternative meaning of "tartar", referring to the nomadic tribes of Asian Tartary, also comes into play.[12] Apparently, the foundational appeasement of the

7 Aristotle, *The Physics*, translated by Philip H. Wicksteed and Francis Cornford, Cambridge, MA: Harvard University Press; and London: Heinemann, 1963, pp. 90–93 [192a].

8 See *DC* 248/249.

9 John Rogers, *The Matter of Revolution: Science, Poetry, and Politics in the Age of Milton*, Ithaca, NY: Cornell University Press, 1996, p. 133.

10 Rogers, *The Matter of Revolution,* p. 135. John Rogers also assumes that the existence of these strange dregs contradicts the assumption that the universe of *Paradise Lost* is a monist creation *ex deo*. According to Rogers, a latent Manicheanism, or polytheism is suggested, a depletion of Milton's "theodicial force" that Rogers speculatively connects to the poet's political disillusionment after the failure of the English Republic (Rogers, *The Matter of Revolution*, pp. 134–142).

11 See the fourth chapter, pp. 143–162.

12 Walter S. H. Lim, "John Milton, Orientalism, and the Empires of the East in *Paradise Lost*", in: *The English Renaissance, Orientalism, and the Idea of Asia*, ed. Debra Johanyak and Walter S. H. Lim, New York: Palgrave Macmillan, 2010, p. 218. See also the reference to the "roving Tartar" (3.432).

cosmic hubbub was not enough: divine creation constantly requires the subtractive work of physiological and social expulsion. In this context it should be remembered that Chaos is not lifeless, but endowed with a strange, belligerent kind of vitality that differs from that of the cosmos mainly by violating the hierarchical boundaries of elemental and organic differentiation. These very bounds of elementality are affirmed by the Son's next act:

> [He] then founded, then conglobed
> Like things to like, the rest to several place
> Disparted, and between spun out the air,
> And earth self-balanced on her centre hung.
> (7.239–242)

After drawing the distinction between chaos and cosmos, God proceeds to differentiate between the elements, of which only air and earth are explicitly mentioned here. This act appears to be homogenizing, bringing together "like things" and arranging them in a common sphere ("conglobing"), excluding the things that are "unlike". It remains unclear, however, whether this act of differentiation results in the traditional, hierarchical order of the Aristotelian cosmos. Is the "conglobing" of the elements focused on a common centre? Raphael says that earth is able to keep her balance by "hanging on her centre", but nowhere does he indicate that this centre is also the centre of the cosmos: the structure of the developing cosmos remains elusive. Furthermore, it is remarkable that Earth, as a matter of course, receives a female pronoun here; it will soon become obvious that she is not only an element and a heavenly body, but also a person. Like Nature, she appears as a divinity and is thus associated with yet another Hesiodic goddess, namely Gaia. According to Hesiod, Gaia was generated out of Chaos; she is the primordial female and the mother of the hills, the sea, Godfather Uranus, the Titans, the Cyclops, the Erinyes and others.[13] Traditionally, Physis/Natura and this earth-mother Gaia/Terra are often identified, for example by Macrobius, who also equates both of them with Isis.[14] In Milton, Nature is without a doubt more prominent and elevated than Earth: she precedes the cosmos, and her powers have already made themselves felt in heaven and in hell; but she also remains a more elusive figure.

After the elements have been differentiated, God has finally reached the stage at which he can utter his primordial biblical command:

13 Hesiod, *Theogonie, Griechisch/Deutsch*, trans. and ed. by Otto Schönberger, Stuttgart: Reclam, 1999, pp. 12–15 [116–153].

14 "Isis iuncta religione celebratur, quae est vel terra vel natura rerum subiacens soli"./ "Isis is worshipped in a kindred cult as either earth or the natural order subject to the sun". Macrobius, *Saturnalia,* Vol. 1, ed. and trans. Robert A. Kaster, Cambridge, MA and London: Harvard University Press, 2011, pp. 276/277 [1.20.18].

> Let there be light, said God, and forthwith light
> Ethereal, first of things, quintessence pure
> Sprung from the deep […].
> (7.243–245)

In the third book, the narrator has already hinted at his suspicion that light might not have been created at all, but instead is "of the eternal co-eternal" (3.2), just like the "eternal Night" of Chaos (3.18). It is all the more interesting that the light of the cosmos does not spring directly from the "excessive bright" (3.380) of God and his word, but instead is called forth from the dark depths of matter. Light is pre-existent *in potentia* within ὕλη as the fifth, ethereal element ("quintessence"; see also 3.716), and the word of God individuates it by naming it. One might consider this differentiation not only as a commandment but also as an evaluation: God calls forth light *because* light is good (whereas tartar is bad). Thus God's primordial act of illumination can also be ascertained as a judgment that provides the opportunity for further judgments. After the separation of the quintessence follows the separation of the waters:

> The waters underneath from those above
> Dividing: for as earth, so he the world
> Built on circumfluous waters calm, in wide
> Crystálline ocean, and the loud misrule
> Of Chaos far removed, lest fierce extremes
> Contiguous might distemper the whole frame:
> And Heaven he named the firmament […].
> (7.268–274)

The mysteries of this passage derive from Milton's need to stay close to the Book of Genesis. Gen. 1.7 asserts that God creates the world as a bubble of air and light in a vast expanse of dark waters.[15] In *Paradise Lost*, this vast expanse is already filled by battling, chaotic proto-elements, so Milton has to confine the waters of the firmament to an intermediary buffer zone, a water wall that protects the differentiated elements of the cosmos from the disintegrative intrusion of Chaos.[16] Milton also closely follows Gen. 1.8 ("And God called the firmament Heaven"), with the result that the term "heaven"

15 "As Rashi perceived, the text pictures a territory formed in the middle of the watery chaos, a giant bubble of air surrounded on all sides by water. Once the land is created, the universe as pictured in Genesis is a habitable bubble, with land and seas at its base, surrounded by a mass of water". Richard Elliott Friedman, *Commentary on the Torah with a New English Translation*, San Francisco and New York: HarperSanFrancisco, 2001, p. 7.

16 There is a slight problem, however, with designating the firmament as an "expanse of liquid": the outer wall of the cosmos on which Satan walks around in the third and tenth book seems to be firm, not fluid – if we are not to assume that Satan is able to walk on water.

becomes equivocal, designating both the watery firmament and also the Father's empire that existed before the creation of the cosmos.[17]

After this elemental and vaguely organic order has been established and shored up against Chaos, God proceeds to the creation of particular objects. These objects seem to spring forth from the organic latency of the cosmos. In the words of John Reichert: "Milton presents creation as the response of that which is as if already alive, embryonic, submerged, or dormant".[18] God mainly uses his encoding order words in the process, but he seems to call forth the creatures from a region of pre-existence rather than determining their forms and their very existence by his utterance. The creation of the cosmos appears as collaborative rather than as solitary work. More fundamental than the divine speech seems to be the divine sexuality, most notably the fact that the Holy Spirit has already impregnated the cosmos. The pregnancy itself is described as an odd double process:

> The Earth was formed, but in the womb as yet
> Of waters, embryon immature involved,
> Appeared not: over all the face of Earth
> Main ocean flowed, not idle, but with warm
> Prolific humour softening all her globe,
> Fermented the great mother to conceive,
> Satiate with genial moisture [...].
> (7.276–282; capitalization added)

It is remarkable that, at this stage, Earth is described both as an embryo maturing in the cosmic waters and also as an expectant mother, inseminated by God, or, more precisely, by the waters that God has fertilized. The shady double duty that Nature fulfils – sometimes taking the role of God's wife-mother, sometimes that of his daughter – is also ascribed to Earth. The birth of land from the nutrient waters is described as her emergence from latency, following the pattern of divine command and creaturely obedience (7.282–300).[19] And Earth instantly proceeds to give birth on God's order:

> Let the Earth
> Put forth the verdant grass, herb yielding seed,

17 The word *shāmayim* (שָׁמַיִם) that is used in the original Hebrew text of Gen. 1.8 has been endowed with the same ambiguity (Rüdiger Bartelmus, "Šāmayim", in *Theological Dictionary of the Old Testament*, Vol. 15, ed. G. Johannes Botterweck, Helmer Ringgren and Heinz-Josef Fabry, trans. David E. Green, Grand Rapids and Cambridge: Eerdmans, 2006, pp. 204–225).

18 John Reichert, *Milton's Wisdom: Nature and Scripture in* Paradise Lost, Ann Arbor: University of Michigan Press, 1992, p. 130.

19 It is hard to gauge whether the resultant migrations of the waters are due to their natural inclinations and the shifting lay of the land or to an introduction of a new natural law, as in Basil the Great's interpretation of the same biblical passage. (See Chapter 1, pp. 47–48.)

> And fruit tree yielding fruit after her kind;
> Whose seed is in herself upon the Earth.
> He scarce had said, when the bare Earth, till then
> Desert and bare, unsightly, unadorned,
> Brought forth the tender grass whose verdure clad
> Her universal face with pleasant green [...].
> (7.309–316)

And so it goes on: after all the plants have been created/born, the fishes and reptiles spring from the waters and the mammals from earth's "fertile womb" (7.454) on the command of God. Even when Milton's God creates the heavenly bodies "to give light on the earth" (7.345), Milton uses a partly organicist vocabulary to describe this act: the Son "framed" the planets (7.355), but he "sowed" the stars (7.358). In all of these cases, the same oscillation between creation by word, creation by hand and creation by natural, sexualized co-generation prevails. For example, the statements that "God created the great whales and each/ Soul living" (7.391) and that the "waters generated" (7.393) them all, stand only two lines apart. Again, it is claimed both that the order word has by itself produced a reality and that it has merely channelled the generative dynamics of Nature and Chaos. This tension can already be found in the Bible: in Gen. 1.20 and Gen. 1.24, Elohim also orders sea and earth to bring forth creatures, as opposed to creating them entirely by himself. The Bible's creation theology is complex, so we will not try to summarize it in this context.[20] It should be noted, however, that Milton, once again, supplements his creation narrative with fragments from pagan mythology and philosophy. The remarkable similarities between the seventh book of *Paradise Lost* and the creation myth in the first book of Ovid's *Metamorphoses* have already been pointed out by Maggie Kilgour and others.[21] Furthermore, the representation of Earth as a great mother who is fertilized by heavenly waters and gives birth to the plants and animals liberally paraphrases Lucretius.[22] And Milton emphasizes the exuberantly fertile femininity of the Earth even more than these pagan authors do. That God is the ultimate, metaphysical cause of the Earth's teeming is not apparent; his full control of the situation must be a matter of belief again.

One might suppose that the natural dynamic of earth is also involved in the creation of Adam and Eve, so that the dust from which they are formed is no mere passive receptacle of the divine spirit, but an active, creative force.

20 See e.g. the interesting opinions of St. Bede on this subject in: Bede the Venerable, *Commentary on Genesis: Book 1*, in *Ancient Christian Texts: Commentaries on Genesis 1–3*, trans. Carmen Hardin, ed. Michael Glerup, Downer Grove, IL: IVP Academic, 2010, pp. 125–128.

21 See e.g. Maggie Kilgour, *Milton and the Metamorphosis of Ovid*, Oxford and New York: Oxford University Press, 2012.

22 Barbara Kiefer Lewalski, Paradise Lost *and the Rhetoric of Literary Forms*, Princeton, NJ: Princeton University Press, 2014, p. 134, referring to the fifth book of *De Rerum Natura*.

This is not explicitly spelled out in *Paradise Lost*, but hints can be found elsewhere: in the *Doctrina Christiana*, Milton asserts that the creation of man was not an altogether supernatural event. From the fact that God's creative power was involved in man's creation, it does not follow "that natural causes [causas naturales] have not brought their usual force to bear on the procreation of the body" (*DC* 306/307). It is not even a privilege of man that he was infused with the divine *ruach*; this force of God has inseminated and pervaded creation so thoroughly that matter and spirit cannot be neatly separated anywhere.[23]

> Nam et halitum vitae caeteris quoque animantibus, ut supra, Deus inspiravit, et inspiratum ita materiae penitus immiscuit, ut non secus atque formas caeterae, humana quoque forma ex potentia materiae a Deo indita propagaretur et produceretur.
>
> For not only did God infuse the breath of life into the other animate creatures too, as above, but also, having infused it, he mixed it in matter so thoroughly that, no differently from the other forms, human form too would be propagated and produced from the power implanted in matter by God.
>
> (*DC* 308/309)

In this context, all sexual reproduction is understood to be an expression of divine creative power. Raphael echoes these notions obscurely, for example when he addresses the bodily Adam as a "living soul" (7.528), and not as a corporeal being that is inhabited by an immortal soul. While Milton mostly refrains from more explicit anthropological assertions in *Paradise Lost*, Adam and Eve are always regarded by themselves and by the angels as co-products of God and Nature, as if this cooperation was self-evident (see e.g. 8.534–538; 8.561–562). Thus, no part of the cosmos can positively be said to have been created without the support of Nature's latent counterforce.

7.2 The great cycle and the Keplerian world picture

In the *Doctrina Christiana*, Milton emphasizes that the divine work of creation came to an end on the seventh day; the rest is "propagation by natural order" (*DC* 305). God does not leave the cosmos to its own devices, however: besides the palpable surveillance and sentry duty of the angels, the preserving, structuring, vitalizing and judgmental force of God is said to still flow through the cosmos (see e.g. the prayer hymn of Adam and Eve in 5.153–208). Thus

23 In the *Doctrina Christiana*, the soul of man is said to be inseparable from his body, if not identical with it: "totum hominem esse animam, et animam hominem; corpus nempe sive substantiam individuam, animatam, sensitivam, rationalem […]"./ "The whole man is soul, and the soul is man; namely a body or substance which is individual, animated, sensitive, and rational […]". (*DC* 302/303). See also Phillip J. Donnelly, "'Matter' versus 'Body': The Character of Milton's Monism", *Milton Quarterly* 33.3 (1999), p. 82.

God's power is still found to influence the world, enacting his will within the processes of nature. One of the forms it takes is light dissemination, dispersing the chaotic powers of darkness. "[A]bove them all" (3.571), it is the light of the sun which is "predominant in heaven" (8.160) and "of this great world both eye and soul" (5.171). All other light sources are derivative: "Hither as to their fountain other stars/ Repairing, in their golden urns draw light" (7.364–365). Adam tells Eve that the things that grow on earth also "receive/ Perfection from the sun's more potent ray" (4.672–673). The sun is connected to God metonymically, as the most direct manifestation of his power. But their relation is also metaphorical: as Satan makes explicit, the sun represents God within the cosmos: it is "like the God/ Of this new world" (4.33–34). Like God, it is most emphatically male and feminizes the rest of the cosmos: the sun "to each inward part/ With gentle penetration, though unseen,/ Shoots invisible virtue" (3.584–586).[24] Besides being the source of cosmic light and growth, it is also the all-seeing "lordly eye" (3.578). The traditional image of the eye of God (which subsequently became the eye of law)[25] is also invoked in this context because the sun is used as a surveillance centre from which archangel Uriel observes the cosmos (3.650–651).[26]

However, the divine norms that are installed in creation demand that no creature remain purely passive: God must be compensated for the influx of structuring and sustaining power that he sends into the universe as his radiating goodness. And on earth, as in heaven, he is paid by obedience and praise; unfallen Adam and Eve pay this debt each day. But this is not all, as Raphael explains: all created things are material to some degree, and so some material sacrifice must also be made to the divine. At the dinner table of Paradise, conversing after their meal, Raphael unfolds how the higher orders are to receive an "alimental recompense" (5.424) from the lower ones:

> O Adam, one almighty is, from whom
> All things proceed, and up to him return,
> If not depraved from good, created all
> Such to perfection, one first matter all,
> Indued with various forms, various degrees
> Of substance, and in things that live, of life;
> But more refined, more spirituous, and pure,
> As nearer to him placed or nearer tending
> Each in their several active spheres assigned,

24 The sexual meaning of "penetration" was already prominent in Milton's time. See "penetration, n.", *OED Online*. Oxford University Press, June 2016. Web. 20 August 2016.

25 See Michael Stolleis, *Das Auge des Gesetzes: Geschichte einer Metapher*, Munich: Beck, 2004.

26 For an approved representative of divine foresight, however, Uriel proves staggeringly ineffective: not only does he recognize Satan far too late; when he finally has identified him, he instantly loses sight of him, subsequently failing to report his discovery until about six hours have passed.

Till body up to spirit work, in bounds
Proportioned to each kind. So from the root
Springs lighter the green stalk, from thence the leaves
More airy, last the bright consummate flower
Spirits odorous breathes: flowers and their fruit
Man's nourishment, by gradual scale sublimed [...].
(5.469–483)

Thus, an all-embracing dietetics is sketched, in which the higher, more spiritual forms of life nourish themselves in cosmic food chains on lower, coarser, more material ones.[27] Similar statements are dispersed throughout the epic. For example, when Adam awakens for the first time, he finds that the sun feeds on his "moisture" (8.256). Milton's narrator and most of his protagonists posit a continuum in which there is no substantial difference between the most elevated supreme beings and the most ordinary material objects: all are but "degrees of substance" which subsume and absorb those of lesser degree:

and food alike those pure
Intelligential substances require
As doth your rational; and both contain
Within them every lower faculty
Of sense, whereby they hear, see, smell, touch, taste,
Tasting concoct, digest, assimilate,
And corporeal to incorporeal turn.
(5.407–413)

A double movement, simultaneously downward and upward, is thus posited in nature, consisting of a constant influx of spiritual, ordering forces into matter on the one hand, and a constant ascent of material forces into more spiritual realms on the other. Under ideal circumstances, both motions converge to form an infinite, encompassing process. It stands to reason that this process is to be regarded as both metabolic and adjudicative, since Milton's cosmos is represented both as an organism and also as a law court. Both components of the operation are most effectively synthesized when the food chains are described as sacramental: Raphael eating his dinner, for example, is said to "transubstantiate" his food (5.438). Just as the priest may turn bread into the body of Christ, the angel can turn fruits into an angelic body. Of course, Milton did not believe in the Catholic doctrine of transubstantiation, as he made unmistakably clear in the *Doctrina* and other places (see, most prominently, *DC* 760–763), but this is perfectly compatible with what he does in this passage: he naturalizes the Eucharist. From an extraordinary,

27 Empson wryly remarks that Milton's angels are therefore in constant danger of being "gobbled up" by God. See William Empson, *Milton's God*, Westport, CT: Greenwood Press, 1978, p. 139.

supernatural event, it becomes the most normal of processes.[28] Milton thus levels the distinction between natural and supernatural events, a distinction that Aquinas emphasizes most strongly in his statement about the Eucharist:

> Haec tamen conversio non est similis conversionibus naturalibus, sed est omnino supernaturalis, sola Dei virtute effecta.
>
> Yet this change is not like natural changes, but is entirely supernatural, and effected by God's power alone.[29]

The cosmos is improved upon by a metabolic process of transubstantiation for which Raphael uses a vaguely alchemical vocabulary of purification. The narrator even suggests in this context that alchemy, supposing it works, must be a regular transformational process in nature, not a miracle:

> nor wonder; if by fire
> Of sooty coal the empiric alchemist
> Can turn, or holds it possible to turn
> Metals of drossiest ore to perfect gold [...].
> (5.439–442)

By way of this constant sacramental purge, the cosmos functions as its own purgatory, so to speak. The natural sacrifice subsumes the sacrament and its juridical component. For the sacrament was thought to entail a divine verdict since Late Antiquity: bread and wine serve as bearers of Christ's spirit, and their consumption fills the faithful with this spirit, thus absorbing them into the mystical body of Christ.[30] But if members of the congregation are unworthy to receive the Eucharist, their pre-existent guilt is enhanced, and God's Supper turns into a divine judgment that makes them ill or kills them, as Paul had already pointed out in his first letter to the Corinthians:

> ὥστε ὃς ἂν ἐσθίῃ τὸν ἄρτον ἢ πίνῃ τὸ ποτήριον τοῦ Κυρίου ἀναξίως, ἔνοχος ἔσται τοῦ σώματος καὶ τοῦ αἵματος τοῦ Κυρίου. δοκιμαζέτω δὲ ἄνθρωπος ἑαυτόν, καὶ οὕτως ἐκ τοῦ ἄρτου ἐσθιέτω καὶ ἐκ τοῦ ποτηρίου πινέτω. ὁ γὰρ ἐσθίων καὶ πίνων κρίμα ἑαυτῷ ἐσθίει καὶ πίνει μὴ διακρίνων τὸ σῶμα. διὰ τοῦτο ἐν ὑμῖν πολλοὶ ἀσθενεῖς καὶ ἄρρωστοι καὶ κοιμῶνται ἱκανοί.

28 For further details see, Björn Quiring, "'With Real Hunger To Transubstantiate': Die Dispersion der Eucharistie in John Miltons 'Paradise Lost'", in *Mitteilungen des Sonderforschungsbereichs 573, "Pluralisierung und Autorität in der Frühen Neuzeit"* 1 (2011).

29 Thomas Aquinas, *Summa Theologiae Tertia Pars, 60–90*, Latin/English Edition, trans. Laurence Shapcote, Lander, WY: Aquinas Institute, 2012, p. 206 [3.75.4].

30 Christopher Elwood, *The Body Broken: The Calvinist Doctrine of the Eucharist and the Symbolization of Power in Sixteenth-Century France*, Oxford and New York: Oxford University Press, 1999, p. 20.

> Wherefore whosoever shall eat this bread, and drink this cup of the Lord, unworthily, shall be guilty of the body and blood of the Lord. But let a man examine himself, and so let him eat of that bread, and drink of that cup. For he that eateth and drinketh unworthily, eateth and drinketh damnation to himself, not discerning the Lord's body. For this cause many are weak and sickly among you, and many sleep.
>
> (1. Cor. 11.27–30)

"Sleep" in this context is a euphemism for "death",[31] and it is in accordance with this doctrine that the gospel narratives on the institution of the Eucharist were always interpreted.[32] Milton's naturalization does not eliminate this divine judgment ritual, but universalizes it: in the eleventh book, Michael sketches an alimental ethics according to which wrong eating habits will incur divine punishment (11.515–537).

Similar natural flows from God to creation and back were frequently outlined in medieval and early modern "natural philosophies", often appropriating Neoplatonic and Stoic cosmologies.[33] Milton modernizes the topos, mostly through the systematic introduction of uncertainty. The result conforms to a general decentring trend of the seventeenth century which Alexandre Koyré has described.[34] Other historians of science have pointed out that the development of the natural sciences was much less unidirectional and more ambivalent and heterogeneous than Koyré assumed.[35] Geocentrism, heliocentrism and a "teleological, theocentric [...] view of nature" persisted almost everywhere and continued to do so for a long time.[36] Despite the validity of these criticisms, Koyré nevertheless points out an uncontested tendency within the complex processes of the Scientific Revolution. Milton's ambivalence concerning these developments is most obvious in his representation of Galileo Galilei, whom Milton proudly claimed to have met during his Grand Tour in Italy.[37] The "Tuscan artist" is mentioned by name once, and on two further occasions, he and his telescope are alluded to.[38] He is the only

31 Ernst Dietzfelbinger, ed., *Das Neue Testament, Interlinearübersetzung Griechisch-Deutsch*, Neuhausen: Hänssler, 1998, p. 751.

32 See Kenneth Hein, *Eucharist and Excommunication: A Study in Early Christian Doctrine and Discipline*, Bern and Frankfurt am Main: Peter Lang, 1973.

33 See e.g. Peter Harrison, *The Bible, Protestantism, and the Rise of Natural Science*, Cambridge and New York: Cambridge University Press, 1998, p. 148. See also Marcia L. Colish, *Medieval Foundations of the Western Intellectual Tradition 400–1400*, New Haven: Yale University Press, 1997, p. 179, referencing Bernardus Silvestris.

34 See e.g. Alexandre Koyré, *Newtonian Studies*, London: Chapman and Hall, 1965, pp. 6–7.

35 See e.g. Steven Shapin, *The Scientific Revolution*, Chicago: University of Chicago Press, 1996, esp. pp. 62–64, 169–170 and 203.

36 Harinder Singh Marjara, *Contemplation of Created Things: Science in* Paradise Lost, Toronto: University of Toronto Press, 1992, p. 8.

37 *Areopagitica*, *CPW* 2:538.

38 "[T]he moon, whose orb/ Through optic glass the Tuscan artist views/ At evening from the top of Fesole,/ Or in Valdarno, to descry new lands,/ Rivers or mountains in her spotty

contemporary of Milton's to be thus honoured. And his presence makes itself felt in other places, too; for example, one can find an indirect, affirmative allusion to him in Raphael's remark that "the morning planet gilds his horns;/ By tincture or reflection" (7.366–367). By way of the telescope, Galileo had ascertained that the morning star, Venus, waxes and wanes like the moon; thus it sports "horns" from time to time.[39] But references such as these supplement numerous terms from Ptolemaic astronomy which also appear in the epic, such as "ecliptic" (3.740), "epicycle" (8.84), "eccentric" (3.575), and so on. Raphael also warns Adam that astronomy might be the symptom of a dangerous hubris (8.66–8.178) and the narrator has the tendency to concur. The metaphors that surround Galileo's telescope suggest that it is a rather dubious utensil; it is even associated with Satan twice (1.287–291; 3.588–590). *Paradise Lost* thus demonstrates both interest in and resentment toward the natural sciences, an ambivalence that also feeds upon the epic's double-edged concept of "nature". Milton's ambivalent cosmology entails an epistemological compromise formation.[40]

Sometimes, Milton's laxity in establishing coherence between ancient and modern worldviews seems almost provocative. For example, one crucial point of Galileo's discovery is that it qualifies and relativizes the distinction between above and below. Conventionally, the lowest point of the cosmos was thought to be the earth's centre. In medieval cosmologies, all heavenly bodies float in the firmament because they are made of a sublime fifth element, the ether, which is lighter and nobler than the other four.[41] When Galileo pointed the telescope at the moon though, he saw irregularities: craters, mountains and rills, which he took to be rivers. The moon resembled earth so much that one could feel entitled to assume that it is not made of ether, but of the four terrestrial elements.[42] But then the question arose as to why the moon does not fall to earth. Thus, the similarity suggested that the earth may not be the lowest point of the universe and that the cosmos may not be so strictly hierarchical as generally had been assumed.[43] In *Paradise Lost*, both the old and the new view are embraced, although they are mutually exclusive: it is strongly suggested that the sun consists of metals and precious stones; it is

globe" (1.287–1.291). "There lands the fiend, a spot like which perhaps/ Astronomer in the sun's lucent orb/ Through his glazed optic tube yet never saw" (3.588–3.590). "As when by night the glass/ Of Galileo, less assured, observes/ Imagined lands and regions in the moon" (5.261–5.263).

39 Laura Fermi and Gilberto Bernardini, *Galileo and the Scientific Revolution*, New York: Basic Books, 1961, pp. 52–55.

40 For the term "Kompromißbildung", see e.g. Sigmund Freud, *Die Traumdeutung,* Frankfurt am Main: Fischer, 1991, p. 464.

41 See e.g. Edward Grant, *Planets, Stars and Orbs: The Medieval Cosmos, 1200–1687*, Cambridge: Cambridge University Press, 1996, pp. 422–428.

42 See e.g. Stephen P. Maran and Laurence A. Marschall, *Galileo's New Universe: The Revolution in our Understanding of the Cosmos*, Dallas, TX: BenBella Books, 2009, pp. 32–35.

43 Alexandre Koyré, *From the Closed World to the Infinite Universe*, p. 96.

a place where, for example, "rivers run/ Potable gold" (3.607–607); but it is also called "ethereal" (3.716). Accordingly, it is sometimes personified, sometimes not; in most cases, the personal pronoun "he" is used to refer to the sun (e.g. 4.395; 4.643; 8.124), but the impersonal pronoun "it" also appears (8.95). The stars are caught in a similar intermediate zone: according to Ptolemy, the stars are all confined to the stellar sphere, close to the edge of the cosmos; but according to some Copernicans such as Thomas Digges, the stars are freely distributed throughout space.[44] Uriel, in turn, speaks of

> stars
> Numberless, as thou seest, and how they move;
> Each had his place appointed, each his course,
> The rest in circuit walls this universe.
> (3.718–721)

Thus he asserts that countless stars float independently through the depths of cosmic space, but there is also a Ptolemaic stellar sphere at the edge of the cosmos to which the rest of them is fixed.

One of the most confusing issues in the universe of *Paradise Lost* is that of gravity. The narrator seems to assume that there is an upside and a downside to the cosmos and a uniform force of weight that draws things downward. Otherwise, Uriel's quintessential means of transportation would prove useless: he glides from the sun to earth on a light beam when the setting sun is still above the earth's horizon, and he glides back on the same beam after the sun has set. It is expressly said that

> Uriel to his charge
> Returned on that bright beam, whose point now raised
> Bore him slope downward to the sun now fallen
> Beneath the Azores […].
> (4.589–592)

Thus, neither the earth nor the sun is the cosmic centre to which all things are naturally drawn; rather, their forces of attraction seem to depend on their relative height in the cosmos. The same theocentric and morally charged laws of gravity seem to apply within the cosmos as outside: the throne of God is the uppermost point of the universe, high "above all height" (3.58). So when a body ascends upward, it always ascends toward God, and when it falls, it falls away from him, down into the infinity of chaotic space – or, if one happens to be within the cosmos, toward the edge of it that is farthest from the pearly gates. The same natural and divine force that made Satan and his minions fall

44 Hans Blumenberg, *The Genesis of the Copernican World*, trans. Robert M. Wallace, Cambridge, MA: MIT Press, 1987. p. 631.

into hell would thus also allow the angels to surf from planet to planet. The circumstance that the earthly creatures do not fall off the earth when they are positioned on its downside can easily be explained by sympathetic forces through which God and Nature keep them in their appointed space: dust remains attached to self-balanced dust.

Before we pursue this as yet somewhat speculative line of thought further, we must confront a rather surprising event: the first man is introduced to Copernicanism and its consequences by an angel. At first, Adam upholds the Ptolemaic worldview, but he also articulates doubts about it. These doubts do not spring from lunar observations he has made, but from the immensity of the cosmos he computes, which contradicts his conception of a reasonable and economical Nature:

> When I behold this goodly frame, this world
> Of heaven and earth consisting, and compute
> Their magnitudes, this Earth a spot, a grain,
> An atom, with the firmament compared
> And all her numbered stars, that seem to roll
> Spaces incomprehensible (for such
> Their distance argues and their swift return
> Diurnal) merely to officiate light
> Round this opacous Earth, this punctual spot,
> One day and night; in all their vast survey
> Useless besides, reasoning I oft admire,
> How Nature wise and frugal could commit
> Such disproportions, with superfluous hand
> So many nobler bodies to create,
> Greater so manifold to this one use,
> For aught appears, and on their orbs impose
> Such restless revolution day by day
> Repeated, while the sedentary earth,
> That better might with far less compass move,
> Served by more noble than herself, attains
> Her end without least motion […].
> (8.15–35; capitalization added)

Raphael thereupon introduces an assortment of Copernican and Keplerian topoi – not on the level of gospel truth, but on the level of hypotheses:

> What if the sun
> Be centre to the world, and other stars
> By his attractive virtue and their own
> Incited, dance about him various rounds?
> Their wandering course now high, now low, then hid,
> Progressive, retrograde, or standing still,

> In six thou seest, and what if seventh to these
> The planet earth, so steadfast though she seem,
> Insensibly three different motions move?
> (8.122–130)

Raphael also theorizes that other parts of the cosmos besides the earth might be inhabited, a speculation that was explored, first and foremost, by Giordano Bruno:[45]

> and other suns perhaps
> With their attendant moons thou wilt descry […]
> Stored in each orb perhaps with some that live.
> (8.148–152)

Furthermore, Raphael asserts that the earth is "[n]ot unconform to other shining globes" (5.259) and situated "between worlds and worlds" (5.268), thus evoking another favourite topic of Giordano Bruno: the multitude of worlds.[46] The devils and the godforsaken, on the other hand, rely on Aristotelian physics in the second book of *Paradise Lost*, and try to convince themselves that the cosmos is thoroughly Ptolemaic in the third.[47] Although the angels remain vague and ambiguous on the question, their general preference for a Copernican/Keplerian view of the cosmos is suggested. One gets the impression that Milton saturates his cosmos with as many cosmologies as he can. As Anita Lawson and Daniel Danielson have pointed out, the Miltonian cosmology perhaps most closely resembles that of Kepler.[48] This resemblance is caused by the fact that both Milton and Kepler are syncretists: Kepler's cosmology has been characterized as a compromise formation between natural magic and the budding natural sciences, "between animism and geometry".[49]

45 Giordano Bruno, *Von der Ursache, dem Prinzip und dem Einen*, trans. Adolf Lasson, Hamburg: Meiner, 1983, p. 27. See also Michael J. Crowe, "Extraterrestrial Intelligence", in *History of Astronomy: An Encyclopedia*, ed. John Lankford, New York and London: Garland, 1997, p. 207.

46 Giordano Bruno, *Von der Ursache, dem Prinzip und dem Einen*, p. 27.

47 "[I]n our proper motion we ascend/ Up to our native seat: descent and fall/ To us is adverse" (2.75–77). The inhabitants of the Paradise of Fools picture a medieval cosmos that is incompatible with the rest of the epic: "They pass the planets seven, and pass the fixed,/ And that crystalline sphere whose balance weighs/ The trepidation talked, and that first moved;/ And now Saint Peter at heaven's wicket seems/ To wait them with his keys" (3.481–485).

48 Anita Lawson, "'The Golden Sun in Splendor Likest Heaven': Johannes Kepler's *Epitome* and *Paradise Lost*, Book 3", *Milton Quarterly* 21.2 (1987), pp. 46–51; Dennis Richard Danielson, Paradise Lost *and the Cosmological Revolution*, Cambridge and New York: Cambridge University Press, 2014, pp. 138–139. It has been speculated that Milton might have read Kepler's *Harmonices mundi*. See Hans Oskar Wilde, *Miltons geistesgeschichtliche Bedeutung*, Heidelberg: C. Winter, 1933, pp. 98–99.

49 Giorgio Stabile, "Natur" in *Historisches Wörterbuch der Philosophie*, Vol. 6, ed. Joachim Ritter, Karlfried Gründer et al., Darmstadt: Wissenschaftliche Buchgesellschaft, 1984, col. 464.

The same applies to Milton; maybe that is why they both assume a cosmic cycle of mutual obligation and nourishment between the sun and the other heavenly bodies.[50]

7.3 The scales: a disappearing miracle

Within this syncretistic mixture, it is all the harder to determine how Nature and God coordinate their administrative acts. For example, how and under what conditions does God interfere with the natural, organic workings of the cosmos? Milton certainly is no deist; he might have deistic tendencies,[51] but disbelief in God's occasional interventions in the functioning of the natural world is not among them. According to the *Doctrina Christiana*, God's extraordinary providence may manifest itself in occasional miracles, which serve first and foremost a polarizing function of judgment:

> Finis miraculorum est potentiae divinae patefactio, fideique nostrae confirmatio. [...] Et incredulorum gravior condemnatio.
>
> The aim of miracles is the manifestation of divine power, and the confirmation of our faith. [...] And [its aim is] a sterner condemnation of unbelievers.
>
> (*DC* 340/341)

Miracles, just like the regular ways of the world, are a device with which to separate the wheat from the chaff on the cosmic threshing floor.

In *Paradise Lost*, there is one particularly striking example of a miraculous divine intervention in the unfallen cosmos, and it is, once again, a judgment involving natural forces. One might call it the Strange Case of Libra: when Satan has been discovered by Ithuriel and Zephon and confronts Gabriel and his troops, west of Eden, a mighty battle looms:

> now dreadful deeds
> Might have ensued, nor only Paradise
> In this commotion, but the starry cope
> Of heaven perhaps, or all the elements
> At least had gone to wreck, disturbed and torn
> With violence of this conflict, had not soon
> The eternal to prevent such horrid fray
> Hung forth in heaven his golden scales, yet seen
> Betwixt Astrea and the Scorpion sign,
> Wherein all things created first he weighed,
> The pendulous round earth with balanced air

50 Danielson, Paradise Lost *and the Cosmological Revolution*, pp. 138–139.

51 See Joseph Frank, "John Milton's Movement toward Deism", *Journal of British Studies* 1.1 (1961), pp. 38–51.

In counterpoise, now ponders all events,
Battles and realms: in these he put two weights
The sequel each of parting and of fight;
The latter quick up flew, and kicked the beam.
(4.990–1004)

By this act, the Father installs the zodiacal sign of Libra, as can be easily ascertained by its placement "betwixt Astrea [i.e. Virgo] and the Scorpion" where it has remained ever since. This act is peculiar in almost every way. First, it is unusual insofar as the Father seems to execute it all by himself; this certainly strengthens the impression that he has a body of his own that is material enough to interact with the elements of the cosmos. There is thus no need of the Son's mediation and accommodating representation even within the cosmos. Second, the divine use of balances is slightly unusual in a Christian context. There are scattered biblical precedents in the Old Testament (Isaiah 40.12–15; Prov. 16.2; and the famous verdict on Belshazzar in Daniel 5.27); but in all these cases, the balance is either used in God's cosmic engineering work or in the judgment of his creatures' moral behaviour. Sometimes both functions seem to blend into each other (e.g. in Job 28.23–26), but they are never associated with success in life's battles. Milton's real precedent is pagan: leaving aside the use of balances in Egyptian and other antique final judgments,[52] the most obvious instance appears in Homer's *Iliad*. In its eighth book, Zeus weighs the fates of the Trojans and the Greeks at a day of fighting, after he has prohibited the other gods to interfere in the battle:

ἦμος δ' Ἠέλιος μέσον οὐρανὸν ἀμφιβεβήκει,
καὶ τότε δὴ χρύσεια πατὴρ ἐτίταινε τάλαντα:
ἐν δ' ἐτίθει δύο κῆρε τανηλεγέος θανάτοιο
Τρώων θ' ἱπποδάμων καὶ Ἀχαιῶν χαλκοχιτώνων,
ἕλκε δὲ μέσσα λαβών: ῥέπε δ' αἴσιμον ἦμαρ Ἀχαιῶν.
αἳ μὲν Ἀχαιῶν κῆρες ἐπὶ χθονὶ πουλυβοτείρῃ
ἑζέσθην, Τρώων δὲ πρὸς οὐρανὸν εὐρὺν ἄερθεν:
αὐτὸς δ' ἐξ Ἴδης μεγάλ' ἔκτυπε, δαιόμενον δὲ
ἧκε σέλας μετὰ λαὸν Ἀχαιῶν: οἳ δὲ ἰδόντες
θάμβησαν, καὶ πάντας ὑπὸ χλωρὸν δέος εἷλεν.

But when the sun had bestrode mid heaven, then it was that the Father lifted up his golden scales, and set in them two fates of grievous death, one for the horse-taming Trojans, and one for the brazen-clad Achaeans; then he grasped the balance by the middle and raised it, and down sank

52 See John Gwyn Griffiths, *The Divine Verdict: A Study of Divine Judgement in the Ancient Religions*, Leiden and New York: Brill, 1991, pp. 221, 224–225.

> the day of doom of the Achaeans. So the Achaeans' fates settled down on to the bounteous earth and those of the Trojans were raised aloft toward wide heaven. Then himself he thundered aloud from Ida, and sent a blazing flash into the army of the Achaeans; and at the sight of it they were struck with wonder, and pale fear seized them all.[53]

The same happens again later, in the decisive single combat between Achilles and Hector:

> ἀλλ' ὅτε δὴ τὸ τέταρτον ἐπὶ κρουνοὺς ἀφίκοντο,
> καὶ τότε δὴ χρύσεια πατὴρ ἐτίταινε τάλαντα,
> ἐν δ' ἐτίθει δύο κῆρε τανηλεγέος θανάτοιο,
> τὴν μὲν Ἀχιλλῆος, τὴν δ' Ἕκτορος ἱπποδάμοιο,
> ἕλκε δὲ μέσσα λαβών: ῥέπε δ' Ἕκτορος αἴσιμον ἦμαρ,
> ᾤχετο δ' εἰς Ἀΐδαο, λίπεν δέ ἑ Φοῖβος Ἀπόλλων.
>
> But when for the fourth time they had come to the springs, then it was that the Father lifted up his golden scales, and set in them two fates of grievous death, one for Achilles, and one for horse-taming Hector; then he grasped the balance by the middle and raised it; and down sank the day of doom of Hector and went away to Hades; and Phoebus Apollo left him.[54]

Both passages are rather similar to each other, perhaps referring to a ritual formula.[55] For Homer's Zeus seems to engage in a ritualized divine oracle that is amalgamated with an ordeal by battle.[56] The battle is decided by the ascertainment of the oracle's result, enacted by the god. This way of determining a battle outcome must seem unproblematic, insofar as antique, medieval and early modern chronicles all use the commonplace of war as a synecdoche of divine judgment.[57] Hence, every military conflict is regarded as a trial by combat; consequently, officers tend to appeal to God before battles, as to the

53 Homer, *Iliad*, Vol. 1, trans. A. T. Murray and William F. Wyatt, Cambridge, MA: Harvard University Press, 1999, pp. 356/357 [8.68–77].

54 Homer, *Iliad*, Vol. 2, trans. A. T. Murray and William F. Wyatt, Cambridge, MA: Harvard University Press, 1999, pp. 466–469 [22.208–213].

55 A passage in Virgil's *Aeneid* quotes the topos, too. See Virgil, *Aeneis*, trans. and ed. Johannes Götte and Maria Götte, Düsseldorf: Artemis und Winkler, 2002, pp. 546/547 [12.725–727].

56 Most Homer scholars regard Zeus' consultation of the scales as a mere rhetorical device, not as a genuine oracle; but not all of them agree. And those that do agree frequently employ arguments that look unconvincing to the non-expert. For example, it is never explicitly said that anyone but Zeus witnesses the movements of those scales; thus, it seems very doubtful that he employs them merely for representational purposes. See B. C. Dietrich, "The Judgment of Zeus", *Rheinisches Museum für Philologie* N. F. 117 (1964), p. 99 et passim. See also Hartmut Erbse, *Untersuchungen zur Funktion der Götter im homerischen Epos*, Berlin and New York: Walter de Gruyter, 1986, p. 89.

57 See e.g. Sigurd Burckhardt, *Shakespearean Meanings,* Princeton, NJ: Princeton University Press, 1968, p. 171.

judge who dispenses a higher justice through war.[58] The battle ordeal generally shows a law in action in which punishment expresses either destiny or divine inclination: who wins, wins because he is favoured by Zeus, God or Fate. In the *Iliad* nothing suggests that one party or the other deserve their fate by their previous behaviour; the oracular judgment in Homer is "stripped of any moral implication".[59] Furthermore, the oracular judgment is apparently not the sovereign judgment of heaven's supreme ruler. Why would Zeus consult the balances, if he himself could decide on the outcome of the battle autonomously? Once again, the force of Fate seems to prescribe his actions; only after consulting the scales does he support the winning side of the Trojans, with the repeated use of thunderbolts.

Is a similar restriction on the allegedly supreme being implied when Milton's God hangs his scales into the heavens? This question is difficult to answer. Just as in the Homeric scene, it is not even clear whether the "sequels" in the balance "are meant to be active agents or passive lots, since one may argue in favour of either belief".[60] What force is responsible for the lifting and lowering of the scales? While their hanging is certainly a miraculous divine intervention, their subsequent movement may be a natural phenomenon. If God is the supreme cause of these movements, the balance would merely be a symbol to convey a divine warning; but if other, possibly independent forces such as Fate, Nature and Gravity are also involved, then the shifting scales would acquire the additional weight of proto-scientific oracular evidence. It has been pointed out by Malabika Sarkar that the narrator might describe a regular natural process when he relates the movement of the balance: Satan and Gabriel meet some time after midnight, at springtime, when the sun is in Aries (10.329). At that time of the year, Libra would be positioned nearest the zenith around midnight, its "beam" (4.1004) almost parallel to the horizon. Subsequently, while the morning approaches, it would move from the south toward the southwest and incline toward the horizon, so that the left/eastern "scale" seems to rise in relation to the right/western one.[61] The divine miracle blends seamlessly with what ever since has happened regularly in the natural cause of events. And, indeed, it might even have happened before: when Satan enters the cosmos for the first time and surveys it, he already gets to see the "eastern point/ Of Libra" (3.557–558) which therefore must already hang in the firmament. Some interpreters say that Libra therefore must already have been positioned at its place before the events of the fourth book occur, and that Gabriel and Satan merely become aware of its presence at this point in

58 See Frederick H. Russell, *The Just War in the Middle Ages,* Cambridge: Cambridge University Press, 1979, p. 26.
59 Dietrich, "The Judgment of Zeus", p. 125.
60 Dietrich, "The Judgment of Zeus", p. 105.
61 Malabika Sarkar, *Cosmos and Character in* Paradise Lost, New York: Palgrave Macmillan, 2012, p. 129.

the story.[62] But since the narrator expressly says that God hangs the scales in the firmament after the quarrel between Gabriel and Satan threatens to turn violent, this point of view is not convincing. The contradiction between the miraculous and the regular nature of Libra remains unresolved.

Furthermore, the literary precedents for the Miltonian use of the divine scales also differ in the meaning ascribed to their rising and sinking. In the biblical case of Daniel 5.27, the lifted scale foreshadows defeat and divine displeasure for the party that has been considered too light ("Thou art weighed in the balances, and art found wanting"). But in Homer, the scale that rises announces victory and divine support for the party it represents: it is not found too light, but light enough to be "raised aloft toward wide heaven". So must the lifting of the "sequel of fight" therefore be interpreted as an argument for or against a battle in Milton's syncretistic cosmos? How are God's creatures to know what significance God has ascribed to his symbolic intervention? The lifting of the scale remains a mystery not only to the reader, but also to Gabriel and Satan, as we can gather from the subsequent events:

> Which Gabriel spying, thus bespake the fiend.
> Satan, I know thy strength, and thou knowest mine,
> Neither our own but given; what folly then
> To boast what arms can do, since thine no more
> Than heaven permits, nor mine, though doubled now
> To trample thee as mire: for proof look up,
> And read thy lot in yon celestial sign
> Where thou art weighed, and shown how light, how weak,
> If thou resist. The fiend looked up and knew
> His mounted scale aloft: nor more; but fled
> Murmuring, and with him fled the shades of night.
> (4.1005–1015)

It thus seems that Gabriel interprets the divine miracle wrongly: instead of identifying the two scales, as the narrator does, with two possible courses of action that both Satan and Gabriel might decide to take, he identifies the one scale with the "lot" of Satan in battle ("thou art weighed, and shown how light"), thus implicitly associating the other scale with the military fortunes of the angelic crew. In the turning of the balance, he does not read a proclamation of God's mysterious will, but a divine approbation of his own manly virtue, confirming his heavenly narcissism. It is even more peculiar that Satan, the master of suspicion who tends to distrust all of God's statements, seems to accept as truthful both God's oracular statement and Gabriel's questionable interpretation without seriously considering the alternatives. On closer

62 See e.g. Frank Harper Moore, "Astraea, The Scorpion, and the Heavenly Scales", *ELH* 38.3 (1971), pp. 355–356; and Sarkar, *Cosmos and Character in* Paradise Lost, p. 129.

inspection, this acceptance appears doubtful, however. Neil Forsyth has pointed out that Satan's murmuring and departure does not necessarily imply that he approves of Gabriel's interpretation: he might also read the raising of "his" scale in the Homeric fashion, as the sign of his ultimate victory.[63] In this case, however, it would make perfect sense for him to fight Gabriel. And even if he envisages eventual defeat in this battle, his abstention from further altercations is somewhat baffling. For the worst that Gabriel can threaten him with is to drag him "back to the infernal pit" after a wreckful battle (4.965). And first ruining the cosmos and then returning to hell is exactly what Satan supposedly wants: one of his declared objectives was to "waste his [God's] whole creation" (2.365). So even if he should lose the battle, he would accomplish his mission. His behaviour can only be explained if one assumes that his proclaimed desire to "partake" (2.374) with man and to drag him down to hell (4.373–385) has overruled all other considerations. The wreck of the cosmos would leave man homeless, but still immortal and unfallen.[64] And no party, except the humans themselves, seems to be interested in that scenario: neither God, who slowly unfolds his guilt-inducing scheme, nor companionable Satan, nor the angels, whose stunning inefficiency once again betrays either dull disinterest in human affairs or suppressed malignancy: after having received Uriel's delayed report on Satan, Gabriel lets three further precious hours pass while doing nothing (4.776–777), then commands almost all his troops to parade along the outside of the Paradise walls, although he knows full well that these walls cannot have posed an obstacle for Satan (4.582–583). He leaves it to merely two soldiers of lower rank to scour the wide wildernesses of Paradise. Thus, Gabriel as well as Satan seem to refrain from battle not because they have to, but because they want to: they accommodate God's miraculous sign to their wishes. The immediate effect of God's oracular intervention is that Satan remains on earth, free to achieve man's Fall.

The balance has long been a symbol of the law, but in this case, it suspends the official goal of God's legal ordinances: Satan is not punished for his escape from hell; he is not prevented from further transgressions; and the cosmic order that is God's declared ideal is not achieved. The result of the miraculous judgment is neither retribution nor prevention nor reconciliation: it is another judgment, namely the "stern condemnation" of mankind. Furthermore, the appearance of the balance is asserted to be an intervention from above, but it strangely blends with the natural course of events. The stellar representation of the scales asserts itself not as a law-positing message from beyond, but, in all its opaqueness, it functions as an uncertain, entangling phenomenon whose status and meaning must be determined by a questionable allegoresis.

63 Neil Forsyth, *The Satanic Epic*, p. 343.

64 As William Empson remarks: "In the age of the Cobalt Bomb, one is inclined to find [the prevention of the fight] rational and sympathetic of God; but, still, if he is going to send nearly all of us to Hell as a result of Adam's Fall, we cannot be expected to agree with him that it was less important than the scenery". See Empson, *Milton's God*, p. 113.

Brute facts and highest justice meet to form an enigma in the skies, that the children of God and Nature must, but cannot, figure out.

7.4 Man's symbolic knowledge

Although they do not witness the hanging of the scales, humans are also caught in this bafflement, posited in an uncertain region between immanence and transcendence. The *inclinatio naturalis* toward the divine that pervades the cosmos is most evident in Adam. As a creature made both of dust and the breath of God, it soon becomes obvious that Adam's mind at birth is anything but a blank slate. Like language, the desire for ascent and transcendence seems to be hard-wired into him; this is clearly discernible in his description of his very first awakening to life, right after his creation:

> Straight toward heaven my wondering eyes I turned,
> And gazed a while the ample sky, till raised
> By quick instinctive motion, up I sprung,
> As thitherward endeavouring, and upright
> Stood on my feet; about me round I saw
> Hill, dale, and shady woods, and sunny plains,
> And liquid lapse of murmuring streams; by these
> Creatures that lived, and moved, and walked, or flew,
> Birds on the branches warbling; all things smiled,
> With fragrance and with joy my heart o'erflowed.
> Myself I then perused, and limb by limb
> Surveyed, and sometimes went, and sometimes ran
> With supple joints, as lively vigour led:
> But who I was, or where, or from what cause,
> Knew not; to speak I tried, and forthwith spake,
> My tongue obeyed and readily could name
> Whate'er I saw. Thou Sun, said I, fair light,
> And thou enlightened Earth, so fresh and gay,
> Ye hills and dales, ye rivers, woods, and plains,
> And ye that live and move, fair creatures, tell,
> Tell, if ye saw, how I came thus, how here?
> Not of myself; by some great maker then,
> In goodness and in power pre-eminent;
> Tell me, how may I know him, how adore,
> From whom I have that thus I move and live,
> And feel that I am happier than I know.
>
> (8.257–282)

After a vain attempt to jump right into heaven (in the double sense of the word), he repeats the same endeavour on a symbolic level, immediately desiring knowledge beyond the empirical. His beautiful environment and his own empirical self are both instinctively perceived as overcoded signs, pointing to their invisible source in an external, primordial and personified cause. Immediately, it becomes his aspiration to adore this transcendent cause in the appropriate manner, but about this manner he finds no information either within himself or in the outside world (8.285). To a certain degree, it seems to spring spontaneously from his affects, however, as can be seen when he, "[r]ejoicing, but with awe" (8.314), falls at the feet of God's representative as soon as he appears on the scene. Thus Adam follows the law that is "grafted" into him, as Milton explains in the *Doctrina*:

> Legis nomine primario hic intelligitur, ilia hominis menti insita et innata: deinde illa ore Dei prolata [...].
>
> By the name of law is understood here primarily that which is grafted onto man's mind and inborn; next, that which was uttered by God's mouth [...].
>
> (*DC* 412/413)

Hence it seems that the human being in its most primal and innocent state is by lawful passion directed toward the approbation of the sovereign ruler of the universe, transcending natural phenomena in the process, or, more precisely, naturally interpreting them as signs pointing toward the beyond.[65] Milton's Adam behaves like a native proponent of natural theology, deducing the existence of God from the experience of nature as his dominion.[66] Raphael holds out the prospect that this approach will get him closer to heaven: "In contemplation of created things/ By steps we may ascend to God" (5.511–512). Milton seems to have shared this belief in natural theology, as far we can deduce it from a crucial passage in the *Doctrina*:

> [T]ot tamen clara indicia sui Deus in mente humana, tot per omnem penitus naturam sui vestigia impressit, ut ignorare Deum esse, nemo non insanus possit. [...] Certe quae in mundo sunt omnia, pulcherrimo ordine, fini alicui bonoque facta, testantur prasextitisse summum aliquem efficientem qui finem sibi in his omnibus proposuerit.
>
> God has imprinted so many clear signs of himself in the human mind, and so many traces of himself throughout all nature, that no sane person can be unaware of God's existence. [...] Surely all the world's contents,

65 Milton here draws on a central topos of the humanist Renaissance: it is man's nature to transcend nature. See e.g. Giovanni Pico della Mirandola, *Oration on the Dignity of Man*, eds. Francesco Borghesi, Michael Papio and Massimo Riva, New York: Cambridge University Press, 2012.

66 For a more extensive analysis of this circumstance, see Katherine Calloway, "'His Footstep Trace': The Natural Theology of *Paradise Lost*", *Milton Studies* 55 (2014), pp. 53–85. For a general overview of natural theology, see Russell Re Manning, John Hedley Brooke and Fraser N. Watts, eds., *The Oxford Handbook of Natural Theology*, Oxford: Oxford University Press, 2013.

made in orderly beauty for some purpose and benefit, attest the pre-existence of some sovereign agent who in all these things set himself a purpose. (*DC* 24/25)

This natural, innate craving to know and worship God does not seem to be common to absolutely all humans, however, but to depend on character and/or on sex: when Eve awakes to life, we hear of no similar religious endeavours; according to her memory, her very first action is to spontaneously question herself "where/ And what I was, whence thither brought, and how" (4.451–452), but she comes to no pious conclusions and soon loses herself among the things of this world, first and foremost her own image. Thus, the religious drive seems to be more developed in some people than in others; it is not altogether clear whether the gender divide is responsible for this gap. In any case, Adam takes it upon himself to bridge it and teach Eve natural theology, fervently and constantly engaging in this pedagogical project. When Satan and the reader are confronted with the first couple for the first time, Adam is already busy with an address to Eve, relating the manifest beauties of Paradise to the invisible generosity of its creator:

Sole partner and sole part of all these joys,
Dearer thyself than all; needs must the power
That made us, and for us this ample world,
Be infinitely good, and of his good
As liberal and free as infinite [...].
(4.409–413)

And throughout the rest of the epic, admonishing instructions such as this remain the central component of conversation on earth. At this point we have to confront a vexed and vexing question in Milton criticism: what is the relation between the divine language of natural performativity and (prelapsarian) human language? As Zwi Werblowsky has pointed out, Denis Saurat's association of *Paradise Lost* with kabbalistic and other mystical teachings, which tend to ontologize language, is not altogether convincing.[67] Milton's God uses performative language in his interactions with Chaos and creation, but there is no univocal evidence that language pre-exists these interactions – or that it does not pre-exist them: it has already been mentioned that Milton leaves the question open whether God created or merely appropriated language.[68] Again, this openness is helpful in establishing an ambiguity: the laws of language can be represented as God's invention or as a necessity to which God himself must submit. But it is not this metaphysical uncertainty, but God's

67 Denis Saurat, *Milton: Man and Thinker*, New York: Dial Press, 1925. For Werblowsky's well-argued refutation, see R. J. Zwi Werblowsky, "Milton and the Conjectura Cabbalistica", *Journal of the Warburg and Courtauld Institutes* 18.1/2 (1955): pp. 90–113.

68 See Chapter 3, pp. 141–142.

undeniable political power to code and recode the material world, which stands at the centre of Milton's theological linguistics. Accordingly, Milton seems to be remarkably uninterested in the question as to which of the current languages might most closely resemble the primordial language of God – a question that was hotly debated in his time.[69] Likewise, the extent of similarities and differences between the heavenly and the Edenic idiom is of no great concern to the narrator of *Paradise Lost*. What matters is the pious passivity of man in his relation to language: soon after he has been created and has addressed the creation, Adam encounters the Son who instantly uses his legislative position in order to pronounce a ban on the Tree of Knowledge (8.323–336). This is followed by Adam's naming of the animals. Eve later names the flowers (11.277), and both humans can designate anorganic objects, such as "hills", "dales" and "rivers" (8.275) immediately after their creation. At first, it seems that the creative power that man wields over language manifests itself in these acts of denomination. However, it should be kept in mind that even the naming of the animals is marked as a trial, culminating in a judgment on Adam's faculty of judgment: the animals seem to have been "for trial only brought,/ To see how thou couldst judge of fit and meet" (8.447–448). The case is decided in Adam's favour: the Son claims that the animals have been "rightly named" by him (8.439). As Umberto Eco has shown, the issue of "correct naming" already concerns the early reception and translation history of the biblical text:

> The Vulgate has Adam calling the various animals "nominibus suis", which we can only translate, "by their own names". [...] But Adam might have called the animals "by their own names" in two senses. [...] The names that Adam gave the animals are either the names that each animal intrinsically ought to have been given or simply the names that the nomothete arbitrarily and *ad placitum* decided to give them.[70]

Paradise Lost without doubt gravitates towards the former standpoint: Adam has to accommodate himself to a divine language in which he is immersed and which he cannot control. *Paradise Lost* suggests that man cannot freely dispose of language; and it is not even clear that God himself can do so. He has doubtlessly created heaven and earth by structuring his "dark materials" through his codings and territorializations. However, God had to engage with the intrinsic dynamics of Chaos and nature in this process of creation. And all the differentiating terms he introduces still bear the marks of these – always potentially conflictual – engagements in a chaotic "hubbub" (2.951). In Milton's work, the question of language always remains very closely connected to the vexed question of physical and political power.

69 Umberto Eco, *The Search for the Perfect Language*, trans. James Fentress, Malden, MA and Oxford: Blackwell, 1995, pp. 73–116.

70 Eco, *Perfect Language*, p. 8.

Even though God's work of creation-by-designation has thus to engage with conditions that are apparently not of his own making, he is obviously not altogether determined by these restrictions. There is still great latitude for him to make arbitrary decisions. And there is no reason to suppose that there is not also a certain leeway for the other characters. Arguably, John Leonard's carefully reasoned verdict is still the most accurate: between sheer arbitrariness and pure mimesis, the linguistics of Milton and his protagonists occupy a "middle ground of wise arbitrary impositions in which both nature and convention play a part".[71] In his study, Leonard rightly points out that language is, first and foremost, a medium of sound judgment within Milton's cosmos; but he tends to neglect how closely these judgments remain connected to questions of power politics. For the power to designate seems to be dependent on one's place in the divine Chain of Being. Most strikingly, man participates in the divine power of language merely to the degree that he has the ability and allowance to designate all things that are positioned beneath him in the cosmic hierarchy. Directly after his creation, Adam can name the things of this world, including himself (7.510); but the limits of his dominion also turn out to be the limits of his inbred nomenclature. Thus, the original power of human words remains restricted to earthly things; even the stars seem to be too close to heaven and thus to pose a difficulty for Adam and Eve: we never witness them calling a star or a constellation by name; they merely use demonstrative pronouns (see e.g. 4.655) and the most generic denominations. Nor do they know the names of Raphael and Michael, and they do not learn them either, since the angels never introduce themselves to them. Nor do they ever get to know a name of the Godhead; all the Son says to introduce himself is: "Whom thou soughtest I am" (8.316). Thus, when Adam addresses him, he can only use tentative terms, repeatedly articulating a certain distress about his inability to call upon the Messiah by rightful name:

> O, by what name, for thou above all these,
> Above mankind, or aught than mankind higher,
> Surpassest far my naming, how may I
> Adore thee, author of this universe,
> And all this good to man [...].
>
> (8.357–361)

This ignorance of the personnel and governmental spaces beyond earth blends with his ignorance of the periods beyond his own position in time; he knows that he lives, but not the origin of his life ("for who himself beginning knew", 8.251). But while Adam's innate capacities may not disclose knowledge of celestial things, they do disclose God as a hidden primordial cause

71 John Leonard, *Naming in Paradise: Milton and the Language of Adam and Eve*, Oxford: Clarendon Press, 1990, p. 6.

for which names are lacking – an absent third transcending mankind and the intellectual instruments over which it disposes. Indeed, this creaturely ignorance of origins may be regarded as the legitimating seal of God's power; it cements God's performative precedence. Accordingly, man is even kept in the dark about the nature of this ignorance: whether it is constitutive and insurmountable or whether it can be overcome by the acquisition of additional knowledge. Raphael's depiction of the cosmic cycle seems to suggest that the latter option is the correct one; but how exactly are men to overcome their ignorance? Obviously, the cosmos they know and partly rule must become a means through which to learn more about the world beyond. Raphael encourages this idea by introducing the venerable topos of the book of nature into his conversation with Adam:[72]

> To ask or search I blame thee not, for heaven
> Is as the book of God before thee set,
> Wherein to read his wondrous works, and learn
> His seasons, hours, or days, or months, or years [...].
> (8.66–69)[73]

Raphael here restricts the book metaphor to the skies, but earth is also repeatedly designated as a symbol of transcendence by its comparison to religious architecture. For example, the narrator calls earth and/or its vegetation a "great altar" (9.195), the smoke of whose sacrifices constantly rises heavenward. When Adam and Eve want to come to terms with their information deficit, they have to hang on to tropes such as these. A world of signs opens before them, pointing them toward the divine. In this respect, their position is similar to the one of the devils in hell, yet it is more fortunate in that the signs with which unfallen man is confronted still belong to the kingdom of the God they designate. Whereas the devils are constantly surrounded by glyphs of their own damnation which confirm their connection to the divine, but at the same time assert that it is irretrievably lost, the cosmos, which is to function as man's "book" and "temple", is an integral part of the Father's dominion. In other words: while the fallen angels are confined to the uncomfortable realm of allegory in which all true names are lost, Adam and Eve are kept in a realm of symbols.[74] One of the most prominent symptoms of this cosmic pansymbolism is the circumstance that Raphael's speech on the Cycle of Nature (5.479–482) uses a metaphor in which the vehicle is gradually absorbed by the

72 For the history of this topos see Erich Rothacker, *Das Buch der Natur: Materialien und Grundsätzliches zur Metapherngeschichte*, ed. Wilhelm Perpeet, Bonn: Bouvier, 1979. See also Hans Blumenberg, *Die Lesbarkeit der Welt,* Frankfurt am Main: Suhrkamp, 1986.

73 Incidentally, it is hard to see how Adam might have learned in Paradise what a book is. God seems to have endowed his "sudden apprehension" with that snippet of information too.

74 See Gerhard Kurz, *Metapher, Allegorie, Symbol*, Göttingen: Vandenhoeck and Ruprecht, 1982, p. 70 ff.

tenor. Coleridge and Gordon Teskey have already referred to the passage as a prime example of symbolism:

> The growing plant is the figure, the simile (beginning with "So") that the angel Raphael employs when he is explaining to Adam how nature works. Note that the simile is never formally closed. When it ends on the words "last the bright consummate flower/ Spirits odorous breathes" (5.481–482), the figural structure is not left behind as a figure standing apart from what it refers to. It is instead reassimilated to the whole. It is small wonder Coleridge placed the entire passage at the head of the thirteenth chapter of *Biographia Literaria* to affirm that the symbol differs from the allegorical sign by participating in what it refers to.[75]

Will allegory turn out to be the truth of symbolism, as Benjamin assumes?[76]

7.5 Learning the mysteries of Nature

Adam and Eve have no innate conception of hell; they do not know anything about Satan before Raphael tells them his story (5.512–518). But among the concepts that are either hard-wired in man's mind or soon discovered by his autonomous deductions is that of Nature: she is mentioned in the hymn of Adam and Eve which addresses the elements as "the eldest birth/ Of Nature's womb" (5.180–181). Apparently, the prelapsarian Adam and Eve also know about Nature's dark, uncertain, vaguely female ancestor Ancient Night, consort of Chaos. For they fear that

> total Darkness should by Night regain
> Her old possession, and extinguish life
> In Nature and all things […].
> (4.665–667)

In Milton's world, at least as seen by Adam and Eve, darkness is an active, autonomous power (and a threat to Nature), as the philosophy of Jacob Böhme also suggests.[77] Their knowledge of the great monarchs Night and

75 Gordon Teskey, *The Poetry of John Milton*, Cambridge, MA and London: Harvard University Press, 2015, p. 364, referring to S. T. Coleridge, *Biographia Literaria*, in *The Major Works*, ed. H. J. Jackson, Oxford and New York: Oxford University Press, 2000, p. 307.

76 Walter Benjamin, *The Origin of German Tragic Drama*, trans. John Osborne, London: Verso, 1998, pp. 175–176.

77 See e.g. Jakob Böhme, *Beschreibung der drei Principien göttlichen Wesens*, Amsterdam: Betkio, 1660, p. 88 ff. Milton and Böhme contradict the theological mainstream on this issue. Since Augustine, darkness was seen as inessential, a mere lack of light. (See e.g. Augustine, *Confessions*, Vol. 2, trans. William Watts, London and New York: Heineman and Macmillan, 1912, pp. 290–293 [12.3].) The natural philosophers of the seventeenth century generally adapted this view, including Newton. (See Roy Sorensen, *Seeing Dark Things: The Philosophy of Shadows,* New York: Oxford University Press, 2008, p. 141.)

Chaos seems to be a natural, intuitive knowledge, and its veracity is borne out by the whole of *Paradise Lost*. However, the inhabitants of Milton's heaven apparently do not want Adam and Eve to think this way: Raphael generally represents the mutable, androgynous entity Chaos as a dominated feminine (7.216–242). He/she/it is fixed, at least verbally, in a female, deficient and passive form which God as the ultra-male dominates. The tension between God and Chaos that is at the base of creation is represented within the cosmos as the polarity of male and female. The gender difference is therefore supposed to be cosmic; even the sun, the moon and the other heavenly bodies are gendered, according to Raphael. The angel hints that the cosmos may be sprinkled with many suns and their "attendant" moons, all of which are

> Communicating male and female light,
> Which two great sexes animate the world,
> Stored in each orb perhaps with some that live.
> (8.150–152)

Apparently, light is considered female when it is passively reflected, such as the light of the feminized moon. This association of activity/passivity with the dichotomy of male and female will cause problems for Adam and Eve, first and foremost concerning the question of human ethics. Are they supposed to transcend this dichotomy or to cherish it? On the one hand, Raphael depicts the separation of the sexes and other cosmic hierarchies as insurmountable. On the other hand, he describes the cosmos as dynamic and evolutionary, endowed with an inherent tendency of progress and advancement. In this context, the angel holds out the prospect of a spiritualizing ascent toward the almighty by way of obedience. Does this evolution involve the abolition of the difference between the sexes? After all, angelhood implies a flexible hermaphroditism whose couplings remain sterile and in which each partner can "either sex assume, or both" (1.424). But if their true goal is to "at last turn all to spirit" (5.497), neither to marry nor to be given in marriage, what about their mission to breed and repopulate the decimated fields of heaven? Apparently, they are all first to propagate, then to spiritualize and become angels. But this attempt at reconciling two contradictory orders is bound to pose another problem in the long run: since Nature is breeding in the cosmos as it does in hell, the human population has the potential for infinite growth. And since all men are immortal, this unlimited propagation, if not checked, is bound to generate so many future angels that they will outnumber their originals and finally break the confines not only of a delimited cosmos, but also of a delimited, static heaven. Is it, perhaps, this prospect that makes the angels generally treat Adam and Eve in such a resentful manner? Significantly, after the creation of the cosmos has been perfected on the sixth day, the angels sing devout hymns praising God and his marvellous work; but in their praises, man is exclusively represented as a static entity and his world as self-enclosed

(8.602–632). The function of the cosmos as a breeding ground and launching pad for future angels is never mentioned; it seems that the original inhabitants of heaven do not like to commemorate it.

As a result of these diverse forces at work in and on the cosmos, the *Lebenswelt* in which Adam and Eve find themselves turns out to be complicated, metaphysically as well as ethically. To be morally justified, it is not sufficient to follow God's seemingly unambiguous prohibition to eat the fruits of a certain tree – officially man's "sole pledge of [...] obedience" (3.95). Raphael, Michael, the Father and the Son repeatedly express approbation and disapprobation of many other of Adam's actions, hinting at the fact that these actions may help or hinder him on his ordained path toward God. Hence, the law of natural inclinations that is grafted into Adam and Eve turns out to be insufficient in itself, if one wishes to attain divine justification and advancement. Generally, Adam and Eve are supposed to navigate between two extremes that must be avoided: to consider themselves as mere earth-bound men and to consider themselves as future angels. (Some Puritans found themselves in the same predicament.)[78] Raphael hints at the fact that God punishes not only the creatures who deny the deity their love, but also those who love him not wisely but too well and thus try to approach him with an ambitious spirit that is above their station (see e.g. 8.167–174). A double bind results from this construction: man is told that his advancement toward God's inner circle is obligatory, but also barred. This contradiction finds one of its most pregnant expressions in the ambiguity of the word "bounds": when Raphael affirms that bodies must and will "up to spirit work, in bounds/ Proportioned to each kind" (5.478–479), the term "bounds" designates both the borders between clearly demarcated ranks in the cosmic hierarchy and also a leap across these borders, a move up a rung on the career ladder of salvation.[79] Formulations such as these must leave Adam and Eve in doubt as to what exactly God demands of them. In the uncertain period after the Son has brought them together and before Raphael has visited them, the only way open to the first couple is to enquire into themselves and their natural environment in order to gain indirect knowledge of God and about their appropriate behaviour. This is what Adam does when he asserts that, "as Nature wills, night bids us rest" (4.633),[80] or when he states that

78 See e.g. Laura Sangha, *Angels and Belief in England, 1480–1700,* London: Routledge, 2016, pp. 81 ff.

79 See John Leonard, *Faithful Labourers: A Reception History of* Paradise Lost, *1667–1970,* Oxford: Oxford University Press, 2013, p. 245.

80 Adam is also affirming rhetorical commonplaces here. Quintilian speaks of night as the time which "nature itself gave us for rest and recuperation" ("tempora ab ipsa rerum natura ad quietem refectionemque nobis data"). (Quintilian, *Ausbildung des Redners: Lateinisch und deutsch,* Vol. 2, trans. and ed. Helmut Rahn, Darmstadt: Wissenschaftliche Buchgesellschaft, 1995, p. 506 [10.3.26]; English translation BQ.)

> Nature multiplies
> Her fertile growth, and by disburdening grows
> More fruitful, which instructs us not to spare.
> (5.318–320)

However, these symbolic instructions are partial in every sense: on other occasions, Nature strikes Adam not as luxuriously exuberant, but as "wise and frugal" (8.26). When Adam asks Raphael how Nature "could commit/ Such disproportions" (8.26–27) as the immense, prodigal size of the cosmos in comparison to earth, it can be read as an admission that his own attempts at natural theology have failed and he is therefore forced to question the angel about the intelligibility of natural processes. But once again the angel proves spectacularly unhelpful, presumably because he must support the ambiguously transcendentalizing political theology of the Father: he urges Adam to inquire into the cosmos and its causes, but he also asserts that Adam must remain largely ignorant about them (8.66–178). This, in itself, might be considered as an admonition that man should use, but not overestimate, his cognitive capacities. But Raphael undermines the force of his argument since he vacillates on the question as to whether Adam is to continue in his ignorance because of an insurmountable ontological necessity or because of a contingent ethical imperative. Would Adam be capable of understanding the inner workings of nature if they were revealed to him? Raphael admonishes:

> nor let thine own inventions hope
> Things not revealed, which the invisible king,
> Only omniscient, hath suppressed in night,
> To none communicable in earth or heaven [...].
> (7.121–124)

Even though he generally rejected the teachings of the church fathers,[81] Milton here perpetuates an Augustinian topos: Augustine, in the *Enarrationes in Psalmum XLV* and elsewhere, disapproves of the theological implications of a comprehensible natural world, as Hans Blumenberg expounds:

> Wenn es für Augustin keine authentisch menschliche Erkenntnis der Natur gibt, so ist auch dies eine Nebenfolge seiner Abwehr der Gnosis. Denn von den gnostischen Systemen läßt sich sagen, daß sie wenigstens *eine* platonische Voraussetzung aufrecht erhalten: die der objektiven Einsichtigkeit des Kosmos. Mit den Augen des christlichen Denkers gesehen, wäre der platonische Ideenkosmos das entäußerte Weltgeheimnis des göttlichen Schöpfers gewesen. Die Selbständigkeit des Ideenkosmos, seine Objektivität, bedeutete jetzt, daß in den Bauplan

81 See Barbara Kiefer Lewalski, *The Life of John Milton: A Critical Biography*, Oxford and Malden, MA: Blackwell, 2003, p. 65.

> der Welt von Unbefugten Einblick genommen werden konnte. Auch ein Dämon konnte so zum Welturheber werden und aus der vorgegebenen Materie das machen, was durch seine falsche Vollkommenheit die darin gefangenen Menschenseelen als Kosmos zu blenden vermochte.[82]
>
> When Augustine denies that authentically human knowledge of Nature can exist, this denial is to be regarded as a side effect of his rejection of Gnosticism. For it characterizes Gnostic systems that they uphold at least one presupposition of Platonism: they assume that the universe is objectively comprehensible. Seen with the eyes of the Christian thinker, the Platonic cosmos of ideas would have to be identified with the externalized world-mystery of the divine creator. That the cosmos of ideas possessed an independent, objective existence implied that unauthorized eyes were able to pry into the construction plan of the universe. Even a demon might thus be enabled to create the world and to turn preexistent matter into a false, but seemingly perfect cosmos with the power to fascinate the human souls that were caught within it.[83]

However, is not easy to reconcile an absolute unintelligibility of the cosmos with Milton's monism. The result is another uneasy compromise formation: that God felt the need to suppress the workings of Nature in night suggests that they would not be mysterious and incommunicable if he had not done so. Further problems result immediately: throughout the epic, the official discourse has represented personified Night as a passive, but potentially dangerous force that must be constantly subdued. Here, all of a sudden, she/it is claimed as God's accomplice or perhaps even his spouse: the keeper of his intimate secrets. Raphael furthermore states:

> From man or angel the great architect
> Did wisely to conceal, and not divulge
> His secrets to be scanned by them who ought
> Rather admire […].
>
> (8.72–75)

That God conceals his secrets again implies that lesser beings might figure them out if the deity would not prevent it. And since this concealment is said to affect "man or angel", Raphael is indirectly questioning the trustworthiness of his own cosmological statements: when all is said and done, he also cannot be certain of the things he is talking about.[84] In his conversations with Adam, Raphael is under the same predicament as Adam in his relationship with Eve: since his place in the hierarchy obliges him to function as the

82 Blumenberg, *Die Lesbarkeit der Welt,* p. 50.

83 Translation BQ.

84 See on this topic also Martin Kuester, *Milton's Prudent Ambiguities: Words and Signs in His Poetry and Prose*, Lanham, MD: University Press of America, 2009.

mouthpiece of God, he has to give his insecure knowledge an assertive, revelatory form. In sum, Raphael asserts that Adam's inquiry into the structure of the universe is meritorious, but also that it is hubristic and blameworthy. It is blameworthy for two reasons: on the one hand, Adam is altogether incapable of delving into these mysteries; on the other hand, he might delve into them and find out things that he is not supposed to know. In order to reconcile the two dogmas that God keeps communicating with his creatures in every sense and that God's intentions cannot possibly be comprehended, the incomprehensibility itself is interpreted as a message:

> And for the heaven's wide circuit, let it speak
> The maker's high magnificence, who built
> So spacious, and his line stretched out so far;
> That man may know he dwells not in his own;
> An edifice too large for him to fill,
> Lodged in a small partition, and the rest
> Ordained for uses to his Lord best known.
> (8.100–106)

Man is to receive the impression that he lives "not in his own", although, in a way, he does, since the stunning display of God's immensity is a message that is conveyed especially to him. The incomprehensibility of the cosmos is to be read by him as a clear sign of God's boundless superiority. In other words: Raphael interprets the cosmos as a manifestation of sublimity, geared towards man's intellectual and aesthetic faculties. The sublime and its relation to the absolute was a prominent topos in the seventeenth century, even in the field of Protestant theological hermeneutics.[85] Milton included the text by Pseudo-Longinus in his pedagogical canon,[86] so he must have approved of his treatment of sublimity at least to a certain degree. But Raphael's use of sublime topoi in *Paradise Lost* subtly undermines the angel's official statements according to which God is completely transcendent: it seems that God has to resort to artistic, theatrical and rhetorical devices as well as to political sanctions in order to impress upon man the ineffability of his ways. God is incomprehensible mainly because he renders himself inaccessible, as Raphael emphasizes yet once again:

> God to remove his ways from human sense,
> Placed heaven from earth so far, that earthly sight,

85 See e.g. Dietmar Till, "The Sublime and the Bible: Longinus, Protestant Dogmatics, and the 'Sublime Style'", in *Translations of the Sublime: The Early Modern Reception and Dissemination of Longinus'* Peri Hupsous *in Rhetoric, the Visual Arts, Architecture and the Theatre,* eds. Caroline van Eck, Stijn Bussels, Marteen Delbeke and Jürgen Pieters, Boston: Brill, 2012, pp. 55–64.

86 Milton, *Of Education*, *CPW* 2:403.

If it presume, might err in things too high,
And no advantage gain.
(8.119–122)

Raphael refers Adam to two constant symbols of God's unfathomable power in the human environment: light and the immensity of the cosmos. But in another volte-face he also asks his interlocutor to consider

that great
Or bright infers not excellence: the earth
Though, in comparison of heaven, so small,
Nor glistering, may of solid good contain
More plenty than the sun that barren shines […].
(8.90–94)

After Raphael has instructed Adam to admire inconceivable greatness and life-giving brightness, he straightaway advises him not to be too impressed with them; this must confuse Adam all the more since these two attributes have hitherto been used to characterize not only the cosmos and the heavenly bodies, but also God and the heavens. Furthermore, as if all these contradictions were not yet sufficient, Raphael also undermines the anthropocentric sublimity he has just propagated: Nature and God's high magnificence may not be as prodigal of light and empty vastnesses as it seems, for there might be other worlds in the cosmos that are also inhabited by rational beings.

For such vast room in Nature unpossessed
By living soul, desért and desolate,
Only to shine, yet scarce to cóntribute
Each orb a glimpse of light, conveyed so far
Down to this habitable, which returns
Light back to them, is obvious to dispute.
(8.153–158; capitalization added)

In short, Raphael's way of justifying the inscrutable ways of God strongly resembles the defensive argument in an old joke quoted by Freud concerning a man who was accused of having returned a borrowed kettle in a damaged condition. He "asserted, first, that he had given it back undamaged; secondly that the kettle had a hole in it when he borrowed it; and, thirdly, that he never borrowed a kettle […] at all".[87] Apparently, it is the task of God's creatures to accept contradictory statements such as these as double, or, more precisely, triple binds, obliging each of them to act as if all divinely sanctioned assertions were true simultaneously, since at least one of them must be and

87 Sigmund Freud, *The Interpretation of Dreams*, in *The Standard Edition of the Complete Psychological Works*, Vol. 4, ed. and trans. James Strachey, London: Hogarth Press, 1953, p. 119.

they cannot know which. It is these very dilemmas that enable and perpetuate the enactment of divine law as a law beyond the capacities of the human intellect: Raphael's final response to Adam's cosmological questions is the non-committal admonition:

> Solicit not thy thoughts with matters hid,
> Leave them to God above; him serve and fear;
> Of other creatures, as him pleases best,
> Wherever placed, let him dispose: joy thou
> In what he gives to thee, this Paradise
> And thy fair Eve; heaven is for thee too high
> To know what passes there; be lowly wise:
> Think only what concerns thee and thy being [...].
> (8.167–174)

After the angel, as the representative of transcendence, has mapped out man's supranatural destiny, he commands him to give in to his natural inclinations and to be more interested in profane, libidinal things. The narrator takes the same line, addressing the post-coital human couple with the words: "O yet happiest if ye seek/ No happier state, and know to know no more" (4.774–775). But how can man be prevented from stumbling upon potentially illicit knowledge, when he is obliged to relate hermeneutically to the cosmos by reading within the works of God the unknown messages that may be directed to him? Furthermore, the narrator himself unapologetically emphasizes that he has crossed the boundary that Raphael and he have set: Regina Schwartz has already indicated that the heavenly Muse Urania whom the narrator invokes in the seventh book (7.1–12) is the ancient Muse of astronomy and supralunar things, hence the Muse of a knowledge that Raphael has categorized as both vain and illicit.[88] In this confusion, which must envelop both the first couple and the reader, Adam still tries to draw a lesson from Raphael's discourse, sounding almost desperate in his attempt to find a common denominator. He claims to have learned

> That not to know at large of things remote
> From use, obscure and subtle, but to know
> That which before us lies in daily life,
> Is the prime wisdom [...].
> (8.191–194)

88 Regina M. Schwartz, *Remembering and Repeating: Biblical Creation in Paradise Lost*, Cambridge: Cambridge University Press, 1988, p. 59. And the (inspired, yet postlapsarian) narrator even claims to have been uplifted by her "into the heav'n of heav'ns" (7.13), making full use of the term's ambiguity.

However, in order to arrive at this coherent conclusion, Adam has to distort Raphael's words: Raphael has not exactly ordered Adam to *know* the things that immediately surround him, but to *enjoy* those that God wants him to enjoy ("joy thou/ In what he gives to thee", 8.170–171). As sources of this obligatory joy, Paradise – with its sensual pleasures and fair fruits – and "fair Eve" (8.172) are listed. A *sacrificium intellectus* seems thus to be demanded of Adam: he is supposed to delight in Nature, not understand it. However, Raphael does not hesitate to also bring up the Stoical commonplace that this natural enjoyment (which might be designated as a Lacanian *jouissance* because of its association with a superego command)[89] must be curbed by reason if it is not to turn into low "carnal pleasure" (8.593) which is also "vouchsafed/ To cattle and each beast" (8.581–582). True delight is in rational, conjugal love, which must be subordinated to the love of God; it is "the scale/ By which to heavenly love thou mayst ascend" (8.591–592). But how can celestial love provide a measure and a guiding light to human enjoyments within the bounds of reason when celestial affairs have just been said to surpass human reason altogether? Raphael's elucidations of divine law turn the ways of heaven, as well as the ways of the world, into a mystery, and discomfort results not only from the unfathomability of the cosmos, but also from the suspicion that this unfathomability may merely be a trick by which to satisfy God's political interests and his anthropomorphic passions – most of all his demands for amusement: Raphael accordingly hints at the fact that God's impenetrably spacious and complex design of the cosmos might be due to his great wish to mock all human attempts to explain it:

> he his fabric of the heavens
> Hath left to their disputes, perhaps to move
> His laughter at their quaint opinions wide [...].
> (8.76–8.78)

Since disputes on the "book of God" cannot be altogether avoided, it must also be considered a form of religious obedience to good-naturedly play the potential butt of God's "eerie jokes".[90] This divine laughter exemplifies that the law that Adam and Eve must obey belongs to a category that Derrida has called "intangible":

> Intangible: by this I understand inaccessible to contact, impregnable, and ultimately ungraspable, incomprehensible – but also that which we have not the right to touch.[91]

89 "The superego is the imperative of jouissance – Enjoy!" See Jacques Lacan, *Encore: On Feminine Sexuality, The Limits of Love and Knowledge*, Seminar 20 (1972–1973), trans. Bruce Fink, New York and London: Norton, 1998, p. 3.

90 Empson, *Milton's God*, p. 108.

91 Jacques Derrida, "Before the Law", in *Acts of Literature*, ed. Derek Attridge, New York: Routledge, 1992, p. 211.

Full comprehension of God's law is declared to be both impossible and prohibited, and it cannot be fathomed whether an impossibility has in this context taken on the rhetorical form of a prohibition or vice versa. A decision for either of the two options would lead into difficulties: if the grounds of the intangibility of divine law are to be found in a divine prohibition to approach it and in nothing else, this implies that God would not be intangible if the prohibition did not exist. This variant strongly suggests a monist universe in which the Machiavellian/Hobbesian Father's performative acts remain inherently intelligible for his creatures. The devils suspect that this may be the true structure of the universe. And they also point out that in such a world the privileged position of God as sole lawgiver would be unjustifiable – except of course, by his superior capacity to enforce it, thus once again via the notion that might makes right. However, if the prohibition to pry into the laws of God would merely express man's insurmountable inability to do so, this strongly implies that man lives in a universe, in which the divine essence of things naturally transcends the human faculties altogether, so that it is bound to remain forever inconceivable. In that case, however, the divine order would also be posited beyond the human conception of good and evil, and any attempt to reconcile them, as Raphael constantly does, would therefore be inappropriate and blasphemous. A divine law of the cosmos that can constitutively never be apprehended by the creatures cannot be obeyed and enforced by them either; it must take care of itself.

Since both a decision for the comprehensibility and for the incomprehensibility of prelapsarian divine law would lead the narrator into moral and logical difficulties, he has to leave the question open. In order for the whole cosmic legal system to function, a point must be supposed to exist where the law that moves the stars and the creatures' natural inclinations is linked to the divine positive law according to which all acts within the world are judged. But since the revelation of this point of juncture would subvert the cosmic legal order in one way or another, it must be imagined to be inaccessible, at least for now.[92] The intersection must remain the intangible holy of holies at the heart of divine jurisdiction, and perhaps all jurisdiction.[93] Man is confronted with a law that bars his access to the law and that consolidates itself as law by this prohibition. Its most foundational commandment is: "Thou shalt not know me", or, more precisely, "I order you not to come to me",[94] or more precisely still, "It is possible for you to come to me, but not now". Adam's position before the law thus resembles that of the man from the country in Kafka's tale "Before the Law". However, the readers of *Paradise Lost* at first sight seem to be in a slightly less desperate situation than that of Kafka's heroes, Kafka's

92 For a discussion of the general problem, see e.g. Alexander Passerin d'Entrèves, *Natural Law: An Introduction to Legal Philosophy*, New Brunswick, NJ and London: Transaction, 1996, pp. 93–107.

93 Derrida, "Before the Law", pp. 181–220.

94 Derrida, "Before the Law", p. 203.

readers and Adam: by the narrator's divine revelation, they are granted at least a few glimpses over the threshold to where natural and positive law converge in divine law; they seem to see more than merely the "radiance that streams forth inextinguishably from the door of the Law".[95]

But on closer inspection it is questionable whether these glimpses are indeed helpful: rather, they seem to entangle its recipients even further into the law's constitutive aporias. Most importantly, there is one significant snippet of information that is rigorously kept from Adam and Eve, but offered to Milton's readers, namely the circumstance that God predicts that the first couple, overcome by the law in their members, shall transgress the one positive law he has given them. While all the angels know about this proclamation since they have witnessed it, Raphael is apparently never once tempted to tell Adam and Eve about it. Rather, his profuse admonishments suggest that their case has not yet been decided. Apparently, it must be guarded as a secret that God has already written off the human race and condemned them as "ingrates" (see e.g. 3.97) before the fact. It is easy to see that this divine divination must remain hidden in order for the Fall to function as it does. Exposure in one form or another would threaten God in his unfathomable legislative position. If Adam and Eve would after this revelation somehow manage to refrain from transgressing, would this refusal not constitute an act of disobedience on another level? Thus, must the transgression not also be considered as an act of obedience? More generally: how exactly are they supposed to reconcile the unfathomable law of natural, cyclical inclinations with their capacity to freely transgress or not to transgress God's positive law? In order to find out, we must take a closer look at the Fall of Man and its Edenic conditions.

95 Franz Kafka, *The Trial: A New Translation Based on the Restored Text*, trans. Breon Mitchell, New York: Schocken, 1998, p. 216. "Glanz, der unverlöschlich aus der Türe des Gesetzes bricht." Id., *Der Proceß*, ed. Hans-Gerd Koch, Frankfurt am Main: Fischer, 2008, p. 227.

8 The process of Paradise

8.1 Panoptic Eden

Traditionally, Paradise is first and foremost a garden.[1] Milton's version is also a stronghold, just like his heaven: God has positioned the Garden of Eden on top of earth's highest mountain (5.261) offering a wide, strategically advantageous view, and he has enclosed it by a high wall, sometimes also designated as a "cliff" (4.546). There is only one gateway to the outside world, and it is heavily guarded by angels. Nature also plays a part in the defence of Eden: the slopes of the mountain are covered by her wildly proliferating plants:

> a steep wilderness, whose hairy sides
> With thicket overgrown, grotesque and wild,
> Access denied [...].
>
> (4.135–137)

This fortification of Paradise and its isolation from the rest of creation is a curious phenomenon: officially, these measures have been taken in order to protect its inhabitants against Satan and his devils – exclusively, since no other tangible enemies are supposed to exist. But it is instantly acknowledged by the chief guardian angel Gabriel that all the Edenic defences are of very limited use against the Arch-fiend:

> hard thou knowst it to exclude
> Spiritual substance with corporeal bar.
>
> (4.584–585)

Accordingly, Satan has no problems whatsoever to enter Paradise, as if these bounds were just proportioned in order to be bounded over:

1 On the general history of Paradise see Jean Delumeau, *Une histoire du paradis,* Vol. 1: *Le jardin des délices*, Paris: Fayard, 1992.

Due entrance he disdained, and in contempt,
At one slight bound high overleaped all bound
Of hill or highest wall, and sheer within
Lights on his feet.

(4.180–183)

And since Satan can render himself invisible (10.443–448), he might have spared himself even that effort. Perhaps all these maximum security efforts are actually not intended to keep out intruders, but to prevent the residents of Paradise from escaping? It is never made clear how the angels might react if Adam and Eve would actually attempt to leave Paradise before they are commanded to do so, and the human pair may be uncertain about that question too. But the Garden of Eden certainly resembles a luxurious prison, not least because Adam and Eve already stand in judgment, in the shadow of their divine pre-condemnation as "ingrates". There is no denying, however, that the conditions of Adam's and Eve's prelapsarian detention seem to be very favourable. Eden is depicted as a privileged place, not only for man but also for personified Nature; for she is very much present and active in Eden, unfolding her full potential. References to her abound in the paradisiacal passages more than in all the others. Her "whole wealth" is said to be stored in Paradise (4.207). Like a zoo or a natural history museum, Eden displays the life forms of the world: all earthly "growth" (5.319), namely all animals and plants are here assembled, "all sorts are here that all the earth yields" (7.541). Accordingly, the narrator calls Eden a "sylvan scene" (4.140) and a "woody theatre/ Of stateliest view" (4.140–141). (The terms "museum" and "theatrum" were often used interchangeably in early modern times.)[2] The garden is described as an inversely structured amphitheatre, in which the most elevated view is from the centre, not from the periphery. As such, Eden is both a place from which to be seen from above and from which to see what lies below. Adam and Eve are thus offered a platform from which to survey their somewhat empty dominion, but it is first and foremost their own life that is eminently theatrical: they always have to be aware of the "regard of heaven" and of the complex multi-level surveillance it has instituted "on all [their] ways" (4.620). In this context, the epic employs a prominent Christian metaphor, favoured by Calvinist and Puritan discourses in particular: in a considerable number of Protestant tractates, man's life is conceived as a "spectaculum" with God as both dramatist and supreme spectator of its plots and executions.[3] In the *Doctrina Christiana*, Milton uses the idea that the world is a representational space in order to explain some biblical passages that

2 See e.g. Eva Schulz, "Notes on the History of Collecting and of Museums", in *Interpreting Objects and Collections*, ed. Susan M. Pearce, London and New York: Routledge, 1994. p. 178.

3 See e.g. Björn Quiring, "Introduction", in *"If Then the World a Theatre Present…": Revisions of the Theatrum Mundi Metaphor in Early Modern England*, ed. Björn Quiring, Berlin: Walter de Gruyter, 2014.

otherwise appear baffling: in the Book of Exodus and other texts, God occasionally hardens the hearts of those who are already in sin and so leads them further toward their punishment (see e.g. Exod. 9.12). Milton explains that such divine impulsions toward evil – "that they may stumble on, and deeper fall" (3.201) – serve the goal of uncovering evil in the public sphere (*DC* 334/335).[4] The limits of Paradise, like those of hell, are clearly structured to facilitate just such a constant "patefactio": Adam and Eve are largely confined to a space in which the mythical temptation of the forbidden tree is always close by, as a *corpus delicti in spe*. And that tree remains continuously unguarded, although it is the only object that it would actually make sense to guard, if the divine goal really was the prevention of Satan's triumph. The heavenly host is apparently not supposed to intervene in the set-up, and should keep communication with the trial subjects to a minimum. Man's unworthiness can thus be successfully demonstrated – not so much to God, since he claims to already know his creatures' inner workings, but to Eve and Adam themselves, to the angels and to Nature. Her sighing (9.783) and groaning (9.1001) upon Man's transgression implies that she figures as a witness to the events in the garden and accedes to the celestial verdict by her non-resistance.[5]

But Nature is not merely a passive audience member in Paradise; she is also actively involved in its generation and regeneration, most obviously as a force of growth and fertility. The narrator states, for example, that she pours forth flowers "profuse on hill and dale and plain" (4.243). God may be the "sovereign planter" (4.691) of Paradise, but again it appears that he is merely administrating and legislating forces that are not completely under his control. Richard Strier has pointed out that the narrator of *Paradise Lost* constantly emphasizes that Nature enjoys a considerable amount of autonomy in her horticultural works: "Edenic nature is notably not rulebound".[6] As one of the most important passages to corroborate this statement, he quotes the following lines:

> A wilderness of sweets; for Nature here
> Wantoned as in her prime, and played at will
> Her virgin fancies, pouring forth more sweet,
> Wild above rule or art; enormous bliss.
> (5.294–97; capitalization added)

Nature's wild, unbounded vitality is not following the rules of God's positive law.[7] Her "will" in this context is a faculty that suggests "happy

4 See also Chapter 6, pp. 200–201.

5 One may think back to the Orphic hymn in which Nature is addressed as the goddess who sees everything. See also Pierre Hadot, *The Veil of Isis: An Essay on the History of the Idea of Nature*, Cambridge, MA and London: Belknap Press of Harvard University Press, 2006, p. 27.

6 Richard Strier, "Milton's Fetters, or, Why Eden is Better Than Heaven", *Milton Studies* 38:1 (2000), p. 188.

7 Strier, "Milton's Fetters", p. 188.

spontaneity, not deliberation" or obedience. What is particularly striking in these representations of Nature is the suggestion that she behaves in ways that are intrinsically good, even though they are untouched by any ethical consideration.[8] It is an involuntary generosity, a teeming *magna mater* goodness, in which Nature's generative faculties are not "free/ To act or not" (7.171–172), but are involuntarily, passionately overflowing. That is why her benignity tends to produce more than is reasonable and why man must constantly "[h]elp to disburden Nature of her birth" (9.624; capitalization added).

If Nature demonstrates her overwhelming generosity in Paradise, it must be said that the abundance of her gifts seems poorly calibrated: most of Eden's wanton growth turns out to be useless or even incommodious and oppressive to Adam and Eve. Almost all of its produce either keeps "hanging incorruptible" (9.622) or "uncropped falls to the ground" (4.731), where it must either decay or suffocate the garden in the long run. The abundant growth thus impairs the first couple's comfort as well as their aesthetic sense of paradisiacal beauty; Adam points out that it leads to the accumulation of fallen "blossoms also, and those dropping gums,/ That lie bestrewn unsightly and unsmooth" and do not allow them to "tread with ease" (4.630–632). That the sun also provides "more warmth than Adam needs" (5.302) enforces the impression that the "enormous bliss" (5.297) with which he is endowed proves somewhat suffocating and is bound to induce cloying discomfort. Milton hints at a stifling side to Nature's all-too-generous embrace of man.

This seems to be an involuntary blunder rather than malignancy on Nature's part, but can we be altogether certain, given her uncertain status between the Father and Chaos? Might God and Nature be involved in a metaphysical good cop/bad cop routine, be it inadvertent or not? Is the first couple supposed to be crushed between an indebting God-Father and an infantilizing Mother Nature in a pincer movement from which Adam and Eve can only escape by an act of guilt-inducing self-assertion? Before jumping to premature conclusions, we ought to take a closer look at the relation between the works of God and Nature in Paradise and the ways in which the human pair is supposed to behave toward them.

The narrator emphasizes the artless naturalness of human life in the garden. Adam and Eve never use fire or metals; only the most primitive, almost untreated tools from organic materials, such as rinds of fruits from which to drink (4.334–335) and "gardening tools as art yet rude,/ Guiltless of fire had formed" (9.391–392). Their chairs and tables are not made of wood, but of moss and peat (5.391–395), and the interior decoration of their bower consists exclusively of flowers. Adam, shortly after the Fall, will prove perfectly capable to spontaneously conceive of a method by which to build a fire (10.1067–1081), so this primitivism must be intentional. They seem to be wary of impinging on the lifestyle that their natural environment

8 Not even the adjective "wanton" appears to be denunciatory. Strier, "Milton's Fetters", p. 188.

prescribes to them: if they would illumine Eden with torches, Nature and Night would bid them rest somewhat less imperiously (4.632), and so their obedience might slacken. The ways of Nature are frequently contrasted with those of art, and, throughout *Paradise Lost*, the term "art" has negative connotations.[9] The treacherous artfulness of the devils' products (such as empty rhetoric, cannons, the highway to hell and the vast splendours of Pandemonium) is constantly stressed; and the beauties of paradisiacal nature are said to trump all enticements of art and culture. But on the other hand, Paradise itself is described as an artwork that was created and keeps being re-created by Nature.[10] She "paints her colours" (5.24) in Eden. Blossoms and fruits have been "enamelled" with gay tints (4.149), and the river banks are "damasked with flowers" (4.333). Metaphors of artifice cluster most densely in descriptions of Adam and Eve's bower:

> the roof
> Of thickest covert was *inwoven* shade
> Laurel and myrtle, and what higher grew
> Of firm and fragrant leaf; on either side
> Acanthus, and each odorous bushy shrub
> *Fenced* up the verdant *wall*; each beauteous flower,
> Iris all hues, roses, and jessamin
> Reared high their flourished heads between, and *wrought*
> *Mosaic*; underfoot the violet,
> Crocus, and hyacinth with rich *inlay*
> *Broidered* the ground, more coloured than with stone
> Of *costliest emblem* [...].
>
> (4.692–703; italics added)

Apparently, the lost natural beauties of Eden can only be elucidated to the reader by equating them with products of an artfulness that has previously been denigrated as devilish. It is all the more difficult to see how the creativity of God and Nature is supposed to differ from the artfulness of the devils. *Prima facie*, God and Nature seem to prefer the gentle fertilizing and forming of growing, organic materials, whereas the devils work exclusively by the violent rearrangement of inorganic stuff, first and foremost the "precious bane" (1.692) of metals and minerals – substances that are designated by the

9 Peter M. McCluskey, "'Nature Taught Art': The Topos of Art and Nature in *Paradise Regained*", in *Spokesperson Milton: Voices in Contemporary Criticism*, eds. Charles W. Durham and Kristin Pruitt McColgan, Selinsgrove, PA: Susquehanna University Press 1994, p. 220.

10 As often, Milton seems to echo Ovid's *Metamorphoses* here: "[S]imulaverat artem/ ingenio natura suo; nam pumice vivo/ et levibus tofis nativum duxerat arcum [...]". "But Nature by her own cunning had imitated art; for she had shaped a native arch of the living rock and soft tufa" (Ovid, *Metamorphoses*, Vol. 1, trans. Frank Justus Miller, London: Heinemann; and Cambridge, MA: Harvard University Press, 1971, pp. 134/135 [3.158–160]).

narrator as "treasures better hid" (1.688), so that only their metaphorical use seems to remain permissible. But on a closer look, things turn out to be more complicated, for throughout the descriptions of Eden, we find passages such as these:

> How from that sapphire fount the crispèd brooks,
> Rolling on orient pearl and sands of gold [...].
> (4.237–238)

> blooming ambrosial fruit
> Of vegetable gold [...].
> (4.219–220)

> fruit burnished with golden rind
> Hung amiable, Hesperian fables true,
> If true, here only [...].
> (4.249–251)

John Reichert has pointed out that in all these instances, it is not altogether clear whether we are confronted with literal or metaphorical riches.[11] Do the paradisiacal rivers happen to flow from an actual sapphire bowl, or is their water so clear that it looks like sapphire? Are there real pearls decorating the riverbanks, or merely sand which is so fine that it shimmers nacreously? Do the rinds of some Edenic fruits actually contain particles of gold, or do they just emit sparkles of deep yellow when the sun shines on them? This ambiguity befits the status of Edenic objects as symbols, and it also allows the narrator to suggest that Adam and Eve inhabit a realm both of frugal natural virtue and of all-encompassing natural abundance.

These ambiguities in Milton's descriptions of art and nature are complemented by another similarly contradictory vocabulary that has received more attention: the narrator frequently uses words that seem to suggest the presence of sin and other nominally postlapsarian conditions within the lower, irrational life forms of prelapsarian Paradise. Some animals that caper around Adam and Eve in spontaneous reverence display odd characteristics. Most prominently, the as-of-yet uncorrupted serpent is already "sly" (4.347) and "insinuating" (4.348), giving proof of an inherent "fatal guile" (4.349). The plants and the entire landscape also behave ominously: the trees display a "wanton growth" (4.629) that mocks any effort to cultivate them, and their "pampered" (5.214) boughs engage in "[f]ruitless embraces" (5.215). The vines are "[l]uxuriant" (4.260), and the whole vegetation "[l]uxurious" (9.209), "luxury" having originally been associated with "lechery".[12] Even the rivers

11 John Reichert, *Milton's Wisdom: Nature and Scripture in* Paradise Lost, Ann Arbor: University of Michigan Press, 1992, p. 107.

12 See "luxury, n.", *OED Online*. Oxford University Press, June 2016. Web. 20 August 2016.

are said to run "with mazy error" (4.239) – just like the "erring" (6.173) devils, "in wandering mazes lost" (2.561). These imputations of organic, subrational transgressions have been read in diverse ways: do they hint at an inherent sinfulness of the natural world that is already ripe for the Fall without being aware of it?[13] According to Stanley Fish, this would be a grievous misreading: that we postlapsarian readers are irritated by expressions such as these should rather alert us to our own fallen state:

> If there are any moments in the poem which should be free of evil or even of the suggestion of evil, surely they are when Paradise is put before our eyes [...]. Mrs. McCaffrey seems almost to attribute the "sense of danger" we feel in the presence of innocence [...] to a potential for evil in nature. But Milton everywhere insists that "matter ... proceeded incorruptible from God, and even since the fall it remains incorruptible". [Fish here quotes from the *Doctrina*.] Again one must exclude (consciously) the tainted meaning, rejecting with it the idea of a guilty nature. The serpent too must be pronounced innocent. He is chosen to accompany "error" only because his physical aspect (accidentally) resembles the movement being described, which is also innocent. Evil exists only in the fallen mind which makes a naturally good universe the reflection of its own corruption. [...] By confronting the reader with a vocabulary bearing the taint of sin in a situation that could not possibly harbour it, Milton leaves him no choice but to acknowledge himself as the source, and to lament.[14]

Fish's general method of establishing a code of doubtful, yet forceful univocities is clearly discernible in this passage: on the grounds of a reference to the *Doctrina*, Fish asserts the unconditional goodness of all matter and deduces the unconditional goodness of Paradise from it. At the base of this deduction is a terminological conflation: in the quoted passage, Fish straightforwardly equates matter and nature, whereas Milton is far from doing so. The oddities of nature can be ignored, because the question-begging *doxa* are already firmly established. Alternative attempts to account for Milton's use of these ambivalent characterizations of Paradise have been made, for example by Reichert; according to him, they do indeed signal the inherent presence of sin in Paradise, but merely as a potential, contained and sublated within a multiplicity of others: if the Book of Nature is meant to report on God's generosity, it also has to confront his creatures with their freedom and its possible consequences.[15]

13 See e.g. Isabel G. MacCaffrey, *Paradise Lost as "Myth"*, Cambridge, MA: Harvard University Press, 1959, p. 165.

14 Stanley E. Fish, *Surprised By Sin: The Reader in* Paradise Lost, Cambridge, MA: Harvard University Press, 1997, pp. 135–136.

15 Reichert, *Milton's Wisdom*, p. 116.

To get a better grip on this problem, another irritating feature of Milton's descriptions of Paradise must also be considered, since it is closely related: introducing an abundant amount of classical references, the narrator enumerates diverse idyllic gardens from ancient history and from pagan mythologies, in which sin is manifestly very much present. One of them, for example, is the site of the rape of Proserpina (4.268–272). On the one hand, these referrals to pagan wickedness within the confines of Eden do not constitute a problem, since they remain contained and subsumed. Officially, they are only listed in order to be judged and denigrated as secondary and deficient in comparison to Paradise. But on the other hand, Eden is evidently basking in the glory of these references: pagan mythology starts to seep into the garden and raises its temperature, even though the narrator puts it *sous rature.* The postlapsarian similes flow so freely that they "disrupt our sense of time as well as of place".[16] Manifestly, this intrusion is not merely a rhetorical contraption by which sinful readers are reminded of their fallen state, for it does not remain restricted to the rhetorical level: there is one point in particular at which an accident seems to happen, whereby the pagan mythological similes break the bonds of figurative speech and directly invade the diegetic space. For it is said that in Eden

> airs, vernal airs,
> Breathing the smell of field and grove, attune
> The trembling leaves, while universal Pan
> Knit with the Graces and the Hours in dance
> Led on the eternal Spring.
> (4.264–268; capitalization added)

The presence of this particular God in prelapsarian Eden is particularly striking: not only is Pan associated with illicit sexuality, as well as other forms of temporary transgression and disorder, but he also belongs to the train of the God Dionysos who, in the works of Euripides, raises these transgressions to the status of natural laws.[17] And Dionysos figures not merely as the supreme legislator of this law, but also as its bloody executor.[18] In medieval writings, Pan was frequently identified with Satan,[19] a tradition that Milton seems to endorse in other passages of *Paradise Lost*; it might, for example, have influenced his decision to call the city of the devils "Pandæmonium" (1.756). Considering these circumstances, the jolly dance of Pan and his entourage in the Garden of Eden must be considered a rather uncanny occurrence.

16 Reichert, *Milton's Wisdom*, p. 104.

17 See e.g. Frank Brommer, "Pan", in *Paulys Realencyclopädie der classischen Altertumswissenschaft*, Supplementband 8, ed. Konrat Ziegler, Munich: Druckenmüller, 1956, col. 969.

18 See Chapter 1, p. 25.

19 Brommer, "Pan", col. 1007–1008.

Most Milton critics have chosen to ignore this embarrassment;[20] Alastair Fowler and others have tried to allegorize and de-paganize the pagan deity by identifying him as a manifestation of "universal nature"; but they have avoided all questions that result from this identification.[21] For example, even if we accord a merely allegorical status to Pan and his train, the passage still remains problematic and slightly scandalous since allegory, in its ineradicable inauthenticity, is a trope that *Paradise Lost* strongly associates with hell and Satan. Either way, the paradisiacal processes of exuberance seem to entail what they purport to exclude, and the remarkably smooth transitions between literal and metaphorical expressions – which are characteristic for the use of symbols – are found to be partly responsible for this. The narrator describes Eden as a dynamic place, caught up in diverse types of organic flux. Hence, Paradise is also a somewhat shifty location, a place of vertigo and uncertainty even in and by its beauty. Finding one's way within it turns out to be rather hard, not only on the level of ethics, but even on the more concrete level of spatial orientation within its landscapes. Reichert has analysed how Milton strings together images of streams, meadows, valleys, hillocks, groves, and other areas, but does not allow the reader to gauge their relation to each other (often connecting them with an "or", in a verbal gesture suggesting both abundance and disorientation).[22] The only orientation is offered by the outside walls, the amphitheatrical structure and by the "the middle tree" at the centre of Paradise, namely the Tree of Life, with the Tree of Knowledge positioned right next to it. Apart from these decisive features, the reader is refused any insight into the general layout of the garden; and even its size remains unclear. Its inhabitants, however, almost never seem to lose their orientation within the mazes of Eden: Adam and Eve seem to have adapted well to Paradise – indeed, so well that they are, to a certain degree, also caught up in its natural flux and its smooth transitions between metaphor and metonymy. Apparently, the bodies of Adam and Eve are endowed with a vegetable life, especially their hair: Adam has "hyacinthine locks" (4.301), and the ringlets of Eve wave "[a]s the vine curls her tendrils" (4.307). This tendency of human "vegetabilization" is complemented by the anthropomorphization of Edenic vegetation, for example "the flowery lap/ Of some irriguous valley" which/who "spread[s] her store" (4.254–255) and the "hairy" sides of the paradisiacal mountain (4.135). By association, some depictions of Eve's body also employ a vocabulary that suggests unruliness and moral deficiency, just like the "luxurious" growths of Paradise: for example she is said to display "wanton" and "dishevelled" locks (4.306). The clear distinction between organic growth and rational – and therefore

20 One exception is Neil Forsyth, referring to Fowler's attempt to contain the accident by allegoresis. See Neil Forsyth, *The Satanic Epic*, Princeton, NJ: Princeton University Press, 2003, pp. 130, 250.

21 See Alastair Fowler, ed. *Paradise Lost*, p. 235.

22 Reichert, *Milton's Wisdom*, p. 108.

legally accountable – actions is subtly undermined by figures such as these. This becomes even more obvious when one considers the way the narrator first introduces the bodies of Adam and Eve. He describes them as symbols of the cosmic and political hierarchy for which they were created, but this description seems to encounter certain limits: the narrator not only asserts a normativity that inheres in the bodies of Adam and Eve, but also suggests that these bodies are nevertheless capable of a proliferating growth that threatens to transgress these norms (see especially 4.296–310). The female body in particular seems to harbour the same maternal capacity of involuntary and abundant (hence dubitable) generosity, a teeming goodness just like that of Edenic Nature. There is a general tendency in *Paradise Lost* to depict woman as a symbol of the whole of Nature; one of its most elaborate similes develops a situation in which the delight in a natural scene is "summed up" in the delight one takes in the sight of a "fair virgin" who is passing through that scene:

> As one who long in populous city pent,
> Where houses thick and sewers annoy the air,
> Forth issuing on a summer's morn, to breathe
> Among the pleasant villages and farms
> Adjoined, from each thing met conceives delight,
> The smell of grain, or tedded grass, or kine,
> Or dairy, each rural sight, each rural sound;
> If chance, with nymphlike step fair virgin pass,
> What pleasing seemed, for her now pleases more,
> She most, and in her look sums all delight [...].
> (9.445–454)

Likewise, Adam asserts that "what seemed fair in all the world" (8.472) appears in Eve "summed up, in her contained" (8.473). Eden is a "wilderness of sweets" (5.294), a labyrinth of burgeoning goodness out of bounds, and Eve more than Adam is not only a lab animal who has to navigate this maze, but is also declared to be part of the maze. God has given her and her husband the task of cultivating Eden (8.319–320), which turns out to be a complex mission involving self-cultivation. They are custodians who must shape and reshape themselves and their garden according to the will of God and the inclination of Nature, finding the appropriate balance between both parties. Different forms of goodness must be weighed, not all of which are hard-wired into them. Is sufficient grace provided from above so that they can accomplish this task?[23]

23 Joanna Picciotto, *Labors of Innocence in Early Modern England*, Cambridge, MA and London: Harvard University Press, 2010, p. 486.

8.2 The republic of the sexes

God and the angels do not fail to turn Adam's enjoyment not only of Eve, but also of Edenic beauty into a commandment (8.170–172); man is not supposed to dislike Paradise. God "ordains" the bliss of man in more than one sense (4.728–729). Like an absent parent who relentlessly showers the kids with expensive toys, God officially clears himself of all blame by reference to Nature's boundless generosity. It allows him to claim that "ingrate" Adam "had of me/ All he could have" (3.97–98). Adam receives more than he ever could want or need from both Nature and God, thus indebting him immeasurably to his two keepers whose interests and demands do not always seem to coincide. Some of the unwanted gifts with which he is smothered prove dangerous; this is most clearly articulated in the case of his "last best gift", Eve (5.19). The only gift that Adam actually asks of God is the fellowship with an equal, "fit to participate/ All rational delight" (8.390–391). The companion he gets, however, is Eve, thus attaining as a surplus the attractions of sexual difference, another unsought bliss that the Son orders him to be pleased about ("What next I bring shall please thee, be assured", 8.449). Although Adam instantly begins to praise Eve's beauty and continues to do so throughout the epic, one might remember that he did not actually beg for beauty and the opportunity of sexual pleasure with his companion, but for equality. And he soon is led to doubt her equality, especially since the Son and Raphael keep pointing out her inferiority to him. Even Eve herself insists that she is not his equal, addressing Adam with the words: "thou/ Like consort to thyself canst nowhere find" (4.447–448).

Adam's original wish seems to have been denied, but at a second glance, things are somewhat less clear. For it is not easy to perceive in what exactly her intellectual inferiority is supposed to consist. The narrator certainly does not depict Eve as stupid (see e.g. 8.48–50); rather, the essential difference between her way of thinking and his seems to lie elsewhere. Adam clearly endeavours to think exclusively within the distinctly coded, static categories with which the representatives of heaven have provided him. In his utterances, the world is represented as an arrangement of symbols that remind him of his indebtedness to and his duties toward God. As well as his first utterance after his birth, which has been quoted in the preceding chapter, his first utterance within the epic (4.410–438) makes this orientation sufficiently clear: his enjoyment of the Edenic lunch break with Eve causes him to repeat once more the law that conditions it and the list of his divine debts. While Adam thus always seeks for the general and eternal within the particular and temporal, Eve seems to be more interested in particularities for themselves, "the fleeting moments and sensations".[24] There is nothing in Adam's utterances to compare to her hymn to the transformations in nature in the course of the day:

24 Reichert, *Milton's Wisdom*, p. 119.

Sweet is the breath of morn, her rising sweet,
With charm of earliest birds; pleasant the sun
When first on this delightful land he spreads
His orient beams, on herb, tree, fruit, and flower,
Glistering with dew; fragrant the fertile earth
After soft showers; and sweet the coming on
Of grateful evening mild, then silent Night
With this her solemn bird and this fair moon […].
(4.641–648; capitalization added)

For our purposes, one thing is particularly striking about these lines: what Eve describes here as the most endearing and pleasant of all things (except Adam) are not so much clear-cut natural objects such as beautiful plants and animals, but diffuse, ephemeral processes: the "rising" of the "breath of morn", the "glistening" of dew on blossoms, birdsong, fragrance, and "the coming on" of Night. All of these are volatile occurrences that percolate through space and time and diffuse the clear-cut boundaries that separate one thing from another. This tendency toward Whiteheadian process thought[25] – as well as her resultant interest in natural events that cannot be easily fitted into the distinctive codes and hierarchies by which God has structured the world – may be the main reason why her intellect is considered inferior by those in high places: it is more intimately related to the deterritorializing, dark side of Edenic nature which borders on the dynamic, "unthinged" processuality of Chaos that always threatens to swallow it.[26]

At this juncture, it bears repeating that the truly primordial woman, the very first rational creature who cannot "either sex assume" (1.424), is not Eve, but Sin. In Milton's cosmos, the emergence of an unalterable female sex is the result of a disabling punishment. Accordingly, it is fair to say that the chastisements of hell have already symbolically entered the world of Adam and Eve by the mere fact of their stable sexual difference. After the Fall, when he is in a particularly nasty mood, Adam himself explicitly designates this sexuation as an deprivation and calls it a "fair defect/ Of nature" (10.891–892). As usual, Adam cannot bring himself to explicitly accuse God in this context (although he comes as close to the brink of questioning his unfathomable decrees as he ever was), and so he ends up laying the blame on flawed Natura. Once more, the Great Mother must be incriminated in order to achieve an exoneration of the Father.

But Adam occasionally also seems intent to overcome this natural flaw. He is told that he stands alone on his rung of the cosmic ladder – inferior to the angels and the Godhead, but superior to Eve. But since Adam has also been

25 See e.g. Alfred North Whitehead, *The Concept of Nature*, Minneola, NY: Dover, 2004, pp. 165–167.

26 On the notion of the "unthinged" see Iain Hamilton Grant, *Philosophies of Nature after Schelling*, London and New York: Continuum, 2006, pp. 137–138.

told that this ladder is a career ladder on which positions are not fixed once and for all, it is only reasonable that he does not give up on a certain striving for equality, driven as he is by the desire for a companion to whom he does not have to talk down all the time. For example, he keeps addressing her as "my other self" or with similar terms (10.128). It seems that Milton himself would have been sympathetic to this wish, judging from the divorce pamphlets in which he emphasizes that not procreation, but rather "a meet and happy conversation" between compatible partners is the chief end of marriage (*Doctrine and Discipline of Divorce*, *CPW* 2.246). In the *Tetrachordon*, he even allows for the possibility that in some extraordinary cases the wife may hold the superior position:

> Not but that particular exceptions may have place, if she exceed her husband in prudence and dexterity, and he contentedly yield, for then a superior and more natural law comes in, that the wiser should govern the less wise, whether male or female.
>
> (*Tetrachordon*, *CPW* 2:589, spelling modernized)

The formulation "a more natural law" is striking, suggesting that there is a scale of naturalness according to which the gender hierarchy cannot be considered quite as natural as the partners' "prudence and dexterity". And that is indeed what his tractates suggest: Milton finds a compromise between the assertion that the relation between male and female is hierarchical and the statement that they should be considered as equals: her inferior position must be voluntarily acknowledged by the subordinate party, in a political act that supplements the dictates of nature.[27] This is just what Eve constantly does, apparently only too happy to indulge in her ancillary role, claiming to enjoy "far the happier lot" (4.446) by submitting to Adam's pre-eminence. The "modest pride" (4.310) that is ascribed to her exemplifies this attitude of voluntary servitude, but the formulation also raises doubts about the hierarchy between her modesty and her pride. Might she withdraw her acquiescence and thus attain the role of an equal? Does her official subjection allow her to rule over Adam on another level, in a dialectical turn? In this uncertainty, oscillating between unquestioned subjugation to her superior and latent resistance, Eve seems to embody the contradictions of paradisiacal Nature and of sexuation-by-subjugation. And this turns out to be exactly her assigned role: if Paradise is a theatre, the male is called to represent God within it, his bodily features declaring "absolute rule" (4.300), while Eve is cast as one in whom the beauties of Nature are "summed up" (8.473). By this move, the difficult relation between God and Nature is bound to determine the relation between Adam and Eve. Just as the whole of cosmic creation

27 See also Victoria Silver, *Imperfect Sense: The Predicament of Milton's Irony*, Princeton, NJ: Princeton University Press, 2001, p. 311.

participates in their union (8.510–520), they are called to represent it. Raphael explains to them both that the cosmos is involved in a partly conflictual, partly harmonious sexual relationship between an active, male deity and a shady, femininized force, which is sometimes represented as an autonomous person and sometimes not, and sometimes seems to have preceded God and sometimes to have been preceded by him. All the resultant problems are put squarely on the shoulders of Adam and Eve. And the main issues turn out to raise far more political problems than just the appropriate relationship between the sexes. The task of mediating between equality and hierarchy is addressed in most of Milton's political writings, not just in those that focus on gender issues. In his theologico-political pamphlets, he frequently reflects on the respective value of acquiescence in a given theocratic order on the one hand and of republican, humanist self-determination on the other. Milton tends to conceive his ideal society as a harmonious power relationship with flexible laws – a hierarchy, but a hierarchy that naturally allows for a certain amount of liberty of all its members, just like a happy family. Around the time when he was writing *Paradise Lost*, Milton also promoted an elitist republicanism based on the core unit of the patriarchal family, thus mingling *oikos* and *polis*.[28] The relationship between Adam and Eve should thus be seen as a blueprint of Milton's ideal commonwealth. Christopher Kendrick was among the first to have pointed out this metaphorical dimension of marriage in *Paradise Lost*: the wedded love of Adam and Eve prefigures the bonds that hold together the whole of society.[29] Eve is dependent upon Adam, and Adam is also dependent upon Eve; their "conversation" constitutes the first human society, a hierarchical one, but one that is to a certain extent open to negotiation – which gives an even stronger poignancy to the question of how Adam and Eve are supposed to relate to each other and to the Nature that determines them from within and without.

Because of heaven's restrictive information policy, the first couple has to experiment with a variety of approaches. They affirm male supremacy, but make it depend on a political consent to keep within their gender expectations. In their interactions, they assume their male and female sexes like roles that have been assigned to them, thus allowing for a certain amount of distance both from their ordained equality and also from their ordained hierarchy. When push comes to shove, however, Adam seems remarkably unwilling to trust in his superior position and impose his will on Eve by sovereign command: "force upon free will hath here no place" (9.1174), he says when Eve herself reproaches him for his reluctance to restrict her and to treat her authoritatively. It is symptomatic that his superior rank is never enforced or even tacitly treated as evident in and of itself, but constantly needs to be

28 See e.g. *The Readie and Easie Way to Establish a Free Commonwealth (Second Edition)*, *CPW* 7:407–463, esp. 458–461.

29 Christopher Kendrick, *Milton: A Study in Ideology and Form*, New York and London: Methuen, 1986, p. 192.

proclaimed and staged by both parties. That is probably the reason for Adam's tedious inclination to speak didactically to Eve on every possible occasion, constantly promulgating commonsensical maxims and proverbs. But male supremacy is artificially constructed by Eve too – for example when she walks away from the conversation with the angel, although she is interested in it and perfectly capable of understanding it: she does this in order to give Adam another opportunity to shower her with his superior wisdom later on (8.40–57), and perhaps also in order to save him from potential embarrassment about his former treatment of a related cosmological question (4.656–671). Eve's tendency to begin her statements with exuberant praise of Adam's superiority must spring from the same source; significantly, she tends to overdo it by gushing forth in ecstatic adoration of his higher faculties even after Adam's most basic, pedestrian statements. On one occasion, for example, she exclaims in enthralled obedience:

> My author and disposer, what thou bidst
> Unargued I obey; so God ordains,
> God is thy law, thou mine: to know no more
> Is woman's happiest knowledge and her praise.
> (4.635–638)

All this after Adam's rather banal assertion that evening has come and it is therefore time to go to bed. The lady does protest too much, thereby casting a strange, histrionic light on male supremacy; Adam and Eve enact a divine (and quite Hobbesian) comedy of the sexes in which the male is mainly experienced as superior because the female is willing to relate to him as such. Thus, they treat the uncertain relation between equality and hierarchy as an issue that is subject to their own negotiating power and therefore not altogether determined by God and Nature. A problem results, however: the play they keep staging runs the risk of developing a dynamic that inadvertently starts interfering with the hard-edged intellective and affective hierarchies of the cosmos. Officially, their sexual love and its "mysterious law" must be regarded as a function of the primal couple's permanent role as God's and Nature's priestly representatives. The union of the most eminent active and the most eminent passive element of the cosmos, in the forms of Adam and Eve, is described as a prelapsarian sacrament, "the rites/ Mysterious of connubial love" (4.742–743), destined to symbolize God's original creation by his fertilization of Chaos/Night which has supposedly generated Nature. It is only consequent that the narrator describes the "mysterious parts" (4.312) of Adam and Eve's bodies as "nature's work" (4.314). Against this background, it is easy to see how their negotiable role-playing might become problematic for their keepers: in the ideology of heaven, a generative union that symbolizes divine creation cannot be a relationship between equals, since that would inadmissibly imply an equality between the parties of primordial generation.

Furthermore, every love between equals that is not firmly overcoded by their common love of God must be regarded as illicit in Milton's universe.[30]

Of course, the denigration of sexuality, even within the bounds of a fertile marriage, has been a common topic of Christian thought since Paul (see e.g. 1 Corinthians 7.8–9). But *Paradise Lost* seems to be more specifically connected to a particular phenomenon of the late seventeenth century: Niklas Luhmann has pointed out that, around this period, the relation between the sexes within the bourgeoisie turned out to be no longer subsumable under the traditional household hierarchies and the stratifications of "religious cosmology".[31] In the course of economic dynamization and secularization, "the asymmetry of domestic order" and of property relations was weakened.[32] Subsequently, marriage based on mutual love slowly became *de rigueur* in England. Luhmann even mentions Milton's *Doctrine and Discipline of Divorce* as an important, if premature, contribution to this development.[33] It is only logical that, in Milton's time of transition, the competition between the love for God and the love for one's spouse became particularly fierce. Certainly, it is in this context that characters like the Calvinist Archibald Johnston must be understood, who, when he got into bed with his wife, always felt the need to loudly assure God that he preferred His face to hers.[34] More eloquent elaborations of the same theme can be found in some of Donne's "Holy Sonnets", first and foremost in Sonnet 17.[35] In *Paradise Lost*, the angel Raphael is the first visitor from the celestial realm to speak the resultant verdict on Adam and Eve's relationship: he famously contracts his brow when Adam sings the praises of Eve to him (8.560). In the angelic castigation that follows, Raphael admonishes Adam for not sufficiently affirming his superior position, but carefully chooses to ignore any suggestion that Eve may not be so inferior after all, or at least that Adam would like to think so. Adam in his dialogue with Raphael not only waxes ecstatic about Eve's apparent bodily attractions, but also about her apparent intellectual achievements:

> All higher knowledge in her presence falls
> Degraded, wisdom in discourse with her
> Loses discount'nanced, and like folly shows [...].
> (8.551–553)

30 William Empson, *Milton's God*, Westport, CT: Greenwood Press, 1978, p. 107.

31 Niklas Luhmann, *Love as Passion: The Codification of Intimacy*, trans. Jeremy Gaines and Doris L. Jones, Stanford, CA: Stanford University Press, 1982, p. 5.

32 Luhmann, *Love as Passion*, p. 80.

33 Luhmann, *Love as Passion*, p. 130.

34 Simon Schama, *A History of Britain*, Vol. 2: *The British Wars 1603–1776*, London: The Bodley Head, 2009, p. 74.

35 See William Empson, "Donne in the New Edition", in *Essays on Renaissance Literature*: Vol. 1: *Donne and the New Philosophy*, ed. John Haffenden, Cambridge and New York: Cambridge University Press, 1993, p. 152.

An argument might well be made that this appraisal is not merely a symptom of Adam's infatuation: Eve's questioning discourse, with its insistence on diffuse, ephemeral and hardly categorizable processes can reasonably be considered more perceptive than the rigid wisdom which has been handed down to Adam and which he is obliged to repeat. Adam oscillates on the issue, but he seems reluctant to accept the verdict from heaven without reservations. In his cautious resistance, he also discreetly hints at the fact that the strange mixture of symmetry and asymmetry in his companionship with Eve was not something he asked for, but something that was inexplicably imposed upon him. He questions whether the fault is altogether his own, or whether perhaps some mistake in his construction might have been made:

> Or Nature failed in me, and left some part
> Not proof enough such object to sustain,
> Or from my side subducting, took perhaps
> More than enough; at least on her bestowed
> Too much of ornament [...].
> (8.534–538; capitalization added)

Knowing that the mere suggestion that God might have failed is altogether inadmissible, he once more ascribes the mistake to his "deputy" Nature. The euphemism is transparent, however; after all, it was not Nature who extracted the rib from Adam's side. By propounding that it was Nature who has either fashioned Eve too attractive or fashioned himself too attracted, Adam promptly enters into another discursive danger zone, though. For the proposal suggests that Nature may have contributed to the creation of man in ways that are not under the firm control of the sovereign Godhead. If her cooperation would create effects that have not been ordained by God, divine omnipotence would be thrown into doubt. Raphael answers this timid challenge with a double rebuke:

> Accuse not Nature, she hath done her part;
> Do thou but thine [...].
> (8.561–562; capitalization added)

Once more, it seems that Raphael's order word aims at getting Adam to shut up and stop tackling inconvenient issues; it certainly is not helpful in answering Adam's doubts. Raphael suggests that Nature – in contributing to man's creation – has just obediently done "her part", that is, the duty that God has assigned to her. However, the Nature whom Adam knows is more than an obedient recipient of divine orders; she has a considerable leeway to cavort around in Paradise and make things grow "[w]ild above rule or art" (5.297), following nothing but her "will" (5.295) and her "virgin fancies" (5.296). If Adam were really to take her as his role model, then a fanciful, abundantly generous devotion to Eve would be an appropriate imitation of Nature's ways. And has Raphael not just told him that an inherent, virtuous striving for the Godhead expresses itself in all natural processes, even in the growth of plants? (5.469–499). So what exactly does Adam's duty to "do his part" encompass? Raphael skirts the question and engages in the easier task of denouncing Adam's passion as ungodly, sensual and bestial. In his both accusatory and pastoral speech, he uses the usual commonplaces that have been employed against the indulgence of "carnal pleasure" in Christian tractates, even though they prove strangely inappropriate to this particular occasion:

> For what admir'st thou, what transports thee so,
> An outside? Fair no doubt, and worth well
> Thy cherishing, thy honouring, and thy love,
> Not thy subjection [...].
> But if the sense of touch whereby mankind
> Is propagated seem such dear delight
> Beyond all other think the same vouchsafed
> To cattle and each beast; which would not be
> To them made common and divulged, if aught
> Therein enjoyed were worthy to subdue
> The soul of man, or passion in him move.
> What higher in her society thou findst
> Attractive, human, rational, love still;
> In loving thou dost well, in passion not [...].
> (8.567–570/579–588)

Raphael both states that love must first and foremost be dedicated to God and that it must not be passionate but remain within the limits of reason. Thus, he echoes commonplaces of a Christianized Stoicism of which Augustine is one of the most prominent exponents:[36] whereas lawful affects reinforce the virtuous soul's general movement towards God, the unruly emotions (called passions) distract it from this straight and narrow path and lead it down toward the things of this world and the entangling senses.[37] Milton also echoes this commonplace in the *Doctrina Christiana*:

> Gaudium ita est temperandum, ut de rebus bonis, prout quidque antecellit, ita gaudeamus; de caeteris quantum par est [...].

36 Concerning Augustine's adoption and revision of Stoic psychology and ethics, see e.g. Marcia L. Colish, *The Stoic Tradition from Antiquity to the Early Middle Ages,* Vol. 2: *Stoicism in Christian Latin Thought Through the Sixth Century*, Leiden: Brill, 1990, pp. 221–224.

37 Thomas Dixon, *From Passions to Emotions: The Creation of a Secular Psychological Category*, Cambridge and New York: Cambridge University Press, 2003, pp. 26–61.

> Joy should be so regulated that we rejoice about good things in proportion to the excellence of each, [and] about the rest so far as is reasonable [...].
>
> (*DC* 1066/1067)

The Stoics first asserted that only rational, lawful inclinations may be considered natural; all passions in their irrational vehemence are therefore not only directed against reason, but also against nature.[38] We can perceive an echo of this notion in Raphael's assertion that Nature has done "her part" and that the rest is up to Adam. But still, the rhetoric of *Paradise Lost* suggests that wild Nature and passion must be associates rather than antipodes. The double bind under which Adam and Eve labour manifests itself in the form of a double-headed Nature who is bound to sustain them and to shower them with pleasures, but who is also bound to reprimand them for these enjoyments.

When confronted with Raphael's elucidation of this ominous arrangement, Adam shows some uncharacteristic stirrings of resistance. He does not submit to Raphael's rebuke, at least not unreservedly; he is not abashed by it, but only "half abashed" (8.595). And he guardedly contradicts the angel: according to Adam, the true focus of his passion is not Eve's animal sex appeal, but her moral excellence and the intimacy of their conversation, and therefore his transports cannot be considered low:

> Neither her outside formed so fair, nor aught
> In procreation common to all kinds
> (Though higher of the genial bed by far,
> And with mysterious reverence I deem)
> So much delights me, as those graceful acts,
> Those thousand decencies that daily flow
> From all her words and actions, mixed with love
> And sweet compliance, which declare unfeigned
> Union of mind, or in us both one soul;
> Harmony to behold in wedded pair
> More grateful than harmonious sound to the ear.
> Yet these subject not; I to thee disclose
> What inward thence I feel, not therefore foiled,
> Who meet with various objects, from the sense
> Variously representing; yet still free
> Approve the best, and follow what I approve.
>
> (8.596–611)

38 Marcia L. Colish, *The Stoic Tradition from Antiquity to the Early Middle Ages*, Vol. 1: *Stoicism in Classical Latin Literature*, Leiden: Brill, 1990, p. 42.

This description affirms that the union of the first human couple is essentially sustained by the communication of words and of significant actions that give proof of interior virtues and of the harmony between the spouses. Thus, Adam claims that at the centre of their relationship stands the exchange of affectionate signs and symbols, and therefore neither beastly intercourse nor their common devotion to God. His assertion is obviously conditioned by the circumstance that the first humans treat their matrimony like a strange sort of mini-republic in which they assume representative functions. Among themselves, they constantly regenerate their hierarchy by way of acknowledgements, exchanging signs of approval (and, rarely, disapproval). That their respective place in the cosmic web must be staged in this way implies that it can be negotiated: by cultivating the small dramatic space that God has left to them, they make each other aware of their narrow fringe of autonomy. It stands to reason that these negotiations are therefore experienced as inherently pleasurable and are sought as ends in themselves. Their forces of judgment and enjoyment intermingle. Adam designates his inclination toward Eve as rational and judicious, but he has also called it a passion, and he does not retract the latter term. His utterances amount to the claim that his joy in the negotiations with Eve is a reasonable and therefore virtuous passion – a phrase that the Stoicist angel must consider a *contradictio in adiecto*. Their relationship, in which passion and the search for the appropriate affect are intertwined inextricably, is no longer neatly localizable in the grand divine web of unquestionable superiorities and inferiorities. By their rational infatuation, Adam and Eve inadvertently escape the centralized grid of divine hierarchy – and the resultant universally enforced narcissism. Raphael peddles the latter, in order to get Adam back on track:

> Weigh with her thyself;
> Then value: Oft-times nothing profits more
> Than self-esteem, grounded on just and right
> Well managed [...].
>
> (8.570–573)

But Adam's lukewarm response suggests that this proposal sounds not all that convincing to him.

By finding joy in their negotiations of hierarchy, the first couple has figured out how to use the ambiguity of the natural "bounds" to their own advantage. That Nature is both a hierarchy and an abundant force that transcends this hierarchy is not only a problem for them, but also a stimulant to their sense of self-worth and mutual attraction. In this function, their negotiations must become a thorn in the side of their guardians, since the game of mutual acknowledgement even allows for the (rather Lucretian) vision of its universalization, namely a universal republicanism involving natural processes. This appropriation of the celestial rhetoric seems to baffle Raphael, since he breaks off his series of admonishments and advice at this point and leaves – after having opposed earthly sexuality to an angelic sexuality that is less problematic, but also strangely unattractive.[39] Adam and Eve are left with an unresolved dilemma: the open dynamic of their relationship, oscillating between equality and hierarchy, may have turned out to offer them some advantages, but it can also be used against them.

8.3 Exercising Adam and Eve

It is not only the relationship between Adam and Eve that proves difficult, but also their common relation to their world, that is, first and foremost, to the feminized Garden of Eden. For Paradise is presented to them as a means to get to heaven, as well as an end in and of itself. Paradise is a breeding ground for new angels, but this very imperative to breed threatens to subvert their prospective angelhood. In the words of Christopher Kendrick: "Paradise, that is, both strives toward utopia and attempts to posit itself as utopia: it is both process and would-be end in this respect".[40] Even in this respect, Adam and Eve are supposed to bridge the internal contradictions of the cosmos. That is the reason why they are given the infinite task of cultivating the garden, that is, imposing divine order and discipline on it (5.211–219). It is easy to see that their work of "reform[ing]" (4.625) Eden is mainly symbolical, though:

> On to their morning's rural work they haste
> Among sweet dews and flowers; where any row
> Of fruit-trees over-woody reached too far
> Their pampered boughs, and needed hands to check
> Fruitless embraces: or they led the vine
> To wed her elm; she spoused about him twines
> Her marriageable arms, and with him brings
> Her dower the adopted clusters, to adorn
> His barren leaves.
>
> (5.211–219)

When Adam and Eve trim the trees that get too close to each other, the excessive proximity is described with a sexually charged expression that echoes an anterior characterization of prostitution (4.766–767); and when they attach climbing plants to the trees, the narrator represents this work as a marriage. The terminology implies that they direct the sexual energy of Edenic vegetation into the appropriate legal channels. As the narrator does not fail to emphasize, this work is just as vain as that of the angels; they are no match for the garden's proliferating exuberance. Adam states that the branches "mock

39 See Chapter 5, pp. 185–186.
40 Christopher Kendrick, *Milton: A Study in Ideology and Form*, p. 190.

our scant manuring, and require/ More hands than ours to lop their wanton growth" (4.628–629).

But this excessive growth poses no real problem, since their work is not actually agricultural and productive. It merely serves to impose a moral symbolism on the garden, so it is not the result that counts, but their moral intention and show of obedient discipline. Their work is symbolic insofar as it remains included in a divine ordering process that it represents. However, the fact that the human couple must constantly prevent vegetable prostitution seems to undermine both this celestial symbolism and Raphael's accompanying notion of natural theology. Nature's transcendental orientation within God's hierarchical order turns out not to be pre-existent within the "consummate flowers", but has to be imposed on them from above, by human aid. Adam and Eve do God's work in nature, but even within their delimited dominion they can only repeat symbolically what he has achieved, namely, to locally restrain the persistent natural remnants of Chaos by the application of codes: male – female; fruitful – fruitless; species A – species B. Their task is essentially an exemplary policing of nature.

There is an evident gap between the workings of God and the workings of Nature in Eden; and by their police work, Adam and Eve have been assigned the task of making this gap invisible and thereby harmonizing the conflicting forces, at least *in effigie*. They thus assert the dominion of God in an area where this dominion is less than evident, helping to bolster the Father's claim to absolute power. However, their work has thereby constantly to engage with a counterforce whose origins lie in unruly Chaos. Apparently, it is the task of God's creatures to accept the contradictions of the Father's rule and take responsibility for their containment, since these very contradictions perpetuate the divine order.

Such containments turn out to be Adam and Eve's main occupation to which all others are subservient: the first human couple has to uphold the codes on which the whole cosmos is said to subsist, in an environment in which these codes are implicitly threatened to be watered down or subverted. Another facet of this problem deserves to be mentioned here: Eden is a largely homogeneous and domesticated space. In this habitat, Adam, who is for "valour formed" (4.297), has but little opportunity to demonstrate his valiant strength and hence his masculinity. His stated ideal of a husband who guards and protects his wife "or with her the worst endures" (9.269) reduces to mere vaporizing since it is not based on experience.[41] His superior, masculine role in which he is supposed to represent God within creation must therefore remain restricted to one task: the doubtful, but obligatory, privilege of naming, instructing and judging inferior creatures. Just as every act of Adam is subject to judgment by

41 Furthermore, he will prove unable to measure up to it at the earliest available opportunity: when the Son comes down from heaven and accuses him of original sin, Adam – apologetically, but instantly – tries to exculpate himself by deflecting the accusation to Eve (10.125–143), even though he will later claim the opposite (10.930–938).

his superiors, Adam is bound to evaluate the lesser ranks of creation. Milton's Paradise is a Paradise of judging in which not only the Son and the angels, but also the first humans, judge incessantly, almost feverishly. Eden echoes with assessments, normative statements and verdicts far more numerous than "this apple should not be eaten". The conversations within it almost always revolve around the question: what is due to whom, and do all get what they are owed? The conversations between Adam and Eve, which are both juridical and joyful, are only one fraction of this general effusion. Both also judge the growths of Eden and their uses according to "pure nature's healthful rules" (11.523). In the process, the humans must also judge to what extent Nature in Paradise has been entitled by God to regulate the behaviour of men (see e.g. 9.940). William Empson has pointed out that there is a polyvalence in the Miltonian concept of Edenic Nature which puts her "above, equal to and below man".[42] By the use of his reason, man has to figure out to what extent each natural object he encounters is merely a passive piece of matter at the mercy of his own superior will and to what extent it conveys authoritative messages, such as the setting sun by which Nature "bids us rest" (4.633) or the abundantly growing plants by which Nature "instructs us not to spare" (5.320). In this context, it is worthwhile taking a closer look at the morning prayer service that Adam and Eve hold in the fifth book (5.153–208), for its contents remain firmly rooted in the natural world: only in eleven out of 56 total lines of the prayer do Adam and Eve address God directly and praise him for his works, which declare his "goodness beyond thought and power divine" (5.159). The remaining 45 lines are addressed not to the deity, but rather to all nonhuman creatures and phenomena: the angels (four lines), stars (five lines), the sun (four lines), moon and other planets (five lines), the elements (seven lines), the animals (five lines) and the plants (two lines) are also called upon to sound God's praise and witness the praise of man. Curiously, it is the least palpable class of entities – namely weather phenomena such as mists, showers and winds – that Adam and Eve call upon most extensively over the course of nine lines:

> Ye mists and exhalations, that now rise
> From hill or steaming lake, dusky or gray,
> Till the sun paint your fleecy skirts with gold,
> In honour to the world's great author rise;
> Whether to deck with clouds the uncoloured sky,
> Or wet the thirsty earth with falling showers,
> Rising or falling still advance his praise.
> His praise, ye winds, that from four quarters blow,
> Breathe soft or loud; and, wave your tops, ye pines,
> With every plant, in sign of worship wave.
>
> (5.185–194)

42 William Empson, *Some Versions of Pastoral*, New York: New Directions, 1974, p. 187.

The orison is thus converted into an obliging hymn to the creation more than to the creator. And the cited passage also shows how the call to prayer subtly oscillates between description and directive in the process: it remains unclear whether the exhalations, the breaths of wind and the wavings of the pines are already duly expressing the mute praise of God or whether the human couple admonishes them to do so. Do Adam and Eve lend creation their voice, or are they dictating to it? They both articulate a religious demand on all natural objects and suggest that the demand is already constantly being met by the sheer persistence of natural processes. Thus, they once more discretely close the gap between the positive law of God and the inherent law of Nature.

But what happens in cases where this closure is not easily attainable? The only decisive criterion Adam and Eve are left with is an explicit judgment by God or his messengers. The commanding word of the Greatest Creditor must *a priori* be true and lawful. Inversely, God and his acts must not be subjected to judgment, as Adam demonstrates when he anxiously avoids the mere hypothetical suggestion that God might have failed in his administrative works. Under these circumstances, Adam's task to represent God within Eden turns out to be unenviable: he must always be right, while being engaged with a world he is neither meant to control nor to understand. It is no wonder he tries to cover up his uncertainties in drab commonplaces when talking to Eve. Despite his nagging impression that *deus sive natura* may have "failed" in him "and left some part/ Not proof enough" (8.534–535), he asserts:

> O woman, best are all things as the will
> Of God ordained them, his creating hand
> Nothing imperfect or deficient left
> Of all that he created, much less man […].
> (9.343–346)

Just like Milton's heaven, Milton's Paradise is a Hobbesian environment in which God takes the role of the absolute sovereign whose rule must never be questioned or opposed under any circumstances. However, there are exceptions even to that rule: in some cases, obedience also implies subservience to the promptings of inner inspiration, even if they seem to contradict God's word.[43] The main example of the latter case is the first discussion in the history of earth, in which Adam humbly demands the joys of a companion, and God, speaking through the Son, reacts by refuting the plea:

> What callst thou solitude, is not the earth
> With various living creatures, and the air

43 Accordingly, Milton states in *Tetrachordon*: "Men of most renowned virtue have sometimes by transgressing most truly kept the law; and wisest magistrates have permitted and dispensed it" (*Tetrachordon*, *CPW* 2: 588, spelling modernized).

Replenished, and all these at thy command
To come and play before thee, knowst thou not
Their language and their ways, they also know,
And reason not contemptibly; with these
Find pastime, and bear rule; thy realm is large.
(8.369–375)

Instead of humbly obeying the decree that God has thus officially promulgated, Adam contradicts him and engages in further discussion:

Hast thou not made me here thy substitute,
And these inferior far beneath me set?
Among unequals what society
Can sort, what harmony or true delight?
Which must be mutual, in proportion due
Given and received [...].
(8.381–386)

After some further haggling, God gives in, maintaining that this fulfilment of Adam's inclination was his intention all along:

I, ere thou spak'st,
Knew it not good for man to be alone,
And no such company as then thou sawst
Intended thee, for trial only brought,
To see how thou couldst judge of fit and meet [...].
(8.444–448)

God thus reveals that the dialogue was a "trial" and that Adam has been judged favourably since he was ready to oppose God's official command and argue reasonably for the judiciousness of his own desires. This implies that, when conflicts arise between God's positive legislation and the natural inclinations that are grafted into Adam, the latter in some cases should have more weight than the former. The understanding of God's law has turned into a *double-entendre.* However, it is hard to understand how Adam and Eve are supposed to tell when exactly a divine decree is merely a ruse. For they have been advised that the cogitations of God are so far above their ken that they should not even try to use their sorely limited reason to understand them. They thus have to make their decisions in a void, but the precedent suggests to them they should be daring in following the reasonable dictates of their hearts. This lesson will have consequences, since it will serve as a contributing cause of the Fall.

8.4 The ascent to the bait of law

The double jurisdiction that God has established in Paradise could theoretically function without the tree: Adam and Eve are already immeasurably obliged and indebted to the natural and supernatural God. Their sinless state is only sustainable when they keep repaying their debt with the help of a frantic *ad hoc* jurisdiction – based on their sense of reason and justice – that must always try to give to God what he is owed in every conceivable sense. The system of divine law therefore seems to be already sustained, if not fulfilled, within Eden. So what is the additional prohibition of the tree at the heart of the garden good for? Adam and Eve are confronted with it as with a mystery, inviting and refuting interpretation, since no reason is given. They find themselves in a situation that is analogous to that of the angels when they witness the Father's baffling proclamation of the Son's begetting and the attendant threat of dire punishment, whereby an enigma is elevated to the status of a law, by a decree that is bound to be perceived as a provocation. Just as it is never made altogether clear from where or what the privileged status of the Son derives, neither Adam nor Eve nor the reader are conclusively informed whether the forbidden fruit has inherent properties that differ from those of all other apples. Throughout the history of theology, this question of the forbidden fruit's nature has been posed, and it has received very different answers:[44] Milton never definitely decides on any definite theory in *Paradise Lost*. However, he does spell out a position on the subject when he discusses the general significance of the forbidden tree in his *Doctrina Christiana*. (It bears repeating that statements from the *Doctrina* are not necessarily binding upon the world of *Paradise Lost*, but can nevertheless illuminate certain aspects of the epic.) According to the *Doctrina*, the Tree of Knowledge must be understood as a "kind of memorial of obedience" ("monumentum quoddam obedientiae", *DC* 358/359). Of course, it subsequently turns out to be a monument of disobedience, proving man's depravity and thus turning man's indebtedness into guilt. It is a "symbolum" that man has fallen from God's law (*DC* 360), and that might be its primordial function. But the divine command that has not been obeyed in the process deserves a closer look: was God's prohibition part of a natural or of a supernatural law? Interestingly, Milton describes the divine prohibition of the tree as a decisionist supplement of natural law:

> Opera autem Adamo nulla mandantur, unum duntaxat prohibetur. Unum autem saltem aut prohibendum erat, aut imperandum, atque id maxime quod neque bonum in se esset, neque malum, ut inde hominis obedientia constaret. Cum enim homo suopte ingenio bene ageret, essetque natura

44 See e.g. Philip C. Almond, *Adam and Eve in Seventeenth-Century Thought*, Cambridge and New York: Cambridge University Press, 1999, p. 192.

> bonus et sanctus, certe nec necesse erat, quod sponte quis faceret, ullo ad id foederis vinculo constringi; neque ullum ex bonis operibus obsequium ostendisset, cum ad ea, sine ullo mandate, naturali prorsus ductu ferretur. Mandatum autem quodvis, vel Domini vel magistratus, etiam praemio et poena proposita, non est continue foedus dicendum, sed edictum potius imperium.
>
> No works [i.e. no works that would disagree with his nature, BQ] are in fact commanded of Adam [and] only one thing is banned. But one thing at least had to be either banned or enjoined and in particular what was of a type neither good nor bad in itself, so that man's obedience might thereby be established. For since by his own disposition man behaved well, and was by nature good and holy, then surely neither was it necessary for anyone to be constrained by any bond of a covenant to [do] what he would be doing voluntarily, nor would any of his good works have shown obedience since, without any command, he was brought to them entirely by a natural inclination. Any command at all, moreover, whether God's or a magistrate's, even with prize and penalty proffered, should not automatically be called a covenant, but rather a declaration of authority. (*DC* 358/359)

Indeed, it is easy to see that eating an apple cannot be considered a morally reprehensible act in and of itself since Adam and Eve were permitted to eat the fruits of all the other trees that did not look especially different to them. Milton deduces that the "edictum" concerning the tree is a decree by which the sovereignty of God affirms itself as a Hobbesian authority that needs no justification in the given order of things. By obeying this divine law, man acknowledges that the legislation of God is above natural law. Accordingly, Milton proceeds to explain:

> Quoniam autem homo ad imaginem Dei factus, totam naturae legem ita secum natam, et in sese insitam habuit, ut nullo ad eam praecepto indigeret, hinc etiam efficitur, si qua ille praeterea, sive de arbore scientiae, sive de conjugio mandata accepit, ea non ad legem naturae pertinuisse, quae rectae rationi consentanea, (i.e.) per se bona quae sunt, satis ipsa docet, sed ad ius tantummodo, quod aiunt, positivum; quo Deus, aut quis alius iusta potestate praeditus ea iubet aut vetat, quae nisi is iussisset aut vetuisset, per se quidem neque bona fuissent neque mala; ideoque neminem obligassent.
>
> But since man, made after God's image, had the whole law of nature born with him and implanted in him in such a way that he needed no directive towards it, it also follows from this that if he received any further commands either about the tree of knowledge or about marriage, they applied not to the law of nature – which itself teaches well enough the things that are agreeable to right reason, that is, those that are intrinsically good – but simply and solely to what they term positive right, by

> which God, or anyone else possessed of just power, orders or else forbids those things which, unless he had ordered or else forbidden them, would, intrinsically at any rate, have been neither good nor evil, and would therefore have bound no one.
>
> (*DC* 360/361)

Here, Milton implicitly posits the general axiom that divinely promulgated, positive law should override inherent, natural law, not because it is more ethical and just, but merely because it is endowed with authority. God's law annuls that of Nature, according to which all apples may be freely eaten; so God and Nature obviously do not "bid the same" here, as Abdiel has previously asserted. Or do they? Another passage in the *Doctrina* asserts that the act of eating the fruit of the forbidden tree must be considered intrinsically, naturally bad, indeed as the sum of all transgressions, for the precise reason that God has forbidden it:

> Et si quis attentius paulo animadvertat, atrocissimum, et totius legis transgressionem haud iniuria dixerit. Sub hoc enim quid non perpetravit homo, credulitate in Satanam, incredulitate in Deum iuxta damnandus, infidelis, ingratus, inobsequens, gulosus, uxorius hic, mariti illa inobservantior, uterque suae prolis, totius generis humani, parricida, fur, et alieni raptor, sacrilegus, fallax, divinitatis insidiosus et indignus affectator, superbus, arrogans.
>
> And anyone who looked at it [the sin of the first parents] a bit more carefully would quite rightly call the sin most atrocious, and a transgression of the whole law. For under this head what did man not perpetrate – to be damned equally for his trustfulness towards Satan and for his trustlessness towards God; faithless, ungrateful, disobedient, gluttonous; he uxorious, she all too heedless of her husband; each of them a killer of their own progeny (the whole human race), a thief, and a preyer on what was not theirs; sacrilegious, deceitful, a crafty and unworthy pretender to divinty, haughty and arrogant?
>
> (*DC* 412/413)

By way of God's sovereign, arbitrary and unquestionable command, the whole fabric of natural ethical obligations is refocused on a formerly indifferent act whose avoidance symbolizes obedience to God and thence the foundation of all other virtues. Thus, natural law is officially subsumed by divine positive law. The tree turns out to be a place from which the rest of the territory is overcoded: it is part of the garden, but it is also a representative of its divine order.[45]

45 On similar structures, see Gilles Deleuze and Félix Guattari, *A Thousand Plateaus*, trans. Brian Massumi, Minneapolis and London: University of Minnesota Press, 2005, p. 382.

As has been pointed out before, this theological decisionism is strangely at odds with some other passages in Milton's prose work, especially in the regicide and divorce tractates.[46] For example, Milton frequently, and always affirmatively, refers to Hugo Grotius, whose work asserts that even God is bound by the laws of reason and nature and is therefore powerless to change any deed that is inherently good into one that is inherently evil and vice versa.[47] If we consider the whole of Milton's prose work, we find no explicit, unambiguous answer as to which branch of God's double legislature he accords greater weight. The same hesitancy also pervades *Paradise Lost*. The many contradictory strands of divine natural jurisdiction entwine in the tree. In God's first proclamation of the prohibition, their divergences already articulate themselves:

> But of the tree whose operation brings
> Knowledge of good and ill, which I have set
> The pledge of thy obedience and thy faith,
> Amid the garden by the Tree of Life,
> Remember what I warn thee, shun to taste,
> And shun the bitter consequence: for know,
> The day thou eatst thereof, my sole command
> Transgressed, inevitably thou shalt die;
> From that day mortal, and this happy state
> Shalt loose, expelled from hence into a world
> Of woe and sorrow.
>
> (8.323–833; capitalization added)

God in this statement leaves open the question of whether the evil effect of the tree would stem from an inherent, natural property of its fruits or from the divine condemnation and punishment that must legally follow upon the latter's consumption. On the one hand, he calls the prohibition a "pledge of obedience", just as Milton does in the *Doctrina*,[48] thus implying that the object of the prohibition may be indifferent. On the other hand, the Father speaks of the tree's own "operation", which produces "inevitable" consequences, thus suggesting that it is equipped with an inherent, possibly poisonous, power that is not accorded to the other plants in the garden. God leaves it deliberately ambiguous as to whether the forbidden fruit has any occult properties, and he also leaves it unclear as to whether those properties, provided they exist, would have been instilled in the fruit by himself or by some other party. In this

46 See e.g. John Rogers, "The Political Theology of Milton's Heaven", in *The New Milton Criticism*, eds. Peter C. Herman and Elizabeth Sauer, Cambridge: Cambridge University Press, 2012, p. 77.

47 See Chapter 1, pp. 88–89; Chapter 5, pp. 178–180.

48 Milton uses the term "pignus", meaning, first and foremost, "security for a debt" (see *DC* 358/359).

context, it should be remembered that the prohibited object is a product of natural growth, and that, according to Raphael's account of cosmic genesis, natural growth may be a force over which God has no absolute control, since Chaos and her/his daughter Nature also contribute to its dynamics. Thus, the human couple is confronted with an incomprehensible law, about whose status they remain in the dark: it may be incomprehensible because it is an arbitrary affirmation of authority or because it has a comprehensible (e.g. defensive) function within the whole of nature which God cannot or prefers not to divulge to them. Therefore the claim of Timothy Rosendale that the tree is a manifestation of a transcendent demand within immanence needs to be qualified. He writes:

> What makes the Tree a pure and transcendent sign is the fact that it finally refers to nothing but absolute difference. Between God and even prelapsarian humanity there is an unbridgeable and inexpressible gulf, and the very arbitrariness of the sign insists upon this. [...] It symbolizes not knowledge, but the impossibility of a particular knowledge, the inscrutable fact that God cannot be truly and fully comprehended by humans, even before the fall.[49]

However, a confrontation with absolute difference is not what the divine prohibition actually entails. For Adam and Eve cannot be sure of the law's "very arbitrariness". They have to make their decisions in a darkness that is so pervasive that they do not even know whether God's law is indeed irredeemably obscure and radically Other. For all they are permitted to know, the deity may have good pragmatic reasons to deny them access to the tree, and *per se* there is nothing blasphemous or disobedient in this supposition. The tree comes to stand for that very uncertainty: just like the natural law that inheres in the cosmos, the positive law that is entangled with and represents it commands, first and foremost: "I order you not to come to me".[50] To this command of ignorance, God adds another twist by designating the tree as the object "whose operation brings/ Knowledge of good and ill" (8.323–324). For this statement ironically suggests that the consumption of the forbidden fruit may itself be able to solve the legal mystery it represents. The law itself is thus used as a decoy, baiting a legal trap.[51] It is only with the installation of this trap that the cosmos becomes saturated with divine law, in other words turned into a court room in which God can judge life unrestrainedly.

49 Timothy Rosendale, "Milton, Hobbes, and the Liturgical Subject", *Studies in English Literature 1500–1900*, 44:1 (2004), p. 156.

50 Jacques Derrida, "Before the Law", in *Acts of Literature*, ed. Derek Attridge, New York: Routledge, 1992, p. 203.

51 On law as decoy, see also Walter Benjamin, "An Werner Kraft", 12 November 1934, in *Briefe*, Vol. 2, ed. Gershom Scholem and Theodor W. Adorno, Frankfurt am Main: Suhrkamp, 1978, p. 629.

Although seemingly rather minimal, the prohibition of the tree turns out to be not such an "easy charge" to keep (4.421). Because of the tension between natural and positive law, Adam and Eve are obliged to second-guess God's true legislative intentions, and they end up adopting different interpretations: Adam, who carries the stronger fear of God within him, accepts almost all decrees that are propounded by his superiors without worrying too much about their internal logic. His eager acquiescence, however, sometimes sounds exaggerated; this becomes most obvious when his praise for God's law ends up to be counterfactual: for example, Adam zealously justifies the prohibition of the tree as a law that is "so just" (5.552). It may be easy to observe, as he stresses in the fourth book, but there is nothing that can be conceivably called "just" about it, for Adam knows nothing about the forbidden fruit and about what may or may not distinguish it from other fruits that he is allowed to eat. He may mean to say that the divine decree involves an appropriate acknowledgement of God's sovereign right to dispose of his creation any natural or unnatural way he sees fit. But in this case, any divine prohibition whatsoever would be "just" by definition – thus, this praise of supreme justice rings rather hollow. When all is said and done, Adam's enthusiastic endorsements, which are supposed to demonstrate his affinity to God's law, instead demonstrate his alienation from it.

Eve adopts a different attitude: she assumes that the natural law includes or trumps positive law and that the innocent workings of her inclinations will therefore be sufficient to keep her from all transgression. In her discussion with Adam about the division of their labours, she asserts:

> Let us not then suspect our happy state
> Left so imperfect by the maker wise,
> As not secure to single or combined.
> Frail is our happiness, if this be so,
> And Eden were no Eden thus exposed.
> (9.337–341)

From her innocent and blissful state, she deduces that her natural inclinations must be sufficient to ward off evil both inside and outside. It is the legal promise that the just will be happy in God's world that thus renders her vulnerable.

On the day of the Fall, this division in the attitudes of Adam and Eve toward the divine law manifests itself. Their separation is due to the initiative of Eve, who, all of a sudden, demonstrates an eagerness to do more cultivation work than is actually required of them, so that "the hour of supper" may not come "unearned" (9.225): apparently, she tries to gain divine favour. If one seeks an explanation for this new attitude, one is bound to find it in the events of the preceding day, namely her dream of flight and the conversation with Raphael. Empson's rather convincing guess is that Eve wants to be "able to do space-travel" and that Raphael's narration has contributed to this desire as much as her Satanic dream.[52] The cosmological accounts of the angel have legitimated this desire to fly and also suggested that airworthiness may be awarded to her and Adam if they are consistently found obedient. After Raphael's denigration of sexuality, Eve may feel that a more severe work ethic (reducing the distance between God and Nature) combined with a more chaste lifestyle may win additional divine favours, thereby lifting her to the skies. This impression is reinforced when she adds that any temptation she might encounter on the way would only redound to her "double honour" when refuted (9.332). Her zest contrasts with Adam's altogether reactive behaviour: her husband admits that they will be more effective if separate, but also more endangered (9.227–269). Thus, he provokes Eve's complaint: "How are we happy, still in fear of harm?" (9.326). According to Eve, Paradise cannot really be Paradise, if it is threatened. This triggers a panic reaction in Adam: "fervently" (9.342) trying to get her back in line, he somewhat confusedly insists both on positive law and also on the need to use reason:

> Reason, is free, and reason he made right,
> But bid her well beware, and still erect,
> Lest by some fair appearing good surprised,
> She dictate false, and misinform the will
> To do what God expressly hath forbid.
> (9.352–356)

Adam urges Eve to use her intellect and asserts that she can only fail God's law when she errs from the road of reason; but he also implies that God's prohibition must never be questioned and is *a priori* reasonable, even though he and his spouse manifestly cannot figure out its sense. Thus, his praise of reason mingles with an admittance that a *sacrificium intellectus* is also in order since God's might makes unquestionably right. It is all the more surprising that Adam seems to be reluctant to use his supreme determining force against Eve, even though he is entitled to do so by the divine hierarchical order (9.364–375). Thus, Eve will encounter the serpent alone.

All that Satan in the form of the serpent subsequently needs to do is to exploit the contradictions of divine legislation. Against God's double law, he pursues a double line of argumentation, suggesting that he may be able to resolve the cosmic ambiguities under which Eve labours. On the one hand, the serpent questions a positive law that serves no discernible purpose, but supposedly obstructs the attainment of knowledge. He suggests that Eve might obey a more fundamental unwritten law by virtuously transgressing the official positive law and thus be "found obedient" in a new and deeper way:

> will God incense his ire
> For such a petty trespass, and not praise

52 Empson, *Milton's God*, p. 154.

Rather your dauntless virtue, whom the pain
Of death denounced, whatever thing death be,
Deterred not from achieving what might lead
To happier life, knowledge of good and evil […]?
(9.692–697)

Thus Satan represents the eating of the forbidden fruit as a morally commendable act, worthy of a divine reward in the form of an ascent toward the celestial realms. Eve might have to follow the implanted law of her inner nature in order to be really found obedient. This must sound all the more convincing to her if she has heard of the dialogue between the Son and Adam on the human need for fellowship in which it was Adam's task to oppose, according to his inborn inclinations, the official divine command to be content with the company of the animals. Satan implies that the prohibition of the fatal fruit may be an analogous "trial": maybe the tree was forbidden in the hope that somebody might transgress this law, thus demonstrating both supreme courage and an indomitable urge to ascend toward the higher spheres. Under theses auspices, Eve appears as reasonable and law-abiding when she assumes that the transgression of an official, inscrutable command might get her closer to heaven.

But Satan also traces a second line of argument: if we on the other hand assume that God genuinely prohibits the consumption of the knowledge-conveying fruit, instead of benevolently playacting, why would he do so? The prohibition then must be due to some natural property of the tree that God cannot control (see e.g. 9.727–728). In this vein, Satan can build on Raphael's words to Adam and Eve:

And from these corporal nutriments perhaps
Your bodies may at last turn all to spirit,
Improved by tract of time, and winged ascend
Ethereal, as we […].
(5.496–499)

This is exactly Satan's assumption when he represents the tree as a mediating device that can overcome the difference between heaven and earth. When he asserts that its fruit has wonderful natural powers, elevating everybody to a more evolved state, and presents himself as an example, he also insinuates that Nature is more powerful than God. Forces seem to inhere in the universe to which God must submit and which work toward an evolution of all living things. If God wants to hinder this process by his legislation, he must be jealous and afraid of potential competition, which in turn would portend that he is not the thoroughly transcendent entity he claims to be, but rather similar to his creatures in essence: not a supernatural ruler, but an usurpator. The argument is rhetorically strengthened by Satan's tendency to refer to the inhabitants of heaven using the plural "gods" (9.547;

9.716–719). This is no mere Satanic perversion, since celestial discourse employs the term in the same way.[53] Satan only needs to emphasize that the forbidden fruit is a product of natural growth from the earth and imply that Nature is superior to the gods in order to complete this second line of argumentation:

> The gods are first, and that advantage use
> On our belief, that all from them proceeds;
> I question it, for this fair earth I see,
> Warmed by the sun, producing every kind,
> Them nothing: if they all things, who enclosed
> Knowledge of good and evil in this tree,
> That whoso eats thereof, forthwith attains
> Wisdom without their leave?
>
> (9.718–725)

These are the two arguments of Satan in their pure form, which he sums up in the formula: "God therefore cannot hurt ye, and be just" (9.700): either God is who he claims to be and will not condemn, but rather praise Eve for eating the apple (whether inherently exceptional or not), or his behaviour would be reprehensibly unethical, and therefore not divine. In either case, it seems that the mysterious double jurisdiction that troubles Eve would finally have to reveal its true, univocal face by the consumption of the forbidden fruit. The subsequent eating of the apple is therefore not motivated by Eve's deluded aspiration to Godhead, as the heavenly jurisdiction purports,[54] but by an urgent epistemological desire: first and foremost, she is just trying to learn what the divine law actually means and whether it is legitimate and hence binding. Immediately before the consumption of the forbidden fruit, Eve inwardly ponders the risks and potential rewards of her deed, demonstrating that she longs not so much for illicit powers or celestial pleasures as for certainty about the law. Even the potential pleasures of flight and angelic adoration are no longer on her mind:

> What fear I then, rather what know to fear
> Under this ignorance of good and evil,
> Of God or death, of law or penalty?
> Here grows the cure of all, this fruit divine […].
>
> (9.773–776)

53 God himself has already articulated the latent polytheism that pervades *Paradise Lost* by addressing his faithful angels as "gods" (3.341).

54 See Book 3, The Argument: "man hath offended the majesty of God by aspiring to Godhead, and therefore with all his progeny devoted to death must die […]".

Given the circumstances, the only way for her to learn whether the natural or the positive law is more binding is the transgression of the only positive law she knows. And she is willing to take the attendant risk upon herself, not least because she already assumes that either God or Nature must be an altogether benevolent and omnipotent entity.[55] It does not enter Eve's mind that God might actually preserve the mystery by upholding both laws, even though they contradict one another. Thus she falls, whereupon Adam follows her out of love, even though he does not share her optimism. In his case, it is not faith in God's or Nature's ultimate benevolence that prompts him to eat of the apple, but solidarity with a loved one whom he assumes to be already "[d]efaced, deflowered" (9.901) and "lost" (9.900). He claims this solidarity to be natural:

> if death
> Consort with thee, death is to me as life;
> So forcible within my heart I feel
> The bond of Nature draw me to my own […].
> (9.953–956; capitalization added)

What does he mean by "the bond of Nature" in this context? One might suppose that he refers to his *inclinatio naturalis*, and the narrator reinforces this impression when he avers that Adam is "fondly overcome by female charm" (9.999). However, his "resolution" (9.907) to face the same punishment as Eve describes itself as unrelated to expectations of sexual pleasure or progeny; it is an affirmation of his loyalty to her as a distinctive individual and as a fellow member of their mini-republic:

> Should God create another Eve, and I
> Another rib afford, yet loss of thee
> Would never from my heart […].
> (9.911–913)

Adam assumes that Eve has grievously sinned; therefore his solidarity is not conditioned upon her ethical behaviour, as heaven's is. Rather, he demonstrates the same overabundant, involuntary support beyond ethics that "wanton" Nature has already exhibited in Paradise. Perhaps his reference to the "bond of Nature" alludes to this circumstance?

55 Again, Stanley Fish propounds a disposable half-truth when he states that Eve falsely imagines God to be worse than he is. (See Stanley Eugene Fish, *How Milton Works*, Cambridge, MA: Belknap Press of Harvard University Press, 2001, p. 520.) Admittedly, Eve echoes the Satanic suspicion that God might be a dubious character who cannot control the growths of Paradise (9.805–807). But on the other hand, she also guesses that God might be willing to emancipate his creatures and thereby to show himself more benevolent and generous than he actually turns out to be. See also Empson, *Milton's God*, p. 163.

In his representation of the Fall, Milton rearticulates an old theological dilemma: the origin of human sinfulness is one of the central problems of dogmatics, for, according to the trenchantly paradoxical formulation of Théodore de Bèze, it is "necessarium sed tamen voluntarium",[56] both necessary and freely chosen. This dilemma has found no satisfactory solution despite being intensely discussed: either the Fall is part of God's original plan, meaning that Man cannot really be blamed for it; or it deviates from his plan, which seems to contradict either his omniscience or his omnipotence.[57] The introduction of a creaturely free will into the equation is supposed to shift the moral blame from God, but in *Paradise Lost* it explains nothing: Milton's Adam and Eve are not represented as trespassing wilfully, but as impelled to do so by an ignorance which suggests that the fatal act might be the most ethical thing they can do under the circumstances. Insistently, the narrator of *Paradise Lost* shows that the Fall springs from human lack of knowledge rather than from free disobedience and might therefore be considered as the catastrophe of a classical tragedy in the Aristotelian sense.[58] The narrator indeed announces that the Fall is to be considered "tragic" (9.6); and his representation is altogether consistent with Benjamin's definition of ancient tragedy according to which tragic conflict springs from a confrontation of the protagonist with the demonic ambiguities of law.[59] An indebting unity underlying both facets of God's law is supposed to exist, but it remains mysterious. *Paradise Lost* confronts us with a Janus-headed divine jurisdiction, entrapping its defendants in the dead zone between its allegorical and its organic interpretation, claiming both limited and unlimited powers in the process. The subjects thereupon transgress the contradictory law in search for the one true law, their primordial guilt becoming actionable in the process.[60] In Milton's world, Calvin's statement that the purpose of natural law is to render man inexcusable[61] also applies to prelapsarian jurisdiction.

56 Théodore de Bèze, *Tractationes Theologicae*, Vol. 1, Geneva: Crispinum, 1570, p. 176.

57 See e.g. Peter White, *Predestination, Policy and Polemic: Conflict and Consensus in the English Church from the Reformation to the Civil War*, Cambridge: Cambridge University Press, 1992, p. 19 et passim.

58 See also Derek N. C. Wood, "Aristotle and Milton's Poetics", in *Renaissance-Poetik/Renaissance Poetics*, ed. Heinrich F. Plett, Berlin and New York: Walter de Gruyter, 1994, p. 371.

59 Walter Benjamin, *Ursprung des deutschen Trauerspiels*, in *Gesammelte Schriften*, Vol. 1, ed. Rolf Tiedemann, Frankfurt am Main: Suhrkamp, 1977, pp. 288, 298. Translated in *The Origin of German Tragic Drama*, trans. John Osborne, London: Verso, 1998, pp. 109, 118.

60 Once again assuming the role of a Protestant preacher and voicing the supposed position of God, Stanley Fish declares that it is better for the reader not to probe too deeply into the divine prohibition: "The freedom of the Fall (and therefore man's responsibility for it) is a point of doctrine, and the reader must resist the temptation to submit it to the scrutiny of reason, just as Adam and Eve must maintain the irrelevancy of reason to the one easy prohibition" (Fish, *Surprised by Sin*, p. 244). Somewhat stunningly, Fish thus reformulates the *sacrificium intellectus* as a hermeneutical imperative for the twentieth-century reader.

61 Jean Calvin, *Institutes of the Christian Religion*, trans. Ford Lewis Battles, ed. John T. McNeill, Louisville, KY: Westminster John Knox Press, 2006, p. 282 [2.2.22].

9 The infinite judgment of creation

9.1 Contagious justice

Not only is the law surrounding the Tree of Knowledge hard to fathom, but so is the punishment that arises from the law's transgression: does man become degenerate and mortal by the mere consumption of the forbidden fruit, or is an additional divine intervention needed to enact the punishment? The narrator obviously wants to leave this issue undecided too: on the one hand, the Fall is described as an inverted sacrament that instantly bestows death instead of life: "Greedily she engorged without restraint,/ And knew not eating death" (9.791–792). And the first results of the consumption also suggest an organic effectiveness of the fruit's inherent properties: before the transgression of Adam and Eve has been made known in heaven and the appropriate celestial decrees have been uttered, a meteorological change of their interior nature is already in evidence:

> high winds worse within
> Began to rise, high passions, anger, hate,
> Mistrust, suspicion, discord, and shook sore
> Their inward state of mind, calm region once
> And full of peace, now tossed and turbulent [...].
> (9.1122–1126)

Later on, the narrator mentions that the fruit has also "bred" an obstructive film on Adam's eyes (11.412–414). According to these descriptions, it seems that Adam and Eve, just like the serpent, have been "vitiated in nature" (10.169) by the act of consumption and are now subject to an organic jurisdiction that is built into nature and automatically enforced. There is still another indication that seems to point in the same direction: even though only Adam and Eve have sinned, their children – who "never touched/ The excepted tree" (11.425–426) and must therefore be considered as legally innocent – will also suffer all the dire consequences. The sin of the first human couple, like a disease, seems to spread organically, by contagion. Yet, on the other hand, an official trial of Adam and Eve does subsequently take place, and the most drastic changes in the cosmic order are only implemented afterwards. The prohibition of the tree was introduced as a positive law that supplemented natural law. It is only consequential that the epic also allows the reader to interpret the purported instant changes in postlapsarian nature as illusionary or rhetorical: the "eaten death" might only be a metonymy for the subsequent condemnation; and the "high winds" that rise "within", might also be an expression of agitated consciences, of disorientation and fear. Even the first couple's brief period of collective tipsiness (9.1007–1045) might be caused not so much by a slightly intoxicating effect of the fruit (9.1047), but rather by a self-aggrandizing euphoria that follows their joint act of transgression. The knowledge conveyed by the Tree of Knowledge is apparently reducible to the knowledge that they have eaten the fruit of the tree and have thereby transgressed: a remark by hungover Adam affirms this:

> our eyes
> Opened we find indeed, and find we know
> Both good and evil, good lost, and evil got [...].
> (9.1070–1072)

And his God seems to concur with him: snarky as always, the Father reveals to his angels that man by his transgression mainly has attained "knowledge of good lost, and evil got" (11.87).

The ambiguity of these statements about the tree's natural properties does not result from oversight, but is deliberately produced. This becomes obvious if one considers Milton's treatment of the other mysterious plant in Eden, the Tree of Life. On the one hand, the narrator castigates Satan for merely perching on the tree, instead of eating its fruit:

> Thence up he flew, and on the tree of life,
> The middle tree and highest there that grew,
> Sat like a cormorant; yet not true life
> Thereby regained, but sat devising death
> To them who lived; nor on the virtue thought
> Of that life-giving plant, but only used
> For prospect, what well used had been the pledge
> Of immortality. So little knows
> Any, but God alone, to value right
> The good before him, but perverts best things
> To worst abuse, or to their meanest use.
> (4.194–204)

Milton's formulations again leave the effectiveness of the tree open to doubt: it is both asserted that its fruit has "life-giving" virtues and that it is merely a "pledge of immortality". Still more peculiar is the narrator's attendant reprimand of Satan's blindness: even if Satan knew about the tree's doubtful effectiveness, it would prove redundant in his case, since the devil already is immortal. And if he were not, one supposes that the narrator would not actually endorse a Satanic attempt to attain deathlessness in this manner. The narrator's remark only makes sense if the image of the fiend on the Tree of Life is considered as an allegorical emblem, abstracted from the diegetical situation in which Satan and the tree happen to find themselves. Again, literal and tropological senses entangle one another, producing uncomfortable, condemning hybrids. Another passage makes it even more obvious that the complexifying obscurity surrounding both trees is deliberately manufactured. For Milton has chosen to change the biblical wording, apparently just in order to leave open the possibility that the Tree of Life differs from any other Edenic tree merely by its designation: the God of the Bible justifies the expulsion of the first couple from Eden by the circumstance that man might otherwise "take also of the tree of life and eat and live for ever" (Gen. 3.22). The Miltonic Father, however, is more exacting:

> Lest therefore his now bolder hand
> Reach also of the tree of life, and eat,
> And live for ever, dream at least to live
> For ever, to remove him I decree [...].
> (11.93–96)

Not only does this remark leave open the possibility that the postlapsarian immortality induced by the Tree of Life might be merely an illusion, but it also suggests that even man's temporary delusion of postlapsarian immortality is so offensive to Milton's God that he feels entitled to prevent it by adding exile from Eden to the other condemnations to which man has already been subjected.

By the production of abeyance and ambiguity, the divine order is systematically posited as both inherent within nature and also as transcendent to it. An indebting unity underlying both facets of God's law is supposed to exist, but it remains mysterious, to the reader as well as to Eve and Adam. However, it soon becomes obvious that the first couple, by its transgression, has entered into a new relation with the judicial sphere. Once more, it is useful to first consult the *Doctrina Christiana* on the legal effects of the Fall: Milton here asserts that the guilt that mankind has incurred is a form of death which binds it "fast to judgement and punishment":

> Primum est reatus; quae quamquam imputatio Dei est, in nobis tamen velut inchoata mors seu mortis quoddam exordium est, quo quasi nexu quodam ad judicium et poenam obstringimur. [...] Totus exinde homo pollutus redditur [...].
>
> First, there is Guilt, which, though it is God's charge on our account, nevertheless exists in us like an incipient death or a kind of opening flourish of death, by which, as if by a kind of knot, we are bound fast to

> judgement and punishment. [...] As a result the whole man is rendered defiled [...].
>
> (*DC* 430/431)

Of course, man was previously bound by the divine law, but this binding did not necessarily include punishment. Milton here combines the theologico-juridical imagery of guilt as a binding fetter with that of guilt as a polluting infection, spreading within man and manifesting his death-in-life. In this medical conception of transgression, corrupting sin and its punishment by God become almost indistinguishable, with conscience bridging the gap. And Milton appropriately adds a few lines later that "sin itself is its own punishment" ("peccatum sui poena", *DC* 432/433). The result is a "lessening of the majesty of the human countenance, and a base degradation of the mind" (*DC* 431). This legal degeneration removes humankind ever farther from their prescribed ways. While man keeps sliding further down a spiral of guilt accumulation and degeneration, God and His law keep ascending out of his reach, becoming ever more transcendent. Adam, perceiving "[a]ll things with double terror" (10.850), laments:

> O Conscience, into what abyss of fears
> And horrors hast thou driven me; out of which
> I find no way, from deep to deeper plunged!
> (10.842–844; capitalization added)

Man's abjection and descent into darkness makes God's law shine all the brighter and all the more encompassingly. Thomas Aquinas has articulated and Richard Hooker has repeated the theological commonplace that the original sin was an offence against an infinite being and therefore worthy of infinite punishment.[1] Punishment in *Paradise Lost* is infinite on almost every level: it is eternal in time, since the flames of hellfire will never be extinguished, but it is also quite boundless in scope. Not only mankind, the cosmos and Satan, but also all the devils in hell are devoted to divine vengeance as a result of Satan's seduction of Adam and Eve (10.519–577). This divine enforcement of kin liability to the nth degree, although already considered archaic before Milton's time, is explicitly endorsed in the *Doctrina*:

> Certe si non omnes in Adamo peccarunt, cur omnium ab eius lapsu conditio facta deterior est? Respondent moderni quidam, physica ilia imminutio, non moralis fuit. At, inquam insontes non minus iustum fuit

1 Thomas Aquinas, *Summa Theologiae Prima Secundae, 74–144*, Latin/English Edition, trans. Laurence Shapcote, Lander, WY: Aquinas Institute, 2012, pp. 166 [Summa 2.1, Quaestio 87, Art. 4]. Richard Hooker, *Of the Laws of Ecclesiastical Polity, Books 6, 7, 8*, ed. Paul G. Stanwood, Cambridge, MA and London: Belknap Press of Harvard University Press, 1981, pp. 52–53 [6.5.2].

> perfectione sua physica quam morali multare; praesertim cum in hanc, id est, in mores tam potenter agat. Haec autem non solum perpetua divinae iustitiae ratio est, verum etiam ius vetustissimum apud omnes gentes Deorumque religiones, ut qui rem sacram violasset, (sacra autem erat arbor ista) non ipse solum, sed omnis etiam progenies eius piacularis et devota fieret.
>
> Surely it is not the case that all sinned in Adam, why was the condition of all made worse by his fall? Certain contemporaries answer: that impairment was physical, not moral. But I say: it was not less just to penalize the guiltless with the loss of physical than of moral perfection, especially since [the former] impinges so powerfully on the latter, that is, on morals. But this is not only divine justice's enduring principle, but also a very ancient law among all races and cults of the Gods, that anyone who had violated a sacred object (and that tree was sacred) should not only become liable for atonement and a marked man himself, but so should all his posterity too.
>
> (*DC* 414/415)[2]

Milton approvingly cites many biblical applications of collective punishment, among them some that cross the species boundary, for example, Joshua 6.21 in which "even the beasts of burden were being marked out for slaughter with their masters" (*DC* 415). He adds further examples from Thucydides, Virgil and unnamed "iurisconsulti", thus extending the principle to pagan and secular jurisdiction (*DC* 418). In *Paradise Lost*, Michael likewise suggests that the "vicious race" of Ham rightly pays for the sin of its ancestors by its perpetual enslavement, echoing proto-racist commonplaces about the rightness of black slavery (12.104).[3] In this context, Milton chooses to ignore passages in the Bible that question this archaic notion of kin liability, most prominently Ezekiel 18, in which it is unambiguously affirmed that the son "will not die for his father's sin; he will surely live" (Ezek. 18.17). Milton's supreme legislator does not delimit his retributions; their endlessness is an inverted image of his own infinite sovereignty, suggesting the cosmos was created so that its corruption might proclaim divine justice and magnificence. God's prosecutions therefore do not only concern mankind, but also all created beings. Raphael, the narrator and even Satan have repeatedly pointed out that man must

2 Significantly, Milton speaks of "the loss of physical than of moral perfection" where one would expect "the loss of moral than of physical perfection". According to the editors of the Oxford edition of the *Doctrina*, the commutation of "physical" and "moral" in this sentence is to be estimated as a "Litotes gone wrong" (*DC* 415).

3 See David M. Whitford, *The Curse of Ham in the Early Modern Era: The Bible and the Justifications for Slavery*, Farnham and Burlington, VT: Ashgate, 2009.

be considered the supreme creature within the cosmos and therefore its supreme representative: the whole is "summed up" (9.113) in him. Under conditions of kin liability, it stands to reason that the whole cosmos and even the whole of nature can be punished for his deeds. Nature may already be enacting divine punishments in hell and elsewhere, but that does not mean that she is granted immunity from prosecution. Nature herself, who has gotten to know her Father/Son better than Adam and Eve, seems to discern the general predicament immediately: her instantaneous reaction to the Fall is remarkably passive and emotional; she seems to have a premonition of what is in store for her:

> Nature from her seat
> Sighing through all her works gave signs of woe,
> That all was lost.
> (9.782–784; capitalization added)

This total loss has to be specified: while there is obviously still natural growth in postlapsarian nature, it is henceforth subject to boundless divine punishment. Nature's sighing and groaning warns of a cosmic state of exception that will soon be declared. She is seconded by some meteorological and geodynamic events which the narrator represents as symptoms of a mourning creation: the sky begins to weep, in other words it starts to rain (9.1002–1003); the earth trembles with pain and fear (9.1000–1001);[4] and lastly, the sun changes his course out of horror or disgust:

> At that tasted fruit
> The Sun, as from Thyéstean banquet, turned
> His course intended […].
> (10.687–689)

All of these natural events can be interpreted as prodigious (they resemble the miracles that occur at the death of Jesus in Matthew 27.45–51). But they also might be within the regular order of things; even the turning of the sun might be perfectly normal: Milton stresses that the Fall occurs around noon (9.739), so the turning of the sun might just indicate that it/he has passed the zenith and hence has turned from rising to descending. Just like the scales that God hangs in the sky, the symptoms of Nature's mourning are situated in the uncertain zone between brute facts and the "signs portentous" of a missing unity; this is the area of allegoresis, which now slowly starts to encroach upon the cosmos from the confines of hell.

4 This trembling cannot be very pronounced though, since neither Adam nor Eve seem to notice it.

9.2 The show trial at the dawn of history

After man has been successfully caught in the act, his transgression is followed by a trial that has all the markings of a show trial. The angels seem to witness the proceedings directly or indirectly: God proclaims that "from them I will not hide/ My judgements" (11.68–69), and the readers of *Paradise Lost* are certainly also called to attend. Of course, the term "show trial" is an anachronism: apparently, it was only coined in the 1920s, by an American journalist who wrote about the Stalinist Shakhty trials.[5] But the England of Milton's time already had a history of what we would nowadays call show trials, the condemnation of Charles I being one of them.[6] Incidentally, Elizabeth A. Wood has pointed out that the religious plays of early modern Russia frequently took the form of primordial court proceedings; prominent among them was a staged trial of Adam and Eve from the seventeenth century which imitated all the forms and structures of a contemporary Russian law court.[7] Wood has further demonstrated that from these early modern Russian-Orthodox plays a continuous line of succession runs to a tradition of Tsarist and early Soviet mock trials and from there on to the notorious Moscow Trials.[8] Fittingly, Milton's Son of God, in his role as Edenic prosecutor and judge, uses many theatrical flourishes; most prominently, he frequently engages in derisive irony, a rhetorical device that future colleagues such as Vyshinsky and Freisler will also employ.[9] (Empson's comparison of Milton's God to Stalin is borne out in this context.)[10] Milton endows the divine utterances he adopts from Gen. 3.9–19 with a stronger sense of sarcasm: after the Son has come down to Paradise, he almost instantly starts to pose ironic questions:

> come I less conspicuous, or what change
> Absents thee, or what chance detains?
>
> (10.107–108)

> Was she thy God, that her thou didst obey
> Before his voice […]?
>
> (10.145–146)

5 Elizabeth A. Wood, *Performing Justice: Agitation Trials in Early Soviet Russia*, Ithaca, NY and London: Cornell University Press, 2005, p. 193.

6 Some historians have used the term in this context. See e.g. Christopher Durston, *Charles I*, London and New York: Routledge, 1998, p. 40.

7 For details see Wood, *Performing Justice*, pp. 17–18.

8 Wood, *Performing Justice*, pp. 34, 194, 208 et passim.

9 See e.g. Slavoj Žižek, *Die bösen Geister des himmlischen Bereichs: Der linke Kampf um das 21. Jahrhundert,* trans. Frank Born, Frankfurt am Main: Fischer, 2011, p. 204; and Walter Wagner, *Der Volksgerichtshof im nationalsozialistischen Staat,* Munich: Oldenbourg, 2011, pp. 746–780.

10 William Empson, *Milton's God*, Westport, CT: Greenwood Press, 1978, p. 146.

The circumstances of the whole fact-finding interrogation ritual are in and of themselves ironical because of their obvious redundancy: the Son already knows the right answers to all his questions, as Adam points out:

> though should I hold my peace, yet thou
> Wouldst easily detect what I conceal [...].
> (10.135–136)

It is an interrogation for interrogation's sake (a favourite pastime of totalitarian executive organs).[11] Another irony is discernible in the Father's assertion that the accused committed the deed voluntarily, his "free will, to her own inclining left/ In even scale" (10.46–47). Both God and the guardian angels he addresses at this moment must be aware that it was chiefly his own hanging of the "golden scales" that prevented the angels from expelling Satan from the cosmos just a few days before.[12] Irony at the same time posits and undermines. It is not limited to saying *x* and meaning *y*, but displays what is meant and what is said as opposites, emphasizing both the distance and also the connection between the two.[13] As such, it is a mode in which the Janus-faced power of Milton's God can express itself clearly. In this respect, irony appears as a variant of the allegorical, as Walter Benjamin has suggested.[14] The divine sarcasm prefigures an earth that will undergo allegoresis and become more infernal in the process.

The serene ironies of heaven contrast with a frightened literalism on the defendants' side: Adam and Eve truncate the narrative of their deeds to the point of misrepresentation. Adam attempts to divert the accusation by a blunt: "She gave me of the tree, and I did eat" (10.143). And all Eve can do is to shift the blame further: "The serpent me beguiled, and I did eat" (10.162). They seem to be too intimidated to even plead extenuating circumstances, let alone to put forward a proper defence. If Adam would proclaim that he only ate of the apple because he was determined to die with Eve, or if Eve would avow that she ate of the apple partly because it seemed to be the most ethical thing to do at the time, these statements would steal some of the Son's thunder. Instead, Adam invents aggravating circumstances and deplores a non-existent hubris that caused him to eat of the apple: quite enthusiastically, but inaccurately, he proceeds to denounce himself as one "who sought/ Forbidden knowledge by forbidden means" in his subsequent dialogue with

11 On this topic see Aron Ronald Bodenheimer, *Warum? Von der Obszönität des Fragens,* Stuttgart: Reclam, 1984.

12 See Empson, *Milton's God*, pp. 116–117. However, Empson, in a conciliatory mood, prefers to interpret the allusion as a symptom of God's bad conscience.

13 See Wayne C. Booth, *A Rhetoric of Irony*, Chicago and London: University of Chicago Press, 1975.

14 Walter Benjamin, *Ursprung des deutschen Trauerspiels*, in *Gesammelte Schriften*, Vol. 1, ed. Rolf Tiedemann, Frankfurt am Main: Suhrkamp, 1977, p. 364. Translated in *The Origin of German Tragic Drama*, trans. John Osborne, London: Verso, 1998, p. 188.

Michael (12.278–279). Rather than question the justice of the divine verdict, he prefers to make himself guiltier than he is. Comparable to the defendants in Stalinist show trials, he might choose this self-sacrificial comportment in order to justify and support the regime that accuses him, desperate for the vindication of God's Great Cause.[15] As in many other forms of primordial judgment, the more Adam obeys and assents, the guiltier he becomes, because accumulating guilt is his present duty.

The subsequent verdict not only proclaims that man will henceforth be mortal, as previously threatened, but it also surprisingly announces that his natural environment will now behave in a hostile manner toward him: organic growth is transformed in ways that negatively impact man's well-being: first, by the curse on female fertility, which is to become a painful affair, and second on the soil, which is now due to bring forth thorns and thistles (10.193–208). Divine jurisdiction is thus enacted with the help of Nature, who turns out to be both a medium of additional punishment and a co-defendant who will herself be impacted negatively by God's decrees. The most baffling of natural condemnations passes on the serpent, who is no longer possessed by Satan. In heaven, the Son has expressly affirmed that "[c]onviction to the serpent none belongs", playing on the double sense of the word (10.84). After his touchdown in Eden and Eve's brief testimony, however:

> without delay
> To judgment he proceeded on the accused
> Serpent though brute, unable to transfer
> The guilt on him who made him instrument
> Of mischief, and polluted from the end
> Of his creation; justly then accursed,
> As vitiated in nature: more to know
> Concerned not Man (since he no further knew) [...].
> (10.163–170)

Alistair Fowler seeks to render this verdict more comprehensible by the assertion that the punishment of animals "had been common" in Milton's time.[16] Admittedly, there have indeed been trials against animals and inanimate objects in medieval and early modern times, asserting a claim on law's dominion over the whole of nature.[17] The parallel is certainly interesting but

15 For parallel behaviour in the Stalinist trials, see e.g. Robert Conquest, *The Great Terror: A Reassessment*, Oxford and New York: Oxford University Press, 2008, pp. 117–120.

16 See Alastair Fowler, ed., *Paradise Lost*, p. 548.

17 Despite some criticism, the work on the subject that is still most quoted is E. P. Evans, *The Criminal Prosecution and Capital Punishment of Animals*, New York: E. P. Dutton, 1906. It is, by the way, remarkable how often clerics were involved in these attempted impositions of boundless justice, inflicting a mixture of secular and ecclesiastical punishments. See e.g. Sadakat Kadri, *The Trial: A History, from Socrates to O. J. Simpson*, New York: Random House, 2005, pp. 152–185.

problematical, insofar as Fowler supposes that these animal trials directly influenced Milton. While such trials did occur, they were rare and apparently never took place in England.[18] Furthermore, they were frequently denounced as superstitious both by jurists and by divines:

> Europe's theologians and lawyers always agreed that innocence and guilt depended on the rational exercise of free will [...]. Philippe de Beaumanoir was already stating the obvious when he observed in the late thirteenth century that "punishment is lost on [animals]", and his contemporary, Thomas Aquinas, was recapitulating equally conventional wisdom when he explained why penalties could have no moral basis. Human laws applied only to those "who know what they are about and have the alternative of doing a thing or leaving it undone", qualities that were "proper to the rational creature only".[19]

In *Paradise Lost*, it is also not suggested that the serpent intends to corrupt Adam and Eve; the animal appears as a passive victim rather than a transgressor, overwhelmed while sleeping and violated by a force it cannot resist. Like Sin, the serpent is thus afflicted with guiltless guilt, a ban whose apparent injustice is even acknowledged by the Son himself. At this point, it is no longer surprising that the narrator justifies the curse on the serpent by way of two complementary arguments of which the first is allegorical, the second biopolitical. First, the narrator implies that the judgment is actually directed against the already-condemned Satan:

> yet God at last
> To Satan first in sin his doom applied
> Though in mysterious terms, judged as then best.
> (10.171–173)

According to this statement, the curse on the serpent merely prefigures a penalty that Satan will receive after Christ's resurrection (see also 10.179–185). To the question of why this allegorical scapegoating (by which the real serpent will eat real dust) is necessary, the narrative answers that either God or the serpent (for the sentence structure admits both readings) is "unable to transfer/ The guilt on him who made him [the serpent] instrument/ Of mischief" (10.165–167). Whether it is ascribed to God or the serpent, this supposed inability is a strange phenomenon: concerning God, it is hardly conceivable why he should be unable to transfer the guilt to the proper culprit, especially because the subsequent development actually demonstrates that he is perfectly capable of doing so, subjecting Satan and his followers to an

18 Keith Thomas, *Man and the Natural World: Changing Attitudes in England, 1500–1800*, London: Penguin, 1984, pp. 97–98.

19 Kadri, *The Trial*, p. 159.

annual brutalization in order to dash their "pride, and joy for man seduced" (10.577). Or is it rather the serpent that is deemed to be unable to shake off the guilt? Of course, it is indeed impossible for the snake to divert the blame that Eve has laid on it to Satan; but one would also think it unnecessary, for God is supposedly informed about the identity of the guilty party. Once again, God exercises a jurisdiction rife with contradictions.

In this context, another strange statement of the Son about Satan should be considered: in heaven, after announcing that he will now descend to earth and judge Adam and Eve, the Son adds the remark that he does not intend to judge the devil on this occasion: "the third best absent is condemned,/ Convíct by flight, and rebel to all law" (10.82–83). This remark is baffling since one would think that Satan has been sufficiently convicted because his transgression has been witnessed by God's all-seeing eye, not because he has subsequently fled. The Son acts as if the trial were an earthly trial in which no omniscient and omnipotent institution exists. All of a sudden, the deity does not present himself as an utterly transcendent entity anymore, but as *primus inter pares* again, Zeus rather than Yahweh. For if his power and knowledge were represented as truly boundless, his condemnation of the serpent would be harder to justify. However, the narrator still gives a second, even more instructive reason for the curse on the snake: the beast has been "vitiated in nature" by its Satanic possession and is therefore rightfully transformed into a grovelling, dust-eating and hated creature (10.175–181). This justification of the heavenly jurisdiction supposes that the proper nature of an irrational animal is contaminated if diabolically violated, making it subject to further sanctions.[20] The narrator's legal approach is here obviously incompatible with a jurisdiction based on ethical considerations of mental capacity and fairness. Rather, he speaks the language of biopolitical pragmatics, extending the principle of collective punishment in order to contain a defilement: again, a vaguely medical terminology of pollution and contamination is used according to which the mere contact with transgressors corrupts the physical being of any thing that comes too close to them. This notion has many predecessors, among them the legal repercussions of the biblical distinction between purity and impurity and of the Greek notion of "miasma".[21] One striking medieval example of this sort of purificatory legislation can be found in a German legal code from about 1275, the so-called *Schwabenspiegel*: according to this document, all people and animals have to be killed in any house into which a woman has been abducted in order to be raped; furthermore, the whole house has to be demolished:

20 Stanley Fish considers only this second argument of the Son and, after a rather superficial analysis, does not fail to find it completely convincing (Stanley Fish, *Surprised By Sin: The Reader in* Paradise Lost, Cambridge, MA: Harvard University Press, 1997, pp. 154–155).

21 Mary Douglas, *Purity and Danger: An Analysis of the Concepts of Pollution and Taboo*, London and New York: Routledge, 2003, p. 134 ff. See also Robert Parker, *Miasma: Pollution and Purification in Early Greek Religion*, Oxford: Clarendon Press, 1983.

man sol allez daz toeten, daz in dem hûse ist gewesen, liute unde vie, ros unde rinder, hunde unde kazen, gense unde hüenre [...]. unde daz hûs dâ ez dâ inne ist geschehen, daz sol man ûf die erden slahen.

Thou shalt kill everything that has been in the house, men and animals, horses and cattle, dogs and cats, geese and chickens [...]. And the house in which it happened shall be razed to the ground.[22]

This work of destruction also resembles what God does to postlapsarian Nature as a whole: instead of immediate repair and containment of the pollution, further damage is inflicted on the whole of the earthly creatures, an act that is taken to be both a form of symbolic justice and a form of hygiene.[23] It should be noted in this context that the idea of a summary trial and punishment of Nature can also be found in early modern liturgical drama. In a mystery play which was performed in some areas of continental Europe (and called *Le procès du Paradis* in France), personfied Nature herself is accused by the personified "Wrath of God" for her many sins; she is defended by "Compassion" but finally sentenced to exile by "Judgment".[24] The punishments that Milton's God and his Cherubim inflict on Nature in the name of Nature with the help of Nature, however, are much more encompassing than mere expulsion.

9.3 Wrecking the natural world: the conquests of sin and death

In Canto 28 of the *Purgatorio*, Dante encounters Matilda of Tuscany in the Garden of Eden, and she explains some properties of the place to him.[25] One lesson is clearly to be drawn from her remarks: even though Man has lapsed, Paradise remains unfallen and henceforth functions as a link between heaven and earth. (Consequently, it can serve as launch pad for Dante's subsequent ascent to the celestial spheres.) Things stand very differently in *Paradise Lost*: with man falls the whole cosmos, including Paradise. However, Milton's

22 *Der Schwabenspiegel in der ältesten Gestalt*, Vol. 1, ed. Wilhelm Wackernagel, Zurich and Frauenfeld: Beyel, 1840, p. 201; quoted in Ramona Sickert, "'durch die vnuernünfftigen thier geschleyfft ...': Tiere in mittelalterlichen Rechtspraktiken und Schandritualen", in *Tiere, Bilder, Ökonomien: Aktuelle Forschungsfragen der Human-Animal Studies*, ed. Chimaira – Arbeitskreis für Human-Animal Studies, Bielefeld: transcript, 2013, p. 174. Translation BQ.

23 This divine contribution to the devastation of the biosphere is usually conveniently ignored in ecocritical readings of *Paradise Lost*. See e.g. Diane Kelsey McColley, *Poetry and Ecology in the Age of Milton and Marvell*, Aldershot and Burlington, VT: Ashgate, 2007, p. 223 ff. On more general problems of McColley's selective and generalizing approach see Christopher Tilmouth, Review of *Poetry and Ecology in the Age of Milton and Marvell* by Diane Kelsey McColley and *Renaissance Ecology: Imagining Eden in Milton's England* edited by Ken Hiltner, *The Seventeenth Century*, 25:1 (2010), pp. 173–176. See also William Shullenberger, Review of *Poetry and Ecology in the Age of Milton and Marvell* by Diane Kelsey McColley, *Milton Quarterly*, 43:1 (2009), pp. 64–68.

24 Wood, *Performing Justice*, p. 17.

25 Dante, *Purgatorio*, trans. Jean Hollander and Robert Hollander, New York: Random House, 2003, pp. 626–629 [28.88–144].

epic also distances itself from Lutheran and Calvinist notions according to which the Fall entails an essential denigration of all natural objects.[26] There is no hint that the elements themselves degenerate in *Paradise Lost.* And in the *Doctrina Christiana*, Milton expressly emphasizes that the essence of matter remains uncorrupted (*DC* 292/293). Rather, the Fall entails a rearrangement of these incorruptible elements – to this extent one might speak of a change in the laws of nature. Having passed his sentence, the Father commands his angels to wreck the old cosmic order and thus to change its dynamics, subjecting creation to new, harsher inherent rules. Ceri Sullivan has pointed out the orderly manner in which the angels go about this task: things do not fall apart since the centre can no longer hold, but they move into new, clearly defined positions.[27] At no point are the "embryon atoms" of Chaos allowed to enter the cosmos. Instead, the angels merely change the ways in which the divine influence that constantly pours into creation is distributed: by rearranging the orbits of the planets and stars, their light and other influx is given a "noxious efficacy" (10.660). And they tilt the axis of the earth in relation to the sun, so that the divine light that is concentrated in the sun hits the earth's surface in new angles. Consequently, the weather becomes too hot in the southern parts and too cold in the northern ones (10.668–687). Among the further results are the "[o]utrage from lifeless things" (10.707), for example destructive tempests (doubling the "high winds worse within", 9.1122), and warfare among the living, irrational creatures:

> through fierce antipathy
> Beast now with beast gan war, and fowl with fowl,
> And fish with fish; to graze the herb all leaving,
> Devoured each other; nor stood much in awe
> Of man, but fled him; or with countenance grim
> Glared on him passing […].
>
> (10.709–714)

So the punishment of the Fall indirectly causes the instant violent death not of man, but of many animals, although they seem to be even more guiltless than the serpent. It remains unclear whether this generation of a nature "red in tooth and claw" is just an organic side effect of the divine sentence or a crucial (though unspoken) stipulation of it. One thing is certain, however: the aberration of Adam and Eve is punished by the production of even more aberration. "The bent of nature" (11.597) now leads even further astray than before, as if God could demonstrate the extent of his dominion over his daughter/mother only by perverting her formerly virtuous ways. In this context, it is

26 See Chapter 1, pp. 83–84.

27 Ceri Sullivan, *Literature in the Public Service: Sublime Bureaucracy*, Basingstoke and New York: Palgrave Macmillan, 2014, p. 57.

particularly suggestive that the Son clothes Adam and Eve with furs immediately after the sentencing. Rephrasing Gen. 3.21, it is said about the Son:

> As father of his family he clad
> Their nakedness with skins of beasts, or slain,
> Or as the snake with youthful coat repaid [...].
> (10.216–218)

By this act of mercy, which supplements the divine law, the Son demonstrates both his humility and his sovereignty. Its officially stated purpose is to protect the human couple from the imminent alterations in nature, "the air, that now/ Must suffer change" (10.212–213). It is left unsaid, but prominent in the biblical reception history of early modern times, that these rags are also meant to cover another effect of the Fall, namely illicit desire and its symptoms, the other law that reigns in their members, as Paul expresses it (Romans 7.23).[28] Clothes will both cover and denote their shame. So far, so conventional. But Milton's narrator gives additional poignancy to this topos when he speculates that the hides did belong to animals that were slain. This is an odd surmise, since animal mortality and animal aggression officially only enter the world later on, with the aforementioned cosmic changes wrought by the angels; there is no obvious organic reason for these deaths at this point. The most obvious solution to this mystery is that the Son slays those beasts himself, thus prefiguring animal mortality; this theory has indeed been discussed.[29] Again, Milton offers an alternative theory that does not rely on direct divine intervention, but on the natural processes of Eden: the skins could also be remnants of animal processes of rejuvenation. According to this notion, all animals were apparently able to shed their skin and thus prolong their life before the Fall. There is one oddity about this scenario, however: the snake is the only animal that is considered to have retained this capacity – and thus the trappings of immortality – even after the Fall.[30] Exactly the animal that was instrumental to the Fall and whose life has been divinely cursed to be both miserable and dangerous to man seems to be relatively unaffected by the death-bringing forces that afflict all postlapsarian creation, as if mysterious culpability and punishment were the only things meant to survive God's verdict and live forever. Thus, the two stories about the origin of apparel demonstrate that human life is henceforth intimately entangled with the propagation of guilt and violence and that the use of clothes emblematizes this entangling.

28 See e.g. Philip C. Almond, *Adam and Eve in Seventeenth-Century Thought*, Cambridge and New York: Cambridge University Press, 1999, p. 199.

29 See Fowler, ed. *Paradise Lost*, p. 531.

30 James Charlesworth, "The Symbology of the Serpent in the Gospel of John", in *John, Jesus, and History,* Vol. 2: *Aspects of Historicity in the Fourth Gospel*, eds. Paul N. Anderson, Felix Just and Tom Thatcher, Atlanta, GA: Society of Biblical Literature, 2009, pp. 66–67.

Generally, the wrecking of the cosmos produces an emblematic environment. Nature no longer communicates an ambiguous law; instead, she communicates to Adam and Eve that this law has been transgressed, emitting "mute signs" of consequent exclusion:

> Nature first gave signs, impressed
> On bird, beast, air, air suddenly eclipsed
> After short blush of morn; nigh in her sight
> The bird of Jove, stooped from his airy tower,
> Two birds of gayest plume before him drove:
> Down from a hill the beast that reigns in woods,
> First hunter then, pursued a gentle brace,
> Goodliest of all the forest, hart and hind;
> Direct to the eastern gate was bent their flight.
> (11.182–190; capitalization added)

Adam and Eve observe huntings that poignantly demonstrate the disharmonious state of fallen nature: the beasts only follow the laws in their members, but these laws can no longer organize them into a harmonious whole.[31] Adam seems to be largely uninterested in these developments by themselves; instead, he focuses on their allegorical impact as prefigurations of mankind's own destiny:

> O Eve, some further change awaits us nigh,
> Which heaven by these mute signs in nature shows
> Forerunners of his purpose, or to warn
> Us haply too secure of our discharge
> From penalty, because from death released
> Some days; how long, and what till then our life,
> Who knows, or more than this, that we are dust,
> And thither must return and be no more.
> Why else this double object in our sight
> Of flight pursued in the air and o'er the ground
> One way the self-same hour?
> (11.193–203)

This interpretation abstracts from the concrete situation and conjectures that the autodigestion of Eden is meant to figure man's own predicament, present and future. Adam reads the pursuits of the animals as emblems of man's endangered, dust-like status in a fallen world,[32] but they obviously also

31 See Romans 7.23: "But I see another law in my members, warring against the law of my mind, and bringing me into captivity to the law of sin which is in my members".

32 See also Karen Edwards, "Milton's Reformed Animals: An Early Modern Bestiary, D-F", *Milton Quarterly* 40:2 (2006), p. 101.

prefigure a heavenly verdict that is still to be added to that of human mortality, namely man's imminent expulsion from Paradise.[33] Thus, the natural lawlessness manages to emblematize the unceasing enactment of a divine law of which Adam and Eve have proven themselves to be unworthy. Karen Edwards hints at this ambiguity, but, on a questionable interpretive basis, she tries to resolve it by separating the sanctioned eagle, "enacting God's judgment", from the beastly lion "embodying injustice against the innocent".[34] The text, however, does not oppose one beast of prey to the other, but parallelizes them. And the violence of both animals refers Adam to a law he can no longer keep: a legal order from which he has been excluded, but which still applies to him. The law of nature out of bounds has been subjected to the divine law of sovereign exception; the cosmos begins to resemble hell as a consequence.

Additionally, hellish allegory also enters Paradise with the arrival of personified Sin and Death who introduce yet another layer to the joint jurisdiction of God and Nature. The hellish pair seems to be estranged from Nature, living beyond the "farthest verge" of her officially designated domain, in the free fire zone of allegory (2.1038). Yet, interestingly, Sin herself ascribes their journey to earth to the effects of a "connatural force" which affects her:

> Methinks I feel new strength within me rise,
> Wings growing, and dominion given me large
> Beyond this deep; whatever draws me on,
> Or sympathy, or some connatural force
> Powerful at greatest distance to unite
> With secret amity things of like kind
> By secretest conveyance.
>
> (10.243–249)

According to this notion, the sinful, deadly act of Adam and Eve draws Sin and Death by natural sympathy toward the fallen cosmos. Once more, the epic plays with the strange status of Sin, which oscillates between that of an incarnated abstraction and that of an individual protagonist: if she were merely an allegorical figure whose task it is to represent sinfulness, she might do her job most appropriately at the entrance of hell. Her journey to earth would be redundant in this case, since sin has already manifested itself in the cosmos before her arrival. But she is also Satan's natural daughter and therefore interested in the expansion of the "infernal empire" (10.389). Consequently, the language with which she describes her new calling is that of a political representative: as one of her father's "substitutes" (10.403), she will take possession of the fallen cosmos and rule it as her "dominion" (10.400). However, she also insists on her allegorical role, for example when she asserts that Death must accompany

33 See also Fowler, ed. *Paradise Lost*, p. 608.

34 Edwards, "Milton's Reformed Animals", p. 138.

her, "[f]or Death from Sin no power can separate" (10.251). And their subsequent construction of a bridge from hell to earth has, of course, heavily allegorical overtones, alluding to Matthew 7.13. Nevertheless, building this hellish "highway" is depicted as a very concrete, material process: they aggregate (10.293) and petrify (10.294) the proto-elemental "dark materials" (2.916) of Chaos into the "cold and dry" (10.294) element of earth – a creative act one would have imagined to be a divine prerogative, since it is thought to distinguish him from his creatures.[35] Sin and Death even presume to hover "upon the waters" (10.285), in a blatant parody of Genesis 1.2. And just like the Father, they choose to ignore the great Anarch Chaos, instead of attempting to fight or cooperate with him: while the devils gain access to the cosmos by Satan's success, Chaos does not; its/his/her waves of "embryon atoms" keep crashing in vain against the works of God and of the devils:

> Disparted Chaos overbuilt exclaimed,
> And with rebounding surge the bars assailed,
> That scorned his indignation […].
> (10.416–418; capitalization added)

Upon their arrival on earth, Sin gives Death a blueprint of their future governance:

> Thou therefore on these herbs, and fruits, and flowers
> Feed first, on each beast next, and fish, and fowl,
> No homely morsels, and whatever thing
> The scythe of Time mows down, devour unspared,
> Till I in man residing through the race,
> His thoughts, his looks, words, actions, all infect
> And season him thy last and sweetest prey.
> (10.603–609; capitalization added)

It is striking to what extent this speech echoes Raphael's speech on eating as evolution: just like the angel, Death feeds on the works of Nature and "transsubstantiates" them into himself. There is one significant difference, however: the corrupting consumption of Sin and Death is not part of the theocentric cosmic cycle; hence, it is not restitutive, but parasitic. That is why Sin uses not only an alimentary vocabulary, but also one of illness and infection. It is all the more surprising when the Father subsequently claims that all this corruption is part of his own design:

> See, with what heat these dogs of hell advance
> To waste and havoc yonder world, which I

35 See Chapter 4, p. 144.

So fair and good created, and had still
Kept in that state, had not the folly of man
Let in these wasteful furies, who impute
Folly to me [...]
And know not that I called and drew them thither
My hell-hounds, to lick up the draff and filth
Which man's polluting sin with taint hath shed
On what was pure [...].
(10.616–621/629–632)

This passage has not been much analysed, but it is remarkable for several reasons. God here proclaims Sin and Death to be his servitors, unwittingly and unmeritoriously executing his justice. He emphasizes the involuntary character of their contribution to his Great Work by animalizing them, though somewhat less palpably than the other devils, namely by referring to them as "his hell-hounds". One might claim that he thus for the first time openly acknowledges the presence of pagan mythology in his world, for there is no hell-hound in the Bible, though Cerberus was Christianized by Dante.[36] Two other implications of this animalization are more peculiar still: God claims ownership over Sin and Death by calling them "*my* hell-hounds". But the owners of Cerberus and his equivalent in Nordic mythology, Garm, have traditionally been the underworld gods Hades/Pluto, resp. Hela.[37] Both Homer and Hesiod emphasize this relation.[38] Thus the property claim seems to associate God with the deities of the underworld. Of course, God controls all natural and unnatural proceedings in hell by punitive measures, therefore he might justly call himself its sovereign. But the very term "hell-hound" also points out that his reign over hell is a peculiar one; for the official task of all Greek, Roman and Scandinavian hell-hounds was to guard the entrance of the underworld. The same exact task was also assigned to Sin and Death (2.850–855), but, unlike their pagan counterparts, they were allowed to abandon their post at the first opportunity and thus extend hell's domain. They are no longer watching at the border between the living and dead; instead, they proclaim the boundlessness of death's reign for which the living merely serve as fuel.

God proclaims this seeming desertion to be a part of evil's unwitting obedience to the ways of the supreme legislator. That would also entail that Sin is deceived when she ascribes her earthbound journey to "connatural forces", or

36 Dante, *Inferno*, trans. Jean Hollander and Robert Hollander, New York: Random House, 2000, pp. 114/115 [6.13–18].

37 See e.g. Boria Sax, *The Mythical Zoo: An Encyclopedia of Animals in World Myth, Legend, and Literature*, Denver and Santa Barbara: ABC-Clio, 2001, p. 87.

38 Homer, *Odyssey*, Vol. 1, trans. A. T. Murray, Cambridge, MA: Harvard University Press and London: Heinemann, 1945, pp. 430/431 [11.623–625]. Hesiod, *Theogonie, Griechisch/Deutsch*, trans. and ed. Otto Schönberger, Stuttgart: Reclam, 1999, pp. 26/27 [310–312].

at least that she does not look far enough, namely to the sovereign of Nature. In other passages of *Paradise Lost*, the forces of Nature appear as more autonomous and problematical, so that God ends up vaguely distancing himself from her (see again, first and foremost, 11.49); one may wonder why he does not do so at this point in the epic. It certainly would serve the cause of justifying his ways much better if he would just leave responsibility with the free will of his creatures; his express contribution to the situation seems to be redundant at best. But God at this point seems to be driven by a will to reassert himself as the transcendent cause of all the proceedings – a determination that will cause problems. For the passage cited above sketches two contradictory scenarios: according to the first scenario, it was man's free lapse that caused Sin and Death to enter the cosmos in order to waste and pollute it. According to the second, God led them on in order to correct that same lapse and pollution inherent in it. Sin is thus considered both incidentally polluting (as a product of human folly) and providentially cleansing (as a product of divine wisdom). This double role obviously depends on the supplementary allegorical function of Satan's daughter: on the one hand, she is Sin incarnate, but on the other hand, she is also cast as the avenger of sin, the problem coming to coincide with its own solution. It is possible to interpret this contradiction allegorically, giving a new meaning to Milton's statement that "sin is its own punishment" (*DC* 432/433). But on the diegetic level, this does not solve the problem that Satan's daughter ends up incarnating and perpetuating the very transgression she supposedly punishes. Transgression itself is thus given free rein in the cosmic theatre of its punishment, and God declares himself the originator of this messy situation. The Father pretends that Sin and Death merely accumulate and absorb the pre-existent sins of man, but they produce ever more of it, infecting "his thoughts, his looks, words, actions all" (10.608), complementing the "noxious" influences (10.660). Just like hellish justice, postlapsarian cosmic justice is enacted as a feedback loop of destruction, with no inherent end to its endless self-enhancement. This absolutization of allegory turns out to be an effective governmental strategy: the cosmos becomes a theatre of judgment without boundaries, representing the sublimity of the divine law – which will subsequently come around to punish Sin and Death for their clean-up too (10.632–637).

Death, like his mother, comes to play a double role in this presentation. For God proceeds to justify the unbinding of Death in yet another way: not as an appropriate punishment, disciplinary measure or hygienic requirement, but as a boon:

> I at first with two fair gifts
> Created him [man] endowed, with happiness
> And immortality: that fondly lost,
> This other served but to eternize woe;
> Till I provided death: so death becomes
> His final remedy […].
>
> (11.57–62)

According to this representation, human mortality is not to be regarded as a negative consequence of the Fall, but as a supplementary gift of grace, eliminating postlapsarian unhappiness. However, God has also declared death (not the loss of happiness) to be the punishment of sin (e.g. in 8.329–331), and thus the divine argumentation turns aporetic once more: God makes man mortal in order to avoid that he must forever mourn his lost immortality. The Father's argument is all the more surprising since he instantly affirms that death will actually not be the end of man (11.62–66): Adam and Eve with their descendants will still be immortal, but this immortality is "seasoned" by death.

Adam's postlapsarian lamentation in the tenth book concerns precisely this point: Death will not cut short his life, as he had vaguely assumed and accepted, but will make it persist in a double infinity of undying punishment:

> But say
> That death be not one stroke, as I supposed,
> Bereaving sense, but endless misery
> From this day onward, which I feel begun
> Both in me, and without me, and so last
> To perpetuity? Ay me, that fear
> Comes thundering back with dreadful revolution
> On my defenceless head; both death and I
> Am found eternal, and incorporate both,
> Nor I on my part single, in me all
> Posterity stands cursed […].
> (10.808–818)

When he speaks of the "endless misery without", Adam is not so much referring to non-human nature about which he seems largely unconcerned; he speaks of his posterity. In his lamentation, he bewails two forms of immortal life: the immortality of his personal, individual self and the immortality of his lineage. Both of them persist, but are vitiated by the influence of death. He has understood that his guilt and the attendant mortality will be passed on to all his sons and daughters – a biopolitical extension of divine legislation of which the Son had not explicitly informed him. But the main subject of his complaints is his own status as an individual being between finitude and infinity. Adam has first tried to comfort himself with the thought that, qua finite being, he can only be condemned to a finite extent of suffering; but then he starts to doubt his delimited nature:

> Yet one doubt
> Pursues me still, lest all I cannot die,
> Lest that pure breath of life, the spirit of man
> Which God inspired, cannot together perish
> With this corporeal clod; then in the grave

Or in some other dismal place, who knows
But I shall die a living death?
(10.782–788)

Adam has been surrounded by "strange contradictions" from the very beginning of his life, and they all converge on this one: a living, incorporate death. He starts to question whether this phenomenon is in accord with the law of nature:

Will he draw out,
For anger's sake, finite to infinite,
In punished man, to satisfy his rigour,
Satisfied never? That were to extend
His sentence beyond dust and nature's law [...].
(10.801–805)

Adam here still refers to Nature as to a unifying force, generating harmony between the tendencies of each singular thing and the general state of the cosmos by her legislation. But after the Fall, this harmony has officially been abrogated, insofar as it ever existed. Just like hell, the cosmos has become a place "[w]here all life dies, death lives" (2.624) and where Nature breeds monstrosities, incarnate contradictions. The natural inclination of each thing is thus thwarted; the thing can never be what it is, for the enduring life of the whole order now entails an overpowering of individual life. If God can "make death" within Adam and Eve "live" (10.1028), this is due to a life within and without them that exceeds them, namely the double-headed life of a law that is the "juridical form assumed by the infinite debt" of all creatures.[39] Adam accepts his debt and guilt, even though he no longer purports to comprehend God's law: "Inexplicable/ Thy justice seems" (10.754–755). In this situation, Adam and Eve reconcile, accept the dismal situation and decide to pray for divine mercy from their "hearts contrite" (10.1104). Remarkably enough, the Father subsequently asserts that the cause of this genuine contrition is his own divine intervention in Adam's interior life:

He sorrows now, repents, and prays contrite,
My motions in him, longer than they move,
His heart I know, how variable and vain,
Self-left.
(11.90–93)

39 Gilles Deleuze and Félix Guattari, *Anti-Oedipus: Capitalism and Schizophrenia*, trans. Robert Hurley, Helen R. Lane and Mark Seem, Minneapolis: University of Minnesota Press, 1983, p. 213.

What is most peculiar about this statement is, again, its contrast with the narrator's own description of the events. In the preceding book, the narrator has extensively described the gradual process that led Adam from utter despair and resentment to a gentle reconciliation with Eve, which thus allows for their subsequent discussion of mankind's future prospects (10.714–965). And from this discussion springs logically their decision to return to the place where the Son has judged them and to beg humbly for mercy (10.966–1104). From a psychological standpoint, it is one of the most tightly-woven sequences in the epic, and so a miraculous divine intervention in Adam's inner life is nowhere in evidence.[40] Again, God claims to be the effective cause of a positive development, confirming his former declaration that postlapsarian men by definition owe "all [...] deliverance" exclusively to him (see 3.175–182). Some critics have wondered about the Father's lines though, since they apparently sever man from his own free will to which heaven heretofore seemed to attach such a crucial importance.[41] Harold Skulsky put it most strongly:

> God himself flouts his earlier libertarian ideal of grace: he cuts off the "variableness" of Adam's heart by refusing to leave the heart to itself; in short, he cuts off Adam's power to "vary" by choosing wrong.[42]

However, God does not explicitly state that he actively interferes with the processes occurring naturally within the heart of Adam; by using the possessive pronoun, the Father only asserts that they belong to him in one way or another. That, of course, is a truism of his official theology: he generally claims to be the ultimate possessor and causal origin of absolutely everything in the universe. And since the motions that have been aroused in Adam and Eve are good motions, and since all goodness is said to come from God, it is compulsory that they should be ascribed to himself. If read in this way, God would make a somewhat empty, propagandist statement, but not one that would contradict the official doctrine of free will. Again, a double reading of a divine utterance is possible which muddies the issue whether God intervenes in human lives in natural or in supernatural ways – an ambiguity that helps to keep heaven's theologico-juridical edifice together. It is all the more astonishing that the passage with which this study opened and in which the Father refers to the Law of Nature as to a force that restricts him is just a few lines away:

40 Neil Forsyth, *The Satanic Epic*, Princeton, NJ: Princeton University Press, 2003, p. 294.

41 Efforts have been made in order to reconcile this passage with Milton's emphasis on free will, referring to Milton's Arminianism in the process. Benjamin Myers sketches why one might find these efforts unconvincing. See Benjamin Myers, *Milton's Theology of Freedom*, Berlin and New York: Walter de Gruyter, 2006, p. 161.

42 Harold Skulsky, *Milton and the Death of Man: Humanism on Trial in* Paradise Lost, Newark and London: University of Delaware Press, 2000, p. 205.

> But longer in that Paradise to dwell,
> The law I gave to nature him forbids:
> Those pure immortal elements that know
> No gross, no unharmonious mixture foul,
> Eject him tainted now, and purge him off
> As a distemper, gross to air as gross,
> And mortal food, as may dispose him best
> For dissolution wrought by sin, that first
> Distempered all things, and of incorrupt
> Corrupted.
>
> (11.48–57)

It is a remarkable passage in which all the ambiguities we have treated so far converge; and it should be emphasized that it mainly serves to justify a further proliferation of the ever-proliferating divine judgment, by way of a further aggravation of man's penalty.

9.4 A new earth in the old: politics, history and the redemption of Christ

When God sends Michael down to drive Adam and Eve out of Eden, he also instructs him to teach Adam a lesson about the new allegorical world order in which he now finds himself. The instruction mainly concerns the history of mankind, and it is rather unrelievedly bleak. It contrasts strongly with the historical reflections in Milton's political pamphlets from the time of the Commonwealth, which tend to exude an optimistic, almost chiliastic faith in progress and human reason.[43] Most strikingly, those pamphlets occasionally hold out the prospect that the acquisition of humanist knowledge may be able to repair the Fall at some point in the future. As a result, man will come to resemble both Adam and God:

43 Milton in this period declares that, despite the Fall, all men are still born to command, hanging on to a set of laws that are both natural and divine. "[F]rom the root of Adam's transgression", people may be inclined to do violent wrongs. But "foreseeing that such courses must needs tend to the destruction of them all, they agreed by common league to bind each other from mutual injury" (*The Tenure of Kings and Magistrates*, *CPW* 3:199, spelling modernized). The people are the ultimate source of sovereignty; rulers are just deputies entrusted by them to enforce this league. "Here, as to some people's assertion that magistrates must be obeyed not only when they are god-fearing but even when they are tyrants commanding wicked things, by no scriptural authority is that confirmed" (*DC* 1237). Hence, the social contract that binds the citizens and their rulers can be revoked at any time, when the ruler proves to neglect his duties and the demands of reason. However, on the most reasonable form of this social contract, Milton remains a bit vague. "There may be no pamphlet written in this period [1649–1660] in which Milton does not assert contradictory positions on the constitution of the ideal political organization" (John Rogers, *The Matter of Revolution: Science, Poetry and Politics in the Age of Milton*, Ithaca, NY and London: Cornell University Press, 1996, p. 109).

> The end of learning is to repair the ruins of our first parents by regaining to know God aright, and out of that knowledge to love him, to imitate him, to be like him, as we may be nearest by possessing our souls of true virtue […].
>
> (*Of Education*, *CPW* 2:366–367, spelling modernized)

After the restoration of the monarchy, Milton's political statements assume a darker tone. Accordingly, Michael's history lesson leaves not much hope for human self-amelioration:

> Since thy original lapse, true liberty
> Is lost, which always with right reason dwells
> Twinned, and from her hath no dividual being […].
>
> (12.83–85)

This is not to say that the human mind is completely darkened. Some uncorrupted light persists, particularly in those of "peculiar grace" (3.183); it takes the form of an unwritten law code that is engraved in the hearts of men and frequently personified as the "umpire conscience" (see 3.195; see also 12.489 and *DC* 811). There are passages in the *Doctrina* which emphasize that salvation is not a natural process, that is, not based on natural inclination (*DC* 555); nonetheless, conscience is frequently designated as a natural law:

> Lex Dei est non scripta vel scripta. Non scripta est naturalis illa primo homini data, cuius reliquiae et quoddam lumen omnium mortalium cordibus permansit; in regeneratis vero Spiritus Sancti opera indies ad perfectionem primaevam renovatur.
>
> The Law of God is [either] unwritten or written. The unwritten law is that law of nature given to the first man, of which remnants and a certain gleam have persisted in the hearts of all mortals; in the regenerate, however, it is daily renewed in the direction of its pristine perfection by the working of the holy spirit.
>
> (*DC* 674–677)

The both natural and supernatural law written in the heart is the decisive *corpus iuris* from the beginning to the end of human history; and the outline of history that Michael presents is intended to demonstrate this. There is thus already a law on earth long before Noah and Moses. That explains, for example, why the sacrifice of Cain is not accepted (11.432–443; see also *DC* 677).[44] The ability to perceive and obey the inborn law is closely connected

44 Incidentally, one may speculate about the consequences of Michael's theatre of cruelty on Adam's family life: the first man may not treat his firstborn in a very loving manner after he has learned that Cain will become the murderer of his brother. This resentment could

to the concept of grace;[45] and grace is depicted as strangely material and organic: an "implanted" grace (11.23), bearing "[f]ruits of more pleasing savour, from thy [God's] seed/ Sown with contrition in his heart"(11.26–27). Empson, referring mainly to the Son's rhetoric, points out that "it is thus presented as like a seed, presumed to grow by itself", acting "in a kind of biological way",[46] referring back to the cosmic cycle developed by Raphael. But so too grows man's unfolding sinfulness that is interlinked with God's curse: evil is also supposed to develop and multiply according to inexorable organic laws. In Michael's history lesson, the most prominent exemplification of this latter circumstance is the vision of the "lazar-house" in which bodily illness figures as punishment for original sin. That he may know "[w]hat misery the inabstinence of Eve/ Shall bring on men" (11.476–477), Adam is shown a "sad, noisome, dark" (11.478) place:

> A lazar-house it seemed, wherein were laid
> Numbers of all diseased, all maladies
> Of ghastly spasm, or racking torture, qualms
> Of heart-sick agony, all feverous kinds,
> Convulsions, epilepsies, fierce catarrhs,
> Intestine stone and ulcer, colic pangs,
> Demoniac frenzy, moping melancholy
> And moon-struck madness, pining atrophy,
> Marasmus, and wide-wasting pestilence,
> Dropsies, and asthmas, and joint-racking rheums.
> (11.479–488)

Adam thereupon weeps and asks why man cannot be exempted from these pains "for his maker's image sake", if for nothing else (11.514). Again, he finds it safer to appeal to God's self-interest rather than to his compassion (see also 9.938–945). Michael refutes him with an argumentation that is rather strange, even though its general structure is already familiar at this point:

> Their maker's image, answered Michael, then
> Forsook them, when themselves they vilified
> To serve ungoverned appetite, and took
> His image whom they served, a brutish vice,
> Inductive mainly to the sin of Eve.

contribute to a feeling of deprivation and fraternal envy on Cain's side, finally erupting in an act of violence. Thus Michael's prophecy might turn out to be self-fulfilling.

45 See, for a more detailed description of the connection in Milton's work, Stephen M. Fallon, *Milton's Peculiar Grace: Self-Representation and Authority,* Ithaca, NY: Cornell University Press, 2007.

46 Empson, *Milton's God*, p. 168.

Therefore so abject is their punishment,
Disfiguring not God's likeness, but their own,
Or if his likeness, by themselves defaced
While they pervert pure Nature's healthful rules
To loathsome sickness, worthily, since they
God's image did not reverence in themselves.
(11.515–525; capitalization added)

On the one hand, this passage perpetuates the commonplace that all mankind must indefinitely pay for Eve's infinite sin. The likeness which men had to God has forsaken them (11.516), and they are henceforth exposed to the "noxious" (10.660) influences of a hostile environment and of a contaminated, brutish interiority. But on the other hand, Michael reproaches them for having themselves actively forsaken the maker's image. And it is not their unwillingness to love God and their neighbour as themselves that is at issue here, but their unhealthy diet: human beings have been created in God's likenesses and so their lack of biopolitical self-care is a blasphemy to be punished with sickness – that is, with even more sickness than has already been given to them as a punishment for the sin of Eve. This statement implies that they receive natural punishments for not being something postlapsarian man is altogether incapable of being: an unfallen creature in harmony with Nature. Accordingly, the formulation at the end of the quoted passage implies that the perversion of "pure Nature's healthful rules" is both man's sin and his punishment for sin. Once again, Nature must be wrecked in the name of Nature in an endless punitive feedback loop. Adam submits meekly to the sublime announcement, acknowledging the self-enhancement of infinite debt: "I yield it just, said Adam, and submit" (11.526).

Michael thereupon proceeds to unveil the future proceedings on earth, which unfold in two complementary narratives: a steady process of collective degeneration is accompanied by episodes of the individual salvation of a few elect. The overwhelming majority of mankind is described as a perverted community, following their evil inclinations, first and foremost licentious sexuality and violence. They are ruled by ministers of death who threaten to "dispossess/ Concord and law of Nature from the earth" (12.28–29). These princes are doing God's work, although this does not exonerate them:

Therefore, since he [man] permits
Within himself unworthy powers to reign
Over free reason, God in judgment just
Subjects him from without to violent lords;
Who oft as undeservedly enthral
His outward freedom: tyranny must be,
Though to the tyrant thereby no excuse.
(12.90–96)

The godly, by contrast, who hang on to God's punishing ways – less by accomplishing good deeds than by castigating sinners and militiating against the degenerate times – are always a small elite, normally a minority of one (male and well-to-do) individual.[47] History unfolds as a long line of their interventions and their failed attempts to build resilient collectivities: first Enoch, the "only righteous in a world perverse" (11.701) preaches "judgment from above" (11.668) and suffers violent attacks for his pains; then Noah, "only son of light/ In a dark age" (11.808–809), preaches to his contemporaries, "denouncing wrath to come/ On their impenitence" (11.815–816), and retreats into the ark when his efforts prove fruitless; Abraham, the "one faithful man", leaves the evil idols of Mesopotamia and becomes the father of a nation that soon falls off from his godly ways (12.113); Moses is "sent from God to claim/ His people from enthralment" and imposes the law on an unwilling Israel (12.170–171); and so on, up to Milton himself, who has already inscribed himself into this lineage by his autobiographical excursions and invocations.[48]

The fate of the "One Just Man" keeps repeating itself throughout history, accentuating the isolation of the virtuous punishers and the hopelessness of collectives. At best, strictly delimited groups gather around the outstanding individual and form his extended family, but their fickle inconstancy is always emphasized. By definition, societies and states seem to be dubious institutions in a postlapsarian world; mankind is split up into its individual members, because everyone will be judged individually. In a degenerated commonwealth, the faithful will mainly distinguish themselves by their ability to denounce and fight the general rot. Indeed, the whole line of Just Men seems to be committed to a warrior ethic: according to Michael's narration, their godliness is not contingent on their virtuous life, but on their zeal, that is, their aptitude to condemn the sinful conduct of their environment. According to Thomas Luxon, this is a general tendency in seventeenth-century Puritan ethics: a piety is promoted "in which the faithful Hebrew prophet (Isaiah, Daniel, and especially David) is the model for Christian faithfulness – wayfaring and warfaring".[49] By their zeal, they advance to the status of godly judges and thus to an apocalyptic form of *imitatio dei* – even though David for instance is not exactly a paragon of saintly virtue. In the *Doctrina Christiana*, Milton explicitly associates the position of the human judge with that of the supreme being:

47 Apparently, it is important to Michael, for example, that Abraham on his way to Canaan is "[n]ot wandering poor" (12.133), but equipped with "a cumbrous train/ Of herds and flocks, and numerous servitude" (12.131–132).

48 See David Loewenstein, *Milton and the Drama of History: Historical Vision, Iconoclasm, and the Literary Imagination*, Cambridge: Cambridge University Press, 1990, pp. 101–102.

49 Thomas H. Luxon, "'Not I, But Christ': Allegory and the Puritan Self", *ELH* 60:4 (1993), p. 918.

> Iudicibus idcirco impertitum est Dei nomen, quod ii vices Dei in iudiciis exercendis quodammodo gerant.
>
> The name of God is bestowed on judges for this reason, that in a way they take the place of God when they administer judgments.
>
> (*DC* 168/169)

As Thomas Corns has pointed out: "Judgment, reward and punishment remain after the Fall the most important roles of the deity"[50] – both before and after the apocalypse. And the godly follow him on his path; their condemnations are figurations of the First and Last Judgment; this is made most explicit in a reference to the biblical *shofetim*, Moses' successors, whose exploits are narrated in the Book of Judges. Michael stresses that the first of these judges is a prefiguration of Christ:

> Joshua whom the gentiles Jesus call,
> His name and office bearing, who shall quell
> The adversary serpent [...].
>
> (12.310–312)

The judges' and prophets' condemnations are apocalyptic unveilings that bring to light what was hidden, the badness of the bad, growing toward damnation, as well as the goodness of the good, growing toward salvation. History is an enactment of divine judgment, both pointing back to the Fall (of Satan as well as of Man) and pointing forward to Final Judgment. William Kerrigan has pointed out the resultant suspension of historical time: "Christian typology, filling the instant with past and future events, contracts linear time; the future is in the present, the conclusion is in the premise".[51] Therefore, history in *Paradise Lost* is strikingly repetitive: it recurs as slight variations on the ever-identical tableau of damnation and salvation, presented as a natural unfolding of fallen life.[52] Similarly, Milton's *Eikonoklastes* – which enumerates the countless historical precedents that justify the execution of Charles I – does not situate the English Civil Wars within history, but instead imbues their proceedings with the aura of timelessness and inevitability.[53] Insofar as history deviates from the prescribed theologico-dramatic pattern, it can only end up as a fruitless vanity, a miscarriage of nature. Those who fail to

50 Thomas Corns, *Regaining* Paradise Lost, London and New York: Longman 1994, p. 4.

51 William Kerrigan, *The Prophetic Milton*, Charlottesville: University of Virginia Press, 1974, p. 226.

52 See also Anselm Haverkamp, "A Narrow Thing Within One Word: The Foreclosure of Nature in Post-Shakespearian Worlds and Times", in *"If Then the World a Theatre Present...": Revisions of the Theatrum Mundi Metaphor in Early Modern England*, ed. Björn Quiring, Berlin: Walter de Gruyter, 2014, p. 143.

53 John Milton, *Eikonoklastes*, *CPW* 3.337–601.

participate in the cosmic trial pattern land on the scrapyard of history that is the Paradise of Fools:

> All who have their reward on earth, the fruits
> Of painful superstition and blind zeal,
> Nought seeking but the praise of men, here find
> Fit retribution, empty as their deeds;
> All the unaccomplished works of Nature's hand,
> Abortive, monstrous, or unkindly mixed,
> Dissolved on earth, fleet hither, and in vain,
> Till final dissolution, wander here [...].
> (3.451–458; capitalization added)

In Michael's typological interpretation, history appears as a gigantic succession of tropes, a steady *re-troping* of Nature's trials.[54] The truth to which all these figures refer is, however, situated outside of history: a beginning and an end that transcends the cosmos. History can only ever exemplify a nature that is made to feel its deserved pains. By this method of allegoresis, history becomes what Benjamin has called "Natur-Geschichte" ("nature-history")[55] and has associated with the image of the ruin:

> Die allegorische Physiognomie der Natur-Geschichte [...] ist wirklich gegenwärtig als Ruine. [...] Allegorien sind im Reiche der Gedanken was Ruinen im Reiche der Dinge.[56]
>
> The allegorical physiognomy of nature-history [...] is present in reality in the form of the ruin. [...] Allegories are, in the realm of thoughts, what ruins are in the realm of things.[57]

The postlapsarian cosmos of *Paradise Lost* is a ruin in precisely this sense. Fittingly, Michael stresses that the political engagement of the One Just Man tends to be vindicated by interventions in and by Nature; the righteous receive support from elements and animals: Enoch is saved from his persecutors when a cloud carries him away (11.670–671); Noah's admonitions are, of course, corroborated when a great expiatory rain drowns the rest of mankind (11.738–753); and Michael's representation of the life of Moses focuses on the escape from Egypt, and most intensely on the ten miraculous "signs and judgements dire" (12.175) – frogs, lice, locusts, hail and so on – visited upon

54 See John Guillory, *Poetic Authority: Spenser, Milton, and Literary History*, New York: Columbia University Press, 1983, p. 150.

55 Walter Benjamin, *Ursprung des deutschen Trauerspiels*, p. 353. Id, *The Origin of German Tragic Drama*, p. 177.

56 Walter Benjamin, *Ursprung des deutschen Trauerspiels*, pp. 353–354.

57 Walter Benjamin, *The Origin of German Tragic Drama*, trans. John Osborne, London: Verso, 1998, pp. 177–178 (translation modified).

the "lawless" Pharaoh who finally drowns in the inrushing waters of the Red Sea (12.173–199).

If the eternal True Law is already written into the hearts of men and women and its force enacted by and on Nature, it stands to reason that the Law of Sinai does not make much of a difference in the course of things. Positive law in general and Mosaic law in particular now only serve as reminders of man's fallen state:

> And therefore was law given them to evince
> Their natural pravity, by stirring up
> Sin against law to fight [...].
> (12.287–289)

In his prose works, Milton also affirms the Pauline saying that no mortal can satisfy the Mosaic law (see e.g. *DC* 914–917): "Now we know that what things soever the law saith, it saith to them who are under the law: that every mouth may be stopped, and all the world may become guilty before God" (Rom. 3.19). In this context, Milton asserts that the Mosaic law serves the same function as the natural law, namely to demonstrate that fallen man cannot keep it and is therefore condemnable (*DC* 680–683). Thus all the insistently repeated legal proceedings of history only serve to indicate the need for a salvation through a celestial act of mercy, and so Christ enters the stage.

According to Michael, the function of the Mosaic law, and first and foremost the sacrificial law, is to prefigure the one true sacrifice of Christ:

> that when they see
> Law can discover sin, but not remove,
> Save by those shadowy expiations weak,
> The blood of bulls and goats, they may conclude
> Some blood more precious must be paid for man,
> Just for unjust, that, in such righteousness
> To them by faith imputed, they may find
> Justification towards God, and peace
> Of conscience [...].
> (12.289–297)

Michael minimizes the difference between the Israelites and the other nations, except for this legal premonition of the messianic salvation that will truly fulfil the divine law.

> he, who comes thy saviour, shall recure,
> Not by destroying Satan, but his works
> In thee and in thy seed: nor can this be,
> But by fulfilling that which thou didst want,
> Obedience to the law of God, imposed

On penalty of death, and suffering death,
The penalty to thy transgression due [...].
(12.393–399)

Milton agrees with Paul, St. Anselm and others that an innocent party, not the guilty one, has to be sacrificed for the purpose of reconciliation between man and God (see 12.294; 2 Cor. 5.21; and *Cur deus homo*,[58] respectively). This salvific fulfilment of the law turns out to be an ambiguous blessing, however: on the one hand, it breaks the vicious cycle of endlessly contaminating guilt, but on the other hand it aggravates it. Some theologians have assumed that the fleshly union of God with Man in Christ – the Θεάνθρωπος – short-circuits the sacrificial logic of endlessly proliferating human guilt by making creditor/judge and debtor/defendant coincide.[59] However, that is not the road Milton takes: Milton's Christology is complicated, but it is fair to say that the payment of the "rigid satisfaction, death for death" (3.212) does not subvert but reassert the bondage of cosmic debt. In the *Doctrina Christiana*, Milton refutes the notion that the Son is co-substantial with the Father precisely on the grounds that the crucifixion could not effectuate God's satisfaction in this case:

> Hoc tamen fateor, me non videre quo pacto qui filium eiusdem cum Patre essentiae esse volunt, eius vel incarnationem, vel satisfactionem possint satis expedire.
>
> At the same time I do admit not seeing how those who claim that the Son is of the same essence as the Father can adequately explain either his incarnation or his satisfaction.
>
> (*DC* 520–521)

William Empson wryly comments:

> What Milton is thinking has to be: "God couldn't have been satisfied by torturing himself to death, not if I know God; you could never have bought him off with that money: he could only have been satisfied by torturing somebody else to death".[60]

Milton accordingly proposes a more political solution, which does not short-circuit but further complicates the entanglements of human suffering, divine law and divine pleasure. For this purpose, the Son himself has already "interpreted" the first human couple's first pleas for mercy, affirming that

58 St. Anselm, *Cur deus homo*, ed. F. S. Schmitt, Bonn: Hanstein, 1929. Translated as *Why God Became Man* in St. Anselm, *The Major Works*, eds. Brian Davies and G. R. Evans, Oxford and New York: Oxford University Press, 1998.

59 See e.g. John Stott, *The Cross of Christ*, Downers Grove, IL: InterVarsity Press, 2006, p. 153.

60 Empson, *Milton's God*, p. 208.

their ultimate wish is to be redeemed by himself and to be "[m]ade one" with him (11.33–44). In the *Doctrina*, the procedure of this unification is explained more extensively: the true Christians become the "members of Christ", being engrafted into one salvific body, also called the "invisible church" (as opposed, of course, to all institutionalized churches, and to the Holy Roman Catholic Church in particular; see *DC* 596/597, 644/645). The constitution of this new communal *corpus* is obviously conceived as a subjection under Christ as king. However, the sovereign Son demands more of his engrafted believers than mere obedience to a new code of law: he asks for their total abandonment of self-will, so that they will live only insofar as he lives in them. The *Doctrina* clarifies that this entails a constant self-denial ("abnegatio sui", *DC* 598/599). A similar scenario is sketched in *Paradise Lost*:

> thy merit
> Imputed shall absolve them who renounce
> Their own both righteous and unrighteous deeds,
> And live in thee transplanted, and from thee
> Receive new life.
> (3.290–294)

Due to Milton's monism, this procedure of incorporation differs from the traditional Pauline doctrine: it is more pragmatic and less mysterious. Again, one may perceive similarities to Hobbes' *Leviathan*, which also emphasizes that the constitution of a sovereign state through its future citizens involves a "real unity of them all in one and the same person" and an abandonment of their rights.[61] That the Hobbesian governing body is a modernization of the *corpus mysticum* has already been stated by diverse authors, among them Carl Schmitt.[62] Due to the similar theologico-political focus, Milton's rhetoric sometimes suggests that the mere event of the incarnation and the subsequent engrafting of the invisible church members should be sufficient for man's justification and salvation; accordingly, the crucifixion is treated rather perfunctorily. Milton, like Hobbes and Calvin, generally seems to distance himself from the idea of the Son's sacramental humiliation and suffering.[63]

61 See Thomas Hobbes, *Leviathan*, ed. J. C. A. Gaskin, Oxford: Oxford University Press, 1998, p. 114 [2.17.13].

62 See e.g. Carl Schmitt, *The Leviathan in the State Theory of Thomas Hobbes: Meaning and Failure of a Political Symbol*, trans. George Schwab and Erna Hilfstein, Westport, CT: Greenwood Press, 1996, p. 62. See also: Johan Tralau, *Thomas Hobbes and Carl Schmitt: The Politics of Order and Myth*, London: Routledge, 2011, pp. 48–49.

63 According to Hobbes, the essence of the Christian doctrine is that "Jesus is the Christ", i.e. the Son of God; that he sacrificed himself for the sins of man appears to be rather secondary. (See Hobbes, *Leviathan*, pp. 321–324, 394 [2.41.2–4, 2.43.11].) On Calvin's account of Christ's suffering on the cross, see Jean Calvin, *Institutes of the Christian Religion,* trans. Ford Lewis Battles, ed. John T. McNeill, Louisville, KY: Westminster John Knox Press, 2006, pp. 515–516 [II.16.10].

His lyrical fragment "The Passion"[64] could be considered paradigmatic in this context, for the alleged topic of the poem is almost systematically avoided.[65] The same applies to Milton's other poetical works. In this context, it is worth pointing out that *Paradise Regained*, despite its title, does not treat Christ's self-sacrifice on the cross, but his temptation through Satan in the desert and his altogether painless, even effortless, success in this trial of faith. In *Paradise Lost*, the crucifixion also appears occluded to the point of docetism:[66] the epic's rather brief and abstract description of Christ's life and death carefully avoids any direct reference to physical pain.[67] Instead, it focuses on the insults that the Son's honour has to bear; what interests Michael in the death on the cross is that it is "shameful and accursed" (12.413). And he instantly, almost anxiously, points out that this death will only be a temporal absence – hence not a real death. And the Son himself also knows that he will but temporarily die (3.247). When all is said and done, Michael represents the crucifixion as another show trial at the end of which man is burdened with a new form of guilt and God has expanded his legal claim on him even further. For humankind comes to owe the Son no less than eternal life, even though they have murdered him. After this act of love, rejection of divine guidance and persistence in the sinful ways of man is all the more unforgivable (3.198–202). And the legislator is henceforth an inner voice that is more demanding than any other lawgiver, even though the Mosaic law already proved impossible to fulfil:

> A Christianis enim non minus perfecta vita requiritur, immo perfectior potius, quam ab iis qui sub lege erant; id quod omnia praecepta Christi sonant. Hoc tantum interest, quod Moses literam sive externam legem

64 John Milton, "The Passion", *CPEP*, pp. 31–33.

65 See Björn Quiring, "'The Greatest Share of Endless Pain': The Spectral Sacramentality of Pain in Milton's *Paradise Lost*", in *Passions and Subjectivity in Early Modern Culture*, eds. Brian Cummings and Freya Sierhuis, Farnham and Burlington, VT: Ashgate, 2013, pp. 258–259.

66 There are some docetist representations of the crucifixion which insist that the true messiah, who was purely spiritual and had no physical body, stood laughing at the foot of the cross. See e.g. the apocryphal *Apocalypse of Peter*: "He whom you see beside the tree glad and laughing, this is the living Jesus. But he into whose hands and feet they drive the nails is his fleshly likeness, the 'ransom', which alone they are able to put to shame" (*The Apocalypse of Peter*, quoted in Fred Lapham, *An Introduction to the New Testament Apocrypha*, London and New York: T. and T. Clark International, 2003, p. 106).

67 It is notable that the most intense of all painful passions has traditionally been ascribed to Jesus Christ. (See e.g. Esther Cohen, *The Modulated Scream: Pain in Late Medieval Culture*, Chicago: University of Chicago Press, 2010, p. 205 ff.). Since Milton's thoroughly victorious Messiah certainly no longer fulfils this function of the representative sacrificial victim on whom all the pains of the world must alight, the role is apparently taken over by Milton's Satan. For Satan is burdened not only with the primal, but also with the most intense pain ever felt, or at least that is what he himself asserts by claiming "the greatest share/ Of endless pain" in Pandæmonium (2.29–30). For a more extensive treatment of this topic, see Quiring, "'The Greatest Share of Endless Pain'".

> imponebat vel invitis; Christus internam Dei legem per Spiritum suum fidelium cordibus inscribit, volentesque ducit [...].
>
> For from Christians no less perfect a life is required – rather, indeed, a *more* perfect life – than from those who were under the law, as all Christ's precepts shout out. This only is different: that Moses used to impose the letter or external law even on the unwilling, [whereas] Christ writes God's internal law through his spirit on the hearts of the faithful, and leads those who are willing.
>
> (*DC* 714/715)

Freedom from condemnation can only be achieved if the creature surrenders and henceforth "lives in Christ", willingly matching the law in their members to the divine law and fusing them into one, thus echoing and internalizing the horticultural work of Adam and Eve. And even though all good Christians must constantly exert themselves to "pray, repent, and bring obedience due" (3.190), the results are not meritorious, since men owe nothing of it to their own will and everything to God's grace, *per definitionem* (3.174–182). Michael suggests that only a small part of mankind will in this way be absorbed into the saviour – and that only this fraction will be saved from the living death of hell. Those who accomplish it are insistently called "the just". But the "far greater part,/ Will deem in outward rites and specious forms/ Religion satisfied" (12.533–535). As the Paradise of Fools interlude makes clear, this "far greater part" will not go to heaven. It will be either dissolved or burn in hell forever. Universal salvation therefore turns out to be very restricted: most women and men will remain "alienate from God" (5.877), so their future will still be an existence of eternal torture or utter annihilation; no forgiveness of the sinner qua sinner and no apocatastasis is to be expected according to Michael (nor according to Milton in the *Doctrina*; see *DC* 892/893). It turns out that the Son, in his role as saviour, saves what has assimilated itself to him and thus to a condemnatory law that has remained a mystery.

In every other respect, nature-history will go on just like before: after Christ's resurrection, men's legal status has changed, but that does not entail that the conditions of their detention will be ameliorated. The same degenerative pattern as before will persevere: the Christian church will be corrupted almost immediately after the death of the apostles, and "grievous wolves" will henceforth use the institution for the further persecution of Just Men:

> heavy persecution shall arise
> On all who in the worship persevere
> Of spirit and truth; [...]
> so shall the world go on,
> To good malignant, to bad men benign,
> Under her own weight groaning [...].
>
> (12.531–539)

Real hope for the redeemed can only be expected from the return of Christ, the day "of respiration to the just,/ And vengeance to the wicked" (12.540–541).

9.5 At the end of history: the bliss of eternal judgment

The universe that is delineated in *Paradise Lost* is already under the spell of the continuous judgment of Nature, which has been overcoded by God in diverse ways. What can the Son's Return and the Final Judgment contribute to this process? This question is difficult to answer: the reader is confronted with a strange blend of continuities and discontinuities. On the one hand, the apocalypse is conceived as a break with pre-apocalyptic existence and as a new start, making "all things new" (11.912, quoting Rev. 21.5), but on the other hand, it is represented as merely the culmination of processes that already inhere in creation. This is, of course, nothing peculiar to Milton: there is a long and venerable pedigree to the idea that divine judgment is not only an event at the end of history, but also an ongoing process that pervades fallen nature and history. It stretches from remarks in the gospels (e.g. Luke 17.20–21) to treatises by some church fathers[68] and medieval and modern millennialists[69] all the way to Blake[70] and Kafka.[71] Milton resembles the latter two authors, insofar as some of the most interesting sections of his treatments of the apocalypse attain what Benjamin has called an "Überspannung der Transzendenz"/"overstretching of transcendence".[72] Milton's monism and his strong emphasis on free will results in a Last Judgment that overflows its conventional boundaries and presents itself as something unexpectedly rich and strange. Suggestions that every man's life on earth, and particularly his afflictions, are a trial of that man's moral qualities is one of the most conventional expression of this topic (see e.g. 11.63–64). Somewhat rarer (though not altogether unprecedented) is a synchronization of the ascension of Christ and the legendary Harrowing of Hell[73] with Satan's binding (Rev. 20.1–3) in

68 See Hans Blumenberg, *Die Legitimität der Neuzeit*, Frankfurt am Main: Suhrkamp, 1996, pp. 53–57.

69 See e.g. Jean Delumeau, *Une histoire du paradis*, Vol. 2: *Mille ans de bonheur*, Paris: Fayard, 1995.

70 See William Blake's notes to his painting *A Vision of the Last Judgment*: "[W]henever any Individual Rejects Error & Embraces Truth a Last Judgment passes upon that Individual". William Blake, "A Vision of The Last Judgment", in *The Complete Poetry and Prose*, ed. David V. Erdman, New York: Doubleday, 1988, p. 562.

71 "Nur unser Zeitbegriff läßt uns das Jüngste Gericht so nennen, eigentlich ist es ein Standrecht." "It is only our conception of time that makes us call the Last Judgment by that name, in fact it is a permanent court-martial." Franz Kafka, "Aphorismen", in *Beim Bau der chinesischen Mauer und andere Schriften*, eds. Malcolm Pasley and Jost Schillemeit, Frankfurt am Main: Fischer, 1994, p. 235; and id., *Shorter Works*, Vol. 1, trans. Malcolm Pasley, London: Secker and Warburg, 1973, p. 90.

72 Benjamin, *Ursprung des deutschen Trauerspiels*, p. 246; translation BQ, since Osborne's translation is flawed.

73 The legend of the Harrowing of Hell has a shaky scriptural basis in 1 Peter 3.19–20. See Henry A. Kelly, "Hell with Purgatory and Two Limbos", in *Hell and Its Afterlife: Historical*

12.451–460, which Cheryl Fresh has pointed out.[74] This temporal collapse makes all the more biblical sense because the binding of Satan is immediately followed by Christ's reign of a thousand years in Revelation (20.4–6). Millennarian views of history were indeed not uncommon in Milton's time, at least among some Protestant groups.[75] But Milton adds another twist to the story by conflating millennium and Last Judgment – implicitly in *Paradise Lost*, expressly in the *Doctrina*. As he explains, what awaits mankind at the end of time will be a Thousand-Year-Judgment:

> Iudicii huius extremi tempore (neque enim unius diei spatio tot angelorum hominumque myriades sisti et iudicari posse verisimile est, et dies pro quovis tempore saepe intelligitur) ab initio, inquam, huius iudicii ad finem usque et aliquanto post finem, promissum illud toties Christi cum sanctis suis regnum in terris gloriosum videtur futurum; quoad hostes eius omnes debellati erunt.
>
> At the time of this last judgment – for indeed it is unlikely that so many myriads of angels and people could be assembled and judged in the space of a single day, and "day" is often understood as any indefinite period of time whatever – from the beginning, I say, of this judgement until its end, and for some time after its end, it appears that that so often promised glorious kingdom of Christ with his saints will come into being on earth; until all his enemies have been vanquished.
>
> (*DC* 882/883)

The passage intimates that the divine judgment may not only take a thousand years, but even longer, an "indefinite period of time". Indeed, Milton ends up affirming that the completion of the cosmic trial may have to be postponed indefinitely, so that the jurisdiction turns into a work of governance and administration:

and Contemporary Perspectives, eds. Isabel Moreira and Margaret Toscano, Farnham and Burlington, VT: Ashgate, 2010, pp. 123–125.

74 "In his descent to death lies the Son's own individual triumph over Death through the Resurrection, but in the Son's descent is also guaranteed the triumph of redeemed humanity through the Harrowing of Hell. Both typified by and implicated in this shared temporal triumph, however, is that eternal triumph to be established by the Last Judgment. Developing his revelation of the timeless implications of the Passion, the Son's voice irresistibly and ever more powerfully modulates into prophetic registers, collapsing into simultaneity and merging into identity the first separation of the redeemed from the damned, to be effected by the Harrowing, and the final apocalyptic separation of the redeemed from the damned [...]" (Cheryl Fresh, "Milton and Blake: Visualizing the Expulsion", in *"All in All": Unity, Diversity and the Miltonic Perspective*, eds. Charles W. Durham and Kristin A. Pruitt, Selinsgrove, PA: Susquehanna University Press, 1999, p. 170).

75 See Keith Thomas, *Religion and the Decline of Magic: Studies in Popular Beliefs in Sixteenth- and Seventeenth-Century England*, London: Penguin, 1991, pp. 166–171.

> Videtur hoc iudicium non diurnum sed diuturnum, non tam iudiciarium quam moderatorium; quo sensu Gedeon, Iephtes et reliqui iudices per multos annos iudicasse dicuntur.
>
> This judgment appears not [just] day-long, but long-lasting, and not so much judicial as governmental, in which sense Gideon, Jephthah, and the remaining Judges are said to have "judged" [Israel] for many years.
>
> (*DC* 884/885)

One may assume that during a court case of such gigantic proportions, men and angels will find occasions to commit new sins and perhaps even generate new defendants, thus necessitating ever new judgments indefinitely. Thus, the divine law court will never close but keep absorbing the life of the creatures. Fittingly, as John Rogers has already remarked, the apocalyptic separation of the sheep from the goats in *Paradise Lost* is often described as a natural process of absorption and excretion, as "digestive actions of salutary assimilation and purgation".[76] Michael, quoting Revelation, keeps repeating that fire shall "purge all things new" (11.900). By the predominant digestive metaphors, the apocalyptic fire is associated with the "interior fire" that was thought to consume food within the belly, an idea going back to Plato and perpetuated in early modern physiology.[77] Accordingly, Michael leaves it unclear whether the cleansing fire will eventually die out or whether it will keep illuminating the "conflagrant mass" (12.548) of the new heaven and new earth. In this context, the reader should remember Raphael's cosmological sketches in which he states that even prelapsarian nature is pervaded by a metabolic, purifying and judicial process.[78] Post-apocalyptic time blends into apocalyptic and pre-apocalyptic times. Consequently, the epic remains ambiguous on the question of whether Nature and Earth themselves will be annihilated by the conflagration, or whether the natural processes will merely be amplified and intensified. And in the *Doctrina*, Milton likewise prefers not to commit himself:

> De huius mundi fine et conflagratione [...] utrum ad substantiae abolitionem an ad qualitatum duntaxat immutationem futura sit, incertum est et nostra parum refert [...].
>
> Concerning the end and conflagration of this world, [...] it is uncertain and of little concern to us whether it will lead to the abolition of its substance or only to the changing of its qualities.
>
> (*DC* 888/889)

76 Rogers, *The Matter of Revolution*, p. 133.

77 Plato, *Timaios*, in *Werke*, Vol. 7, ed. Gunther Eigler, Darmstadt: Wissenschaftliche Buchgesellschaft, 1972, pp. 176/177 [80e]. This notion was cited approvingly by Ficino; see Marsilio Ficino, *All Things Natural: Ficino on Plato's* Timaeus, trans. Arthur Farndell, London: Shepheard-Walwyn, 2010, p. 100.

78 See Chapter 7, pp. 231–234.

An abolition of the cosmic substance would entail the annihilation of any cosmic dynamism; but a mere change in its qualities would entail its persistence. The second option would leave open the possibility that cosmic Nature still influences God in his dealings with mankind, whereas the first option denies that possibility. Hence, the blanket statement that the destiny of the cosmic substance should be "of little concern to us" serves to once more obscure the crucial double role Nature plays in the double-headed self-legitimation of divine jurisdiction. And just as it remains ambiguous how the apocalypse will affect Nature, the perspective for the blessed and the damned likewise remains unclear. When the Father speaks to the Son about it, he suggests that the apocalypse will largely be a purgative trial, effectively eliminating the wicked from the earth, sending them downward, like the "tartareous dregs":

> Then all thy saints assembled, thou shalt judge
> Bad men and angels, they arraigned shall sink
> Beneath thy sentence [...].
>
> (3.330–332)

The further destiny of the damned, following this "dread tribunal" (3.326), is obscure, however. On the one hand, it is confidently stated that they all will be condemned to hell, which will thereupon be "for ever shut" (3.333). But on the other hand, the Last Judgment holds out the prospect of annihilation for at least some sinners – exactly the "utter dissolution" (2.127) that Moloch had hoped for as the better alternative to the hell in which Nature breeds ever new miseries (2.93–94). Michael announces that the Son will "dissolve" Satan, instead of forcing him back to the place of endless pain (12.546–547). And the occupants of the "Fool's Paradise" on the "backside" (3.494) of the cosmos also seem to face extinction, in the form of "final dissolution", rather than eternal tortures (3.458). In this perspective, the vaporized sinners might finally come to join the "embryon atoms" of Chaos (2.900) and thus be reabsorbed into the "dark materials" (2.916) from which new worlds can be created.[79] The fortunes of the just men, that is, the "saints", turn out to be equivocal in much the same way: will they ascend to heaven and accommodate themselves to angelhood, as Raphael promised, or will they remain on earth, an alternative that Michael introduces (12.463)? Might they even be (re)absorbed into the Godhead, as the Father sometimes seems to suggest in predicting that God shall "be all in all" (3.341) when all is subjected to him?[80] Or is the Father

79 It should be remarked that the idea of a final dissolution of the damned is rejected in the *Doctrina* – in a tone of snarky irony that seems to echo that of the Father in *Paradise Lost* (see *DC* 892/893).

80 Milton here quotes 1 Cor. 15.28, a passage on which he comments more extensively in the Doctrina (*DC* 889). However, it is still far from clear what is meant by "all in all" in this context; the passage has therefore been subjected to numerous contradictory interpretations. Robert Myers assumes that it implies the erasure of hell, Robert Fallon vehemently denies it

merely using theologico-political rhetoric again in this passage? Whether saint or sinner, humankind's ultimate destiny is marked by a vacillation that has already characterized its prelapsarian life.

The story of the cosmos does not achieve closure in *Paradise Lost*, and perhaps one decisive reason can be found in the enormous importance of free will in Milton's work. According to Augustine's *City of God*, man will no longer be able to sin, once he has been admitted into heaven:

> Deus natura peccare non potest: particeps vero Dei ab illo accepit, ut pecare non possit. Servandi autem gradus erant divini muneris, ut primum daretur liberum arbitrium, quo non peccare homo posset, novissimum, quo peccare non posset [...].[81]
>
> The inability to sin belongs to God's nature, while he who partakes of God's nature receives the impossibility of sinning as a gift from God. Moreover, the stages of the divine gift had to be preserved. Free will was given first, with the ability to sin; and the last gift was the inability to sin.[82]

Augustine's theology has been criticized for this assumption, since it is incompatible with his doctrine of original sin. For he has formerly explained that the possibility of evil was a necessary result of providing man with a free will; but here he contradicts this statement, asserting that God has the option to provide man with a more excellent sort of freedom that does not contradict the incapacity to sin.[83] As for Milton, he never thematizes the creatures' ability to sin after the apocalypse, but his unrelenting insistence on man's free will as a necessary condition of his humanity and dignity make it highly unlikely that

(Robert M. Myers, "'God Shall Be All In All': The Erasure of Hell in *Paradise Lost*", *The Seventeenth Century*, 5.1 (1990), pp. 43–53; Robert Thomas Fallon, *Divided Empire: Milton's Political Imagery*, University Park: Pennsylvania State University Press, 1995, pp. 155–159). Christopher Hill compares it to the Marxist topos of the "withering away of the state", Diana Treviño Benet speculates that it might imply the abolition of personal identity (Christopher Hill, *Milton and the English Revolution*, Harmondsworth: Penguin, 1979, p. 304; Diana Treviño Benet, "'All in All': The Threat of Bliss", in *"All in All": Unity, Diversity, and the Miltonic Perspective*, eds. Charles W. Durham and Kristin Pruitt McColgan, Selinsgrove, PA: Susquehanna University Press and London: Associated University Press, 1999, pp. 48–66). One of the most interesting and generous, but also most questionable readings is that of William Empson. According to him, God is tired of his tyrannical position. He plans to abdicate and to "dissolve into the landscape", leaving his sovereign post to the Son, i.e. to the unfallen angels and the just men who constitute the Son's body (Empson, *Milton's God*, p. 133). However, several good objections have been raised against this interpretation. (See e.g. Kenneth Borris, *Allegory and Epic in English Renaissance Literature: Heroic Form in Sidney, Spenser, and Milton*, Cambridge and New York: Cambridge University Press, 2000, p. 307.)

81 Augustine, *Der Gottesstaat/De Civitate Dei*, Vol. 2, trans. Carl Johann Perl, Paderborn: Ferdinand Schöningh, 1979, p. 870 [22.30].

82 Augustine, *Concerning the City of God Against the Pagans*, translated by Henry Bettenson, London and New York: Penguin, 2003, p. 1089 [22.30].

83 See e.g. Gareth B. Matthews, *Augustine*, Oxford and Malden, MA: Blackwell, 2005, p. 113.

he would have taken the road of Augustine. In *Areopagitica*, he confidently asserts that a human creature that cannot sin would be a mere automaton:

> Many there be that complain of divine providence for suffering Adam to transgress, foolish tongues! When God gave him reason, he gave him freedom to choose, for reason is but choosing; he had been else a mere artificial Adam, such an Adam as he is in the motions.
>
> (*CPW* 2:527, spelling modernized)

And in *Paradise Lost*, Raphael explains that the state of the blessed angels must always be an endangered state:

> Myself and all the angelic host that stand
> In sight of God enthroned, our happy state
> Hold, as you yours, while our obedience holds;
> On other surety none […].
>
> (5.535–538)

The creatures cannot be deprived of their capacity to sin without depriving them of their moral worth, which is a necessary constituent of their participation in the realm of God.[84] However, if all the inhabitants of heaven retain their free will, they still harbour a potential for disobedience and sin. And thus the whole story of creaturely rebellion may start all over again, despite the redemptive trials of mankind. Salvation is always uncertain, for heaven must retain the potential to rid itself of unruly inhabitants; only hell provides its residents with a permanent citizenship and can confidently be assumed to keep growing forever. Under these circumstances, one can easily see why the Last Judgment must be perpetual.

But how does this never-ending trial relate to the proclaimed "eternal bliss" of heaven, the "golden days, fruitful of golden deeds,/ With joy and peace triumphing, and fair truth" (3.337–338)? According to the *Doctrina Christiana*, the end of the apocalypse is the delight of the just (*DC* 897); and there are strong indications that the eternal judgment in and of itself may already constitute their greatest delight. For it is assumed that they will actively participate in it:

> Iudicium extremum est, quo Christus cum sanctis gloria atque potentia patris instructus malos angelos, hominumque genus universum iudicabit.
>
> The last judgment is that in which Christ, with the saints, equipped with the father's glory and power, will judge the evil angels and the entire human race.
>
> (*DC* 881)

84 See also Harold Skulsky, *Milton and the Death of Man*, p. 212.

It has already been pointed out that the love that Father and Son profess to harbour for mankind remains strangely abstract and pale, and that the joys of celestial brotherhood among the angels appear rather questionable. First and foremost, the inhabitants of heaven get emotionally involved, and their language becomes colourful and lively, when they refer to scenes in which they judge and subdue their enemies (see e.g. 10.633–637). St. Paul seems to have been the first to claim that the Christian saints will be the world's judges:

> ἢ οὐκ οἴδατε ὅτι οἱ ἅγιοι τὸν κόσμον κρινοῦσιν; [...] οὐκ οἴδατε ὅτι ἀγγέλους κρινοῦμεν [...].
>
> Do ye not know that the saints shall judge the world? [...] Know ye not that we shall judge angels?
>
> (1 Cor. 6.2–3)

It is a common topic among medieval and early modern theologians that the condemnation of the bad contributes to the well-being of the good. Thomas Aquinas and others have explicitly stated that an important component of the saints' delight will be their witnessing of hell's tortures:

> [A] beatis nihil subtrahi debet quod ad perfectionem beatitudinis eorum pertineat. Unumquodque autem ex operatione contrarii magis cognoscitur; quia "contraria juxta se posita magis elucescunt" [Rhet. 3.2] Et ideo, ut beatitudo sanctorum eis magis complaceat, et de ea uberiores gratias Deo agant, dantur eis ut poenam impiorum perfecte intueantur.[85]
>
> To the blessed, nothing should be denied that belongs to their beatitude's perfection. Now all things are better acknowledged if the contrary is also perceived; for "contraries that are juxtaposed become more conspicuous" [Aristotle, Rhetoric 3.2]. And therefore, that the beatitude of the saints may please them more, and that they may thank God more copiously, it is given to them that they may perfectly clearly behold the sufferings of the faithless.[86]

De Doctrina Christiana sketches a more republican ideal of divine punishment: instead of being reduced to the position of onlookers, the saints may participate in the condemnation of the wicked when they, by "peculiar grace", have ascended through the ranks from the status of defendants to that of associate judges.[87] The chosen ones are those for whom the joys of judgment

85 *Summa Theologica: Die deutsche Thomas-Ausgabe,* Vol. 26*: Supplement, Quaestiones 87–99*, trans. Dominicans and Benedictines of Germany and Austria, Heidelberg: Kerle and Cologne: Styria, 1961, pp. 181 [Supplement, Quaestio 94. Art. 2].

86 Translation BQ.

87 The task of judging angels was also dwelt upon by other British Protestants at that time, for example the minister Christopher Wyvill in a sermon on Christian magistrates: "You cannot be ignorant that you shall judge even angels, and therefore you are now much more worthy of inferior seats of judgment, to judge of matters which pertain to this life. He [Paul

surpass all other joys, and God has promised to provide for them so that they can never lack. All flesh will chant the praises of their justice, directly or allegorically. In this scenario, participating in salvation equals participating in the differentiation between the "just" and the "unjust" – a process that goes on forever. The never-ending, but joyful, administrative work that Adam and Eve have performed in prelapsarian Paradise can be read as a prefiguration of these saintly labours in the kingdom of God: both enact the endless eradication of the distance between God and Nature, reconciling them to each other, that is, sublating their difference by acts of allegorical overcoding. This is the eternal bliss of the true saints and angels in their ideal commonwealth: judgment, in Milton's world, turns out to be not the means to an end, but the end and perfection of life itself, and God's unceasing apotheosis.

Still, Nature's limitless ancestor Chaos is bound to remain an active force in the universe. There is no sign that the inherent movement of the "embryon atoms" will be controlled and their internal battles be pacified once and for all, even after the apocalypse. This circumstance guarantees that the work of divine judgment is never done: beyond the eternal administration process "is all abyss", as Adam says (12.555), namely the deterriorializing "dark unbottomed infinite abyss" of Chaos (2.405), whose forces will go on assailing the bars of God's iron prison world. This may provide a job guarantee for the saints, but on the other hand the vivacious void that surrounds them is a constant reminder that their glorious eternity might find an inglorious end: Chaos might still turn out to be Nature's grave.

9.6 Beyond the Fall

Michael thus grants Adam a vision of the first and last judgment of God and Nature. For the representative of mankind, despite his vauntings, it is not a pleasant sight: the sacrifices and self-sacrifices keep accumulating with no end in sight. Adam apparently also perceives this, since he desperately tries to find edification in Michael's history lesson. Whereas Michael's official mission is to console Adam (11.113), he turns the lesson into yet another trial, using every occasion to test his pupil and snub him for his misinterpretation of the things that are revealed to him. Adam is obviously nervous about this examination as well as under strain caused by the prospect of mankind's bleak future. He becomes subject to strong mood swings, alternately crying and rejoicing (11.448–12.386). Thus, Michael manipulates him into total submission: when Adam finally tries to draw moral lessons from the theatre of cruelty with which he has been confronted, one is left with the impression that he only tries to say what the angel wants to hear. As John Carey expresses it: "Adam's elation over the wonderful cleverness of this plan only makes us feel that he has had all the

in 1 Cor 6.2–3] attributes, you see, a sort of a judicature to the saints hereafter, and therefore would have them to be judges now [...]". Christopher Wyvill, *Of Christian Magistracy*, London: Aylmer, 1697, p. 3, spelling modernized.

stuffing knocked out of him by God's tricks".[88] After Michael has explained how the salvation through Christ shall work, Adam exclaims:

> Oh goodness infinite, goodness immense!
> That all this good of evil shall produce,
> And evil turn to good; more wonderful
> Than that which by creation first brought forth
> Light out of darkness! Full of doubt I stand,
> Whether I should repent me now of sin [...].
> (12.469–474)

Obviously, he is trying to describe his transgression as a *felix culpa* and to see the sublime beauty of the whole legal process by which the infinite accumulation and condemnation of the bad comes to define the good. The problem is, as Empson remarks, that Michael, by his representation of the Fall as fortunate, admits that the transgressions of Adam and Eve turn out to be part of an ulterior divine plan:

> What [Adam] is really saying, apart from the emotional condition he has been reduced to, is "Oh, so you did want us to eat the apple after all? Well, I'm pleased to hear that, because Eve rather thought you did, at the time". It would mean that there is no reason for all the evils Adam has just been shown on earth, let alone the pains of Hell. The doctrine of the Fortunate Fall, it seems clear, removes from God the last rag of excuse for his plot to corrupt the whole race of mankind.[89]

Adam's effusion is rife with (advertent or inadvertent) ironies, starting from the exclamation "O goodness infinite, goodness immense!", in a situation in which the finitude of divine goodness, strictly delimited by "endless pain" (2.30), is only all too obvious. Adam now is reduced to a state in which he is compelled to Christianize himself (12.572–573) by embracing the divine vision of human history to the point of self-abnegation. His surrender is comparable to that of Job in the ashes, humbling himself when confronted with the accusatory voice from the whirlwind (Job 42.2–6); and a similar subdued irony has been discerned in Job's repentance.[90] Since his "last rag of excuse" is gone at this point, Milton's God presents himself to Adam as sheer overbearing force, successfully asserting himself as a completely transcendent and omnipotent entity. His quest for absolute dominion is accomplished; he stands revealed and untouchable. The universe has become a courtroom in which the judgmental Father has transcended all laws and is advanced to a

88 John Carey, *Milton*, London: Evans Brothers, 1969, p. 81.

89 Empson, *Milton's God*, pp. 191–192.

90 See e.g. David Robertson, "The Book of Job: A Literary Study", *Soundings: An Interdisciplinary Journal* 56.4 (1973): pp. 446–469, esp. pp. 465–467.

sublime non-actionability beyond any notion of human justice. Adam only has the choice to either turn into one of the castigating zealots who execute God's unquestionable will or to become one of the condemned bodies who complement and glorify God's absolute surplus of power with their absolute lack of power.[91]

The immediate effect of this divine triumph is strange, however: Adam still retains his official devotion to God and voices pious commonplaces when taking sad leave of Michael and Paradise (12.557–573), but the epic conveys the impression that his relationship to the deity has shifted. One indication is the circumstance that something is left unsaid when Adam reencounters Eve in the next few lines: comforted by a dream conveying the hope of salvation, she tells him that she can well bear to leave Paradise as long as he keeps her company. Adam apparently wants to say something at this point, but decides to keep his silence because Michael is listening in:

> Adam heard
> Well pleased, but answered not; for now too nigh
> The archangel stood [...].
> (12.624–626)

This is a rather mysterious remark: if he wants to cheer his wife with a godly or loving proclamation, why would he be afraid to be overheard by the angel? One possible interpretation is that he has learned another lesson of which he cannot speak as long as he walks as in God's presence (12.563). In this context, it is worth remembering a remark of the narrator who affirms that the last part of *Paradise Lost* is "tragic" (9.6). The fate of Adam and Eve might be said to follow the rules of tragedy in a specifically Benjaminian sense: according to Benjamin, in the crucial Athenian tragedies, the hero recognizes at the end that he is more just and good than his gods, by the standards which the immortals themselves have propagated. And this realization strikes him dumb:

> [D]ie Tragödie, die da gewidmet schien dem Gerichte über den Helden, wandelt sich zur Verhandlung über die Olympischen, bei der jener den Zeugen abgibt [...] [I]n der Tragödie besinnt sich der heidnische Mensch, daß er besser ist als seine Götter, aber diese Erkenntnis verschlägt ihm die Sprache, sie bleibt dumpf. Ohne sich zu bekennen sucht sie heimlich ihre Gewalt zu sammeln [...].[92]

> [T]he tragedy which appeared to be devoted to the judgment of the hero is transformed into a hearing about the Olympians in which the latter appears as a witness [...]. [I]n tragedy pagan man realizes that he is better

91 See Michel Foucault, *Discipline and Punish: The Birth of the Prison*, trans. Alan Sheridan, New York: Vintage Books, 1979, p. 29.

92 Benjamin, *Ursprung des deutschen Trauerspiels*, pp. 288–289.

> than his gods, but this realization strikes him dumb, and it remains unarticulated. Without declaring itself, it secretly endeavours to gather strength [...].[93]

A similar inarticulate realization, though of a different kind, seems to dawn at the conclusion of *Paradise Lost*: the Father has transcended all laws and in the process become both indefensible and unassailable. All moral and logical contradictions inherent in his rule can henceforth only contribute to its further consolidation. But it is exactly at this point of the Father's most glorious victory that his supreme, all-pervasive reign recedes into a strange distance. He remains an overbearing legal and political force, but in his both indefensible and unassailable status he has attained a status beyond good and evil and therefore become morally indifferent. An indication of this transformation is the strange undertone of worldliness in the epic's last lines, presenting "solitary" Adam and Eve on the "subjected plain":

> Some natural tears they dropped, but wiped them soon;
> The world was all before them, where to choose
> Their place of rest, and Providence their guide:
> They hand in hand with wandering steps and slow,
> Through Eden took their solitary way.
> (12.645–649; capitalization added)

Providence has hitherto both been defined as a divine command that pervades the cosmos and been associated with Fate and Nature.[94] Since this divine/natural force is asserted to be still with the first couple and to offer them guidance, the statement sounds orthodox enough, even though God's precedence over Nature/Fate/Providence may frequently have been called into doubt by the epic. However, it should be noted that the narrator has introduced a grammatical ambiguity: the sentence can either mean that the world was all before them and that providence was their guide through it, helping them to orient themselves in the new environment, or the phrase can be taken to mean that Adam and Eve have the whole world before them, and in their explorations might or might not choose to accept divine providence for their guide, just as they can sensibly choose their place of rest among many potential resting places.[95] A supplementary ambiguity, which has been much commented on since Richard Bentley, is that of "Eden" in the last line.[96] Of course, "Eden" also denotes the tract of land around the garden, as well as the garden itself; but the line nevertheless contains a hint that Paradise has not been altogether

93 Benjamin, *The Origin of German Tragic Drama*, pp. 109–110.
94 See Chapter 1, pp. 32, 38, 40; Chapter 3, pp. 140–141.
95 See Forsyth, *The Satanic Epic*, p. 298.
96 See e.g. Richard Bentley, "Emendations to Paradise Lost", in John Milton, *The Critical Heritage, Vol. 2: 1732–1801*, ed. John T. Shawcross, London: Routledge, 1995, p. 49.

lost to the human couple. Of course, there is the "paradise within" (12.587) that Michael has promised Adam as a prize for good conduct. But the epic also introduces a "paradise in-between" which grows from the interactions between Eve and Adam, constituting their miniature republic. The last words that are spoken in the epic are spoken by Eve, and they contain a love declaration that equates the company of Adam with her presence in Paradise:

> In me is no delay; with thee to go,
> Is to stay here; without thee here to stay,
> Is to go hence unwilling; thou to me
> Art all things under heaven [...].
> (12.615–618)

It has frequently been pointed out that *Paradise Lost* can be regarded as the last European epic – and as an epic that demonstrates that the form of the epic is no longer sustainable.[97] The new literary form which will largely replace it already makes its presence felt: in *Paradise Lost*, the conventional plot of the eighteenth- and nineteenth-century novel is foreshadowed, namely the formation, conflict and reconciliation of a heterosexual couple.[98] A fair amount of the agony and ecstasy that formerly was associated with the relation between mankind and the celestial realm will henceforth be rather expected to result from the interactions between man and woman – and from the political relationship between superiors and inferiors which the bond between Adam and Eve also prefigures.[99] The infinite, unilateral debt towards God gets increasingly overlaid by a network of bilateral debts between humans.

When Adam and Eve walk out of *Paradise Lost*, the divine hero of the epic is fading from view, a victim of his own success, left behind in the great theologico-juridical beyond he has built for himself over the course of twelve books.[100] But the first human couple does not have the option to also leave

97 See e.g. Tobias Gregory, *From Many Gods to One: Divine Action in Renaissance Epic*, Chicago: University of Chicago Press, 2006, pp. 217–220.

98 See e.g. Neil H. Keeble, "Milton and Puritanism", in *A Companion to Milton*, ed. Thomas N. Corns, Oxford and Malden, MA: Blackwell, 2003, pp. 139–140.

99 See e.g. Niklas Luhmann, *Love as Passion: The Codification of Intimacy*, Cambridge, MA: Harvard University Press, 1986, pp. 65, 173.

100 As John Cowper Powys has pointed out, Milton's God also lives on in evangelical theology, a complement of secularism: "One feels, as one reads Milton, that his ultimate view of the universe is a great chaotic battlefield, amid the confused elements of which rise up the portentous figures of 'Thrones, Dominations, Principalities, and Powers', and in the struggle between these, the most arbitrary, the most tyrannical, the most despotic, conquers the rest, and, planting his creative Gonfalon further in the Abyss than any, becomes 'God'; the God whose personal and unrestrained Caprice creates the Sun, the Moon and the Stars, out of Chaos; and Man out of the dust of the Earth. Thus it is brought about that what this God wills is 'Good', and what his strongest and most formidable antagonist wills is 'Evil'. Between Good and Evil there is no eternal difference, except in the eternal difference between the conquering Personality of Jehovah and the conquered Personality of Lucifer. So, far from it being true

behind the guidance and judgment of Nature altogether, for it still structures their world, "everywhere weaving together partial natures with wholes". After being led out of Paradise, man and woman weep "natural tears", that is, tears that spring from their individual thwarted inclinations, but that are also the best symbolic expression of a split Nature. Since the beginnings of the genre, tears and laments have played a substantial role in the heroic narrative poem: "the resolution of tears […] ends most of the European poems that we commonly describe as epics".[101] The tears of Priam and Achilles are particularly prominent examples, but one might also invoke the tears of Penelope and Ulysses, of Turnus, Aeneas and Dido, of Dietrich and Etzel, of Rinaldo and Armida. The object of their laments is, in one form or another, always the cost of naturally born empires of law, empires no one completely controls and no one seems to be able to escape. In the history of the novel, these tears have never stopped flowing,[102] indicating that the problem of natural demands has not been solved but only updated in modernity. The rhetoric of accountability is still saturated with double binds, resulting from an entanglement of facts and norms, of things-as-they-are and things-as-they-should-be. Nature's metaphorical law court persists as a sustaining pillar of the social order, but also as a threatening void with which legal thought has been forced to engage ever since.

In *Paradise Lost*, an internal, inadmissible split is discernible that law needs in order to function. The cosmic legal system turns out to consist of two contradictory laws, both with their own judicial apparatuses, judging the world and judging one another. And secularization apparently has not been able to overcome this internal split. The attempt to absorb positive law into natural law has so far always ended in catastrophic aporias.[103] And even though the reference to a judgment beyond the bounds of human discretion appears increasingly archaic, no attempt to get rid of the concept of natural law completely has proven enduringly successful either. All attempts seem contaminated by

that Milton is the dull transcriber of mere traditional Protestantism, a very little investigation reveals the astounding fact that the current popular Evangelical view of the origin of things and the drama of things is based, not upon the Bible at all, but upon Milton's poem." John Cowper Powys, *Visions and Revisions: A Book of Literary Devotions*, New York: G. Arnold Shaw and London: William Rider, 1915, pp. 92–93. On evangelicalism as complement of secularism, see Christian Smith, *American Evangelicalism: Embattled and Thriving*, Chicago: University of Chicago Press, 1998, pp. 178–217.

101 Thomas M. Greene, "The Natural Tears of Epic", in: *Epic Traditions in the Contemporary World: The Poetics of Community*, ed. Margaret Beissinger, Jane Tylus and Susanne Wofford, Berkeley [etc.]: University of California Press, 1999, p. 192.

102 See e.g. Tom Lutz, *Crying: The Natural and Cultural History of Tears*, New York and London: Norton, 1999, pp. 251–286; Gisela Berkenbusch, *Zum Heulen: Kulturgeschichte unserer Tränen*, Berlin: Transit, 1985.

103 See e.g. Hanna Arendt, *The Origins of Totalitarianism*, San Diego and New York: Harcourt, 1985. See also Björn Quiring, *Shakespeare's Curse: The Aporias of Ritual Exclusion in Early Modern Royal Drama*, trans. Michael Winkler and Björn Quiring, New York: Routledge, 2014, pp. 167–251.

the assumptions they want to overcome. The most prominent example is legal positivism, which claims to formulate a new, decisionist paradigm beyond natural law, but largely ends up reformulating and updating the latter.[104] Thus, one of the most prominent and thoughtful theorists of the positivist tradition, Hans Kelsen, concedes in a few passages of his work that his theories can still be regarded as a perpetuation of the natural law doctrine.[105] Analogously, the most prominent British representative of twentieth-century legal positivism, H. L. A. Hart, asserts that there is "a core of indisputable truth in the doctrines of natural law".[106] Even anarchist thought which opposes not only positive law, but the very form of law seems only capable of doing so at the price of imputing the existence of its supplement within nature.[107] Normativity has a way of surviving its demise: the abolition and even the foreclosure of law tends to take a legal form, a performative contradiction to which any discourse decreeing the end of natural or positive law must fall prey.[108] In that respect, the borders between law and lawlessness tend to dissolve on closer inspection, but the pervasive attachment to legal forms apparently cannot be annihilated by the mere recognition of this uncomfortable fact.

By describing the cosmic legal system as a double-headed process of absorption and excretion and at the same time as the true goal of all creation, Milton's epic sheds light on this both unjustifiable and inescapable dimension of law. The image of jurisdiction that emerges resembles the emblem of

104 See e.g. Erik Wolf, *Das Problem der Naturrechtslehre: Versuch einer Orientierung*, Karlsruhe: Müller, 1964, p. 25.

105 Hans Kelsen, *Das Problem der Souveränität und die Theorie des Völkerrechts: Beitrag zu einer reinen Rechtslehre*, Reinheim: Scientia Aalen, 1960, p. 252. See also Jochen von Bernstorff, *The Public International Law Theory of Hans Kelsen: Believing in Universal Law*, trans. Thomas Dunlap, Cambridge: Cambridge University Press, 2010, p. 116. Thomas Olechowski, "Kelsens Rechtslehre im Überblick", in *Hans Kelsen: Eine politikwissenschaftliche Einführung*, ed. Tamara Ehs, Baden-Baden: Nomos, 2009, p. 58.

106 H. L. A. Hart, *The Concept of Law*, eds. Penelope A. Bulloch and Joseph Raz, Oxford: Oxford University Press, 2012, p. 181.

107 See e.g. Emma Goldman's statement: "A natural law is that factor in man which asserts itself freely and spontaneously without any external force, in harmony with the requirements of nature. For instance, the demand for nutrition, for sex gratification, for light, air, and exercise, is a natural law. But its expression needs not the machinery of government, needs not the club, the gun, the handcuff, or the prison. To obey such laws, if we may call it obedience, requires only spontaneity and free opportunity." (Emma Goldman, "Anarchism: What It Really Stands For", in *The Political Theory Reader*, ed. Paul Schumaker, Chichester and Malden, MA: Wiley-Blackwell, 2010, p. 49.) See also C. Alexander McKinley, *Illegitimate Children of the Enlightenment: Anarchists and the French Revolution, 1880–1914*, New York: Peter Lang, 2008, pp. 101–110. Lysander Spooner, *Natural Law or the Science of Justice: A Treatise on Natural Law, Natural Justice, Natural Rights, Natural Liberty and Natural Society, Showing That all Legislation Whatsoever is an Absurdity, a Usurpation, and a Crime*, Boston: A. Williams, 1882.

108 See e.g. the mystical anarchism of Peter Lamborn Wilson in his *Scandal: Essays in Islamic Heresy*, New York: Autonomedia, 1987. On the legal form of law's foreclosure, see e.g. Anika Lemaire, *Jacques Lacan*, Sprimont: Mardaga, 1977, pp. 281–282.

the double ouroboros: two serpents, endlessly consuming one another's tails, forming a circle.[109] It is certainly a vivid portrait of the horror of universal law which renders infinite justice indistinguishable from absolute violence. And since we as legal subjects are apparently still caught within this voracious circle, the best we seem to be able to do is renegotiate and expand the limited open area between the two laws again and again, doing the endless work of allegoresis.

Meanwhile, at the point where the two laws collide and produce double binds, a scream still rises. And Walter Raleigh has pointed out that one may discern it in *Paradise Lost*, more clearly than almost anywhere else:

> But in the midst of all this vast rivalry of interests and jar of opposed systems, a cry is heard [...]. It is the cry of the human soul, left homeless and derelict in a universe where she is the only alien. For her the amaranth of the empyreal Heaven is as comfortless as the adamant of Hell.[110]

But it may not only be the scream of a human soul "thrashing about in exasperation"[111] one can hear in *Paradise Lost*, but also that of the rest of creation, even the sound of Nature and of God himself, screaming into the tumultuous void: "What pleasure I from such obedience paid?" For moments, this scream can render perceptible the forces acting on an endless body, compulsively inflicting pain on itself in the name of transcendent justice.[112] It might be useful to listen intently to it, rather than to the edifying stories we like to tell ourselves about nature's trials.

109 The ouroboros has also been associated with misrule and with the paradisiacal serpent. See Hans-Werner Schütt, *Auf der Suche nach dem Stein der Weisen: Die Geschichte der Alchemie*, Munich: Beck, 2000, pp. 128–130. See also *Emblemata: Handbuch zur Sinnbildkunst des 16. und 17. Jahrhunderts*, ed. Arthur Henkel and Albrecht Schöne, Stuttgart and Weimar: Metzler, 1996, cols. 652–659.

110 Walter Raleigh, *Milton*, London: Edward Arnold, 1900, p. 118.

111 Empson, *Milton's God*, p. 115.

112 On the scream that renders perceptible a field of forces, see Gilles Deleuze, *Francis Bacon: The Logic of Sensation*, trans. Daniel W. Smith, London and New York: Continuum, 2003, pp. 60–61.

Bibliography

Achinstein, Sharon, *Milton and the Revolutionary Reader*, Princeton, NJ: Princeton University Press, 1994.

Achtner, Wolfgang, *Vom Erkennen zum Handeln: Die Dynamisierung von Mensch und Natur im ausgehenden Mittelalter als Voraussetzung für die Entstehung naturwissenschaftlicher Rationalität*, Göttingen: Vandenhoeck und Ruprecht, 2008.

Adamson, Peter, "State of Nature: Human and Cosmic Rulership in Ancient Philosophy", in *Menschennatur und politische Ordnung*, edited by Andreas Höfele and Beate Kellner, Paderborn: Wilhelm Fink, 2016.

Aeschylus, *Prometheus Bound*, in *Persians. Seven against Thebes. Suppliants. Prometheus Bound*, edited and translated by Alan H. Sommerstein, Cambridge, MA and London: Harvard University Press, 2008.

Agamben, Giorgio, *Die Beamten des Himmels: Über Engel. Gefolgt von der Angelologie des Thomas von Aquin*, translated by Andreas Hiepko, Frankfurt am Main: Verlag der Weltreligionen, 2007.

———, *Herrschaft und Herrlichkeit: Zur theologischen Genealogie von Ökonomie und Regierung*, translated by Andreas Hiepko, Frankfurt am Main: Suhrkamp, 2010.

———, *Homo Sacer: Sovereign Power and Bare Life*, translated by Daniel Heller-Roazen, Stanford, CA: Stanford University Press, 1998.

———, *The Time that Remains: A Commentary on the Letter to the Romans*, translated by Patricia Dailey, Stanford, CA: Stanford University Press, 2005.

Agnew, Jean-Christophe, *Worlds Apart: The Market and the Theater in Anglo-American Thought*, Cambridge: Cambridge University Press, 1986.

Alan of Lille, *De Planctu Naturae*, edited by Nikolaus M. Häring, Spoleto: Centro italiano di studi sull'alto medioevo, 1978.

———, *The Plaint of Nature*, translated by James J. Sheridan, Toronto: Pontifical Institute of Mediaeval Studies, 1980.

Allen, D. C., "Some Theories of the Growth and Origin of Language in Milton's Age", *Philological Quarterly* 28 (1949).

Almond, Philip C., *Adam and Eve in Seventeenth-Century Thought*, Cambridge and New York: Cambridge University Press, 1999.

Anaximander, "Fragment", in *Introductory Readings in Ancient Greek and Roman Philosophy*, edited by C. D. C. Reeve and Patrick L. Miller, Indianapolis: Hackett, 2006.

———, "Fragment 110", in *Die vorsokratischen Philosophen*, edited by G. S. Kirk, J. E. Raven and M. Schofield, translated by Karlheinz Hülser, Stuttgart and Weimar: J. B. Metzler, 2001.

Anderson, Charles A., *Philo of Alexandria's Views of the Physical World*, Tübingen: Mohr Siebeck, 2011.

Anselm of Canterbury, *Cur deus homo*, edited by F. S. Schmitt, Bonn: Hanstein, 1929.

———, *Why God Became Man*, in *The Major Works*, edited by Brian Davies and G. R. Evans, Oxford and New York: Oxford University Press, 1998.

Antiphon the Sophist, *The Fragments*, edited by Gerard J. Pendrick, Cambridge: Cambridge University Press, 2002.

Apollodorus, *The Library*, Vol. 1, translated by James George Frazer, London: Heineman and New York: Putnam's Sons, 1921.

Aquinas, Thomas, *De Physico Auditu*, in *In Aristotelis Stagiritae Nonnullos Libros Commentaria*, Parma: Petrus Fiaccadorus, 1865.

———, *On Love and Charity: Readings from the Commentary on the Sentences of Peter Lombard*, Washington, DC: Catholic University of America Press, 2008.

———, *Summa Contra Gentiles/Summe gegen die Heiden*, Vol. 3.2, edited and translated by Karl Allgaier, Darmstadt: Wissenschaftliche Buchgesellschaft, 1996.

———, *Summa Theologica: Die deutsche Thomas-Ausgabe,* Vol. 26: *Supplement, Quaestiones 87–99*, translated by Dominicans and Benedictines of Germany and Austria, Heidelberg: Kerle and Cologne: Styria, 1961.

———, *Summa Theologica: Die deutsche Thomas-Ausgabe,* Vol. 32: *Supplement, Quaestiones 17–40*, translated by Dominicans and Benedictines of Germany and Austria, Graz [etc.]: Styria, 1985.

———, *Summa Theologiae Prima Pars, 1–49*, Latin/English Edition, translated by Laurence Shapcote, Lander, WY: Aquinas Institute, 2012.

———, *Summa Theologiae Prima Pars, 50–119*, Latin/English Edition, translated by Laurence Shapcote, Lander, WY: Aquinas Institute, 2012.

———, *Summa Theologiae Prima Secundae, 71–114*, Latin/English Edition, translated by Laurence Shapcote, Lander, WY: Aquinas Institute, 2012.

———, *Summa Theologiae Secunda Secundae, 1–91*, Latin/English Edition, translated by Laurence Shapcote, Lander, WY: Aquinas Institute, 2012.

———, *Summa Theologiae Tertia Pars, 60–90*, Latin/English Edition, translated by Laurence Shapcote, Lander, WY: Aquinas Institute, 2012.

———, *Über die Herrschaft der Fürsten*, translated by Friedrich Schreyvogl, Stuttgart: Reclam, 1990.

Arendt, Hannah, "Approaches to the German Problem", in *Essays in Understanding: 1930–1954*, edited by Jerome Kohn, New York: Harcourt, Brace and Co., 1994.

———, *Between Past and Future: Six Exercises in Political Thought*, New York: Viking, 1961.

———, *The Human Condition:* Second Edition, Chicago and London: University of Chicago Press, 1998.

———, *Der Liebesbegriff bei Augustin: Versuch einer philosophischen Interpretation*, Olms: Hildesheim, 2006.

———, *The Origins of Totalitarianism*, San Diego and New York: Harcourt, 1985.

———, *The Promise of Politics*, edited by Jerome Kohn, New York: Schocken, 2005.

———, *Vita activa oder vom tätigen Leben*, Munich and Zurich: Piper, 1987.

———, *Zur Zeit: Politische Essays*, translated by Eike Geisel, edited by Marie Luise Knott, Berlin: Rotbuch, 1986.

Aristotle, *The Art of Rhetoric*, translated by John Henry Freese, Cambridge, MA: Harvard University Press and London: Heinemann, 1967.

———, *Generation of Animals*, translated by A. L. Peck, Cambridge, MA: Harvard University Press and London: Heinemann, 1943.

———, *The Metaphysics*, translated by Hugh Tredennick, Cambridge, MA: Harvard University Press and London: Heinemann, 1961.

———, *The Nicomachean Ethics*, translated by H. Rackham, Cambridge, MA: Harvard University Press and London: Heinemann, 1962.

———, *Parts of Animals/Movement of Animals/Progression of Animals*, translated by A. L. Peck and E. S. Foster, London: Heinemann and Cambridge, MA: Harvard University Press, 1956.

———, *The Physics*, translated by Philip H. Wicksteed and Francis Cornford, Cambridge, MA: Harvard University Press and London: Heinemann, 1963.

———, *Poetik*, translated by Manfred Fuhrmann, Stuttgart: Reclam, 1994.

———, *Poetics*, translated by Stephen Halliwell, in id., *Poetics*, Longinus, *On the Sublime*, Demetrius, *On Style*, Cambridge, MA: Harvard University Press, 1999.

———, *Politics*, translated by H. Rackham, Cambridge, MA: Harvard University Press and London: Heinemann, 1944.

———, *The Art of Rhetoric*, translated by John Henry Freese, Cambridge, MA: Harvard University Press and London: Heinemann, 1967.

Armogathe, Jean-Robert, "Deus Legislator", in *Natural Law and Laws of Nature in Early Modern Europe: Jurisprudence, Theology, Moral and Natural Philosophy*, edited by Lorraine Daston and Michael Stolleis, Farnham and Burlington, VT: Ashgate, 2008.

Arndt, Johann and Anne-Charlott Trepp, "Natural Order and Divine Salvation: Protestant Conceptions in Early Modern Germany (1550–1750)", in *Natural Law and Laws of Nature in Early Modern Europe: Jurisprudence, Theology, Moral and Natural Philosophy*, edited by Lorraine Daston and Michael Stolleis, Farnham and Burlington, VT: Ashgate, 2008.

Auerbach, Erich, *Mimesis: Dargestellte Wirklichkeit in der abendländischen Literatur*, Tübingen and Basel: Francke, 2001.

———, *Mimesis: The Representation of Reality in Western Literature*, translated by Willard Trask, Princeton, NJ: Princeton University Press, 1953.

Augustine, *The City of God Against the Pagans*, edited and translated by R. W. Dyson, Cambridge and New York: Cambridge University Press, 1998.

———, *Concerning the City of God Against the Pagans*, translated by Henry Bettenson, London and New York: Penguin, 2003.

———, *Confessions*, Vol. 2, translated by William Watts, London and New York: Heineman and Macmillan, 1912.

———, *De Trinitate (Bücher VIII–XI, XIV–XV)*, edited by Johann Kreuzer, Hamburg: Meiner, 2001.

———, *Der Gottesstaat/De Civitate Dei*, Vol. 2, translated by Carl Johann Perl, Paderborn: Ferdinand Schöningh, 1979.

———, *Logik des Schreckens: die Gnadenlehre von 397*, translated and edited by Kurt Flasch, Mainz: Dieterich, 1990.

———, *On Genesis*, in *Works* 1.13, translated by Edmund Hill, edited by John E. Rotelle, Hyde Park, NY: New City Press, 2002.

Aylmer, G. E., *The State's Servants: The Civil Service of the English Republic: 1649–1660*, London and Boston: Routledge and Kegan Paul, 1973.

Bacon, Francis, *The Advancement of Learning*, in *The Major Works*, edited by Brian Vickers, Oxford and New York: Oxford University Press, 2008.

———, "The Case of Impeachment of Waste", in *The Works*, Vol. 7, edited by James Spedding, Robert Leslie Ellis and Douglas Denon Heath, London: Longman [etc.], 1861.

———, *Neues Organon, Lateinisch-deutsch*, edited by Wolfgang Krohn, Hamburg: Meiner, 1999.

———, *New Atlantis and The Great Instauration*, edited by Jerry Weinberger, Arlington Heights, IL: H. Davidson, 1989.

———, *The New Organon*, edited by Lisa Jardine and Michael Silverthorne, Cambridge and New York: Cambridge University Press, 2000.

———, *Of the Dignity and Advancement of Learning*, in *The Works*, Vol. 4, edited by James Spedding, Robert Leslie Ellis and Douglas Denon Heath, London: Longman [etc.], 1858.

———, *Valerius Terminus: Of the Interpretation of Nature*, in *The Works*, Vol. 3, edited by James Spedding, Robert Leslie Ellis and Douglas Denon Heath, London: Longman [etc.], 1854.

Baker, John Hamilton, *An Introduction to English Legal History*, London: Butterworths, 1979.

Barbour, Julian B., *The Discovery of Dynamics: A Study from a Machian Point of View of the Discovery and the Structure of Dynamical Theories*, Oxford: Oxford University Press, 2001.

Barmeyer, Eike, *Die Musen: Ein Beitrag zur Inspirationstheorie*, Munich: Wilhelm Fink, 1968.

Barnett, Pamela R., *Theodore Haak, F. R. S. (1605–1690): The First German Translator of Paradise Lost*, The Hague: Mouton, 1962.

Bartelmus, Rüdiger, "Šāmayim", in *Theological Dictionary of the Old Testament*, Vol. 15, edited by G. Johannes Botterweck, Helmer Ringgren and Heinz-Josef Fabry, translated by David E. Green, Grand Rapids, MI and Cambridge: Eerdmans, 2006.

Basil of Caesarea, *The Hexaemeron*, in *Letters and Select Works*, *Nicene and Post-Nicene Fathers:* Second Series, Vol. 8, edited by Philip Schaff and Henry Wallace, New York: Cosimo, 2007.

———, *Homilien zum Hexameron*, New Series, *Die griechischen christlichen Schriftsteller der ersten Jahrhunderte*, Vol. 2, edited by Emmanuel Amand de Mendieta and Stig Y. Rudberg, Berlin: Akademie, 1997.

Bateson, Gregory, *Steps to an Ecology of Mind: Collected Essays in Anthropology, Psychiatry, Evolution, and Epistemology*, Chicago and London: University of Chicago Press, 2000.

Bede the Venerable, *Commentary on Genesis: Book 1*, in *Ancient Christian Texts: Commentaries on Genesis 1–3*, translated by Carmen Hardin, edited by Michael Glerup, Downer Grove, IL: IVP Academic, 2010.

Benet, Diana Treviño, "'All in All': The Threat of Bliss", in *"All in All": Unity, Diversity, and the Miltonic Perspective*, edited by Charles W. Durham and Kristin Pruitt McColgan, Selinsgrove, PA and London: Susquehanna University Press and Associated University Press, 1999.

Benjamin, Walter, "An Werner Kraft", 12 November 1934, in *Briefe*, Vol. 2, edited by Gershom Scholem and Theodor W. Adorno, Frankfurt am Main: Suhrkamp, 1978.

———, "Critique of Violence", translated by Edmund Jephcott, in *Selected Writings*, Vol. 1, edited by Marcus Bullock and Michael Jennings et al., Cambridge, MA: Belknap Press, 1996.

———, "Fate and Character", translated by Edmund Jephcott, in *Selected Writings*, Vol. 1, edited by Marcus Bullock, Michael Jennings et al., Cambridge, MA: Belknap Press, 1996.

———, *The Origin of German Tragic Drama*, translated by John Osborne, London: Verso, 1998.

———, *Ursprung des deutschen Trauerspiels*, in *Gesammelte Schriften*, Vol. 1, edited by Rolf Tiedemann, Frankfurt am Main: Suhrkamp, 1977.

Bentley, Richard, "Emendations to *Paradise Lost*", in *John Milton: The Critical Heritage,* Vol. 2: *1732–1801*, edited by John T. Shawcross, London: Routledge, 1995.

———, *The Works, Vol. 3, Theological Writings*, edited by Alexander Dyce, London: Macpherson, 1838.

Berkenbusch, Gisela, *Zum Heulen: Kulturgeschichte unserer Tränen*, Berlin: Transit, 1985.

Bernstorff, Jochen von, *The Public International Law Theory of Hans Kelsen: Believing in Universal Law*, translated by Thomas Dunlap, Cambridge: Cambridge University Press, 2010.

Bezio, Kristin M. S., *Staging Power in Tudor and Stuart English History Plays: History, Political Thought, and the Redefinition of Sovereignty*, Farnham: Ashgate, 2015.

Bianchi, Emanuela, *The Feminine Symptom: Aleatory Matter in the Aristotelian Cosmos*, New York: Fordham University Press, 2014.

Blake, William, "A Vision of The Last Judgment", in *The Complete Poetry and Prose*, edited by David V. Erdman, New York: Doubleday, 1988.

———, "The Marriage of Heaven and Hell", in *The Complete Poetry and Prose*, edited by David V. Erdman, New York: Doubleday, 1988.

Bloom, Harold, *The Anatomy of Influence: Literature as a Way of Life*, New Haven, CT: Yale University Press, 2011.

———, "Introduction", in *John Milton: Bloom's Modern Critical Views*, edited by Harold Bloom, New York and Philadelphia: Chelsea House, 2004.

———, *A Map of Misreading*, Oxford and New York: Oxford University Press, 2003.

Blumenberg, Hans, *Arbeit am Mythos*, Frankfurt am Main: Suhrkamp, 2006.

———, *Ästhetische und metaphorologische Schriften*, edited by Anselm Haverkamp, Frankfurt am Main: Suhrkamp, 2001.

———, "'Imitation of Nature': Toward a Prehistory of the Idea of the Creative Being", translated Anna Wertz, *Qui Parle* 12:1 (2000).

———, *Geistesgeschichte der Technik*, Frankfurt am Main: Suhrkamp, 2009.

———, *The Genesis of the Copernican World*, translated by Robert M. Wallace, Cambridge, MA: MIT Press, 1987.

———, *The Legitimacy of the Modern Age*, translated by Robert M. Wallace, Cambridge, MA: MIT Press, 1985.

———, *Die Legitimität der Neuzeit*, Frankfurt am Main: Suhrkamp, 1996.

———, *Die Lesbarkeit der Welt*, Frankfurt am Main: Suhrkamp, 1986.

———, *Paradigmen zu einer Metaphorologie*, Frankfurt am Main: Suhrkamp, 1998.

———, *Paradigms for a Metaphorology*, translated by Robert Savage, Ithaca, NY: Cornell University Press, 2010.

———, *Work on Myth*, translated by Robert M. Wallace, Cambridge, MA: MIT Press, 1990.

Bobbio, Norberto, *Thomas Hobbes and the Natural Law Tradition*, Chicago: University of Chicago Press, 1993.

Bodenheimer, Aron Ronald, *Warum? Von der Obszönität des Fragens*, Stuttgart: Reclam, 1984.

Bodmer, Johann Jacob, *Critische Abhandlung von dem Wunderbaren in der Poesie und dessen Verbindung mit dem Wahrscheinlichen*, Zurich: Conrad Orell, 1740.

Böhme, Jakob, *Beschreibung der drey Principien göttlichen Wesens*, Amsterdam: Betkio, 1660.

———, *Der Weg zu Christo*, Amsterdam: n.p., 1682.

Boethius, *Consolatio Philosophiae/Trost der Philosophie*, edited and translated by Ernst Gegenschatz and Olof Gigon, Zurich: Artemis und Winkler, 2004.

———, *The Theological Tractates: The Consolation of Philosophy*, translated by H. F. Stewart and E. K. Rand, London: Heinemann, 1973.

Bohlender, Matthias, *Die Rhetorik des Politischen. Zur Kritik der politischen Theorie*, Berlin: Akademie, 1995.

Boileau, Nicolas, "L'Art poétique", in *Art poétique, épîtres, poesies diverses, odes, et epigrammes*, edited by Sylvain Menant, Paris: Flammarion, 1969.

Bonta, Mark and John Protevi, *Deleuze and Geophilosophy: A Guide and Glossary*, Edinburgh: Edinburgh University Press, 2006.

Booth, Wayne C., *A Rhetoric of Irony*, Chicago and London: University of Chicago Press, 1975.

Borris, Kenneth, *Allegory and Epic in English Renaissance Literature: Heroic Form in Sidney, Spenser, and Milton*, Cambridge and New York: Cambridge University Press, 2000.

Borzeszkowski, Horst-Heino und Renate Wahsner, *Die Natur technisch denken? Zur Synthese von* technē *und* physis *in der Newtonschen Mechanik oder das Verhältnis von praktischer und theoretischer Mechanik in Newtons Physik*, Berlin: Max-Planck-Institut für Wissenschaftsgeschichte/Preprint, 1998.

Boyle, Robert, *The Excellency of Theology Compared with Natural Philosophy*, in *The Works*, Vol. 4, edited by Thomas Birch, London: J. and F. Rivington [etc.], 1777.

———, *A Free Enquiry into the Vulgarly Received Notion of Nature*, edited by Edward B. Davis and Michael Hunter, Cambridge: Cambridge University Press, 1996.

Brague, Rémi, *The Law of God: The Philosophical History of an Idea*, translated by Lydia G. Cochrane, Chicago: University of Chicago Press, 2007.

Bremer, Dieter, "Von der Physis zur Natur: Eine griechische Konzeption und ihr Schicksal", *Zeitschrift für philosophische Forschung* 43:2 (1989).

Brommer, Frank, "Pan", in *Paulys Realencyclopädie der classischen Altertumswissenschaft*, Supplementband 8, edited by Konrat Ziegler, Munich: Druckenmüller, 1956.

Brundage, James, "Sin, Crime, and the Pleasures of the Flesh: The Medieval Church Judges Sexual Offences", in *The Medieval World*, edited by Peter Linehan and Janet L. Nelson, London and New York: Routledge, 2003.

Bruno, Giordano, *Von der Ursache, dem Prinzip und dem Einen*, translated by Adolf Lasson, Hamburg: Meiner, 1983.

Buchanan, Ian, *Deleuze and Guattari's* Anti-Oedipus*: A Reader's Guide*, London and New York: Continuum, 2008.

Buci-Glucksmann, Christine, *Baroque Reason: The Aesthetics of Modernity*, London and Thousand Oaks, CA: Sage Publications, 1994.

Budick, Sanford, *The Dividing Muse: Images of Sacred Disjunction in Milton's Poetry*, New Haven, CT: Yale University Press, 1985.

———, *Kant and Milton*, Cambridge, MA: Harvard University Press, 2010.

Burckhardt, Sigurd, *Shakespearean Meanings*, Princeton, NJ: Princeton University Press, 1968.

Burke, Peter, *The Fabrication of Louis XIV*, New Haven, CT: Yale University Press, 1992.

Burns, Tony, *Aristotle and Natural Law*, London and New York: Continuum, 2011.

———, "Sophocles' *Antigone* and the History of the Concept of Natural Law", *Political Studies* 50:3 (2002).

Butler, Judith, *Antigone's Claim: Kinship Between Life and Death*, New York: Columbia University Press, 2000.

Cain, William E., "Reflections on the Milton Industry", *Modern Language Notes* 96:5 (1981).

Calloway, Katherine, "'His Footstep Trace': The Natural Theology of *Paradise Lost*", *Milton Studies* 55 (2014).

Calvin, John, *Institutes of the Christian Religion*, translated by Ford Lewis Battles, edited by John T. McNeill, Louisville, KY: Westminster John Knox Press, 2006.

———, *Institutio Christianae Religionis in Libros Quattuor*, Geneva: Robert Estienne, 1559.

Campbell, Gordon and Thomas N. Corns, *John Milton: Life, Work and Thought*, Oxford: Oxford University Press, 2008.

Campbell, Gordon, Thomas N. Corns, John K. Hale and Fiona J. Tweedie, *Milton and the Manuscript of* De Doctrina Christiana, Oxford: Oxford University Press, 2007.

Carey, John, *Milton*, London: Evans Brothers, 1969.

Carlyle, Thomas, "Shakespeare", in *Selections*, edited by A. H. R. Ball, Cambridge: Cambridge University Press, 2014.

Chapman, Alison A., *The Legal Epic:* Paradise Lost *and the Early Modern Law*, Chicago and London: University of Chicago Press, 2017.

Charlesworth, James, "The Symbology of the Serpent in the Gospel of John", in *John, Jesus, and History,* Vol. 2: *Aspects of Historicity in the Fourth Gospel*, edited by Paul N. Anderson, Felix Just, and Tom Thatcher, Atlanta, GA: Society of Biblical Literature, 2009.

Chaucer, Geoffrey, *The Parliament of Fowls*, in *Dream Visions and Other Poems*, edited by Kathryn L. Lynch, New York and London, W. W. Norton and Co., 2007.

Chester, Robert, *Love's Martyr or Rosalin's Complaint*, edited by Alexander B. Grosart, London: Trubner, 1878.

Cicero, Marcus Tulius, *Cato Maior*, in *Cato Maior und Laelius, Lateinisch-deutsch*, edited by Rainer Nickel, Berlin: Akademie, 2011.

———, *De Natura Deorum*, in *De Natura Deorum/Academica*, translated by Harris Rackham, Cambridge, MA: Harvard University Press and London: Heinemann, 1967.

———, *De Natura Deorum/Über das Wesen der Götter: Lateinisch/Deutsch*, translated and edited by Ursula Blank-Sagemeister, Stuttgart: Reclam, 1995.

———, *De Re Publica/The Republic*, in *De Re Publica/De Legibus*, translated by C. W. Keyes, Cambridge, MA: Harvard University Press, 1943.

———, *On the Laws*, in *On the Republic/On the Laws*, translated by C. W. Keyes, Cambridge, MA and London: Harvard University Press, 2000.

Claudian, *On Stilicho's Consulship*, in *Works*, Vol. 2, edited by Maurice Platnauer, Cambridge, MA and London: Harvard University Press, 1922.

Clay, Jenny Strauss, *Hesiod's Cosmos*, Cambridge: Cambridge University Press, 2003.

———, *The Wrath of Athena: Gods and Men in the* Odyssey, London: Rowman and Littlefield, 1997.

Cohen, Esther, *The Modulated Scream: Pain in Late Medieval Culture*, Chicago: University of Chicago Press, 2010.

Cohen, Jeremy, *Be Fertile and Increase, Fill the Earth and Master It: The Ancient and Medieval Career of a Biblical Text*, Ithaca, NY: Cornell University Press, 1989.

Colebrook, Claire, *Milton, Evil and Literary History*, London and New York: Continuum, 2008.

Coleridge, Samuel Taylor, *Biographia Literaria*, in *The Major Works*, edited by H. J. Jackson, Oxford and New York: Oxford University Press, 2000.

Colish, Marcia L., *Medieval Foundations of the Western Intellectual Tradition 400–1400*, New Haven: Yale University Press, 1997.

———, *The Stoic Tradition from Antiquity to the Early Middle Ages,* Vol. 1: *Stoicism in Classical Latin Literature*, Leiden: Brill, 1990.

———, *The Stoic Tradition from Antiquity to the Early Middle Ages,* Vol. 2: *Stoicism in Christian Latin Thought Through the Sixth Century*, Leiden: Brill, 1990.

Collier, John, *Milton's* Paradise Lost*: Screenplay for Cinema of the Mind*, New York: Alfred A. Knopf, 1973.

Collins, Jeffrey R., *The Allegiance of Thomas Hobbes*, Oxford and New York: Oxford University Press, 2005.

Condren, Conal, *Argument and Authority in Early Modern England: The Presupposition of Oaths and Offices*, Cambridge: Cambridge University Press, 2006.

Conquest, Robert, *The Great Terror: A Reassessment*, Oxford and New York: Oxford University Press, 2008.

Cook, Arthur B., *Zeus: A Study in Ancient Religion*, Cambridge: Cambridge University Press, 1925.

Copernicus, Nicolaus, *De revolutionibus I*, in *Das neue Weltbild, Lateinisch-Deutsch*, Hamburg: Meiner, 1990.

Coquillette, Daniel R., *Francis Bacon*, Stanford, CA: Stanford University Press, 1992.

Cornford, F. M., *From Religion to Philosophy: A Study in the Origins of Western Speculation*, Princeton, NJ: Princeton University Press, 1991.

Corns, Thomas, *Regaining* Paradise Lost, London and New York: Longman 1994.

Courtenay, William J., *Capacity and Volition: A History of the Distinction of Absolute and Ordained Power*, Bergamo: P. Lubrina, 1990.

Cross, Richard, *The Metaphysics of the Incarnation: Thomas Aquinas to Duns Scotus*, New York and Oxford: Oxford University Press, 2002.

———, "Natural Law, Moral Constructivism, and Duns Scotus's Metaethics: The Centrality of Aesthetic Explanation", in *Reason, Religion, and Natural Law: From Plato to Spinoza*, edited by Jonathan A. Jacobs, Oxford and New York: Oxford University Press, 2012.

Crowe, Michael Bertram, *The Changing Profile of the Natural Law*, The Hague: Nijhoff, 1977.

Crowe, Michael J., "Extraterrestrial Intelligence", in *History of Astronomy: An Encyclopedia*, edited by John Lankford, New York and London: Garland, 1997.

Curtius, Ernst Robert, *Europäische Literatur und lateinisches Mittelalter: Götter – Menschen – Rituale*, Bern and Munich: Francke, 1965.

———, *European Literature and the Latin Middle Ages*, translated by Willard R. Trask, Princeton, NJ: Princeton University Press, 2013.

———, "Die Musen im Mittelalter, Erster Teil: Bis 1100", *Zeitschrift für romanische Philologie* 59:1 (1939).

Damaška, Mirjan R., *The Faces of Justice and State Authority: A Comparative Approach to the Legal Process*, New Haven, CT: Yale University Press, 1986.

Danielson, Dennis Richard, Paradise Lost *and the Cosmological Revolution*, Cambridge and New York: Cambridge University Press, 2014.

Dante Alighieri, *Inferno*, translated by Jean Hollander and Robert Hollander, New York: Random House, 2000.

———, *Paradiso*, translated by Jean Hollander and Robert Hollander, New York: Random House, 2007.

———, *Purgatorio*, translated by Jean Hollander and Robert Hollander, New York: Random House, 2003.

Darbishire, Helen, *The Early Lives of Milton*, London: Constable and Co., 1932.

Daston, Lorraine and Fernando Vidal, "Doing What Comes Naturally", in *The Moral Authority of Nature*, edited by Lorraine Daston and Fernando Vidal, Chicago and London: University of Chicago Press, 2004.

———, and Katharine Park, *Wonders and the Order of Nature, 1150–1750*, New York: Zone Books and Cambridge, MA: MIT Press, 1998.

Davis, Rebecca, Piers Plowman *and the Books of Nature*, Oxford: Oxford University Press 2017.

De Bèze, Théodore, *Tractationes Theologicae*, Vol. 1, Geneva: Crispinum, 1570.

Deitz, Luc, "Einleitung zum ersten Buch", in *Poetices libri septem: Sieben Bücher über die Dichtkunst*, Vol. 1, by Julius Caesar Scalinger, edited by Luc Deitz and Gregor Vogt-Spira, Stuttgart-Bad Cannstatt: Frommann-Holzboog, 1994.

Deleuze, Gilles, *Critique et clinique*, Paris: Minuit, 1990.

———, *Francis Bacon: The Logic of Sensation*, translated by Daniel W. Smith, London and New York: Continuum, 2003.

Deleuze, Gilles and Félix Guattari, *Anti-Oedipus: Capitalism and Schizophrenia*, translated by Robert Hurley, Helen R. Lane and Mark Seem, Minneapolis: University of Minnesota Press, 1983.

———, *Mille Plateaux*, Paris: Éditions de Minuit, 1980.

———, *A Thousand Plateaus*, translated by Brian Massumi, Minneapolis and London: University of Minnesota Press, 2005.

———, *What is Philosophy?*, translated by Hugh Tomlinson and Graham Burchell, New York: Columbia University Press, 1994.

Della Mirandola, Giovanni Pico, *Oration on the Dignity of Man*, edited by Francesco Borghesi, Michael Papio and Massimo Riva, New York: Cambridge University Press, 2012.

Delumeau, Jean, *Une histoire du paradis,* Vol. 1: *Le jardin des délices*, Paris: Fayard, 1992.

———, *Une histoire du paradis,* Vol. 2: *Mille ans de bonheur*, Paris: Fayard, 1995.

De Mundo, translated by E. S. Forster, Oxford: Clarendon Press, 1914.

Derrida, Jacques, "Before the Law", in *Acts of Literature*, edited by Derek Attridge, New York: Routledge, 1992.

———, "Khōra", in *The Derrida Reader: Writing Performances*, translated by Ian McLeod, edited by Julian Wolfreys, Lincoln: University of Nebraska Press, 1998.

Descartes, René, *Correspondance avec Arnauld et Morus*, edited by Geneviève Lewis, Paris: J. Vrin, 1953.

———, *The Philosophical Writings, Vol. 3: The Correspondence*, translated by John Cottingham, Robert Stoothoff, Dugald Murdoch and Anthony Kenny, Cambridge: Cambridge University Press, 1991.

———, *Principia Philosophiae*, Amsterdam: Elsevier, 1644.

Des Chene, Dennis, "Forms of Art in Jesuit Aristotelianism (with a Coda on Descartes)", in *The Artificial and the Natural*, edited by Bernadette Bensaude-Vincent and William R. Newman, Cambridge, MA: MIT Press, 2007.

———, *Physiologia: Natural Philosophy in Late Aristotelian and Cartesian Thought*, Ithaca, NY and London: Cornell University Press, 1996.

Dietrich, B. C., "The Judgment of Zeus", *Rheinisches Museum für Philologie* N. F. 117 (1964).

Diogenes Laertius, *Leben und Meinungen berühmter Philosophen*, translated by Otto Apelt and Hans Günter Zekl, edited by Klaus Reich, Hamburg: Meiner, 2015.

Dixon, Thomas, *From Passions to Emotions: The Creation of a Secular Psychological Category*, Cambridge and New York: Cambridge University Press, 2003.

Donnelly, Phillip J., "'Matter' versus 'Body': The Character of Milton's Monism", *Milton Quarterly* 33:3 (1999).

Douglas, Mary, *Purity and Danger: An Analysis of the Concepts of Pollution and Taboo*, London and New York: Routledge, 2003.

Dreier, Ralf, *Zum Begriff der "Natur der Sache"*, Berlin: Walter de Gruyter, 1965.

Drozdek, Adam, *Greek Philosophers as Theologians: The Divine* Arche, Aldershot and Burlington, VT: Ashgate, 2007.

Drummond, C. Q., *In Defence of Adam: Essays on Bunyan, Milton and Others*, edited by John Baxter and Gordon Harvey, Norfolk: Brynmill Press/Edgeway Books, 2004.

Du Bartas, Guillaume, *La Sepmaine ou Création du Monde*, Paris: Pour Michel Gadouleau, 1583.

Dumézil, Georges, *The Destiny of a King*, translated by Alf Hiltebeitel, Chicago and London: University of Chicago Press, 1973.

Duran, Angelica, *A Concise Companion to Milton*, Oxford and Malden, MA: Blackwell, 2007.

Durkheim, Émile, *The Division of Labour in Society*, translated by W. D. Halls, Basingstoke and London: Macmillan, 1984.

Durston, Christopher, *Charles I*, London and New York: Routledge, 1998.

Eco, Umberto, *The Search for the Perfect Language*, translated by James Fentress, Malden, MA and Oxford: Blackwell, 1995.

Economou, George D., *The Goddess Natura in Medieval Literature*, Cambridge, MA: Harvard University Press, 1972.

Edwards, Karen, "Milton's Reformed Animals: An Early Modern Bestiary, D–F", *Milton Quarterly* 40:2 (2006).

Elledge, C. D., *Resurrection of the Dead in Early Judaism, 200 BCE–CE 200*, Oxford: Oxford University Press, 2017.

Éluard, Paul, *Capitale de la douleur*, Paris: Gallimard, 1966.

Elwood, Christopher, *The Body Broken: The Calvinist Doctrine of the Eucharist and the Symbolization of Power in Sixteenth-Century France*, Oxford and New York: Oxford University Press, 1999.

Emblemata: Handbuch zur Sinnbildkunst des 16. und 17. Jahrhunderts, edited by Arthur Henkel and Albrecht Schöne, Stuttgart and Weimar: Metzler, 1996.

Empson, William, "Donne the Space Man", in *Essays on Renaissance Literature*, Vol. 1: *Donne and the New Philosophy*, edited by John Haffenden, Cambridge and New York: Cambridge University Press, 1993.

———, "Donne in the New Edition", in *Essays on Renaissance Literature,* Vol. 1: *Donne and the New Philosophy,* edited by John Haffenden, Cambridge and New York: Cambridge University Press, 1993.

———, *Milton's God,* Westport, CT: Greenwood Press, 1978.

———, *Seven Types of Ambiguity*, New York: New Directions, 1947.

———, *Some Versions of Pastoral*, New York: New Directions, 1974.

Erbse, Hartmut, *Untersuchungen zur Funktion der Götter im homerischen Epos*, Berlin and New York: Walter de Gruyter, 1986.

Eriugena, John Scotus, *Expositiones super Ierarchiam caelestem S. Dionysii*, in *Opera*, Vol. 1, edited by Heinrich Joseph Floss, Paris: Migne, 1865.

———, *Divisione della Natura*, edited and translated by Nicola Gorlani, Milan: Bompiani, 2013.

Esterhammer, Angela, *Creating States: Studies in the Performative Language of John Milton and William Blake*, Toronto: University of Toronto Press, 1994.

Euripides, *Bacchae*, in *Bacchae/Iphigenia at Aulis/Rhesus*, edited and translated by David Kovacs, Cambridge, MA: Harvard University Press, 2002.

———, *Fragments: Aegeus-Meleager*, edited and translated by Christopher Collard and Martin Cropp, Cambridge, MA: Harvard University Press, 2008.

Eusebios of Caesarea, *La préparation évangelique*, Livre VII, translated by Guy Schroeder, Paris, 1975.

Evans, E. P., *The Criminal Prosecution and Capital Punishment of Animals*, New York: E. P. Dutton, 1906.

Evans, J. Martin, *Milton's Imperial Epic:* Paradise Lost *and the Discourse of Colonialism*, Ithaca, NY: Cornell University Press, 1996.

Fallon, Robert Thomas, *Divided Empire: Milton's Political Imagery*, University Park: Pennsylvania State University Press, 1995.

Fallon, Stephen M., *Milton Among the Philosophers: Poetry and Materialism in Seventeenth-Century England*, Ithaca, NY: Cornell University Press, 1991.

———, *Milton's Peculiar Grace: Self-Representation and Authority*, Ithaca, NY: Cornell University Press, 2007.

Fermi, Laura and Gilberto Bernardini, *Galileo and the Scientific Revolution*, New York: Basic Books, 1961.

Fernández-Santamaría, J. A., *Natural Law, Constitutionalism, Reason of State, and War: Counter-Reformation Spanish Political Thought*, Vol. 2, New York: Peter Lang, 2006.

Festa, Thomas, "God as Geometer and Architect in *Paradise Lost*", in *Their Maker's Image: New Essays on John Milton*, edited by Mary C. Fenton and Louis Schwartz, Selinsgrove, PA: Susquehanna University Press, 2011.

Fiaschi, Giovanni, "The Power of Words: Political and Theological Science in Thomas Hobbes", *Hobbes Studies* 26 (2013).

Ficino, Marsilio, *All Things Natural: Ficino on Plato's* Timaeus, translated by Arthur Farndell, London: Shepheard-Walwyn, 2010.

Fish, Stanley E., *How Milton Works*, Cambridge, MA: Belknap Press of Harvard University Press, 2001.

———, *Surprised By Sin: The Reader in* Paradise Lost, Cambridge, MA: Harvard University Press, 1997.

Flannagan, Roy, *John Milton: A Short Introduction*, Oxford and Malden, MA: Blackwell, 2002.

Flasch, Kurt, "Ars imitatur naturam: Platonischer Naturbegriff und mittelalterliche Philosophie der Kunst", in *Parusia: Studien zur Philosophie Platons und zur*

Problemgeschichte des Platonismus: Festgabe für Johannes Hirschberger, edited by Kurt Flasch, Frankfurt am Main: Minerva, 1965.

Flaxman, Gregory, *Gilles Deleuze and the Fabulation of Philosophy: Powers of the False,* Vol. 1, Minneapolis and London: University of Minnesota Press, 2012.

Foljanty, Lena, *Recht oder Gesetz: Juristische Identität und Autorität in den Naturrechtsdebatten der Nachkriegszeit*, Tübingen: Mohr Siebeck, 2013.

Forsyth, Neil, Review of *The Ruins of Allegory: Paradise Lost and the Metamorphosis of Epic Convention*, by Catherine Gimelli Martin, *International Journal for the Classical Tradition* 7:3 (2001).

———, *The Satanic Epic*, Princeton, NJ: Princeton University Press, 2003.

Fortescue, John, *De Natura Legis Naturae*, in *Works*, edited by Thomas Fortescue, Lord Claremont, London: Private, 1869.

Foucault, Michel, *Abnormal: Lectures at the Collège de France, 1974–1975*, translated by Graham Burchell, edited by Valerio Marchetti and Antonella Salomoni, New York: Picador, 2003.

———, *Discipline and Punish: The Birth of the Prison*, translated by Alan Sheridan, New York: Vintage Books, 1979.

———, *Security, Territory, Population: Lectures at the Collège de France, 1977–78*, translated by Graham Burchell, edited by Michel Senellart, François Ewald and Alessandro Fontana, Basingstoke and New York: Palgrave Macmillan, 2007.

Frank, Joseph, "John Milton's Movement Toward Deism", *Journal of British Studies* 1:1 (1961).

Fresh, Cheryl, "Milton and Blake: Visualizing the Expulsion", in *"All in All": Unity, Diversity and the Miltonic Perspective*, edited by Charles W. Durham and Kristin A. Pruitt, Selinsgrove, PA: Susquehanna University Press, 1999.

Freud, Sigmund, *Aus der Geschichte einer infantilen Neurose*, in *Zwei Krankengeschichten*, Frankfurt am Main: Fischer, 1996.

———, *The Interpretation of Dreams*, in *The Standard Edition of the Complete Psychological Works*, Vol. 4, edited and translated by James Strachey, London: Hogarth Press, 1953.

———, *Totem und Tabu: Einige Übereinstimmungen im Seelenleben der Wilden und der Neurotiker*, Stuttgart: Fischer, 1991.

———, *Die Traumdeutung*, Frankfurt am Main: Fischer, 1991.

Friedman, Richard Elliott, *Commentary on the Torah with a New English Translation*, San Francisco and New York: HarperSanFrancisco, 2001.

Friedrich, Hugo, *Die Rechtsmetaphysik der Göttlichen Komödie*, Frankfurt am Main: V. Klostermann, 1942.

Galilei, Galileo, *Dialogues Concerning Two New Sciences*, translated by Henry Crew and Alfonso de Salvio, New York: Cosimo Classics, 2010.

———, *Opere*, Vols. 5 and 6, edited by Antonio Favaro, Florence: Barbèra, 1968.

Genette, Gérard, *Narrative Discourse: An Essay in Method*, translated by Jane E. Lewin, Ithaca, NY: Cornell University Press, 1980.

Goldman, Emma, "Anarchism: What It Really Stands For", in *The Political Theory Reader*, edited by Paul Schumaker, Chichester and Malden, MA: Wiley-Blackwell, 2010.

Goldstein, Jürgen, *Nominalismus und Moderne: Zur Konstitution neuzeitlicher Subjektivität bei Hans Blumenberg und Wilhelm von Ockham*, Freiburg and Munich: Karl Alber, 1998.

Goodchild, Philip, "Why Is Philosophy so Compromised with God?" in *Deleuze and Religion*, edited by Mary Bryden, London and New York: Routledge, 2001.

Grant, Edward, *Planets, Stars and Orbs: The Medieval Cosmos, 1200–1687*, Cambridge: Cambridge University Press, 1996.

Grant, Iain Hamilton, *Philosophies of Nature after Schelling*, London and New York: Continuum, 2006.

Graves, Neil D., "'The Whole Fulness of the Godhead Dwells in Him Bodily': The Materiality of Milton's God", *Christianity and Literature* 52:4 (2003).

Greenblatt, Stephen, *Shakespearean Negotiations*, Berkeley, CA: University of California Press, 1988.

Greene, Thomas M., "The Natural Tears of Epic", in *Epic Traditions in the Contemporary World: The Poetics of Community*, edited by Margaret Beissinger, Jane Tylus and Susanne Wofford, Berkeley, CA: University of California Press, 1999.

Gregerson, Linda, *The Reformation of the Subject: Spenser, Milton, and the English Protestant Epic*, Cambridge and New York: Cambridge University Press, 1997.

Gregory, Tobias, *From Many Gods to One: Divine Action in Renaissance Epic*, Chicago: University of Chicago Press, 2006.

———, "In Defense of Empson: A Reassessment of *Milton's God*", in *Fault Lines and Controversies in the Study of Seventeenth-Century English Literature*, edited by Claude J. Summers and Ted-Larry Pebworth, Columbia and London: University of Missouri Press, 2002.

Griffiths, John Gwyn, *The Divine Verdict: A Study of Divine Judgement in the Ancient Religions*, Leiden and New York: Brill, 1991.

Groh, Dieter, *Göttliche Weltökonomie: Perspektiven der wissenschaftlichen Revolution vom 15. bis zum 17. Jahrhundert*, Berlin: Suhrkamp, 2010.

Grotius, Hugo, *De jure belli ac pacis: Libri tres, in quibus jus naturae et gentium, item juris publici praecipua explicantur*, Amsterdam: Joan Blaeu, 1646.

———, *On the Law of War and Peace*, translated by Francis Kelsey, edited by Stephen C. Neff, Cambridge and New York: Cambridge University Press, 2012.

Gruber, Howard E., "Darwin's 'Tree of Nature' and Other Images of Wide Scope", in *Creativity, Psychology and the History of Science*, edited by Howard E. Gruber and Katja Bödeker, Boston Studies in the Philosophy of Science, Dordrecht: Springer, 2005.

Guattari, Félix, *The Anti-Oedipus Papers*, translated by Kélina Gotman, edited by Stéphane Nadaud, New York: Semiotext(e) and Cambridge, MA: MIT Press, 2006.

Guillory, John, *Poetic Authority: Spenser, Milton, and Literary History*, New York: Columbia University Press, 1983.

Gunkel, Hermann, *Creation and Chaos in the Primeval Era and the Eschaton*, translated by K. William Whitney Jr., Grand Rapids, MI: W. B. Eerdmans, 2006.

Guthrie, William Keith Chambers, *A History of Greek Philosophy,* Vol. 3: *The Fifth-Century Enlightenment*, Cambridge and New York: Cambridge University Press, 1969.

———, *A History of Greek Philosophy,* Vol. 6: *Aristotle: An Encounter*, Cambridge: Cambridge University Press, 1981.

Haas, Alois M., *Mystik als Aussage: Erfahrungs-, Denk- und Redeformen christlicher Mystik*, Frankfurt am Main: Suhrkamp, 1996.

Hadot, Pierre, *The Veil of Isis: An Essay on the History of the Idea of Nature*, translated by Michael Chase, Cambridge, MA: Belknap Press of Harvard University Press, 2006.

Hager, F. P., "Natur", in *Historisches Wörterbuch der Philosophie*, Vol. 6, edited by Joachim Ritter and Karlfried Gründer, Darmstadt: Wissenschaftliche Buchgesellschaft, 1984.

Hale, John K., *Milton's Languages: The Impact of Multilingualism on Style*, Cambridge: Cambridge University Press, 1997.

Hale, John K. and J. Donald Cullington, "Preface" to *De Doctrina Christiana*, in *The Complete Works*, Vol. 8., by John Milton, edited by John K. Hale, J. Donald Cullington, Gordon Campbell and Thomas N. Corns, Oxford: Oxford University Press, 2012.

Halewood, Michael, *A. N. Whitehead and Social Theory: Tracing a Culture of Thought*, London and New York: Anthem, 2011.

Hamacher, Werner, "Wilde Versprechen: Die Sprache *Leviathan*", in *Die Ordnung des Versprechens*, edited by Manfred Schneider, Munich: Wilhelm Fink, 2005.

Hampe, Michael, *Eine kleine Geschichte des Naturgesetzbegriffs*, Frankfurt am Main: Suhrkamp, 2007.

Han, Sui, *Der Begriff des Nichtseienden bei Plotin*, Wiesbaden: Springer VS, 2016.

Hardie, Philip, "The Presence of Lucretius in *Paradise Lost*", *Milton Quarterly* 29:1 (1995).

———, *Rumour and Renown: Representations of Fama in Western Literature*, Cambridge and New York: Cambridge University Press, 2012.

Harrington, James, *The Censure of the Rota upon Mr. Milton's Book, Intitled* The Ready and Easie Way to Establish a Free Commonwealth etc., London: Paul Giddy, 1660, in John Milton, *The Ready and Easy Way to Establish a Free Commonwealth*, edited by Evert Mordecai Clark, New Haven, CT: Yale University Press, London: Humphrey Milford and Oxford: Oxford University Press, 1915.

Harrison, Peter, *The Bible, Protestantism, and the Rise of Natural Science*, Cambridge and New York: Cambridge University Press, 1998.

Hart, D. Bentley, "Matter, Monism and Narrative: An Essay on the Metaphysics of *Paradise Lost*", *Milton Quarterly* 30:1 (1996).

Hart, H. L. A., *The Concept of Law*, edited by Penelope A. Bulloch and Joseph Raz, Oxford: Oxford University Press, 2012.

Haverkamp, Anselm, "Distant Information: Die komparatistische Bedeutung Miltons", *Deutsche Vierteljahrsschrift für Literaturwissenschaft und Geistesgeschichte* 68:4 (1994).

———, "A Narrow Thing Within One Word: The Foreclosure of Nature in Post-Shakespearian Worlds and Times", in *"If Then the World a Theatre Present...": Revisions of the Theatrum Mundi Metaphor in Early Modern England*, edited by Björn Quiring, Berlin: Walter de Gruyter, 2014.

Hawkes, David, *John Milton: A Hero of Our Time*, Berkeley, CA: Counterpoint, 2009.

Heidel, Alexander, *Babylonian Genesis: The Story of the Creation*, Chicago: University of Chicago Press, 1972.

Hein, Kenneth, *Eucharist and Excommunication: A Study in Early Christian Doctrine and Discipline*, Bern and Frankfurt am Main: Peter Lang, 1973.

Heinrich, Klaus, *Gesellschaftlich vermitteltes Naturverhältnis: Begriff der Aufklärung in den Religionen und der Religionswissenschaft*, Dahlemer Vorlesungen 8, Frankfurt am Main: Stroemfeld/Roter Stern, 2007.

Helmholz, R. H., *Natural Law in Court: A History of Legal Theory in Practice*, Cambridge, MA and London: Harvard University Press, 2015.

Henry, John, "The Scientific Revolution in England", in *The Scientific Revolution in National Context*, edited by Roy Porter und Mikuláš Teich, Cambridge: Cambridge University Press, 1992.

Heraclitus, "Fragment 112", in *Die Fragmente der Vorsokratiker, griechisch und deutsch*, Vol. 1, edited by Hermann Diels, Berlin: Weidmann, 1906.

———, "Fragment 123", in *Die vorsokratischen Philosophen*, edited by G. S. Kirk, J. E. Raven and M. Schofield, translated by Karlheinz Hülser, Stuttgart and Weimar: J. B. Metzler, 2001.

Herman, Peter C., "C. S. Lewis and the New Milton Criticism", *Milton Quarterly* 45:4 (2011).

———, "*Paradise Lost*, the Miltonic 'Or', and the Poetics of Incertitude", *Studies in English Literature 1500–1900* 43:1 (2003).

Herodotus, *The Persian Wars*, Vol. 1, translated by A. D. Godley, London: Heinemann and New York: Putnam's Sons, 1920.

Herzog, Tamar, *A Short History of European Law: The Last Two and a Half Millennia*, Cambridge, MA and London: Harvard University Press, 2018.

Hesiod, *Theogonie, Griechisch/Deutsch*, translated and edited by Otto Schönberger, Stuttgart: Reclam, 1999.

———, *Works and Days*, in *Theogony, Works and Days, Testimonia*, translated and edited by Glenn W. Most, Cambridge, MA and London: Harvard University Press, 2006.

———, "The Shield" in *The Shield, Catalogue of Women, Other Fragments*, translated and edited by Glenn W. Most, Cambridge, MA: Harvard University Press, 2007.

Hill, Christopher, *Milton and the English Revolution*, Harmondsworth: Penguin, 1979.

Hirsch, Eric Donald, *Wordsworth and Schelling: A Typological Study of Romanticism*, New Haven, CT: Yale University Press, 1960.

Hoagwood, Terence Alan, Review of *Creating States: Studies in the Performative Language of John Milton and William Blake*, by Angela Esterhammer, *Modern Language Review* 91:4 (1996).

Hobbes, Thomas, "The Answer to the Preface", in *The Works*, by William Davenant, London: T. N. for Henry Herringman, 1673.

———, *Behemoth, or The Long Parliament*, edited by Paul Seaward, Oxford: Clarendon Press, 2010.

———, *Leviathan*, edited by J. C. A. Gaskin, Oxford: Oxford University Press, 1998.

———, *Leviathan, sive De Materia, Forma et Potestate Civitatis Ecclesiasticae et Civilis*, in *Opera Philosophica Omnia*, Amsterdam: Joan Blaeu, 1668.

———, *On the Citizen*, edited and translated by Richard Tuck and Michael Silverthorne, Cambridge: Cambridge University Press, 1997.

——, and John Bramhall, *On Liberty and Necessity*, edited by Vere Chappell, Cambridge and New York: Cambridge University Press, 1999.

Homer, *Iliad*, Vol. 1, translated by A. T. Murray and William F. Wyatt, Cambridge, MA: Harvard University Press, 1999.

———, *Iliad*, Vol. 2, translated by A. T Murray and William F. Wyatt, Cambridge, MA: Harvard University Press, 1999.

———, *Odyssey*, Vol. 1, translated by A. T. Murray, Cambridge, MA: Harvard University Press and London: Heinemann, 1945.

Hooker, Richard, *Of the Laws of Ecclesiastical Polity: Preface, Book 1 and 8*, edited by Arthur Stephen McGrade, Cambridge: Cambridge University Press, 1989.

———, *Of the Laws of Ecclesiastical Polity: Books 6, 7, 8*, edited by Paul G. Stanwood, Cambridge, MA and London: Belknap Press of Harvard University Press, 1981.

Horace, *Oden und Epoden: Lateinisch/Deutsch*, translated and edited by Bernhard Kytzler, Stuttgart: Reclam, 2000.

Hume, David, *A Treatise on Human Nature*, Vol. 1, edited by David Fate Norton, Oxford: Clarendon Press, 2007.

Hutton, Margaret-Anne, *Testimony from the Nazi Camps: French Women's Voices*, London and New York: Routledge, 2005.

Hyde, Edward, Earl of Clarendon, *A Brief View and Survey of the Dangerous and Pernicious Errors to Church and State in Mr. Hobbes's Book, entitled Leviathan*, Oxford: Printed at the Theater, 1676.

Irenaeus of Lyon, *Adversus Haereses*, Vol. 3, translated and edited by Norbert Brox, Freiburg: Herder, 1995.

Jacobs, Jonathan A., "Introduction", in *Reason, Religion, and Natural Law: From Plato to Spinoza*, edited by Jonathan A. Jacobs, Oxford and New York: Oxford University Press, 2012.

Javitch, Daniel, *Proclaiming a Classic: The Canonization of* Orlando Furioso, Princeton, NJ: Princeton University Press, 1991.

Jenkins, Joseph S., *Inheritance Law and Political Theology in Shakespeare and Milton: Election and Grace as Constitutional in Early Modern Literature and Beyond*, Burlington, VT: Ashgate, 2012.

John of Salisbury, *The Metalogicon: A Twelfth-Century Defense of the Verbal and Logical Arts of the Trivium*, translated by Daniel D. McGarry, Philadelphia: Paul Dry Books, 2009.

Johnston, Douglas M., "The Heritage of Political Thought in International Law", in *The Structure and Process of International Law: Essays in Legal Philosophy, Doctrine, and Theory*, edited by Ronald St. John Macdonald and Douglas M. Johnston, The Hague and Boston: Nijhoff, 1983.

Jonas, Hans, *Gnosis: Die Botschaft des fremden Gottes*, edited by Christian Wiese, Frankfurt am Main and Leipzig: Insel, 1999.

Jones, Christopher P., *Between Pagan and Christian*, Cambridge, MA: Harvard University Press, 2014.

Jonson, Ben, *The Complete Masques*, edited by Stephen Orgel, New Haven, CT: Yale University Press, 1969.

Justinian's Institutes, translated by Peter Birks and Grant McLeod, London: Duckworth, 1987.

Kadri, Sadakat, *The Trial: A History, from Socrates to O. J. Simpson*, New York: Random House, 2005.

Kafka, Franz, *Beim Bau der chinesischen Mauer und andere Schriften*, edited by Malcolm Pasley and Jost Schillemeit, Frankfurt am Main: Fischer, 1994.

———, *Der Proceß*, edited by Hans-Gerd Koch, Frankfurt am Main: Fischer, 2008.

———, *Shorter Works*, Vol. 1, translated by Malcolm Pasley, London: Secker and Warburg, 1973.

———, *The Trial: A New Translation Based on the Restored Text*, translated by Breon Mitchell, New York: Schocken, 1998.

Kahn, Victoria, "Allegory, the Sublime, and the Rhetoric of Things Indifferent in *Paradise Lost*," in *Creative Imagination: New Essays in Renaissance Literature in Honor of Thomas M. Greene*, edited by David Quint, Margaret W. Ferguson, G. W. Pigman III and Wayne Rebhorn, Binghamton, NY: Medieval and Renaissance Texts and Studies, 1992.

Kalimtzis, Kostas, *Aristotle on Political Enmity and Disease: An Inquiry into Stasis*, Albany: State University of New York Press, 2000.

Kant, Immanuel, *Critique of Pure Reason*, translated by Werner S. Pluhar, Indianapolis: Hackett, 1996.

———, *Kritik der praktischen Vernunft/Grundlegung zur Metaphysik der Sitten*, edited by Wilhelm Weischedel, Frankfurt am Main: Suhrkamp, 1974.

———, *Kritik der reinen Vernunft*, edited by Wilhelm Weischedel, Frankfurt am Main: Suhrkamp, 1974.

Kantorowicz, Ernst, *The King's Two Bodies: A Study in Mediaeval Political Theology*, Princeton, NJ: Princeton University Press, 1997.

———, "The Sovereignty of the Artist: A Note on Legal Maxims and Renaissance Theories of Art", in *De artibus opuscula XL: Essays in Honor of Erwin Panofsky*, edited by Millard Meiss, New York: New York University Press, 1961.

Keeble, Neil H., "Milton and Puritanism", in *A Companion to Milton*, edited by Thomas N. Corns, Oxford and Malden, MA: Blackwell, 2003.

Kelley, Theresa M., *Reinventing Allegory*, Cambridge and New York: Cambridge University Press, 1997.

Kelly, Henry A., "Hell with Purgatory and Two Limbos", in *Hell and Its Afterlife: Historical and Contemporary Perspectives*, edited by Isabel Moreira and Margaret Toscano, Farnham and Burlington, VT: Ashgate, 2010.

Kelly, John Norman Davidson, *Altchristliche Glaubensbekenntnisse: Geschichte und Theologie*, Göttingen: Vandenhoeck und Ruprecht, 1972.

Kelsen, Hans, *Das Problem der Souveränität und die Theorie des Völkerrechts: Beitrag zu einer reinen Rechtslehre*, Reinheim: Scientia Aalen, 1960.

———, "Die Staatslehre des Dante Alighieri", in *Veröffentlichte Schriften 1905–1910 und Selbstzeugnisse*, edited by Matthias Jestaedt, Tübingen: Mohr Siebeck, 2007.

Kemp, Wolfgang, *Natura: Ikonographische Studien zur Geschichte und Verbreitung einer Allegorie*, Dissertation, Tübingen, 1973.

Kendrick, Christopher, *Milton: A Study in Ideology and Form*, New York and London: Methuen, 1986.

Kensky, Meira Z., *Trying Man, Trying God: The Divine Courtroom in Early Jewish and Christian Literature*, Tübingen: Mohr Siebeck, 2010.

Kerrigan, William, *The Prophetic Milton*, Charlottesville: University of Virginia Press, 1974.

———, *The Sacred Complex: On the Psychogenesis of* Paradise Lost, Cambridge, MA and London: Harvard University Press, 1983.

Keßler, Eckhard, "Naturverständnisse im 15. und 16. Jahrhundert", in *Naturauffassungen in Philosophie, Wissenschaft, Technik*, Vol. 2, edited by Lothar Schäfer and Elisabeth Ströker, Freiburg and Munich: K. Alber, 1994.

Kilgour, Maggie, *Milton and the Metamorphosis of Ovid*, Oxford and New York: Oxford University Press, 2012.

King, John N., *Milton and Religious Controversy: Satire and Polemic in* Paradise Lost, Cambridge and New York: Cambridge University Press, 2000.

Klein, Jacob, "Stoic Eudaimonism and the Natural Law Tradition", in *Reason, Religion, and Natural Law: From Plato to Spinoza*, edited by Jonathan A. Jacobs, Oxford and New York: Oxford University Press, 2012.

Kloft, Hans, *Mysterienkulte der Antike*, Munich: Beck, 2003.

Knowlton, Edgar C., "The Goddess Nature in Early Periods", *The Journal of English and Germanic Philology* 19:2 (1920).

———, "Nature in Middle English", *The Journal of English and Germanic Philology* 20:2 (1921).

Knox, John, *Chapters in a Life of Paul*, Revised Edition, edited by Douglas Hare, Macon: Mercer University Press, 1987.

Koerner, Joseph Leo, *Bosch and Bruegel: From Enemy Painting to Everyday Life*, Princeton, NJ: Princeton University Press, 2016.

Konradt, Matthias, *Gericht und Gemeinde: Eine Studie zur Bedeutung und Funktion von Gerichtsaussagen im Rahmen der paulinischen Ekklesiologie und Ethik im 1 Thess und 1 Kor*, Berlin and New York: De Gruyter, 2003.

Koyré, Alexandre, *From the Closed World to the Infinite Universe*, Baltimore: Johns Hopkins University Press, 1957.

———, *Galileo Studies*, translated by John Mepham, Atlantic Highlands, NJ: Humanities Press, 1978.

———, *Newtonian Studies*, London: Chapman and Hall, 1965.

Kuester, Martin, *Milton's Prudent Ambiguities: Words and Signs in His Poetry and Prose*, Lanham, MD: University Press of America, 2009.

Kurz, Gerhard, *Metapher, Allegorie, Symbol*, Göttingen: Vandenhoeck and Ruprecht, 1982.

Labriola, Albert, "The Begetting and Exaltation of the Son: The Junius Manuscript and Milton's *Paradise Lost*", in *Milton's Legacy*, edited by Kristin A. Pruitt, and Charles W. Durham, Selinsgrove, PA: Susquehanna University Press, 2005.

Lacan, Jacques, *Encore: On Feminine Sexuality, The Limits of Love and Knowledge*, Seminar 20 (1972–1973), translated by Bruce Fink, New York and London: Norton, 1998.

Lakshmanan, Ar and J. J. S. Wharton, *Wharton's Concise Law Dictionary*, Delhi: Universal Law Publishing, 2009.

Landau, Peter, "Der biblische Sündenfall und die Legitimität des Rechts", in *Die Begründung des Rechts als historisches Problem, Schriften des Historischen Kollegs 45*, edited by Dietmar Willoweit and Elisabeth Müller-Luckner, Munich: Oldenbourg, 2000.

Lang, Bernhard, *Jesus der Hund: Leben und Lehre eines jüdischen Kynikers*, Munich: Beck, 2010.

Langland, William, *Piers Plowman: A Modern Verse Translation*, translated by Peter Sutton, Jefferson, NC: McFarland, 2014.

———, *Piers Plowman, A Parallel-Text Edition of the A, B, C and Z Versions*, Vol. 1, edited by A. V. C. Schmidt, London and New York: Longman, 1995.

Lapham, Fred, *An Introduction to the New Testament Apocrypha*, London and New York: T. and T. Clark International, 2003.

Latour, Bruno, *Politics of Nature: How to Bring the Sciences into Democracy*, translated by Catherine Porter, Cambridge, MA: Harvard University Press, 2004.

Lawson, Anita, "'The Golden Sun in Splendor Likest Heaven': Johannes Kepler's *Epitome* and *Paradise Lost,* Book 3", *Milton Quarterly* 21:2 (1987).

Lefebvre, Alexandre, *The Image of Law: Deleuze, Bergson, Spinoza*, Stanford, CA: Stanford University Press, 2008.

Lehnhof, Kent R., "Deity and Creation in the *Christian Doctrine*", *Milton Quarterly* 35 (2001).

Leijenhorst, Cees, "Sense and Nonsense about Sense: Hobbes and the Aristotelians on Sense Perception and Imagination", in *The Cambridge Companion to Hobbes's* Leviathan, edited by Patricia Springborg, Cambridge: Cambridge University Press, 2007.

Leisegang, Hans, "Physis", in *Paulys Realencyclopädie der classischen Altertumswissenschaft*, Half-Volume 39, edited by Georg Wissowa, Wilhelm Kroll and Karl Mittelhaus, Stuttgart: Druckenmüller, 1941.

———, "Sophia", in *Paulys Realencyclopädie der classischen Altertumswissenschaft*, Second Series, Fifth Half-Volume, edited by Georg Wissowa, Wilhelm Kroll and Karl Mittelhaus, Munich: Druckenmüller, 1927.

Lemaire, Anika, *Jacques Lacan*, Sprimont: Mardaga, 1977.

Lemke, Thomas, *Biopolitics: An Advanced Introduction*, New York and London: New York University Press, 2011.

Leonard, John, *Faithful Labourers: A Reception History of* Paradise Lost, *1667–1970*, Oxford: Oxford University Press, 2013.

———, *Naming in Paradise: Milton and the Language of Adam and Eve*, Oxford: Clarendon Press, 1990.

Leslie, Charles, "Leslie on Milton's Theology", in *John Milton: The Critical Heritage,* Vol. 1: *1628–1731*, edited by John T. Shawcross, London: Routledge, 1970.

Lévi-Strauss, Claude, *The Elementary Structures of Kinship*, translated by James Harle Bell, John Richard von Sturmer and Rodney Needham, Boston: Beacon, 1969.

———, *Le Totémisme aujourd'hui*, Paris: Presses universitaires de France, 1965.

Lewalski, Barbara Kiefer, *The Life of John Milton: A Critical Biography*, Oxford and Malden, MA: Blackwell, 2003.

———, Paradise Lost *and the Rhetoric of Literary Forms*, Princeton, NJ: Princeton University Press, 2014.

Lewis, C. S., *A Preface to* Paradise Lost, Oxford: Oxford University Press, 1969.

———, *Studies in Words*, Cambridge: Cambridge University Press, 1967.

Lewis, Ewart, *Medieval Political Ideas*, Vol. 1, Abingdon and New York: Routledge, 2013.

Lim, Walter S. H., "John Milton, Orientalism, and the Empires of the East in *Paradise Lost*", in *The English Renaissance, Orientalism, and the Idea of Asia*, edited by Debra Johanyak and Walter S. H. Lim, New York: Palgrave Macmillan, 2010.

Linguiti, Alessandro, "Physis as Heimarmene: On Some Fundamental Principles of the Neoplatonic Philosophy of Nature", in *Physics and Philosophy of Nature in Greek Neoplatonism*, edited by Riccardo Chiaradonna and Franco Trabattoni, Leiden and Boston: Brill, 2009.

Little, Lester K., *Benedictine Maledictions: Liturgical Cursing in Romanesque France*, Ithaca, NY and London: Cornell University Press, 1993.

Livesley, Graham, "Assemblage", in *The Deleuze Dictionary*, Revised Edition, edited by Adrian Parr, Edinburgh: Edinburgh University Press, 2005.

Lloyd, Geoffrey E. R., *Aristotelian Explorations*, Cambridge and New York: Cambridge University Press, 1999.

———, "Greek Antiquity: The Invention of Nature", in *Nature: Critical Concepts in the Social Sciences*, Vol. 1, edited by David Inglis, John Bone and Rhoda Wilkie, London and New York: Routledge, 2005.

Loewenstein, David, *Milton and the Drama of History: Historical Vision, Iconoclasm, and the Literary Imagination*, Cambridge: Cambridge University Press, 1990.

Long, A. A., *Stoic Studies*, Berkeley, CA and London: University of California Press, 1996.

Lorris, Guillaume de and Jean de Meun, *Le Roman de la Rose*, Vol. 4, edited by Ernest Langlois, Paris: Firmin-Didot, 1922.

———, *Le Roman de la Rose*, Vol. 5, edited by Ernest Langlois, Paris: Firmin-Didot, 1924.

———, *The Romance of the Rose*, translated by Charles Dahlberg, Princeton, NJ: Princeton University Press, 1995.

———, *The Romance of the Rose*, translated by Frances Horgan, Oxford and New York: Oxford University Press, 1999.

Lovejoy, Arthur O., "'Nature' as Aesthetic Norm", *Modern Language Notes* 42:7 (1927).

Lucretius, *De rerum natura*, translated by W. H. D. Rouse and Martin Ferguson Smith, Cambridge, MA: Harvard University Press, 1992.

Luhmann, Niklas, *Love as Passion: The Codification of Intimacy*, translated by Jeremy Gaines and Doris L. Jones, Stanford, CA: Stanford University Press, 1982.

———, *Paradigm Lost: Die ethische Reflexion der Moral*, Festvortrag anlässlich der Verleihung des Hegel-Preises der Landeshauptstadt Stuttgart am 23. November 1988 im Neuen Schloß Stuttgart, Stuttgart: Enke, 1988.

———, "Über Natur", in *Gesellschaftsstruktur und Semantik: Studien zur Wissenssoziologie der modernen Gesellschaft*, Vol. 4, Frankfurt am Main: Suhrkamp, 1995.

Luig, Klaus, "Leibniz's Concept of Jus Naturale and Lex Naturalis – Defined 'with Geometric Certainty'", in *Natural Law and Laws of Nature in Early Modern Europe: Jurisprudence, Theology, Moral and Natural Philosophy*, edited by Lorraine Daston and Michael Stolleis, Farnham and Burlington, VT: Ashgate, 2008.

Lumpkin, Ben Gray, "Fate in *Paradise Lost*", *Studies in Philology* 44:1 (1947).

Luther, Martin, *The Bondage of the Will*, translated by J. I. Packer and A. R. Johnston, Old Tappan, NJ: Revell, 1957.

———, *On the Creation: A Critical and Devotional Commentary on Genesis*, Vol. 1, translated by Henry Cole and John Lenker, Minneapolis: Lutherans in All Lands, 1904.

———, "Predigt 41" (1534), in *Werke: Kritische Gesamtausgabe*, Vol. 37, edited by O. Brenner, Weimar: Böhlau, 1910.

———, "Die Schmalkaldischen Artikel", in *Luther Deutsch: Die Werke Martin Luthers in neuer Auswahl für die Gegenwart,* Vol. 3: *Der neue Glaube*, edited by Kurt Aland, Göttingen: Vandenhoeck and Ruprecht, 1983.

———, *The Schmalkald Articles*, translated by William R. Russell, Minneapolis: Fortress, 1995.

———, *Text der Genesisvorlesung*, in *Werke: Kritische Gesamtausgabe*, Vol. 42, edited by G. Koffmane and Otto Reichert, Weimar: Böhlau, 1911.

Lutz, Tom, *Crying: The Natural and Cultural History of Tears*, New York and London: Norton, 1999.

Luxon, Thomas H., "'Not I, But Christ': Allegory and the Puritan Self", *ELH* 60:4 (1993).

Lydgate, John, *Reson and Sensuallyte*, edited by Ernst Sieper, London: Kegan Paul, Trench, Trübner and Company, 1901.

Lyly, John, *The Woman in the Moon*, edited by Leah Scragg, Manchester and New York: Manchester University Press, 2006.

MacCaffrey, Isabel G., *Paradise Lost as "Myth"*, Cambridge, MA: Harvard University Press, 1959.

Macé, Arnaud, "La naissance de la nature en Grèce ancienne", in *Anciens et Modernes par-delà nature et société*, edited by Arnaud Macé und Stéphane Haber, Besançon: Presses universitaires de Franche-Comté, 2012.

Mack, Maynard. *Milton*, Englewood Cliffs, NJ: Prentice-Hall, 1961.

Mackenzie, W. Roy, "A Source for Medwall's *Nature*", *PMLA* 29:2 (1914).

Macrobius, *Saturnalia*, Vol. 1, Books 1–2, edited and translated by Robert A. Kaster, Cambridge, MA and London: Harvard University Press, 2011.

Manning, Russell Re, John Hedley Brooke and Fraser N. Watts, eds., *The Oxford Handbook of Natural Theology*, Oxford: Oxford University Press, 2013.

Maran, Stephen P. and Laurence A. Marschall, *Galileo's New Universe: The Revolution in our Understanding of the Cosmos*, Dallas, TX: BenBella Books, 2009.

Margolus, Norman, "Looking at Nature as a Computer", *International Journal of Theoretical Physics* 42:2 (2003).

Marjara, Harinder Singh, "Angelic Motion and Moloch's False Rhetoric", *Milton Quarterly* 19:3 (1985).

———, *Contemplation of Created Things: Science in* Paradise Lost, Toronto: University of Toronto Press, 1992.

Marlowe, Christopher, *The Tragical History of Doctor Faustus*, in *English Renaissance Drama: A Norton Anthology*, edited by David Bevington, New York and London: W. W. Norton and Company, 2002.

Marquard, Odo, *Abschied vom Prinzipiellen: Philosophische Studien*, Stuttgart: Reclam 1991.

Marshall, David J., "John Calvin", in *Augustine Through the Ages: An Encyclopedia*, edited by Allan D. Fitzgerald, Grand Rapids, MI: W. B. Eerdmans, 1999.

Martin, Catherine Gimelli, *Milton Among the Puritans: The Case for Historical Revisionism*, Farnham and Burlington, VT: Ashgate, 2010.

———, *The Ruins of Allegory:* Paradise Lost *and the Metamorphosis of Epic*, Durham, NC: Duke University Press, 1998.

Masek, Rosemary, "Desiderius Erasmus", in *A Milton Encyclopedia*, Vol. 3, edited by William B. Hunter Jr., Lewisburg, PA: Bucknell University Press and London: Associated University Presses, 1978.

Matthews, Gareth B., *Augustine*, Oxford and Malden, MA: Blackwell, 2005.

May, Gerhard, "Creatio Ex Nihilo: The Doctrine of 'Creation out of Nothing'" *in Early Christian Thought*, translated by A. S. Worrall, London and New York: T. and T. Clark International, 2004.

Mayer, Thomas F., *The Roman Inquisition: A Papal Bureaucracy and Its Laws in the Age of Galileo*, Philadelphia: University of Pennsylvania Press, 2013.

McCluskey, Peter M., "'Nature Taught Art': The Topos of Art and Nature in *Paradise Regained*", in *Spokesperson Milton: Voices in Contemporary Criticism*, edited by Charles W. Durham and Kristin Pruitt McColgan, Selinsgrove, PA: Susquehanna University Press, 1994.

McColley, Diane Kelsey, *Poetry and Ecology in the Age of Milton and Marvell*, Aldershot and Burlington, VT: Ashgate, 2007.

McGee, C. E., "'The Visit of the Nine Goddesses': A Masque at Sir John Crofts's House", *English Literary Renaissance* 21:2 (1991).

McGrath, Alister E., *The Intellectual Origins of the European Reformation*, Malden, MA: Blackwell, 2004.

McKinley, C. Alexander, *Illegitimate Children of the Enlightenment: Anarchists and the French Revolution, 1880–1914*, New York: Peter Lang, 2008.

Merchant, Carolyn, *Autonomous Nature: Problems of Prediction and Control from Ancient Times to the Scientific Revolution*, New York and London: Routledge, 2016.

Miles, Jack, *God: A Biography*, New York: Alfred A. Knopf, 1995.

Miller, Henry, *Sexus*, New York: Grove Press, 1965.

Miller, Perry and Thomas H. Johnson, "Introduction", in *The Puritans: A Sourcebook of Their Writings*, edited by Perry Miller and Thomas H. Johnson, Mineola/New York: Dover, 2001.

Minkinnen, Panu, *Thinking Without Desire: A First Philosophy of Law*, Oxford: Hart Publishing, 1999.

Mitchell, J. Allan, "Reading God Reading 'Man': Hereditary Sin and the Narrativization of Deity in *Paradise Lost,* Book 3", *Milton Quarterly* 35:2 (2001).

Mittelstraß, Jürgen, "Das Wirken der Natur: Materialien zur Geschichte des Naturbegriffs", in *Naturverständnis und Naturbeherrschung, Philosophiegeschichtliche Entwicklung und gegenwärtiger Kontext*, edited by Friedrich Rapp, Munich: Wilhelm Fink, 1981.

Modersohn, Mechthild, *Natura als Göttin im Mittelalter: Ikonographische Studien zu Darstellungen der personifizierten Natur*, Berlin: Akademie, 1997.

Moloney, Pat, "Leaving the Garden of Eden: Linguistic and Political Authority in Thomas Hobbes", *History of Political Thought*, 18:2 (1997).

Monahan, Arthur P., *The Circle of Rights Expands: Modern Political Thought after the Reformation, 1521 (Luther) to 1762 (Rousseau)*, Montreal and Ithaca, NY: McGill-Queen's University Press, 2007.

Moore, Frank Harper, "Astraea, The Scorpion, and the Heavenly Scales", *ELH* 38:3 (1971).

Morand, Paul Phelps, *De Comus à Satan: L'Oeuvre poétique de John Milton expliquée par sa vie*, Paris: H. Didier, 1939.

Morrison, Sarah R., "When Worlds Collide: The Central Naturalistic Narrative and the Allegorical Dimension to *Paradise Lost*", in *Living Texts: Interpreting Milton*, edited by Kristin A. Pruitt and Charles W. Durhamp, Selingsgrove, PA: Susquehana University Press and London and Cranbury, NJ: Associated University Presses, 2000.

Müller, Reinhard, *Jahwe als Wettergott: Studien zur althebräischen Kultlyrik anhand ausgewählter Psalmen*, Berlin and New York: Walter de Gruyter, 2008.

Murphy, James Bernard, *The Philosophy of Positive Law: Foundations of Jurisprudence*, New Haven and London: Yale University Press, 2005.

Myers, Benjamin, *Milton's Theology of Freedom*, Berlin and New York: Walter de Gruyter, 2006.

Myers, Robert M., "'God Shall Be All In All': The Erasure of Hell in *Paradise Lost*", *The Seventeenth Century* 5:1 (1990).

Naddaf, Gerard, *The Greek Concept of Nature*, Albany, NY: State University of New York Press, 2005.

Nagy, Gregory, *Homer the Preclassic*, Berkeley and Los Angeles: University of California Press, 2010.

Nesselrath, Heinz-Günther, "Wenn Zeus an seine Grenzen kommt: Die Götter und das Schicksal bei Homer", in *Vorsehung, Schicksal und göttliche Macht: Antike Stimmen zu einem aktuellen Thema*, edited by Reinhard G. Kratz and Hermann Spieckermann, Tübingen: Mohr Siebeck, 2008.

Das Neue Testament, Interlinearübersetzung Griechisch-Deutsch, translated by Ernst Dietzfelbinger, Neuhausen: Hänssler, 1998.

Newman, Barbara, *God and the Goddesses: Vision, Poetry and Belief in the Middle Ages*, Philadelphia: University of Pennsylvania Press, 2003.

Nicholas of Cusa, *De coniecturis*, in *Philosophisch-theologische Werke*, Vol. 2, edited by Winfried Happ and Josef Koch, Hamburg: Meiner, 2002.

———, *Idiota de mente*, in *Philosophisch-theologische Werke*, Vol. 2, edited by Renate Steiger, Hamburg: Meiner, 2002.

Nicolai, Friedrich, *Leben und literarischer Nachlass*, edited by Leopold von Göckingk, Berlin: Nicolaische Buchhandlung, 1820.

Nietzsche, Friedrich, *Zur Genealogie der Moral*, in *Zur Genealogie der Moral/Götzen-Dämmerung*, edited by Claus-Artur Scheier, Hamburg: Meiner, 2013.

Nilles, Jean-Claude, "Approche mythique du Bien, du Phytourgos et du Démiurge", *Revue Internationale de Philosophie* 40:1 (1986).

Nonnos, *Dionysiaca*, Vol. 1, translated by W. H. D. Rouse, London: Heinemann and Cambridge, MA: Harvard University Press, 1940.

Novak, David, *Natural Law in Judaism*, Cambridge and New York: Cambridge University Press, 1998.

Nussbaum, Martha C., "Philosophy and Literature", in *The Cambridge Companion to Greek and Roman Philosophy*, edited by David Sedley, Cambridge and New York: Cambridge University Press, 2003.

Nuttall, A. D., *Overheard by God: Fiction and Prayer in Herbert, Milton, Dante, and St. John*, London: Methuen, 1980.

Oakeshott, Michael, *Hobbes on Civil Association*, Indianapolis: Liberty Fund, 2000.

Oakley, Francis, "Medieval Theories of Natural Law: William of Ockham and the Significance of the Voluntarist Tradition", *Natural Law Forum/The American Journal of Jurisprudence* 6:1 (1961).

———, *Natural Law, Laws of Nature, Natural Rights: Continuity and Discontinuity in the History of Ideas*, New York: Continuum, 2005.

Oldenburg, Henry, "A Preface to the Third Year of These Tracts", in *Philosophical Transactions of the Royal Society* 2 (1666).

Olechowski, Thomas, "Kelsens Rechtslehre im Überblick", in *Hans Kelsen: Eine politikwissenschaftliche Einführung*, edited by Tamara Ehs, Baden-Baden: Nomos, 2009.

Ong, Walter J., *Ramus, Method, and the Decay of Dialogue: From the Art of Discourse to the Art of Reason*, Chicago: University of Chicago Press, 2004.

Origen, *Contra Celsum, Books II–VIII*, translated by Frederick Crombie, Edinburgh: T. and T. Clark, 1872.

Orphic Hymns, edited by Apostolos N. Athanassakis, Missoula, MT: Scholars Press for the Society of Biblical Literature, 1977.

Ovid, *Metamorphoses*, Vol. 1, translated by Frank Justus Miller, London: Heinemann and Cambridge, MA: Harvard University Press, 1971.

———, *Metamorphoses*, Vol. 2, translated by Frank Justus Miller, London: Heinemann and New York: Putnam's Sons, 1916.

Palmer, Ada, *Reading Lucretius in the Renaissance*, Cambridge, MA: Harvard University Press, 2014.

Parker, Robert, *Miasma: Pollution and Purification in Early Greek Religion*, Oxford: Clarendon Press, 1983.

Parkin, Jon, *Science, Religion and Politics in Restoration England: Richard Cumberland's* De Legibus Naturae, Woodbridge: Royal Historical Society/Boydell Press, 1999.

Partee, Charles, *Calvin and Classical Philosophy*, Leiden: Brill, 1977.

Passerin d'Entrèves, Alexander, *Natural Law: An Introduction to Legal Philosophy*, New Brunswick and London: Transaction, 1994.

Pattaro, Enrico, *The Law and the Right: A Reappraisal of the Reality that Ought to Be*, Dordrecht: Springer, 2005.

Pausanias, *Description of Greece*, edited by W. H. S. Jones, Cambridge, MA: Harvard University Press, 1918.

Pearson, Roger, *Unacknowledged Legislators: The Poet as Lawgiver in Post-Revolutionary France*, Oxford: Oxford University Press, 2016.

Peppard, Michael, *The Son of God in the Roman World: Divine Sonship in its Social and Political Context*, Oxford: Oxford University Press, 2011.

Peters, Julie Stone, "A 'Bridge over Chaos': *De Jure Belli*, *Paradise Lost*, Terror, Sovereignty, Globalism, and the Modern Law of Nations", *Comparative Literature* 57:4 (2005).

Phillips, Edward, "The Life of Milton", in *Complete Poems and Major Prose*, by John Milton, edited by Merritt Y. Hughes, Indianapolis: Sheridan Books, 2003.

Phillips, Philip Edward, *John Milton's Epic Invocations: Converting the Muse*, New York: Peter Lang, 2000.

Philo of Alexandria, *Quod deterius potiori insidiari soleat*, edited by Irène Feuer, Paris: Éditions du Cerf, 1965.

Picciotto, Joanna, *Labors of Innocence in Early Modern England*, Cambridge, MA and London: Harvard University Press, 2010.

Piccolino, Marco and Nicholas J. Wade, *Galileo's Visions: Piercing the Spheres of the Heavens by Eye and Mind*, New York and Oxford: Oxford University Press, 2014.

Pindar, "Zweite Olympische Ode", in *Oden*, translated by Eugen Dönt, Stuttgart: Reclam, 1986.

Pinomaa, L. and U. Dierse, "Gericht", in *Historisches Wörterbuch der Philosophie*, Vol. 3, edited by Joachim Ritter, Darmstadt: Wissenschaftliche Buchgesellschaft, 1989.

Plato, *Gorgias*, in *Werke*, Vol. 2, edited by Gunther Eigler, Darmstadt: Wissenschaftliche Buchgesellschaft, 1973.

———, *Gorgias*, translated by W. D. Woodhead, in *The Collected Dialogues*, edited by Edith Hamilton and Huntington Cairns, Princeton, NJ: Princeton University Press, 1973.

———, *Kratylos*, in *Werke*, Vol. 3, edited by Gunther Eigler, Darmstadt: Wissenschaftliche Buchgesellschaft, 1974.

———, *Nomoi*, in *Werke*, Vol. 8:2, edited by Gunther Eigler, Darmstadt: Wissenschaftliche Buchgesellschaft, 1977.

———, *Politeia*, in *Werke*, Vol. 4, edited by Gunther Eigler, Darmstadt: Wissenschaftliche Buchgesellschaft, 1971.

———, *Der Sophist*, in *Werke*, Vol. 6, edited by Gunther Eigler, Darmstadt: Wissenschaftliche Buchgesellschaft, 1970.

———, *Sophist*, translated by F. M. Cornford, in *The Collected Dialogues*, edited by Edith Hamilton and Huntington Cairns, Princeton, NJ: Princeton University Press, 1973.

———, *Timaeus*, translated by Donald J. Zeyl, Indianapolis: Hackett, 2000.

———, *Timaios*, in *Werke*, Vol. 7, edited by Gunther Eigler, Darmstadt: Wissenschaftliche Buchgesellschaft, 1972.

Plotinus, "On the Movement of Heaven", in *Ennead II*, translated by A. H. Armstrong, Cambridge, MA: Harvard University Press and London: W. Heinemann, 1966.

———, "On Nature and Contemplation and the One", in *Ennead III*, translated by A. H. Armstrong, Cambridge, MA and London: Harvard University Press, 1967.

Plutarch, "To an Uneducated Ruler", in *Moralia*, Vol. 10, translated by Harold North Fowler, Cambridge, MA: Harvard University Press and London: Heinemann, 1969.

Pointon, Marcia R., *Milton and English Art*, Manchester: Manchester University Press, 1970.

Poole, William, "The Early Reception of *Paradise Lost*", *Literature Compass* 1:1 (2004).

Pope, Alexander, "The Dunciad", in *The Poems: A One-Volume Edition of the Twickenham Text with Selected Annotations*, edited by John Butt, New Haven, CT and London: Yale University Press, 1963.

———, "Windsor Forest", in *The Poems: A One-Volume Edition of the Twickenham Text with Selected Annotations*, edited by John Butt, New Haven, CT and London: Yale University Press, 1963.

Powys, John Cowper, *Visions and Revisions: A Book of Literary Devotions*, New York: G. Arnold Shaw and London: William Rider, 1915.

Proclus, *Commentary on Plato's* Timaeus, Vol. 1, translated by Harold Tarrant, Cambridge: Cambridge University Press, 2006.

———, *In Platonis Timaeum Commentaria*, Vol. 1, edited by Ernst Diehl, Leipzig: Teubner, 1903.

Protevi, John, "The Organism as the Judgment of God: Aristotle, Kant and Deleuze on Nature (that is, on Biology, Theology and Politics)", in *Deleuze and Religion*, edited by Mary Bryden, London and New York: Routledge, 2001.

Pullan, Brian, *The Jews of Europe and the Inquisition of Venice: 1550–1620*, London: Tauris, 1997.

Puttenham, George, *The Art of English Poesy: A Critical Edition*, edited by Frank Whigham and Wayne A. Rebhorn, Ithaca, NY and London: Cornell University Press, 2007.

Quilligan, Maureen, *The Language of Allegory: Defining the Genre*, Ithaca, NY: Cornell University Press, 1979.

Quintilian, *Ausbildung des Redners: Lateinisch und deutsch*, Vol. 2, translated and edited by Helmut Rahn, Darmstadt: Wissenschaftliche Buchgesellschaft, 1995.

Quiring, Björn, "A Consuming Dish: Supplementing Raffield", *Law and Literature* 17:3 (Fall 2005).

———, "The Greatest Share of Endless Pain: The Spectral Sacramentality of Pain in Milton's *Paradise Lost*", in *Passions and Subjectivity in Early Modern Culture*, edited by Brian Cummings and Freya Sierhuis, Farnham and Burlington, VT: Ashgate, 2013.

———, "Introduction", in *"If Then the World a Theatre Present…": Revisions of the Theatrum Mundi Metaphor in Early Modern England*, edited by Björn Quiring, Berlin: Walter de Gruyter, 2014.

———, "Milton's God and Hobbes' Leviathan: Elective Affinities", in *Natur und Herrschaft: Analysen zur Physik der Macht*, edited by Kay Peter Jankrift, Alexander Kagerer, Christian Kaiser and María Ángeles Martín Romera, Berlin and Boston: Walter de Gruyter, 2016.

———, *Shakespeare's Curse: The Aporias of Ritual Exclusion in Early Modern Royal Drama*, translated by Michael Winkler and Björn Quiring, New York: Routledge, 2014.

———, "With Real Hunger to Transubstantiate': Die Dispersion der Eucharistie in John Miltons *Paradise Lost*", in *Mitteilungen des Sonderforschungsbereichs 573, "Pluralisierung und Autorität in der Frühen Neuzeit"* 1 (2011).

Rabelais, François, *Pantagruel*, in *Oeuvres complètes*, edited by Mireille Huchon, Paris: Gallimard, 1994.

Raleigh, Walter, *Milton*, London: Edward Arnold, 1900.

Raunio, Antti, "Divine and Natural Law in Luther and Melanchthon", in *Lutheran Reformation and the Law*, edited by Virpi Mäkinen, Leiden and Boston: Brill, 2006.

Reesing, John, "The Materiality of God in Milton's *De Doctrina Christiana*", *Harvard Theological Review* 1:3 (1957).

Reichert, John, *Milton's Wisdom: Nature and Scripture in* Paradise Lost, Ann Arbor: University of Michigan Press, 1992.

Reisner, Noam, *Milton and the Ineffable*, Oxford and New York: Oxford University Press, 2009.

Reiwald, Paul, *Die Gesellschaft und ihre Verbrecher*, Zurich: Pan, 1948.

Ricks, Christopher, "Introduction", in *Paradise Lost*, by John Milton, edited by Christopher Ricks, London: Penguin, 1989.

Ricoeur, Paul, *Finitude et culpabilité II: La symbolique du mal*, Paris: Aubier, 1960.

Ripa, Cesare, *Iconologia*, Rome: Lepido Faci, 1603.

Robertson, David, "The Book of Job: A Literary Study", *Soundings: An Interdisciplinary Journal* 56:4 (1973).

Rogers, John, *The Matter of Revolution: Science, Poetry and Politics in the Age of Milton*, Ithaca, NY and London: Cornell University Press, 1996.

———, "The Political Theology of Milton's Heaven", in *The New Milton Criticism*, edited by Peter C. Herman and Elizabeth Sauer, Cambridge: Cambridge University Press, 2012.

Rose, Herbert J., *Griechische Mythologie: Ein Handbuch*, Munich: Beck, 1982.

Rosenblatt, Jason P., "Milton, Natural Law, and Toleration", in *Milton and Toleration*, edited by Sharon Achinstein and Elizabeth Sauer, Oxford and New York: Oxford University Press, 2007.

Rosendale, Timothy, "Milton, Hobbes, and the Liturgical Subject", *Studies in English Literature 1500–1900* 44:1 (2004).

Rosler, Andrés, "Odi et Amo? Hobbes on the State of Nature", in *Hobbes Studies* 24 (2011).

Ross, George MacDonald, *Starting with Hobbes*, London and New York: Continuum, 2009.

Rothacker, Erich, *Das Buch der Natur: Materialien und Grundsätzliches zur Metapherngeschichte*, edited by Wilhelm Perpeet, Bonn: Bouvier, 1979.

Rumrich, John P., *Milton Unbound: Controversy and Reinterpretation*, Cambridge: Cambridge University Press, 1996.

———, "Milton's God and the Matter of Chaos", *PMLA* 110:5 (1995).

Russell, Frederick H., *The Just War in the Middle Ages*, Cambridge and New York: Cambridge University Press, 1979.

Russell, Jeffrey Burton, *A History of Heaven: The Singing Silence*, Princeton, NJ: Princeton University Press, 1997.

———, *The Prince of Darkness: Radical Evil and the Power of Good in History*, Ithaca, NY: Cornell University Press, 1992.

Sangha, Laura, *Angels and Belief in England, 1480–1700*, London: Routledge, 2016.

Santangelo, Federico, "Law and Divination in the Late Roman Republic", in *Law and Religion in the Roman Republic*, edited by O. Tellegen-Couperus, Leiden and Boston: Brill, 2012.

Sarkar, Malabika, *Cosmos and Character in* Paradise Lost, New York: Palgrave Macmillan, 2012.

Saurat, Denis, *Milton: Man and Thinker*, New York: Dial Press, 1925.

Savage, J. B., "Freedom and Necessity in *Paradise Lost*", in *ELH* 44:2 (1977).

Sax, Boria, *The Mythical Zoo: An Encyclopedia of Animals in World Myth, Legend, and Literature*, Denver and Santa Barbara: ABC-Clio, 2001.

Scaliger, Julius Caesar, *Poetices libri septem: Sieben Bücher über die Dichtkunst*, Vol. 1, edited by Luc Deitz and Gregor Vogt-Spira, Stuttgart-Bad Cannstatt: Frommann-Holzboog, 1994.

Scattola, Merio, *Das Naturrecht vor dem Naturrecht: Zur Geschichte des* ius naturae *im 16. Jahrhundert*, Tübingen: Niemeyer, 1999.

Schama, Simon, *A History of Britain,* Vol. 2: *The British Wars 1603–1776*, London: The Bodley Head, 2009.

Schein, Seth L., "Introduction", in *Reading the* Odyssey*: Selected Interpretive Essays*, edited by Seth L. Schein, Princeton, NJ: Princeton University Press, 1996.

Schelling, Friedrich Wilhelm Joseph, *Vorlesungen über die Methode des akademischen Studiums*, edited by Walter E. Ehrhardt, Hamburg: Meiner, 1974.

Schiller, Friedrich, "The Stage Considered as a Moral Institution", in *Sources of Dramatic Theory, Vol. 2: Voltaire to Hugo*, edited by Michael Sidnell, translated by Jean Wilson, Cambridge: Cambridge University Press, 2014.

———, "Was kann eine gute stehende Schaubühne eigentlich wirken?", in *Die Entwicklung des bürgerlichen Dramas im 18. Jahrhundert: Ausgewählte Texte*, edited by Jürg Mathes, Tübingen: Niemeyer, 1974.

Schmidt-Biggemann, Wilhelm, *Philosophia Perennis: Historical Outlines of Western Spirituality in Ancient, Medieval and Early Modern Thought*, Dordrecht: Springer, 2004.

Schmitt, Carl, *The Leviathan in the State Theory of Thomas Hobbes: Meaning and Failure of a Political Symbol*, translated by George Schwab and Erna Hilfstein, Westport, CT: Greenwood Press, 1996.

———, *The Nomos of the Earth in the International Law of the Jus Publicum Europaeum*, translated by G. L. Ulmen, New York: Telos Press, 2003.

———, *Political Theology: Four Chapters on the Concept of Sovereignty*, translated by George Schwab, Cambridge, MA and London: MIT Press, 1985.

———, *Politische Theologie: Vier Kapitel zur Lehre von der Souveränität*, Berlin: Duncker und Humblot, 1996.

Schnelle, Udo, *Apostle Paul: His Life and Theology*, translated by M. Eugene Boring, Grand Rapids: Baker, 2005.

Schofield, Malcolm, *The Stoic Idea of the City*, Chicago: University of Chicago Press: 1999.

Scholem, Gershom, *Die jüdische Mystik in ihren Hauptströmungen*, Frankfurt am Main: A. Metzner, 1957.

Schott, Heinz, "Natur und Gott im Menschenbild des Paracelsus", in *Nova Acta Paracelsica 19*, edited by Urs Gantenbein and Pia Holenstein, Bern: Peter Lang, 2005.

Schulz, Eva, "Notes on the History of Collecting and of Museums", in *Interpreting Objects and Collections*, edited by Susan M. Pearce, London and New York: Routledge, 1994.

Schütt, Hans-Werner, *Auf der Suche nach dem Stein der Weisen: Die Geschichte der Alchemie*, Munich: Beck, 2000.

Schwarte, Ludger, *Vom Urteilen: Gesetzlosigkeit, Geschmack, Gerechtigkeit*, Berlin: Merve, 2012.

Schwartz, Regina M., *Remembering and Repeating: On Milton's Theology and Poetics*, Cambridge and New York: Cambridge University Press, 1988.

———, *Sacramental Poetics at the Dawn of Secularism: When God Left the World*, Stanford, CA: Stanford University Press, 2008.

Schweiger, Cornelia, *Die Naturrechtskonzeption des Antoninus von Florenz OP: Ein Spiegel theoretischen Erbes oder praktischer Erfordernisse?*, Berlin: Lit, 2012.

Scotus, John Duns, "Ordinatio 1, Distinctio 44", in *Opera Omnia*, Vol. 6, Vatican City: Typis Polyglottis Vaticanis, 1963.

———, "Ordinatio 1, Distinctio 44", in *On the Will and Morality*, translated and edited by Allan B. Wolter and William A. Frank, Washington, DC: Catholic University of America Press, 1997.

———, "Ordinatio 2, Distinctio 6", in *Commentaria Oxoniensa*, Vol. 4:2, Florence: Ad Claras Aquas, 1914.

———, "Ordinatio 2, Distinctio 6", in *On the Will and Morality*, translated and edited by Allan B. Wolter and William A. Frank, Washington, DC: Catholic University of America Press, 1997.

Selden, John, *The Table Talk*, edited by Samuel Harvey Reynolds, Oxford: Clarendon, 1892.

Sellars, John, *Stoicism*, Berkeley, CA: University of California Press, 2006.

Seneca, *De Beneficiis*, in *Moral Essays*, Vol. 3, translated by John W. Basore, Cambridge, MA: Harvard University Press, 1935.

———, *Naturales Quaestiones/Naturwissenschaftliche Untersuchungen*, translated and edited by M. F. A. Brok, Darmstadt: Wissenschaftliche Buchgesellschaft, 1995.

Septuaginta, edited by Alfred Rahlfs, Stuttgart: Deutsche Bibelgesellschaft, 1979.

Seznec, Jean, *The Survival of the Pagan Gods: The Mythological Tradition and its Place in Renaissance Humanism and Art*, Princeton, NJ: Princeton University Press, 1981.

Shakespeare, William, "Sonnet 11", in *The Norton Shakespeare*, edited by Stephen Greenblatt, New York and London: W. W. Norton and Co., 1997.

Shapin, Steven, *The Scientific Revolution*, Chicago: University of Chicago Press, 1996.

Shaviro, Steven, *The Universe of Things: On Whitehead and Speculative Realism*, Minneapolis: University of Minnesota Press, 2014.

Shuger, Deborah, *Sacred Rhetoric: The Christian Grand Style in the English Renaissance*, Princeton, NJ: Princeton University Press, 1988.

Shullenberger, William, Review of *Poetry and Ecology in the Age of Milton and Marvell* by Diane Kelsey McColley, *Milton Quarterly*, 43:1 (2009).

Shults, F. LeRon, *Iconoclastic Theology: Gilles Deleuze and the Secretion of Atheism*, Edinburgh: Edinburgh University Press, 2015.

Sickert, Ramona, "'durch die vnuernünfftigen thier geschleyfft…': Tiere in mittelalterlichen Rechtspraktiken und Schandritualen", in *Tiere, Bilder, Ökonomien: Aktuelle Forschungsfragen der Human-Animal Studies*, edited by Chimaira – Arbeitskreis für Human-Animal Studies, Bielefeld: transcript, 2013.

Sidney, Philip, "The Defence of Poesy", in *Sidney's "The Defence of Poesy" and Selected Renaissance Literary Criticism*, edited by Gavin Alexander, London and New York: Penguin, 2004.

Silver, Victoria, *Imperfect Sense: The Predicament of Milton's Irony*, Princeton, NJ: Princeton University Press, 2001.

Silvestris, Bernardus, *Cosmographia*, edited by Peter Dronke, Leiden: Brill, 1978.

———, *The Cosmographia of Bernardus Silvestris*, translated by Winthrop Wetherbee, New York and London: Columbia University Press, 1973.

Skinner, Quentin, "The Ideological Context of Hobbes's Political Thought", *The Historical Journal* 9:3 (1966).

Skulsky, Harold, *Milton and the Death of Man: Humanism on Trial in* Paradise Lost, Newark and London: University of Delaware Press, 2000.

Smith, Christian, *American Evangelicalism: Embattled and Thriving*, Chicago: University of Chicago Press, 1998.

Smith, Mark S., *God in Translation: Deities in Cross-Cultural Discourse in the Biblical World*, Grand Rapids, MI: W. B. Eerdmans, 2010.

Song, Eric B., *Dominion Undeserved: Milton and the Perils of Creation*, Ithaca, NY and London: Cornell University Press, 2013.

Sophocles, *Antigone*, in *Antigone, The Women of Trachis, Philoctetes, Oedipus at Colonus*, translated and edited by Hugh Lloyd-Jones, Cambridge, MA and London: Harvard University Press, 1994.

———, *Oedipus at Colonus*, in *Antigone, The Women of Trachis, Philoctetes, Oedipus at Colonus*, translated and edited by Hugh Lloyd-Jones, Cambridge, MA and London: Harvard University Press, 1994.

Sorensen, Roy, *Seeing Dark Things: The Philosophy of Shadows*, New York: Oxford University Press, 2008.

Spencer, Herbert, *Social Statics*, in *Nineteenth-Century Science: A Selection of Original Texts*, edited by Alan S. Weber, Peterborough, ON and Orchard Park, NY: Broadview Press, 2000.

Spenser, Edmund, *The Faerie Queene*, edited by A. C. Hamilton, Harlow: Longman, 2001.

Spinoza, Baruch de, *Ethica/Die Ethik*, translated by Jacob Stern, Stuttgart: Reclam, 1977.

———, *The Letters*, edited by Steven Barbone, Lee Rice and Jacob Adler, translated by Samuel Shirley, Indianapolis: Hackett, 1995.

———, *Theological-Political Treatise*, translated by Michael Silverthorne and Jonathan Israel, Cambridge: Cambridge University Press, 2007.

———, *Tractatus Theologico-Politicus*, in *Oeuvres*, Vol. 3, edited by Fokke Akkerman and Pierre-François Moreau, translated by Jacqueline Lagrée and Pierre-François Moreau, Paris: Presses universitaires de France, 1999.

Spooner, Lysander, *Natural Law or the Science of Justice: A Treatise on Natural Law, Natural Justice, Natural Rights, Natural Liberty and Natural Society, Showing That all Legislation Whatsoever is an Absurdity, a Usurpation, and a Crime*, Boston: A. Williams, 1882.

Stabile, Giorgio, "Natur", in *Historisches Wörterbuch der Philosophie*, Vol. 6, edited by Joachim Ritter, Karlfried Gründer et al., Darmstadt: Wissenschaftliche Buchgesellschaft, 1984.

Stachniewski, John, *The Persecutory Imagination: English Puritanism and the Literature of Religious Despair*, Oxford: Oxford University Press, 1991.

Stallard, Matthew S., "Editorial Preface", in *Paradise Lost: The Biblically Annotated Edition*, by John Milton, edited by Matthew S. Stallard, Macon, GA: Mercer University Press, 2011.

Steadman, John M., *Moral Fiction in Milton and Spenser*, Columbia, MO: University of Missouri Press, 1995.

Stein, Jürgen, "Excommunication", in *The Encyclopedia of Christianity*, Vol. 1, edited by Erwin Fahlbusch and Geoffrey William Bromiley, Grand Rapids, MI: W. B. Eerdmans and Leiden: Brill, 2001.

Steinle, Friedrich, "The Amalgamation of a Concept: Laws of Nature in the New Sciences", in *Laws of Nature: Essays on the Philosophical, Scientific and Historical Dimensions*, edited by Friedel Weinert, Berlin and New York: Walter de Gruyter, 1995.

———, "From Principles to Regularities: Tracing 'Laws of Nature' in Early Modern France and England", in *Natural Law and Laws of Nature in Early Modern Europe: Jurisprudence, Theology, Moral and Natural Philosophy*, edited by Lorraine Daston and Michael Stolleis, Farnham and Burlington, VT: Ashgate, 2008.

Steppich, Christoph J., *Numine afflatur: Die Inspiration des Dichters im Denken der Renaissance*, Wiesbaden: Harrassowitz, 2002.

Stillman, Robert E., *Philip Sidney and the Poetics of Renaissance Cosmopolitanism*, Aldershot and Burlington, VT: Ashgate, 2008.

Stoicorum Veterum Fragmenta, edited by Johannes von Arnim, Stuttgart: Teubner, 1964.

Stoll, Elmer Edgar, "Give the Devil His Due: A Reply to Mr. Lewis", *Review of English Studies* 20 (1944).

Stolleis, Michael, *Das Auge des Gesetzes: Geschichte einer Metapher*, Munich: Beck, 2004.

Stone, Gregory B., *The Ethics of Nature in the Middle Ages*, New York: St. Martin's Press, 1998.

Stott, John, *The Cross of Christ*, Downers Grove, IL: InterVarsity Press, 2006.

Strier, Richard, "Milton's Fetters, or, Why Eden is Better Than Heaven", *Milton Studies* 38:1 (2000).

Suárez, Francisco, *Tractatus de gratia Dei*, in *Opera Omnia*, Vol. 7, edited by Charles Berton, Paris: Vives, 1857.

———, *Tractatus de legibus et legislatore Deo*, in *Opera Omnia*, Vol. 5, edited by Charles Berton, Paris: Vives, 1856.

Sullivan, Ceri, *Literature in the Public Service: Sublime Bureaucracy*, New York: Palgrave Macmillan, 2013.

Summers, Joseph H., *The Muse's Method: An Introduction to* Paradise Lost, London: Chatto and Windus, 1962.

Tasso, Torquato, *Jerusalem Delivered (Gerusalemme liberata)*, translated by Anthony M. Esolen, Baltimore: Johns Hopkins University Press, 2000.

Taubes, Jacob, *Ad Carl Schmitt: Gegenstrebige Fügung*, Berlin: Merve, 1987.

Taylor, George Coffin, *Milton's Use of Du Bartas*, Cambridge, MA: Harvard University Press, 1934.

Tertullian, *Adversus Praxean/Treatise against Praxeas*, edited by Ernest Evans, London: SPCK, 1948.

Teskey, Gordon, *Allegory and Violence*, Ithaca, NY: Cornell University Press, 1996.

———, *Delirious Milton*, Cambridge, MA and London: Harvard University Press, 2006.

———, *The Poetry of John Milton*, Cambridge, MA and London: Harvard University Press, 2015.

Thomas, Keith, *Man and the Natural World: Changing Attitudes in England, 1500–1800*, London: Penguin, 1984.

———, *Religion and the Decline of Magic: Studies in Popular Beliefs in Sixteenth- and Seventeenth-Century England*, London: Penguin, 1991.

Thür, Gerhard, "Oaths and Dispute Settlement in Ancient Law", in *Greek Law in its Political Setting*, edited by Lin Foxhall and A. D. E. Lewis, Oxford: Clarendon Press, 1996.

Ticciati, Susannah, *A New Apophaticism: Augustine and the Redemption of Signs*, Leiden and Boston: Brill, 2013.

Till, Dietmar, *Das doppelte Erhabene: Eine Argumentationsfigur von der Antike bis zum Beginn des 19. Jahrhunderts*, Tübingen: Niemeyer, 2006.

———, "The Sublime and the Bible: Longinus, Protestant Dogmatics, and the 'Sublime Style'", in *Translations of the Sublime: The Early Modern Reception and Dissemination of Longinus'* Peri Hupsous *in Rhetoric, the Visual Arts, Architecture and the Theatre*, edited by Caroline van Eck, Stijn Bussels, Marteen Delbeke and Jürgen Pieters, Boston: Brill, 2012.

Tilmouth, Christopher, Review of *Poetry and Ecology in the Age of Milton and Marvell* by Diane Kelsey McColley and *Renaissance Ecology: Imagining Eden in Milton's England*, edited by Ken Hiltner, *The Seventeenth Century*, 25:1 (2010).

Tournu, Christophe, "Louis XIV", in *The Milton Encyclopedia*, edited by Thomas N. Corns, New Haven, CT: Yale University Press, 2012.

Tralau, Johan, *Thomas Hobbes and Carl Schmitt: The Politics of Order and Myth*, London: Routledge, 2011.

van Woudenberg, René, "A Brief History of Theodicy", in *The Blackwell Companion to the Problem of Evil*, edited by Justin P. McBrayer and Daniel Howard-Snyder, Chichester: Wiley-Blackwell, 2013.

Veyne, Paul, *Did the Greeks Believe in Their Myths? An Essay on the Constitutive Imagination*, translated by Paula Wissing, Chicago: University of Chicago Press, 1988.

Vico, Giambattista, *The New Science*, translated by Thomas Bergin and Max Fish, Ithaca, NY and London: Cornell University Press, 1984.

Virgil, *Aeneis*, translated and edited by Johannes Götte and Maria Götte, Düsseldorf: Artemis und Winkler, 2002.

Vodola, Elisabeth, *Excommunication in the Middle Ages*, Berkeley: University of California Press, 1986.

Vöhler, Martin, Bernd Seidensticker and Wolfgang Emmerich, eds., *Mythenkorrekturen: Zu einer paradoxalen Form der Mythenrezeption*, Berlin and New York: Walter de Gruyter, 2005.

Vossenkuhl, Wilhelm, "Vernünftige Kontingenz: Ockhams Verständnis der Schöpfung", in *Die Gegenwart Ockhams*, edited by Wilhelm Vossenkuhl and Rolf Schönberger, Weinheim: VCH Acta Humaniora, 1990.

Wagner, Walter, *Der Volksgerichtshof im nationalsozialistischen Staat*, Munich: Oldenbourg, 2011.

Waldock, A. J. A., Paradise Lost *and Its Critics*, Cambridge: Cambridge University Press, 1966.

Walker, William, "On Reason, Faith, and Freedom in *Paradise Lost*", *Early Modern Literary Studies* 10:1 (2004).

Waltke, Bruce K., *Creation and Chaos: An Exegetical and Theological Study of Biblical Cosmogony*, Portland, OR: Western Conservative Baptist Seminary, 1974.

Warren, Christopher N., "John Milton and the Epochs of International Law", *The European Journal of International Law* 24:2 (2013).

———, *Literature and the Law of Nations, 1580–1680*, Oxford: Oxford University Press, 2015.

Weber, Max, *Wirtschaft und Gesellschaft: Grundriß der verstehenden Soziologie*, Tübingen: Mohr, 1972.

Welsford, Enid, *The Court Masque: A Study in the Relationship Between Poetry and the Revels*, Cambridge: Cambridge University Press, 1927.

Werblowsky, R. J. Zwi, "Milton and the Conjectura Cabbalistica", *Journal of the Warburg and Courtauld Institutes* 18:1/2 (1955).

Westfall, Richard S., *Never At Rest: A Biography of Isaac Newton*, Cambridge: Cambridge University Press, 1980.

White, Peter, *Predestination, Policy and Polemic: Conflict and Consensus in the English Church from the Reformation to the Civil War*, Cambridge: Cambridge University Press, 1992.

Whitehead, Alfred North, *The Concept of Nature*, Mineola, NY: Dover, 2004,

———, *Process and Reality: An Essay in Cosmology: Gifford Lectures Delivered in the University of Edinburgh During the Season 1927–28*, edited by David Ray Griffin and Donald W. Sherburne, New York: Free Press, 1985.

Whitford, David M., *The Curse of Ham in the Early Modern Era: The Bible and the Justifications for Slavery*, Farnham and Burlington, VT: Ashgate, 2009.

Wilde, Hans Oskar, *Miltons geistesgeschichtliche Bedeutung*, Heidelberg: C. Winter, 1933.

William of Ockham, "A Dialogue", in *A Letter to the Friars Minor and Other Writings*, edited by Arthur Stephen McGrade and John Kilcullen, Cambridge: Cambridge University Press, 1995.

———, *Scriptum in librum primum sententiarum, Ordinatio, Distinctiones XIX–XLVIII*, edited by Girard Etzkorn and Francis Kelley, New York: The Franciscan Institute of St. Bonaventure University, 2000.

Williams, Raymond, "Nature", in *Keywords: A Vocabulary of Culture and Society*, Oxford and New York: Oxford University Press, 1983.

Wilson, Catherine, "From Limits to Laws: The Construction of the Nomological Image of Nature in Early Modern Philosophy", in *Natural Law and Laws of Nature in Early Modern Europe: Jurisprudence, Theology, Moral and Natural Philosophy*, edited by Lorraine Daston and Michael Stolleis, Farnham and Burlington, VT: Ashgate, 2008.

Wilson, Peter Lamborn, *Scandal: Essays in Islamic Heresy*, New York: Autonomedia, 1987.

Wise, M. Norton and Crosbie Smith, "Work and Waste: Political Economy and Natural Philosophy in Nineteenth Century Britain (3)", *History of Science* 28:3 (1990).

Wittreich, Joseph, "Milton's Transgressive Maneuvers: Receptions (Then and Now) and the Sexual Politics of *Paradise Lost*", in *Milton and Heresy*, edited by Stephen Dobranski and John Rumrich, Cambridge: Cambridge University Press, 1998.

Wolf, Erik, *Das Problem der Naturrechtslehre: Versuch einer Orientierung*, Third Edition, Karlsruhe: Müller, 1964.

Wood, Derek N. C., "Aristotle and Milton's Poetics", in *Renaissance-Poetik/ Renaissance Poetics*, edited by Heinrich F. Plett, Berlin and New York: Walter de Gruyter, 1994.

Wood, Elizabeth A., *Performing Justice: Agitation Trials in Early Soviet Russia*, Ithaca, NY and London: Cornell University Press, 2005.

Wright, B. A., Review of *A Preface to* Paradise Lost by C. S. Lewis, *The Review of English Studies* 20:77 (1944).

Wyvill, Christopher, *Of Christian Magistracy*, London: Aylmer, 1697.

Zilsel, Edgar, *Die sozialen Ursprünge der neuzeitlichen Wissenschaft*, edited by Wolfgang Krohn, Frankfurt am Main: Suhrkamp, 1976.

Žižek, Slavoj, *Die bösen Geister des himmlischen Bereichs: Der linke Kampf um das 21. Jahrhundert*, translated by Frank Born, Frankfurt am Main: Fischer, 2011.

Index

www.ingramcontent.com/pod-product-compliance
Lightning Source LLC
LaVergne TN
LVHW021117300926
849160LV00010B/756
9780367653859